SQL —
THE STANDARD HANDBOOK

SQL —
THE STANDARD HANDBOOK

based on the new SQL standard

(ISO 9075:1992(E))

S.J. Cannan
G.A.M. Otten

McGRAW-HILL BOOK COMPANY

London · New York · St Louis · San Francisco · Auckland · Bogotá · Caracas
Hamburg · Lisbon · Madrid · Mexico · Milan · Montreal · New Delhi · Panama
Paris · San Juan · São Paulo · Singapore · Sydney · Tokyo · Toronto

Published by
McGRAW-HILL Book Company Europe
Shoppenhangers Road, Maidenhead, Berkshire, SL6 2QL, England
Telephone 0628 23432
Fax 0628 770224

British Library Cataloguing in Publication Data
Cannan, Stephen John
SQL:Standard Handbook – Based on the New
SQL Standard IS 9075:1992(E)
I. Title II. Otten, Gerard A. M.
005.756

ISBN 0-07-707664-8

Library of Congress Cataloging-in-Publication Data
Cannan, Stephen J. (Stephen John),
SQL--the standard handbook / Stephen J. Cannan, Gerard A.M. Otten.
p. cm.
Includes bibliographical references and index.
ISBN 0-07-707664-8 :
1. SQL (Computer program language)
I. Otten, Gerard A.M. . II. Title.
QA76.73.S67C35 1992
005.75′6--dc20 92-2176
CIP

1234 CUP 9543

Typeset by Perfect Service, Schoonhoven, Holland
and printed and bound in Great Britain at the University Press, Cambridge

Contents

Foreword xi

Acknowledgements xiii

Part I – Introduction

1 Introduction 3
1.1 What is SQL? 3
1.2 The History of SQL 4
1.3 Why a Standard? 5
1.4 The Standardization Process 6
1.5 The Importance of SQL 8
1.6 How to Read this Book 9

2 Some Basic Concepts 15
2.1 Environment 16
2.2 Information System 16
2.3 Database Management System 16
2.4 Database 16
2.5 Database Definition 17
2.6 Database Manipulation 21
2.7 Conventions Used 21

Part II – The SQL Language

3 Basic Language Elements 27
3.1 Characters 27
3.2 Tokens 28
3.3 Identifiers 29
3.4 Names 31
3.5 Literals 33
3.6 Values and Targets 33
3.7 Data Types 34

4 Data Definition 49
4.1 CREATE SCHEMA 49
4.2 CREATE TABLE 52
4.3 CREATE DOMAIN 66
4.4 CREATE VIEW 68
4.5 CREATE ASSERTION 70
4.6 CREATE CHARACTER SET 71
4.7 CREATE COLLATION 72
4.8 CREATE TRANSLATION 75

5 Schema Manipulation 77
5.1 The DROP Statements 77
5.2 The ALTER Statements 84

6 Non-Cursor Operations 91
6.1 INSERT 91
6.2 Single Row SELECT 93
6.3 UPDATE Searched 93
6.4 DELETE Searched 95
6.5 Data Assignment Rules 96

7 Cursor Operations 99
7.1 DECLARE CURSOR 101
7.2 OPEN 104
7.3 FETCH 104
7.4 UPDATE Positioned 105
7.5 DELETE Positioned 108
7.6 CLOSE 109

8 Access Control 111
8.1 GRANT 113
8.2 REVOKE 116
8.3 Ripple Effects of the GRANT Statement 117
8.4 Cascade Effects of the REVOKE Statement 117
8.5 Checking the Privileges 119

9 Derived Tables 121
9.1 Row Value Constructors 121
9.2 Table Value Constructors 122
9.3 Query Expression 122
9.4 Table Expression 138
9.5 Query Specification 141
9.6 Subqueries 144

10 Predicates and Search Conditions 145
10.1 Search Conditions 145
10.2 Predicates 147

11 Functions and Expressions 159
11.1 Value Expressions 159
11.2 Scalar Functions 165
11.3 Conditional Value Expressions 176
11.4 Set Functions 178

12 Transaction Management 181
12.1 Some Basic Concepts 181
12.2 Initiating a Transaction 184
12.3 Control Statements in SQL 185

13 Environment Management 189
13.1 SET CATALOG 189
13.2 SET SCHEMA 190
13.3 SET NAMES 190
13.4 SET SESSION AUTHORIZATION 191
13.5 SET CONSTRAINTS MODE 191
13.6 SET TIME ZONE 192

14 Session Management 195
14.1 CONNECT 196
14.2 SET CONNECTION 197
14.3 DISCONNECT 197

15 Error Handling and Diagnostics 199
15.1 The GET DIAGNOSTICS Command 200
15.2 Diagnostic Area 200
15.3 SQLSTATE 204
15.4 SQLSTATE Codes 205
15.5 Whatever Happened to SQLCODE? 208

16 The Module Language 209
16.1 Modules 210
16.2 DECLARE LOCAL TEMPORARY TABLE 211
16.3 Procedures 212
16.4 Parameters 214
16.5 A Complete Example 218

17 The Embedded Languages 221
17.1 The Supported Languages 223
17.2 Exception Control 227
17.3 Inserting SQL Commands into the Host Language 228
17.4 A Complete Example 229

18 Dynamic SQL 233
18.1 Why Dynamic SQL? 233
18.2 The Basic Structure of Dynamic SQL 234
18.3 EXECUTE IMMEDIATE 235
18.4 PREPARE 235
18.5 DEALLOCATE PREPARE 237
18.6 DESCRIBE 237
18.7 USING 238
18.8 ALLOCATE DESCRIPTOR 239
18.9 DEALLOCATE DESCRIPTOR 243
18.10 GET DESCRIPTOR 244
18.11 SET DESCRIPTOR 245
18.12 EXECUTE 247
18.13 Dynamic DECLARE CURSOR 247
18.14 Dynamic ALLOCATE CURSOR 247
18.15 Dynamic OPEN CURSOR 248
18.16 Dynamic CLOSE CURSOR 248
18.17 Dynamic FETCH CURSOR 249
18.18 Dynamic DELETE Positioned 249
18.19 Dynamic UPDATE Positioned 249
18.20 Preparable Dynamic DELETE Positioned 250
18.21 Preparable Dynamic UPDATE Positioned 250
18.22 A Complete Example 250

19 Direct Invocation of SQL 255
19.1 Permitted Statements 256
19.2 Direct Select : Multiple Rows 256

20 The Information Schema 257
20.1 The Definition Schema 258
20.2 The Information Schema 279
20.3 Extracting the Information 293

Part III – Using the SQL Language

21 Database and Application Analysis 297
21.1 From Conceptual to Physical Using Data and Function 298
21.2 Database and Application Analysis Issues 298
21.3 Correctness Aspects 304
21.4 Security Aspects 307
21.5 Current Trends 308
21.6 Data Driven Programming 311

22 Integrity Control 313
22.1 Definition 313
22.2 Domain Integrity 314
22.3 Entity Integrity 316
22.4 Referential Integrity 317
22.5 User Integrity 320
22.6 The Implementation of Relationships — Examples 323
22.7 Combinations of Relationships 340
22.8 Management 345

23 Using the Datetime Facilities 351
23.1 Basic Facilities 351
23.2 A Taxonomy of Time 352
23.3 Time Zones 365

24 Handling Missing Information 369
24.1 Missing: Applicable and Inapplicable Markings 370
24.2 SQL and Three-Valued Logic 370
24.3 Predicates and Missing Information 373
24.4 Set Functions and Missing Information 373
24.5 More Than Three-Valued Logic 374
24.6 Tautological and Absurd Queries 376
24.7 DEFAULT <literal> or CASE for NULL 377
24.8 Replace NULL by Value Always 379

25 Translating Natural Language Queries 381
25.1 The Steps in the Query Formulation Method 381
25.2 A Query Transformation Example 385
25.3 General Remarks 391
25.4 Background Information 395
25.5 Additional Information for Natural Language Translation 398

26 Usage of Views 403
26.1 Enhancing Accessibility and User Access 403
26.2 Limiting Access to Data 407
26.3 Mapping to Host Language Conventions 409

26.4 Enhanced Physical Environment Support 409
26.5 Using the WITH CHECK Options 410
26.6 Conclusions on Views 413

27 Distributed Databases 415
27.1 Definition of Terms in Distributed Databases 416
27.2 A Four-Step Method for Data Distribution 418
27.3 A Worked Example 430

28 Performance Aspects 437
28.1 Physical Data and Application Design Approach 439
28.2 Disk Access Structures 442
28.3 Disk Storage and Main Memory Organization 446
28.4 Query Access Planning 448

Appendices

A The Example Database 453

B BNF Syntax Notation 467

C BNF Syntax Diagrams 471

D Key Words 531

E Levels and Conformance 535

F Differences between SQL-1992 and SQL-1989 539

G Glossary 543

H References 561

I Analytical Table of Contents 565

Index 577

Foreword

As Editor of the *Data Base Newsletter*, I have spent a considerable amount of time over the years reading formal standards documents. These sparse, highly stylized documents are not for the typical practitioner. This is why I find the authors' work in this book so valuable. What they have done is fill in the gaps with bountiful explanations and examples — in other words, to make accessible a highly precise and technical body of work.

For a subject as important as SQL, this is no insignificant matter. Lest anyone need reminding, SQL is currently without rival as a standard database language. Every major supplier currently provides database products that are either based on SQL or have an SQL interface. Among the major players are IBM's SAA, DEC's NAS, CA's CA/90's, UNISYS's UA and many others, including virtually every vendor in the client-server arena. Not only software vendors but also users are now heavily investing in SQL. SQL has also, of course, been adopted as a Federal Information Processing Standard.

Besides being a standard in its own right, SQL also provides an important tool — a building block — for defining other key standards. Such areas include ISO's Information Resource Directory System Standard, Remote Data Access Standard and the X/Open Portability Guide. Ultimately, some of these areas are likely to prove as important as or even more important than SQL itself.

Most important research on database technology has been centred on SQL since the mid seventies in both the academic community and industry research labs. In that context, it has been a focal point for investigating such crucial technological issues as query optimization, data distribution and distributed processing. It continues in this leading research role for newer innovations such as object-orientation and declarative specification of constraints.

Be that as it may, for the average database user, the real advantage of SQL lies not so much with its power as a database sub-language (although that is apparent) but rather simply with the fact that it *is* a standard. Anybody who has ever plugged an electric cord into a wall outlet can readily appreciate the inestimable benefits of workable standards. Indeed, with respect to electrical power, the very fact that we seldom even think about such access (until something goes wrong) is a sure sign of just how fundamentally important a successful standard can be.

I do not mean to suggest that SQL is as simple as an electrical plug. Indeed, it most certainly is not. Like a plug, however, it provides access to many sources of power and productivity that would otherwise prove either elusive or prohibitively expensive. I think in particular of all the various portability issues plaguing companies today — portability not just of applications and software tools, but of skills and knowledge as well. A standard means reusability — of *people* as well as software components. For the long term, use of a good standard means the greatest possible return on investment.

With respect to the labours the authors have put into this book, I have very high admiration. If the work seems authoritative, this should come as no surprise — the authors have been involved in the ISO SQL standardization process since its inception and have either drafted or assisted in the drafting of major sections of the current standard. I believe readers will find their product-independent and non-commercial approach quite appealing. I congratulate them on an outstanding work.

Ronald G. Ross
Editor/Publisher
Data Base Newsletter

Boston, Massachusetts

Acknowledgements

This book would not have been written without the help and support of a number of people and organizations. In the first place, without the support of DCE Nederland b.v. over many years in providing us with the time and the finances, as well as the incentive, to participate in the standardization process at national and international level, attending dozens of meetings in countries all round the globe, we would not have been in a position to write the book at all.

Our thanks are also due to the many participants in the standardization process, from all over the world, without whom there would have been nothing to write about. There are far too many of these to name them all individually, but special recognition must go to the current editor of the standard, Jim Melton, who tirelessly strove to make coherent text from our proposals and the Rapporteur, Len Gallagher, who always sought the consensus vital to the progression of the work.

We are grateful for the many valuable criticisms and suggestions received from those who read all or part of the various drafts and in particular for those of Eleanor Cannan and Fred Ras. Thanks are due to Desirée Hendriks who drew the more difficult diagrams for us in DrawPerfect and also to Wordperfect Nederland who kindly supplied us both with free copies of Wordperfect 5.1 and DrawPerfect 1.1 with which to produce the book.

Last, but not least, our thanks must go to our wives for their patience and uncomplaining support. They may have seen rather less of us than they might have hoped but then they have learned rather more about SQL than they dreamed possible.

Part I
Introduction

1

Introduction

The objective of this book is to provide a reference work explaining and describing the SQL standard (ISO 9075) in a much less formal and very much more readable way than the standard itself. This is not a criticism of the standard which is, by its nature, a formal document with the emphasis on precision. It does not include examples or other tutorial material to explain the usage of commands or constructs, but we hope we have provided sufficient examples and explanatory material so that even someone without previous knowledge or experience of SQL will be able to understand the principles of the language, its facilities and its usage. The book is not, however, intended as a tutorial. Since it is based on the standard and not on a particular implementation's dialect of the language it is a useful reference for users of all conforming implementations. Since the trend is towards conformance the information will therefore become increasingly relevant. The version of the standard described is the International Standard dated 1992 (ISO, 1992a).

Before we start, however, we would like to explain a little about what SQL is and what it is not, its history, the process by which it has become a standard and how the standard is maintained. We will say something about why SQL is important and must be taken seriously by everybody in the database world, and we will end by explaining how the book is structured and is intended to be read.

1.1 What is SQL?

SQL as such is a database sub-language, which means that it is not a complete language in its own right since it contains no control commands. SQL provides definitional language facilities for data definition, for integrity constraint definition and, to some extent, for access control definition. For data manipulation, it provides a module language that consists of procedures containing statements that can retrieve, store and modify data in various ways. Extensions to standard programming languages such as COBOL are defined as embedded SQL languages, so called because the SQL is inserted or embedded in the existing languages. SQL can also be used directly but the exact means used to achieve this is not defined by the standard. SQL contains only these definitional and manipulative commands; it contains no control commands. There are therefore no IF THEN ELSE, GO TO, DO WHILE or other commands to provide a flow of control. These must be implemented with existing programming languages or through the decisions of the 'direct' user.

1.2 The History of SQL

The history of SQL can probably be said to have started with the publication of the paper 'A relational model for large shared data banks' by E.F. Codd (1970), then working at IBM's Research Laboratory in San Jose. In 1974 D.D. Chamberlain, also from the IBM San Jose Laboratory, defined a language called the 'Structured English Query Language' or SEQUEL. A revised version SEQUEL/2 was defined in 1976-7 but the name was subsequently changed to SQL for legal reasons. An IBM research project implementation, 'System R', was based on SEQUEL/2 and became operational in 1977. Also in the late 1970s the database system ORACLE was produced by what is now the ORACLE Corporation and was probably the first commercial implementation. IBM then introduced products based on their experience with System R, which were announced as SQL/DS for the DOS/VSE and VM/CMS environments in 1981 and 1982 respectively and as DB2 for the MVS environment in 1983.

In 1982 the American National Standards Institute, ANSI, began work on a Relational Database Language, or RDL, based on a concept paper from IBM. The International Organization for Standardization (ISO) picked up the work started by ANSI in 1983 and together they defined a standard for SQL. The name RDL was dropped in 1984 and the draft standard reverted to a form that was more like the existing implementations of SQL. Today there are literally dozens of implementations of SQL or SQL-like interfaces to existing database systems.

The first SQL standard was published by ISO in 1987 as ISO 9075:1987(E) (ISO, 1987) (the ANSI version, technically identical, was published at the end of 1986 as X3.135); in 1989 ISO published an addendum which defined an 'integrity enhancement feature'. The combined document was then called ISO 9076:1989(E) (ISO,1989). Also in 1989, ANSI published X3.168, standardizing the embedded SQL languages which in the previous ANSI and ISO standards had been merely 'informative' annexes, i.e. recommendations rather than norms.

The initial, 1987, standard attracted a considerable degree of criticism from such well-known database personalities as C.J. Date (Date, 1987a). Much of the criticism was valid and had been appreciated by the standards bodies before the standard was published. It had been decided, however, that it was more important to get a standard out quickly in order to establish a common base from which the language and the implementations could develop than to wait until all the features that people felt should be present could be defined and stabilized. A quick peek at *Appendix F Differences between SQL-1992 and SQL-1989* will give you a good idea of the number of facilities felt to be missing which have now been stabilized and will also give you an idea of what people still feel needs to be done. With hindsight, the decision to go for a quick and minimal standard was almost certainly correct.

In 1992 the first major revision to the standard took place and the result is described in this book. Although some features have been defined in the standard for the first time, many of these have already been implemented, in part or in a similar but not necessarily identical form in one or more of the many SQL implementations.

1.3 Why a Standard?

What is the purpose of a standard? A standard can provide many benefits, not all of which will be applicable for everybody all the time but always for some people, some of the time. The advantages of a standard are:

- Open development. The demands on systems nowadays are increasingly complex so that it is increasingly difficult to find a single package that meets all the requirements and impossible for suppliers to cater for all needs. For innovative developers to have a chance of success they need to be able to interface rapidly with a stable and known situation and to build on what is already present without reinventing the wheel. The existence of standard interfaces helps them to build bridges to existing software with relatively little cost. The area of CASE tools is an excellent example of the need for standardization.
- People portability. People are increasingly the expensive part of any development activity. Standards help to decrease the training effort because training based on standards gives a greater chance that those so trained can work effectively with different products, all of which conform to the standard.
- Application portability. Applications can be developed using standard tools and languages or using the standard aspects of particular tools and languages. This means that the application can be transferred to any other environment where the same platform of standard tools and languages exists. Even if a complete correspondence does not exist the use of standards will minimize the conversion necessary. At the moment, since there is no complete standard platform, complete portability is not possible, but again it minimizes the differences between platforms and increases the number of possible choices.

- Increased inter-operability. Distribution of data and processing is an increasing necessity when designing a technical infrastructure. The reasons for this can be many but might include scalability, resilience, local autonomy, etc. It is also frequently the case that the existing situation must be incorporated and this, together with the different needs that exist at different locations, leads to heterogeneous hardware and software being linked. The existence of common languages and protocols for communication between the nodes is essential and standardization at all levels improves the chances of success.
- Reference point. In a world full of choice it is difficult to judge the benefits and disadvantages of so many products. One becomes involved in N^2 comparisons. The existence of a standard can help the process by reducing it to N comparisons, all comparisons against a common base — the standard.
- Preservation of investment. Applications of increasing complexity are being developed and the development consumes large sums of money. The continuity of the language and flexibility of choice of implementation provided by a standard increases the chance that investments in software development will be recovered.

Why do we not just leave it to the market place to determine what the language is? Primarily because the interests of the users are not necessarily the same as the interests of the suppliers and standards are one way in which the users can exercise some influence. Also, standards reduce the scope for manipulation of the market by one or a small number of suppliers to their own advantage.

This is not to say that standardization is perfect. There is also a down side. Standards are never perfect and they cannot remain fixed. Like everything else in this world they must either grow or die. They can provide a degree of stability but must never enforce stagnation. A good standard will always leave room for bright people to improve and extend it in developing products and will adopt the best ideas in revisions of the standard. This process can be clearly seen in this new version of the SQL standard.

1.4 The Standardization Process

The standardization process which led to the SQL discussed in this book was controlled by the Joint Technical Committee 1 (JTC1) of the International Organization for Standardization (ISO) and the International Electrotechnical Commission (IEC). The work was actually done by a number of groups of individuals working at international and national level. The authors of this book have participated in these groups at both levels.

The International Organization for Standardization is divided into a number of Technical Committees. In the case of JTC1 this is a joint committee with the IEC and is responsible for 'Information Technology'. Each Technical Committee has a number of subcommittees, the relevant subcommittee in the case of SQL being SC21 whose responsibility is 'Information Retrieval, Transfer and Management for Open Systems Interconnection' (OSI). It is also responsible for the well-known seven-layer OSI communications architecture. Within SC21 there are a number of Working Groups, of which the third (WG3) is responsible for all matters 'Database'. WG3 is itself divided into rapporteur groups, each of which looks after one or more projects. The 'Database Languages' rapporteur group looks after the development of the SQL database language and the NDL database language (which was based on the CODASYL network ideas).

The members of ISO are the national standards bodies such as ANSI (American National Standards Institute), BSI (British Standards Institute), NNI (Nederlands Normalisatie-instituut), JISC (Japanese Industry Standards Committee), AFNOR, DIN, SCC, etc. However, at the working group level the participants are individuals, deemed 'experts', active in the relevant field. Some of these are sponsored by their national body or by their governments but many are sponsored by their employer.

Within the national standards bodies there is normally a rough parallel to the ISO structure and within these bodies there may be individual standardization effort, either separate from or parallel to that which takes place in ISO. An example in the case of SQL occurs within ANSI which has a large committee developing SQL in close co-operation with the international community in ISO.

How is a standard arrived at? It begins, normally, with a proposal for a 'New Work Item' by a member body. If this is accepted then the item is assigned to a working group and a development plan is made for the standard to be developed. The first stage is a 'Working Draft', a document that goes through numerous revisions, with additions, deletions and modifications as a result of proposals submitted by the national bodies or individuals in the attempt to find a definition that is acceptable to the vast majority of the participants. The intention is always to find a consensus within the working group or rapporteur group on what will make the best standard. This is a long process; the first SQL standard (ISO 9075:1987) took approximately three years to complete. The submissions from national bodies will have already been submitted to a similar process within the national working groups. Eventually a document is developed that everybody can agree is a suitable basis for a standard, but before it becomes one it must pass a number of hurdles. The Working Draft must be accepted by a vote of all the participating national bodies for registration as a Committee Draft. Following registration the Committee Draft is circulated to all national bodies for a three month ballot, to give time for the complete proposal to be reviewed by interested parties in all the member nations. Following the ballot, a meeting is held to resolve comments and objections and if at the end of the meeting 75 per cent of the voting national bodies agree the document passes to the next stage. If not, it will normally be referred back to the working group for further work before repeating the process. Assuming that it has received a 75 per cent yes vote it is promoted to a 'Draft International Standard' and the, possibly revised, document is again circulated, this time for a six month ballot. The editing process is repeated and when successful the document is sent to the ISO secretariat to be published as a full 'International Standard'.

Following publication the document is maintained by an editing committee that deals with queries regarding interpretation and attempts to fix any errors or ambiguities that may be discovered in the standard.

Most standards in the information technology area are subject to periodic revision which may take place in one of two ways. First, if a new feature is required and can be reasonably easily added to the existing document within a short period of time then an 'addendum' may be defined for the standard. An addendum goes through the same stages as a standard but when finally published is treated as part of the original standard. This was done with the 'integrity enhancement feature' which was issued in 1989 as an addendum to the 1987 standard. The second alternative is a complete revision. These are not normally issued within five years of the previous standard as one of the objectives of standardization is stability. Revisions take the existing standard as their working draft and work their way through the process exactly like a new standard except that on publication they supersede the previous standard. This is the route taken by the latest SQL standard which is the subject of this book.

1.5 The Importance of SQL

SQL is an important language as it is the first and so far only standard database language to gain wide acceptance. The only other standard database language, NDL, based on the CODASYL network model, has few followers. Nearly every major current supplier provides database products based on SQL or with an SQL interface and nearly all are represented in one or other of the standard making bodies. There is a huge investment in the language both by suppliers and by users. It has become part of application architectures such as IBM's SAA, DEC's NAS or UNISYS's UA and is the strategic choice of many large and influential users. SQL has also become a Federal Information Processing Standard to which conformance is required for all sales of databases to the American Government. The SQL standard language is used in other standards or developing standards as a definitional tool. Examples include ISO's Information Resource Directory System Standard, Remote Data Access Standard and the X/Open portability guide. The development of the language is supported by considerable academic interest, providing both a theoretical basis for the language and the techniques needed to implement it successfully. This is especially true in the areas of query optimization, distribution of data, privacy and security. Hardware support is developing with the availability of database machines. Specialized implementations of SQL are beginning to appear directed at new markets, such as on-line transaction processing. Long-term planning for future enhancements has already taken place and these should include facilities or support for distributed processing, object-oriented programming, user-defined extensions, etc.

1.6 How to Read this Book

Since this book is written with the aim of functioning as a reference book on SQL, we have designed several mechanisms to enable you to find the description of the topic you want. Furthermore, though not the primary function of this book, we have tried to make it readable from beginning to end. Should you choose this option you will occasionally have to search forward for the explanatory text, since the sequence of the topics does not always support this mode.

1.6.1 The Structure of the Book

This book contains four major parts, each with a specific purpose:

- Introduction
- The SQL Language
- Using the SQL Language
- Appendices

1.6.1.1 Introduction

This part gives background information on the production and use of standards, the historic development of SQL as a data sub-language and provides useful insight into this book. The major concepts of database technology insofar as they are pertinent to SQL and the standards world are illustrated and act as a basis for the entire book.

1.6.1.2 The SQL Language

This part provides a dissertation on the various constructs and elements of the SQL language identified in the international standard ISO 9075:1992(E). The sequence of treatment of the SQL syntax is slightly different from that in the standard in order, we hope, to make the book more accessible. The entire SQL standard is treated in sufficient depth for use by SQL programmers, database analysts, database designers and teachers of information technology and related subjects. For those employees of computer manufacturers and software vendors who are responsible for implementing SQL in a database package the standard is still a necessary evil for the in-depth descriptions needed to understand fully esoteric topics such as conformance levels.

The SQL language syntax consists of a number of separate syntax hierarchies which are sequenced in a sensible fashion (*see Table 1.1*). We treat some basic language concepts first and then discuss the data definition language (DDL) syntax. Then we discuss the schema manipulation syntax by means of which modifications can be made to existing definitions. The data manipulation language (DML) syntax is discussed in two chapters, on cursor and non-cursor operations. Non-cursor operations are in principle the set-oriented commands everybody thinks of when talking about SQL, whereas the cursor operations are the commands used in languages that do not directly support set-oriented constructs. The following chapter deals with controlling access to the database. The

Table 1.1 Chapter overview for the SQL language

Topic	*Description*	*Chapters*
The basic components of the language	The tokens, recognition of which enables the character strings that make up the SQL language to be broken up into the components which form the syntax of the language. Data types, literals, identifiers and other such basic concepts are also described	Basic Language Elements (3)
The creation and manipulation of the meta-data (DDL)	The language statements that enable the various objects of SQL, tables, views, domains, etc., to be described, altered and deleted	Data Definition (4) Schema Manipulation (5)
The creation, modification, deletion and retrieval of application data (DML)	The language statements that enable the application data to be stored in tables, updated, deleted and retrieved in various ways and forms	Non-Cursor Operations (6) Cursor Operations (7)
The protection of the privacy and security of data	The language statements that enable the use of the various SQL objects to be controlled with regard to the types of actions that may be performed on them and any application data that they contain	Access Control (8)
The constructs that are common to both DDL and DML	The language components that occur in both the DDL and the DML statements. These components include predicates, value expressions, derived table definitions, etc.	Derived Tables (9) Predicates and Search Conditions (10) Functions and Expressions (11)
The environment	The language statements that enable programs (etc.) to control their environment, success points and data access, etc.	Transaction Management (12) Environment Management (13) Session Management (14)
Handling error situations and warnings	The error codes returned by SQL and the diagnostic information that is associated with various classes of error together with the means of retrieving this information	Error Handling and Diagnostics (15)
The binding methods of the SQL language	The various ways in which the SQL language can be used and presented to the DBMS	The Module Language (16) The Embedded Languages (17) Dynamic SQL (18) Direct Invocation of SQL (19)
The catalogue	The meta data of SQL	The Information Schema (20)

following three chapters describe the so-called ‘common elements’. These elements are language constructs used for formulating parts of DDL and DML operations. A good understanding of these chapters gives you the right to claim an understanding of SQL. The three chapters on transaction, environment and session management explain how the running of SQL programs in a computer environment can be controlled. Then a chapter on error handling shows how to deal with error situations and which errors the standard defines. Four chapters present four different forms of the SQL language: the module language, which can be considered as a subroutine implementation; the embedded language, where SQL is mixed with host language operations; dynamic SQL, which allows construction and execution of SQL statements during program execution; and finally direct invocation of SQL, probably the form that is expected to be the default variant but is probably the least well defined. Finally, once you think you understand SQL you can check your knowledge against the contents of the Information Schema chapter, which describes the capabilities of the SQL language in terms of a database description. The database description is, of course, in SQL and makes use of many of the constructs.

1.6.1.3 Using the SQL Language

This part provides a tutorial description of a number of important topics related to database management systems, and the analysis, design and operational control and usage of database systems. These topics are treated from the perspective of actually using the SQL language. Sometimes different solutions are possible with differing effects upon the maintainability or some other aspect. In other cases the current standard SQL language may offer, as yet, no (easy) solution. For some simple concepts it may be necessary to use many different language constructs in a well-co-ordinated manner and at other times complex concepts can be treated in a simple fashion within the SQL language.

Each chapter in this part is fully self-contained and uses the language descriptions as explained in the SQL language part of the book.

1.6.1.4 Appendices

This part contains a variety of items such as the complete description of our example database used throughout the book, the complete SQL language syntax diagrams, problems and differences with previous SQL standards, references to other works and the Glossary.

1.6.2 Access Mechanisms

This book is designed to be easily accessible (*see Figure 1.1*). The various access mechanisms are described below.
There are four major entry points to the book:

- The Analytical Table of Contents
- The Glossary
- The BNF Syntax Diagrams
- The Index

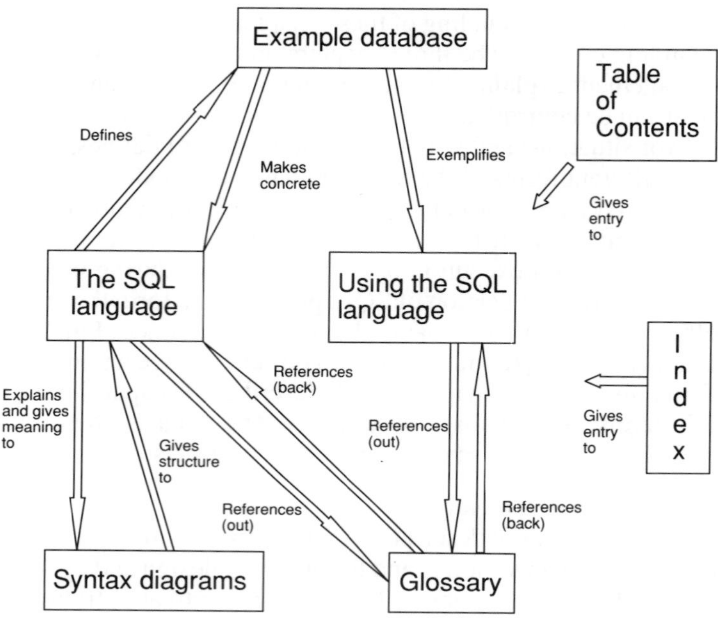

Figure 1.1 *Structure of the book*

The Table of Contents provides access to the major topics covered in the book. There are two Tables of Contents, a synoptic one at the front of the book and one containing *all* section headings in *Appendix I Analytical Table of Contents*. These are naturally arranged in the order in which they appear in the book and describe a logical way of approaching the complete material. A reader interested in a complete major topic should be able to find the general topic in the Table of Contents and proceed from there. In some places within the text reference is made to other sections and these references take the form (*see Section 1.6.2 Access Mechanisms*).

The second major entry point is the Glossary. The Glossary consists of an alphabetically sorted set of definitions of the important terms used within SQL. Together with the short definition and description of the use of the term are a set of references to the chapters and sections of the book where the complete description of the term occurs and to the major places where the term is used. To enable the reader to determine whether a term occurs in the Glossary all occurrences of terms are in bold type as follows: **search condition**. Frequently terms that occur in the Glossary are also the names of major syntax productions. This is not always the case and the converse is certainly not true, i.e. the names of all syntax productions are not defined in the Glossary. However, to enable the reader to find a description of the appropriate syntactic production an Appendix is provided (*see Appendix C BNF Syntax Diagrams*) that contains all the syntax productions, listed in alphabetical order, together with a reference to the place in the text where the major productions are described.

The last access mechanism is the Index which provides access to things that are neither in the Glossary nor the syntax productions. The Index provides no clue to the use of the item at the place indexed so we would recommend first looking in the Glossary and then at either the syntax productions or the index or both.

2

Some Basic Concepts

Before proceeding to the SQL language we will describe some basic terminology to avoid unnecessary confusion on words. The purpose of this chapter is to make the reader familiar with the terminology used in the International Organization for Standardization (ISO) in the area of database-related standards such as SQL.

SQL is seen as belonging to the family of languages that describe facilities for relational database management systems and it should be understood that these are different from the relational database model which describes the characteristics of management of data according to relational principles. The relational principles are derived from mathematics and set theory, but need continuous adaptation and change to fit the current and maturing thinking on database-related issues. One such issue is the treatment of NULL, which received interesting but widely varying and inconsistent attention from many database academicians and practitioners.

Implementors then create products that exhibit features contained in the relational model. Each such implementation uses a language to transfer the concepts involved in defining and manipulating data. SQL is such a database sub-language. The definition of these languages must ensure that practitioners can enjoy effective and efficient data handling, often requiring practical solutions to issues that have not been satisfactorily solved in the relational model. The relational model evolves as theory is further developed and the community of database practitioners should understand the concepts clearly and apply them sensibly. The pragmatic solving of problem areas may sometimes be seen as theoretically wobbly and non-relational. From that point of view SQL is not entirely relational, but that is not a claim which ISO wants to make, since the word relational has not been used in standardization efforts since the mid eighties.

In this book we will talk about what is directly possible in SQL given the set of features available from an SQL international standard. We will also discuss a number of issues and provide directions for resolving them in the part of the book dealing with the use of SQL.

2.1 Environment

An environment is simply a grouping of data, processes and processing capacity, all of which are in some way related to one another, or can be mutually aware. You may need to think of an environment as a single isolated computer or a complete distributed network depending on the circumstances.

2.2 Information System

The term information system is used to represent the combination of database, the database management system and the application programs. In some approaches the humans using the system are also included. In this book the information system is confined to the boundaries of the computer system.

2.3 Database Management System

The maintenance of data in computers can only be performed through the use of an agent, called a database management system (DBMS). The SQL language describes how this agent can be addressed, i.e. which syntax to use when communicating with the DBMS, and what the functionality exhibited will be, i.e. which meaning or semantics are involved. A DBMS can be implemented in many ways, but the SQL standard does not require a specific configuration provided that the syntax and semantics as described in the standard are observed. In numerous instances the standard explicitly allows implementors to make their own decisions such as the design of the user interface and interface arrangements to the operating system components and file system.

2.4 Database

An object maintained by a database management system is called a database. A database consists of two parts, a definition part and a data part. SQL provides language facilities that enable the definition of data and language facilities for maintaining the defined data in computer systems to be made. These two parts can be seen as a closely linked pair. The definition part is also known as the schema, the meta-data, the database definition, the database description or the database structure. SQL always uses the term schema for the definition part. The data part, which cannot exist without the definition part, contains the data and is often loosely referred to as simply *the* database, the physical database or the data(base) files.

Application database definition
Application database data

The two parts of a database

In the early days of databases it was always considered that a single database was described by a single definition element or schema. Nowadays we need to consider programs that access data on many different computers in a network. Not all of these computers need to be under the control of the same organization and thus it is both impossible and undesirable to have a single schema that defines all of the data in a database. Indeed, in some large networks consisting of several thousand nodes it may be impossible to determine what the complete definition of all the data stored is, as it is highly likely that not all the nodes of the network are available at any given moment in time. SQL deliberately uses a rather vague definition of database in order to avoid this conceptual problem. In SQL a database is defined as being 'the collection of all the data described by all the schemas in all the catalogs referenced in an SQL-session'. If we assume for now that a session (*see Chapter 14 Session Management*) is an execution of an application program, we see that a database is all the data defined by all the definitions (or better, groups of definitions — catalogs) that happen to be accessed by a program. Thus the SQL database may change radically between executions of a program but this is not of interest to any particular execution. An SQL database is therefore all things to all men; in the simplest case you can think of it as the data defined by a single schema and in complex cases you may need to consider data described by many schemata on many computers scattered over the whole world.

2.5 Database Definition

Part of the SQL language consists of the data definition language (DDL) which allows the definition of data structures, the specification of access control, so enabling the population of the database definition part. The SQL objects and concepts associated with this part of the language are primarily tables, rows and columns, although several others also exist.

2.5.1 Table

The basic concept of an SQL database is a table. The official definition of a table is 'A table is a multi-set of rows. A row is a non-empty sequence of values ...'. An example is shown in Figure 2.1. This looks just like a matrix with rows and columns and indeed those are the terms we will use. The four lines are the 'multi-set of rows', a multi-set being a collection that does not exclude **dupli-**

Patel	5 Lauder Road	+44(0)34-291-5644
Smith	12 Greenbank Avenue	+44(0)71-349-9906
...	...	...
Jones	71 High Street	+44(0)71-765-2132

Figure 2.1 *An example of a basic table*

cates. Duplicates may be bad practice but they are not excluded from SQL. This is a practicality which the relational model would not tolerate, but SQL offers facilities to allow or exclude duplicates. Including duplicates in your database design may require specific mechanisms to govern the correct functioning of the information system.

The purpose of a table is to hold structured data about things, whether they be past, current or future, real or imagined. Some examples are: Employees, Invoices, Projects, Inventions, Equipment. Each row in a table consists of a number of values, one in each column. Each row has the same number of columns; the number of columns is called the degree, which in this case is 3. The number of rows in the table is sometimes called its cardinality.

This is a fairly common way of representing data and is the only way in SQL. All data in SQL exist in one or another table and all queries are made against the data in one or more tables. Thus the essence of SQL is very simple but the language allows many complex ideas to be expressed in terms of these simple concepts.

As we will see later, there are several different kinds of table: base tables, temporary tables, views and derived tables. These tables all have the same form and the differences will be explained in the appropriate sections of the book.

A row of a table is the smallest unit of data that may be inserted into or deleted from a table. Most tables have an explicit name, and all tables can be assumed to possess a name of some sort, even if it is only one generated by the database management system itself.

The table has one or more columns which are designed to hold particulars about the items. Each column has a name, again mostly explicitly provided, but in any case the columns must be identifiable by the DBMS. The discussion above indicates that the example table is rather naked and needs some more 'meta-data' to become complete. The names of tables and columns are vital parts of the meta-data. Let us call the table 'Employee' and the columns 'name', 'address' and 'home_telno'. The table could now be presented as shown in Figure 2.2 where the database definition items are shaded and the database data are clear. This will be the format of a table throughout the book, with the names of tables starting with an upper-case character and the names of columns with a lower-case character.

The intersection of row and column forms a container, or field, holding the actual data. Here the container holds information, e.g. 'Patel', about a specific characteristic, e.g. 'name' (a column), for a specific object of interest, e.g. an

Employee			
name	*address*	*home_telno*	*deptcd*
Patel	5 Lauder Road	+44(0)34-291-5644	SLS
Smith	12 Greenbank Avenue	+44(0)71-349-9906	PER
...	...	...	...
Jones	71 High Street	+44(0)71-765-2132	MKT

Figure 2.2 *Format of a table*

Employee (a row of the table). The table name provides the name of the object of interest, while individual objects are described by rows. The values in fields are often constrained for good reasons.

Characteristics like birth dates, salaries, age and many more have 'intrinsic' constraints. Languages like SQL offer possibilities for describing such constraints. The allowable set of values is defined in a domain. A domain is a set of permissible values. In theory, every column has a domain, e.g. in the column home_telno (*see Figure 2.2*) I might expect to be able to use the characters '+', '(', ')', '–' and the digits '0' to '9' inclusive but not the characters 'A' to 'Z', etc. Every column has a defined maximum length, size, precision, etc., and thus there is always a finite set of possible values, though the set may be very large. In SQL we restrict the use of the term domain to a named definition of a domain. These named domains may be used in the definition of columns, which are otherwise defined in terms of data types with certain characteristics that imply the actual domain.

Further limitations can be the result of relationships between tables as expressed in referential integrity specifications. The referential integrity concept deals with dependencies between things of one kind — like Employees — on the one hand and things of (possibly) another kind — like Department — on the other hand. In a given application an Employee always works in a Department; thus no Employee can exist without the Department worked in. This relationship is reflected in an SQL database by means of symbolic keys. Each Department has a unique identifier, called the primary key, and this identifier, in our case deptcd, is used for each dependent Employee to reflect the dependence. The permissible values of the deptcd for each Employee is restricted to the actual values of deptcd in the Department table.

A key is a column or a collection of columns whose values identify a unique row in a table. There are several kinds of keys:

Candidate key. A candidate key is a collection of columns in a table whose values uniquely identify the rows of that table. There may be more than one candidate key in a table. For example, in a person table the following may be candidate keys:

- Tax number
- Employee number
- Full name + date of birth
- Social Security number

Primary key. The primary key is one of the candidate keys of a table which has been chosen as the primary identification of the rows in the table. Whereas a table may have multiple candidate keys, it may have only one primary key.

Foreign key. A foreign key is a collection of one or more columns in a table which, if not null, uniquely identify a row in (another) table.

2.5.2 Schema

The purpose of a schema is to collect together SQL objects, tables, views, domains, etc., that are in some way related to each other. All the objects in a database are described in one schema or another. You can think of a schema as being a collection of objects, all of which are owned by the same person (where person is a loose concept, and not necessarily a human being). The relationship between all the objects manifests itself in the naming of the objects, all of which have the same prefix to their name. Thus the ownership of an object is clearly seen.

2.5.3 Catalog

A catalog in SQL is a named collection of schemata in an environment. All of the schemata in a catalog have the catalog name as a prefix to their names. The grouping of schemata may be done for several reasons, for example, the schemata may be grouped for purely administrative purposes or on the basis of physical placement, and the schemata at each node in the network may be grouped into one catalog. The schemata in a single catalog describe the smallest unit that can be called a database. The meta-data of a schema that describes a portion of a database may itself be considered as data. SQL adopts this approach and each catalog always contains a special schema, INFORMATION_SCHEMA, which describes the meta-data of all the schemata in the catalog. The catalog is thus a kind of database within a database. In some senses the catalog can be compared to a data dictionary system or an information resource dictionary system, although these systems will normally possess more information than is held in the catalog.

One could visualize the catalog database as:

Catalog data definition
Catalog database data

However, since the catalog database data defines the schemata, which in turn describe the application data we could draw the following picture:

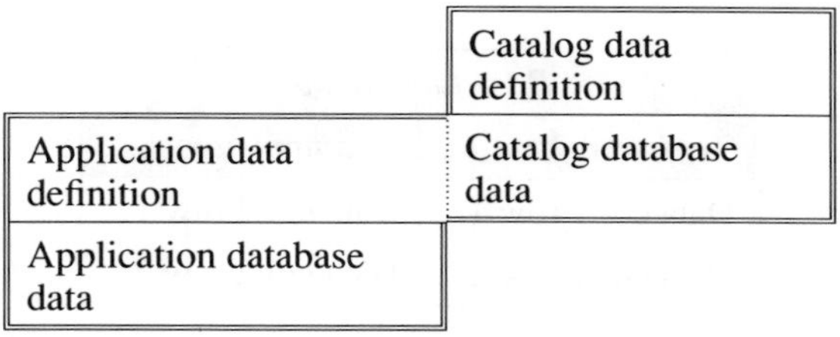

Catalog data definition

Application data definition | Catalog database data

Application database data

The individual pairs of each database are interlocked, since the definition of the database structure of an individual (application) database can be found as an application description in the catalog database data. The catalog database is controlling the application database. We have two interlocking pairs offering in total three levels of data: application data, dictionary or catalog data and catalog definition data. The functionality of an application database is determined by the application database structure as defined in the catalog in the next level up. The functionality of the catalog is determined by the catalog database structure as defined yet another level up. This could continue for a further one or two additional levels, as the Reference Model for Data Management (ISO, 1992b) specifies. This concept of interlocking pairs is one of the cornerstones of the emerging ISO standards on the Information Resource Dictionary System (IRDS) and the Reference Model for Data Management. Since the development of standards does not take place completely in sync there are a few differences between the SQL model and those in the other standards. For the purpose of this book these differences are irrelevant.

2.6 Database Manipulation

The other important part of the SQL language contains the data manipulation language (DML). This is the language that is used to instruct the DBMS on how to manipulate the actual data stored, according to the definitions, in the database. Using this language data may be inserted, deleted, updated or retrieved in various ways.

2.7 Conventions Used

Throughout this book, for the definition of SQL statements, we have made use of basically the same syntax conventions as those to be found in the standard. These are a modified form of **BNF** (Backus Naur Form or Backus Normal Form) (*see Appendix C BNF Syntax Diagrams*).

For the presentation of the contents of tables we have a diagrammatic form that indicates the type of table. The three types are shown in Figure 2.3,

Figure 2.4 and Figure 2.5. For **data structure diagrams**, etc. we have used the conventions shown in Figure 2.6 to show entities and relationships.

Base table name	
column name 1	*column name 2*
Data col 1 row 1	Data col 2 row 1
Data col 1 row 2	Data col 2 row 2

Figure 2.3 *Diagrammatic convention — base tables*

View/derived table name	
column name 1	*column name 2*
Data col 1 row 1	Data col 2 row 1
Data col 1 row 2	Data col 2 row 2

Figure 2.4 *Diagrammatic convention — derived tables*

Cursor name

column name 1	*column name 2*
Data col 1 row 1	Data col 2 row 1
Data col 1 row 2	Data col 2 row 2

Figure 2.5 *Diagrammatic convention — cursors*

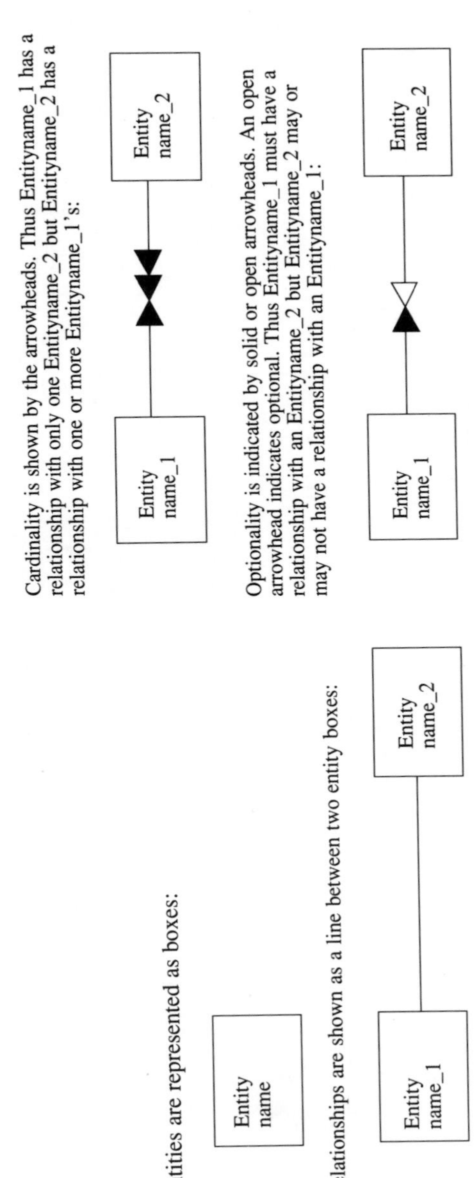

Entities are represented as boxes:
Entity name
Relationships are shown as a line between two entity boxes:
Entity name_1
Entity name_2
Cardinality is shown by the arrowheads. Thus Entityname_1 has a relationship with only one Entityname_2 but Entityname_2 has a relationship with one or more Entityname_1's:
Entity name_1
Entity name_2
Optionality is indicated by solid or open arrowheads. An open arrowhead indicates optional. Thus Entityname_1 must have a relationship with an Entityname_2 but Entityname_2 may or may not have a relationship with an Entityname_1:
Entity name_1
Entity name_2

***Figure 2.6** Data structure diagram conventions*

Part II
The SQL Language

3

Basic Language Elements

This chapter defines a number of basic language elements which are used extensively in the subsequent chapters. These are the valid characters, the tokens, identifiers, data types and literals.

3.1 Characters

The simplest and most basic language element is the character. Every SQL implementation has one character set called SQL_TEXT which defines all the characters that may be used in that implementation. The Information Schema contains the definition of this character set. The SQL standard defines a set of characters that must be present in the SQL_TEXT of all conforming implementations. Basically, this minimum set is those characters that are required to write all of the commands of the language.

The basic set consists of all the simple Latin upper-case letters, A, B, C, ..., Z, all the corresponding simple Latin lower-case letters, a, b, c, ..., z, the digits 0, 1, 2, ..., 9, and a number of special characters.

These special characters are:

. ; ( ) , : % _ ? ' " + – * / < > = & |

and in addition the 'space' character. These are later referred to as the BASIC SQL set as it is a defined set of characters in the SQL language, even if the implementation does not provide it as an explicit character set for the user.

3.2 Tokens

Tokens are the lexical units of the language. These lexical units are the next level up from the character level in the language and provide the building blocks for the syntax described in the later chapters. The tokens allow the implementation to decide how the string of characters that constitutes a statement is to be broken up. There are two kinds: delimiter tokens and non-delimiter tokens. In addition to tokens there are separators. A delimiter token may be followed by any number of separators, another delimiter token or a non-delimiter token. A non-delimiter token must be followed by any number of separators or a delimiter token. If the syntax does not allow for a non-delimiter token to be followed by a delimiter token then it must be followed by at least one separator.

A separator consists of a space character, a new line indication or a comment. The new line indication is implementation defined and a comment consists of any sequence of two or more consecutive hyphens (minus signs) followed by any number of characters terminating with the first new line indication. As far as the rest of the language is concerned every comment and every new line (not part of a comment) is treated as if it was a single new line indication.

A delimiter token is one of the following:

. ; ( ) , : % _ ? ’ " + – * / < > = & | <> >= <= || [ ]

or one of:

a delimited identifier
a character string literal

The first is discussed in *Section 3.3 Identifiers* and the second in *Section 3.5 Literals*.

A non-delimiter token is one of the following:

a regular identifier
a key word
an unsigned numeric literal
a date string
a time string
a timestamp string
an interval string
a national character string literal
a bit string literal
a hex string literal

The first is discussed in *Section 3.3 Identifiers*, the list of key words can be found in *Appendix D Key Words* and the remainder are discussed in *Section 3.5*

Literals. We should make the point that although the key words are always written in this book in upper-case, e.g. TABLE, the lower-case version, e.g. table, would also be accepted as a key word. Most key words are also reserved words, i.e. they may not be used as identifiers by a user. The exceptions are the single letter key word, C, and some others which, when used, cannot be confused with identifiers.

3.3 Identifiers

An identifier is a name or part of a name. These names serve to identify the various objects in an SQL database, e.g. the tables, columns and views. There are many kinds of name in SQL but they are all made up of one or more identifiers linked together with periods. Each identifier has the following basic structure:

[_<character set name>] <actual identifier>

The <character set name> is used to select an alternative character set from which the characters of the <actual identifier> are taken. If the <character set name> is specified then all the characters in the <actual identifier> must come from the named character set. Otherwise the characters must come from the BASIC SQL set of characters, excluding the special characters (*see Section 3.1 Characters*), or from the character set identified by the module or schema that contains the identifier. This means that, where the implementation supports several character sets, you have access to two sets without having to specify them explicitly and additional sets if you use the " _<character set name> " prefix to the identifier.

An <actual identifier> can be either a regular identifier or a delimited identifier. A regular identifier consists of a string of 128 or fewer characters from the specified set where each character represents either a letter, a digit (except as the first character), an underscore (also except as the first character), a syllable or an ideograph (i.e. it is not a space or other punctuation character). Every lower-case letter in a regular identifier is treated as though it were replaced by the equivalent upper-case letter; this upper casing goes further than the UPPER function in that it replaces *all* lower-case letters from whatever alphabet and not just the simple Latin letters. No (converted) regular identifier may **compare equal** to a reserved word (*see Section D.1 Reserved Words*). A delimited identifier consists of any string of 128 or fewer characters taken from the complete character set, excluding the " character, but surrounded by a pair of " characters. Within the string a " can be represented by a pair of characters, i.e. "". Thus if we are writing identifiers in a module that has the Russian alphabet defined as its default character set the following would be valid identifiers (assuming that the implementation supports Russian, Greek and the BASIC SQL set only):

```
Gerard
MIЯ
_Russian Поездка
_Greek Ξενοδοχείο
"TABLE"
C
"Stephen"
"A delimited identifier including a single "" symbol"
"% _ ."
An_extremely_long_identifier_which_is_much_longer_than_
any_reasonable_person_is_ever_likely_to_specify_as_it_is_
exactly_128_long
```

whereas the following are not:

`My_Επάγγελμα`
not characters from either of the two sets and not prefixed with the character set name

`אשכוליות`
not characters from any valid character set

`World_MIЯ`
characters from more than one valid character set (i.e. not wholly in one set)

`_Hebrew קיבוצים`
invalid character set name

`"MIЯ"`
delimited identifier with characters not from the BASIC SQL set

`9teen`
identifiers may not start with a digit

`_Malayalam`
identifiers may not start with an underscore as it could be confused with the prefix

`"Jim"s"`
delimited identifier may not contain a " character

```
abcdefghijabcdefghijabcdefghijabcdefghijabcdefghijabcdefghij
abcdefghijabcdefghijabcdefghijabcdefghijabcdefghijabcdefghij
123456789
```
identifier longer than 128 characters

`TABLE`
identifier may not be a reserved word

The reason for delimited identifiers, such as "TABLE", is that the equivalent regular identifier, TABLE, would be treated as a reserved word and not as an identifier.

Two identifiers are equal if, when treated as character strings (without the "'s if one or both is a delimited identifier) the comparison predicate would report them as equal. Thus Fred is the same as FRED (regular identifiers are always upper-cased) and also "FRED", but "FRED" is only equal to "Fred" in the unlikely event that the implementation defined collating sequence for the SQL_TEXT character set ignores case. However, a smart collating sequence might equate "Strasse" and "Straße".

3.4 Names

The purpose of a name is to provide a 'handle' for the various concepts and constructs in the SQL world. The following is a list of the various kinds of names found in SQL:

(a) Unqualified names
- catalog name
- authorization identifier
- correlation name
- module name
- procedure name
- parameter name
- cursor name
- dynamic cursor name
- SQL statement identifier

(b) Names qualified by catalog name
- schema name

(c) Names qualified by schema name
- domain name
- table name
- column name
- constraint name
- character set name
- collation name
- translation name
- conversion name

Qualification means preceding it with the qualifier and a period. For example an unqualified schema name might be:

```
Company
```

but the qualified name (assuming the default catalog name of `CATALOG`) would be:

```
CATALOG.Company
```

Similarly the table name of the Dept table might be any of:

```
Dept
Company.Dept
CATALOG.Company.Dept
```

This gives the so-called three-level naming. In most cases the qualifiers are simply defaulted in a consistent manner but may always be specified if desired. The default schema name for an unqualified name is determined as follows. If the name is contained within a schema definition the name of the schema is used and if it is in an SQL command being executed either directly or dynamically the session defaults are used (*see Chapter 13 Environment Management*), otherwise the default schema name associated with the module is used. The default catalog name for an unqualified schema name is determined as follows. If it occurs in a module header it is implementation defined, if it occurs in a schema definition but not in the part that names the schema the explicit or implicit catalog part of the schema name is used and if it is in an SQL command being executed dynamically then the session defaults are used (*see Chapter 13 Environment Management*); otherwise the default catalog name associated with the module is used.

The few oddities with names are:

- A table name, instead of being qualified with a schema name, may be qualified with the word `MODULE`, in which case it identifies a declared temporary table.
- An SQL statement identifier and a dynamic cursor name, as well as being identifiers, may be an extended name which is a parameter or a host language variable containing a character string which has the format of an identifier. If the program has not provided a valid string then an error is raised. In addition, an extended name may have a scope declaration of GLOBAL or LOCAL. A LOCAL scope is the **module** in which the extended name is defined and a GLOBAL scope is all modules being used in an SQL **session**. The default is LOCAL. Descriptor names are also extended names with the scope options but have no identifier alternative.
- A character set name may consist only of simple Latin letters, digits and underscores.
- The actual permitted values of an authorization identifier are dependent on the implementation environment since user authentication is not part of SQL.
- Character set names, collation names, conversion names and translation names that are not qualified with a schema name are assumed to have a schema qualifier of `INFORMATION_SCHEMA`. This means that all user-defined **character sets**, **translations** and **collations** must always be referenced by a qualified name (conversions cannot be user defined).

This ensures that a new standard or implementation defined name cannot override a previously defined user name. Incidentally, all these standard and implementation defined objects in INFORMATION_SCHEMA have privileges granted to PUBLIC with the grant option, so they may be freely used; any objects built using them can be passed on to others (*see Chapter 8 Access Control*).

3.5 Literals

Literals are means of specifying constant values or constants in the SQL language. They can be used to provide values for input to the database, to compare to other values in the database, etc. There are different forms of literal available for every data type supported by SQL, to enable such constants to be expressed. Each literal has the normal characteristics of the data type with which it is associated. The specific forms are described together with the characteristics of the data types themselves (*see Section 3.7 Data Types*).

3.6 Values and Targets

A value in SQL is used in many places: it can be used to supply a value to a column in the database, to compare to the value of a column in the database, to position a cursor, etc. A value can be a literal (*see Section 3.5 Literals*), a parameter specification, a dynamic specification (*see Section 18.3 EXECUTE IMMEDIATE*), a host language variable specification or one of the system supplied values USER, CURRENT_USER, SESSION_USER or SYSTEM_USER. For the other special value *see Section 4.3.3 Domain Constraints*. In the BNF a value is normally derived from the production <value specification>.

A parameter specification takes the form:

<parameter name> [[INDICATOR] <parameter name>]

and a host language variable specification takes the form:

<embedded variable name> [[INDICATOR] <embedded variable name>]

In both cases the second <parameter name> or <embedded variable name> which follows the key word INDICATOR if provided must have a data type of exact numeric with a scale of zero (i.e. effectively an integer) and is used to provide a NULL status. Any negative value in this parameter or host language variable indicates that the value in the first parameter (host language variable) is to be ignored and the NULL states used instead. A positive or zero value indicates that the value of the first parameter (host language variable) is to be used. These are called the indicator parameters or indicator variables.

The special system supplied values USER and CURRENT_USER provide the value of the current authorization identifier, that is either the explicit module authorization identifier if the current module has one or the current session authorization identifier. SESSION_USER provides the current authorization identifier for the session irrespective of any explicit module authorization and

SYSTEM_USER provides the value of the operating system's identification of the user who is operating the session regardless of whether the user has assumed another identity within the session or is in a module with an explicit authorization identifier. Both values are either fixed or varying character strings of implementation defined length. In the BNF <unsigned value specification> is sometimes used if the value may not be signed; otherwise it is identical to <value specification>.

A target in SQL is used to receive data from some source, either the database or some other SQL construct such as a descriptor area (*see Section 18.6 DESCRIBE*) or the diagnostics area (*see Chapter 15 Error Handling and Diagnostics*). A target can be a parameter specification or a host language variable specification and have the same format as shown above. The indicator variable or parameter is also used in a target situation to provide an indication of actual length of a truncated string (*see Section 6.5.1 Retrieval Assignment*). In the BNF <simple value specification> and <simple target specification> are used if the value or target may not be NULL. This is the case, for example, in cursor positioning or in the get diagnostics statement. In these cases the second name and the key word INDICATOR must be omitted.

3.7 Data Types

In this section we will look in some detail at all of the SQL data types that are available and explain their characteristics and differences and the ways of specifying constants or literals in those data types. There are six SQL data types and these are:

character
bit
exact numeric
approximate numeric
datetime
interval

Sometimes for manipulation and conversion purposes the data types 'character' and 'bit' are collectively referred to as 'string' data types and 'exact numeric' and 'approximate numeric' are referred to as 'numeric' data types since they share similar properties.

3.7.1 The Character Data Type

The character data type is used for defining character strings. A character string is a sequence of characters each of which is drawn from a defined set of characters. This set of characters is called a character repertoire and an implementation may support several different repertoires. Each character repertoire has a name. An implementation may support, for example, three repertoires, the 'BASIC' SQL character repertoire, a repertoire that supports all the languages of the European Community and a repertoire that supports the Japanese Kanji set of characters. Because there are widely different numbers of characters in each repertoire it may not be efficient to use the same encoding mechanism for each repertoire and if the implementation knows the appropriate repertoire of a character set it may optimize its storage. These various encodings are called forms-of-use. A character set is a named combination of a repertoire and a form-of-use. Within each character set there may be a number of collating sequences. There are, for example, several ways of sorting Japanese characters and within Europe each language is different with regard to the correct ordering of words. Each character set has a default collating sequence.

We may define a character string as being of fixed or of varying length. Every character string has a length that is the number of characters in the string. If the character string is of fixed length then it is that length; if the character string is of varying length then it can be either zero or any positive number up to a defined maximum. The maximal maximum length is an implementation defined limit.[1] The length is a logical length and independent of an encoding mechanism. Functions are provided to determine the physical characteristics of all strings (including the bit string), but these physical characteristics play no role in the specification of the strings.

The syntax for specifying character data types is as follows:

```
CHARACTER [ VARYING ] [ ( <length> ) ]
    [ CHARACTER SET <character set name> ]
```

The length must be specified for a varying character string but is optional for a fixed length character string, in which case it defaults to (1). The " CHARACTER SET " specification is optional and if omitted it defaults to the one explicitly or implicitly specified for the schema if used in a column or domain definition and in other cases to an implementation defined one. Thus we may define character data types such as:

`CHARACTER`
a single character from the schema's default set

`CHARACTER VARYING (200)`
a varying length character string with a maximum length of 200 characters, again taken from the schema's default set

`CHARACTER (40) CHARACTER SET Kanji`
a fixed length character string, of length 40, with characters taken from the 'Kanji' set

`CHARACTER VARYING (1000) CHARACTER SET Latin_1`
a varying length character string with a maximum length of 1000 characters, taken from the Latin_1 character set

---

1. Although the standard does not define any minimal maximum lengths, groups such as 'the SQL Access group' which is made up of several implementors of SQL systems, have agreed a definition of such minima. Anyone intending to write portable programs would be well advised to check these beforehand.

Some shorthand ways of writing the specifications are provided in the standard:

CHAR (x)	≡	CHARACTER (x)
VARCHAR (x)	≡	CHARACTER VARYING (x)
NATIONAL CHARACTER (x)	≡	CHARACTER (x) CHARACTER SET r where r is an implementation defined character set name
NCHAR (x)	≡	NATIONAL CHARACTER (x)

NATIONAL CHARACTER is provided as a shorthand to conform to previous Japanese SQL standards in an upwardly compatible manner.

3.7.2 Character Literals

The character literal is used to represent character strings. A character string is a sequence of characters, each of which is drawn from a defined set of characters. Each character literal has the following basic structure:

```
[ _<character set name> ] ' [ <character>... ] '
    [ { <separator>... ' [ <character>... ] ' }... ]
```

An optional character set name prefix, as in identifiers, is followed by a string of characters enclosed in quotes. The literal may be very long and impossible to fit on one line. In these cases it may be split into separate strings enclosed in quotes with separators (spaces, comments and new lines) between them. At least one separator must be a new line. Note that the character set name is not repeated and effectively any ' `<separator>...` ' constructions are deleted before interpreting the literal.

As in identifiers, the character set name is used to select an alternative character set from which the characters of the string are taken. If the character set name is specified then all the characters in the actual literal must come from the named character set. Otherwise the characters must come from the BASIC SQL set of characters or from the character set identified by the module or schema which contains the literal. One additional rule is that each quote character is represented within the string by two quote characters, e.g. ''. This does not change the length of the string but disambiguates the quote as character from the quote as string terminator. The length of the string is the number of characters in the string. For details of variations on length *see Section 11.2.2 String Functions.*

Examples of character literals (assuming again that Russian is the default character set):

```
'Otten'
'Яблоко от яблони нецалеко пацает'
_Greek 'Αυτή είναι η τράπεζα του και ο αριθμός λογαριασμού μου'
'"TABLE"'
'''Cannan'''
_Hebrew 'התפוח אינו נופל רחוק מן העץ'
'+44(Ø)71-549-9925'
'A fairly long literal string which it' -- Comment here
   ' might have been inconvenient to have had to place'
   ' on one line which is better written on'
   ' several lines. This also allows for'
   ' comments to be placed at the start of the literal.'
```

There is one special case where instead of using a normal character set name the prefix 'N' is used as a shorthand to indicate the use of an implementation defined 'national character set'. For example if the implementation defined national character set just happened to be Greek then the following two literals are identical:

```
N'Πού μπορώ να ενοικιάσω ένα αυτοκίνητο;'
_Greek 'Πού μπορώ να ενοικιάσω ένα αυτοκίνητο;'
```

3.7.3 The Bit Data Type

The bit data type is used to define bit strings. A bit string is a sequence of binary digits (bits), each having either the value 0 or the value 1.

The bit data type is intended to allow for data whose structure is unknown or is not supported by SQL to be stored in SQL tables. The advantage of using 'bit' over 'character' is that with character there is always the possibility that the data will be converted from one character set to another (and thus corrupted) during operations or exchange of data between two heterogeneous database management systems. With bit data types this will not happen because both database management systems will know that the data are to be treated simply as a string of bits and will not try to attribute meaning to them. Furthermore, the length of a character is dependent on the implementation (always greater than the length of a bit) and this will frequently lead to surplus and unwanted bits being added to the end of the string as well as making programs non-portable.

We may define a bit string as being of fixed or of varying length. Every bit string has a length which is the number of bits in the string. If the bit string is of fixed length then it is that length; if the bit string is of varying length then it can be either zero or any positive number up to a defined maximum. The maximal maximum length is an implementation defined limit.

The syntax is similar to that of the character data type, e.g.

BIT [VARYING] [(<length>)]

so, for example, we may define data types such as:

```
BIT
BIT (10)
BIT VARYING (30000)
```

The <length> must be specified for a varying bit string but is optional for a fixed length bit string, in which case it defaults to (1).

3.7.4 Bit String Literals

The bit string literal is used to represent bit strings, a sequence of binary digits (bits), each having either the value 0 or the value 1. Bit string literals take one of two forms, similar to the national character set form. These are:

B' [<bit>...] ' [{ <separator>... ' [<bit>...] ' }...]
X' [<hexdigit>...] ' [{ <separator>... ' [<hexdigit>...] ' }...]

where <bit> is 0 or 1 and <hexdigit> is one of 0, 1, 2, 3, 4, 5, 6, 7, 8, 9, A, B, C, D, E, F, a, b, c, d, e or f. The lower-case letters are treated as identical to the upper-case letters. Each <hexdigit> is interpreted as a quartet of bits. Thus 0 ≡ 0000, 1 ≡ 0001, 2 ≡ 0010, 3 ≡ 0011, 4 ≡ 0100, 5 ≡ 0101, 6 ≡ 0110, 7 ≡ 0111, 8 ≡ 1000, 9 ≡ 1001, A ≡ 1010, B ≡ 1011, C ≡ 1100, D ≡ 1101, E ≡ 1110, F ≡ 1111. The length of the string is the number of bits in the string (*see Section 11.2.2 String Functions*).

Examples of bit string literals:

```
B'001001101'
X'c4'
X'1FFE'
B'0101010101010101010'          -- a bit string literal
    '11111010101001100l'        -- spread over two lines
```

3.7.5 The Exact Numeric Data Type

The exact numeric data type is used to define numbers that have an exact representation. Examples are the integers or currency values (such as $ and ¢ or £ and p).

Every exact numeric data type has a precision and a scale, although this is sometimes implementation defined. The precision is a positive integer which defines the maximum number of significant digits in a particular radix (binary or decimal) which are to be kept regardless of sign. Scale is a non-negative integer. If the scale is n and the integer value of the digits of the value is i then $i*10^n$ is the exact numeric value. There are several ways of specifying exact numeric data types. These are:

<exact numeric type> ::=
NUMERIC [(<precision> [, <scale>])]
DECIMAL [(<precision> [, <scale>])]
INTEGER
SMALLINT

The radix is always decimal for NUMERIC and DECIMAL. For NUMERIC the implementation must provide exactly the precision requested but for DECIMAL it may provide a precision that is greater than or equal to the requested precision. For INTEGER and SMALLINT it may be either binary or decimal at the implementation's choice but must be the same for both. The reason for allowing a binary radix is that the implementation may not provide a precision greater than that requested, and since many computers use binary storage representation addition checking would be required at every storage operation to check that no logical overflow (more than the permitted number of significant digits) had occurred. This checking is frequently not required and in those cases where it is it may be done with a check constraint.

The default scale is always zero and the default precision is always implementation defined. The precision of SMALLINT and INTEGER is always implementation defined but the precision for SMALLINT may not be greater than that for INTEGER, though it may be the same. The scale of these two data types is by definition always zero.

Two shorthand ways of writing the specification are provided:

INT	≡	INTEGER
DEC (p,s)	≡	DECIMAL (p,s)

Examples of exact numeric data types are:

```
INTEGER
DECIMAL (6,2)
NUMERIC (5)
SMALLINT
NUMERIC (5,2)
DECIMAL (11)
```

3.7.6 Exact Numeric Literals

The exact numeric literal is used to represent numbers that have an exact representation, such as integers or currency values (e.g. $ and ¢ or £ and p). Exact numeric literals may be signed or unsigned. A signed exact numeric literal is simply an unsigned literal preceded by a plus sign or a minus sign.

An exact numeric literal is simply a decimal number with or without a decimal point. Standard SQL does not support the decimal comma notation as in 100,00 or editing separators between the digits as in 100,000.00 as these would lead to ambiguities in the rest of the language. Many implementations do, however, support these concepts but impose additional rules on the syntax of the language over and above the rules of SQL itself.

The following are valid exact numeric literals:

```
12
06
100.3
.003
7.
005.
+0.7
4.300
-.2
-200.75
```

3.7.7 The Approximate Numeric Data Type

The approximate numeric data type is used for defining numbers that do not always have an exact representation, such as real numbers. Every approximate numeric data type consists of a mantissa and an exponent. It has a precision for the mantissa which may be implementation defined and which specifies the number of significant digits in the binary radix that are to be kept in the mantissa. The exponent is a signed integer which gives the power of 10 by which the mantissa should be multiplied to obtain the value. If the exponent is e and the exact numeric value of the mantissa is m then the approximate numeric value is $m*10^e$.

There are several ways of specifying approximate numeric data types. These are:

<approximate numeric type> ::=
FLOAT [(<precision>)]
REAL
DOUBLE PRECISION

The <precision> controls the precision of the mantissa. The implementation may provide a precision greater than that requested, and the maximum supported precision is implementation defined. The precision of REAL and DOUBLE PRECISION is always implementation defined, but the precision for DOUBLE PRECISION must be greater than that for REAL.

The maximum and minimum permitted values of the exponent are always implementation defined and need not have the same absolute value, i.e. –127, +128 are acceptable limits. Examples of approximate numeric data types are:

```
DOUBLE PRECISION
FLOAT
FLOAT (24)
REAL
```

3.7.8 Approximate Numeric Literals

The approximate numeric literal is used to represent numbers that do not always have an exact representation, such as real numbers. Approximate numeric literals may be signed or unsigned. A signed approximate numeric literal is simply an unsigned literal preceded by a plus sign or a minus sign. An approximate numeric literal has the following format:

<mantissa>E<exponent>

where the <mantissa> is an exact numeric literal and the <exponent> is an exact numeric literal without a decimal point (i.e. an integer). This is the normal, so called, 'scientific' notation.

The following are valid approximate numeric literals:

```
10E3
+57.4E5
-.2E-9
-7E+16
```

3.7.9 The Datetime Data Type

The datetime data type is used to define points in time to a certain degree of accuracy. Examples are dates, times and times of day. Every datetime data type consists of a contiguous subset of the fields:

YEAR	The year in the Gregorian calendar including the century (e.g. 1991).
MONTH	The month within the year (e.g. 05, May).
DAY	The number of the day within the month (e.g. 16)
HOUR	The hour within the day, in the 24 hour clock (e.g. 22)
MINUTE	The minute within the hour (e.g. 07)
SECOND	The second and any fractions of a second within the minute (e.g. 47.9538)
TIMEZONE_HOUR	The hour part of the time zone offset from UTC (e.g. +07)
TIMEZONE_MINUTE	The minute part of the time zone offset from UTC (e.g. 30)

The above fields, from YEAR to SECOND, have a significant order and are listed in that order, i.e. YEAR is more significant than MONTH which in turn is more significant than DAY (*see Table 3.1*).

Three kinds of datetime data type are supported, namely:

DATE
TIME
TIMESTAMP

The precise syntax is:

```
<datetime type> ::=
      DATE
    | TIME [ ( <time precision> ) ] [ WITH TIME ZONE ]
    | TIMESTAMP [ ( <time precision> ) ] [ WITH TIME ZONE ]
```

Table 3.1 Datetime fields and their range of valid values

Field	*Valid values*
YEAR	0001 to 9999. This permits the specification of years prior to the invention of the Gregorian calendar and assumes that the rules of the Gregorian calendar can be applied retrospectively
MONTH	01 to 12
DAY	01 to 31, with the restriction that the combination of YEAR and MONTH may further restrict the maximum to 30, 29 or 28 according to the well-known rules of the Gregorian calendar
HOUR	00 to 23
MINUTE	00 to 59
SECOND	00 to 61.9(*n*), where *n* is restricted to the number of digits specified by the precision of the time. The normal range is 00 to 59.9 but the specified range allows for up to 2 leap seconds
TIMEZONE_HOUR	–12 to +13. The normal range is –11 to +12 but the extended range allows for political variations, such as daylight saving time in the time zones on either side of the international date line
TIMEZONE_MINUTE	00 to 59. (In combination with TIMEZONE_HOUR only values between –12:59 and +13:00 inclusive are allowed)

The DATE data type supports the fields YEAR, MONTH and DAY, the TIME data type supports the fields HOUR, MINUTE and SECOND and the TIMESTAMP data type supports all the fields from YEAR to SECOND. Thus DATE and TIMESTAMP represent unique points in time (with different degrees of accuracy) and TIME either represents a unique point in time (for which the date is implicit) or it represents a recurring point of time.

With both the TIME and the TIMESTAMP data types it is possible to specify a precision, i.e. the number of decimal places of accuracy to which th

SECOND field will be kept. If this is not specified TIME defaults to a precision of zero (i.e. whole seconds only) and TIMESTAMP defaults to six (i.e. microseconds). The maximum precision is implementation defined but must be the same for both TIME and TIMESTAMP and is naturally at least 6.

Both the TIME and the TIMESTAMP data types may have a WITH TIME ZONE option. If the option is not specified the values of the data type are assumed to be always in the current default time zone of the SQL_user session. If the option is specified then the values of the data type include the TIMEZONE_HOUR and TIMEZONE_MINUTE fields which specify the offset of the time zone of the rest of the value from Universal Coordinated Time (which used to be called Greenwich Mean Time). Thus the values 20:07:00–5:00 and 01:07:00+0:00 represent the same absolute time except that the first is stored as Eastern Standard Time (which is five hours behind Universal Coordinated Time) and the latter as Greenwich Mean Time. Note that to adjust a time to Universal Coordinated Time we need to subtract the time zone offset of the original time; thus in this example we subtract –05:00, i.e. add 5 hours, and obtain a time of 25:07:00 which is more correctly expressed as 01:07:00 but on the following day. For example we can define datetime data types such as the following:

`DATE`
a date (year, month and day)

`TIME (3) WITH TIME ZONE`
a time complete with time zone offset from Universal Coordinated Time (hour, minute, second and milliseconds, timezone-hour and timezone-minute)

`TIMESTAMP (6)`
a date and time (year, month, day, hour, minute, second and microseconds) which is always in the current session's time zone

`TIME`
a time (hour, minute and second) which is always in the current session's time zone.

There is a set of functions provided to return the current date and time to the required precision and a command to change the current default time zone.

3.7.10 Datetime Literals

The datetime literal is used to represent a defined point in time with a certain accuracy. Examples are dates, times and times of day. Datetime literals come in three kinds, again to match the equivalent data types. They take the forms:

DATE'<year>-<month>-<day>'
TIME'<hour>:<minute>:<second> [<time zone interval>]'
TIMESTAMP'<year>-<month>-<day> <hour>:<minute>:<second>
    [<time zone interval>]'

where <year>, <month>, <day>, <hour>, <minute>, <second> represent the component parts of time under the Gregorian calendar represented as two-digit integers, except for <year> and <second>. <year> must be a four-digit integer. <second> may include a fractional part (i.e. it has the format of an unsigned approximate numeric literal). The optional <time zone interval> specifies the time zone offset in hours and minutes within the range –11:59 to +12:00.

The following are valid datetime literals:

```
DATE'1900-01-01'
DATE'0001-01-01'
TIME'23:59:59.999999-05:00'
TIME'00:00:00'
TIME'12:00:00.000000001'
TIMESTAMP'1949-05-16 22:00:00+11:30'
TIMESTAMP'1957-07-23 05:00:15.'
```

The rules for date literals enforce the rules for Gregorian dates; the rules for time literals follow the 24 hour clock. The following are illegal literals:

```
DATE'1968-4-31'
DATE'92-01-31'
DATE'1988-004-13'
DATE'1967-02-29'
TIME'24:00:00'
TIME'17:00:00-13:00'
TIMESTAMP'03:0:00+12:30'
```

For more details of permissible values *see Section 3.7.9 The Datetime Data Type*.

3.7.11 The Interval Data Type

The interval data type is used to represent periods of time. If time is thought of as a line then an interval value represents a segment of that line whereas a datetime value represents a point (or points) on that line. Every interval data type consists of a contiguous subset of the fields:

YEAR	Years
MONTH	Months
DAY	Days
HOUR	Hours
MINUTE	Minutes
SECOND	Seconds and any fractions of a second

The fields have the same ordering as with datetime. There are two classes of interval data types, *year-month* intervals and *day-time* intervals. The *year-month* class may only contain the YEAR and/or the MONTH fields and the *day-time* class may only contain a contiguous selection from DAY, HOUR, MINUTE and SECOND. The reason for this is that when you start to do arithmetic with intervals and dates the results become indeterminate if the interval is specified as, for example, so many months plus so many days. The precise syntax for an interval data type is:

```
<interval type> ::= INTERVAL
    { { <start field> TO <end field> } | <single datetime field> }

<start field> ::= <non-second datetime field>
    [ ( <interval leading field precision> ) ]

<end field> ::=
      <non second datetime field>
    | SECOND [ ( <fractional seconds precision> ) ]

<single datetime field> ::=
      <non-second datetime field> [ ( <interval leading field precision> ) ]
    | SECOND [ ( <interval leading field precision>
        [ , <fractional seconds precision> ] ) ]

<non-second datetime field> ::= YEAR | MONTH | DAY | HOUR | MINUTE
```

In all cases the first field has an <interval leading field precision>, which defaults to 2 and may not exceed the implementation defined maximum precision for an interval leading field precision. Thus in the simplest cases we can specify interval data types such as:

`INTERVAL YEAR (4)`
an interval of years with a value between 0 and 9999

`INTERVAL DAY`
an interval of days with a value between 0 and 99 (the default precision is 2)

`INTERVAL SECOND (6,0)`
an interval of seconds with a value between 0 and 999999 (the precision of 2 and the fractional precision of 0 have been explicitly set, i.e. only whole seconds)

`INTERVAL SECOND`
an interval of seconds with a value between 0.000000 and 99.999999 (the default precision is 2 and the default fractional precision is 6)

More complicated interval data types can be defined:

`INTERVAL YEAR (2) TO MONTH`
an interval with a value between 0 years 0 months and 99 years 11 months

`INTERVAL DAY TO HOUR`
an interval with a value between 0 days 0 hours and 99 days 23 hours

```
INTERVAL HOUR TO SECOND (6)
```
an interval with a value between 0 hours 0 minutes 0 seconds and 99 hours 59 minutes 59.999999 seconds

In these two examples we see the use of the " TO <end field> " construction which allows the specification of a range of fields in the interval. Only in the case of SECONDS, as for datetime data types, can we also specify a precision. In the example above we have specified microseconds.

Table 3.2 Interval fields and their range of valid values

End field	*Valid values*
MONTH	1 to 11 (not 12 as 12 months = 1 year)
HOUR	0 to 23
MINUTE	0 to 59
SECOND	0 to 59.9(*n*), where *n* is restricted to the number of digits specified by the precision of the time

3.7.12 Interval Literals

The interval literal is used to represent a period of time. If time is thought of as a line then an interval value represents a segment of that line whereas a datetime value represents a point (or points) on that line. The format of an interval literal is:

INTERVAL [+ | -] '<value string>' <interval qualifier>

where the <interval qualifier> has the format:

<start field> [(<precision>)] [TO <end field>]

where

- <start field> and <end field> are one of " YEAR ", " MONTH ", " DAY ", " HOUR ", " MINUTE " or " SECOND [(<fractional precision>)] ".
- The <fractional precision> specification, e.g. SECOND(6), allows for the specification of the accuracy of the seconds field, in this example microseconds. However, if " SECOND " is also a <start field> the <fractional precision> and the <precision> are combined as in SECOND(4,6). The default <fractional precision>, if not specified, is 6.
- <precision> is the number of significant digits to be held for the first field. The default precision is 2.
- <end field>, if present, must be different from <start field> and must be to the right of the <start field> in the list of valid values. Also the sub-list from <start field> to <end field> inclusive must not contain both MONTH and DAY, as this might cause anomalies in arithmetic with the interval and datetime values.

- The <value string> is similar to a timestamp literal, except that only the parts relevant to the interval qualifier are present.

The attributes of the data type that the literal assumes are defined by the interval qualifier. The following are annotated examples of valid interval literals:

```
INTERVAL '1990' YEAR(4)
```
an interval of one thousand nine hundred and ninety years which is not a date but a period of time

```
INTERVAL -'1-1' YEAR TO MONTH
```
an interval of minus one year and one month

```
INTERVAL +'100 0:0:0.1' DAY(3) TO SECOND
```
an interval of 100 days and one-tenth of a second

```
INTERVAL '0:0:0.0' HOUR TO SECOND(9)
```
an interval of zero nanoseconds (but specified as having a data type of INTERVAL HOUR TO SECOND(9)

```
INTERVAL '100000.001' SECOND(6,3)
```
an interval of one hundred thousand seconds and one millisecond

```
INTERVAL -'10' MINUTE
```
an interval of minus ten minutes

```
INTERVAL '1:1' HOUR(6) TO MINUTE
```
an interval of 61 minutes

The following are annotated examples of invalid interval literals:

```
INTERVAL '1-0-0' YEAR TO DAY
```
range specified by start and end fields includes both MONTH and DAY

```
INTERVAL '1' DAY TO DAY
```
start and end fields the same

```
INTERVAL '1000' MINUTE
```
value greater than the precision (default 2)

```
INTERVAL '+100' DAY(3) TO SECOND
```
an incorrect number of sub-fields

For more details of permissible values *see Section 3.7.11 The Interval Data Type*.

4

Data Definition

The data definition commands of SQL permit the creation of schemata and all the objects that go to make up a schema, such as tables, views, domains, collations, etc. We will describe the data definition language (DDL) syntax using parts of the company database example in *Appendix A The Example Database*. At the end of this chapter, and for the rest of the book, we assume the example database to be completely defined and the structure description to be in place in the Information Schema. We will also assume that a quantity of data has been loaded into the database.

4.1 CREATE SCHEMA

A schema is a named collection of database objects. The name of the collection forms part of the name of all the included objects. All the objects in a schema have the same owner and share a number of defaults. The schema definition statement has the following syntax:

```
CREATE SCHEMA <schema authorization clause>
    [ <schema character set specification> ]
    [ <schema element>... ]
```

Of the three component parts of a schema definition statement only the first component is mandatory. It names the schema and both identifies the catalog in which it is to reside and the owner of the schema. The remaining components are all optional. The second component declares the default character set for columns and domains in the schema that do not explicitly define one. The third and last component consists of as few or as many CREATE statements for tables, views, domains, etc., as are required to define the schema. Initially a schema may be empty and commands, called schema manipulation commands, are provided to add, remove and alter the components of a schema.

4.1.1 Authorization

The <schema authorization clause> has the following syntax:

```
<schema authorization clause> ::=
    <schema name>
  | AUTHORIZATION <authorization identifier>
  | <schema name> AUTHORIZATION <authorization identifier>
```

<schema name> is itself a qualified name, with the catalog name being the qualifier. If the catalog name is omitted from the schema name then the default implementation defined catalog name is used. If the schema name is omitted it is assumed to be the same as the <authorization identifier> and if the authorization identifier is omitted it is assumed to be that of the executing user. Thus in its simplest form we can write:

```
CREATE SCHEMA cannan
```

which creates an empty schema that uses the default character set. The schema is called ' `cannan` '; it is owned by the user who issued the command and resides in the implementation defined catalog since the schema name is unqualified.

If we assume that the implementation defined catalog is called ' `CATALOG` ' and that the executing user is ' `cannan` ' then the following are all equivalent statements:

```
CREATE SCHEMA cannan
CREATE SCHEMA AUTHORIZATION cannan
CREATE SCHEMA cannan AUTHORIZATION cannan
CREATE SCHEMA CATALOG.cannan
CREATE SCHEMA AUTHORIZATION cannan
CREATE SCHEMA CATALOG.cannan AUTHORIZATION cannan
```

4.1.2 Schema Default Character Set

The <schema character set specification> clause takes the form:

```
DEFAULT CHARACTER SET <character set name>
```

where <character set name> is any of the implementor defined character sets or a user-defined character set.

The role of the schema character set specification is to provide a default character set for columns and domains in the schema that do not have one explicitly specified. If the clause is omitted then ' `DEFAULT CHARACTER SET imple-`

mentation_defined_character_set ' is assumed where ' implementation_defined_character_set ' is an implementation defined character set.

4.1.3 Schema Elements

The remaining clause is <schema element>. This clause defines a schema element. There can be as many of these clauses as required and they may be specified in any order. The objects which may be defined as schema elements are:

tables
domains
views
assertions
character sets
collations
translations
privileges

These are all the objects that can be defined in a schema and the syntax implies that the schema CREATE SCHEMA statement encompasses all the other definition statements. However, we will treat these separately in the following sections, and indeed there is no reason why one should not begin as we have with the creation of an empty schema and add to it piece by piece. The only disadvantage is that when adding objects one at a time the resulting schema after each addition must be complete and consistent whereas when it is all done in one statement (the CREATE SCHEMA) then only the final result of the schema definition needs to be consistent. This is due to the general principle that the database, including the Information Schema, must be consistent after the execution of every SQL statement. As we will see later, a user may temporarily disable some consistency checks within the scope of a transaction for his or her own data, but this is not permitted for the Information Schema.

Thus, for example, a more complete example of a schema definition might be:

```
CREATE SCHEMA example AUTHORIZATION cannan
   DEFAULT CHARACTER SET BASIC
```

which defines everything except any schema elements. The " DEFAULT CHARACTER SET " clause identifies the character set for the schema. ' BASIC ' is assumed to be a set which includes all of the characters that are needed to write standard SQL language, and in any case these characters must be included in the implementation default.

The individual schema elements are discussed in the following sections of this chapter except for the GRANT statement which defines **privileges** and which is discussed in a separate chapter (*see Chapter 8 Access Control*).

4.2 CREATE TABLE

The table definition statement or CREATE TABLE statement is used to define either created temporary tables or base tables. Created temporary tables are tables that have a permanent definition but no permanent contents while base tables are the heart of an SQL database and have not only a permanent definition but also permanent contents.

A table is an ordered collection of one or more columns, and a set of zero or more constraints. The syntax for CREATE TABLE is:

```
CREATE [ { GLOBAL | LOCAL } TEMPORARY ] TABLE <table name>
    ( <table element> [ { , <table element> }... ] )
    [ ON COMMIT { PRESERVE | DELETE } ROWS ]
```

where

```
<table element> ::= <column definition> | <table constraint definition>
```

The two optional clauses, " { GLOBAL | LOCAL } TEMPORARY " and " ON COMMIT { PRESERVE | DELETE } ROWS ", go together and the second cannot be specified unless the first is also specified. If neither " GLOBAL " nor " LOCAL " is specified then the table created is a base table; otherwise it is a temporary table. The two alternatives define the scope of the table. A GLOBAL temporary table has one copy for each application program and is available to every module in that program, whereas a LOCAL temporary table has one copy for every module of every program.

The " ON COMMIT " clause determines what happens to the rows of a temporary table when a transaction successfully terminates. " PRESERVE " indicates that the rows remain and " DELETE " indicates that the table is made empty after every transaction.

All tables are created empty. When a table is created a complete set of privilege descriptors is created for the owner of the table so that the owner may perform all possible data manipulations and use the table in all other permitted ways.

Although the remaining clauses, the <table element>s, are dealt with in the following sections, we will give an example of a complete table definition here. In our example database, the simplest entity is probably the `Dept` entity which represents the company's departments. This entity has two attributes, a name and a code. Thus in tabular form the department data might look like:

SLS	Sales
PER	Personnel
...	...
TRA	Travel

We define such a table as follows:

```
CREATE TABLE Dept
(
deptcd  CHARACTER (3),
deptnm  CHARACTER (12)
)
```

Here we can see that the table has been given a name, ' `Dept` ', and two columns called ' `deptcd` ' and ' `deptnm` ', which represent the attributes 'code' and 'name' respectively. The order of the columns does not matter in most cases and we have simply chosen, in this case, to place the smallest one first. The column order *is* important in some syntax constructions but we will cover that when it occurs.

Both columns have been given a character data type; 'deptcd' has been restricted to being exactly 3 characters long and 'deptnm' to exactly 12 characters long. Fixed length character columns are automatically padded with spaces or have trailing spaces truncated when required during storage, retrieval or comparison. Thus it does not matter that a department name may be shorter than 12 characters. We will discuss the details of column definitions and data types shortly. The owner of the table receives all possible **privileges** on the table. Our table then looks like that shown in Figure 4.1.

Dept	
code	*name*
SLS	Sales
PER	Personnel
...	...
TRA	Travel

Figure 4.1 *Dept table*

If we take one of the more complex entities, such as Employee, the data structure diagram of that part of the example is shown in Figure 4.2, and our description of the associated ' `Employee` ' table would look something like this:

```
CREATE TABLE Employee
(
empnr         NUMERIC (5),
name          CHARACTER (40) NOT NULL,
address       CHARACTER VARYING (200),
sex           CHARACTER NOT NULL,
home_telno    telno,
...
work_telno    telno UNIQUE,
salary        NUMERIC (6) NOT NULL,
```

```
commission   NUMERIC (6,2),
vehicleid    CHARACTER (7),
constituency CHARACTER (4),
CHECK (sex IN ('M','F')),
PRIMARY KEY (empnr),
CHECK ((vehicleid, empnr) MATCH
   (SELECT vehicleid, empnr FROM Vehicle)),
FOREIGN KEY (empnr) REFERENCES Emp_Ext,
FOREIGN KEY (deptcd) REFERENCES Dept,
FOREIGN KEY (constituency) REFERENCES Constituency
)
```

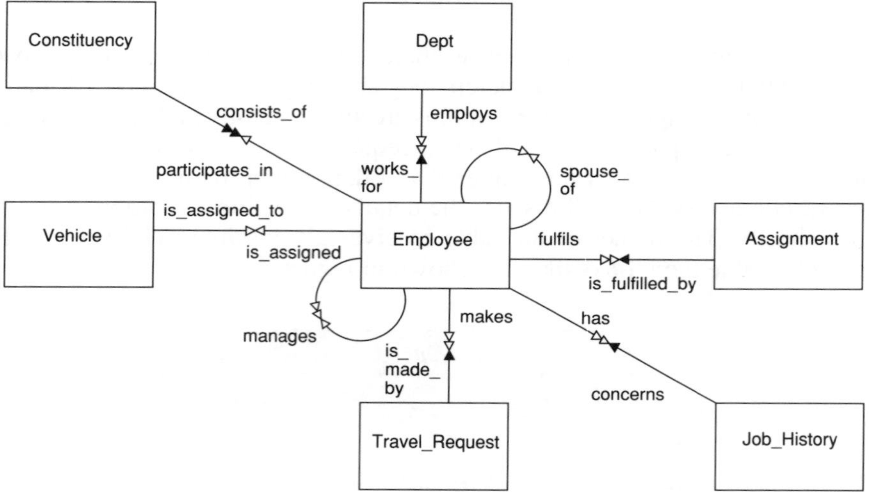

Figure 4.2 *Data structure diagram (Employee entity)*

and the database table would look like that shown in Figure 4.3.

This definition contains not only column definitions but also some necessary table constraints which will be discussed shortly (*see Section 4.2.1.2 Column Constraints and 4.2.2 Table Constraints*). Since we have chosen to split the Employee entity into two tables, Employee and Emp_Ext, not all of the attributes of the Employee entity are present in the table. On the other hand, in order to model the relationships properly it is necessary to include attributes taken from the related entities. The process of converting from a data structure diagram to a set of SQL tables is discussed in the third part of the book, 'Using the SQL Language' (*see specifically Chapters 21 Database and Application Analysis and 22 Integrity Control*). We can see from the above examples that the SQL basics for defining data are really very simple and straightforward. With these basics we can go on and build databases. The rest of the book will show how to make use of the tables defined in this way and explain how the more advanced features of SQL allow you to control and monitor your data to reflect the real world.

Employee										
empnr	*name*	*address*	*sex*	*home_ telno*	...	*work_ telno*	*salary*	*com- mis- sion*	*vehicle_id*	*consti- tuency*
12345	Patel	5 Lauder Road	F	+44(0)34-291-5644	...	+44(0)71-211-2012	25000	0	XW-99-TS	N/A
23456	Smith	12 Green-bank Avenue	M	+44(0)71-349-9906	...	+44(0)71-211-2047	12000	0	AA-51-KL	Grp 2
...	...	...	...	...	...	...	...	...	...	...
56789	Jones	71 High Street	M	+44(0)71-765-2132	...	+44(0)71-211-3014	9000	N/A	N/A	Grp 4

Figure 4.3 *Employee table*

4.2.1 Column Definition

The column definition clauses define the columns of a table, and in principle the order of the columns is that in which they are defined. The syntax of a column definition is:

```
<column name> { <data type> | <domain name> }
    [ <default clause> ]
    [ <column constraint definition>... ]
    [ <collate clause> ]
```

We will leave the full discussion of the <domain name> alternative to <data type> until we have discussed the definition of domains. Suffice it to say at this moment that <domain name> can be thought of as an indirect specification of <data type> and fall-back values for <default clause>, <column constraint definition> and <collate clause>. If the column definition contains a <default clause> and/or a <collate clause>, and a <domain name> was specified, then the definitions in the <column definition> override those of the domain definition. A <collate clause> can only be specified if the data type of the column has a character string data type.

4.2.1.1 Defaults

The default clause permits the specification of a value which will be used when a row is inserted into a table and no value is provided for the column. The syntax is:

```
DEFAULT {
      <literal>
    | <datetime value function>
    | USER
    | CURRENT_USER
    | SESSION_USER
    | SYSTEM_USER
    | NULL }
```

The NULL option is the default if no default clause is specified and a domain default is not applicable. The key word USER or CURRENT_USER indicates that the value of the current authorization identifier, i.e. either the explicit module authorization identifier if the current module has one or the current session authorization identifier, is to be used. SESSION_USER indicates that the current authorization identifier for the session irrespective of any explicit module authorization is to be used and SYSTEM_USER indicates that a string representing the identity of the user as known to the operating system is to be substituted; NULL indicates the NULL status. The datetime value functions cause the substitution of values from the system clocks (*see Section 11.2.1 Datetime Functions*) and literals specify constant values.

In all cases the data types of the values to be substituted must be such that they match the data type defined for the column and that the value can be represented in the column without loss of significance or precision. In the case of fixed length character or bit string literals the value may be extended as necessary on the right with spaces or 0 bits respectively. In the case of 0 bit padding a warning will be raised.

The interaction of column and domain defaults is given in Table 4.1.

Table 4.1 Effective default clause for a column

Column based on domain	*Domain default specified*	*Column default specified*	*Effective default*
Yes	Yes	Yes	Column Default
Yes	Yes	No	Domain Default
Yes	No	Yes	Column Default
Yes	No	No	Default Domain Default — NULL
No	No	Yes	Column Default
No	No	No	Default Column Default — NULL

4.2.1.2 Column Constraints

Column constraints are used to control the values that may be stored in a single column. The control may involve only the column that is to be controlled or a column that is the referenced column in a foreign key constraint. For controlling values in multiple columns a table constraint must be used.

There are four column constraints, namely:

not null constraint
unique constraint
foreign key constraint
check constraint

The full syntax is:

<column constraint> ::= [CONSTRAINT <constraint name>]
{ NOT NULL
| <unique specification>
| <references constraint>
| <check constraint definition> }
[<constraint attributes>]

<constraint attributes> ::=
[NOT] DEFERRABLE [INITIALLY IMMEDIATE | INITIALLY
DEFERRED]
| { INITIALLY IMMEDIATE | INITIALLY DEFERRED }
[[NOT] DEFERRABLE]

where the optional <constraint name> provides a unique identification for the constraint which can later be used to reference the constraint and which is available in the diagnostic information should violations of the constraint need to be reported. If the name is not specified then the constraint is given one by the database management system.

Unless otherwise specified, constraints are effectively checked after every SQL command has been executed; i.e. although the implementation will not actually check *every* constraint explicitly because it can determine which of the several constraints might be affected, it could do so if it wished and obtain the same result. A constraint may be defined as either INITIALLY IMMEDIATE, the default, or INITIALLY DEFERRED. This determines which mode the constraint assumes at the beginning of each **transaction**. The mode may or may not be subsequently changed by a <set constraints mode statement> depending on whether DEFERRABLE or NOT DEFERRABLE is specified. NOT DEFERRABLE is the default, except when INITIALLY DEFERRED is specified as these are naturally mutually exclusive.

4.2.1.2.1 NOT NULL

The not null constraint is specified by use of the key words NOT NULL appended to the column definition. An example of this can be seen in the Employee table columns: name, sex and salary

```
CREATE TABLE Employee
(
empnr          NUMERIC (5) CONSTRAINT Employee_PK PRIMARY KEY,
name           CHARACTER (40) NOT NULL,
address        CHARACTER VARYING (200),
sex            CHARACTER NOT NULL,
home_telno     telno,
work_telno     telno CONSTRAINT Emp_work_telno_U UNIQUE,
salary         NUMERIC (6) NOT NULL,
commission     NUMERIC (6,2),
)
```

NOT NULL means simply what it says, that the column must always have a valid value. In the Employee example this means that we cannot store an Employee row until we at least know the name, sex and salary of that employee, whereas other attributes such as address are not considered so important. The decision to define a column as NOT NULL or not will depend mainly on the logical characteristics of the data, but in some implementations additional storage space is needed to handle NULL and so performance trade-offs may lead to columns being defined as NOT NULL where allowing NULLs would have been the logical choice.

Specification of NOT NULL is equivalent to a table constraint in the form:

```
CHECK (col IS NOT NULL)
```

where 'col' is taken to be the column name of the column in which the NOT NULL appears. The appropriate NOT DEFERRABLE or DEFERRABLE option is also assumed.

4.2.1.2.2 UNIQUE

The unique constraint is specified by use of the key word UNIQUE or the key words PRIMARY KEY appended to the column definition. An example of this can be seen in the Employee table columns, empnr and work_telno, shown previously. The unique constraint controls the values in the column such that no two rows in the same table may have the same value. This does not prevent any number of rows having null status, as null is not a real value. PRIMARY KEY is actually a shorthand for NOT NULL UNIQUE. It may, however, only occur once in a table as a column or a table constraint. UNIQUE and the combination NOT NULL UNIQUE may be specified as many times as needed in any one table definition.

You will have noticed that unlike the NOT NULL constraints these two constraints have been given names in the example. Specification of UNIQUE is equivalent to a table constraint in the form:

```
UNIQUE (col)
```

and specification of PRIMARY KEY is equivalent to a table constraint in the form:

```
PRIMARY KEY (col)
```

where 'col' is taken to be the column name of the column in which the UNIQUE or PRIMARY KEY appears. In either case the appropriate NOT DEFERRABLE or DEFERRABLE option is also assumed.
For example:

```
deptcd        CHARACTER (3) PRIMARY KEY
```

is equivalent to:

```
deptcd        CHARACTER (3),
PRIMARY KEY (deptcd)
```

and

```
work_telno    telno UNIQUE,
```

is equivalent to:

```
work_telno    telno,
UNIQUE (work_telno)
```

4.2.1.2.3 REFERENCES

The references clause allows the logical connection of two tables through what is called a foreign key constraint. This is specified by the use of the key word REFERENCES appended to the column definition. The foreign key constraint means that every non-null value in the column must have an equivalent value in another column of some table, the referenced table, and that column in the referenced table must be the subject of a unique constraint. Thus there can only be a single associated row in the referenced table. If we add a column 'deptcd' to the Employee table previously shown, in order to maintain information about the department in which the employee works, then this would be a foreign key that references the Dept table. The Dept and Employee tables might now look like:

```
CREATE TABLE Dept
(
deptcd          CHARACTER (3) PRIMARY KEY,
deptnm          CHARACTER (12)
)

CREATE TABLE Employee
(
empnr           NUMERIC (5) PRIMARY KEY,
name            CHARACTER (40) NOT NULL,
address         CHARACTER VARYING (200),
sex             CHARACTER NOT NULL,
home_telno      telno,
deptcd          CHARACTER (3) REFERENCES Dept (deptcd),
work_telno      telno UNIQUE,
salary          NUMERIC (6) NOT NULL,
commission      NUMERIC (6,2),
)
```

The full format of the constraint is:

REFERENCES <table name> [(<reference column list>)]
  [MATCH { FULL | PARTIAL }]
  [<triggered action>]

The <reference column list>, in our example ' `(deptcd)` ', is optional but in that case the table referenced must have a PRIMARY KEY which is then assumed to be the target. Thus we could have written:

```
deptcd          CHARACTER (3) REFERENCES Dept
```

to obtain the same effect.

The MATCH option is discussed in *Section 4.2.2.2 References* and although it may be specified in a column constraint it is irrelevant due to there being only one column. The triggered actions are similarly discussed in *Section 4.2.2.2 References* and can be specified here without additional restriction.

Specification of foreign key constraint ' `REFERENCES ...` ' is equivalent to a table constraint of the form:

```
FOREIGN KEY (col) REFERENCES ...
```

where ‘col’ is taken to be the column name of the column in which the references constraint appears.

4.2.1.2.4 CHECK

The check constraint is specified by use of the key word CHECK appended to the column definition. An example of this can be seen in the Employee table column sex, as shown below:

```
CREATE TABLE Employee
(
empnr          NUMERIC (5) PRIMARY KEY,
name           CHARACTER (40) NOT NULL,
address        CHARACTER VARYING (200),
sex            CHARACTER NOT NULL CHECK (sex IN ('M','F')),
home_telno     telno,
deptcd         CHARACTER (3) REFERENCES Dept (deptcd),
work_telno     telno UNIQUE,
salary         NUMERIC (6) NOT NULL,
commission     NUMERIC (6,2),
)
```

The full syntax is:

CHECK (<search condition>)

and is equivalent to a table constraint with the same syntax, including the specification of deferrable or not. The only restriction on the <search condition> over and above those of the table constraint is that the only column that may be referenced is the column in whose definition it occurs.

4.2.1.3 Collation

The <collate clause> defines for a column with a character data type what the collating sequence is to be for comparisons of data in that column. This comparison can occur in predicates, character value expressions, group by clauses and order by clauses. The syntax is simply:

COLLATE <collation name>

where <collation name> identifies either an implementation defined collation definition or one defined using the CREATE COLLATION statement. If a collate clause is not specified for a column with a character data type then the default collating sequence for the data type is used.

4.2.2 Table Constraints

Whereas column constraints are restricted to checking the values of a column in isolation, table constraints may check the values of several columns together. As we have seen, all of the column constraints can be expressed as table constraints and thus the column constraints are merely an alternative syntax. The syntax of a table constraint is:

```
<table constraint definition> ::= [ CONSTRAINT <constraint name> ]
    { <unique constraint definition>
    | <referential constraint definition>
    | <check constraint definition> }
    [ <constraint attributes> ]
```

where the optional <constraint name> provides a unique identification for the constraint which can later be used to reference the constraint and which is available in the diagnostic information should violations of the constraint need to be reported.

Unless otherwise specified, constraints are effectively checked after every SQL command has been executed; i.e. although the implementation will not actually check *every* constraint explicitly because it can determine which of the several constraints might be affected, it could do so if it wished and obtain the same result. A table constraint may be defined with attributes and these have the same meaning and restrictions as the constraint attributes for column constraints.

Both the CHECK and the FOREIGN KEY constraints permit or possess references to tables other than the table in which they are defined. The restrictions are described in Table 4.2. Furthermore, if the referenced table is defined with ON COMMIT DELETE ROWS then the referencing table must also be defined with ON COMMIT DELETE ROWS.

Table 4.2 Permitted types of tables referenced in constraints

Type of table containing the constraint	*Types of tables which may be referenced*
Base	Base, view
Global temporary	Global temporary
Local temporary	Global temporary, local temporary
Declared local temporary	Global temporary, local temporary, declared local temporary

4.2.2.1 Unique

The syntax of the unique constraint is:

```
<unique constraint definition> ::=
    <unique specification> ( <column name> [ { , <column name> }... ] )

<unique specification> ::= UNIQUE | PRIMARY KEY
```

where the list of column names must identify columns of the table in which the constraint exists and may not be repeated. Furthermore, the same set of column names may not be specified in any other unique constraint for this table.

The unique constraint definition controls the values in the column such that no two rows in the same table may have the same value. The UNIQUE does not prevent any number of rows having null status, as null is not a real value. The exact check is specified using the unique predicate as follows:

```
CHECK (UNIQUE (SELECT unique_column_list FROM T))
```

where unique_column_list is the specified list of column names and T is the name of the table for which it is defined.

The PRIMARY KEY option may only be specified once for a table, either as a column constraint or as a table constraint, and it is identical in effect to a check constraint of the form:

```
CHECK (    UNIQUE (SELECT unique_column_list FROM T)
           AND
           (unique_column_list) IS NOT NULL)
```

For example:

```
UNIQUE (vehicle_id)
PRIMARY KEY (empnr)
```
both from the Employee table in the example database

```
UNIQUE (empnr, request_date)
```
from the Itinerary table

4.2.2.2 References

The referential constraint definition allows the creation of a foreign key relationship between two tables. The foreign key relationship means that every non-null value in a list of columns must have an equivalent value in another set of columns in the same or another table, and that set of columns in the other, referenced, table must be the subject of a unique constraint. Thus there can only be a single associated row in the referenced table. The requirement that there be a unique constraint means that the referenced table must also be a base table.

The syntax of the constraint definition is:

FOREIGN KEY (<referencing columns>)
  REFERENCES <referenced table and columns>
  [MATCH { FULL | PARTIAL }]
  [<referential triggered action>]

<referencing columns> ::= <column name> [{ , <column name> }...]

<referenced table and columns> ::= <table name> [(<referenced columns>)]

<referenced columns> <column name> [{ , <column name> }...]

<referential triggered action> ::=
    <update rule> [<delete rule>]
  | <delete rule> [<update rule>]

<update rule> ::= ON UPDATE <referential action>

<delete rule> ::= ON DELETE <referential action>

<referential action> ::=
{ CASCADE | SET NULL | SET DEFAULT | NO ACTION }

where the <table name> in <referenced tables and columns> must be any base table. The referenced columns must be the subject of a unique constraint which has an explicit or implicit NOT DEFERRABLE attribute. If <referenced columns> is omitted, the referenced table must have a primary key, whose columns are taken to be the referenced columns. Within each list of columns, the column names must be unique and the pairs of columns, from the referencing and the referenced lists, must have the same data types. Although foreign keys frequently have primary keys as their target, which are by their nature NOT NULL, when the target is not a primary key the only requirement is that the column or columns be defined as UNIQUE. Even the referenced columns may have NULL status but any that do can never be referenced by a referencing row.

A referential constraint is satisfied if the referencing columns in a row are all non-null and there is a row in the referenced table whose referenced columns contain the same non-null values. The MATCH options provide additional constraints. In the case of the MATCH FULL option, the columns in the referencing columns list must all be null or must all have values, and in the case of the MATCH PARTIAL option, if any columns are non-null, there must be at least one row in the referenced table that could satisfy the constraint if the other null values were correctly substituted.

The ON DELETE referential action works on each row of the referencing table, which had values that matched those in a row which was deleted from the referenced table, as follows:

CASCADE is specified	The matching rows are deleted.
SET NULL is specified	The referencing columns of the matching rows are set to the null status.
SET DEFAULT is specified	The referencing columns of the matching rows are set to the default value specified for each column.
NO ACTION	No special action is taken. This is the default if ON DELETE is not specified.

The ON UPDATE referential action works on each row of the referencing table, which had values that matched (the matching is done before the update) those of a row in the referenced table which was updated to a value **distinct** from the original value. It works as follows:

CASCADE is specified	The referencing columns of the matching rows, which correspond to updated referenced columns, are set to the same value as the corresponding referenced column.

SET NULL is specified	The referencing columns of the matching rows, which correspond to updated referenced columns, are set to the null status. If the MATCH FULL option was specified then all referencing columns are set to the null status in order to preserve the MATCH FULL constraint.
SET DEFAULT is specified	The referencing columns of the matching rows, which correspond to updated referenced columns, are set to the default value specified for each column.
NO ACTION	No special action is taken. This is the default if ON UPDATE is not specified.

In the case of the PARTIAL option for ON DELETE and ON UPDATE, only rows in the referencing table that match *only* the row being deleted or updated in the referenced table are affected by the triggered actions. This is because if there is more than one possible matching row in the referenced table we cannot be sure that the selected row is *the* row.

The triggered actions themselves cause either updates or deletions to take place and these may in turn cause the triggering of further referential triggered actions. Note that if a row to be updated or deleted has already been deleted or updated through a still open cursor then a warning is raised.

It is possible to conceive of cycles or networks of triggered actions that might result in conflicting or order-dependent actions to be performed on a single row as the result of some update or deletion. The database management system must check for this and will return an error if such conflicting changes occur. In order to minimize the possibility of interaction any cascaded deletes are deferred until the end of the statement so that any cascaded updates may pass through them to other tables.

A simple example of referential constraints and triggered actions is given in the following three table definitions. The middle table has referential constraints on both the other tables. The first is expressed without the explicit use of a referenced column list as the referenced columns are also the primary key. In the case of the second this is not so and a referenced column list is explicitly stated. In the first case triggered actions are defined with the effect that if an order is deleted then all associated order lines are also deleted, and if an order has its order number updated the order lines also have their order numbers updated accordingly. In the second case no actions are defined so no row in the Product table may be deleted, or have its product_code changed, if there are orders that reference it.

```
CREATE TABLE Order
(
ordernr       NUMERIC (5),
suppliernr    NUMERIC (5) NOT NULL,
date_issued   DATE NOT NULL,
PRIMARY KEY (ordernr)
)

CREATE TABLE Order_Line
(
ordernr       NUMERIC (5),
order_linenr  NUMERIC (5),
product_code  NUMERIC (5) NOT NULL,
quantity      NUMERIC (5) NOT NULL,
PRIMARY KEY (ordernr, order_linenr),
FOREIGN KEY (ordernr) REFERENCES Order
   ON DELETE CASCADE
   ON UPDATE CASCADE,
FOREIGN KEY (product_code) REFERENCES Product (product_code)
)

CREATE TABLE Product
(
product_code  NUMERIC (5) UNIQUE,
name          CHARACTER (20),
PRIMARY KEY (name)
)
```

4.2.2.3 Check

The check clause allows the specification of an arbitrary condition which must hold for the table. The syntax is simply:

CHECK (<search condition>)

with a few basic restrictions on the contents of the search condition. It must not contain anything that might vary over time or is undefined at certain points in time (e.g. USER, CURRENT_USER, SESSION_USER, SYSTEM_USER or any of the datetime functions such as CURRENT_DATE). This is necessary since otherwise a database that was perfectly correct could become incorrect without any changes having taken place. Furthermore, it must not contain a query that is possibly indeterminate. An indeterminate query can arise as a result of the way **compare equal** works on a character string, i.e. non-identical values may compare equal depending on, for example, the collation. Thus queries involving DISTINCT, GROUP BY, MIN, MAX, INTERSECT, EXCEPT or UNION (without the ALL option) on character columns are potentially indeterminate. The rules as specified in the standard are over broad in that they designate some deterministic situations as potentially indeterminate. The intent is clear but the execution is not; the standard itself contains (in its terms) potentially indeterminate queries in the constraints of the DEFINITION_SCHEMA. We must hope that the implementors, in this case, implement the intent and not the letter of the standard. There is a hierarchy of tables — base, global, local, declared local (*see Chapter 16 The Module Language*), and this first constraint means that the check clauses of a table may only reference tables of the same sort or higher, i.e. base tables may only reference base tables, global temporary tables may only reference base tables and global temporary tables. Secondly, set functions may only be contained in subqueries, i.e.

```
CHECK ((SELECT COUNT(*) FROM Order) < 100)
```

is valid, but

```
CHECK (COUNT(*) < 100)
```

is not, even if specified in the Order table.

A check constraint is satisfied if there is no row in the table for which the search condition is false. It does *not* have to be true for every row — it can very well be unknown — but the constraint is still satisfied. One interesting side effect of this is that if the table is empty a check constraint is always satisfied. Thus pure minimum cardinality constraints on the table, for example ' `CHECK ((SELECT COUNT(*) FROM DEPT) > 1)` ' must be specified as assertions. The reason for this is obvious when we consider that a check constraint, C, on a table, T, whose <search condition> is SC, is equivalent to an assertion of the form:

```
CREATE ASSERTION C
        CHECK (NOT EXISTS(SELECT * FROM T
        WHERE NOT (SC)))
```

For example there is a check clause in the Vehicle table definition:

```
CREATE TABLE Vehicle
(
vehicleid          NUMERIC (5),
empnr              NUMERIC (5),
acquisition_date   DATE NOT NULL,
PRIMARY KEY (vehicleid),
CHECK ((empnr, vehicleid) MATCH
   (SELECT empnr, vehicleid FROM Employee))
)
```

4.3 CREATE DOMAIN

A domain is a set of permissible values. Every value in a column must belong to a domain which may be specified in terms of a domain name or in terms of a simple data type specification, which is itself a kind of domain specification in that it limits the permissible values. The domain specification itself permits the definition of domains in terms of a data type together with, optionally, a number of domain constraints or CHECK clauses, a DEFAULT definition and a collating sequence. The advantage of a domain specification is that the same complex definition of data type, check clauses, etc., can be reused in many columns and those columns are then guaranteed to have the same definition. Also, if the check clauses or default clauses are altered then the new specifications automatically apply to all associated columns, which significantly reduces the cost of maintenance of these definitions.

The syntax of a domain definition is:

```
<domain definition> ::=
    CREATE DOMAIN <domain name> [AS] <data type>
        [ <default clause> ]
        [ <domain constraint>... ]
        [ <collate clause> ]

<domain constraint> ::=
    [ CONSTRAINT <constraint name> ]
    <check constraint definition>
    [ <constraint attributes> ]
```

A domain name, defined by a domain definition, can be used in column definitions in place of a data type. When this is done the column acquires the data type of the domain, together with a number of column constraints based on the domain constraints (with the appropriate substitution), and if the column does not have its own default and/or collate clauses these are also taken from the domain definition. A domain constraint may be defined with attributes, and these have the same meaning and restrictions as the constraint attributes for column constraints.

A USAGE privilege descriptor is created for the owner of the domain and this privilege is grantable if and only if the owner has a grantable REFERENCES privilege on every column referenced in any domain constraint and a grantable USAGE privilege on every collation, character set, domain and translation used in the domain definition. For example:

```
CREATE DOMAIN telno AS CHARACTER (14)
   CHECK (    VALUE LIKE '+%(_)%-%-%'
           OR VALUE LIKE '+%-%-%-%'
           OR VALUE LIKE '%-%'
           OR VALUE LIKE '___')

CREATE DOMAIN acquisition_date AS DATE DEFAULT CURRENT_DATE
```

4.3.1 Defaults

The default specification for a domain is identical to that for a column. Remember, however, that the domain default clause is overridden by a column default clause if one is specified.

4.3.2 Collation

The collate clause for a domain is identical to that for a column. Remember, however, that the domain collate clause is overridden by a column collate clause if one is specified.

4.3.3 Domain Constraints

A domain constraint is identical to a column check constraint except that the search condition may not contain any domain names whose definitions contain a reference to this domain, either directly or through references to other domains (i.e. no cyclic definitions), and can only reference base tables. The key word VALUE is used to represent the column name of whichever column uses the domain. The check is applied to each column defined in terms of the domain with the column name substituted for VALUE.

4.4 CREATE VIEW

The create view statement defines a table. The table defined is not a physical, base, table like those defined by create table but a derived table defined in terms of a query expression on one or more base tables or, recursively, on views. Unlike other derived tables, query expressions, query specifications, etc., a view is a permanent object and in addition to the permanent definition has an optional update control clause. It has **privileges** associated with it which can be granted to other people. This does not, however, mean that the data available through a view must be regarded as a separate permanent storage structure; in fact it is always generated from underlying permanent objects.

The syntax of the view definition is:

```
CREATE VIEW <table name> [ ( <view column list> ) ]
    AS <query expression>
    [ WITH [ LOCAL | CASCADED ] CHECK OPTION ]
```

where

```
<view column list> ::= <column name> [ { , <column name> }... ]
```

View definitions may not be self-recursive, i.e. the view name of the view being defined may not be used directly or indirectly in the definition. In other words, the view name being defined must not occur in the definition itself or in the definition of any component used in the definition.

The view column list is optional only if all the columns resulting from the query expression are explicitly named (i.e. none of them has an implementation supplied name) and these names are unique; otherwise the view column list must be specified and name every column in the query expression uniquely.

The WITH CHECK OPTION may only be specified if the view is updatable and a view is updatable only if the query expression is updatable. The owner of the view is granted select privileges on the table. If the view is updatable and the owner has insert, update, delete and references privileges on the table and/or columns from which the view and its columns are derived, then the owner is also granted the equivalent privileges on the view and its columns. These privileges are grantable if and only if the equivalent privileges are also grantable. Note that to acquire references privileges on a column requires references privileges on all tables and columns that are either used to provide the values for the column or are involved in some way in the selection. For example:

```
CREATE VIEW Hq_Tel_List (name, telno, staffnr)
   AS
   SELECT name, work_telno, empnr
     FROM Employee
     WHERE deptcd = 'HDQ'
```

results in the table shown in Figure 4.4.

Hq_Tel_List		
name	*telno*	*staffnr*
jones	+44(0)71-211-3014	30
smith	+44(0)71-211-2047	102

Figure 4.4 *Hq_Tel_List table*

If we assume that the creator had select and insert privileges on the Employee table, together with update privileges on the work_telno and empnr columns then the creator will receive select and insert privileges on the view together with update privileges on the telno and staffnr columns of the view. If in addition the creator had references privileges on work_telno and deptcd then the creator would also acquire a reference privilege on the column telno of the view. A reference privilege on just work_telno alone is not sufficient. The WITH CHECK OPTION provides a degree of control on the updates that may be done through the view. In general, if a WITH CHECK OPTION is specified then no insert or update statement may result in a row being created that will not appear in the view. If the LOCAL option is used then the constraint specifically provides that, if the row appears in the directly underlying table or view after the change, it must also appear in the view itself. If the CASCADED option is specified (the default if a WITH CHECK OPTION is used without either alternative), then the same check is carried out for each underlying view regardless of whether it has a WITH CHECK OPTION and of which sort. For example, given the following view:

```
CREATE VIEW Non_hq_tel_list (name, telno, staffnr, deptcd)
   AS
   SELECT name, work_telno, empnr, deptcd
     FROM Employee
     WHERE deptcd <> 'HDQ'
     WITH CHECK OPTION
```

these commands would not be valid:

```
INSERT INTO Non_hq_tel_list
   VALUES ('patel', '+1-854-1111-3678', 127, 'HDQ')
UPDATE Non_hq_tel_list SET deptcd = 'HDQ'
     WHERE name= 'brown'
```

If a view is defined in terms of a view and the lower level view has a WITH CHECK OPTION, no operations may be done through it that would violate its WITH CHECK OPTION, even if the higher level view does not have its own WITH CHECK OPTION. A fuller explanation of these alternatives and their use can be found in *Chapter 26 Usage of Views*.

Although the view is a permanent object its structure is determined at the time at which it is created. If, for example, the <query expression> had been of the form ' `SELECT * FROM T ...` ' then the * means all the columns of T that are defined at the moment the create view is executed. If columns are subsequently added to T then these will not appear in the view, unless the view is dropped and recreated.

4.5 CREATE ASSERTION

An assertion is an integrity constraint that is not directly coupled with a table definition. It has the syntax:

CREATE ASSERTION <assertion name> CHECK (<search condition>)
[<constraint attributes>]

From this it can be seen that it is similar to a table constraint of the check type. Indeed, the assertion name is treated as a constraint name and so must not be the same as that of any other constraint. An assertion may be defined with attributes and these have the same meaning and restrictions as the constraint attributes for column constraints. There is little effective difference between an assertion and a check constraint in a *base* table definition. The emphasis is on base because assertions may not reference temporary tables. One reason for using assertions in place of table constraints is that constraints sometimes involve more than one table and the constraint must either be duplicated or placed with an arbitrary table from the set of possible tables. The use of assertions makes for a cleaner and more accessible definition. The other reason is when minimum cardinality constraints are required, as this cannot be checked in a table constraint.

For example, see the following assertion which is taken from the Information Schema definition:

```
CREATE ASSERTION UNIQUE_CONSTRAINT_NAME
  CHECK (1 =
        (SELECT MAX (OCCURRENCES)
          FROM (SELECT COUNT (*) AS OCCURRENCES
            FROM (SELECT CONSTRAINT_CATALOG,
                         CONSTRAINT_SCHEMA,
                         CONSTRAINT_NAME
                         FROM DOMAIN_CONSTRAINTS
                      UNION ALL
                         SELECT CONSTRAINT_CATALOG,
                         CONSTRAINT_SCHEMA, CONSTRAINT_NAME
                            FROM TABLE_CONSTRAINTS
                      UNION ALL
                         SELECT CONSTRAINT_CATALOG,
                                CONSTRAINT_SCHEMA,
                                CONSTRAINT_NAME
                                   FROM ASSERTIONS)
             GROUP BY CONSTRAINT_CATALOG, CONSTRAINT_SCHEMA,
                    CONSTRAINT_NAME)))
```

which is a check which ranges over three tables. The assertion ensures that the same constraint name (a combination of catalog, schema and unqualified constraint name) is not used more than once in any table constraint, domain constraint or assertion. It does this by UNIONing the three name columns selected from the DEFINITION_SCHEMA tables DOMAIN, TABLE_CONSTRAINT and ASSERTION, and then doing a COUNT(*) of the rows in each group of rows having the same name (i.e. **duplicate** rows) and checking that the maximum count (the maximum number of times a name is used) is equal to 1.

4.6 CREATE CHARACTER SET

A create character set statement defines a logical set of characters and a physical encoding for those characters. This is a combination of a character repertoire and a form-of-use. The facility is limited in that only implementation defined character sets may be used as a basis for the definition and the only changes that can be made are those relating to the default collating sequence. The statement has the following syntax:

```
CREATE CHARACTER SET <character set name>
    [ AS ] GET <character set name>
    [ COLLATE <collation name> | COLLATION FROM <collation source> ]
```

where the second <character set name> identifies the character set that is to be used as the basis for this set. The <collation source> provides all the options that are available in collation definition.

A new character set is created with the same characters as those in the set named by the second <character set name> and with a default collating sequence that is either specified by a collation definition identified by <collation name> or specified by <collation source>. If nothing is specified then COLLATION FROM DEFAULT is assumed.

A USAGE privilege descriptor is created for the owner of the character set and this privilege is grantable. For example:

```
CREATE CHARACTER SET Rev_ASCII AS GET ASCII COLLATION
   FROM DESC (ASCII)
```

4.7 CREATE COLLATION

A create collation statement defines a set of rules for comparing character strings. These rules are used to determine whether two strings are equal and, if not, which comes before the other in a sorted sequence. A collating sequence is specific to a character set but there may be many collating sequences defined for a character set, although in string comparison only one can obviously be in use for each comparison. The facility is limited in that only implementation defined collation rules may be used as a basis for the definition. The definition command has the following syntax:

```
CREATE COLLATION <collation name> FOR <character set name>
   FROM <collation source> [ NO PAD | PAD SPACE ]

<collation source> ::=
     DEFAULT
   | <collation name>
   | DESC ( <collation name> )
   | EXTERNAL ( ' <external collation name> ' )
   | TRANSLATION <translation name>
        [ THEN COLLATION <collation name> ]
```

where <character set name> identifies the associated character set. An external collation name must be one that is supplied by the implementation. Any other <collation name> referred to in the FROM part must exist and be defined in the specified character set. In principle the user must have USAGE privilege on the external collation name, but since all implementation defined collations are granted to PUBLIC this never matters.

A USAGE privilege descriptor is created for the owner of the collation definition and this privilege is grantable if, and only if, the owner also has a grantable USAGE privilege on the associated character set. The collation rules defined depend on the option specified with FROM and are as follows:

DEFAULT — The collation is performed using the order of the characters as they appear in the character repertoire.

<collation name> — The collation is performed as specified by the <collation name>.

DESC — The collation is performed in the reverse order to that specified by the <collation name> in parentheses.

EXTERNAL — The collation is performed using the rules of the implementation or standard defined collation definition identified by <external collation name>.

TRANSLATION — The character string is effectively translated using the translation identified by <translation name> and the result is collated using the default collation of the character set specification of the result or, if THEN COLLATION is specified, the collation identified by the <collation name> following THEN COLLATION.

The padding options, NO PAD, PAD SPACE, allow the creator to determine whether space padding on the right is to occur when comparison of unequal strings takes place. The default is the padding option of the <collation name> of the <collation source>, if there is one; otherwise it is PAD SPACE. Note that the default collation sequence for standard character repertoires, e.g. ISO 646, is always PAD SPACE; for implementation defined repertoires it may be either. For example:

```
CREATE COLLATION Reverse_ASCII FOR SQL_TEXT FROM DESC
   (ASCII)
CREATE COLLATION My_Seq FOR My_Set FROM EXTERNAL ('EBCDIC')
CREATE COLLATION My_Def_Seq FOR My_Set FROM DEFAULT NO PAD
```

Every character string has a coercibility attribute defining which collating sequence is to be used when two strings with different collating sequences are compared and which combinations are illegal. The coercibility attribute is also used in determining which collating sequence and coercibility attribute the result of an operation on a character string has. All columns have a coercibility attribute of *Implicit* and the collating sequence explicitly or implicitly defined for the column. Literals, parameters and host language variables have a coercibility attribute of *Coercible* and the collating sequence that is the default for its character set. Specification of a COLLATE clause in a character value expression or a GROUP BY clause gives the string to which it applies a coercibility attribute of *Explicit* and the collating sequence that the COLLATE clause specifies.

Monadic operations, e.g. SUBSTRING, do not change the coercibility attribute or the collating sequence of character strings. The resulting coercibility attribute and collating sequence from dyadic operations on strings and the collating sequence to be used when comparing two strings are given in Table 4.3. Note that in some cases the resulting character string may have no appropriate collating sequence or coercibility attribute.

Table 4.3 Coercibility and collating sequences resulting from dyadic operations and for use in comparisons

First operand (coercibility, collating sequence)	*Second operand (coercibility, collating sequence)*	*Coercibility*	*Collating sequence*	
		Dyadic operation	*Dyadic operation*	*Comparison*
Coercible, character repertoire default	Coercible, character repertoire default	Coercible	Character repertoire default	Character repertoire default
Coercible, character repertoire default	Implicit, *y*	Implicit	*y*	*y*
Coercible, character repertoire default	None	None	None	Error – illegal syntax
Coercible, character repertoire default	Explicit, *y*	Explicit	*y*	*y*
Implicit, *x*	Coercible, character repertoire default	Implicit	*x*	*x*
Implicit, *x*	Implicit, *x*	Implicit	*x*	*x*
Implicit, *x*	Implicit, *y* , *y* <> *x*	None	None	Error – illegal syntax
Implicit, *x*	None	None	None	Error – illegal syntax
Implicit, *x*	Explicit, *y*	Explicit	*y*	*y*
None	Any except explicit	None	None	Error – illegal syntax
None	Explicit, *y*	Explicit	*x*	*x*
Explicit, *x*	Coercible, character repertoire default	Explicit	*x*	*x*
Explicit, *x*	Implicit, *y*	Explicit	*x*	*x*
Explicit, *x*	None	Explicit	*x*	*x*
Explicit, *x*	Explicit, *x*	Explicit	*x*	*x*
Explicit, *x*	Explicit, *y* , *y* <> *x*	Error – illegal syntax	Error – illegal syntax	Error – illegal syntax

4.8 CREATE TRANSLATION

A create translation statement defines a translation from one character set to another. It is a very limited facility in that it permits the definition of a translation from one character set to another only in terms of IDENTITY or of an implementation defined translation. The syntax is as follows:

```
CREATE TRANSLATION <translation name>
   FOR <source character set name>
   TO  <target character set name>
   FROM {    IDENTITY
         | <translation name>
         | EXTERNAL (' <external translation name> ') }
```

where <translation name> must be an existing translation name and <external translation name> must be an implementation defined translation name. In principle the user must have USAGE privilege on the external translation name, but since all implementation defined translations are granted to PUBLIC this never matters.

Specifying IDENTITY translates from one character set to another without changing the characters (it requires that the two character sets must share the same character repertoire and is equivalent to a conversion); otherwise the characters are translated using the implementation defined rules.

A USAGE privilege descriptor is created for the owner of the translation and this privilege is grantable if, and only if, the owner has a grantable USAGE privilege on both of the character sets involved. For example:

```
CREATE TRANSLATION Invert FOR ASCII TO Rev_ASCII
   FROM IDENTITY
CREATE TRANSLATION A_to_E FOR ASCII TO EBCDIC
   FROM EXTERNAL ('ASCII_EBCDIC')
```

5

Schema Manipulation

Once a schema has been created it is then possible to modify that schema by adding or deleting any of the component parts or by modifying certain constructs in place. Adding objects to the schema is accomplished using exactly the same statements as those used to create schemata in the first place, e.g. CREATE TABLE, CREATE VIEW, etc. The target schema for the modification is identified by the schema name portion of the identifier of the object being added. Deletion and modification of existing objects within a schema are accomplished by the DROP and ALTER commands described in the following sections.

In order to be able to manipulate any part of a schema the current authorization must be that of the owner of the schema, i.e. the authorization identifier that was explicitly or implicitly specified in the

AUTHORIZATION <authorization identifier>

clause of the CREATE SCHEMA command. The assumption of an authorization identifier by a user is outside the control of SQL and the possibilities for group users, etc. depends on the operating system and security system in use.

All the examples of schema manipulation in this chapter are based on an example schema (*see Appendix A The Example Database*) but each example is treated separately and does not depend on previous examples.

5.1 The DROP Statements

Most of the DROP commands require an explicit statement as to whether their actions are to be cascaded or not. Those that have no such specification are non-cascading, by default. For non-cascading commands, i.e. those with the

RESTRICT option, if there are any other objects that depend for their existence on the continued existence of the object to be dropped, the command will be rejected. Commands that request cascading will automatically issue DROP commands, also with the CASCADE option, for the dependent objects. This is necessary because these objects may themselves have dependent objects which also cannot be allowed a continued existence. The total effect of a DROP with the CASCADE option can thus be very extensive and careful inspection of the contents of the Information Schema is required before issuing such a command to determine its total scope. In principle, there is no need for the RESTRICT option as the absence of the CASCADE could have implied RESTRICT but many implementations, and indeed the X/OPEN portability guides assume a default cascading action. The standard has therefore been required to demand an explicit specification of intent for both options.

5.1.1 DROP SCHEMA

This command is used to destroy a schema, i.e. to delete all of the associated data and definitions. Since the SQL standard does not define any storage structures, the effect of *all* the DROP commands on these structures is also not defined by the standard and remains implementation dependent. The command syntax is:

DROP SCHEMA <schema name> { RESTRICT | CASCADE }

If RESTRICT is specified then the schema must be empty, i.e. it must not contain any domain definitions, table definitions, view definitions, assertion definitions, character set definitions, collation definitions or translation definitions. Thus an attempt to execute

```
DROP SCHEMA Company RESTRICT
```

would fail as the schema, in our example, contains tables, among other objects.

If CASCADE is specified actions take place in the following order:

1. For every table in the schema,
   `DROP TABLE t CASCADE`
   where t is the name of the table, is executed.
2. For every view in the schema,
   `DROP VIEW v CASCADE`
   where v is the name of the view, is executed.
3. For every domain in the schema,
   `DROP DOMAIN d CASCADE`
   where d is the name of the domain, is executed.
4. For every assertion in the schema,
   `DROP ASSERTION a CASCADE`
   where a is the name of the assertion, is executed.

5. For every collation definition in the schema,
   ```
   DROP COLLATION co
   ```
   where co is the name of the collation definition, is executed.
6. For every translation definition in the schema,
   ```
   DROP TRANSLATION tr
   ```
   where tr is the name of the translation definition, is executed.
7. For every character set definition in the schema,
   ```
   DROP CHARACTER SET c
   ```
   where c is the name of the character set definition, is executed.

The effect of these commands is described in the following sections, but if any of them is rejected then the entire DROP SCHEMA command is also rejected and no changes are made to either data or definitions. If no problems have been encountered, the schema with all its associated data and descriptions, including the data about the schema in the Information Schema, is destroyed. Thus, executing

```
DROP SCHEMA Company CASCADE
```

would destroy the entire example database and data definitions.

5.1.2 DROP DOMAIN

This command is used to destroy a domain. The command syntax is:

DROP DOMAIN <domain name> { RESTRICT | CASCADE }

If RESTRICT is specified then the domain must not be used in any existing table definition (including defined temporary table definitions and existing, i.e. active, declared temporary table definitions), view definitions or assertion definitions. Thus an attempt to execute

```
DROP DOMAIN telno RESTRICT
```

would fail as the domain telno is used in the table Employee.

Otherwise, if CASCADE is specified the following actions take place in order:

1. For every column that is defined using the domain the column definition is altered as follows:

   (a) The domain name is replaced by the data type specification of the domain.
   (b) If the domain had a domain constraint then an equivalent column constraint is added if and only if the owner of the table in which the column resides possesses the privileges necessary to create such a column constraint.
   (c) If the column has no default clause then the domain default clause, if any, is added.
   (d) If the column has no collate clause then the domain collate clause, if any, is added if and only if the owner of the table in which the column resides possesses the privilege necessary to have created such a collate clause.

   The effect of this is to define the column in exactly the same way it would have been if the domain had never existed. Having done this no column descriptions are dependent on the domain and thus will not be destroyed when the next step is done. We thus never lose actual data as the result of a DROP DOMAIN command.

2. The following command is executed:

   ```
   REVOKE USAGE ON DOMAIN d FROM u CASCADE
   ```

   where d is the name of the domain and u is the authorization identifier of the owner of the domain. The REVOKE is executed on behalf of the pseudo-user, _SYSTEM, which granted the owner the privileges at the time of the create. This will not only remove the privileges from everybody, including the owner, to use the domain but will also cause a DROP command to be issued for every dependent object (*see Section 8.4 Cascade Effects of the REVOKE Statement*).

Finally the domain and its description, including the data about it in the Information Schema, is destroyed. Thus the execution of:

```
DROP DOMAIN telno CASCADE
```

would result in the redefinition of the work_telno and home_telno columns to be (the relevant privileges exist since the objects come from the same schema):

```
home_telno    CHARACTER (14)
     CHECK (home_telno    LIKE '+%(_)%-%-%'
            OR home_telno LIKE '+%-%-%-%'
            OR home_telno LIKE '%-%'
            OR home_telno LIKE '___'),
work_telno    CHARACTER (14)
     CHECK (work_telno    LIKE '+%(_)%-%-%'
            OR work_telno LIKE '+%-%-%-%'
            OR work_telno LIKE '%-%'
            OR work_telno LIKE '___'),
```

and the destruction of the domain telno.

5.1.3 DROP TABLE

This command is used to destroy a table. The command syntax is:

DROP TABLE <table name> { RESTRICT | CASCADE }

The specified table name must reference a base table, that is one created by a CREATE TABLE command. If RESTRICT is specified then the table must not be referenced in any existing domain definitions, table definitions, view definitions or assertion definitions. Thus an attempt to execute

```
DROP TABLE Dept RESTRICT
```

would fail as the table Dept is referenced in the definition of the Employee table (in a FOREIGN KEY). Otherwise, if CASCADE is specified, the following command is executed:

```
REVOKE ALL PRIVILEGES ON t FROM u CASCADE
```

where t is the name of the table and u is the authorization identifier of the owner of the table. The REVOKE is executed on behalf of the pseudo-user, _SYSTEM, which granted the owner the privileges at the time of the create. This will not only remove the privileges from everybody, including the owner, to use the table but will also cause a DROP command to be issued for every dependent object (*see Section 8.4 Cascade Effects of the REVOKE Statement*).

Finally, the table (i.e. the data) and its description, including all the data about the table in the Information Schema is destroyed. Thus the execution of:

```
DROP TABLE Dept CASCADE
```

would result in the destruction of the Dept table and the dropping of the FOREIGN KEY table constraint in the Employee table.

5.1.4 DROP ASSERTION

This command is used to destroy an assertion. The command syntax is:

DROP ASSERTION <constraint name>

The specified constraint name must reference an assertion. There are no RESTRICT or CASCADE options, and none are in fact needed as there can be no dependent objects.

The assertion and its description, including data in the Information Schema, is destroyed. Thus the execution of:

```
DROP ASSERTION Max_Order_lines
```

would simply result in the destruction of the assertion Max_Order_lines.

5.1.5 DROP VIEW

This command is used to destroy a view. The command syntax is:

DROP VIEW <view name> { RESTRICT | CASCADE }

The specified table name must reference a viewed table, that is one created by a CREATE VIEW command.

If RESTRICT is specified then the table must not be referenced in any existing domain definitions, table definitions, view definitions or assertion definitions. Otherwise, if CASCADE is specified, the following command is executed:

```
REVOKE ALL PRIVILEGES ON TABLE v FROM u CASCADE
```

where v is the name of the view and u is the authorization identifier of the owner of the view. The REVOKE is executed on behalf of the pseudo-user, _SYSTEM, which granted the owner the privileges at the time of the create. This will not only remove the privileges from everybody, including the owner, to use the view but will also cause a DROP command to be issued for every dependent object (*see Section 8.4 Cascade Effects of the REVOKE Statement*).

Finally, the view and its description, including data in the Information Schema, is destroyed. Thus the execution of:

```
DROP VIEW Hq_Tel_List CASCADE
```

would result in the destruction of the Hq_Tel_List view and the dropping of any dependent objects.

5.1.6 DROP COLLATION

This command is used to destroy a collation definition. The command syntax is:

DROP COLLATION <collation name>

The collation must not be referenced in any existing domain definitions, table definitions, view definitions or assertion definitions.

There is no CASCADE option and although character sets may reference collations there is no automatic way of deleting the character set as well. The presence of such a character set does not inhibit the command and if a collation, y, which is dropped, is used in a character set definition, i.e. in a ‘ TRANSLATION x THEN COLLATION y ’, ‘ DESC(y) ’ or ‘ COLLATE y ’, then it is effectively deleted from the definition, leaving just the translation or the default collation.

The following command is executed:

```
REVOKE USAGE ON COLLATION c FROM u CASCADE
```

where c is the name of the collation and u is the authorization identifier of the owner of the collation. The REVOKE is executed on behalf of the pseudo-user, _SYSTEM, which granted the owner the privileges at the time of the create. This will remove the privileges from everybody, including the owner, to use the collation. It will not, however, cause a DROP command to be issued for any dependent object.

The collation and its description, including data in the Information Schema, is destroyed. Thus the execution of:

```
DROP COLLATION Case_independent
```

would simply result in the destruction of the collation Case_independent.

5.1.7 DROP TRANSLATION

This command is used to destroy a translation definition. The command syntax is:

DROP TRANSLATION <translation name>

The translation must not be referenced in any existing domain definitions, table definitions, view definitions, assertion definitions or collation definitions.

There is no CASCADE option and although character sets may reference translations there is no automatic way of deleting the character set as well. The presence of such a character set does not inhibit the command and if a translation, x, which is dropped is used in a character set definition, i.e. in a ‘ TRANSLATION x ’ then it is effectively deleted from the definition, leaving just the default collation.

The following command is executed:

```
REVOKE USAGE ON TRANSLATION t FROM u CASCADE
```

where t is the name of the translation and u is the authorization identifier of the owner of the translation. The REVOKE is executed on behalf of the pseudo-user, _SYSTEM, which granted the owner the privileges at the time of the create. This will remove the privileges from everybody, including the owner, to use the translation, but it will not cause a DROP command to be issued for any dependent object.

The translation and its description, including data in the Information Schema, is destroyed. Thus the execution of:

```
DROP TRANSLATION ASCII_EBCDIC
```

would simply result in the destruction of the translation ASCII_EBCDIC.

5.1.8 DROP CHARACTER SET

This command is used to destroy a character set definition. The command syntax is:

DROP CHARACTER SET <character set name>

The character set must not be referenced in any existing domain definitions, table definitions, view definitions, assertion definitions, translation definitions or collation definitions.

There is no CASCADE option and although collating sequences may reference them there is no automatic way of deleting or modifying them as well.

The following command is executed:

```
REVOKE USAGE ON CHARACTER SET cs FROM u CASCADE
```

where cs is the name of the character set and u is the authorization identifier of the owner of the character set. The REVOKE is executed on behalf of the pseudo-user, _SYSTEM, which granted the owner the privileges at the time of the create. This will remove the privileges from everybody, including the owner, to use the character set but it will not cause a DROP command to be issued for any dependent object.

The character set and its description, including data in the Information Schema, is destroyed. Thus the execution of:

```
DROP CHARACTER SET EBCDIC
```

would simply result in the destruction of the character set EBCDIC.

5.2 The ALTER Statements

There are only two ALTER commands, ALTER DOMAIN and ALTER TABLE, both of which have a number of options. There are no ALTER commands available for schemata, views, character sets, collations or translations. ALTER is not needed for schemata as the DROP and ALTER statements for the other objects perform that function. Assertions also do not require an ALTER as they have no dependent objects and can thus be DROPed and CREATEed again at will. In the case of views, character sets, collations and translations, ALTER would be useful and, with the exception of views, relatively easy to define. Unfortunately, the standard has, so far, ignored this area.

5.2.1 ALTER DOMAIN

The alter domain command is used to modify the attributes of the domain definition. Only those attributes that do not affect the actual data are permitted. Thus the alter domain command has four options:

set domain default
drop domain default
add domain constraint
drop domain constraint

There is no option to change the data type or for that matter the collating sequence, but this latter is just an oversight in the standard as it does not affect the data.

5.2.1.1 Set Domain Default
This command is used to force a default clause on to a domain. The command syntax is:

ALTER DOMAIN <domain name> SET <default clause>

The syntax for <default clause> is identical to that of a default clause in a CREATE DOMAIN command. Whether the domain already possesses a default clause or not is irrelevant.

The default value specified by the added default clause applies to all columns that are defined in terms of the domain and do not have a default clause defined at the column level (*see Section 4.2.1.1 Defaults*). This default, even when applicable at the column level, does not alter any existing values in the database, even if they were inserted as a result of a default specification. The new default value only applies to columns in rows that are subsequently inserted. It should also be noted that it is possible to set a default value such that the value is unacceptable with regard to other constraints. For example, the default default value is NULL which is clearly unacceptable in any column defined as NOT NULL. Alternatively, this unacceptableness might be used as a way of requiring that a value be explicitly provided (even if that value is NULL). For example, the sex column in the Employee table may be NULL or contain 'M' or 'F' which is controlled by a CHECK clause; if the default was set to, say, 'X' then the intended contents of the column would need to be provided with every insert. For example:

```
ALTER DOMAIN telno SET DEFAULT '100'
```

would add the operator's number as the default telephone number to the telno domain.

```
ALTER DOMAIN acquisition_date SET DEFAULT DATE'1990-01-01'
```

would replace the existing default with the date 1 January 1990.

5.2.1.2 Drop Domain Default
This command is used to delete the default clause from a domain. The command syntax is:

ALTER DOMAIN <domain name> DROP DEFAULT

The domain identified by domain name must have an existing default clause. The default clause, which applies to all columns defined in terms of the domain and that do not have a default clause defined at the column level, is dropped. This implies that the default for those columns, and any new column defined using the domain, will use the default default value that is NULL. For example:

```
ALTER DOMAIN acquisition_date DROP DEFAULT
```

would remove the explicit default from the acquisition_date domain. The default for the domain then becomes NULL.

5.2.1.3 Add Domain Constraint

This command is used to add a check constraint to a domain. The command syntax is:

ALTER DOMAIN <domain name> ADD <domain constraint>

The syntax of the <domain constraint> is identical to that of a domain constraint in a CREATE DOMAIN command.

This domain constraint, which consists of a check constraint, is evaluated for every column that is defined in terms of this domain, with any occurrence of the key word VALUE replaced by the name of the column. The situation is then the same as if the domain had been originally defined with that domain constraint.

This constraint does not just apply to new data but to all existing data as well, so it is possible to have the command rejected if the database contains values in any column using this domain that do not satisfy the new constraint. For example:

```
ALTER DOMAIN acquisition_date ADD CONSTRAINT
   CHECK (VALUE > DATE'1990-01-01')
```

would add a constraint to the existing domain that previously did not have one.

5.2.1.4 Drop Domain Constraint

This command is used to delete a check constraint from a domain. The command syntax is:

ALTER DOMAIN <domain name> DROP CONSTRAINT <constraint name>

The domain must have a domain constraint whose name is that specified by <constraint name>.

The domain constraint associated with the domain is destroyed and is no longer checked for any column defined in terms of this domain. The situation is then the same as if the domain had been originally defined without this domain constraint. For example:

```
ALTER DOMAIN telno DROP CONSTRAINT
```

would remove the existing domain constraint.

5.2.2 *ALTER TABLE*

The alter table command is used to modify the structure and attributes of a table. Some of the changes affect attributes that do not result in the data in the database being affected, but some of the changes also cause the data in the database to be changed. The alter table command has six options:

add column
drop column
add table constraint
drop table constraint
set column default
drop column default

5.2.2.1 Add Column

This command is used to add a column to a table. The command syntax is:

ALTER TABLE <table name> ADD [COLUMN] <column definition>

The syntax of the <column definition> is identical to that of a column definition in a CREATE TABLE command.

The new column is added to the end of the table, both in the description and in the database, i.e. it is as if it had been the last column in the original table definition. The new column in the database is filled with the appropriate default value, taken from either the column default clause, if specified, or the domain default clause, if appropriate, or NULL if no default was explicitly specified. If * had been used as the column list in a view definition then this new column is *not* added to the view definition.

Every user who has a table privilege (other than a DELETE privilege) on the table to which the column is added is immediately granted an equivalent column privilege for the new column, with the same attributes (grantor, grantable, action) as the table privilege. This is in fact the purpose of the table privilege, as opposed to a complete set of column privileges, in that it allows users to acquire access to new columns that are defined in the future.

In all other respects the situation is then the same as if the table had been originally defined with that column. For example:

```
ALTER TABLE Vehicle ADD engine_size NUMERIC (4)
```

adds a new column engine size to the existing Vehicle table in our example database; it becomes the fourth (and last) column in the table and that column is filled with NULLs.

5.2.2.2 Drop Column

This command is used to destroy a column in a table. The command syntax is:

ALTER TABLE <table name> DROP [COLUMN] <column name>
{ RESTRICT | CASCADE }

It is not permitted to drop the last remaining column in a table.

If RESTRICT is specified then the column must not be referenced, explicitly or implicitly, in any existing domain definitions, view definitions, assertion definitions or any table constraint definition other than one that references only this column and is defined in the same table (e.g. a NOT NULL constraint). The following command is executed:

```
REVOKE INSERT(c), UPDATE(c), REFERENCES(c)
   ON TABLE t FROM u CASCADE
```

where t is the name of the table, u is the authorization identifier of the owner of the view and c is the name of the column. The REVOKE is executed on behalf of the pseudo-user, _SYSTEM, which granted the owner the privileges at the time of the create. This will not only remove the privileges from everybody, including the owner, to use the column but will also cause a DROP command to be issued for every dependent object (*see Section 8.4 Cascade Effects of the REVOKE Statement*). Any remaining column privilege descriptors that reference the column are deleted.

Finally the column (i.e. the data) and its description, including data in the Information Schema, is destroyed. For example:

```
ALTER TABLE Vehicle DROP acquisition_date RESTRICT
```

removes the column acquisition_date from the Vehicle table. It was the third column and any subsequent column is renumbered, e.g. the engine_size we added in the previous example as the fourth column now becomes the third. In general, one should try not to think in terms of column numbers and always use the names. The order of the columns is, however, sometimes of importance (e.g. in a UNION, INTERSECTION or EXCEPT operation).

5.2.2.3 Add Table Constraint

This command is used to add a table constraint to a table, the syntax is:

ALTER TABLE <table name> ADD <table constraint definition>

The syntax of the <table constraint definition> is identical to that of a table constraint definition in a CREATE TABLE command. The situation is then the same as if the table had been originally defined with that table constraint.

This constraint does not just apply to new data but to all existing data as well, so it is possible to have the command rejected if the database contains values that do not satisfy the new constraint. For example:

```
ALTER TABLE Emp_ext ADD
  CHECK (date_of_birth + INTERVAL'16'
         YEAR < date_of_joining)
```

would add the constraint that no employee may join the firm until they are at least 16 years old. If there are any currently on the staff who did so then this command would be rejected.

5.2.2.4 Drop Table Constraint
This command is used to delete a table constraint from a table. The command syntax is:

ALTER TABLE <table name>
DROP CONSTRAINT <constraint name> { RESTRICT | CASCADE }

If RESTRICT is specified then the constraint identified by constraint name must not be a UNIQUE constraint which is needed by a referential constraint. The target columns of a referential constraint must always be defined as unique and thus it is not permitted to delete the UNIQUE constraint and leave the referential constraint as it is.

If CASCADE is specified and there exist any dependent referential constraints then for each such dependent constraint the following command is executed on behalf of the owner of the dependent constraint:

```
ALTER TABLE t DROP CONSTRAINT c CASCADE
```

where t is the name of the table whose definition contains the dependent referential constraint c.

The table constraint identified by constraint name is destroyed and is no longer checked. The situation is then the same as if the table had been originally defined without that table constraint. For example:

```
ALTER TABLE Order DROP CONSTRAINT
    Order_contains_at_least_one_order_line CASCADE
```

would drop the rule that says that every order specified must have at least one order line:

```
CHECK (Ordernr IN (SELECT ordernr FROM Order_line))
```

We might want to do this if it proves too tedious to handle the cyclic constraints between Order and Order_line, but having done so the schema would no longer be a true model of our Company's data.

5.2.2.5 Set Column Default
This command is used to force a default clause on to a column. The command syntax is:

ALTER TABLE <table name> ALTER [COLUMN] <column name>
SET <default clause>

The default value specified by the replaced or added default clause applies to the column. For example:

```
ALTER TABLE Employee ALTER COLUMN salary SET DEFAULT 8000
```

would provide the salary column in the Employee table with a default value of 8000 pounds.

5.2.2.6 Drop Column Default

This command is used to delete the default clause from a column. The command syntax is:

ALTER TABLE <table name> ALTER [COLUMN] <column name>
DROP DEFAULT

The column identified by column name must have an existing default clause to be dropped. If the column was defined in terms of a domain then the appropriate domain default is used instead. Otherwise the default default value, NULL, is used. For example:

```
ALTER TABLE Employee ALTER COLUMN salary DROP DEFAULT
```

would remove the explicit default inserted above.

6

Non-Cursor Operations

The non-cursor operations are the basic, native, operations of the SQL language. They are mostly set-oriented and provide for the insertion, deletion and updating of sets of rows from tables, as well as the retrieval of a single row from any arbitrarily derived table. The natural retrieval operation would also be set-oriented but due to the limitations of programming languages this command is only available in the direct mode of operation (*see Chapter 19 Direct Invocation of SQL*).

6.1 INSERT

This command is used to insert rows into a table. The command syntax is:

```
INSERT INTO <table name>
    [ ( <column name> [ { , <column name> }... ] ) ] <query expression>
    | DEFAULT VALUES
```

The table identified by the table name must be updateable. Furthermore, unless the table is temporary, the transaction must be a read–write transaction. Even if the transaction is read only it may still insert rows into a temporary table.

Each column name must be a column name of the table and no column name may appear more than once. If no list of column names is provided, then a list consisting of all the columns in the table in the order in which they are defined is assumed. The option DEFAULT VALUES is a special option that specifies a single row consisting entirely of the default values for each column.

The current authorization identifier must have an INSERT privilege on each column in the list. The rows to be inserted are defined by the query expression. The query expression defines a derived table which must have the same number of columns as are specified, or implicit, in the column list and in the same order. If not all of the columns of the table are specified in the list, then the missing columns are added into the derived table in the appropriate position and filled with the appropriate default value. This, possibly modified, derived table is then UNIONed with the specified table. The number of rows in the derived table can be any non-negative number including zero. Attempting to insert zero rows is not an error but does change the completion status from 'successful completion' to 'no data'.

For example to insert a single row into the Vehicle table we can use:

```
INSERT INTO Vehicle VALUES (94, NULL, '1991-07-12')
```

This defines a single row derived table which is then added (inserted/UNIONed) to the Vehicle table. This uses literals to define a constant table but the query expression may be any derived table. If the derived table is based in some way on the target table then the complete set of rows to be inserted is first evaluated, before any row is inserted, so that problems of recursion or indeterminacy are avoided.

If we wanted to initialize the Product_Supply table for a new supplier who can supply all products with a product code greater than 6000 in minimum quantities of 50, then we can write (assuming the new supplier, with a suppliernr of 12017, is already inserted):

```
INSERT INTO Product_supply
   ( SELECT product_code, suppliernr, 50
       FROM Supplier, Product
       WHERE suppliernr = 12017 AND product_code > 6000 )
```

If the default for minimum_order was in fact 50 then we could equally well have written:

```
INSERT INTO Product_supply (product_code, suppliernr)
   ( SELECT product_code, suppliernr
     FROM Supplier, Product
     WHERE suppliernr = 12017 AND product_code > 6000 )
```

Here we have specified a column list of only two columns and modified the query expression to have just two columns as well. The third column then uses the default value for that column. This form must be used if inserts are done into tables where INSERT privileges are not available on all columns in the table. If we define columns with defaults of, say, USER or CURRENT_TIMESTAMP, then not providing INSERT privileges is a useful mechanism for keeping track of the user who inserted a row or the time at which it was inserted, as the values will always be accurately provided by the defaults and cannot be overridden by the actual user or program.

For the rules regarding the transfer of values *see Section 6.5.2 Store Assignment.*

6.2 Single Row SELECT

This command is used to retrieve the values from a single row of a table. The command syntax is:

SELECT [ALL | DISTINCT] <select list>
    INTO <target specification> [{, <target specification> }...]
    <table expression>

This is identical syntax to that of a <query specification> (*see Section 9.5 Query Specification*), except for the interposed INTO phrase. The effect is as if the equivalent <query expression> was evaluated and then the values from the resulting derived table transferred to the targets identified by their target specifications. For the rules on transfer of values *see Section 6.5.1 Retrieval Assignment.*

There must be exactly the same number of targets as there are columns in the derived table and these are matched one to one in the same order. The resulting derived table must not contain more than one row, otherwise an error results. Whether or not the targets contain values from one or other of the possible rows when such an error is returned is implementation dependent, but the user would be well advised not to rely one way or the other on this. If it contains zero rows then a 'no data' warning is returned. The reason for restricting the command to a single row is due to the limitations of current programming languages which are record rather than set-oriented. A multi-row select is available in Direct SQL (*see Chapter 19 Direct Invocation of SQL*).

For example, in order to obtain the name and the total of the salary and commission of the employee with employee number 52 we can say:

```
SELECT name, salary + commission
  INTO :name, :gross
  FROM Employee
  WHERE empnr = 52
```

where :name and :gross are host language variables. We know that, in this case, only one row will be returned because empnr is the primary key of the Employee table. Alternatively, if we want the average salary of all personnel then

```
SELECT AVG(salary) INTO temp FROM Employee
```

will return that information into the parameter temp. Naturally, this is also always a single row.

6.3 UPDATE Searched

This command is used to update rows from a table where the rows to be updated are identified by a search condition. The command syntax is:

UPDATE <table name>
    SET <column name> = { <value expression> | NULL | DEFAULT }
    [{, <column name> = { <value expression> | NULL | DEFAULT } }...]
    [WHERE <search condition>]

The table identified by the table name must be updateable. Furthermore, unless the table is temporary, the transaction must be a read–write transaction. Even if the transaction is read only it may still update rows in a temporary table.

Each column name must be a column name of the table and no column name may appear more than once. The current authorization identifier must have an UPDATE privilege on each column to be updated. The rows to be updated are identified by the search condition. If no WHERE clause is present then all rows of the table are identified.

The number of rows identified can be any number between zero and the total number of rows in the table. Attempting to update zero rows is not an error but does change the completion status from 'successful completion' to 'no data'. Note that if a row to be updated has already been deleted or updated through a still open cursor then a warning is raised. For example, to update a single selected row, if it exists, from the Product_Supply table we can use:

```
UPDATE Product_Supply SET minimum_order = 1000
   WHERE product_code = 10564 AND suppliernr = 12017
```

This identifies a single row as, together, product_code and suppliernr constitute the primary key of the Product_Supply table.

To update multiple rows from a table, say Employee, we could use:

```
UPDATE Employee SET salary = salary + 500
   WHERE salary = ( SELECT MIN (salary) FROM Employee )
```

This will give all employees with the smallest salary a rise of £500.

The search condition references the same table as that in which the updates are to take place. You might think that if the MIN function was repeatedly evaluated this command might actually give all employees a rise, or better still never stop giving employees a rise. Unfortunately, this does not happen as it is a two-stage process: all the rows to be updated are identified with the help of the WHERE clause and subsequently the identified rows are updated.

Similarly, in the previous example the SET phrase both updates and references the same column — salary. I might also have used salary to update more that one column, for example:

```
UPDATE Employee
   SET salary = salary + 500, commission = commission +
      salary/10
```

There might be confusion over the value of the salary to be used in updating the commission column. Is it the one in the original row or the one after the addition of the £500? In such cases the references to a column on the right-hand side of the = is always the value before *any* updating takes place, i.e. the value in the original row. DEFAULT implies the substitution of the current default value defined for the target column. For the rules regarding the transfer of values *see Section 6.5.2 Store Assignment*.

The SET phrase may also specify NULL as the key word if the column is to be updated to the null value. If we wish to register the fact that headquarters staff are not eligible to receive commission, the following statement will do it:

```
UPDATE Employee SET commission = NULL WHERE deptcd = 'HDQ'
```

6.4 DELETE Searched

This command is used to delete rows from a table where the rows to be deleted are identified by a search condition. The command syntax is:

DELETE FROM <table name> [WHERE <search condition>]

The table identified by the table name must be updateable. Furthermore, unless the table is temporary, the transaction must be a read–write transaction. Even if the transaction is read only it may still delete rows from a temporary table.

The current authorization identifier must have a DELETE privilege on the table identified by table name. The rows to be deleted are identified by the search condition. If no WHERE clause is present then all rows of the table are identified. The number of rows identified can be any number between zero and the total number of rows in the table. Attempting to delete zero rows is not an error but does change the completion status from 'successful completion' to 'no data'. For example, to delete a single selected row, if it exists, from the Dept table we can use:

```
DELETE FROM Dept WHERE deptcd = 'SLS'
```

This identifies a single row as deptcd is the primary key of the Dept table.

To delete multiple rows from a table, say Employee, we could use:

```
DELETE FROM Employee
   WHERE commission = ( SELECT MIN (commission)
      FROM Employee )
```

This will 'fire' all employees who receive the least commission, i.e. the bottom-ranking salesmen. Just to encourage the others you understand!

The search condition in this case references the same table as that from which the deletes are taking place. The same rules apply as in the UPDATE Searched so as to avoid the possibility of deleting all of the rows in the table through repeated evaluation of the MIN function. This is a two-stage process. All the rows to be deleted are identified with the help of the WHERE clause and subsequently the identified rows are deleted.

If the table identified is a view, then the rows deleted are the rows in the base table from which the identified rows in the view were derived. Note that if a row to be deleted has already been deleted or updated through a still open cursor then a warning is raised.

6.5 Data Assignment Rules

Where values are transferred from the database to the parameters of a procedure or to host language variables certain conditions must hold and certain actions take place. These rules and actions are common regardless of the command used to carry out the transfer and so they are described here in one place rather than duplicate the text in every place where transfers occur. Similarly, there are rules and actions that hold for transfers in the reverse direction.

6.5.1 Retrieval Assignment

In order to transfer data from the database into a parameter or a host language variable both the source and the target must have compatible data types. Thus, if the source has data type character string, bit string, numeric (exact or approximate), datetime or interval then the target must also have data type character string, bit string, numeric (again, exact or approximate), the identical datetime type or a comparable interval type.

If the value to be transferred is the null value then the indicator parameter (or variable) is set to –1 if it exists; otherwise a warning is raised 'data exception — null value, no indicator parameter'. Unfortunately there is no way of determining which transfer, if there is more than one, had the problem. If the value to be transferred is not null then the indicator parameter, if it exists, is set to 0.

For transfers of numeric values, provided there is no loss of leading significant digits, the value is simply transferred; otherwise an error is raised 'data exception — numeric value out of range'.

For transfers of datetime and interval values, provided there is an exact representation in the target data type of the value of the source, the value is simply transferred; otherwise in the case of interval an error is raised 'data exception — interval field overflow'. Datetime cannot raise an error as the data types of the source and target must be identical.

Transfers of character and bit strings are a little more complicated. Firstly, if the length of the string to be transferred is greater than the target will hold, the indicator parameter, if it exists, is set to the true length of the source string. Subsequently, the characters or bits are transferred. If the target is too small then the string is truncated on the right and a warning condition raised. If the string is too short for a fixed length target then the string is padded on the right with space characters or 0 bits as appropriate. In the case of bit padding a warning is also raised. If the target is variable length its length is adjusted to the length of the string actually transferred.

6.5.2 Store Assignment

In order to transfer data into the database from a parameter or a host language variable both the source and the target must have compatible data types. Thus, if the source has data type character string, bit string, numeric (exact or approximate), datetime or interval then the target, in the database, must also have data type character string, bit string, numeric (again, exact or approximate), the identical datetime type or a comparable interval type.

If the indicator parameter (or variable) exists and is set to –1, or the key word NULL was specified then the value to be transferred is the null value.

For transfers of numeric values, provided there is no loss of leading significant digits, the value is simply transferred; otherwise an error is raised 'data exception — numeric value out of range'.

For transfers of datetime and interval values, provided there is an exact representation in the target data type of the value of the source, the value is simply transferred; otherwise an error is raised 'data exception — datetime field overflow'.

Transfers of character and bit strings are a little more complicated. The characters or bits are transferred. If the target is too small then the string is truncated on the right provided that all the truncated characters are space characters or 0 bits as appropriate, otherwise an error is raised 'data exception — string data, right truncation'. If the string is too short for a fixed length target then a character string is padded on the right with space characters but in the case of a bit string an error is raised 'data exception — string data, length mismatch'. If the target is variable length its length is adjusted to the length of the string actually transferred.

7

Cursor Operations

A cursor is a mechanism that allows a program to step through the rows of a table, whether a base table, a view or any other arbitrarily derived table. This is necessary since the programming languages available for use with SQL work in principle on a record basis and not on a set basis. Cursors provide an interface between the set orientation of SQL and the record orientation of the programming languages.

The standard sequence of commands to declare and manipulate a cursor is as follows:

DECLARE CURSOR — This defines the cursor's characteristics. In principle it does not matter where in the module this declaration takes place but we will proceed as if it was always done at the beginning of the module.

OPEN — This causes the derived table to be defined. The rows that are to form part of the table are identified at this point in time. The derived table may or may not be physically materialized.

FETCH — This command must be the first executed after OPEN and may be repeated many times before the CLOSE is issued. It causes the contents of a particular row from the derived table to be retrieved into the host program and the cursor to have 'position' on that row.

UPDATE / DELETE	These commands are optional and may be issued after a FETCH, i.e. when the cursor actually has a position on a row.
CLOSE	This releases the definition of the derived table and no further processing may take place with the cursor until it is reopened.

A cursor designates a table, an ordering of the rows of that table and a position relative to the rows of the table. The table is defined by a query expression, the ordering is either implicit or is defined by an order by clause and the position is determined by the various commands. The position within a cursor is expressed relative to a row and may be:

before a specified row
on a specified row
after the last row

There is one special case: 'before the first row'. A cursor may be 'before the first row' or 'after the last row' even where the query expression has generated a table of zero rows.

Cursors are automatically closed whenever a transaction terminates, e.g. when a COMMIT or a ROLLBACK command is executed. Although only one cursor with the same name may be open at any one time, during the life of a transaction a particular cursor may be opened, closed, reopened and reclosed many times and because the OPEN command has parameters the cursor effectively created or the rows that participate in the cursor may be different each time.

Cursors have a number of additional attributes (*see Section 7.1 DECLARE CURSOR*). These various attributes affect the commands that may be executed on a specific cursor. Cursors, especially when updating, can be thought of as extended (in time) versions of the equivalent searched update or delete commands. Updates or deletes using cursors also cause the normal triggered actions of referential constraints to take place where appropriate. There are, however, major differences. Firstly, it is possible to insert additional changes to the database between two operations on the same cursor: for example, between two UPDATE WHERE CURRENT cursor commands, a non-cursor searched DELETE might be issued. It is, however, not possible to insert a searched DELETE in the middle of a non-cursor searched UPDATE because a searched SQL command always runs to completion before the next is issued. Secondly, it is possible to mix UPDATE and DELETE commands on a single cursor. Finally, the triggered actions are initiated after each cursor command and not at the CLOSE cursor. This latter is the equivalent to the way triggered actions operate on searched commands. These differences can lead to anomalies and inconsistent results depending on the ordering of rows in the cursor and the sensitivity of the cursor. In order to detect possible problems a warning is issued on opening a cursor and on issuing an insert, a searched update or a searched delete command if conflicts could possibly arise with any (other) open cursors (*see Section 7.2 OPEN*).

7.1 DECLARE CURSOR

This statement is used to define a cursor. If the cursor definition contains any parameters or host language variables the values of these are not substituted until the OPEN is issued. The command syntax is:

```
DECLARE <cursor name> [ INSENSITIVE ] [ SCROLL ] CURSOR
    FOR <query expression>
     [ <order by clause> ]
     [ <updatability clause> ]
```

The most important clause here is the <query expression>. This defines the derived table which is the table of the cursor. This may be as simple as '`SELECT * FROM t`' or it may be a complex query involving joins and sub-queries, etc.

The <order by clause>, or its absence, determines the order in which the rows of the cursor will be presented. The syntax of the <order by clause> is:

```
ORDER BY <sort key> [ { ASC | DESC } ] [, <sort key> [ { ASC | DESC } ] ]...
```

where <sort key> is either a column name or an unsigned integer. The use of the unsigned integer (i), which is equivalent to the use of the column name of the *i*th column, is a deprecated feature and should now no longer be used as all columns may be explicitly named if required.

The left to right ordering of the column names in the ORDER BY clause determines the major to minor sort keys with the normal meaning. The key words ASC and DESC (with ASC being the default if neither is specified) represent ascending and descending order for each sort key respectively. It should be noted that the relative order of rows that have the same values in all their sort key columns is indeterminate and may vary from one opening of the cursor to another, even if no changes to the database or to the parameters of the OPEN have been made. For the purposes of this ordering all null values are treated as being equal, with an effective value which is either less than or greater than any actual value; i.e. nulls either all occur before any actual value or all occur after all actual values. The choice of before or after is dependent on the implementation.

The lack of an ORDER BY clause does not mean that there is no ordering of the rows, only that the implementation is free to choose any ordering it likes. However, having chosen an order for a cursor this must be maintained for the life of the cursor (i.e. until a CLOSE is issued).

The INSENSITIVE option relates to the visibility, within this cursor, of updates not done through this cursor. If INSENSITIVE is specified then the complete collection of rows in the cursor is determined at the time of the OPEN and will remain visible in the cursor, regardless of any changes made to the underlying tables by other commands in the transaction.

The SCROLL option indicates that FETCH commands for this cursor may make use of positioning options other than NEXT. This means that without the SCROLL option all FETCH commands must specify (or imply) NEXT and with the SCROLL option FETCH commands may specify FIRST, LAST, NEXT, PRIOR, RELATIVE or ABSOLUTE (*see Section 7.3 FETCH*).

The <updatability clause> allows additional control over which columns may or may not be updated using the cursor. In practice this clause is frequently unnecessary and can always be omitted, although in some implementations this specification might offer performance improvements as the database management system will know more about the intended usage. An alternative use is to provide additional protection against mistakes within a program. The one case where it is vital is where a cursor with an ORDER BY clause is to be updated.

The syntax of the <updatability clause> is:

```
FOR { READ ONLY
    | UPDATE [ OF <column name> [ {, <column name> }... ] ] }
```

where <column name> is a column name of the base table that underlies the cursor. If the table is updatable then there can only be one possible table, for the updatability rules (*see Section 9.3 Query Expression*). The column names in this clause are not those of the derived table but of the underlying base table. There is no requirement that the columns even appear in the cursor itself. This can be an advantage in that the cursor need contain only the columns necessary to identify and select the desired rows, thereby minimizing the transfer of data between the database and program while still allowing any desired columns to be modified.

Combinations of FOR UPDATE with either INSENSITIVE or SCROLL are illegal as the latter all imply a read only cursor. If the <updatability clause> is not specified then FOR READ ONLY is implicit if INSENSITIVE, ORDER BY or SCROLL is specified or if the derived table resulting from the <query expression> is not updatable (*see Section 9.3 Query Expression*). Otherwise FOR UPDATE is implicit. If FOR UPDATE without OF is specified then it is equivalent to FOR UPDATE OF with a list of all the columns of the underlying base table. READ ONLY means that no UPDATE or DELETE statements may be issued and UPDATE means that only those columns specified may be the subject of UPDATE commands using this cursor. The example:

```
DECLARE Prd_high_earners SCROLL CURSOR FOR
   SELECT name, salary
     FROM Employee
     WHERE deptcd = 'PRD'
         AND
         salary BETWEEN 35000 AND 100000
   ORDER BY name
```

declares a cursor that consists of two columns from selected rows of the Employee table. The rows are ordered by the name column in ascending order (the default). The cursor is not updatable because it has a SCROLL option. As a result of the SCROLL option the positioning options may be used on the FETCH command. The cursor may or may not (depending on the implementation) be sensitive to changes in the Employee table made by the transaction using other cursors or non-cursor commands since the INSENSITIVE option has not been used. The lack of an INSENSITIVE option does not imply sensitivity, only uncertainty. The example:

```
DECLARE Prd_high_earners CURSOR FOR
   SELECT name, salary
     FROM Employee
     WHERE deptcd = 'PRD'
        AND
        salary BETWEEN 35000 AND 100000
   FOR UPDATE salary, commission
```

declares a cursor that consists of the same two columns from selected rows of the Employee table. The rows are ordered in any way that the implementation decides. The cursor is now updatable but only for the salary and commission columns (commission is a column of Employee but not of the cursor), but the only positioning option permitted on FETCH commands is now NEXT. Again the cursor may be sensitive to changes in the Employee table.

The major problem with cursors is one that we have mentioned several times in this section, namely the sensitivity of the cursor to changes made to the underlying tables of the cursor by other commands not operating through the cursor. For instance, if we have the following sequence of commands:

```
DECLARE List_emps SCROLL CURSOR FOR
   SELECT empnr, name, salary
     FROM Employee
     WHERE salary BETWEEN 35000 AND 100000
OPEN List_emps
FETCH FIRST List_emps FROM INTO :progempnr, :progname,
       :progsalary
FETCH NEXT List_emps FROM INTO :progempnr2, :progname2,
        :progsalary2
DELETE Employee WHERE empnr = :progempnr
FETCH FIRST List_emps FROM INTO :progempnr2, :progname2,
        :progsalary2
```

there is no guarantee that the row fetched by the first FETCH is either the same or different from the row fetched by the last FETCH. If the cursor is sensitive then they will be different; if the cursor is insensitive then they will be the same. The sensitivity may even vary within one declared cursor, from one OPEN to the next. Thus great care must always be exercised when using an open cursor in combination with other cursors or data modifying commands.

7.2 OPEN

This command is used to open a cursor. The command syntax is:

OPEN <cursor name>

There must be a DECLARE CURSOR statement in the same module that declares a cursor with the name <cursor name>. There may be only one OPEN statement in the module referencing a specific cursor. The cursor is then opened — it must not be already open. This is achieved by evaluating the derived table definition contained in the DECLARE CURSOR statement. Any parameters that were present in the DECLARE CURSOR are now substituted with the values pertaining at the time of the OPEN. The value of the key words USER, CURRENT_USER, SESSION_USER, SYSTEM_USER and the values of all datetime value functions (e.g. CURRENT_TIME) are evaluated once at the moment of the open and the same value is always used within that cursor definition. The rows selected for the cursor will not change with time. The cursor will be ordered if the DECLARE CURSOR statement contains an ORDER BY clause. If the cursor is declared INSENSITIVE a copy of the derived table is effectively made and used as the cursor. Whether or not one is actually made depends on the implementation and the situation, but it will always appear as if one had been made since no updates made subsequently will be visible through this cursor.

The cursor is positioned before the first row. For example, if we declare a cursor as:

```
DECLARE All_dept CURSOR FOR SELECT * FROM Dept
```

we open it with

```
OPEN All_dept
```

7.3 FETCH

This command is used to retrieve a row from the derived table made available through an open cursor. The command syntax is:

FETCH [[<position>] FROM] <cursor name> INTO <fetch list>

where <fetch list> is a comma separated list of parameters or host language variables with exactly one target for each column in the derived table. Each target specification may include specification of the optional indicator parameters. The <position> option must be one of the following:

NEXT
PRIOR
FIRST
LAST

ABSOLUTE <simple value expression>
RELATIVE <simple value expression>

in which <simple value expression> must be either a literal, a parameter or a host language variable. If not specified, the <position> option defaults to NEXT. The cursor identified by the cursor name must be open.

The cursor is first positioned according to the <position> option. If the <position> option is other than NEXT, then the cursor must have been declared with the SCROLL option. NEXT positions the cursor on the row following the current position (if the cursor is positioned 'before row x', after a FETCH NEXT the cursor will be 'on row x'). PRIOR positions the cursor on the row preceding the current cursor position. FIRST positions the cursor on the first row of the cursor. LAST positions the cursor on the last row of the cursor. ABSOLUTE n positions the cursor on the *n*th row of the cursor counting from the beginning if *n* is positive and counting from the end of the cursor if *n* is negative. Thus ABSOLUTE 1 is equivalent to FIRST and ABSOLUTE –1 is equivalent to LAST. RELATIVE n is equivalent to n NEXT positioning requests if *n* is positive or n PRIOR positioning requests if *n* is negative. If RELATIVE 0 is specified then if the cursor is positioned on a row it remains positioned on that row; otherwise it returns a warning (no data). If there are not enough rows in the table to satisfy the movement then the cursor is positioned before the first row or after the last row as appropriate and a warning is issued (no data). Some positioning requests will always return a warning; e.g. ABSOLUTE 0 is legal but can never identify a row. If the positioning was successful then the values of the columns of the row on which the cursor is now positioned are copied to the target parameters (or host language variables). The order in which this is done is indeterminate and if any error occurs during the transfer the values of all the targets is indeterminate and the position of the cursor remains on the current row. This means that if the same target is used for two columns the actual value that it receives may be that from either of the two columns. Similarly, if an error occurs transferring the value of the third column there is no guarantee that the values of the first two columns have been transferred or that the value of column four (or higher) has not already been transferred. For the rules on transfer of values *see Section 6.5.1 Retrieval Assignment*.

Examples are:

```
FETCH All_dept INTO :progname, :progsalary

FETCH LAST All_dept FROM INTO :progname, :progsalary

FETCH RELATIVE -4 FROM All_dept INTO :progname, :progsalary
```

7.4 UPDATE Positioned

This command is used to update a row in a base table where the row is identified as being the row from which the current row of an open cursor has been derived. The command syntax is:

UPDATE <table name>
SET <object column name> = { <value expression> | NULL | DEFAULT }
[{ <object column name> =
{ <value expression> | NULL | DEFAULT } }...]
WHERE CURRENT OF <cursor name>

The cursor identified by the cursor name must be open, updateable (*see Section 7.1 DECLARE CURSOR*), positioned on a row and the table identified by the table name must be the only table identified in the outermost FROM clause of the cursor specification. Currently, standard SQL has severe restrictions on which cursors (and, indeed, views) may be updated. Furthermore, unless the table underlying the cursor is a temporary table the transaction must be a read–write transaction. Even if the transaction is read only it may still update rows in a temporary table.

The current authorization identifier must have an UPDATE privilege on each column identified by object column name, and the object column must have been explicitly or implicitly included in the updatability clause for the cursor (*see Section 7.1 DECLARE CURSOR*). No object column may occur more than once in the list, and all must be columns of the table identified by the table name. Furthermore, no column that is used in the ORDER BY clause may be updated. There is, however, no requirement that they also be columns visible through the cursor.

The value expressions, if specified, must not contain a set function such as MAX, COUNT, etc. DEFAULT implies the substitution of the current default value defined for the object column. The value expressions are evaluated before the row is updated, so that references to columns of the table (which use values from the object row) take the values before any column is updated. For example, if we declare a cursor as:

```
DECLARE All_dept CURSOR FOR SELECT * FROM Dept
```

and open it with:

```
OPEN All_dept
```

then we might have a cursor which looks like the one shown in Figure 7.1. Depending on the position of the cursor:

```
UPDATE Dept
   SET deptnm = deptcd || '_' || deptnm
       deptcd = SUBSTRING (deptnm FROM 1 FOR 3)
   WHERE CURRENT OF All_dept
```

will have the result shown in Table 7.1.

If any errors occur when deriving the values to be used in the updating or during its assignment then the cursor remains positioned on the row. You can

	All_dept	
	deptcd	*deptnm*
(a) →		
(b) →	SLS	Sales
	PER	Personnel
(c) →		
	...	...
(d) →		
	TRA	Travel
(e) →		

Figure 7.1 *All_dept cursor*

Table 7.1 Cursor position following UPDATE positioned

Position of cursor	*Effect on database/status*	*Final position of cursor*
(a) Before first row	None/invalid cursor state	Implementor defined
(b) On a row (SLS)	A row with deptcd = 'Sal' (not 'SLS') and deptnm = 'SLS_Sales'/successful completion	On the same row
(c) After a row (PER)	None/invalid cursor state	Implementor defined
(d) Before a row (TRA)	None/invalid cursor state	Implementor defined
(e) After last row	None/invalid cursor state	Implementor defined

therefore make a second attempt to get it right. Note that if the row to be updated has already been deleted or updated through another still open cursor, or by some non-cursor statement or even a triggered action from a referential constraint, then a warning is raised. This apparent inconsistency can occur because the visibility, within the cursor, of changes made outside a cursor is implementation dependent. This warning signals that a possible problem has arisen but does not seek to forbid it or take any corrective action. The problem can be largely avoided, but not eliminated, because of the triggered actions, by treating the complete set of operations on a cursor as if it were a searched command (i.e. atomic) by performing only the same update or delete on the current row after each fetch and by not including any other statements, cursor or non-cursor, between the open and close of the cursor.

7.5 DELETE Positioned

This command is used to delete a row from a table where the row is identified as being the row from which the current row of an open cursor has been derived. The command syntax is:

DELETE FROM <table name> WHERE CURRENT OF <cursor name>

The cursor identified by the cursor name must be open, updateable (*see Section 7.1 DECLARE CURSOR*), positioned on a row and the table identified by the table name must be the first, and only, table identified in the outermost FROM clause of the cursor specification. Furthermore, unless the table underlying the cursor is a temporary table the transaction must not be a read only transaction. Even if the transaction is read only it may still delete from a temporary table.

The current authorization identifier must have a DELETE privilege on the table identified by table name. For example: If we declare a cursor as:

```
DECLARE All_dept CURSOR FOR SELECT * FROM Dept
```

and open it with

```
OPEN All_dept
```

then we might have a cursor that looks like the one shown in Figure 7.2.

All_dept

	deptcd	*deptnm*
(a) →		
	SLS	Sales
(b) →	PER	Personnel
(c) →		
	...	...
(d) →		
(e) →	TRA	Travel
(f) →		

Figure 7.2 *A different All_dept cursor*

Depending on the position of the cursor:

```
DELETE FROM Dept WHERE CURRENT OF All_dept
```

will have the result shown in Table 7.2.

Table 7.2 Cursor position following DELETE positioned

Position of cursor	*Effect on database/status*	*Final position of cursor*
(a) Before first row	None/invalid cursor state	Implementor defined
(b) On a row (PER)	Row PER deleted/successful completion	Before the next row
(c) After a row (PER)	None/invalid cursor state	Implementor defined
(d) Before a row (TRA)	None/invalid cursor state	Implementor defined
(e) On last row (TRA)	Row TRA deleted/successful completion	After the last row
(f) After last row	None/invalid cursor state	Implementor defined

Note that if the row to be deleted has already been deleted or updated through another still open cursor, or by some non-cursor statement or even a triggered action from a referential constraint, then a warning is raised. This apparent inconsistency can occur because the visibility, within the cursor, of changes made outside a cursor is implementation dependent. This warning signals that a possible problem has arisen but does not seek to forbid it or take any corrective action. The problem can be largely avoided, but not eliminated, because of the triggered actions, by treating the complete set of operations on a cursor as atomic and not interspersing other statements.

7.6 CLOSE

This command is used to close an open cursor. The command syntax is:

CLOSE <cursor name>

The cursor identified by the cursor name must be open. The cursor is then closed, and the definition (and any materialized contents) of the derived table is destroyed. For example, if we declare a cursor as:

```
DECLARE All_dept CURSOR FOR SELECT * FROM Dept
```

we close it with

```
CLOSE All_dept
```

8

Access Control

Access control in SQL is based on the concept of an authorization identifier. This is a normal SQL identifier, with perhaps some implementation defined limitations, which is used to establish at any given point in time the identity of a user, human or otherwise, for SQL. The limitations are due to the fact that the identifier is not normally chosen within SQL but within the context of a system-wide security system. For all practical purposes we can assume that the identifier is simply a way of uniquely identifying the user. On the basis of the current authorization identifier an SQL compliant Database Management System will determine what objects that user may reference and what actions may be performed on those objects and the data contained in those objects.

Additionally, SQL has a concept of the ownership of objects and a concept of privileges on objects. Each object that is created in SQL has an owner. The owner is identified by the authorization identifier explicitly or implicitly defined in the AUTHORIZATION clause in the schema definition of the schema to which the object belongs. The owner is the only person who may perform certain actions on the object and, without permission, no user other than the owner may perform any actions on the object or, indeed, be able to become aware of the existence of the object. In this case the term person is treated as somebody or something that has or can assume the requisite authorization identifier. For details of how an authorization identifier is assumed (*see Chapter 13 Environment Management*).

In the example schema, for instance, the CREATE TABLE statement that defines the Employee table was successfully executed and the table was created but only the person who was designated the owner of the schema (in the example 'cannan') can access the Employee table or discover that the Employee table exists. The same holds for all the other tables and objects in the example database. Specifically, the owner may reference the Employee table or the columns of the Employee table in select statements or in the search conditions associated with other data manipulation statements, the owner may insert rows into the Employee table, may update the values in the columns of rows of the Employee table and may delete rows from the Employee table, and the owner may reference the Employee table or the columns of the Employee table in constraints that are subsequently defined by the owner, e.g. the FOREIGN KEY in Travel_Req. Furthermore, the owner may execute schema manipulation statements such as DROP TABLE Employee. However, the owner is the only person who may do any of these things and that is not very useful in a normal situation, although ideal for a private database.

To enable others to use tables, etc. that the owner has created the owner must explicitly give them the privilege of doing so. SQL defines and manages these privileges by means of 'privilege descriptors'. There are several sorts of privilege descriptors, namely:

usage privilege descriptors
table privilege descriptors
column privilege descriptors

Each descriptor contains:

- The identification of the object (domain, table, column, character set, collation or translation) to which the privilege applies
- The authorization identifier of the user who gives the privilege, called the grantor in SQL
- The authorization identifier of the user who receives the privilege, called the grantee in SQL
- The identification of the action on the object that is permitted
- An indication of whether the privilege may be given to other users by the receiver of the privilege

The possible actions are:

INSERT
UPDATE
DELETE
SELECT
REFERENCES
USAGE

The action of DELETE and SELECT may only be used when the object is a table; the actions INSERT, UPDATE and REFERENCES may be used with either tables or columns and a USAGE action may only be used when the object is a domain, character set, collation or translation. However, when a SELECT privilege is granted for a table, column privileges are also created for each column in the table. When a user creates an object a complete set of all relevant privilege descriptors is created with an artificial grantor of '_SYSTEM'. '_SYSTEM' is illegal as an authorization identifier and thus nobody can ever assume that identity and remove any privileges from the original owner. The privilege descriptors as described can be seen in the base tables defined in the Information Schema (*see Chapter 20 The Information Schema*).

The standard defines no action to permit the use of any schema manipulation statements on an object. The right to DROP or ALTER an object is reserved exclusively for the owner of the object. It is, however, likely that an implementation would provide extensions to the above list of privileges to control the usage of certain commands, including perhaps the schema manipulation statements, and to enable control of physical resources to be achieved, e.g. allocation of tables to files, etc.

How does a user who owns an object, let us say a table, give another user privileges on that table and how at a later stage can the owner retract that privilege? SQL has two commands, GRANT and REVOKE, which are used, respectively, for those purposes.

8.1 GRANT

Let us assume that the owner, cannan, wishes to grant a fellow employee, with an authorization identifier of OTTEN, read access to the Vehicle table. The owner would then issue a command:

```
GRANT SELECT ON Vehicle TO OTTEN
```

This grants OTTEN the right to reference the Vehicle table and any columns contained in Vehicle in a CREATE VIEW statement and in any of his SQL data manipulation statements so long as they do not attempt to change the data in the Vehicle table. Thus OTTEN may now define his own view on Vehicle which includes only the columns vehicleid and acquisition_date.

However, OTTEN is responsible for the company's vehicle fleet and must be able to insert and delete rows and to modify existing rows in the table. With the currently assigned privileges he could not do this so we must provide these as well:

```
GRANT INSERT, DELETE, UPDATE ON TABLE Vehicle TO OTTEN
```

Notice the use of the optional key word TABLE. He can now insert and update rows in Vehicle but could never store anything except NULL in the column Vehicle.empnr as the combination of constraints defined on the Vehicle table make it impossible to insert a value into the column without also inserting a value into the Employee.vehicleid column. Now assume that we wish to allow that but do not wish to allow OTTEN to update any other columns or otherwise change the Employee table. To do that we need to be able to specify the column (or columns) to which the action applies, as follows:

```
GRANT UPDATE(vehicleid) ON Employee TO OTTEN
GRANT SELECT ON Employee TO OTTEN
```

The SELECT privilege is necessary in order to be able to identify the individual Employee row to be updated.

The qualification by column cannot be applied to the SELECT, DELETE or USAGE actions. In the case of USAGE this is obvious because the objects to which USAGE can be applied do not possess columns and for DELETE it is also clear that one either deletes a row or not: one cannot delete one column from a single row (schema manipulation is a separate topic). However, for SELECT it is not immediately obvious why one cannot qualify the action by a column list as it obviously makes sense to be able to select only certain columns. The argument is that the view mechanism (*see Section 4.4 CREATE VIEW*) is all that is required. Not everyone is convinced this is the right answer and this restriction may well be relaxed in future. In this example if OTTEN was not to be permitted to read all of the Employee table, we would have had to define a special view to restrict access before granting SELECT and UPDATE on that view and not on the base table.

The absence of a column list has one implication that should be remembered. If columns are subsequently added to the table then the same privileges will exist on these new columns. In general this is no problem but if a column that is to hold sensitive data is added to a table then a review of the privileges already granted is vital.

OTTEN now has all the privileges needed in order to carry out his work but cannot delegate any of it to JONES who works in the same department. In order to do that we need to allow OTTEN the privilege to grant his privileges to others. We can do that with the so-called WITH GRANT OPTION:

```
GRANT UPDATE(vehicleid) ON Employee TO OTTEN WITH GRANT
     OPTION
GRANT SELECT ON Employee TO OTTEN WITH GRANT OPTION
GRANT SELECT, INSERT, DELETE, UPDATE ON Vehicle
     TO OTTEN WITH GRANT OPTION
```

SQL is clever enough to recognize that the two sets of privilege descriptors we have just created are identical except for the indicator for the grant option. It will therefore discard the descriptor without the option indicator set. This also applies to complete duplicates. Only one descriptor describing a privilege for some action on some object granted by one user to another may exist at any one time. The attempt to create a duplicate is not an error but is effectively a null action. Privilege descriptors granted by different users, say A and B, are not identical, even when they grant the same action on the same object to the same third user C.

OTTEN has all possible privileges on Vehicle except one, REFERENCES. REFERENCES is an action very similar to SELECT except that it applies to the usage of the table or column in different circumstances. SELECT effectively grants privileges for data manipulation statements whereas REFERENCES grants privileges for data definition statements, i.e. it permits the referencing of those columns in constraints such as the check constraint and the foreign key constraint. The reason for this separation is that while you may freely give SELECT privileges away without restricting what you yourself may do with the data in your tables (you only allow others to read it), the use of your columns in a foreign key constraint in somebody else's table, to which you have no guaranteed access, may stop you from deleting rows in your own table if the other person has not defined an ON DELETE CASCADE triggered action option in the foreign key definition. This significant difference in consequences is the justification for the separation of privileges. If we assume that the owner is happy for OTTEN to use the Vehicle table in any constraints that he may define in his own tables then the owner could have replaced the statement:

```
GRANT SELECT, INSERT, DELETE, UPDATE ON Vehicle
   TO OTTEN WITH GRANT OPTION
```

with the statement:

```
GRANT ALL PRIVILEGES ON Vehicle TO OTTEN WITH GRANT OPTION
```

ALL PRIVILEGES is a shorthand that means all the privileges that the grantor possesses and that he is permitted to grant (i.e. where he or she also has the grant option for that privilege). These may not be all possible privileges. Thus OTTEN might well grant his privileges to JONES using:

```
GRANT ALL PRIVILEGES ON Vehicle TO JONES
GRANT ALL PRIVILEGES ON Employee TO JONES
```

This effectively grants JONES all the actions that OTTEN had on those two tables since all the privileges that OTTEN has are also grantable. The grant option is not granted with this statement, despite the fact that OTTEN possesses it.

It is possible to grant to multiple users in a grant statement, e.g. assume that OTTEN also has two clerks, WHITE and GREY, who should be able to read but not update the Vehicle table. OTTEN would then execute:

```
GRANT SELECT ON Vehicle TO WHITE, GREY
```

There is one further option and that is the use of the pseudo user PUBLIC. If we wish to grant a privilege to everyone then we can use PUBLIC instead of a list of authorization identifiers. This has the additional advantage of automatically granting the privileges to users who may be defined after we issue the grant statement. Since there is no sensitive information in the Dept table we may simply grant read access to everybody:

```
GRANT SELECT ON Dept TO PUBLIC
```

One final comment can be made. It is naturally illegal to attempt to grant privileges that you do not possess to somebody else, but as we have seen earlier it is not illegal to grant privileges several times to the same person. The ALL

PRIVILEGES option is a useful shorthand for avoiding attempting to grant privileges that you do not possess.

8.2 REVOKE

The REVOKE statement performs the reverse of the GRANT statement. The REVOKE has two options, RESTRICT and CASCADE, which operate exactly like those options on the DROP statement for other objects in the schema. We will deal first with the use of commands with the RESTRICT option and then later with the use of the CASCADE option. Let us assume that OTTEN changed his mind about giving GREY privileges on the Vehicle table; then he would issue:

```
REVOKE ALL PRIVILEGES ON Vehicle FROM GREY RESTRICT
```

which in this case is equivalent to:

```
REVOKE SELECT ON Vehicle FROM GREY RESTRICT
```

as SELECT is the only action ever granted. You can only revoke privileges that you have granted. Thus the owner may not issue the REVOKE statement to remove the privilege from GREY; only OTTEN can do that. Because of the RESTRICT option there must not exist any objects, such as views, that GREY has created on the basis of the privilege or privileges to be revoked.

You will notice that there is no requirement for the actual REVOKE statement to mirror the original GRANT statement. One must always think in terms of the privilege descriptors which are effectively the memory of the access control mechanism and not in terms of the GRANT statement which created the access control data. GRANT creates (or updates) privilege descriptors and REVOKE deletes (or updates) privilege descriptors.

In the same way that it is possible to grant a privilege with or without a WITH GRANT OPTION it is also possible to revoke either the entire privilege or only the WITH GRANT OPTION on the privilege. If the owner changes his mind about letting OTTEN pass on his UPDATE privilege on the Employee table then the owner can recall that option with:

```
REVOKE GRANT OPTION FOR UPDATE(vehicleid) FROM OTTEN
       RESTRICT
```

This would only be possible if OTTEN had not yet passed on the UPDATE(vehicleid) privilege to JONES, as otherwise JONES's privilege descriptor would also require deleting and the RESTRICT forbids this. There is a CASCADE option which will allow the forced revocation of JONES privileges, but we will discuss that in the next section.

8.3 Ripple Effects of the GRANT Statement

Given an environment with several schemata, views defined using tables from other schemata or tables defined using domains, etc. from other schemata, a hierarchy of privileges granted on the basis of the WITH GRANT OPTION issuing grant statements may have a ripple effect on privileges on other objects. There are two circumstances where this might occur.

First, when a potentially updatable view is defined by a user and this is based on a table which that user does not own then the privilege descriptors created for the view's creator are restricted to those privileges that the user has on the underlying table. If subsequently that user is granted more privileges on the underlying tables, for example the addition of a delete privilege (the additional privileges must be one of delete, insert or update), then all the additional privileges that would have been available had the view been created under the new situation are automatically added to the privileges defined for the view. If that view itself had been used in other view definitions then the additional privileges ripple through the view hierarchy until the privileges are the same as if all views were to be redefined anew.

Second, when a user like JONES, who has previously made use of a privilege without the WITH GRANT OPTION to create a view, subsequently receives the WITH GRANT OPTION it is added to the appropriate privilege on the view which he holds as the owner. He may then grant those privileges to others. Similarly, if the user has defined a translation or a collation on a character set for which he or she has a usage privilege but no WITH GRANT OPTION, the user is unable to grant usage of those translations or collations to other users. Again, if the user subsequently receives the WITH GRANT OPTION that is added to his or her own usage privilege on the translation or collation he or she may grant that privilege to others.

Similarly, the owner of a domain may not have had the WITH GRANT OPTION on some of the privileges necessary to create the domain and may thus not have received the WITH GRANT OPTION on the USAGE privilege. If the owner subsequently is granted all the necessary WITH GRANT OPTIONs then his USAGE privilege also acquires the WITH GRANT OPTION.

8.4 Cascade Effects of the REVOKE Statement

Since privileges are required in order to be able to use certain objects in the definition of other objects, or to grant privileges received to another, revoking a privilege can remove the authority that allowed the object to be created. The existence of such a dependent object will prevent a revoke from successfully executing unless the CASCADE option is used.

Table 8.1 Privileges required to create schema objects

Object	*Privileges are needed on*
View	Table (at least select, additional privileges determine the extent of the owner's own privileges) Domain Collation Character set Translation
Domain	Collation
Domain constraint	Table/column (references privilege) Domain Collation Character set Translation
Table constraint	Table/column (references privilege) Domain Collation Character set Translation
Assertion	Table/column (references privilege) Domain Collation Character set Translation
Collation	Character set
Translation	Character set
Privilege descriptor	Privilege (used to create (grant) the privilege to which the privilege relates)

Let us look first at what is dependent on what. This is shown in Table 8.1. An object is said to be abandoned if the revoke of a privilege would result in the necessary privileges for the object's creation no longer being present. Any revoke that would result in abandoned translations or collations is rejected. A simple revoke by OTTEN:

```
REVOKE SELECT ON Vehicle FROM GREY RESTRICT
```

is rejected if it would result in any abandoned object such as a view. Privilege descriptors are also treated as objects in this context and a revoke, by cannan, of the WITH GRANT OPTION only, such as:

```
REVOKE GRANT OPTION FOR UPDATE(vehicleid) FROM OTTEN
    RESTRICT
```

can only result in abandoned privilege descriptors being rejected if any such privilege descriptors exist. To handle the case where abandoned privilege descriptors, views, table constraints, domains, domain constraints or assertions exist we need the CASCADE option.

This key word replaces RESTRICT in a revoke statement. For example, a revoke by OTTEN such as:

```
REVOKE SELECT ON Vehicle FROM GREY CASCADE
```

causes all abandoned privilege descriptors to be destroyed and an appropriate DROP statement, with a CASCADE option, to be issued for any abandoned domains, domain constraints, views, table constraints or assertions. We should note that these drop commands may themselves trigger further revoke statements (i.e. for the privileges that have been granted on them), and the cascade process continues until no further objects are abandoned.

A revoke of the WITH GRANT OPTION only with the CASCADE option as in:

```
REVOKE GRANT OPTION FOR UPDATE(vehicleid) FROM OTTEN CASCADE
```

while causing all abandoned privilege descriptors to be destroyed and the appropriate DROP statements to be issued, leaves OTTEN still with the UPDATE(vehicleid) privilege, but now without the WITH GRANT OPTION.

It is possible for the owner of an object to inspect the views of the Information Schema to ascertain the impact of such a CASCADE operation before actually executing it.

8.5 Checking the Privileges

We said at the beginning of the chapter that checking is done on the basis of the current authorization identifier but how is that determined? For every session there is an authorization identifier which is either implementation defined or specified in the connect statement that initiates the session. This authorization identifier may be changed by a set statement. All SQL statements are executed in procedures of modules (in the case of dynamic, direct and embedded SQL the module is fictitious). A module may or may not have an explicit authorization identifier defined for it. If it does, then that authorization identifier is the current identifier for all procedures of that module and is unaffected by the session authorization identifier or any changes to it. If the module does not have an explicit authorization identifier then the current session one is used. It is therefore possible to write modules that can perform actions that the end-user cannot perform for him- or herself. The restrictions on whether a specific user may assume another authorization identifier with the SET SESSION AUTHORIZATION statement and the restrictions on which users may call procedures in modules with explicit module authorization identifiers are implementation defined.

Having established the current authorization identifier for a given SQL command the appropriate privileges must be held by that authorization identifier in order to be able to complete the command successfully. The privilege requirements are as follows:

SELECT privileges are required on all tables used
in a <query expression> of an <insert statement>, a <cursor specification>, a <view definition> or a <direct select statement: multiple rows>,
or in a <table expression> or a <select list> contained in a <select statement: single row>,
or in a <query specification> contained in a <dynamic single row select statement>,
or in a <search condition> immediately contained in a <delete statement> or an <update statement>,
or in a <select list> immediately contained in a <select statement: single row>,
or in a <value expression> immediately contained in an <set clause: searched> or an <set clause: positioned>.

DELETE privilege is required on all tables that are the target of a <delete statement: positioned> or a <delete statement: searched>.

INSERT privileges are required for each column identified in an explicit or implicit <insert column list> of an <insert statement>.

UPDATE privileges are required for each column identified in an <object column: positioned> or an <object column: searched>.

REFERENCES privileges are required on all referenced columns in a <referential constraint definition>, on at least one column of all tables and on all columns referenced in a <search condition> contained in either a <check constraint definition> or an <assertion definition>.

USAGE privilege is required for each domain, collation, character set or translation that is referenced in any command other than the one that creates it.

9

Derived Tables

This chapter describes the various elements of the SQL language that can be used to generate derived tables.

9.1 Row Value Constructors

A row value constructor is an ordered set of values that is regarded as if it was a row in a table. It takes the form:

```
<row value constructor> ::=
    { <value expression> | NULL | DEFAULT }
  | ( { <value expression> | NULL | DEFAULT }
      [ {, <value expression> | NULL | DEFAULT }... ] )
  | <subquery>
```

If <subquery> is specified then it must only return zero or one row. If the <subquery> returns zero rows then the result of the <row value constructor> is a row of nulls; otherwise it is the row returned. The result of the row value constructor is a row of columns with the values of <value expression>, NULL or, if DEFAULT is specified, the current default value specified for the target column. There is a restriction that NULL and DEFAULT may only be specified if the row value construction constitutes part of the input data for an INSERT statement (this is because we cannot determine the data type of the column or the default value, since NULL has no implicit data type and a column that is simply in a row value constructor has no default). The row value constructor does not need to be enclosed in parentheses if there is only one column. For example:

```
empnr
('A text string', NULL, 2.3)
(SELECT * FROM Dept WHERE deptcd ='SLS')
```

9.2 Table Value Constructors

A table value constructor is a set of row value constructors that is regarded as a table. It is a kind of literal, non-updatable table and it takes the form:

<table value constructor> ::=
VALUES <row value constructor> } [{, <row value constructor> }...]

All of the row value constructors must have the same number of values. Each row value constructor is considered a table of one row with the columns having the data types of the corresponding values. The result of the table value constructor is the table that would result from a UNION of all the tables representing the row value constructors.

For example, create a two-row table with the same structure as the Dept table:

```
VALUES ('SLS', 'Sales'), ('TRA', 'Travel')
```

To create a similar table with the same two rows plus the row, if any, from the Dept table whose primary key is 'PRD' gives:

```
VALUES ('SLS', 'Sales'),
       ('TRA', 'Travel'),
       (SELECT * FROM Dept WHERE deptcd = 'PRD')
```

9.3 Query Expression

The query expression is the basic way of defining a derived table. It is the starting point for the declaration of views, cursors and subqueries. There are many options and levels within the syntax for defining a derived table. Two of these intermediate levels are used as starting points for the specification of a derived table in commands. The first of these is a <query specification> which is identical to the <dynamic single row select statement> and, indeed, is the same as a <select statement: single row> without the INTO clause. The <select statement: single row> uses the second form of the derived table — a <table expression>. The reason for this is largely historical and it has been retained to maintain upward compatibility in the syntactic structure of the select statements. Since, as we will see, the query expression, the query specification and the table expression definitions may also contain the other forms as components (i.e. the definitions are recursive), the distinction is not a real problem.

The syntax structure of a query expression is:

<query expression> ::=
<non-join query expression>
| <joined table>

```
<non-join query expression> ::=
     <non-join query term>
   | <query expression> UNION  [ ALL ] [ <corresponding specification> ]
       <query term>
   | <query expression> EXCEPT [ ALL ] [ <corresponding specification> ]
       <query term>

<query term> ::=
     <non-join query term>
   | <joined table>

<non-join query term> ::=
     <non-join query primary>
   | <query term> INTERSECT [ ALL ] [ <corresponding specification> ]
       <query primary>

<query primary> ::=
     <non-join query primary>
   | <joined table>

<non-join query primary> ::=
     <simple table>
   | ( <non-join query expression> )

<simple table> ::=
     <query specification>
   | <table value constructor>
   | TABLE <table name>

<corresponding specification> ::=
    CORRESPONDING [ BY ( <corresponding column list> ) ]

<corresponding column list> ::=
    <column name> [ { , <column name> }... ]
```

Interpreted, this means that a query expression can be one of two types: either a table constructed from join operators or a table constructed from non-join operators. In the first case the operands are simple table names or subqueries and in the second case the operands are subqueries, table value constructors, or query specifications or table names preceded by the key word TABLE. This last form is equivalent to " (SELECT * FROM <table name>) " and needs the key word TABLE in order to avoid parsing ambiguities. In complex query expressions, expressions within parentheses are evaluated first, then joined tables, then, finally, UNION and EXCEPT. UNION and EXCEPT are evaluated left to right.

The syntax and semantics of joined tables are described in *Section 9.3.2.4 JOIN*. The non-join set operators are UNION, INTERSECT and EXCEPT. These are also given separate sections but there are certain rules, etc. that are common and are discussed here. All columns of all tables have a name that is unique within that table. When tables are derived using a query expression the name of a column in the result table is either that of the column from which it is derived or, in the case of UNION, EXCEPT or INTERSECT, the common name of the two columns from which it derives. If the derivation is not simple or if the column names in set operators differ then the system supplies a unique name. The data types of the columns resulting from a non-join operation are determined by a special set of rules (*see Section 9.3.3 Set Operations Result Data Types*).

The derived table resulting from a <query expression> is only updatable if it consists only of a <non-join query primary> (i.e. no set operators are specified) and the specified <simple table> or <non-join query expression> is itself updatable.

The two operand tables for a non-join set operator must have the same number of columns. If the CORRESPONDING option is specified then this is equivalent to the following query expression:

```
(SELECT select_list FROM operand1)
op
(SELECT select_list FROM operand2)
```

where 'op', 'operand1' and 'operand2' are respectively the set operator and the first and the second operand from the original query expression; 'select_list' is derived as follows:

- If no corresponding column list is specified, then it is a list of all the column names that occur in both operand tables, but in the order in which those columns occur in the first operand. It is a requirement that there be at least one common column.
- Otherwise, it is the list of column names given in the corresponding column list, this time in the order given in that corresponding column list. All the specified columns must occur in both operand tables.

It is a requirement that there are no duplicate column names within the individual tables so that no ambiguity arises. This situation would arise, for example, in the derived table ' `A JOIN A` '. The following are all valid query expressions:

```
VALUES ('SLS', 'Sales'), ('TRA', 'Travel')
```

a table value constructor

```
(SELECT * FROM Employee)
EXCEPT CORRESPONDING
(SELECT * FROM Travel_Req)
```

an EXCEPTed table (a single column (empnr) table of all employees who have never submitted a travel requisition)

```
SELECT DISTINCT suppliernr FROM Order
```

a query specification

```
Order NATURAL JOIN Order_Line
```

a joined table

```
(SELECT empnr
   FROM Emp_Ext
   WHERE date_of_birth < CURRENT_DATE - INTERVAL '60' YEAR)
UNION
(SELECT empnr
   FROM Emp_Ext
   WHERE date_of_birth > CURRENT_DATE - INTERVAL '20' YEAR)
```

a UNIONed table (containing employees over 60 as well as employees under 20)

9.3.1 Table References

At several places within queries it is necessary to reference various tables of different sorts, i.e. base tables, views or the derived tables that result from subqueries. It is also possible to couple local names to these tables, either to simplify the writing of the rest of the query or to distinguish between two different uses of the same table.

The syntax of a table reference is:

```
<table reference> ::=
    <table name> [ [ AS ] <correlation name> [ ( <derived column list> ) ] ]
    <table subquery> [ [ AS ] <correlation name> [ ( <derived column list> ) ] ]
    <joined table>

<derived column list> ::= <column name> [ { , <column name> }... ]
```

The AS clauses provide replacement names for tables or derived tables. This is vital if the same table occurs more than once in the list of table references, as we may need to distinguish between them. Once a <correlation name> is attached to a table any other <table name> or <correlation name> with the same value within the scope of the new <correlation name> is hidden and no longer usable. A usable table name or correlation name is said to be *exposed*.

The <derived column list> is an option which permits the renaming, or naming, of columns. The reason for having <joined table> as an extra option, since a '(<joined table>)' is also a table subquery, is because of the naming rules. A <table subquery> has no name, unless explicitly given one by a <correlation name>; thus unless this was done it would be impossible to reference the columns of the <joined table> in a subsequent clause.

The scope of a table or correlation name, or the places where it is valid, is defined as follows:

- If the <table reference> is contained in a <from clause> then it is the innermost <query specification> or <select statement: single row> in which the <from clause> appears.

- If the <table reference> is not contained in a <from clause> then it is the outermost <joined table> that contains the <table reference> without an intervening <derived table>.

9.3.2 Set Operators

Table_1
column_1
a
b
b
d
e
e
e
e

Table_2
column_1
b
c
d
e
e

Figure 9.1 *Tables for set operators*

The only relational operator missing from the standard is the DIVIDE operator. We have included a section, however, that shows how this may be simulated in SQL (*see Section 9.3.2.5 DIVIDE — the missing option*). The following sections describe the effects of each of the set operators in detail. In describing these functions we will use the tables shown in Figure 9.1. These tables are not meaningful in their own right but allow us to demonstrate all the various effects without cluttering up the essentials by the derivation of suitable data from meaningful tables.

Note that in the following sections where **duplicate** rows are eliminated the choice of row to be eliminated in cases where the duplicate rows are not identical (due to the working of the **compare equal** mechanism) is arbitrary.

9.3.2.1 UNION

Basically, the UNION operator takes two sets of rows (*see Figure 9.2*), i.e. the set of rows in the first operand table and the set of rows in the second operand table, and produces a table that contains both sets of rows. There is one option with the UNION operator, ALL. If ALL is not specified then UNION works as a pure set operator, i.e. **duplicate** rows in the result are eliminated. If ALL is specified then UNION works as a multi-set operator and duplicate rows are not eliminated. (This is similar to the ALL option in a <query specification>, but the default option in this case is not ALL but an unspecified 'DISTINCT').

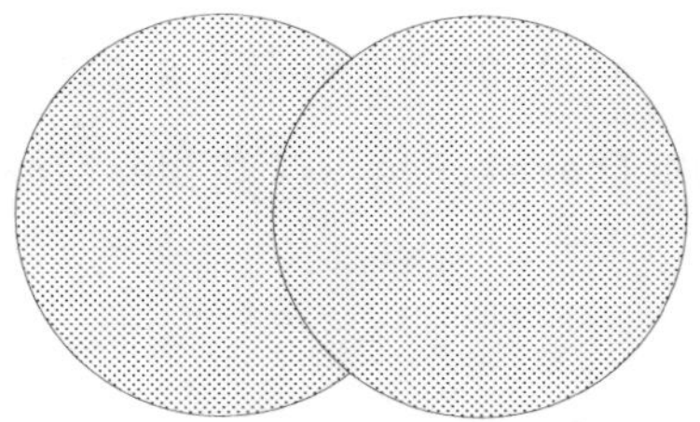

Figure 9.2 The UNION of two sets

column_1
a
b
c
d
e

(a)

column_1
a
b
b
b
c
d
d
e
e
e
e
e
e

(b)

Figure 9.3 UNION result tables

Given the two example tables T1 and T2 in Figure 9.1,

T1 UNION T2

gives the table in Figure 9.3(a) as the result, whereas

T1 UNION ALL T2

gives the table in Figure 9.3(b) as the result.

If, for example, we wanted the list of employees who had either worked on one of the Sullom Voe projects or who had requested travel to Lerwick then we could say:

```
SELECT * FROM
(SELECT empnr FROM Assignment WHERE project_cd LIKE 'SULL%'
 UNION
 SELECT empnr FROM Travel_Req WHERE destination = 'LERWICK')
```

9.3.2.2 EXCEPT

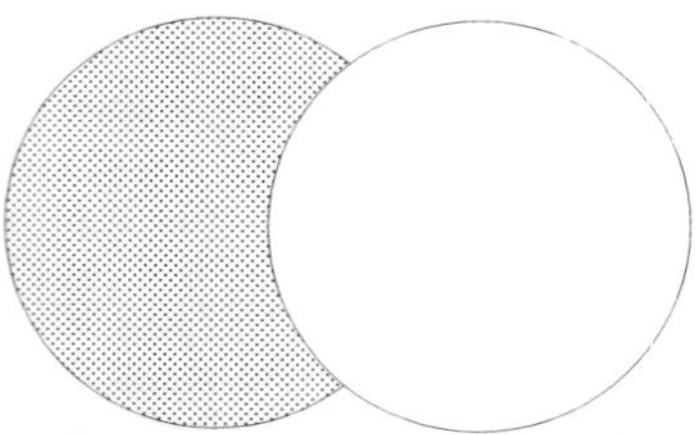

Figure 9.4 *The EXCEPT of two sets (difference)*

Basically, the EXCEPT operator takes two sets of rows (*see Figure 9.4*), i.e. the set of rows in the first operand table and the set of rows in the second operand table, and produces a table that contains the rows from the first set that do not occur in the second set. This is also sometimes referred to as the 'difference' operator. Again there is one option with the EXCEPT operator, ALL. If ALL is not specified then EXCEPT works as a pure set operator, i.e. only a single (non-**duplicate**) row from the first table occurs in the result if no corresponding row exists in the second table. If ALL is specified then EXCEPT works as a multi-set operator and rows in the first table are eliminated if there is a corresponding row in the second table, i.e. if the first table has five rows, R1, which are all duplicates of each other and the second table also has two rows which are R1 duplicates then the resulting table will have three rows which are R1 duplicates. (If ALL was not specified then the result in this case would have no rows.)

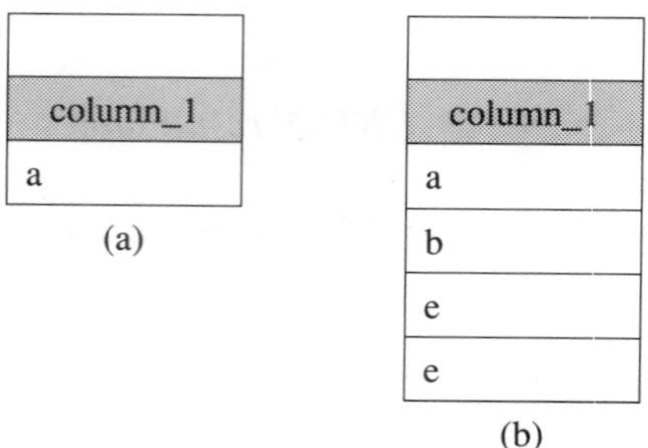

column_1
a

(a)

column_1
a
b
e
e

(b)

Figure 9.5 *EXCEPT result tables*

Given the two example tables T1 and T2 in Figure 9.1,

T1 EXCEPT T2

gives the table in Figure 9.5(a) as the result whereas

T1 EXCEPT ALL T2

gives the result in Figure 9.5(b).

If, for example, we wanted the list of employees who had worked on one of the Sullom Voe projects but who had never requested travel to Lerwick then we could say:

```
SELECT * FROM
(SELECT empnr FROM Assignment WHERE project_cd LIKE 'SULL%'
 EXCEPT
 SELECT empnr FROM Travel_Req WHERE destination = 'LERWICK')
```

9.3.2.3 INTERSECT

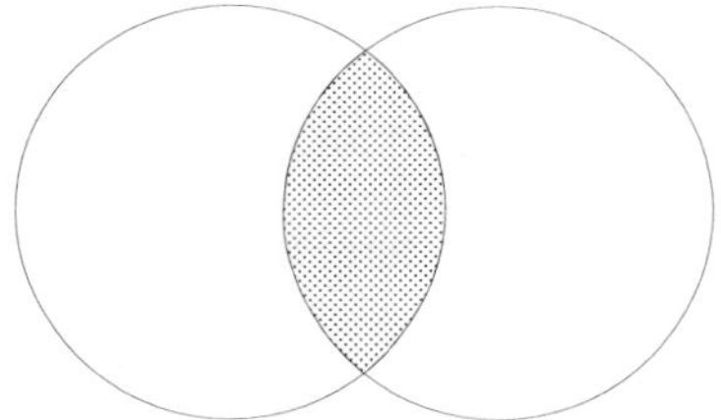

Figure 9.6 *The INTERSECT of two sets*

Basically, the INTERSECT operator takes two sets of rows (*see Figure 9.6*), i.e. the set of rows in the first operand table and the set of rows in the second operand table and produces a table that contains the rows from the first set which also occur in the second set. Again there is one option with the INTERSECT operator, ALL. If ALL is not specified then INTERSECT works as a pure set operator, i.e. **duplicate** rows in the result are eliminated. If ALL is specified then INTERSECT works as a multi-set operator and duplicates are not eliminated, i.e. if the first table has five duplicates of a row and the second table has two duplicates of the same row then the result will have only two duplicates.

Given the two example tables T1 and T2 in Figure 9.1,

T1 INTERSECT T2

gives the table in Figure 9.7(a) as the result whereas

T1 INTERSECT ALL T2

gives the result in Figure 9.7(b).

If we wanted the converse of the previous list, i.e. all those employees who had both worked on one of the Sullom Voe projects and who had requested

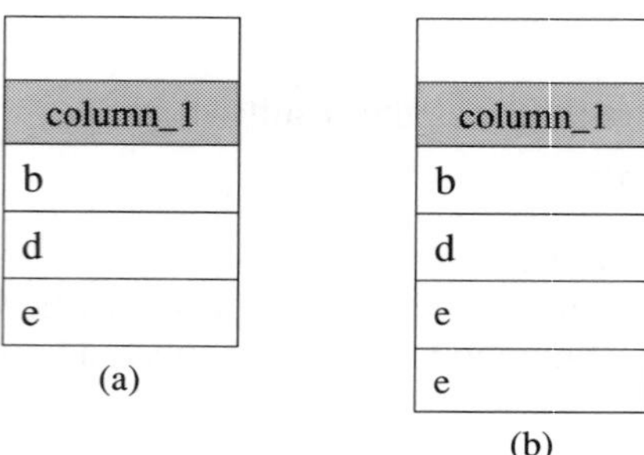

Figure 9.7 *INTERSECT result tables*

travel to Lerwick, then the query is:

```
SELECT *
 FROM
  (SELECT empnr
     FROM Assignment
     WHERE project_cd LIKE 'SULL%'
  INTERSECT
  SELECT empnr FROM Travel_Req WHERE destination =
     'LERWICK')
```

9.3.2.4 JOIN

The JOIN operator has a number of alternatives and options which allow the generation of four major classes of join. These are cross product, inner join, outer join and union join. These classes of join are separately described in the following sections. However, we will look at the overall syntax structure first. The syntax for joined table is as follows:

<joined table> ::=
<cross join>
| <qualified join>
| (<joined table>)

<cross join> ::= <table reference> CROSS JOIN <table reference>

<qualified join> ::= <table reference> [NATURAL] [<join type>] JOIN
<table reference> [<join specification>]

<join type> ::=
INNER
| { LEFT | RIGHT | FULL } [OUTER]
| UNION

<join specification> ::= <join condition> | <named columns join>

<join condition> ::= ON <search condition>

<named columns join> ::= USING (<join column list>)

<join column list> ::= <column name> [{ , <column name> }...]

The options NATURAL, <join specification> and a <join type> of UNION are mutually exclusive. The default for <join type> is INNER. The special effects of the NATURAL option and the <named columns join> option are separately discussed (*see Section 9.3.2.4.5 The NATURAL option*).

The order of evaluation is first, expressions within parentheses and then, from left to right within the constraints of the syntax. The key word JOIN together with either the key word ON or the key word USING also act as a form of brackets when used.

9.3.2.4.1 CROSS

Table_1
col_A
1
2
3

Table_2	
col_B	col_C
1	A
2	B

Result_table		
col_A	col_B	col_C
1	1	A
1	2	B
2	1	A
2	2	B
3	1	A
3	2	B

Figure 9.8 *The CROSS join of two tables*

The CROSS JOIN variant of the join operator is the simplest of the joins and forms the basis for nearly all the other joins. Given two tables (*see Figure 9.8*), the first with n rows each of x columns and the second with m rows each of y columns, it returns a table with $n \times m$ rows each of $x+y$ columns. The rows of the result table are formed by taking each of the rows of the first table in turn and appending a row from the second table. Every row in the second table is appended to each row in the first table.

For example:

```
Product CROSS JOIN Supplier
```

would provide a table of every possible combination of supplier and product. The FROM clause effectively defines a CROSS JOIN of all the tables in that clause. Thus the above example generates the same derived table as:

```
FROM Product, Supplier
```

9.3.2.4.2 INNER

The INNER JOIN variant of the join operator is the next simplest of the joins. Given two tables, the result of the INNER JOIN is the CROSS JOIN with only the rows for which the <join condition> is true retained. For example:

```
Order INNER JOIN Order_Line ON Order.ordernr =
    Order_Line.ordernr
```

would provide a table of every combination of order and associated order line.

The search condition does not need to be an equality test. For example, if we wish to know the order lines that are for more than twice the minimum order for supplier '12017' then we can say:

```
Order_Line
INNER JOIN
(SELECT * FROM Product_Supply WHERE suppliernr = 12017) PS
   ON Order_Line.product_code = PS.product_code
      AND
      Order_Line.quantity > 2 * PS.minimum_order
```

The FROM clause and a WHERE clause together effectively define an INNER JOIN of the tables where the WHERE clause includes a predicate that references both tables. The use of the INNER JOIN syntax is preferable, especially in complex situations, as it clearly separates the join condition from the restriction (selecting rows) function of the WHERE clause.

9.3.2.4.3 OUTER

Sometimes we want to join two tables but not to lose the information from rows that are unmatched. If we use INNER JOIN then the result only contains the rows that matched and we have lost information. Let us assume that we want a list of all employees and the destinations to which they have travelled, but including all employees regardless of whether they have travelled or not. To achieve this we can write the following query:

```
(SELECT empnr FROM Employee)
NATURAL LEFT JOIN
(SELECT empnr, destination FROM Travel_Req)
```

This gives us a two-column table, with columns empnr and destination, with one row for every combination of empnr and destination and one row for every empnr for which there is no empnr, destination combination. In the latter rows the destination column has the null value.

The OUTER JOIN variant has three options, LEFT, RIGHT and FULL, and we have used one option, LEFT, in the above example. In general an OUTER JOIN of two tables T1 and T2 works as follows:

- Let I be the T1 INNER JOIN T2 with the same <join condition>.
- Let R1 be a table containing the rows of T1 which did not contribute to

any of the rows of I, extended on the right with the same number of columns as T2 and all containing the null value.

- Let R2 be a table containing the rows of T2 which did not contribute to any of the rows of I, extended on the left with the same number of columns as T1 and all containing the null value.

LEFT OUTER JOIN is then equivalent to:

```
SELECT * FROM I
UNION ALL
SELECT * FROM R1
```

RIGHT OUTER JOIN is then equivalent to:

```
SELECT * FROM I
UNION ALL
SELECT * FROM R2
```

FULL OUTER JOIN is then equivalent to:

```
SELECT * FROM I
UNION ALL
SELECT * FROM R1
UNION ALL
SELECT * FROM R2
```

Vehicle		
vehicleid	*empnr*	*acquisition_date*
AA-51-KL	23456	1984-02-24
TB-23-TB	N/A	1988-09-02
XW-99-TS	12345	1989-03-02

Employee			
empnr	*name*	...	*vehicleid*
12345	Patel	...	XW-99-TS
23456	Smith	...	AA-51-KL
56789	Jones	...	N/A

Figure 9.9 *Contents of the Vehicle and Employee tables*

Thus the LEFT option preserves unmatched rows from the first table, the RIGHT option preserves unmatched rows from the second and the FULL option preserves the unmatched rows from both tables. For example, assuming that the Vehicle table and the Employee table have the contents shown in Figure 9.9,

Vehicle LEFT JOIN Employee ON (Vehicle.vehicleid = Employee.vehicleid)						
vehicleid	*empnr*	*acquisition_date*	*empnr*	*name*	*...*	*vehicleid*
AA-51-KL	23456	1984-02-24	23456	Smith	...	AA-51-KL
TB-23-TB	N/A	1988-09-02	N/A	N/A	N/A	N/A
XW-99-TS	12345	1989-03-02	12345	Patel	...	XW-99-TS

Figure 9.10 *Result of LEFT JOIN*

then the result of Vehicle LEFT JOIN Employee ON (Vehicle.vehicleid = Employee.vehicleid) is as shown in Figure 9.10, the result of Vehicle RIGHT JOIN Employee ON (Vehicle.vehicleid = Employee.vehicleid) is shown in Figure 9.11 and the result of Vehicle FULL JOIN Employee ON (Vehicle. vehicleid = Employee.vehicleid) is shown in Figure 9.12.

Vehicle RIGHT JOIN Employee ON (Vehicle.vehicleid = Employee.vehicleid)						
vehicleid	*empnr*	*acquisition_date*	*empnr*	*name*	*...*	*vehicleid*
AA-51-KL	23456	1984-02-24	23456	Smith	...	AA-51-KL
N/A	N/A	N/A	56789	Jones	...	N/A
XW-99-TS	12345	1989-03-02	12345	Patel	...	XW-99-TS

Figure 9.11 *Result of RIGHT JOIN*

Vehicle FULL JOIN Employee ON (Vehicle.vehicleid = Employee.vehicleid)						
vehicleid	*empnr*	*acquisition_date*	*empnr*	*name*	*...*	*vehicleid*
AA-51-KL	23456	1984-02-24	23456	Smith	...	AA-51-KL
TB-23-TB	N/A	1988-09-02	N/A	N/A	N/A	N/A
N/A	N/A	N/A	56789	Jones	...	N/A
XW-99-TS	12345	1989-03-02	12345	Patel	...	XW-99-TS

Figure 9.12 *Result of FULL JOIN*

9.3.2.4.4 UNION

UNION JOIN permits a form of union between completely heterogeneous tables; i.e. T1 UNION JOIN T2 is equivalent to the UNION of T1 right extended with as many columns of nulls as T2 has columns and T2 left extended with nulls in the same manner. This provides a mechanism to process tables in the same way as conventional mixed record type sequential files. T1 UNION JOIN T2 is thus equivalent to T1 FULL OUTER JOIN T2 ON 1=2 or any other guaranteed false condition.

We can, for example, UNION JOIN the Travel_Agent table with the Supplier table with

```
Travel_Agent UNION JOIN Supplier
```

This gives us a table with the following columns: travel_agent_id, name, address, suppliernr, name and address. Alternatively, if we were to UNION JOIN the two tables that we used in the CROSS JOIN, Table_1 and Table_2, the result would be as shown in Figure 9.13.

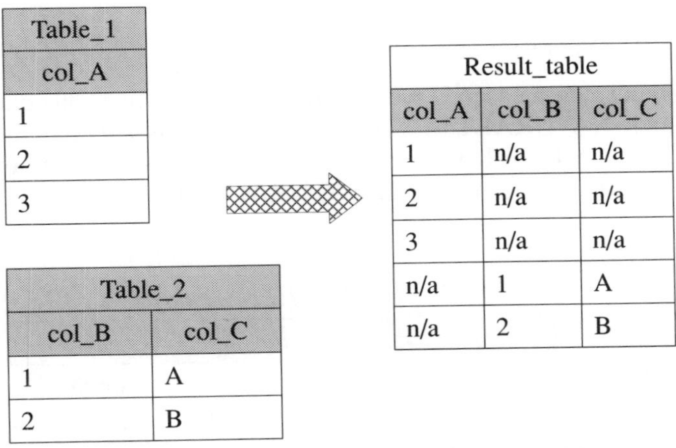

Table_1
col_A
1
2
3

Table_2	
col_B	col_C
1	A
2	B

Result_table		
col_A	col_B	col_C
1	n/a	n/a
2	n/a	n/a
3	n/a	n/a
n/a	1	A
n/a	2	B

Figure 9.13 *The UNION JOIN of two tables*

9.3.2.4.5 THE NATURAL OPTION

The NATURAL option and the <named columns join> are shorthand ways of specifying commonly needed combinations. NATURAL itself is a shorthand for a <named columns join> where the list of column names contains all of the column names that occur in both the operand tables. It is a requirement that there are no duplicate column names within the individual tables so that no ambiguity arises.

The <named column join> option works as follows, assuming T1 is the first operand and T2 is the second operand:

- A select list, SLCC, is created with a derived column for each column name in <join column list>, in the order in which those columns appear in T1, in the form:

```
COALESCE (T1.C, T2.C) AS C
```

- A select list, SLT1, is created with a column for each column name in T1 that is not in <join column list>, in the order in which those columns appear in T1.
- A select list, SLT2, is created with a column for each column name in T2 that is not in <join column list>, in the order in which those columns appear in T2.
- A search condition is created that is a comparison predicate of the form:

```
(T1.C1 , ... , T1.Cn) = (T2.C1, ... , T2.Cn)
```

  where C1, ..., Cn represent each column in the <join column list>.
- Assuming that SLCC has at least one column then a <join condition> containing the above <search condition> is assumed.
- The normal join is done as if NATURAL or named column join had not been specified.
- The final result is the result of the <query specification>:

```
SELECT SLCC, SLT1, SLT2 FROM R
```

  where R is the result table of the normal join.

The difference can be seen if we slightly modify the previous queries. The result of Vehicle NATURAL LEFT JOIN Employee is as shown in Figure 9.14, the result of Vehicle RIGHT JOIN Employee USING (vehicleid) is as shown in Figure 9.15 and the result of Vehicle NATURAL FULL JOIN Employee is as shown in Figure 9.16.

Vehicle NATURAL LEFT JOIN Employee				
vehicleid	*empnr*	*acquisition_date*	*name*	...
AA-51-KL	23456	1984-02-24	Smith	...
TB-23-TB	N/A	1988-09-02	N/A	N/A
XW-99-TS	12345	1989-03-02	Patel	...

Figure 9.14 *Result of NATURAL LEFT JOIN*

Vehicle RIGHT JOIN Employee USING (vehicleid)					
vehicleid	*empnr*	*acquisition_date*	*empnr*	*name*	...
AA-51-KL	23456	1984-02-24	23456	Smith	...
N/A	N/A	N/A	56789	Jones	...
XW-99-TS	12345	1989-03-02	12345	Patel	...

Figure 9.15 *Result of NATURAL RIGHT JOIN*

Vehicle NATURAL FULL JOIN Employee				
vehicleid	*empnr*	*acquisition_date*	*name*	*...*
AA-51-KL	23456	1984-02-24	Smith	...
TB-23-TB	N/A	1988-09-02	N/A	N/A
N/A	56789	N/A	Jones	...
XW-99-TS	12345	1989-03-02	Patel	...

Figure 9.16 *Result of NATURAL FULL JOIN*

9.3.2.5 DIVIDE — the missing option

The division operator takes two sets of rows, i.e. the set of rows in the first operand table and the set of rows in the second operand table, and produces a table that contains the non-**duplicate** rows from the first set for which every row in the second table has a match with a row in the first table.

If we take the example of the Supplier, Product and Product_Supply tables from our standard example database and ask the question 'Who supplies all parts?' then the query is:

```
SELECT suppliernr FROM Product_Supply PS1
  WHERE NOT EXISTS (
     SELECT product_code FROM Product P
       WHERE NOT EXISTS (
          SELECT * FROM Product_Supply PS2
            WHERE PS1.suppliernr = PS2.suppliernr
                  AND
                  PS2.product_code = P.product_code))
```

i.e. give me the suppliernrs from Product_Supply where there is NO product_code in Product for which there is no corresponding product_code in Product_Supply, with the same suppliernr as selected.

9.3.3 Set Operations Result Data Types

When two tables are involved in a set operation the data types of two corresponding columns do not need to be exactly alike. Similarly, in a CASE statement the data types of all the possible results do not need to be exactly alike. If they are not precisely the same then we need to be able to determine which combinations are permissible, what the data type of the result will be and what its attributes such as length, precision, etc., are.

Consider the set of data types that are being UNIONed, etc.; then:

- If all the data types are exact numeric the result is also exact numeric with an implementation defined precision and with a scale equal to the maximum of the scale of the data types in the set.

- If any of the data types is approximate numeric all the other data types must be either exact or approximate numeric and the result is approximate numeric with an implementation defined precision.
- If any of the data types is a datetime data type all the other data types must be the same datetime data type and the result is again the same datetime data type.
- If any of the data types is interval then all the other data types must also be interval. However, if one data type specifies YEAR or MONTH then all the data types must specify only YEAR or MONTH. The result has a data type of INTERVAL with a precision of 's TO e' where s is the most significant of the start fields and e the least significant of the end fields. The precision of the start and end fields is the maximum of the precisions of those start and end fields amongst the data types.
- If any of the data types is bit string then all the data types must be bit string. If they are all of fixed length then the result is also of fixed length with a length equal to the maximum of the lengths of the data types. If any of them is of varying length, then the result is also of varying length with a length equal to the maximum of the length of any fixed length data types in the set and the maximum lengths of the varying length data types.
- If any of the data types is character string then all the data types must be character string and from the same character repertoire. This means that they can have different character set names but the definitions must only differ effectively with regard to the collating sequence. The result is also a character string with the same repertoire. The collating sequence and coercibility attribute of the result is determined by Table 4.3 'Coercibility and collating sequences resulting from dyadic operations and for use in Comparisons' (*see Section 4.7 CREATE COLLATION*). If they are all of fixed length then the result is also of fixed length, with a length equal to the maximum of the lengths of the data types. If any of them is of varying length then the result is also of varying length, with a length equal to the maximum of the length of any fixed length data types in the set and the maximum lengths of the varying length data types.

9.4 Table Expression

The purpose of a table expression is to define a derived table. This differs from a query expression in that the derived table can be grouped; i.e. groups of rows, with some common criteria, can be operated on together. Turning the grouped table back into a normal derived table can be achieved by a query specification (*see Section 9.5 Query Specification*).

The syntax of a table expression is:

<table expression> ::=
  <from clause>
  [<where clause>]
  [<group by clause>]
  [<having clause>]

The <from clause> defines a derived table which may be progressively modified by the succeeding optional clauses. The result of the table expression is the final derived table resulting from the application of all specified clauses.

Because the <table expression> has so many component and interrelated parts, and forms part of the query specification, which is also closely interrelated, examples are not given in this section but a range of examples is provided with the description of query specification.

9.4.1 FROM

The <from clause> is the starting point for a query specification and defines a derived table. The syntax of a from clause is:

<from clause> ::= FROM <table reference> [{ , <table reference> }...]

The derived table, T, is the single table identified by the single table reference or a CROSS JOIN of all the tables identified by a list of table references. The tables that participate in the <from clause> can be simple tables or derived tables (table subqueries or joined tables).

9.4.2 WHERE

This clause creates a new derived table from the derived table, T, defined by the from clause by retaining only selected rows. The syntax is:

<where clause> ::= WHERE <search condition>

The column references in the search condition must reference columns in T or be references to columns in an enclosing derived table definition (outer reference). This occurs where the WHERE clause is part of a nested derived table. The search condition may not contain set functions unless this <where clause> is itself part of a higher level having clause or a select list, in which case it may not reference T, only outer references.

The resulting derived table contains only the rows of T for which the search condition is true. The search condition is theoretically completely re-evaluated for each row of T (although in practice this may not always be necessary).

The book contains numerous examples of WHERE clauses but a specific example that demonstrates an outer reference (Order.ordernr in the second WHERE clause) is:

```
SELECT * FROM Order
  WHERE 10 = (SELECT COUNT(*)
              FROM Order_line
              WHERE Order.ordernr = Order_line.ordernr)
```

9.4.3 GROUP BY

The group by clause takes the table derived from the <from clause>, and the <where clause> if specified, and produces a 'grouped' table. A grouped table is one where the rows are divided up into one or more sets of rows, such that for each set of rows the values in certain specified columns are not **distinct**. This grouping is done such that the number of sets, or groups, is a minimum.

The syntax is as follows:

<group by clause> ::= GROUP BY <column reference> [<collate clause>]
[{ , <column reference> [<collate clause>] }...]

The column references must naturally be ones in the derived table. The <collate clause> is only permissible if the referenced column has a character data type. This clause, if present, changes the collating sequence of the column to the specified sequence with the 'Explicit' attribute. This collating sequence is then used when comparing rows in order to group them.

Whenever reference is made to a grouping column for any row in a group the value of that column is returned. Since certain non-identical values can **compare equal** (especially with the use of collating sequences) the value actually returned may be any of the possible candidates.

Furthermore, subsequent references to columns of the grouped table must be either to a grouping column or be contained within a set function. In this way the group by clause forces the creation of a table with at most one row per group, which provides information about that group and not about the individual elements of that group. The required use of a set function for non-grouping columns reduces these to a single value, the result of the set function.

For example, if we wish to have a list of the departments with a count of their employees we can request:

```
SELECT deptcd, deptnm, COUNT(*)
  FROM Dept LEFT JOIN Employee
  GROUP BY deptcd, deptnm
```

Note that we have included deptnm in the GROUP BY clause simply to avoid having to place it in a set function. In this case the restriction is not logically necessary because deptnm is functionally dependent on deptcd, which is also in the GROUP BY clause. SQL is currently not able to distinguish these special cases. An alternative to placing deptnm in the GROUP BY clause would be to turn it into a MIN(deptnm) or MAX(deptnm) in the select list, either of which would give the same result.

If we wish to have a count of the number of employees of each sex, we can request:

```
SELECT sex, COUNT(*)
  FROM Employee
  GROUP BY sex
```

9.4.4 HAVING

The having clause permits whole groups to be eliminated from the derived table, T, resulting from the preceding <from clause> and any associated <where clause> and <group by clause>. If there was no preceding <group by clause> then the whole derived table is treated as a single group (without any grouping columns). The syntax is:

<having clause> ::= HAVING <search condition>

The column references in the search condition must reference columns in T or be references to columns in an enclosing table definition (outer reference) and, as previously noted, references to a column of T must be either to a grouping column or be contained within a set function. The resulting derived table contains only the groups of T for which the search condition is true. The <search condition> is theoretically completely re-evaluated for each group of T.

For example, if we wish to have a list of the departments with a count of their employees, but in this case only for departments with more than 20 employees, then we can request:

```
SELECT deptcd, MIN(deptnm), COUNT(*)
  FROM Dept LEFT JOIN Employee
  GROUP BY deptcd
  HAVING COUNT(*) > 20
```

or if we wish to know the average order quantity of products for which more than 1000 items have been ordered then we can request:

```
SELECT product_code, AVG(quantity)
  FROM Order_Line
  GROUP BY product_code
  HAVING SUM(quantity) > 1000
```

9.5 Query Specification

The primary function of a <query specification> is to take a projection of a derived table, T, i.e. to select some or all of the columns from the table or grouped table defined by a table expression. In addition to selecting columns the <query specification> can also create columns using value expressions. These value expressions will frequently involve a column or columns of the table in an expression, perhaps with literals as well.

The syntax is of the following form:

<query specification> ::= SELECT [ALL | DISTINCT] <select list>
<table expression>

<select list> ::= * | <select sublist> [{ , <select sublist> }]

<select sublist> ::= <qualifier>.* | <value expression> [[AS] <column name>]

The <select list> defines the columns of the resulting table. There are two shorthands available, * and <qualifier>.*. The first, *, means all columns in the result of the table expression unless the query expression is directly the subject of an exists predicate, when it means a single column which is any arbitrary literal (in this case we are not interested in the columns of the result, only in whether there are any rows). The second, <qualifier>.*, means all columns, except common columns, of the table identified by <qualifier>. The identified table must be one of the component tables in the from clause. It is important to note that the * means the 'all' applicable at the time of execution and is not affected by subsequent additions of columns to base tables. A common column is one that occurred in an explicit or implicit (through use of NATURAL) <join column list> in a joined table. The reason for this is that these columns are derived from a COALESCE function on the columns from both of the joined tables and the original columns are no longer part of the result. Columns can be renamed in the result using the AS option, otherwise they take the name of the equivalent column in the table expression.

The result table produced by a query specification depends on several factors:

- If T is not grouped and the select list includes a set function the whole derived table, T, is the argument to the set function and the result table has only one row. In this case the select list must not reference any columns unless they are the subject of a set function.
- Otherwise, if T is not grouped the result has the same number of rows as T, with each row derived from the select list evaluated for each row of T.
- If T is grouped then the select list may reference columns only if they are grouping columns or the subject of a set function. The argument to each set function is a group. The result table has one row for each group.

Finally, if DISTINCT was specified (the default is ALL) **duplicate** rows are eliminated from the result. Then

```
SELECT ALL empnr FROM Travel_Req
```

will return a result table with one row for every Travel Request whereas

```
SELECT DISTINCT empnr FROM Travel_Req
```

will return a table with a list of employees who have made a Travel Request, but each employee will only occur once regardless of the number of requests made.

The resulting table is updatable only if:

- DISTINCT is not specified.
- Every <value expression> is a simple column reference (i.e. no expressions) and no column appears more than once.
- The from clause has only one table and that table was itself updatable.
- The table expression did not specify a group by or having clause.
- The where clause did not have a subquery that referenced the table in the from clause.

The following are some examples of updatable tables:

```
SELECT * FROM Dept
```
the entire Dept table

```
SELECT empnr, salary, commission
  FROM Employee
  WHERE empnr IN (SELECT empnr
                  FROM Emp_Ext
                  WHERE CURRENT_DATE - date_of_joining
                        BETWEEN INTERVAL 1 YEAR AND
                                INTERVAL 2 YEAR)
```
a subset of the columns of the Employee table, with rows only for employees who have worked with the company for between 1 and 2 years

Examples of non-updatable tables:

```
SELECT DISTINCT destination FROM Travel_Req
```
a list of distinct locations that have been requested as destinations on travel requests.

```
SELECT name
  FROM Employee
  WHERE salary > (SELECT AVG(salary) FROM Employee)
```
a list of employees who earn more than the average salary

```
SELECT name || address FROM Employee
```
a list consisting of the concatenated name and address of all employees (i.e. an expression)

```
SELECT name, name FROM Employee
```
a list with the name of all employees occurring twice

```
SELECT name, CURRENT_TIME FROM Employee
```
a list of employees with the current time (i.e. a function)

```
SELECT suppliernr, Order_line.*
  FROM Order O, Order_Line OL
  WHERE O.ordernr = OL.ordernr
```
a joined table of orders and order lines

```
SELECT deptcd
  FROM Employee
  GROUP BY deptcd
```
a table derived with a GROUP BY, in this case departments with at least one employee

```
SELECT ordernr
  FROM Order_line
  WHERE product_code BETWEEN 6000 AND 7000
  HAVING COUNT(*) > 100
```
orders, if any, that together have more than 100 order lines for products with codes between 6000 and 7000

9.6 Subqueries

Subqueries come in three flavours: scalar, row and table. Each is simply a <query expression> in parentheses. For example:

```
(SELECT deptnm FROM Dept WHERE deptcd = 'TRA')
```

is a scalar subquery as it returns a single column and a single row (i.e. a single value). It can naturally also be treated as a row subquery or a table subquery.

```
(SELECT * FROM Dept WHERE deptcd = 'TRA')
```

is a row subquery as it returns multiple columns but only a single row. Naturally it can also be treated as a table subquery.

```
(SELECT deptnm FROM Dept)
```

is a table subquery, provided the table Dept has more than one row, as it returns multiple rows (the number of columns returned being irrelevant).

A scalar subquery can, in principle, be used wherever a single value is needed. A scalar subquery is an option of the common primary found in the syntax of all the value expressions. A row subquery can be used wherever a row value constructor is needed, mostly in the predicates. A table subquery can be used wherever a table is needed, in, for example, the <from clause> or the IN predicate.

The scalar subquery in a value expression opens up a whole world of ways of expressing queries. In order to illustrate the possibilities, there follow a couple of queries using the facility. To select the names of all programmers, as well as the difference between their current salary and their highest previous salary the following is used:

```
SELECT name, salary -
          (SELECT MAX(salary)
             FROM Job_History
             WHERE Job_History.empnr = Employee.empnr)
  FROM Employee
  WHERE job = 'PROGRAMMER'
```

To increase the salary of all employees by the percentage specified for their job (assume a temporary table containing the job name and the associated raise, i.e. 10 per cent = 0.10) the following is used:

```
UPDATE Employee
   SET salary = salary *
          (1 + (SELECT raise
                  FROM Raises R
                  WHERE R.job = Employee.job))
```

10

Predicates and Search Conditions

This chapter describes the various **predicates** of the SQL language and the ways in which these can be combined in a search condition in order to select rows from a table, or determine their existence or otherwise.

10.1 Search Conditions

A **search condition** is a statement or group of statements joined together by **boolean** operators which are either true, false or unknown. It is used primarily to determine if a row or a group of rows fulfils certain criteria.

The syntax takes the following form:

<search condition> ::= <boolean term> | <search condition> OR <boolean term>

<boolean term> ::= <boolean factor> | <boolean term> AND <boolean factor>

<boolean factor> ::= [NOT] <boolean test>

<boolean test> ::= <boolean primary>
[IS [NOT] { TRUE | FALSE | UNKNOWN }]

<boolean primary> ::= <predicate> | (<search condition>)

In a boolean test an expression of the form ' `x IS NOT y` ' is equivalent to an expression of the form ' `NOT (x IS y)` '.

In a search condition involving more than one predicate the expression is evaluated in the following manner. First, expressions within parentheses are evaluated and then IS is applied before NOT, which is applied before AND, which in turn is applied before OR. Two operators at the same precedence level are applied left to right. The ordering of operators is implicit in the syntax tree shown above.

The results of each of the operators are given in the truth tables in Tables 10.1 to 10.4.

Table 10.1 Truth table for the OR boolean operator

OR	*true*	*false*	*unknown*
true	true	true	true
false	true	false	unknown
unknown	true	unknown	unknown

Table 10.2 Truth table for the AND boolean operator

AND	*true*	*false*	*unknown*
true	true	false	unknown
false	false	false	false
unknown	unknown	false	unknown

Table 10.3 Truth table for the NOT boolean operator

NOT	
true	false
false	true
unknown	unknown

Table 10.4 Truth table for the IS boolean operator

IS	*true*	*false*	*unknown*
true	true	false	false
false	false	true	false
unknown	false	false	true

For example:

1=1 AND 1=0	≡ true AND false	= false
1=1 OR 1=0 AND 1=1	≡ true OR false AND true	
	≡ true OR false	= true

10.2 Predicates

A **predicate** is simply a single statement which can be either true, false or unknown. SQL understands 10 kinds of predicates namely:

a comparison predicate
a between predicate
a like predicate
a null predicate
an in predicate
a quantified comparison predicate
a match predicate
an overlaps predicate
an exists predicate
an unique predicate

All of the predicates can evaluate to true or false and all except four, the null predicate, the exists predicate, the unique predicate and the match predicate, can also evaluate to unknown.

10.2.1 Comparison Predicate

The comparison **predicate** is used to compare two **row value constructors**. These may be actual rows or constant rows built using literals or some combination. The format is:

<x> <op> <y>

where <x> and <y> are both row value constructors of the same degree (number of columns or values present) and where each of the pairs of values, taken from the same position in each of the two row value constructors, is of a comparable data type. Comparable means that both values are one of the following:

character string, taken from the same character repertoire
bit string
numeric (either exact or approximate)
datetime, with the same datetime fields
interval, with the same datetime fields

Since a row value constructor can consist of more than one value the comparison of <row value constructor> is determined by the comparison of the corresponding pairs of values, say 'a' and 'b'.

The simple comparison ‘ a <op> b ’ yields a result of unknown if either a or b is null. Otherwise, depending on the type of <op> it yields results as shown in Table 10.5.

Table 10.5 Comparison operators

<op>	*true if and only if*
a = b	a is equal to b
a <> b	a is not equal to b
a < b	a is less than b
a > b	a is greater than b
a <= b	a is less than or equal to b
a >= b	a is greater than or equal to b

The rules for comparison depend on the **data type** of the operands:

Numeric — Numbers are compared with respect to their algebraic value.

Bit string — Bit strings are compared bit by bit, from left to right. A 1 bit is greater than a 0 bit. If the strings are not of equal length and the strings are equal for the length of the shorter then the shorter compares less than the longer.

Character string — Character strings are compared using the appropriate collating sequence (*see Section 4.7 CREATE COLLATION*). If the strings are not of equal length then, if the collating sequence specifies PAD SPACE, the shorter is extended on the right by space characters to the length of the longer. If NO PAD is specified then if two unequal length strings are compared equal for the length of the shorter then the shorter is assumed to be less than the longer.

Warning: when character strings are compared to determine the MAX or the MIN, or during the selection of DISTINCT rows, or when referencing a grouping column, several different strings can **compare equal** (due to length differences or collation sequence effects); the selected value from among the ‘equal’ strings is arbitrary.

Datetime — Datetime values are compared by subtracting one from the other and comparing the resulting interval with an interval of zero. The precision of the subtraction is dependent on the precision of the least significant datetime field of the operands. The operands must have identical datetime fields, including the precision.

The final result of a comparison between two row value expressions, R1 and R2, depends on the set of comparisons between the corresponding pairs. The results are shown in the following tables:

For all pairs a = b is true			
R1	=	R2	is true
R1	<>	R2	is false
R1	<=	R2	is true
R1	>=	R2	is true
R1	>	R2	is false
R1	<	R2	is false

For at least one pair a <> b is true			
R1	<>	R2	is true
R1	=	R2	is false

For the first pair where a = b is false, a < b is true			
R1	<	R2	is true
R1	<=	R2	is true
R1	>	R2	is false
R1	>=	R2	is false

For the first pair where a = b is false, a > b is true			
R1	>	R2	is true
R1	>=	R2	is true
R1	<	R2	is false
R1	<=	R2	is false

If R1 <op> R2 is neither true nor false then it is unknown. For example, to select all the employees who have a salary greater than 11500 one can say:

```
SELECT empnr FROM Employee
  WHERE salary > 11500
```

To select all the employees who are female and who work in the SLS department one can say:

```
SELECT empnr FROM Employee
  WHERE (sex, deptcd) = ('F', 'SLS')
```

However, to select all the employees who have the same sex as and who work in the same department as the representative for constituency 12 one can say:

```
SELECT empnr
   FROM Employee
   WHERE (sex, deptcd) = ( SELECT sex, deptcd
      FROM Employee I
      WHERE (SELECT representative
         FROM Const
         WHERE constituency = 12) = I.empnr )
```

10.2.2 Between Predicate

The BETWEEN **predicate** tests if the values of one **row value constructor** lie between the values of two other value expressions. It is in fact merely a shorthand form of a combination of Comparison predicates. It takes either the form:

```
x BETWEEN y AND z
```

which is equivalent to:

```
x >= y AND x <= z
```

or the form:

```
x NOT BETWEEN y AND z
```

which is equivalent to:

```
NOT ( x BETWEEN y AND z )
```

or to:

```
x < y OR x > z
```

The predicate adds nothing in the way of functionality to the language but its syntactic style sometimes allows more intuitive statements to be written. For example:

```
salary BETWEEN 9000 AND 25000
```

is easier to read and understand than:

```
salary >= 9000 AND salary <= 25000
```

simply because it reads as a single condition and one does not have to make the connection between the two comparisons oneself.

10.2.3 Like Predicate

The LIKE **predicate** applies only to character strings and tests to see if a string conforms to a specified pattern. The format is:

<x> [NOT] LIKE <y> [ESCAPE <z>]

where <x>, <y> and <z> are all character value expressions.

<x> NOT LIKE <y> [ESCAPE <z>]

is equivalent to:

NOT (<x> LIKE <y> [ESCAPE <z>])

Assuming that NOT was not specified, if either <x> or <y> (or <z> if specified) is null then the predicate evaluates to unknown. Otherwise it evaluates to true if <x> matches the pattern of <y> (under the influence of <z>) and to false if it does not match.

Before we look at the process of matching we need to understand how a pattern is defined. In the character string that is the result of <y>, assuming <z> is not specified, characters have the following meaning:

_	(the underscore)	any single character
%	(the per cent sign)	any sequence of zero or more characters

All other characters stand for themselves.

If <z> is specified then it must evaluate to a single character, called the escape character, which must only appear in the pattern string if it is followed by itself, _ or %. In these cases the pair of characters is taken to represent the single character which is the second of the pair. This allows one to test for _ and % as characters rather than have them adopt their special meaning.

A string matches the pattern if the string can be so divided that each substring compares equal to a substring of the pattern made up of consecutive characters from the pattern that are not _ or %, or is a single character that matches a _ in the pattern, or is an arbitrary substring of length zero or more that matches a % in the pattern. For example:

```
name LIKE 'Can%'
```

is true if the column 'name' contains a string that begins with 'Can'.

```
mark_up LIKE ' 5._#%' ESCAPE '#'
```

is true if the column 'mark_up' contains a string that begins with ' 5.' which is then followed by any character which is itself followed by a % character, e.g. the following values would result in true: ' 5.0%', ' 5.6%'. One special case is that if <x> and <y> are both varying length strings of length 0 the predicate evaluates to true.

When comparing the substrings the normal collating sequence rules are used, so that in a character set that collated upper- and lower-case letters together the following would also be true:

```
'cannan' LIKE 'CAN%N%AN'
```

10.2.4 Null Predicate

The NULL **predicate** tests for the presence of '**null** states' in a **row value constructor**. It has two forms:

x IS NULL

and

x IS NOT NULL

If all of the values of the row value constructor x are NULL then ' `x IS NULL` ' is true; otherwise it is false. If none of the values of the row value constructor x are NULL then ' `x IS NOT NULL` ' is true; otherwise it is false.

Unlike the use of the key word NOT in other predicates, such as LIKE, BETWEEN and IN where the NOT merely inverts the truth value of the predicate without the NOT specified, it is NOT the case that ' `x IS NOT NULL` ' is equivalent to ' `NOT x IS NULL` '. This non-invertibility occurs when some values of x are NULL and some values are not. Table 10.6 shows the value of the predicate for the various different cases.

Table 10.6 Results of the NULL predicate

Values of the components of x	*x IS NULL*	*x IS NOT NULL*	*NOT x IS NULL*	*NOT x IS NOT NULL*
All components NULL	true	false	false	true
Some components NULL and some components not	false	false	true	true
No components NULL	false	true	true	false

The reason this predicate is needed is that a construction such as:

```
commission = NULL
```

is considered illegal, since NULL is not really a value but a state and in general no assumption is made that one null is the same as another. Thus even if the test was permitted it would not produce the result desired. For example, if home_telno and work_telno are both NULL then:

```
(home_telno, work_telno) IS NULL              is true
(home_telno, work_telno) IS NOT NULL          is false
```

If home_telno and work_telno both have values then:

```
(home_telno, work_telno) IS NULL              is false
(home_telno, work_telno) IS NOT NULL          is true
```

However, if home_telno is NULL and work_telno has a value then:

```
(home_telno, work_telno) IS NULL              is false
(home_telno, work_telno) IS NOT NULL          is false
NOT (home_telno, work_telno) IS NULL          is true
NOT (home_telno, work_telno) IS NOT NULL      is true
```

10.2.5 In Predicate

The IN **predicate** tests if a row, defined by a **row value constructor**, exists in the table defined by a **subquery**. The format is:

x [NOT] IN { <subquery> | <in value list> }

where ' `x NOT IN y` ' is equivalent to ' `NOT (x IN y)` '. The <in value list> may only be specified if x is a row value constructor with a degree of 1, i.e. it has only one value or column. In that case the <in value list>, which consists of a comma separated list of value expressions, is considered to be a **table value constructor** where each value expression is a row value constructor. For example:

```
deptcd IN ('HDQ','SAL')
```

is equivalent to:

```
deptcd IN (VALUES 'HDQ','SAL')
```

and (VALUES 'HDQ','SAL') is a valid, if constant, subquery. This alternative is present only to maintain upwards compatibility with the 1987 and 1989 standards, which did not possess the generalized table value constructor capability and required a special syntax in this predicate to express what is in fact a simple table value constructor. The precise meaning of ' `x IN y` ' is the same as that of ' `x = ANY y` ' (*see Section 10.2.6 Quantified Comparison Predicate*).

10.2.6 Quantified Comparison Predicate

The quantified comparison **predicate** is used to test a **row value constructor** against a **table subquery** and return true or false depending on whether any or all of the rows of the table derived from the subquery match the row value constructor. The format is:

<row value constructor> <op> { ALL | { SOME | ANY } } <table subquery>

The number of values in the row value constructor must be the same as the number of columns in the table subquery. <op> may be any of the comparison operators (*see 10.2.1 Comparison Predicate*). SOME and ANY are synonyms so there are effectively just two options, ALL and ANY. *See also* ***quantifiers*** in the Glossary.

If 'rve' is the row value constructor and 'tsr' is a row in the result of the subquery then the comparison predicate ' `rve <op> tsr` ' is done for each row of the subquery. If the subquery is empty or if the comparison predicate is true for every row in the subquery and the quantified predicate specified the ALL option then the predicate is true. If the subquery is empty or if the comparison predicate is false for every row in the subquery and the quantified predicate specified the ANY option then the predicate is false. If the comparison predicate is false for at least one row in the subquery and the quantified predicate specified the ALL option then the predicate is false. If the comparison predicate is true for at least one row in the subquery and the quantified predicate specified the ANY option then the predicate is true.

If none of the above conditions applies then the result of the predicate is unknown. For example:

```
'TRA' = ANY (SELECT deptcd FROM Dept)
```

will evaluate to true if '`(SELECT deptcd FROM Dept)`' yields at least one row containing `'TRA'`. If we wished to find the oldest employee (or employees if more than one) then one way to formulate the query would be:

```
SELECT empnr
  FROM Emp_Ext
  WHERE date_of_birth <= ALL (SELECT date_of_birth
     FROM Emp_Ext)
```

10.2.7 Overlaps Predicate

The OVERLAPS **predicate** tests for overlapping datetime ranges. This ought to be possible with a combination of comparison predicates but would be very messy syntactically and not something that one is likely to get right. The predicate takes the form:

(a, b) OVERLAPS (c, d)

where a and c are both of comparable datetime data types and b and d are either of a datetime data type comparable with a and c respectively, or of an interval data type such that it can be added to a or c respectively. Start time (S1) and end time (E1) for the first period, defined by (a, b), are calculated as follows, where x is a temporary variable:

```
if b is of datetime data type
 then x = b; else x = a + b;
fi
if a < x or b IS NULL
 then S1 = a; E1 = x; else S1 = x; E1 = a;
fi
```

Start time (S2) and end time (E2) for the second period, defined by (c, d), are similarly calculated:

```
if c is of datetime data type
 then x = d; else x = c + d;
fi
if c < x or d IS NULL
 then S2 = c; E2 = x; else S2 = x; E2 = c;
fi
```

The result of the predicate is the result of:

```
(S1>S2 AND NOT (S1>=E2 AND E1>=E2))
OR
(S2>S1 AND NOT (S2>=E1 AND E2>=E1))
OR
(S1=S2 AND (E1<>E2 OR E1=E2))
```

The predicate is deliberately asymmetric in that periods do not overlap if the end of one is exactly the start of another, with the exception of the degenerate case — a pair of points, i.e. where S1=E1=S2=E2, which do overlap. This enables us to define periods that are guaranteed to be contiguous but do not overlap. For more information on how this is used *see Chapter 23 Using the Datetime Facilities*. For example:

```
(DATE'1989-02-01',DATE'1989-05-01')
OVERLAPS
(DATE'1989-05-01',DATE'1989-06-01')
```

is false but:

```
(DATE'1989-06-03',INTERVAL '-3' DAY)
OVERLAPS
(DATE'1989-05-01',DATE'1989-06-01')
```

is true.

10.2.8 Match Predicate

The MATCH **predicate** tests, as the name suggests, for matching rows. It is a form of temporary referential integrity check, and indeed the referential integrity constraint is defined in terms of the MATCH predicate. The format is:

<row value constructor> MATCH [UNIQUE]
[PARTIAL | FULL] <table subquery>

The number of values in the row value constructor must be the same as the number of columns in the table subquery. For example, in the definition of the Vehicle table I have a check constraint:

```
CHECK ( ( empnr, vehicleid )
   MATCH (SELECT empnr, vehicleid FROM Employee ) )
```

For each row in the Vehicle table this takes the values from the columns empnr and vehicleid and, treating that column pair as a row in its own right, looks to see whether one of the values is the null value or whether there is at least one identical row in the table derived from the table subquery '`SELECT empnr, vehicleid FROM Employee`'. If either of those conditions is true then the result of the predicate is true: otherwise it is false.

There are three options in the MATCH predicate, UNIQUE, PARTIAL and FULL. The first option, **UNIQUE**, not only checks to see whether there is a matching row but also whether that matching row is the only matching one. If there is more than one matching row then the result of the predicate is also false. The second and third options, PARTIAL and FULL, concern the checking of the row value constructor for nulls. If neither are specified then the result of the predicate is true if any value in the row value constructor is null. If PARTIAL is specified then the result of the predicate is true if considering only the non-null columns there is a matching row; otherwise it is false. Finally, if FULL is specified, the result of the predicate is true if all of the values are null and false if any of the values is null. If all of the values are not null then the result is true only if a matching row can be found.

10.2.9 Exists Predicate

EXISTS differs slightly from other **predicates** in that, instead of testing a simple value or a row value constructor against something, it returns a result purely on the basis of the characteristics of the result of a **subquery**. The EXISTS predicate tests for an empty table. It has been pointed out by some authors, notably C. J. Date, that the use of the word EXISTS is misleading; it is therefore important that you should understand that the EXISTS predicate is either true or false and is never unknown or **NULL**, as a table is always either empty or not empty but never indeterminate. *See also **quantifiers** in the Glossary.*

The format is:

EXISTS <subquery>

and the result is true if the table that is the result of the **subquery** contains at least one row and is false if it contains no rows. For example:

```
EXISTS (SELECT * FROM Dept)
```

will return true if the dept table contains any rows and is false otherwise, whereas:

```
EXISTS (SELECT * FROM Dept WHERE deptcd = deptcd || 'A')
```

will return false regardless, as the WHERE clause will exclude all possible rows.

The major use of the predicate involves the use of a correlated subquery as in:

```
SELECT *
    FROM Employee E
    WHERE EXISTS ( SELECT *
                       FROM Travel_Req T
                       WHERE E.empnr = T.empnr )
```

which returns the employee data of the employees who have submitted travel requisitions.

It is interesting to note the different meanings of the two usages of * as in ‘ `SELECT *` ’ in this query. In the first case the * stands for a list of all the columns in the table (Employee) whereas in the second case it stands for an arbitrary literal e.g. `'A'` in the select list. In this second case it does not matter what columns are contained within the result of the subquery as we are only interested in the cardinality of the table and not in its contents.

10.2.10 Unique Predicate

UNIQUE, like EXISTS, also differs from other **predicates** in that, instead of testing a simple value or a row value constructor against something, it returns a result purely on the basis of the characteristics of the result of a **subquery**. The UNIQUE predicate tests for the presence of **duplicate**, non-**null** rows in a table. It is a form of temporary unique constraint, and indeed the unique constraint is defined in terms of it.

The format is:

UNIQUE <subquery>

and the result is true if the table that is the result of the subquery contains no **duplicate**, non-**null** rows and is false otherwise. For example:

```
UNIQUE (SELECT deptcd FROM Dept)
```

will return true if the Dept table contains no rows with the same deptcd and is false otherwise.

In this case a row is considered a duplicate of another row if neither row contains any columns that are NULL and if the values of each corresponding column of the two rows compare equal according to the rules of the comparison predicate. In the case of columns with a character data type this does not necessarily mean that they are literally identical. The comparisons are done on the basis of the defined collating sequence for the column and if, for instance, that collating sequence treats upper- and lower-case letters alike then a column containing ‘FRED’ would be ‘equal’ to one containing ‘fred’.

11

Functions and Expressions

This chapter describes the various expressions that can be used to generate and manipulate values and the various scalar and set functions that are provided by the standard language. Most implementations will provide a richer set of functions than are described here, but these can be considered the minimal acceptable set of functions.

11.1 Value Expressions

A value expression provides a value that is derived from a combination of primary values and operators. The primary values can be literals, parameters, host language variables, columns, functions or derived from any of these. There are several kinds of value expression, depending on the data type of the result, which restricts the range of functions and operators that may be specified. There are four basic types of value expression:

<value expression> ::=
<numeric value expression>
<string value expression>
<datetime value expression>
<interval value expression>

The primaries that are valid for all data types we have called common primaries and consist of the following:

<common primary> ::=
<unsigned value specification>
<column reference>
<set function specification>
<scalar subquery>
<case expression>
<cast specification>
(<value expression>)

For examples of <common primary> see either the sections that describe the specific primary or one of the following data type specific sections.

11.1.1 Numeric Value Expressions

A numeric value expression results in a value with a data type that is either exact or approximate numeric. The syntax takes the following form:

<numeric value expression> ::=
<term>
| <numeric value expression> + <term>
| <numeric value expression> – <term>

<term> ::= <factor> | <term> * <factor> | <term> / <factor>

<factor> ::= [+ | –] <numeric primary>

<numeric primary> ::=
<common primary>
| <position expression>
| <extract expression>
| <char length expression>
| <octet length expression>
| <bit length expression>

For example:

```
3.14

quantity + 1000

(SELECT MAX(salary) FROM Employee)
    / (SELECT AVG(salary) FROM Employee)

CHARACTER_LENGTH(address) + CHARACTER_LENGTH(name) + 1
```

The data type of any <common primary> must be numeric.

The data type of the result depends on the operators and the operands. Monadic operators (i.e. + and –) do not change the data type. For dyadic operators (i.e. +, –, * and /) if either of the operands is approximate numeric the result is also approximate numeric but with an implementation defined precision; otherwise the data type is exact numeric with an implementation defined precision. The scale of an exact numeric result is determined as shown in Table 11.1.

Table 11.1 Scale of the result of arithmetic expressions

Operator	*Scale of result*
+	The maximum of the scales of the operands
–	The maximum of the scales of the operands
*	The sum of the scales of the operands
/	Implementation defined

If any of the <numeric primary>s is null or, in the case of a <scalar subquery>, empty the result is null. Otherwise the result is determined using conventional arithmetic. Expressions within parentheses are evaluated first, then the monadic operators (+ and –), then the dyadic operators (* and /) and finally the dyadic operators (+ and –). Two operators at the same precedence level are applied left to right. The ordering of operators is implicit in the syntax tree shown above.

11.1.2 String Value Expressions

A string value expression results in a value with a data type that is either character string or bit string. The syntax takes the following form:

<string value expression> ::=
    <character value expression>
  | <bit value expression>

The syntax of <character value expression> is:

<character value expression> ::=
    <character value expression> || <character primary> [<collate clause>]
  | <character primary> [<collate clause>]

<character primary> ::=
    <common primary>
  | <substring>
  | <upper>
  | <lower>
  | <character translation>
  | <form-of-use conversion>

For example:

```
USER
UPPER ((SELECT MAX(name) FROM Employee))
name || address
name || ', ' || address
```

The data type of any <common primary> and <substring> must be character string. The character repertoires of all <character primary>s in an expression must be the same.

If any of the <character primary>s is null or, in the case of a scalar <subquery>, empty the result is null. The || operator is the concatenation operator and appends the second string to the first. If either of the strings is varying length the result is varying length; otherwise it is fixed length. The length of the string is the sum of the two operand lengths. If this is greater than the implementation defined maximum length then an error occurs unless it can be truncated to the maximum length by deleting only spaces. The collating sequence of the result is determined by the table for dyadic operators (*see Section 4.7 CREATE COLLATION and Table 4.3 Coercibility and collating sequences resulting from dyadic operations and for use in comparisons*).

If the <collate clause> is specified then the associated <character primary> takes the specified collating sequence as an explicit collating sequence. Expressions within parentheses are evaluated first and then the concatenation operators are applied left to right. The syntax of <bit value expression> is:

```
<bit value expression> ::=
    <bit value expression> || <bit primary>
  | <bit primary>

<bit primary> ::=
    <common primary>
  | <substring>
```

For example:

```
X'2F' || B'010101'
```

Unfortunately since the bit data type is only used for attributes such as graphical images it is difficult to provide very 'meaningful' examples. The data type of any <common primary> and <substring> must be bit string.

If any of the <bit primary>s is null, or, in the case of a <scalar subquery>, empty the result is null. The || operator is the concatenation operator and works like that for character strings, except that the truncation test is for zero bits instead of spaces. Expressions within parentheses are evaluated first and then the concatenation operators are applied left to right.

11.1.3 Datetime Value Expressions

A datetime value expression results in a value with a data type that is datetime. The syntax takes the following form:

```
<datetime value expression> ::=
    <datetime term>
  | <interval value expression> + <datetime term>
  | <datetime value expression> { + | – } <interval term>
<datetime term> ::= <datetime primary> [ <time zone> ]
```

<datetime primary> ::=
  <common primary>
  | <current date function>
  | <current time function>
  | <current timestamp function>

<time zone> ::=
  AT { LOCAL | TIME ZONE <simple value specification> }

For example:

```
start_date
INTERVAL '3' MONTH + date_of_joining
date_of_birth - INTERVAL '9' MONTH
Itinerary.return_time
    AT SELECT offset FROM Displacements
    WHERE location = 'London'
```

The data type of any <common primary> must be datetime. Any <interval value expression>s or <interval term>s may contain only datetime fields from the associated <datetime term> or <datetime value expression>. The precision of the result is the precision of the <datetime primary>. If the data type is DATE then <time zone> may not be specified.

If any of the <datetime primary>s is null or, in the case of a <scalar subquery>, empty the result is null. Otherwise, the interval values are added or subtracted from the datetime values using the normal rules for dates and times. Note, however, that if the interval is a year, month or year-month interval then the DAY field of the datetime value is not altered in the result. This may lead to illegal dates being generated, e.g. DATE'1992-01-31' + '1' MONTH generates DATE'1992-02-31', which is clearly not a valid date.

If a <time zone> was specified then the value of the datetime value expression is the result of:

dtpv – tzv

where dtpv is the value of <datetime primary> and tzv is the value of the <simple value specification> or, if LOCAL was specified, the value of the current default time zone offset.

Expressions within parentheses are evaluated first and then the operators are applied left to right. It should be noted that the result of expressions involving intervals that include leap seconds and/or discontinuities in calendars (such as the switch from the Julian to the Gregorian) are implementation defined.

11.1.4 Interval Value Expressions

An interval value expression results in a value with a data type that is interval. The syntax takes the following form:

```
<interval value expression> ::=
      <interval term>
    | ( <datetime value expression> – <datetime term> ) <interval qualifier>
    | <interval value expression> { + | – } <interval term>

<interval term> ::=
      <interval factor>
    | <interval term> * <factor>
    | <interval term> / <factor>
    | <term> * <interval factor>

<interval factor> ::=
    [ + | – ] <common primary> [ <interval qualifier> ]
```

For example:

```
yearly_leave / 12
```
holiday entitlement per month (assumes yearly_leave is of INTERVAL DAY data type)

```
(date_of_joining - date_of_birth) YEAR
```
age at joining

```
MAX((return_date - outward_date) DAY + 1 DAY)
```
longest trip in days

<term> and <factor> are both parts of <numeric value expression>. The optional <interval qualifier> is only permitted when the <common primary> is actually a <dynamic parameter specification>, i.e. a ?, when the <interval qualifier> is used simply to specify the data type which might otherwise be indeterminable (*see Section 18.4 PREPARE*).

The data type of any <common primary> must be interval. If two intervals are present in one interval value expression they must both be year-month or both be day-time intervals. The reason for this is that when you start to do arithmetic with intervals and dates the results become indeterminate if the interval spans months and days. If two datetimes are present in one interval value expression they must both contain the same datetime fields. The result has the same datetime fields as the <interval primary> unless either <interval qualifier> is specified (in which case it has the specified fields) or two interval values are specified (in which case the result has all the fields from the most significant to the least significant field of both operands). If multiplication or division occur then the leading precision is adjusted so as not to lose significant digits in the most significant field.

If any of the <interval primary>s is null or, in the case of a <scalar subquery>, empty the result is null. Otherwise, the interval values or datetime values are added and subtracted or, in the case of interval values, multiplied and divided, using the normal rules for dates and times. Expressions within parentheses are evaluated first and then the operators are applied left to right. It should be noted that the result of expressions involving two datetime values that span leap seconds and/or discontinuities in calendars are implementation defined.

11.2 Scalar Functions

This section describes those functions defined as standard in SQL that take a scalar value as parameter and return a scalar value. These can be used directly in assignments to column, in the appropriate sort of value expressions or in comparisons. A scalar value in the sense used here is one that is non-repeating and not compound — in principle any value that is suitable for assignment to a column.

11.2.1 Datetime Functions

This group of functions either returns a value with a datetime data type or operates on a datetime value. There are four functions, three of which return date and/or time information about the environment and one of which operates on a datetime data type to yield a numeric value. If a single SQL command contains more than one datetime function, values are returned as if all the datetime functions had been evaluated simultaneously at some arbitrary point during the execution of the command.

For example, assume the following update command was issued:

```
UPDATE Timesheet SET timestamp_end = CURRENT_TIMESTAMP
```

If we assume that there are quite a few rows in the table then it will take longer than one microsecond to complete. The actual time of update for the first and last rows will thus be different, and if CURRENT_TIMESTAMP was taken from the system clock at the moment of update the rows would have different values in the timestamp_end column. This is not what is desired, so instead of taking the clock value for each row that is updated the clock value is taken once for the command as a whole so all rows receive the same value.

11.2.1.1 CURRENT_DATE

This function returns the current date in the time zone which is local for the application or user. See the SET TIME ZONE statement. It takes the form:

<current date function> ::= CURRENT_DATE

and the data type of the result is DATE. For example:

```
CURRENT_DATE
```

returns the current date in the local time zone.

11.2.1.2 CURRENT_TIME

This function returns the current time in the time zone which is the current default for the session. See the SET TIME ZONE statement. It takes the form:

<current time function> ::= CURRENT_TIME [(<time precision>)]

and the data type of the result is TIME. The <time precision> parameter determines the precision of the result; the default is zero. See the TIME data type for more details. For example:

```
CURRENT_TIME
```
the current time, with second precision

```
CURRENT_TIME(6)
```
the current time, with microsecond precision

11.2.1.3 CURRENT_TIMESTAMP

This function returns the current date and time in the time zone which is the current default for the session. See the SET TIME ZONE statement. This combination of date and time is referred to as a timestamp as it identifies a unique (within the limits of the precision) point in time. It takes the form:

<current timestamp function> ::=
    CURRENT_TIMESTAMP [(<time precision>)]

and the data type of the result is TIMESTAMP. The <time precision> parameter determines the precision of the result; the default is 6 (i.e. microseconds). See the TIMESTAMP data type for more details. For example:

```
CURRENT_TIMESTAMP(0)
```
the current timestamp, with second precision

```
CURRENT_TIMESTAMP
```
the current timestamp, with microsecond precision

11.2.1.4 EXTRACT

This function returns the value of a specific field from a datetime or interval value. The returned value is null if the datetime or interval value is null; otherwise it is a numeric value. It takes the form:

<extract expression> ::=
    EXTRACT ({ YEAR | MONTH | DAY | HOUR | MINUTE
        | SECOND | TIMEZONE_HOUR | TIMEZONE_MINUTE }
    FROM { <datetime value expression> | <interval value expression> })

For example:

```
EXTRACT (YEAR FROM Employee.date_of_birth)
```
the year in which an employee was born

```
EXTRACT (HOUR FROM Timesheet.overtime_hours)
```
the number of whole hours of overtime worked

```
EXTRACT (TIMEZONE_HOUR FROM Itinerary.outward_time)
```
the hours part of the offset of the timezone in which the outward time of the flight is expressed

A <timezone field> may only be specified with a <datetime value expression> that is a time or timestamp. The resulting value has the same sign as the <interval value expression> or the time zone offset in a <datetime value expression> except for zero values and any non-time zone fields of a <datetime value expression> which are always positive.

11.2.2 String Functions

This group of functions operates on either character strings or bit strings. They return either a string of the same type, i.e. character or bit, or a numeric value. There are four functions, three of which return a numeric value and one of which returns a string. If any of the strings or numeric parameters are null then the result is also null.

11.2.2.1 SUBSTRING

This function returns a substring selected from within a string. It takes the form:

```
<substring> ::=
    SUBSTRING ( <string value expression>
        FROM <start position> [ FOR <string length> ] )
```

where <string value expression> must be an expression that results in either a character string or a bit string and the other two parameters must be exact numeric with scale 0 (integer). The data type of the result is either varying length character string with a maximum length equal to the maximum (or fixed) length of the string value expression and with the same character repertoire, collating sequence and form-of-use or varying length bit string with a maximum length equal to the maximum (or fixed) length of the string value expression depending on the data type of the <string value expression>.

If string length is omitted then it is assumed to be either the length of the string minus the starting position plus one or zero, whichever is greater. The actual or assumed string length must be non-negative but may be zero.

There is no requirement that the start position should identify a character or bit within the string. It may indeed be before the beginning of the string (i.e. negative) or beyond the end of the string. Substring works by assuming an infinite number of cells numbered from $-\infty$ to $+\infty$ with the string positioned with its first character or bit, if any, in cell 1 and the next, again if any, in cell 2, etc. The start position and length thus define a consecutive range of cells numbered from start position through to start position + string length inclusive. The result consists of any characters or bits occupying selected cells. Unoccupied cells are equivalent to the empty string. This way of working allows a substring to be specified without complicated tests for special circumstances.

For example, to obtain the character to the left of the first 'a' in various strings we can say:

```
SUBSTRING ('Gerard' FROM POSITION('a' IN 'Gerard')-1 FOR 1)
```
answer 'r'

```
SUBSTRING ('Stephen' FROM POSITION('a' IN 'Stephen')-1 FOR 1)
```
answer ''

Simpler examples are:

```
SUBSTRING ('Stephen' FROM 5 FOR 3)
```
answer 'hen'

```
SUBSTRING ('Stephen' FROM -3 FOR 8)
```
answer 'Step' (cell 0 is assumed to exist and thus –3 and not –4 is used)

```
SUBSTRING ('Stephen' FROM 9)
```
answer error (implied length is negative, 7 – 9 + 1)

```
SUBSTRING ('Stephen' FROM 8)
```
answer '' (implied length is zero, 7 – 8 + 1)

```
SUBSTRING ('123' FROM 1 FOR 5)
```
answer '123'

Bit string examples are:

```
SUBSTRING (B'1010101' FROM 4)
```
answer B'0101'

```
SUBSTRING (X'F0F0' FROM 3 FOR 8)
```
answer X'C3'

11.2.2.2 CHARACTER_LENGTH

This function returns the length of the string in characters, if the string is a character string or if the string is a bit string, the length of the string in octets (rounded up). The result is independent of whether a one, two or more byte (octet) encoding is used to represent the character internally. It takes the form:

<char length expression> ::=
{ CHAR_LENGTH | CHARACTER_LENGTH } (<string value expression>)

Examples:

```
CHARACTER_LENGTH (X'F0F0')
```
answer 2

```
CHARACTER_LENGTH ('Stephen')
```
answer 7; the answer is always 7 regardless of the number of octets used to store the string

11.2.2.3 OCTET_LENGTH

This function returns the length of the string in octets. The result is equivalent to the smallest integer not less than the quotient of (BIT_LENGTH(S)/8). It takes the form:

```
<octet length expression> ::=
    OCTET_LENGTH ( <string value expression> )
```

Examples:

```
OCTET_LENGTH (X'FØFØ')
```
answer 2, i.e. the same as for CHAR_LENGTH

```
OCTET_LENGTH ('Stephen')
```
answer 7 or 14 or 9 depending on whether a one-octet, a two-octet or a one-octet with case shift encoding was used

11.2.2.4 BIT_LENGTH

This function returns the length of the string in bits. It takes the form:

```
<bit length expression> ::=
    BIT_LENGTH ( <string value expression> )
```

Examples:

```
BIT_LENGTH (X'FØFØ')
```
answer 16

```
BIT_LENGTH ('Stephen')
```
answer 56 if it is a one-octet encoding, 112 if a two-octet encoding and so forth

11.2.3 Character Functions

This group of functions operates on character strings. They return either a character string or a numeric value. There are six functions, one of which returns a numeric value and five of which return a string. If any of the strings is null then the result is also null.

11.2.3.1 POSITION

This function returns the position of one string within another string. Both strings must be from the same repertoire. It takes the form:

```
<position expression> ::=
    POSITION ( <character value expression> IN <character value expression> )
```

where <character value expression> must be an expression that results in a character string. If the first string is of zero length then the result is 1; otherwise the result is the number of the first character within the second string which starts an occurrence of the second string, if any. If no such string exists then the result is 0. For example:

```
POSITION('ar' IN 'Gerard')
```
answer 4

```
POSITION('' IN 'Otten')
```
answer 1

```
POSITION('CEng' IN 'MBCS')
```
answer 0

```
POSITION('r' IN 'Gerard')
```
answer 3

11.2.3.2 TRIM

The TRIM function is used to remove leading and/or trailing characters from a string. It takes the form:

<trim function> ::=
    TRIM ([[{ LEADING | TRAILING | BOTH }]
        [<trim character>] FROM] <trim source>)

<trim source> ::= <character value expression>

<trim character> ::= <character value expression>

<trim source> and <trim character> must have the same character repertoire and the latter must have a length of 1 (if it is not specified it defaults to a single space character).

The result of a trim function is a varying length character string with the same character repertoire, collating sequence and coercibility attribute as <trim source> and with the leading, trailing or both leading and trailing occurrences of the <trim character> removed, depending on whether LEADING, TRAILING or BOTH is specified. If none of LEADING, TRAILING or BOTH is specified BOTH is assumed. For example:

```
TRIM(LEADING '*' FROM '***Error')
```
answer 'Error'

```
TRIM('  T I T L E ' )
```
answer 'T I T L E'

11.2.3.3 UPPER

This function converts lower-case letters into upper-case letters. It takes the form:

<upper> ::= UPPER (<character value expression>)

where <character value expression> must be an expression that results in a character string. The data type of the result is the same as the data type of <character value expression> and with all the same attributes.

Every simple Latin lower-case letter is replaced with the corresponding simple Latin upper-case letter ('a' with 'A' and 'b' with 'B', etc.). This replacement only applies to simple Latin letters; other characters such as é or б will not be replaced by É or Б respectively as one might have hoped. For example:

```
UPPER ('abc')
```
is 'ABC'

```
UPPER ('côté')
```
is 'CôTé'

11.2.3.4 LOWER

This function converts upper-case letters into lower-case letters, i.e. the converse of the UPPER function. It takes the form:

<lower> ::= LOWER (<character value expression>)

where <character value expression> must be an expression that results in a character string. The data type of the result is the same as the data type of <character value expression> and with all the same attributes.

Every simple Latin upper-case letter is replaced with the corresponding simple Latin lower-case letter. Again, this replacement only applies to simple Latin letters. For example:

```
LOWER ('ABC')
```
is 'abc'

```
LOWER ('CÔTÉ')
```
is 'cÔtÉ'

11.2.3.5 TRANSLATE

This function invokes a translation from one character set to another defined by a translation definition. It takes the form:

<character translation> ::=
TRANSLATE (<character value expression> USING <translation name>)

where <character value expression> must be an expression that results in a character string and <translation name> must identify a translation for which the user has USAGE privileges. The data type of the result is of character varying data type with the implementation defined maximal maximum length, the same character repertoire as the target character set specified in the translation definition and no collating sequence attribute.

The string is translated using the algorithm specified by the translation definition. This is a logical character translation and is not concerned with the encodings or physical representation in storage. For example, given a suitable translation routine, say TRANS1, we could translate a string as follows:

```
TRANSLATE ('ЛЕНИН' USING TRANS1)
```

giving 'LENIN'.

11.2.3.6 CONVERT

This function invokes a form-of-use conversion or conversion from one physical representation to another. This enables, for example, conversion from an encoding that uses some compression technique resulting in different numbers of octets being used for different characters to one that uses a fixed number of octets for each and every character. It takes the form:

<form-of-use conversion> ::=
  CONVERT (<character value expression> USING <conversion name>)

where <character value expression> must be an expression that results in a character string and <conversion name> must identify an implementation defined conversion. The data type of the result is of character varying data type with the implementation defined maximal maximum length, the same character repertoire as the character value expression and no collating sequence attribute.

The string is converted using the conversion routine from one form-of-use to another. This is a purely physical translation and is only concerned with the encodings. The primary use of this function is to enable an application program to receive a string in a particular encoding. For example, if an implementation provides a compacted form of use with a variable number of octets per character an application may wish to receive that in a form with a fixed number of octets per character in order to be able to index the string.

```
CONVERT ('Comrade ЛЕНИН' USING CONV1)
```

of course, gives 'Comrade ЛЕНИН' as logically nothing has changed.

The underlying encoding in octets may well have changed from, say, (ISO 10646 one octet compaction[1]):

67,111,109,114,97,100,101,32,153,32,38,57,153,32,38,50,153,32,38,59,
153,32,38,53,153,32,38,59

to (ISO 10646 four octet):

32,32,32,67,32,32,32,111,32,32,32,109,32,32,32,114,32,32,32,97,32,32,32,
100,32,32,32,101,32,32,32,32,32,32,38,57,32,32,38,50,32,32,38,59,32,32,
38,53,32,32,38,59

11.2.4 CAST

The CAST function converts a value expression of one data type into a value in another data type. It takes the form:

CAST ({ <value expression> | NULL } AS { <domain name> | <data type> })

---

1. In 10646 characters are normally encoded as four octets representing the group, plane, row and cell in which the character is to be found. One character compression assumes that the group, plane and row are implicitly all 32, in which row the Latin characters are found. Other characters from the same group can be identified by a 153 character followed by the plane, row and cell octets for the character. The Cyrillic characters are found in plane 32 row 38.

If <domain name> is specified the user must have a USAGE privilege for the domain. The data type of the result is the data type of the domain or data type specified with all the associated characteristics. Obviously, not all transformations are possible, but it is always possible to cast a value as a character string with a character set of SQL_TEXT (i.e. one which includes all supported characters), although the reverse depends on the value of the character string. The character string form being used is that which conforms to the specifications for literals with leading and trailing blanks in the string ignored. Table 11.2 shows which conversions are permitted syntactically. Table 11.3 provides notes on the conversions that take place and any errors raised.

Table 11.2 Permissible data type conversion using CAST

Data type of source	*Data Type of Target*								
	Exact numeric	*Approximate numeric*	*Character*	*Bit*	*Date*	*Time*	*Time-stamp*	*Year-month interval*	*Day-time interval*
Exact numeric	Yes	Yes	Yes	No	No	No	No	If the target has only a single datetime field	If the target has only a single datetime field
Approximate numeric	Yes	Yes	Yes	No	No	No	No	No	No
Character	Yes	Yes	If the character repertoires are the same	Yes	Yes	Yes	Yes	Yes	Yes
Bit	No	No	Yes	Yes	No	No	No	No	No
Date	No	No	Yes	No	Yes	No	Yes	No	No
Time	No	No	Yes	No	No	Yes	Yes	No	No
Timestamp	No	No	Yes	No	Yes	Yes	Yes	No	No
Year-month interval	If the source has only a single date-time field	No	Yes	No	No	No	No	Yes	No
Day-time interval	If the source has only a single date-time field	No	Yes	No	No	No	No	No	Yes
Unknown (i.e. NULL key word specified)	Yes	Yes	Yes	Yes	Yes	Yes	Yes	Yes	Yes

Table 11.3 Notes on data type conversions using CAST (Part 1)

<table>
<tr><th rowspan="2">Data type of source</th><th colspan="6">Data type of target</th></tr>
<tr><th>Exact numeric</th><th>Approximate numeric</th><th>Character varying</th><th>Character (fixed)</th><th>Bit varying</th><th>Bit (fixed)</th></tr>
<tr><td>Exact numeric</td><td colspan="2" rowspan="2">If no leading significant digits are lost after truncation or rounding (the choice is implementation defined), otherwise error</td><td>If the shortest literal representation, with the same scale, is not too long, otherwise error</td><td>If the shortest literal representation, with the same scale, is not too long (if shorter then pad with spaces), otherwise error</td><td colspan="2" rowspan="2">N/A</td></tr>
<tr><td>Approximate numeric</td><td>If the shortest literal representation is not too long, otherwise error. The shortest representation is taken to be 0E0 for zero, and n.mmmm where n is non-zero for the others</td><td>If the shortest literal representation is not too long (if shorter then pad with spaces), otherwise error. The shortest representation is taken to be 0E0 for zero, and n.mmmm where n is non-zero for the others</td></tr>
<tr><td>Character</td><td colspan="2">If the character string conforms to the rules for the appropriate numeric literal, otherwise error</td><td>The source is truncated to the length of the target if necessary and transferred. A warning is raised if truncation occurs</td><td>The source is extended on the right by spaces if it is shorter than the target. The source is then truncated to the length of the target if necessary and transferred. A warning is raised if truncation occurs</td><td rowspan="2">The bit representation of the string is transferred, truncated to the maximum length of the target if necessary. A warning is raised if truncation occurs</td><td rowspan="2">The bit representation of the string is transferred, padded with zero bits on the right if shorter and truncated to the maximum length of the target if necessary. A warning is raised if either truncation or padding occurs</td></tr>
<tr><td>Bit</td><td colspan="2" rowspan="4">N/A</td><td>The bit string is treated as character (padded with zero bits on the right to an exact multiple of the minimum character size) without regard to legal encodings. If necessary the character string is truncated. A warning is raised if either truncation or padding occurs</td><td>The bit string is treated as character (padded with zero bits on the right to an exact multiple of the minimum character size) without regard to legal encodings. If the resulting string is shorter than the target it is padded on the right with characters consisting of all zero bits. If necessary the character string is truncated. A warning is raised if either truncation or padding occurs</td></tr>
<tr><td>Date</td><td rowspan="5">If the shortest literal representation is not too long, otherwise error</td><td rowspan="5">If the shortest literal representation is not too long (if shorter then pad with spaces), otherwise error</td><td colspan="2" rowspan="5">N/A</td></tr>
<tr><td>Time</td></tr>
<tr><td>Timestamp</td></tr>
<tr><td>Year-month interval</td><td rowspan="2">If no leading significant digits are lost, otherwise error</td><td rowspan="2">N/A</td></tr>
<tr><td>Day-time interval</td></tr>
</table>

Table 11.3 Notes on data type conversions using CAST (Part 2)

<table>
<tr><th rowspan="2">Data type of source</th><th colspan="5">Data type of target</th></tr>
<tr><th>Date</th><th>Time</th><th>Timestamp</th><th>Year-month interval</th><th>Day-time interval</th></tr>
<tr><td>Exact numeric</td><td colspan="3" rowspan="2">N/A</td><td colspan="2">If no leading significant digits are lost after truncation or rounding (the choice is implementation defined), otherwise error</td></tr>
<tr><td>Approximate numeric</td><td colspan="2">N/A</td></tr>
<tr><td>Character</td><td colspan="5">If the character string conforms to the rules for the appropriate datetime or interval literal, otherwise error</td></tr>
<tr><td>Bit</td><td colspan="3">N/A</td><td colspan="2" rowspan="4">N/A</td></tr>
<tr><td>Date</td><td>Simple transfer</td><td>N/A</td><td>The year, month and day fields are taken from the source. The remaining fields are set to zero</td></tr>
<tr><td>Time</td><td>N/A</td><td>Simple transfer</td><td>The hour, minute and second fields are taken from the source. The remaining fields are set to values obtained from CURRENT_DATE</td></tr>
<tr><td>Timestamp</td><td>The year, month and day fields are trans- ferred</td><td>The hour, minute and second fields are transferred</td><td>Simple transfer</td></tr>
<tr><td>Year-month interval</td><td colspan="3" rowspan="2">N/A</td><td>If no loss of leading precision in the target, otherwise error</td><td>N/A</td></tr>
<tr><td>Day-time interval</td><td>N/A</td><td>If no loss of leading precision in the target, otherwise error</td></tr>
</table>

In all cases, if the value of the source value expression is null or the key word NULL was specified then the result is null.

If the target was specified by domain name then any domain constraint is checked for the result value. For example:

```
CAST ('100' AS FLOAT)
CAST (1E2 AS INTEGER)
CAST (empnr AS CHARACTER(5))
CAST ((name || address) AS BIT VARYING(1920))
```

11.3 Conditional Value Expressions

A conditional value expression selects a value to return based on a condition or a number of conditions. It should not be confused with condition execution, e.g. the IF THEN ELSE constructs in programming languages, which are absent in SQL. A conditional value expression is a single statement which in principle is completely executed; only the value returned is conditional (on some condition(s)).

SQL has one condition value expression, called the case expression, and a pair of syntactic shorthand ways of expressing two commonly used forms of case expressions. These two shorthands are called NULLIF and COALESCE.

11.3.1 CASE

The case expression returns a value conditional on other values. It takes the form:

```
<case expression> ::=
   CASE [ <case operand> ] <when clause>... [ <else clause> ] END

<case operand> ::= <value expression>

<when clause> ::= WHEN { <search condition> | <when operand> }
      THEN <result>

<else clause> ::= ELSE <result>

<result> ::= { <value expression> | NULL }

<when operand> ::= <value expression>
```

If a <case operand> is specified then every <when clause> must have a <when operand>. The effect is as if the <case operand> had not been specified and every <when operand> had been replaced by a <search condition> of the form ‘ <case operand> = <when operand> ’. Also, at least one of the <result>s must specify some <value expression> and not the key word NULL (this is necessary in order to be able to determine the data type of the result). The data type of the result is determined by rules (*see Section 9.3.3 Set Operations Result Data Types*) based on the data types of all the <value expression>s in the WHEN and ELSE clauses.

The value returned is the value of the first (left most) <result> for which the associated <search condition> is true. If no <search condition> is true then the result is the value of the <result> in the <else clause>, if it exists, and NULL otherwise. For example:

```
CASE sex WHEN 'F' THEN 'Female' WHEN 'M' THEN 'Male' END

CASE WHEN sex = 'F' THEN 'Female'
     WHEN sex = 'M' THEN 'Male' END
```

```
CASE sex WHEN 'F' THEN 'Female'
         WHEN 'M' THEN 'Male'
         ELSE 'Unknown' END

CASE grade WHEN < 12 THEN 'Low'
           WHEN BETWEEN 13 AND 15 THEN 'Medium'
           ELSE 'High' END

CASE WHEN forecast > 1000000 THEN 'Over Ceiling??'
     WHEN (actual-budget)/budget > .2
          THEN 'Horrible Overrun'
     ELSE 'OK' END
```

11.3.2 NULLIF

NULLIF, as the name suggests, substitutes null for a given value if it occurs. It is in fact a 'shorthand' for a particular form of <case expression>. It has the syntax:

NULLIF (<value expression>, <value expression>)

and a statement:

```
NULLIF (v1, v2)
```

is equivalent to:

```
CASE WHEN v1 = v2 THEN NULL ELSE v1 END
```

It can be used to prevent errors such as divide by zero, as in the following example:

```
SELECT salary / (NULLIF(commission, 0) FROM Employee)
```

since salary/NULL is NULL whereas salary/0 would be an error.

11.3.3 COALESCE

COALESCE returns the first non-NULL value from a list of values. It is in fact another 'shorthand' for a <case expression>. It takes the form:

COALESCE (<value expression> { , <value expression> }...)

A statement:

```
COALESCE (v1, v2)
```

is equivalent to:

```
CASE WHEN v1 IS NOT NULL THEN v1 ELSE v2 END
```

and when there are more than two values in the list:

```
COALESCE (v1, v2, ... , vn)
```

is equivalent to:

```
CASE WHEN v1 IS NOT NULL THEN v1 ELSE COALESCE (v2, ... ,vn)
END
```

COALESCE is used in the definition of NATURAL join and is most frequently used in other outer join situations.

11.4 Set Functions

Whereas the scalar functions operated on a single value, the set functions operate on a set of values. The set of values used are all of the values in a column of a table or all of the values from a column in a group of rows of a table. The syntax takes the form:

```
<set function specification> ::=
    COUNT(*)
  | { AVG | MAX | MIN | SUM | COUNT }
      ( [ DISTINCT | ALL ] <value expression> )
```

There are some restrictions: AVG and SUM may not be specified if the value expression has a data type of character, bit or datetime, i.e. they may only be used if it is numeric or interval. Value expression may not itself contain another set function, nor may it contain a subquery. Thus one may not write MIN(MAX(salary)) or AVG(SELECT salary FROM Employee WHERE empnr = 56789), but these are fairly meaningless anyway as a value expression is single valued and we would be attempting a set function on a set of one. If the value expression references a column in a table higher in the nesting sequence (i.e. an outer reference) then the value expression must reference only one column and be contained in either the select list of a query specification or in a HAVING clause, where the table name of the column referenced is part of the FROM clause at the same level as the HAVING clause. This last rule forbids such meaningless constructions as:

```
SELECT c1
  FROM T1 A
  GROUP BY c1
  HAVING EXISTS (SELECT *
                   FROM T2 B
                   WHERE B.c2 = (SELECT SUM(D.c3)
                                   FROM T3 D
                                   WHERE D.c4 = SUM(B.c5)))
```

If neither DISTINCT nor ALL is specified, then ALL is assumed. With the exception of COUNT(*), the set functions ignore rows where the value is null but will return a warning if any such nulls are ignored.

The data type of the result is basically the data type of the value expression with implementation defined precision and a scale not less than that of the value expression, in the case of numeric data types. In the case of COUNT the data type is exact numeric (integer).

11.4.1 COUNT

This function counts rows. There are three options, COUNT(*), COUNT DISTINCT and COUNT ALL. For example:

```
SELECT COUNT(*) FROM Employee
```
is a single row table containing the number of rows in the table Employee

```
SELECT COUNT (ALL destination) FROM Travel_Req
```
is a single row table containing the number of non-null values of the destination column in the table Travel_Req

```
SELECT COUNT (DISTINCT destination) FROM Travel_Req
```
is a single row table containing the number of non-**duplicate** and non-**null** values of the destination column in the table Travel_Req

11.4.2 AVG

This function returns the average of the non-null values. For example:

```
SELECT AVG (ALL salary) FROM Employee
```
is a single row table containing the average salary of employees

```
SELECT AVG (DISTINCT salary) FROM Employee
```
is a single row table containing the average of **distinct** salaries

11.4.3 MIN

This function returns the minimum value. For example:

```
SELECT MIN (ALL salary) FROM Employee
```
is a single row table containing the lowest employee salary

In the case of the MIN function the DISTINCT option makes no difference.

11.4.4 MAX

This function returns the maximum value. For example:

```
SELECT MAX (ALL salary) FROM Employee
```
is a single row table containing the highest employee salary

In the case of the MAX function the DISTINCT option makes no difference.

11.4.5 SUM

This function returns the total of all the non-null values. For example:

```
SELECT SUM (ALL salary) FROM Employee
```

is a single row table containing the total salary bill for the company

```
SELECT SUM (DISTINCT salary) FROM Employee
```

is a single row table containing the sum of all the **distinct** salaries

12

Transaction Management

12.1 Some Basic Concepts

Before we look at the facilities that SQL provides for the management of transactions, we should first define a few terms.

12.1.1 Transaction

In SQL a transaction is defined as 'a sequence of operations, including database operations or schema definition or manipulation operations, that is atomic with respect to recovery'. Thus a transaction is a series of SQL commands together with any additional procedural commands from the host language or other environment.

In addition, a transaction has a number of attributes which may be set by executing SQL statements and which cause it to react differently to statements issued by itself or with regard to changes in the database made by other, concurrent, transactions. The attributes are called the 'access mode' of the transaction and the 'isolation' level of the transaction. The access mode indicates the way in which the transaction is to work itself and the isolation level determines the degree of interaction from other transactions that can be tolerated during the execution of the transaction (Gray, 1981 and Eswaran *et al.*, 1976). A transaction may also sometimes be referred to as a 'success unit', a 'logical unit of work', a 'consistency unit' or even an 'integrity unit'.

12.1.2 Atomicity

In order to make a coherent change to the database it may be necessary to execute more than one data manipulation statement that inspects and changes the database. The classic example, which is always used, is that of a banking transaction that transfers an amount from one account to another. This sample banking transaction must:

1. Inspect the account of the paying client to ensure that sufficient funds are available.
2. Subtract the sum to be transferred from the account of the paying client.
3. Add the sum to the account of the receiving client.

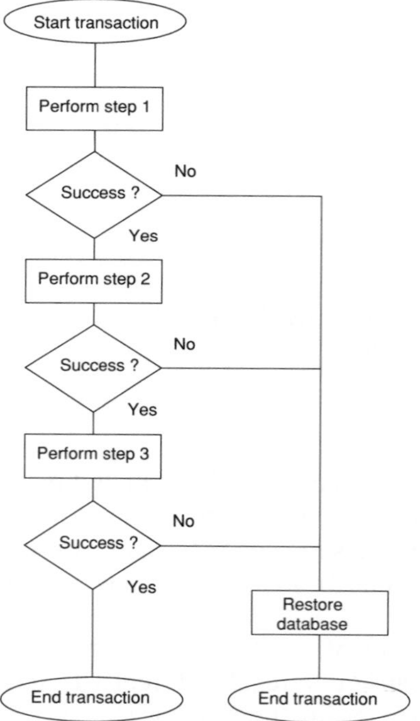

Figure 12.1 *Transaction flow*

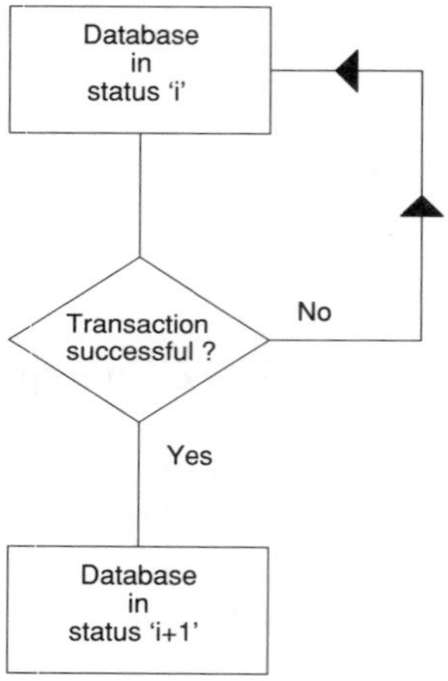

Database in status 'i'
Transaction successful ?
No
Yes
Database in status 'i+1'

Figure 12.2 *Database states changes*

All three steps involve the use of an SQL statement. Steps 2 and 3 involve changing the contents of the database. The exact order in which the statements are executed is not of any great importance in this example; however, the details of the check in step 1 will be different depending on whether it is done before or after step 2. What is of importance is that all three steps are completed successfully or no changes to the database are made. Failure at any stage must abort the transaction. The transaction can thus be structured as shown in Figure 12.1.

The state of the database always changes according to the scheme shown in Figure 12.2. This is the essence of atomicity. Atomicity means that from the point of view of other transactions inspecting the database, a transaction has either successfully completed and all its changes are visible or it is as if that transaction had never run, i.e. only database states 'i' and 'i+1' are visible to anybody except the transaction itself. A transaction that has successfully completed, i.e. committed, cannot be abrogated. It is sometimes said to exhibit the property of being durable. Durable does not mean that the database cannot be changed from the state in which the transaction left it, but that the successful completion cannot be later denied or made as if it had never happened except through the actions of another successfully committed transaction.

12.1.3 Recovery

We can see from the above discussion of atomicity that the database management system will need some facility to 'restore' the database to a previous state with regard to a given transaction or transactions. A transaction may fail for a number of reasons: it may be explicitly requested by the transaction, it may be enforced by the database management system as a result of errors in the transaction that cause a situation in which the transaction cannot succeed, it may occur because of resource allocation problems within the database management system or the computer or application system in general or it may be caused by system or system component failure (either hardware or software). In all of these, and in all other situations where the transaction has not ended successfully, the database management system must be able to effectively remove from the database any changes made by the transaction.

12.1.4 Concurrency

Concurrency is the state of being active at the same time. In a normal database system it is of considerable importance that several transactions should be able to be active at the same time. Where this cannot be the case it is probable that severe queuing would take place and the response times perceived by users of the system would become unacceptable.

There are naturally problems if we allow several transactions to execute at the same time and these transactions access and change the same areas of the database. We can distinguish three types of phenomena that may occur if transactions execute concurrently in an uncontrolled manner. For convenience these have been called, 'Dirty Read', 'Non-repeatable Read' and 'Phantoms'.

Dirty Read occurs, for example, when a transaction, T1, inserts or modifies a row in the database, another transaction, T2, reads that row and then T1 decides to perform a rollback. Transaction T2 will thus have read a row that was never committed and thus was never part of a guaranteed integral database, and logically can be said to have never existed.

Non-repeatable Read occurs, for example, when a transaction, T1, reads a row and then transaction T2 updates or deletes the same row and commits its changes. If T1 then decides to re-read the row it will either receive different values to those it received the first time or it will discover that the row does not now exist.

Phantoms occur when changes in the database made by a transaction, T1, cause the set of rows read by another transaction, T2, to differ between two executions of the same query. In the simplest example assume that we issue a select to find out if an employee exists with empnr 2001 and find that no such employee exists. Subsequently, we attempt to store an employee with that number and find employee 2001 now exists because an employee with that number has just been stored by another shorter transaction. Employee 2001 is then a phantom for the first transaction, T1.

12.1.5 Serializability

Serializability means that it is possible to take a set of transactions that have executed concurrently and find an order in which those transactions could have been executed serially to produce the same result in the database. Serial execution means that each transaction runs to completion before the next transaction starts. Serializability thus guarantees that no interaction has taken place between concurrent transactions which is dependent on the timing of operations within the transactions.

12.2 Initiating a Transaction

Normally a transaction is initiated, if one is not already active, whenever an SQL command is executed. There are, however, some exceptions. Some statements do not initiate a transaction. These are:

any <SQL session statement>
any <SQL transaction statement>
any <SQL environment statement>
a <get diagnostics statement>

Some of these statements may also be executed within a transaction but the following may not, and generate an error if the attempt is made:

a <set transaction statement>
a <set authorization identifier statement>

The following statements may only be executed within a transaction if the implementation permits a transaction to span multiple sessions (*see Chapter 14 Session Management*):

a <connect statement>
a <set connection statement>

We should be aware that in some circumstances an SQL transaction may be part of a larger transaction involving other SQL databases and/or other resource managers, such as message queues, etc. In these cases the transactions may be started explicitly by some other means and committed or rolled back as a result of more global commands. When this happens the actions specified by the COMMIT and ROLLBACK commands will be executed, though not necessarily all at once, even though the application program did not explicitly issue the COMMIT or ROLLBACK command. In fact, if the transaction was started by a non-SQL agent then use of SQL's COMMIT and ROLLBACK commands by the application program is illegal and will generate an error.

12.3 Control Statements in SQL

SQL provides three statements which allow control of the transaction and its execution attributes. These three statements are the commit, rollback and the set transaction statements.

12.3.1 The COMMIT Statement

The commit statement is the command that a transaction must issue in order to attempt the successful end of itself. The statement is very simple and is written:

COMMIT WORK

where even the word WORK is optional.

During the execution of the commit statement and before the successful end of the transaction a number of actions are performed, some of which might lead to rejection of the commit statement, as the database would become non-integral. The vital implicit action has to do with deferred integrity checking. If the checking of any integrity constraint is still deferred, the implicit SET CONSTRAINTS ALL IMMEDIATE statement is executed. If all integrity constraints are satisfied then the commit may proceed; otherwise, since a non-integral database is never permitted, the transaction is aborted, i.e. an implicit rollback is done. One should therefore think very carefully before attempting a commit with constraints in a deferred mode. Good practice indicates always explicitly making constraints immediate before committing.

The other actions implicit in the commit are:

- The deletion of rows from any temporary table associated with the transaction which specifies the ON COMMIT DELETE option.
- The closing of any open cursors.

Following the successful completion of all these actions the changes in the database or the schema definitions made by this transaction are irrevocably saved, i.e. the transaction may no longer change its mind about the changes. They can only be reversed by the independent actions of subsequent transactions.

12.3.2 The ROLLBACK Statement

The rollback statement is the command that a transaction may issue in order to terminate the transaction unsuccessfully. The statement is, again, very simple and is written:

```
ROLLBACK WORK
```

where, again, even the word WORK is optional.

The other action implicit in the rollback is:

- The closing of any open cursors.

Following the completion of all these actions any changes in the database or the schema definitions made by this transaction are cancelled, i.e. the transaction is as if it had never happened.

12.3.3 The SET TRANSACTION Statement

In order to choose the conditions under which a transaction will execute, a SET TRANSACTION statement has been provided to allow transactions to define their 'access mode' as retrieval only or read write transactions, to define their isolation level and to determine the size of the diagnostics area.

This statement is optional, i.e. it does not have to be specified for a transaction and defaults are available for all the options, but if it is executed it must be the first statement executed in the transaction. This prevents a transaction from changing its mind, a circumstance that could make life impossible for a database management system to police.

First let us look at 'access mode'. There are two options, READ ONLY and READ WRITE, and we have used the terms 'read only transaction' and 'read–write transaction' elsewhere to indicate transactions that have these options, implicitly or explicitly specified. READ WRITE is the default case except when isolation level READ UNCOMMITTED (*see later in this section*) is specified when READ ONLY is the default. The statement looks like:

```
SET TRANSACTION READ ONLY
```

Surprisingly READ ONLY does *not* mean that the transaction cannot issue INSERT, DELETE and UPDATE statements but only that it may not issue them against tables unless they are temporary tables. The use of temporary tables may well be useful in a complex reporting program which needs to store intermediate results but not make permanent changes to the database. It is possibly useful for the database management system to know whether permanent changes in the database are ever possible or not as a result of executing the transaction. If they are not, then it may be possible to simplify the locking strategy, etc. as no changes made by a READ ONLY transaction can ever affect another transaction since the temporary tables are local to the transaction.

Secondly, let us look at the isolation level. There are four isolation levels labelled READ UNCOMMITTED, READ COMMITTED, REPEATABLE READ and SERIALIZABLE. We discussed the classes of possible phenomena that could occur as a result of concurrently executing transactions in a previous section (*see Section 12.1.4 Concurrency*). The isolation level allows a transaction to choose which, if any, of these phenomena may occur during execution. Table 12.1 indicates, with a 'Y', which phenomena may occur at each isolation level.

Table 12.1 Permitted phenomena within isolation levels

Level	*Dirty Read*	*Non-repeatable Read*	*Phantoms*
READ UNCOMMITTED	Y	Y	Y
READ COMMITTED	N	Y	Y
REPEATABLE READ	N	N	Y
SERIALIZABLE	N	N	N

The number and type of phenomena against which the database management system must protect can have a significant effect on the performance and response of a system, so it normally makes sense to select the lowest level consistent with the needs of the transaction. You will see that isolation level SERIALIZABLE is necessary if we require *serializable* transactions, and this is always a safe, if expensive, option. Frequently the logic of the application does not require, or cannot afford, this degree of protection and then a lower level should be chosen.

The syntax is simple as the level may only be specified by a literal unsigned integer, e.g.:

```
SET TRANSACTION ISOLATION LEVEL SERIALIZABLE
```

If isolation level READ UNCOMMITTED is specified then the access mode must be READ ONLY, either explicitly or by default. This makes level READ UNCOMMITTED of limited use except for reporting programs that do not require absolute consistency. Otherwise, access mode is not restricted by the isolation level or vice versa.

One final point: an implementation is required to support the specification of all the levels but not necessarily to distinguish between them; i.e. it may always choose to execute a transaction at a higher level than requested, as the transaction will be unable to distinguish the difference. Thus a conforming implementation need only implement level SERIALIZABLE, but you would be well advised to investigate its performance before buying it.

Lastly, let us look at the diagnostics area size. The contents of the diagnostics area are separately discussed (*see Chapter 15 Error Handling and Diagnostics*). The size determines how many diagnostics may be stored. If no value is specified by the transaction then an implementation defined value is used. Otherwise the value specified determines the *maximum* number of diagnostics to be stored though the actual number stored may well be less. This lets the database management system know when it is pointless continuing to look for possible further errors, and restricting this value can thus have a beneficial effect on performance. We can specify the limit using a literal, e.g.:

```
SET TRANSACTION DIAGNOSTICS SIZE 12
```

or using a host language variable or parameter, e.g.:

```
SET TRANSACTION DIAGNOSTICS SIZE :diagsze
```

We can combine all or any of the various options, separated by commas, in any order, e.g. we can write

```
SET TRANSACTION READ WRITE, DIAGNOSTICS SIZE 12,
   ISOLATION LEVEL REPEATABLE READ
```

or

```
SET TRANSACTION ISOLATION LEVEL REPEATABLE READ, READ WRITE,
   DIAGNOSTICS SIZE 12
```

for the same effect.

13

Environment Management

A number of statements allow a transaction to control its environment. These are described in the following sections. Each of these commands is effective only for the SQL session in which it is executed. If a transaction spans multiple sessions the environment management commands executed in one session do not affect commands in another session.

13.1 SET CATALOG

This command is used to set the default catalog name for use in both **dynamic SQL** statements, which are prepared following the execution of this command and direct SQL statements. The command syntax is:

SET CATALOG <value specification>

The value specification must yield a character string that is interpretable as the identifier of a **catalog**. Leading and trailing blanks do not matter. The specified catalog name is used as the catalog name in all schema names that are not explicitly qualified. No check is made on whether the catalog specified actually exists, only that it is a legal name. If no SET CATALOG has been executed then the default catalog name is implementation defined.

This default applies only to dynamic SQL statements. Other SQL statements take the default from the **module** or from the schema definition statement in which they are embedded. For example, if we have two catalogues called TEST and PRODUCTION we can switch between them using the two commands:

```
SET CATALOG PRODUCTION
```

and

```
SET CATALOG TEST
```

13.2 SET SCHEMA

This command is used to set the default **schema** name for use in both **dynamic SQL** statements, which are prepared following the execution of this command and direct SQL statements. The command syntax is:

SET SCHEMA <value specification>

The value specification must yield a character string that is interpretable as the identifier of a schema. Leading and trailing blanks do not matter. The specified schema name is used as the schema name in all object names that are not explicitly qualified. No check is made that the schema specified actually exists, only that it is a legal name. If no SET SCHEMA has been executed then the default schema name is implementation defined.

The schema name may or may not be explicitly qualified with a **catalog** name. If it is, then an implicit SET CATALOG command is issued for the catalog name and the SET SCHEMA is done only on the schema name part of the character string. This default applies only to dynamic SQL statements. Other SQL statements take the default from the module or from the schema definition statement in which they are embedded. For example:

```
SET SCHEMA 'CATALOG'
```

will specify the Information Schema in the default catalog as the default schema whereas

```
SET SCHEMA 'TEST.CATALOG'
```

will set the default catalog to TEST and specify the Information Schema in that catalog as the default schema. The default catalog may subsequently be changed by a SET CATALOG command.

13.3 SET NAMES

This command is used to set the default character set for identifiers and literals used in both **dynamic SQL** statements, which are prepared following the execution of this command and direct SQL statements. The command syntax is:

SET NAMES <value specification>

The value specification must yield a character string that is interpretable as a **character set** name. Leading and trailing blanks do not matter. The specified character set name is used as the character set name for all identifiers and literals with no explicit character set name. No check is made that the character set specified actually exists, only that it is a legal name. If no SET NAMES command has been executed the literals and/or identifiers must entirely consist of either characters in the BASIC SQL character set or characters in the character set defined by the NAMES ARE clause in the module header.

This default applies only to dynamic SQL statements. Other SQL statements take the default from the **schema definition** statement. For example:

```
SET NAMES Latin_1
```

13.4 SET SESSION AUTHORIZATION

This command is used to set the current **authorization identifier**; i.e. it allows the transaction to assume an alias for the current user. The command syntax is:

SET SESSION AUTHORIZATION <value specification>

The value specification must yield a character string that is interpretable as an authorization identifier. The specified authorization identifier is then used as the applicable authorization identifier for all **privilege** checking which takes place until it is again changed by a SET SESSION AUTHORIZATION command. The restrictions that apply and any privileges needed to change from one authorization identifier to another are implementation defined according to the standard. This is because there is no defined standard security mechanism (for user authentication as opposed to data access) and this command must by its nature make use of such an authentication mechanism.

There is, however, a standard error code for an illegal attempt to change the authorization identifier and that is *invalid session authorization specification*. For example, if one of us is permitted two authorization identifiers (CANNAN and DBA), one for a normal programming role and one for database administration, then a switch can be made between them using:

```
SET SESSION AUTHORIZATION 'CANNAN'
SET SESSION AUTHORIZATION 'DBA'
```

Because there would be problems with open **cursors**, deferred **constraints,** etc., if the privileges available to a transaction were to change in the middle of a transaction, this command is restricted to situations when no transaction is active, e.g. after a commit and before the next access to data. Temporary tables would also present a problem but the new authorization identifier is also granted privileges on these tables as a result of this command.

13.5 SET CONSTRAINTS MODE

This command is used to set the **constraint** mode of a constraint within a session of a **transaction** to immediate or deferred. The command syntax is:

SET CONSTRAINTS
{ ALL | <constraint name> [{ , <constraint name> }...] }
{ DEFERRED | IMMEDIATE }

Every constraint has a constraint mode within a session of a transaction. This mode may be either immediate or deferred, with immediate being the default. Some constraints are deferrable and some are not. This is specified when the constraint is defined. Unless otherwise specified, **domain** constraints are not deferrable and other constraints are. The constraint mode for a deferrable constraint may vary between transactions and may be changed within a transaction with the help of this command.

Immediate constraint mode means that the constraint is effectively checked at the end of every SQL command. In fact, this means that the DBMS needs only to check those constraints that it knows to have been possibly compromised by the SQL command. Deferred constraint mode means that the checking of the constraint is delayed until either a COMMIT command is executed or the constraint mode of the constraint is changed back to immediate. Note that in the case of a COMMIT constraint modes in all sessions associated with the transactions are reset to immediate. When either of these happens the deferred constraints are checked and any necessary diagnostics raised. It is the SET CONSTRAINTS command that will be rejected if there are constraint violations and not the command that introduced the problem. In these cases the transaction has the option of correcting the database with the help of the diagnostics available or doing an explicit ROLLBACK of the transaction.

The command allows either the constraint mode of all deferrable constraints to be set with the ALL option or the constraint mode of individually named constraints to be set by using explicit constraint names. In either case, the constraint mode can be set to deferred or immediate, with the DEFERRED or IMMEDIATE option respectively. For example:

```
SET CONSTRAINTS ALL DEFERRED
```

will temporarily suspend any constraint checking, whereas

```
SET CONSTRAINTS Check_1 DEFERRED
```

will only suspend the single constraint 'Check_1' and

```
SET CONSTRAINTS Check_1 IMMEDIATE
```

will only restore the single constraint 'Check_1' provided that no current errors exist in the database, whereas

```
SET CONSTRAINTS ALL IMMEDIATE
```

will reset all constraint checking to immediate provided that no current errors exist in the database.

13.6 SET TIME ZONE

This command is used to define the local **time zone** for the **session** which is then used in time zone adjustment. The command syntax is:

SET TIME ZONE { LOCAL | <interval value expression> }

A SET TIME ZONE statement designates the default time zone for the session for use in evaluating <datetime value expression>s, for instance.

The options have the following meanings:

LOCAL	The value of the default time zone offset for the SQL environment. This is implementation defined. This may, for example, be the offset applicable to the installation, i.e. particular computer system, or the offset applicable to the terminal from which the command is executed or application program started.
<interval value expression>	The value of <interval value expression>, which must have a data type of INTERVAL HOUR TO MINUTE and a value between –12:59 and +13:00.

The value of the local time zone designator remains active across **transaction** boundaries for as long as the session remains active. For example, to set the local time to Central European Time we might say:

```
SET TIME ZONE INTERVAL'+1:00' HOUR TO MINUTE
```

or even

```
SET TIME ZONE LOCAL
```

if the default for the SQL environment just happened to be Central European Time.

14

Session Management

A session is a connection between an application program in an SQL_Client and an SQL_Server. This whole area is left, in the standard, somewhat to the implementation to define. The true scope of an SQL_Client and/or SQL_Server as well as how an implementation will use the information provided by the session management statements to determine the location, identity and required protocols to create a session with that SQL_Server are all implementation defined.

It has been said that these management statements break one of the rules for true distributed databases – location transparency – but while that is admitted, the statements have been standardized to permit a degree of both portability and distribution until true distributed heterogeneous databases become a reality. The session management statements permit an application program to establish connections to several SQL_Servers and to switch between them. Whether or not a transaction may span more than one session, i.e. may a SET CONNECTION or CONNECT be done while a transaction is active, is implementation defined. The standard permits it but does not require it. Implementations that do not permit it must raise a standard error condition if the attempt is made.

An application program within an SQL_Client possesses a single diagnostics area and uses one or more modules. All SQL statements other than GET DIAGNOSTICS and the session management statements execute in an SQL_Server; the exceptions execute only in the SQL_Client. Whenever a connection is made to an SQL_Server and a session established the modules associated with the application program are effectively shipped to that server. Of course, whether or not they are physically shipped or are already known in some way by the server is implementation defined. A server-related SQL statement is always executed in the current session if there is one. If no session is active then if the default session was dormant it is activated. Failing that a CONNECT TO DEFAULT is implicitly executed before the original SQL statement. There is always a default server for every SQL_Client. Again, whether this is local or remote is not of interest.

Each session has a set of context information which is preserved when a session is made dormant and restored when the session is made current. This context information consists of:

the session identifier
the current authorization identifier
the identities of all instances of temporary tables
the position of all open cursors
the identities and contents of all dynamic SQL descriptor areas
the SQL_session module
the current default catalog name
the current default unqualified schema name
the current character set name substitution value
the current default time zone
the current constraint mode for each integrity constraint
the current transaction access mode
the current transaction isolation level
the current transaction diagnostics area limit

It should be noted that transactions that span sessions and connect to the same SQL_Server may generate deadlocks with themselves as changes done through one session are not visible through commands issued in another session, even when these are part of the same transaction.

14.1 CONNECT

This command is used to establish a session between the SQL_Client and an SQL_Server. The command syntax is:

```
CONNECT TO
    { <SQL_Server> [ AS <connection name> ] [ USER <user name> ] }
  | DEFAULT
```

<SQL_Server>, <connection name> and <user name> must be either a literal, a host language variable or a parameter and must have a data type of character. If <user name> is not specified an implementation defined value is used, but if <connection name> is not specified, the default is the value of <SQL_Server>.

DEFAULT is equivalent to the specification of:

```
Server AS connection USER user
```

where Server and connection are the implementation dependent names of the default SQL_Server and associated connection name. The value of user is also implementation defined.

It is illegal to attempt to establish more than one simultaneous session with the same connection name. Implicit in the execution of this command is the command:

```
SET CONNECTION <connection name>
SET SESSION AUTHORIZATION <user name>
```

14.2 SET CONNECTION

This command is used to select a session from among those already established by CONNECT commands and make it the current one. The command syntax is:

SET CONNECTION <connection name> | DEFAULT

DEFAULT is equivalent to the specification of a <connection name> which is the implementation dependent name of the default SQL_Server. The value of <connection name> must identify the current or a dormant session.

The command makes the current session dormant, it saves the session's context information and then makes the session associated with <connection name> active after restoring the appropriate context information. All subsequent executions of procedures take place within the new active session.

14.3 DISCONNECT

This command is used to terminate the connection with an SQL_Server and to terminate a session. The command syntax is:

DISCONNECT { <connection name> | CURRENT | ALL | DEFAULT }

DEFAULT is equivalent to the specification of a <connection name> which is the implementation dependent name of the default SQL_Server. The value of <connection name> must be one of the current or a dormant session. The option CURRENT refers to the current connection and the option ALL refers to all dormant sessions and the current session.

If one of the sessions to be disconnected is active, i.e. a transaction is still active and an SQL command has been executed in that session since the transaction started, then an error is raised. The application must commit or rollback a transaction before disconnecting any session used by that transaction. All sessions identified by the command are terminated. Termination will take place of all specified sessions regardless of errors that may be discovered, although these errors, if any, will be reported in the diagnostics area. If the current session was not one of the sessions whose termination was requested then it remains the current session; otherwise there is no current session.

The actions associated with terminating a session include the dropping of all materializations of temporary tables, deallocation of all system descriptor areas and dropping the rest of the context information. Examples of the effects of the above statements and others on sessions and their status is shown in Table 14.1.

Table 14.1 Effects on sessions and their status

SQL statement	*Active session*	*Dormant sessions*
	N/A	N/A
SELECT * FROM T	DEFAULT	
CONNECT TO S1	S1	DEFAULT
CONNECT TO S2	S2	DEFAULT, S1
DISCONNECT CURRENT	N/A	DEFAULT, S1
SELECT * FROM T	DEFAULT	S1
DISCONNECT S1	DEFAULT	N/A
CONNECT TO S3	S3	DEFAULT
SET CONNECTION DEFAULT	DEFAULT	S3
CONNECT TO S1	S1	DEFAULT, S3
DISCONNECT ALL	N/A	N/A

15

Error Handling and Diagnostics

Whenever an SQL statement is executed one or more status codes are always generated. These status codes and normally a certain amount of diagnostic information are stored in an area called the Diagnostics Area. There is only ever one Diagnostics Area for an application program regardless of how many modules there are or how many sessions the program establishes. The Diagnostics Area is also always effectively part of the SQL_Client. An application program may choose the size of the Diagnostics Area in terms of the number of status codes, but it is always greater than zero. If the application does not choose a specific size then the implementation default size is used.

At the end of the execution of an SQL statement, other than a GET DIAGNOSTICS statement, the Diagnostics Area is cleared and any diagnostics information resulting from the execution is placed into it. In the case of a GET DIAGNOSTICS statement the Diagnostics Area remains unchanged and only the SQLSTATE parameter is altered. If any exceptions or warnings are generated by the execution then the implementation will store them in the Diagnostics Area; if no errors or warnings are generated then a successful completion status code must be stored. It is possible that the execution of a single statement may cause more than one error; e.g. changing a value in a column may cause two or more constraints to be violated. An implementation will store as many exception statuses as it detects, up to the limit of the size of the Diagnostics Area. However, it must be remembered that an implementation is not required to detect all actual errors that might be caused by a statement and thus the number of errors actually stored may be less than the size of the Diagnostics Area, even if it was theoretically possible to detect more errors. The important thing is that the implementation should report all errors that it detects, but it is not required to waste resources looking for extra errors that it might have found, once it has decided to abandon the execution of the command.

15.1 The GET DIAGNOSTICS Command

The GET DIAGNOSTICS command is available to return the additional diagnostic information, about any exception or warning that has occurred, from the Diagnostics Area. The command permits the return of additional information about more than one exception condition which resulted from the execution of an SQL statement, for example the violation of more than one integrity constraint. The sort of information available includes identifiers for the constraints violated, the names of associated tables, columns or cursors and may be extended by an implementor to provide whatever extra information may be available. In cases where information is being returned about an object whose existence is implied by the error and on which the user has no privileges, then the name of the object is suppressed, i.e. replaced by the 0-length string. Any of the items provided in the Diagnostics Area may be retrieved. If we wish to return information about the previous statement executed, the number of exceptions raised into a host language variable, :nelast, for example, then we can say:

```
GET DIAGNOSTICS :nelast=NUMBER
```

The general format is ‘ `target = identifier` ’ where the identifier specifies what information is requested and the target identifies the parameter or variable into which the information is to be placed. We can request more than one item of information about the statement at the same time as in:

```
GET DIAGNOSTICS :nelast=NUMBER, :more=MORE,
   :laststmt=COMMAND_FUNCTION
```

If we wish to retrieve information specific to a particular exception generated by the last command then we must specify the exception number; e.g. to retrieve information about the third exception we say:

```
GET DIAGNOSTICS EXCEPTION 3 :conscat=CONSTRAINT_CATALOG,
   :constsch=CONSTRAINT_SCHEMA,
   :constname=CONSTRAINT_NAME
```

It is not permitted to ask for specific exception information and the general statement information at the same time.

15.2 Diagnostic Area

The information held in the Diagnostic Area is explained in Tables 15.1 to 15.3. All the pieces of information given are returned as CHARACTER VARYING (L) where ‘L’ is the implementation defined length of an identifier with the exception of the following: RETURNED_SQLSTATE which is defined as CHARACTER (5); MORE which is defined as CHARACTER (1); NUMBER and MESSAGE_LENGTH which are both implementation defined with a data type of exact numeric with a scale of 0.

Table 15.1 Statement information in the Diagnostics Area

Identifier	*Information provided*
COMMAND_FUNCTION	This is an identifier for the SQL statement executed. Each SQL statement has a standard identifier, shown in Table 15.3 Values of COMMAND_ FUNCTION, which relates the BNF syntax production name to the specific identifier (*see Appendix C BNF Syntax Diagrams*)
DYNAMIC_FUNCTION	If the SQL statement was executed dynamically then this contains the standard identifier of the dynamic command. The identifier is generated in the same way as those for COMMAND_FUNCTION
ROW_COUNT	The number of rows affected directly by an INSERT, or a non-cursor DELETE or an UPDATE statement, i.e. the number of rows inserted, deleted or updated by the statement. The count does not contain rows indirectly affected by any triggered actions. If the statement was not one of the three above then the value of ROW_COUNT is undefined
NUMBER	The number of exceptions that have been stored in the Diagnostics Area for the last command executed, other than a GET DIAGNOSTICS command. The GET DIAGNOSTICS command may return a status via SQLSTATE without modifying the diagnostics area
MORE	An indication of the completeness of the information contained in the Diagnostics Area. This item may have one of two values, namely: Y More exceptions occurred than are stored. N All exceptions have been stored

Table 15.2 Exception information in the Diagnostics Area

Identifier	*Information provided*
CONDITION_NUMBER	The sequence number of the condition or error being described
RETURNED_SQLSTATE	This is the contents of the SQLSTATE parameter if this status code had been the only status code possible
CLASS_ORIGIN	This is the identification of the issuing authority for the class value part in the RETURNED_SQLSTATE value. In the case of class value defined by the SQL standard this will be 'ISO 9075'. Other class values may be defined by implementations; other standards or groups may be identified by this origin value
SUBCLASS_ORIGIN	This is the identification of the issuing authority for the subclass value part in the RETURNED_SQLSTATE value. In the case of class value defined by the SQL standard this will be 'ISO 9075'. Other subclass values may be defined by implementations; other standards or groups may be identified by this origin value
CONNECTION_NAME	This is the name of the session or connection that was current when the SQLSTATE value was generated. This is normally the session in which the command executed, but in the case of the session management statements (*see Chapter 14 Session Management*) is the session addressed in the command
SERVER_NAME	This is the name of the SQL_server that generated the SQLSTATE value. This is normally the SQL_server on which the command executed, but in the case of the session management statements is the SQL_server addressed in the command
CONSTRAINT_CATALOG	This is the name of the catalog in which the constraint that was violated is defined
CONSTRAINT_SCHEMA	This is the name of the schema, without the catalog qualification, in which the constraint that was violated is defined
CONSTRAINT_NAME	This is the name of the constraint that was violated. It is the unqualified name, i.e. without either catalog or schema name
CATALOG_NAME	This is the name of the catalog in which the table identified in TABLE_NAME is defined
SCHEMA_NAME	This is the name of the schema, without the catalog qualification, in which the table identifier in TABLE_NAME is defined
TABLE_NAME	This is the table name, without the catalog and schema qualification, of the table that is uniquely associated with the exception. For example, if the exception was a table constraint violation then this is the name of the table whose table definition contains the constraint or if the exception was a data exception then this is the table that contains the data that caused the exception

Table 15.2 continued

Identifier	*Information provided*
COLUMN_NAME	This is the column name, without the catalog, schema and table qualification, of the column that is uniquely associated with the exception. For example, if the exception was a table constraint violation that involves only one column then this is the name of that column or if the exception was a data exception then this is the column that contains the data that caused the exception
CURSOR_NAME	This is the name of the cursor that has an invalid state
MESSAGE_TEXT	This is an implementation defined character string that contains either spaces or a readable description of the exception
MESSAGE_LENGTH	This is the length in characters of the text contained in MESSAGE_TEXT
MESSAGE_OCTET_ LENGTH	This is the length in octets of the text contained in MESSAGE_TEXT

Table 15.3 Values of COMMAND_FUNCTION

<SQL statement>	*Identifier*
<allocate cursor statement>	ALLOCATE CURSOR
<allocate descriptor statement>	ALLOCATE DESCRIPTOR
<alter domain statement>	ALTER DOMAIN
<alter table statement>	ALTER TABLE
<assertion definition>	CREATE ASSERTION
<character set definition>	CREATE CHARACTER SET
<close statement>	CLOSE CURSOR
<collation definition>	CREATE COLLATION
<commit statement>	COMMIT WORK
<connect statement>	CONNECT
<deallocate descriptor statement>	DEALLOCATE DESCRIPTOR
<deallocate prepare statement>	DEALLOCATE PREPARE
<delete statement: positioned>	DELETE CURSOR
<delete statement: searched>	DELETE WHERE
<describe statement>	DESCRIBE
<disconnect statement>	DISCONNECT
<domain definition>	CREATE DOMAIN
<drop assertion statement>	DROP ASSERTION
<drop character set statement>	DROP CHARACTER SET
<drop collation statement>	DROP COLLATION
<drop domain statement>	DROP DOMAIN
<drop schema statement>	DROP SCHEMA
<drop table statement>	DROP TABLE

Table 15.3 continued

<SQL statement>	*Identifier*
<drop translation statement>	DROP TRANSLATION
<drop view statement>	DROP VIEW
<dynamic close statement>	DYNAMIC CLOSE
<dynamic delete statement: positioned>	DYNAMIC DELETE CURSOR
<dynamic fetch statement>	DYNAMIC FETCH
<dynamic open statement>	DYNAMIC OPEN
<dynamic update statement: positioned>	DYNAMIC UPDATE CURSOR
<execute immediate statement>	EXECUTE IMMEDIATE
<execute statement>	EXECUTE
<fetch statement>	FETCH
<get descriptor statement>	GET DESCRIPTOR
<grant statement>	GRANT
<insert statement>	INSERT
<open statement>	OPEN
<prepare statement>	PREPARE
<revoke statement>	REVOKE
<rollback statement>	ROLLBACK WORK
<schema definition>	CREATE SCHEMA
<select statement: single row>	SELECT
<set catalog statement>	SET CATALOG
<set connection statement>	SET CONNECTION
<set constraints mode statement>	SET CONSTRAINT
<set descriptor statement>	SET DESCRIPTOR
<set time zone statement>	SET TIME ZONE
<set names statement>	SET NAMES
<set schema statement>	SET SCHEMA
<set transaction statement>	SET TRANSACTION
<set authorization identifier statement>	SET SESSION AUTHORIZATION
<table definition>	CREATE TABLE
<translation definition>	CREATE TRANSLATION
<update statement: positioned>	UPDATE CURSOR
<update statement: searched>	UPDATE WHERE
<view definition>	CREATE VIEW

15.3 SQLSTATE

SQLSTATE is the status parameter that must be provided on every SQL procedure call. It contains one of the RETURNED_SQLSTATE values that was stored in the Diagnostics Area during the execution of the SQL statement. All exception and warning statuses which are defined in the standard also have standardized values for the codes. Provision is also made for implementor defined codes, but in such a way that they are clearly distinguished from the standard codes.

SQLSTATE is a five-character item divided into two sub-fields, Class and Sub-Class. Class is two characters long and Sub_Class is three characters long. The character string has a one-octet form-of-use and is restricted to the digits 0–9 and the simple Latin upper-case characters A–Z.

A class value that begins with a digit between '0' and '4' inclusive or a simple Latin upper-case letter between 'A' and 'H' inclusive is reserved for this or other standards, although only a few are actually in use. Values of sub-classes of these classes which begin with one of the same 13 characters are also reserved for the standards. An implementation defined class or sub-class may take any other legal value. It is possible for a standard class code to be used in combination with an implementation defined sub-class code but not vice versa, with the exception of sub-class '000' which always implies 'no subcode'. In the absence of an appropriate standard or implementation defined sub-class code '000' is returned.

A class value of 'HZ' indicates a condition defined by ISO/DIS 9579-2, Remote Data Access, Part 2:SQL Specialization.

15.4 SQLSTATE Codes

Table 15.4 SQLSTATE values

Condition	*Class*	*Sub-condition*	*Sub-class*
ambiguous cursor name	3C	(no subcode)	000
cardinality violation	21	(no subcode)	000
connection exception	08	(no subcode)	000
		connection does not exist	003
		connection failure	006
		connection name in use	002
		SQL_client unable to establish SQL_connection	001
		SQL_server rejected establishment of the SQL_connection	004
		transaction resolution unknown	007
cursor operation conflict	09	(no subcode)	000
data exception	22	(no subcode)	000
		character not in repertoire	021
		datetime field overflow	008
		division by zero	012
		error in assignment	005
		indicator overflow	022
		interval field overflow	015

Table 15.4 continued

Condition	*Class*	*Sub-condition*	*Sub-class*
data exception (cont.)		invalid character value for cast	018
		invalid datetime format	007
		invalid escape character	019
		invalid escape sequence	025
		invalid parameter value	023
		invalid time zone displacement value	009
		null value, no indicator parameter	002
		numeric value out of range	003
		string data, length mismatch	026
		string data, right truncation	001
		substring error	011
		trim error	027
		unterminated C string	024
dependent privilege descriptors still exist	2B	(no subcode)	000
dynamic SQL error	07	(no subcode)	000
		cursor specification cannot be executed	003
		invalid descriptor count	008
		invalid descriptor index	009
		prepared statement not a cursor specification	005
		restricted data type attribute violation	006
		using clause does not match dynamic parameter specifications	001
		using clause does not match target specifications	002
		using clause required for dynamic parameters	004
		using clause required for result fields	007
feature not supported	0A	(no subcode)	000
		multiple server transactions	001
integrity constraint violation	23	(no subcode)	000
invalid authorization specification	28	(no subcode)	000
invalid catalog name	3D	(no subcode)	000
invalid character set name	2C	(no subcode)	000
invalid condition number	35	(no subcode)	000
invalid cursor name	34	(no subcode)	000

Table 15.4 continued

Condition	*Class*	*Sub-condition*	*Sub-class*
invalid cursor state	24	(no subcode)	000
invalid schema name	3F	(no subcode)	000
invalid SQL descriptor name	33	(no subcode)	000
invalid SQL statement name	26	(no subcode)	000
invalid transaction state	25	(no subcode)	000
invalid transaction termination	2D	(no subcode)	000
no data	02	(no subcode)	000
successful completion	00	(no subcode)	000
syntax error or access rule violation	42	(no subcode)	000
syntax error or access rule violation in direct SQL statement	2A	(no subcode)	000
syntax error or access rule violation in SQL dynamic statement	37	(no subcode)	000
transaction rollback	40	(no subcode)	000
		integrity constraint violation	002
		serialization failure	001
		statement completion unknown	003
triggered data change violation	27	(no subcode)	000
warning	01	(no subcode)	000
		cursor operation conflict	001
		disconnect error	002
		implicit zero-bit padding	006
		insufficient item descriptor areas	005
		null value eliminated in set function	003
		privilege not granted	007
		privilege not revoked	006
		query expression too long for information schema	00A
		search condition too long for information schema	009
		string data, right truncation	004
with check option violation	44	(no subcode)	000

15.5 Whatever Happened to SQLCODE?

The old SQL status parameter, SQLCODE, has not actually been removed from the standard but it has been added to a list of 'deprecated' features. Deprecated features are ones that will be removed at the next revision of the standard. In practice you may use SQLCODE as well as, or instead of, SQLSTATE as the status parameter on a procedure call. However, you would be well advised not to use SQLCODE in any new programs as these may require to be altered when SQLCODE is finally removed. In any case it was virtually impossible to write portable programs with SQLCODE since as a 'standard' error code it is a joke.

In the first place SQLCODE was defined as an integer and thus its possible range of values was implementation defined. In the second place it only had three effective values as shown in Table 15.5.

Table 15.5 SQLCODE values

Value	*Condition*
<0	exception
0	successful completion
100	no data

where it can be seen that all errors are identical as far as a portable program is concerned and no warnings are defined or possible except for 'no data'.

16

The Module Language

The module language consists of a module header definition, some declarative statements and procedure definitions. The procedures provide one of the two standard ways in which standard programming languages can interface with the SQL language. The other way is the embedded SQL language which is discussed later (*see Chapter 17 The Embedded Languages*). In fact, the embedded languages are defined in terms of the module language so this can be seen as the basic interface, even if in practice only a small, but increasing, number of implementors support the module language directly.

How does the interface work? It works exactly as if the SQL procedures were not SQL procedures but normal procedures or subroutines of the language from which they are called. Thus all the normal calling conventions of the host language are obeyed.[1] Since the SQL data types do not always exactly match those of the programming languages some conversions are required and these are described later.

---

1. At the moment there is considerable difficulty in mapping the data types of one language, including SQL, on to those of another language. There is also the problem of the calling conventions to be used. At the moment there is no definitive standard but a working group of the International Organization for Standardization, ISO/IEC JTC1/SC22/WG11, is looking at developing standards for both 'Common Language-Independent Datatypes' and for a 'Language-Independent Procedure Calling Mechanism'.

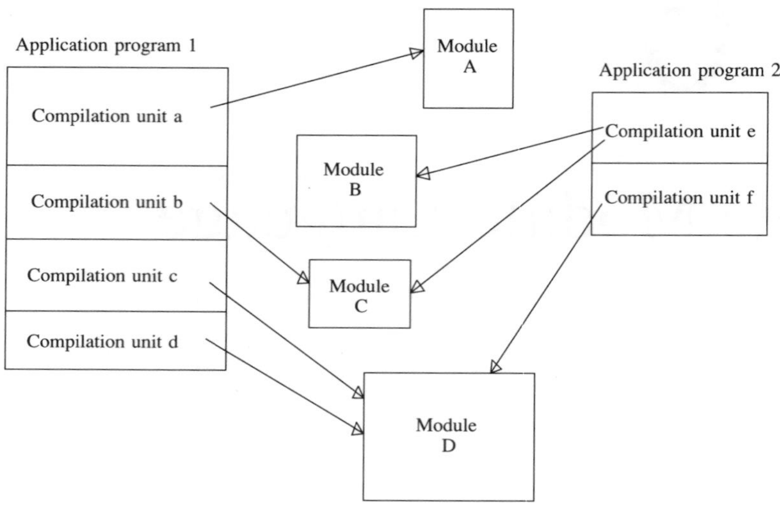

Figure 16.1 *Relationships between application programs, compilation units and modules*

16.1 Modules

A module is associated with zero or more compilation units. A compilation unit may be associated with several modules. All the SQL commands that a single piece of compiled code uses must exist in a module, with each command being an SQL procedure. All the non-dynamic embedded SQL commands in an embedded SQL program are considered to be defined in a single module. Dynamic SQL statements, or rather the statements prepared by a PREPARE or an EXECUTE IMMEDIATE command, are assumed to belong to a separate module. An application program which may be built from several independent compilation units (e.g. a main program and several subroutines) may, therefore, access several modules (*see Figure 16.1*).

The format of a module is:

```
<module> ::=
    <module name clause>
    LANGUAGE { ADA | C | COBOL | FORTRAN | MUMPS | PASCAL | PLI }
    <module authorization clause>
    [ <temporary table declaration>... ]
    <module contents>...

<module name clause> ::=
    MODULE [ <module name> ] [ NAMES ARE <character set name> ]
```

```
<module authorization identifier> ::=
      SCHEMA <schema name>
    | AUTHORIZATION <authorization identifier>
    | SCHEMA <schema name> AUTHORIZATION <authorization identifier>

<module contents> ::=
      <declare cursor>
    | <dynamic declare cursor>
    | <procedure>
```

The module name is optional, and as far as the standard is concerned merely documentation, unless the language is given as ADA, in which case it is mandatory and must be a valid Ada library unit name.

The NAMES ARE clause specifies the character set which may be used for identifiers and literals unless either of these has a character set introducer. Absence of the clause gives an implementation defined set. However, the basic characters needed to write SQL statements may always be used regardless of the character set specification.

The module authorization identifer provides two values, the default schema name (which is used if a name for an object is unqualified) and the authorization identifier to be used for access control. In the same way that the restrictions on whether a specific user may assume another authorization identifier with the SET SESSION AUTHORIZATION statement are implementation defined, so too are the restrictions on which users may call procedures in modules with explicit module authorization identifiers. Either or both of the names may be specified. If the schema name is not specified then the authorization identifier is used for the schema name as well; if the authorization identifier is not specified then the authorization identifier of the user's session at the time is used. The schema name may or may not be itself qualified by the catalog name. If not, then the implementation default is used, and the implicit or explicit catalog name is used as the default catalog name for all unqualified schema names.

Of the module contents, the declare cursor statement is described with the rest of the cursor commands and dynamic declare cursor with the rest of the dynamic commands. The procedures are described in the following sections.

16.2 DECLARE LOCAL TEMPORARY TABLE

The declare local temporary table allows a module to 'create' a temporary table whose scope is limited to the module in which it is declared and which exists only for the duration of the session in which it was declared. When an explicit or implicit CONNECT is done all declared temporary tables are materialized with zero rows.

The syntax is similar to that of the CREATE TABLE and has the form:

```
DECLARE LOCAL TEMPORARY TABLE <table name>
    <table element> [ {, <table element> }... ]
    [ ON COMMIT { PRESERVE | DELETE } ROWS ]
```

The default, if ON COMMIT is not explicitly specified, is ON COMMIT DELETE ROWS.

The declared local temporary table is identical to normal tables except for the following restrictions:

1. In a declared local temporary table, <table name> takes a special form, local table name, which looks like ' `MODULE.`<identifier> '. The reason for this is that the table 'belongs' not to a schema but to the module. The <identifier> part of the name must be different from the <identifier> in any other local table name in the module but different modules may use identical names.
2. It may not be referenced in view or assertion definitions.
3. It may not be referenced in constraint definitions except those of other declared local temporary tables.
4. It may not be altered or dropped.
5. It is not recorded in the Information Schema.
6. Its privileges are not grantable.

In addition, the ON COMMIT options control the contents of the table when a COMMIT is executed. If ON COMMIT DELETE ROWS is specified then on every commit an implicit delete of all rows is executed. In any case when the session ends all rows are deleted and the table definition is destroyed.

The declared local temporary table is a useful tool that a module can use as a private store during the lifetime of a session. It is private in the sense that nothing, except procedures in the same module, can read or update the declared local temporary table.

16.3 Procedures

The procedure must be thought of as a kind of subroutine that substitutes parameter values into a single SQL command, executes that command and returns results again through parameters. In this analogy the compilation unit would be the module. The format of a procedure is:

```
<procedure> ::=
    PROCEDURE <procedure name> ( <parameter> [ { , <parameter> }... ] ) ;
    <SQL statement> ;

<parameter> ::= <parameter name> <data type> | SQLSTATE | SQLCODE
```

The procedure name must be unique within the module for obvious reasons, and if it does not conform to the specific rules for procedure, function or routine names of the specified host language then some implementation defined way of mapping the name on to an acceptable name must exist. Parameters may also be listed without the enclosing '( )' and separating ','s, but this is deprecated and this alternative may well be discarded from any follow-on standard. Similarly, SQLCODE is deprecated and users are advised to use the much more suitable SQLSTATE option. The parameters are discussed in the following section.

The alternatives for <SQL statement> are:

<SQL schema statement>	i.e. all the statements described in Chapters 4 Data Definition, 5 Schema Manipulation and 8 Access Control
<SQL data statement>	i.e. all the statements described in Chapters 6 Non-Cursor Operations and 7 Cursor Operations with the exception of <declare cursor>
<SQL transaction statement>	i.e. all the statements described in Chapter 12 Transaction Management
<SQL session statement>	i.e. all the statements described in Chapter 14 Session Management
<SQL environment statement>	i.e. all the statements described in Chapter 13 Environment Management
<SQL dynamic statement>	i.e. all the statements described in Chapter 18 Dynamic SQL
<SQL diagnostics statement>	i.e. the statement described in Chapter 15 Error Handling and Diagnostics

While <SQL data statement> and <SQL schema statement> may exist in the same module whether or not they may be executed in the same transaction is implementation dependent. If the implementation does not support mixing then an error is raised.

When a procedure executes:

1. If no session is current then
   (a) If no CONNECT statement has been executed previously, there is no default session and the SQL statement is not itself a CONNECT, then an implicit CONNECT TO DEFAULT is executed. This is the case when the first statement is not a CONNECT.
   (b) If no CONNECT statement has been executed previously and there is a default session, then a SET CONNECTION DEFAULT is executed. This is the situation when a program not using its own session management statements has been disconnected by some failure.
   (c) Otherwise an error is raised. This occurs when a program doing its own session management has been disconnected by some failure.
2. If no transaction is active and the command is transaction initiating (*see Section 12.2 Initiating a Transaction*) then a transaction is initiated with read–write access, isolation level SERIALIZABLE and constraint checking immediate for all constraints not initially deferred.
3. The input parameters are initialized.
4. The SQL statement is executed and the output parameters, including the status parameters, are set.

If the status parameters indicate an error then no changes of any kind are made to the database or any schema definition. Certain languages require that output parameters be set in all circumstances, but whether or not any database values are set in the output parameters or any changes made to the SQL descriptor areas is implementation defined.

16.4 Parameters

The format of a parameter name is:

: <identifier>

All of the parameters that occur in the associated SQL statement must be declared in the parameter list and in addition at least one of the status parameters SQLSTATE or SQLCODE must be specified.

The other rules regarding parameters are all language dependent. The Ada language requires that the data types all be declared in an Ada package named SQL_STANDARD which looks like:[1]

```
package SQL_STANDARD is
   package CHARACTER_SET renames csp;
   subtype CHARACTER_TYPE is CHARACTER_SET.cst;
   type CHAR is array (POSITIVE range <>) of CHARACTER_TYPE;
   type BIT is array (NATURAL range <>) of BOOLEAN;
   type SMALLINT is range bs..ts;
   type INT is range bi..ti;
   type REAL is digits dr;
   type DOUBLE_PRECISION is digits dd;
   type INDICATOR_TYPE is t;
   type SQLCODE_TYPE is range bsc..tsc;
   subtype SQL_ERROR is SQLCODE_TYPE range
         SQLCODE_TYPE'FIRST..–1;
   subtype NOT_FOUND is SQLCODE_TYPE range 100..100;
   type SQLSTATE_TYPE is CHAR(1..5);

   package SQLSTATE_CODES is
      AMBIGUOUS_CURSOR_NAME_NO_SUBCLASS:
         constant SQLSTATE_TYPE :='3C000';

      ...
   end SQLSTATE_CODES;
end SQL_STANDARD;
```

1. Bold type here is used to distinguish parameters and does not refer to glossary terms.

where *csp*, *cst*, *bs*, *ts*, *bi*, *ti*, *dr*, *dd*, *bsc*, *tsc*, *t* are implementation defined. *csp* is a package, *cst* is character type, *t* is INT or SMALLINT and the rest are integer values. The package SQLSTATE_CODES contains all the standard specified SQLSTATE codes and any implementation defined codes. Fortunately, conforming implementations are required to generate the code of the Ada library unit package so that is one horrifying task that the programmer is spared.

Table 16.1 Data types of the status parameters

Language	*Status parameter*	
	SQLSTATE	*SQLCODE*
Ada	SQL_STANDARD. SQLSTATE_TYPE	SQL_STANDARD.SQLCODE_TYPE
C	Char[6]	pointer to long
COBOL	PICTURE X(5)	PICTURE S9(pc) USAGE COMPUTATIONAL where 4 <= pc <= 18 (implementation defined)
FORTRAN	CHARACTER*5	INTEGER
MUMPS	VARCHAR (5)	INT
Pascal	PACKED ARRAY [1..5] OF CHAR	INTEGER
PL/I	CHARACTER(5)	FIXED BINARY(pp) where pp >= 15 (implementation defined)

The host language data types of the status parameters are given in Table 16.1 while those corresponding to the parameter data types are given in Table 16.2, with 'pn' used as the parameter name. If a data type is not listed as a parameter data type then it may not be specified. DATE, TIME, TIMESTAMP, INTERVAL are never specified and can only be used in standard programming languages if first explicitly CAST to a character string and back. Some implicit conversion takes place for CHARACTER in all languages (except Ada which supports character sets); the octets of the SQL string are converted into host language characters and back (without regard for legal values). This is the same for BIT in all languages (except Ada and PL/I) where the string is converted into characters of one octet length.

Table 16.2 Host language data types of the SQL parameter data types

Language	*SQL parameter data type*	*Host language data type*
Ada	CHARACTER(l)	SQL_STANDARD.CHAR with P'LENGTH equal to OCTET_LENGTH(pn)
	BIT(l)	SQL_STANDARD.BIT with P'LENGTH equal to BIT_LENGTH(pn)
	INTEGER	SQL_STANDARD.INT
	SMALLINT	SQL_STANDARD.SMALLINT
	REAL	SQL_STANDARD.REAL
	DOUBLE PRECISION	SQL_STANDARD. DOUBLE_PRECISION
C	CHARACTER(l)	char[n] with n equal to OCTET_LENGTH(pn)
	CHARACTER VARYING(l)	char[n] with n equal to OCTET_LENGTH(pn)
	BIT(l)	char[n] with n equal to smallest number of characters that will hold the bit string
	INTEGER	pointer to long
	SMALLINT	pointer to short
	REAL	pointer to float
	DOUBLE PRECISION	pointer to double
COBOL	CHARACTER(l)	PICTURE X(n) with n equal to OCTET_LENGTH(pn)
	BIT(l)	PICTURE X(n) with n equal to smallest number of characters that will hold the bit string
	NUMERIC(p,s)	USAGE DISPLAY SIGN LEADING SEPARATE PICTURE SxVy with x = p–s 9's, and y = s 9's, if y = '' the V is optional
	INTEGER	PICTURE S9(ip) USAGE BINARY with ip implementation defined
	SMALLINT	PICTURE S9(ip) USAGE BINARY with ip implementation defined

Table 16.2 continued

Language	*SQL parameter data type*	*Host language data type*
FORTRAN	CHARACTER(l)	CHARACTER*n with n equal to OCTET_LENGTH(pn)
	BIT(l)	CHARACTER*n with n equal to smallest number of characters that will hold the bit string
	INTEGER	INTEGER
	REAL	REAL
	DOUBLE PRECISION	DOUBLE PRECISION
MUMPS	VARCHAR(l)	N/A[1]
	INT	N/A[1]
	DEC	N/A[1]
	REAL	N/A[1]
Pascal	CHARACTER(l)	PACKED ARRAY[1..n] OF CHAR with n equal to OCTET_LENGTH(pn) or CHAR if OCTET_LENGTH(pn) = 1
	BIT(l)	PACKED ARRAY[1..n] OF CHAR with n equal to smallest number of characters that will hold the bit string or CHAR if only one character is needed
	INTEGER	INTEGER
	REAL	REAL
PL/I	CHARACTER(l)	CHARACTER(n) with n equal to OCTET_LENGTH(pn)
	CHARACTER VARYING(l)	CHARACTER VARYING(n) with n equal to OCTET_LENGTH(pn)
	BIT(l)	BIT(l)
	BIT VARYING(l)	BIT VARYING(l)
	DECIMAL(p,s)	REAL DECIMAL(p,s)
	INTEGER	FIXED BINARY(p) with p implementation defined
	SMALLINT	FIXED BINARY(p) with p implementation defined
	FLOAT(p)	FLOAT REAL BINARY(p)

1. Since in MUMPS variables are not declared this is not relevant. The effective data type of a MUMPS variable is 'CHARACTER VARYING(ml)' where 'ml' is the implementation defined maximum length of a character string.

A parameter is an input parameter if it is used as a value within the SQL statement and is an output parameter if it is used as a target or is a status parameter. In Ada the parameter mode is also set to **in** for input parameters that are not also output parameters, **out** for output parameters that are not also input parameters, **in out** for parameters that are both input and output parameters and **in**, **out** or **in out** for other parameters (i.e. unused ones).

16.5 A Complete Example

The following unlikely example program is written in C and allocates unallocated vehicles to employees with more than *x* years service who currently do not have a vehicle. The employees are processed in order of decreasing length of service to the company until the vehicles run out.

First we give the definition of the module:

```
MODULE AllocV
   LANGUAGE C
   SCHEMA Company AUTHORIZATION Cannan

DECLARE CURSOR Emps AS
   SELECT empnr, name
   FROM Employee NATURAL JOIN Emp_Ext
   WHERE vehicleid IS NULL
         AND
         date_of_joining <
         CURRENT_DATE - CAST (:years AS INTERVAL YEAR)
   ORDER BY date_of_joining ASC

DECLARE CURSOR Veh AS
   SELECT vehicleid
   FROM Vehicle
   WHERE empnr IS NULL
   FOR UPDATE OF empnr

PROCEDURE End_T (SQLSTATE);
   COMMIT;

PROCEDURE Abort_T (SQLSTATE);
   ROLLBACK;

PROCEDURE Open_E (SQLSTATE, :years INTEGER);
   OPEN Emps;

PROCEDURE Close_E (SQLSTATE);
   CLOSE Emps;

PROCEDURE Open_V (SQLSTATE);
   OPEN Veh;
```

```
PROCEDURE Close_V (SQLSTATE);
  CLOSE Veh;

PROCEDURE Fetch_E
   ( SQLSTATE,
     :employee INTEGER,
     :name CHARACTER(40));
  FETCH NEXT FROM Emps
    INTO :employee :name;

PROCEDURE Update_E
   ( SQLSTATE,
     :employee INTEGER,
     :vehicle INTEGER);
  UPDATE Employee
    SET vehicleid = :vehicle
    WHERE empnr = :employee;

PROCEDURE Fetch_V (SQLSTATE, :vehicle INTEGER);
  FETCH NEXT FROM Veh
    INTO :vehicle;

PROCEDURE Update_V (SQLSTATE, :employee INTEGER);
  UPDATE Vehicle
    SET empnr = :employee
    WHERE CURRENT OF Veh;
```

and now the C program itself:

```
#include <stdio.h>

main()
{
  long int employee, vehicle, years;
  char name[40], SQLSTATE[5];
  long int *emp, *veh, *yrs;
  char *nam, *state;

  yrs = &years;
  scanf(u, *yrs);

  state = &SQLSTATE;
  nam = &name;
  emp = &employee;
  veh = &vehicle;
  SQLSTATE = '00000';

  Open_E(state, yrs);
  Open_V(state);
```

```
    do {
        Fetch_E(state, emp, nam);
        if (SQLSTATE <> 'ØØØØØ')
        then break;
        Fetch_V(state, veh);
        if (SQLSTATE <> 'ØØØØØ')
        then break;
        Update_V(state, emp);
        if (SQLSTATE <> 'ØØØØØ')
        then break;
        Update_E(state, veh);
        }
    while (SQLSTATE = 'ØØØØØ');

    if (SQLSTATE = 'ØØ1ØØ')
        then {
       Close_E(state);
       Close_V(state);
       End_T(state);
       }
        else {
       Abort_T(state);
       }
}
```

17

The Embedded Languages

The embedded languages are extensions to standard programming languages. These extensions are called <embedded SQL statement> and <embedded SQL declare section>. It is possible to convert a conforming program written using embedded SQL into a normal standard program together with a standard SQL module, where the standard program makes calls on the procedures of the module instead of having embedded commands. Indeed, the standard defines the functionality of the embedded languages in just that way.

The format of an embedded SQL statement is:

```
<embedded SQL statement> ::=
    <SQL prefix>
        { <declare cursor>
        | <dynamic declare cursor>
        | <temporary table declaration>
        | <embedded exception declaration>
        | <SQL statement>
        } [ <SQL terminator> ]
```

The format of an embedded SQL declare section is:

```
<embedded SQL declare section> ::=
    <SQL prefix> BEGIN DECLARE SECTION <SQL terminator>
        [ SQL NAMES ARE <character set name> ]
        [ <host language variable definition>... ]
    <SQL prefix> END DECLARE SECTION <SQL terminator>
  | <embedded SQL MUMPS declare>
```

```
<embedded SQL MUMPS declare> ::=
      <SQL prefix> BEGIN DECLARE SECTION
        [ SQL NAMES ARE <character set name> ]
        [ <host language variable definition>... ]
      END DECLARE SECTION <SQL terminator>
```

The special case, which is only valid for MUMPS, has only a single prefix and terminator pair round the whole section. This is because MUMPS has no native variable definition statements, though the embedded SQL needs them.

The <SQL statement>s are identical to those of the Module language except that instead of parameters being used, embedded host language variables are used. These have the format:

```
: <host identifier>
```

where <host identifier> is a valid variable, identifier, data name, etc. (depending on the language), in the host language.

The <host language variable definition>s are primarily natural host language variable definitions, with limited options. The detailed options are discussed below in a separate section for each language. Where the syntax differs from that of the host language, for example the BIT host variables in COBOL, they are converted into a legal host language variable. This is primarily converting BIT variables to CHARACTER variables. Each character host language variable definition, except for those of MUMPS, has an option CHARACTER SET IS <character set name>, which is not part of the host language variable definition but a way of specifying to SQL in which character set the characters are to be delivered to the program. This is also used to adjust the length of the variable when necessary. Omission of this option in any language, including MUMPS, indicates that an implementation-defined character set is to be used. The host language variable definitions may include either SQLSTATE or SQLCODE (in FORTRAN, SQLSTATE may be abbreviated to SQLSTA and SQLCODE must be abbreviated to SQLCOD). If either or both are specified they must occur in the program before any SQL statement. If neither is specified then SQLCODE is assumed. This is purely for upwards compatibility of programs since SQLCODE is a deprecated feature. <SQL prefix> and <SQL terminator> depend on the host language (*see Table 17.1*).

Table 17.1 SQL prefixes and terminators by language

Language	*<SQL prefix>*	*<SQL terminator>*
Ada	EXEC SQL	;
C	EXEC SQL	;
COBOL	EXEC SQL	END-EXEC
FORTRAN	EXEC SQL	(none)
MUMPS	&SQL(	)
Pascal	EXEC SQL	;
PL/I	EXEC SQL	;

17.1 The Supported Languages

SQL provides support for seven languages, Ada, C, COBOL, FORTRAN, MUMPS, Pascal (including Extended Pascal) and PL/I, being the standard programming languages as defined by various ISO documents. The relevant standards are given in Table 17.2.

Table 17.2 SQL supported languages

Language	*Standard*
Ada	ISO/IEC 8652
C	ISO/IEC 9899
COBOL	ISO/IEC 1989
FORTRAN	ISO/IEC 1539
MUMPS	ISO/IEC 11756
Pascal	ISO 7185
Extended Pascal	ISO/IEC 10206
PL/I	ISO 6160

17.1.1 Ada

All Ada variable definitions must conform to Ada rules and must also be derivable from the following syntax:

```
<Ada variable definition> ::=
    <Ada host identifier> [ { , <Ada host identifier> }... ] :
    <Ada type specification> [ <Ada initial value> ]

<Ada type specification> ::=
      <Ada qualified type specification>
    | <Ada unqualified type specification>
<Ada qualified type specification> ::=
      CHAR [ CHARACTER SET [IS] <character set name> ] ( 1..<length> )
    | SQL_STANDARD.BIT ( 1..<length> )
    | SQL_STANDARD.SMALLINT
    | SQL_STANDARD.INT
    | SQL_STANDARD.REAL
    | SQL_STANDARD.DOUBLE_PRECISION
    | SQL_STANDARD.SQLCODE_TYPE
    | SQL_STANDARD.SQLSTATE_TYPE
    | SQL_STANDARD.INDICATOR_TYPE
```

```
<Ada unqualified type specification> ::=
      CHAR ( 1..<length> )
    | BIT ( 1..<length> )
    | SMALLINT
    | INT
    | REAL
    | DOUBLE_PRECISION
    | SQLCODE_TYPE
    | SQLSTATE_TYPE
    | INDICATOR_TYPE

<Ada initial value> ::=
    := <character representation>...
```

17.1.2 C

All C variable definitions must conform to C rules and must also be derivable from the following syntax:

```
<C variable definition> ::=
    [ <C storage class> ]
    [ <C class modifier> ]
    { <C numeric variable> | <C character variable> | <C derived variable> } ;

<C storage class> ::= auto | extern | static

<C class modifier> ::= const | volatile

<C numeric variable> ::=
    { long | short | float | double } <C host identifier> [ <C initial value> ]
        [ { , <C host identifier> [ <C initial value> ] }... ]

<C character variable> ::=
    char [ CHARACTER SET [IS] <character set name> ]
        <C host identifier> <C array specification> [ <C initial value> ]
        [ { , <C host identifier> <C array specification> [ <C initial value> ] }... ]

<C array specification> ::= <left bracket> <length> <right bracket>
<C derived variable> ::=
      <C VARCHAR variable>
    | <C bit variable>

<C VARCHAR variable> ::=
    VARCHAR [ CHARACTER SET [IS] <character set name> ]
        <C host identifier> <C array specification> [ <C initial value> ]
        [ { , <C host identifier> <C array specification> [ <C initial value> ] }... ]
```

```
<C bit variable> ::=
    BIT <C host identifier> <C array specification> [ <C initial value> ]
        [ { , <C host identifier> <C array specification> [ <C initial value> ] }... ]

<C initial value> ::=
    = <character representation>...
```

17.1.3 COBOL

All COBOL variable definitions must conform to COBOL rules and must also be derivable from the following syntax:

```
<COBOL variable definition> ::=
    {01|77} <COBOL host identifier> <COBOL type specification>
    [ <character representation>... ] <period>

<COBOL type specification> ::=
      <COBOL character type>
    | <COBOL bit type>
    | <COBOL numeric type>
    | <COBOL computational integer type>
    | <COBOL binary integer type>

<COBOL character type> ::=
    [ CHARACTER SET [IS] <character set name> ]
    { PIC | PICTURE } [IS] { X [ ( <length> ) ] }...

<COBOL bit type> ::=
    { PIC | PICTURE } [IS] { B [ ( <length> ) ] }...

<COBOL numeric type> ::=
    { PIC | PICTURE } [IS]
          S { <COBOL nines> [ V [ <COBOL nines> ] ]
        | V <COBOL nines> }
    [ USAGE [IS] ] DISPLAY SIGN LEADING SEPARATE

<COBOL nines> ::= { 9 [ ( <length> ) ] }...

<COBOL computational integer type> ::=
    { PIC | PICTURE } [IS] S<COBOL nines>
    [ USAGE [IS] ] { COMP | COMPUTATIONAL }

<COBOL binary integer type> ::=
    { PIC | PICTURE } [IS] S<COBOL nines> [ USAGE [IS] ] BINARY
```

17.1.4 FORTRAN

All FORTRAN variable definitions must conform to FORTRAN rules and also be derivable from the following syntax:

```
<FORTRAN variable definition> ::=
    <FORTRAN type specification> <FORTRAN host identifier>
        [ { , <FORTRAN host identifier> }... ]

<FORTRAN type specification> ::=
    CHARACTER [ * <length> ] [ CHARACTER SET [IS]
            <character set name> ]
  | BIT
  | INTEGER
  | REAL
  | DOUBLE PRECISION
```

17.1.5 MUMPS

All MUMPS variable definitions must conform to MUMPS rules and also be derivable from the following syntax:

```
<MUMPS variable definition> ::=
    { <MUMPS numeric variable> | <MUMPS character variable> }
    <semicolon>

<MUMPS character variable> ::=
    VARCHAR <MUMPS host identifier> ( <length> )
        [ { , <MUMPS host identifier> ( <length> ) }... ]

<MUMPS numeric variable> ::=
    {  INT
     | DEC [ ( <precision> [ , <scale> ] ) ]
     | REAL
    } <MUMPS host identifier> [ { , <MUMPS host identifier> }... ]
```

17.1.6 Pascal

Support for Pascal includes support for Extended Pascal. All Pascal variable definitions must conform to Pascal rules and must also be derivable from the following syntax:

```
<Pascal variable definition> ::=
    <Pascal host identifier> [ { , <Pascal host identifier> }... ] <colon>
        <Pascal type specification> <semicolon>
```

```
<Pascal type specification> ::=
      PACKED ARRAY <left bracket> 1..<length> <right bracket> OF CHAR
            [ CHARACTER SET [IS] <character set name> ]
    | PACKED ARRAY <left bracket> 1..<length> <right bracket> OF BIT
    | INTEGER
    | REAL
    | CHAR [ CHARACTER SET [IS] <character set name> ]
    | BIT
```

17.1.7 PL/I

All PL/I variable definitions must conform to PL/I rules and must also be derivable from the following syntax:

```
<PL/I variable definition> ::=
    { DCL | DECLARE }
    {       <PL/I host identifier>
       | ( <PL/I host identifier> [ { , <PL/I host identifier> }... ] )
    } <PL/I type specification> [ <character representation>... ] <semicolon>

<PL/I type specification> ::=
      { CHAR | CHARACTER } [ VARYING ] (<length>)
         [ CHARACTER SET [IS] <character set name> ]
    | BIT [ VARYING ] (<length>)
    | <PL/I type fixed decimal> ( <precision> [ , <scale> ] )
    | <PL/I type fixed binary> [ ( <precision> ) ]
    | <PL/I type float binary> ( <precision> )

<PL/I type fixed decimal> ::=
      { DEC | DECIMAL } FIXED
    | FIXED { DEC | DECIMAL }

<PL/I type fixed binary> ::=
      { BIN | BINARY } FIXED
    | FIXED { BIN | BINARY }

<PL/I type float binary> ::=
      { BIN | BINARY } FLOAT
    | FLOAT { BIN | BINARY }
```

17.2 Exception Control

The <embedded exception declaration> permits the specification of the action to be taken should the status parameter returned by the SQL DBMS indicate anything other than successful completion. The declaration is valid for every embedded SQL statement in the program that occurs after the declaration in the text sequence and before any other declaration specifying the same condition (SQLERROR or NOT FOUND).

The format is:

```
<embedded exception declaration> ::=
    WHENEVER { SQLERROR | NOT FOUND } { CONTINUE | <go to> }

<go to> ::= { GO TO | GOTO } <go to target>

<go to target> ::= {
      : <host label identifier>
    | <unsigned integer>
    | <host PL/I label variable> }
```

If CONTINUE is specified, then no further action takes place on a condition and the program must check explicitly if it needs to know what status values were returned. If a <go to> was specified then, after every embedded SQL statement to which it applies, a host 'GO TO' statement of the appropriate kind is executed whenever the appropriate condition occurs (no data — NOT FOUND; any other except successful completion — SQLERROR). The various options of the <go to target> are to accommodate the various languages. The rule is simply that at the position of every SQL statement to which the condition applies the host language 'GO TO' statement constructed using the <go to target> must be a valid host language statement.

17.3 Inserting SQL Commands into the Host Language

Embedded SQL commands may be inserted into the host language wherever a similar host command could be specified, and if a host command in that place could be labelled or numbered or otherwise given an identity so can the embedded SQL command. One difference for FORTRAN programmers is that spaces are significant within embedded SQL statements. This includes host language variable names used within SQL statements.

In order to capture the status returns from executing SQL commands every host program must contain at least one of the following:

- a host language variable called SQLSTATE (in the case of FORTRAN, SQLSTA)
- a host language variable called SQLCODE (in the case of FORTRAN, SQLCOD)

with a definition which matches that for a parameter in the module language for the same host language.

17.4 A Complete Example

The following unlikely example program is the same example program as was given for the module language but written using embedded COBOL instead of C with a module. It allocates unallocated vehicles to employees with more than *x* years service who currently do not have a vehicle. The employees are processed in order of decreasing length of service to the company until the vehicles run out.

```
IDENTIFICATION DIVISION.
PROGRAM-ID. ALLOCV.

DATA DIVISION.
WORKING-STORAGE SECTION.

EXEC SQL BEGIN DECLARE SECTION END-EXEC.
01 SQLSTATE PICTURE X(5).
01 EMPLOYEE USAGE DISPLAY SIGN LEADING SEPARATE
PICTURE S99999.
01 VEHICLE USAGE DISPLAY SIGN LEADING SEPARATE
PICTURE S99999.
01 NAME PICTURE X(40).
01 YEARS USAGE DISPLAY SIGN LEADING SEPARATE PICTURE S99.
EXEC SQL END DECLARE SECTION END-EXEC.

PROCEDURE DIVISION.
STARTING SECTION.
PARA1.

EXEC SQL
  WHENEVER SQLERROR GO TO :ABORT
END-EXEC.

EXEC SQL
  WHENEVER NOT FOUND GO TO :FINISH
END-EXEC.

ACCEPT YEARS FROM CARD-READER.
MOVE '00000' TO SQLSTATE.
```

```
EXEC SQL
  DECLARE CURSOR Emps AS
    SELECT empnr, name
      FROM Employee NATURAL JOIN Emp_Ext
      WHERE vehicleid IS NULL
            AND
            date_of_joining <
            CURRENT_DATE - CAST ( :years AS INTERVAL YEAR )
    ORDER BY date_of_joining ASC
END-EXEC.

EXEC SQL
  DECLARE CURSOR Veh AS
    SELECT vehicleid
      FROM Vehicle
      WHERE empnr IS NULL
    FOR UPDATE OF empnr
END-EXEC.

EXEC SQL
  OPEN Emps
END-EXEC.

EXEC SQL
  OPEN Veh
END-EXEC.

LOOP SECTION.
PARA4.

EXEC SQL
  FETCH NEXT FROM Emps
    INTO :employee :name
END-EXEC.

IF SQLSTATE NOT = '00000'
  IF SQLSTATE = '00100' GOTO FINISH
     ELSE GOTO ABORT.

EXEC SQL
  FETCH NEXT FROM Veh
    INTO :vehicle
END-EXEC.

IF SQLSTATE NOT = '00000'
  IF SQLSTATE = '00100' GOTO FINISH
    ELSE GOTO ABORT.
```

```
EXEC SQL
  UPDATE Vehicle
    SET empnr = :employee
    WHERE CURRENT OF Veh
END-EXEC.

IF SQLSTATE NOT = '00000' GOTO ABORT.

EXEC SQL
  UPDATE Employee
    SET vehicleid = :vehicle
    WHERE empnr = :employee
END-EXEC.

IF SQLSTATE = '00000' GOTO PARA4
  ELSE GOTO ABORT.

FINISH SECTION.
PARA2.

EXEC SQL
  CLOSE Emps
END-EXEC.

EXEC SQL
  CLOSE Veh
END-EXEC.

EXEC SQL
  COMMIT
END-EXEC.

STOP RUN.

ABORT SECTION.
PARA3.

EXEC SQL
  ROLLBACK
END-EXEC.

STOP RUN.
```

18

Dynamic SQL

Dynamic SQL is a method by which an SQL statement to be executed is presented to the database management system such that the SQL statement does not need to be known before the program from which it is executed is run. In other words the statement may be constructed during program execution.

18.1 Why Dynamic SQL?

In many cases the SQL statement to be executed is fully known at the time that a program is written. The desired statements can then be fully coded using the embedded syntax or using calls on the procedures of a module. Since the statement is known beforehand the number and types of the parameters, both input and output, are also known and can be specified in the program. In some other cases, however, the SQL statement, or a part of it, is not known when the program is coded and must be generated during the program execution. This may occur, for instance, in programs providing a Query-by-Forms interface to the user. In this case virtually nothing can be known about the required statement — not the table name, not the column names, not the search criteria, nothing. Dynamic SQL provides an extension to both the module and embedded languages to permit SQL statements to be constructed and executed. Facilities are provided to enable information about the SQL statement just constructed to be requested from the SQL DBMS. This information relates to the number and types of input parameters of the SQL statement and the number and types of resulting columns from a fetch or select statement. A way of specifying the locations within the program of the actual source and target parameters is also provided.

18.2 The Basic Structure of Dynamic SQL

As we will see, dynamic SQL consists of a number of commands. The relationships between these commands and the various associated pieces of data and storage areas are sketched in Figure 18.1. This picture should be taken as a guide and not a complete description of all the relationships. The complete set of commands available in dynamic SQL is described in some detail in the following sections. However, the three most important commands are PREPARE, DESCRIBE and EXECUTE, and that is the normal sequence of execution. Basically, a character string containing an SQL statement with places where the contents of parameters and host language variables should be substituted marked by ?'s is prepared by a PREPARE command. This is roughly equivalent to the compilation phase. Information about the parameters and the data returned by such a command can be obtained by executing a DESCRIBE command which returns either information about the parameters or the data to be returned into a storage area called an SQL descriptor area. The characteristics of the parameter or result data can be modified by changing the contents of the descriptor areas, which is useful if the host programming language does not support all of the necessary data types itself. The values of the parameters can then be set into the descriptor area and the execution phase of the SQL statement initiated using the EXECUTE command. This takes the parameter values out of a descriptor area and returns any result values into, probably, another

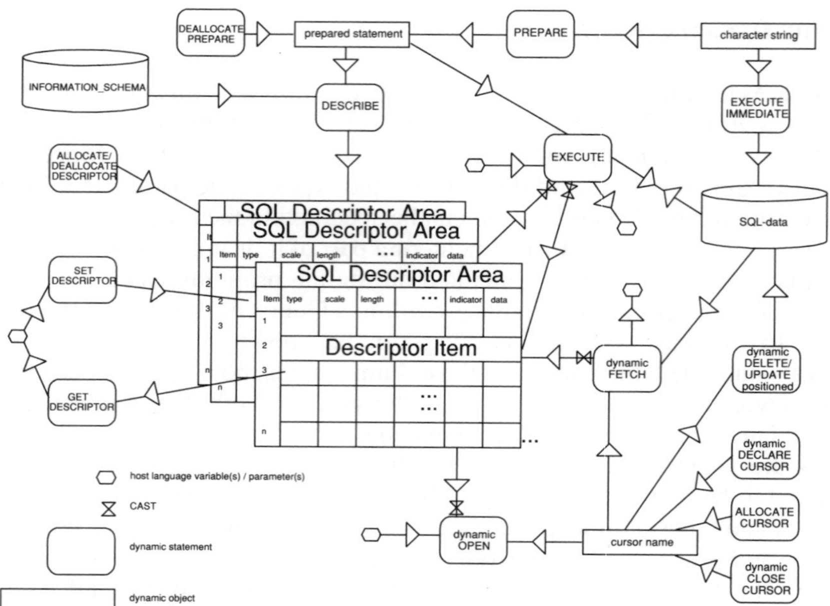

Figure 18.1 Relationships between objects and commands in dynamic SQL

descriptor area. The returned data values can then be inspected in the descriptor area. It is possible to skip the DESCRIBE step and to use the EXECUTE command with normal parameters or host language variables as sources and targets. The advantage of the descriptor area approach is that you do not need to know in advance, i.e. at coding time, anything about the number or types of parameters or resulting values, as would be the case with an EXECUTE coded using host language variables. There are variations of some commands, e.g. EXECUTE IMMEDIATE, that can be used when there are no parameters or resulting data, and a host of supporting commands, for example, allocating and deallocating descriptor areas and, as we have already implied, moving values into and out of these descriptor areas.

18.3 EXECUTE IMMEDIATE

This is the simplest of the dynamic SQL statements. It takes the form:

EXECUTE IMMEDIATE <SQL statement variable>

where <SQL statement variable> is a character string whose contents must be any of the SQL statements which can be prepared by a PREPARE statement without any comments or dynamic parameters (dynamic parameters are question marks (?) in the character string, rather than the ':name' format used in static SQL). There are two exceptions, <dynamic select statement> and <dynamic single row select statement>. The statement contained in the string is executed as if it were a procedure with only an SQLSTATE and SQLCODE parameter. No other parameters exist as there is no way of specifying the values for them. In any case, if necessary they can be edited into the string before the command is issued. For example:

```
EXECUTE IMMEDIATE 'COMMIT'
EXECUTE IMMEDIATE 'DELETE FROM Itinerary WHERE
   itinerary_no = 1065'
EXECUTE IMMEDIATE :Text
```

where :Text contains ' `INSERT INTO Dept VALUES ('EXP')` '.

18.4 PREPARE

The prepare command can be compared to the compilation phase of static, module, SQL. It takes the following form:

PREPARE <SQL statement name> FROM <SQL statement variable>

where <SQL statement variable> is as for EXECUTE IMMEDIATE and <SQL statement name> is either an identifier or an extended name (*see Section 3.4 Names*).

The SQL statement in the SQL statement variable is prepared for execution (a pseudo compilation) and the value of the SQL statement name is attached to the prepared statement for later identification by other dynamic SQL commands (e.g. the EXECUTE command). If the SQL statement name is an identifier then the prepared statement must be referenced by an identifier in an EXECUTE or dynamic DECLARE statement; otherwise it must be referenced as an extended name in an EXECUTE or ALLOCATE CURSOR statement. If the SQL statement name used already refers to a prepared statement then an implicit DEALLOCATE PREPARE is executed for the SQL statement name. A prepared statement is always valid in the transaction in which it is prepared and, depending on the implementation, may also be valid in subsequent transactions.

There are several restrictions on what may be specified in the SQL statement variable. The most important restriction is on the statements that may be specified. These are:

<SQL schema statement>
<SQL transaction statement>
<set catalog statement>
<set schema statement>
<set names statement>
<set authorization identifier statement>
<set constraints mode statement>
<set time zone statement>
<insert statement>
<update statement: searched>
<delete statement: searched>
<dynamic single row select statement>
<preparable dynamic delete statement: positioned>
<preparable dynamic update statement: positioned>
<dynamic select statement>
<preparable implementation defined statement>

These are all the commands described in Chapters 4 Data Definition, 5 Schema Manipulation, 8 Access Control, 12 Transaction Management 13 Environment Management with the exception of the <set transaction statement>, together with all of the commands described in Chapter 6 Non-Cursor Operations with the exception of Single Row SELECT (which is functionally replaced by <dynamic single row select statement>), together with the <dynamic select statement>, which is used as the basis for cursors and any implementation defined extensions. <preparable dynamic delete statement: positioned> and <preparable dynamic update statement: positioned> are syntactically equivalent to the ordinary <delete statement: positioned> and <update statement: positioned> except that they reference cursors defined by a <dynamic declare cursor> and the FROM <table name> and <table name> are optional. Being based on a dynamic cursor these may not be known at the time of writing the text of the statement.

The format of <dynamic single row select statement> is the same as that of <query specification> (i.e. <single row select statement> without the INTO clause) and that of the <dynamic select statement> is the same as that of <cursor specification> (i.e. everything in a DECLARE CURSOR after the key word FOR).

There are some other restrictions in that no comments are permitted in the text and ? parameters are not permitted in places that make it impossible to determine the data type of the ? parameter from the context (e.g. on both sides of a dyadic arithmetic operator, ' ?+? ', an item in a select list or on both sides of a comparison predicate in the same position, ' (X.name, ?) > (Y.name, ?) '). In an attempt to minimize this problem, simplistic assumptions are sometimes made which may not always be true, e.g. in an expression ' BIT_LENGTH(?) ', the parameter is always assumed to be bit string. To avoid these problems the CAST function may be used, as in ' BIT_LENGTH(CAST(? AS CHARACTER)) ', for in these circumstances the data type of ? is assumed to be the data type to which it is being cast, in this case CHARACTER. For example:

```
PREPARE :stat1 FROM 'SELECT * FROM Dept WHERE deptcd = ?'
PREPARE :stat2 FROM :Text
```

18.5 DEALLOCATE PREPARE

Since the retention of many prepared statements can cause unnecessary consumption of resources, a method is provided of releasing these resources and effectively making it as if the prepare had not been done. The format of this statement is:

DEALLOCATE PREPARE <SQL statement name>

where <SQL statement name> identifies a previously prepared statement. If the SQL statement name identifies an open cursor then an error condition is raised; otherwise, after the execution of the command, the identified prepared statement is no longer usable.

For example if statements were prepared with:

```
PREPARE command1 FROM :Text
```

and

```
PREPARE :com1 FROM :Text2
```

they may be destroyed with

```
DEALLOCATE PREPARE command1
```

and

```
DEALLOCATE PREPARE :com1
```

respectively.

18.6 DESCRIBE

The describe statement initializes an SQL descriptor area with information about the input parameters or the output values of a prepared statement. It takes the form:

DESCRIBE [INPUT | OUTPUT] <SQL statement name>
USING SQL DESCRIPTOR <descriptor name>

INPUT implies that information about the input parameters is required and OUTPUT, which is the default if neither is specified, requests information about the select list columns of the result.

The requested information about the parameters or select list columns of the prepared statement identified by <SQL statement name> is placed in the items of the SQL descriptor identified by <descriptor name>. A descriptor name can be specified using a literal, a parameter name or an embedded variable name, and the descriptor area itself must have been previously allocated (*see Section 18.8 ALLOCATE DESCRIPTOR*). For example:

```
PREPARE :stat1 FROM 'SELECT * FROM Dept WHERE deptcd = ?'
DESCRIBE INPUT :stat1 USING SQL DESCRIPTOR :desc1
DESCRIBE OUTPUT :stat1 USING SQL DESCRIPTOR 'descriptor2'
```

18.7 USING

The <using clause> is used to identify either a list of arguments or an SQL descriptor area to be used as parameters or targets for the execution of a dynamic SQL command. It has the format:

<using clause> ::= <using arguments> | <using descriptor>

<using arguments> ::=
{ USING | INTO } <target specification> [{ , <target specification> }...]

<using descriptor> ::=
{ USING | INTO } SQL DESCRIPTOR <descriptor name>

The key word INTO must be used when defining the targets for dynamic fetch and execute statements. In the case of the execute statement the targets must be specified with the key word INTO in order to distinguish them from the parameter specification and in the case of the dynamic fetch statement for maximum compatibility with the syntax of the static fetch statement.

The number of target specifications in a <using arguments> list must equal the number of parameters required or the number of output columns returned in any execute or dynamic fetch statement in which it occurs. When using the <using arguments> alternative the data types of the host language variables or the parameters being used as either the source or the target must match those of the dynamic parameters or the columns being returned in the same way that parameters must match in normal module language. Values are taken directly from or placed directly into the parameters or host language variables. If, however, the <using descriptor> alternative is used then some implicit use of the CAST function takes place. When the <using descriptor> is part of a <dynamic fetch statement> or an <execute statement> and includes the INTO key word then a data item being returned is first cast into the data type specified by the corresponding item descriptor and the data placed into the DATA field of that item descriptor (the fields INDICATOR, RETURNED_LENGTH and RETURNED_OCTET_LENGTH are also set if appropriate). The values of the fields in the item descriptor that define the data type must have been previously set using a <describe statement> or a series of <set descriptor statement>s. The values stored can later be extracted with the <get descriptor statement>. When the <using descriptor> is part of a <dynamic open statement> or an <execute statement> and includes the USING key word then the value used for the dynamic parameter is the value of the DATA field (assuming that INDICATOR does not signify NULL) cast first into the data type that would have been specified by a DESCRIBE INPUT statement on the prepared statement. If DESCRIBE INPUT had been used to initialize the SQL descriptor area and no changes had been made using a <set descriptor statement> then the casts naturally take place between identical data types. If, however, the item descriptor had been built using <set descriptor statement>s or those provided by DESCRIBE had been changed then this cast ensures that there are no mismatches with the data type expected in the dynamic parameter.

The reason for using the descriptor area and this casting mechanism is to allow a program to access data from tables that have a data type not supported by the programming language itself.

18.8 ALLOCATE DESCRIPTOR

To be able to specify an SQL descriptor area in a USING clause it is first necessary to allocate it. This is achieved with the following command:

ALLOCATE DESCRIPTOR <descriptor name> [WITH MAX <occurrences>]

where

```
<occurrences> ::=
        [+] <exact numeric literal>
      | <parameter name>
      | <embedded variable name>
```

If <occurrences> is not specified then an implementation defined value is used; otherwise the value of <occurrences> must be an exact numeric value between 1 and some implementation defined maximum. The number of active descriptor areas is also subject to an implementation limit.

The SQL descriptor area is allocated with the specified name and with at least the specified number of item descriptors, all of which are initially undefined. The names must not be longer than 128 octets. This differs from the 128 character limit for identifiers because most programming languages do not yet support the character set facilities of SQL.

Each descriptor area has a field called COUNT which defines how many items are currently in use, i.e. how many parameters are defined or how many columns there are in the select list of the resulting table/row. Each item describes the input parameters in the order in which they occur in the command and the output columns in the order in which they occur in the select list. A list of the item descriptor fields is given in Table 18.1.

Table 18.1 Item descriptor fields

Field name	*Data type of field*	*Meaning*
NAME	SQL_TEXT character string >= 128 characters	The name of the derived column if it is an output descriptor, otherwise it is implementation dependent.
UNNAMED	Integer	If the value of NAME is an implementation dependent column name then the value of UNNAMED is 1, otherwise the value is 0.
TYPE	Integer	A code that defines the data type (*see Table 18.2 The values of the TYPE descriptor field*).
LENGTH	Integer	This gives the maximum length for string data types, in characters or bits as appropriate. If the data type is datetime then it indicates the length of the datetime type, i.e. DATE is 10, TIME is 8 and TIME WITH TIME ZONE is 14, the last two both plus fractional seconds precision plus 1 if fractional seconds precision > 0, TIMESTAMP is 19 and TIMESTAMP WITH TIME ZONE is 25, again both plus fractional seconds precision plus 1 if fractional seconds precision > 0.
RETURNED_ LENGTH	Integer	This gives the actual length in characters if the item is the result of a dynamic fetch or execute command.
OCTET_ LENGTH	Integer	For character string data types this is the maximum length in octets.
RETURNED_ OCTET_ LENGTH	Integer	This gives the actual length in octets if the item is the result of a dynamic fetch or execute command.
PRECISION	Integer	For exact or approximate numeric data types this gives the precision. For datetime data types it is the time or timestamp precision. For interval data types it is the fractional seconds precision.
SCALE	Integer	For exact numeric data types this gives the scale. For approximate numeric data types it is 0.
COLLATION_ CATALOG	SQL_TEXT character string >= 128 characters	If the data type is character, this gives the catalog name of the associated collating sequence, otherwise it is spaces.
COLLATION_ SCHEMA	SQL_TEXT character string >= 128 characters	If the data type is character, this gives the schema name of the associated collating sequence, otherwise it is spaces.
COLLATION_ NAME	SQL_TEXT character string >= 128 characters	If the data type is character, this gives the unqualified name of the associated collating sequence, otherwise it is spaces.

Table 18.1 continued

Field name	*Data type of field*	*Meaning*
CHARACTER_ SET_ CATALOG	SQL_TEXT character string >= 128 characters	If the data type is character, this gives the catalog name of the associated character set, otherwise it is spaces.
CHARACTER_ SET_SCHEMA	SQL_TEXT character string >= 128 characters	If the data type is character, this gives the schema name of the associated character set, otherwise it is spaces.
CHARACTER_ SET_NAME	SQL_TEXT character string >= 128 characters	If the data type is character, this gives the unqualified name of the associated character set, otherwise it is spaces.
DATETIME_ INTERVAL_ CODE	Integer	If the data type is datetime or interval it indicates the specific type (*see Table 18.3 The values of the DATETIME_INTERVAL_CODE descriptor field for datetime data types and Table 18.4 The values of the DATETIME_ INTERVAL_CODE descriptor field for interval data types*).
DATETIME_ INTERVAL_ PRECISION	Integer	For interval data types it gives the leading field precision.
NULLABLE	Integer	If the column is known not to accept nulls then the value is 0, otherwise it is 1. A discussion of when a column is known not to be nullable can be found below.
INDICATOR	Integer	An indicator of whether the value is null or that contained in DATA. Effectively the same as an indicator parameter in the module language. A negative value indicates NULL.
DATA	Defined by TYPE, LENGTH, OCTET_LENGTH, PRECISION, SCALE	The value of the parameter or the value of the target depending on whether it is an input or output descriptor.

A column, C, of a base table is known not to be nullable if:

- It is part of a primary key or
- It has a constraint that contains at the highest level either a '`C IS NOT NULL`', a '`NOT C IS NULL`', or a '<row value expression> `IS NOT NULL`' where the row value expression contains simply C as one element of the row and these are neither combined using OR with any other expression nor are they combined with another NOT, or
- It is based on a domain that has a domain constraint containing at the highest level a '`VALUE IS NOT NULL`' or a '`NOT VALUE IS NULL`' and this is neither combined using OR with any other expression nor combined with another NOT.

Note that since the column constraint NOT NULL is equivalent to a C IS NOT NULL constraint, that is also included.

Thus the following constraints would yield 'known not nullable' columns:

```
CHECK (c1 IS NOT NULL)
CHECK (NOT c2 IS NULL)
CHECK (c3 IS NOT NULL AND c4 IS NOT NULL AND c5 > 0)
CHECK (VALUE IS NOT NULL)
CHECK ((c5,c6,c7) IS NOT NULL)
```

A column of a derived table is known not to be nullable if:

- It is a column of a joined table that did not specify FULL or UNION and was not a column of the left (right) table if the join specified RIGHT (LEFT) and if the column (or columns in the case of coalesced columns) was also known not be nullable or
- It is a column of a table in a UNION, INTERSECT or EXCEPT and both columns from which it derives are known not to be nullable or
- It is a column in a select list that is derived from a column that is known not to be nullable, or a literal (other than NULL or SYSTEM_USER), or a COUNT set function or an expression that only involves these three elements and does not involve a subquery.

It is sometimes possible to prove that a column that is not 'known to be not nullable' by SQL can never be set to null but the standard has taken the line of only adopting the simpler cases.

Table 18.2 The values of the TYPE descriptor field

Code	*Data type*
<0	Implementation defined
1	CHARACTER
2	NUMERIC
3	DECIMAL
4	INTEGER
5	SMALLINT
6	FLOAT
7	REAL
8	DOUBLE PRECISION
9	DATETIME
10	INTERVAL
12	CHARACTER VARYING
14	BIT
15	BIT VARYING

Table 18.3 The values of the DATETIME_INTERVAL_CODE descriptor field for datetime data types

Code	*Datetime data type*
1	DATE
2	TIME
3	TIMESTAMP
4	TIME WITH TIME ZONE
5	TIMESTAMP WITH TIME ZONE

Table 18.4 The values of the DATETIME_INTERVAL_CODE descriptor field for interval data types

Code	*Interval qualifier*
1	YEAR
2	MONTH
3	DAY
4	HOUR
5	MINUTE
6	SECOND
7	YEAR TO MONTH
8	DAY TO HOUR
9	DAY TO MINUTE
10	DAY TO SECOND
11	HOUR TO MINUTE
12	HOUR TO SECOND
13	MINUTE TO SECOND

For example:

```
ALLOCATE DESCRIPTOR :desc1 WITH MAX 10
ALLOCATE DESCRIPTOR 'descriptor2' WITH MAX 20
```

18.9 DEALLOCATE DESCRIPTOR

This command is used in order to free, or deallocate, an SQL descriptor area. It has the form:

DEALLOCATE DESCRIPTOR <descriptor name>

The descriptor name must, naturally, be an existing, allocated descriptor area. For example:

```
DEALLOCATE DESCRIPTOR :desc1
DEALLOCATE DESCRIPTOR 'descriptor2'
```

18.10 GET DESCRIPTOR

Having described or executed a prepared statement we can obtain information from the SQL descriptor area using the <get descriptor statement>. This takes the form:

```
<get descriptor statement> ::=
   GET DESCRIPTOR <descriptor name> <get descriptor information>

<get descriptor information> ::=
     <simple target specification> = COUNT
   | VALUES <item number>
       <get item information> [ { , <get item information> }... ]

<get item information> ::= <simple target specification> =
   {   NAME | UNNAMED | TYPE | LENGTH | RETURNED_LENGTH |
       OCTET_LENGTH | RETURNED_OCTET_LENGTH | PRECISION |
       SCALE | NULLABLE | INDICATOR | DATA |
       COLLATION_CATALOG | COLLATION_SCHEMA |
       COLLATION_NAME | CHARACTER_SET_CATALOG |
       CHARACTER_SET_SCHEMA | CHARACTER_SET_NAME |
       DATETIME_INTERVAL_CODE |
       DATETIME_INTERVAL_PRECISION
   }

<item number> ::= <simple value expression>
```

The data type of the <simple target specification> must match that of the specified key word, either the one specified in the table above or, in the case of COUNT, it must be of an integer data type. <item number> is an integer that is used to select the required item entry from the descriptor area, and must lie between 1 and the maximum number of items in the area. Note that an attempt to acquire information from an item whose number is greater than the value of COUNT will raise a 'no data' warning. The GET DESCRIPTOR command sets the target specified to the value of the requested attribute of the selected item or to the value of COUNT if that was specified. In the case of DATA, if the value is null, an error is raised if INDICATOR was not specified as well; otherwise there would be no way of indicating that fact. Also, when retrieving the value of DATA the data type of the <simple target specification> must match that given by the values of the item descriptors for that item. For a given TYPE only those relevant attributes are checked: thus for a TYPE of NUMERIC or DECIMAL, SCALE and PRECISION are checked; for FLOAT, PRECISION; for BIT, LENGTH; for CHARACTER, LENGTH, CHARACTER_SET_CATALOG, CHARACTER_SET_SCHEMA and CHARACTER_SET_NAME. For example:

```
GET DESCRIPTOR 'descriptor2' :count = COUNT
GET DESCRIPTOR :desc1 VALUES 2 :col2name = NAME,
               :col2type = TYPE
```

18.11 SET DESCRIPTOR

This command allows the setting of the values in the SQL descriptor area. All of the items specified in <set descriptor information> can be set, although changing the values of TYPE, LENGTH, PRECISION, SCALE, CHARACTER_SET_CATALOG, CHARACTER_SET_SCHEMA, CHARACTER_SET_NAME, DATETIME_INTERVAL_CODE and DATETIME_INTERVAL_PRECISION are subject to the same restrictions as would exist if an attempt was made to CAST the original data type into the new. The command takes the form:

```
<set descriptor statement> ::=
    SET DESCRIPTOR <descriptor name> <set descriptor information>

<set descriptor information> ::=
      COUNT = <simple value specification>
    | VALUES <item number>
        <set item information> [ { , <set item information> }... ]

<set item information> ::=
    {   TYPE | DATETIME_INTERVAL_CODE |
        DATETIME_INTERVAL_PRECISION |  SCALE | PRECISION |
        CHARACTER_SET_CATALOG | CHARACTER_SET_SCHEMA |
        CHARACTER_SET_NAME | LENGTH | INDICATOR | DATA
    } = <simple value specification>
```

The data type of the <simple target specification> must match that of the specified key word, either the one specified in the table above or, in the case of COUNT, it must be of an integer data type. <item number> is an integer that is used to select the required item from the descriptor area, and must lie between 1 and the maximum number of items in the area.

The command sets the specified attribute to the value of the value specification. If multiple attributes are set in one command, the attributes are always set in the order specified in <set item information>, and setting any attribute other than DATA causes the DATA attribute for that item to become undefined. When certain attributes are set other attributes acquire default values. These default values are given in Table 18.5 and are approximately those one would expect if specified as a data type on a column.

When the value of DATA is set values of item descriptors must match those of the data type of the <simple value specification>. For a given TYPE only those relevant attributes are checked: for a TYPE of NUMERIC or DECIMAL, SCALE and PRECISION are checked; for FLOAT, PRECISION; for BIT, LENGTH; for CHARACTER, LENGTH, CHARACTER_SET_CATALOG, CHARACTER_SET_SCHEMA and CHARACTER_SET_NAME. For example:

```
SET DESCRIPTOR 'descriptor2' COUNT = :count
SET DESCRIPTOR :desc1 VALUES 1 LENGTH = 3, DATA = 'TRA',
   INDICATOR = 0
```

Table 18.5 Default item descriptor values set as a result of setting other item descriptor values

Item descriptor set and the value set		*Other item descriptors set and their values*
TYPE =	CHARACTER or CHARACTER VARYING	CHARACTER_SET_CATALOG, CHARACTER_SET_SCHEMA, CHARACTER_SET_NAME = the values for the default character set name of the current SQL session LENGTH = 1 All others are undefined
TYPE =	BIT or BIT VARYING	LENGTH = 1 All others are undefined
TYPE =	DATETIME	PRECISION = 0 All others are undefined
TYPE =	INTERVAL	DATETIME_INTERVAL_PRECISION = 2 All others are undefined
TYPE =	NUMERIC or DECIMAL	SCALE = 0 PRECISION = the implementation defined default value for a DECIMAL or NUMERIC data type respectively All others are undefined
TYPE =	INTEGER or SMALLINT	All others are undefined
TYPE =	FLOAT	PRECISION = the implementation defined default value for a FLOAT data type All others are undefined
TYPE =	REAL or DOUBLE PRECISION	All others are undefined
DATETIME_INTERVAL_CODE (when TYPE = DATETIME)		If DATETIME_INTERVAL_CODE indicates DATE, TIME or TIME WITH TIME ZONE then PRECISION = 0, otherwise PRECISION = 6 (i.e. TIMESTAMP or TIMESTAMP WITH TIME ZONE) All others are undefined
DATETIME_INTERVAL_CODE (when TYPE = INTERVAL)		DATETIME_INTERVAL_PRECISION = 2 If DATETIME_INTERVAL_CODE indicates DAY TO SECOND, HOUR TO SECOND, MINUTE TO SECOND or SECOND the PRECISION = 6, otherwise PRECISION = 0 All others are undefined

18.12 EXECUTE

In order to execute a prepared statement we must use the execute statement. The syntax of this is:

EXECUTE <SQL statement name> [<using clause>] [<using clause>]

where the <SQL statement name> must identify a prepared statement and the first <using clause> is used to specify the targets for the resulting values, if any. These must be specified with an INTO key word and the second <using clause>, with a USING key word, is used to specify the values of any parameters. If the prepared statement being executed returns more than one row then an error is raised; otherwise the prepared statement executes exactly like the equivalent statement in a procedure of a module except that ? parameters are replaced with the values taken from the last <using clause>, the one with the USING key word. The values of the columns of any result table are placed in the targets specified by the <using clause> which contains the key word INTO.

18.13 Dynamic DECLARE CURSOR

The dynamic declare cursor associates a cursor with a statement identifier. This identifier may later be used in a prepare statement to specify the actual cursor to be used. It has the following syntax:

DECLARE <cursor name> [INSENSITIVE] [SCROLL] CURSOR
FOR <statement identifier>

You will notice that <statement identifier> replaces the bulk of the <declare cursor> statement, i.e. everything after the FOR key word; otherwise they are identical. The statement identified by <statement identifier>, when prepared by the PREPARE statement, must contain a <dynamic select statement> which is identical to the missing syntax. This constructed declare statement is then treated as if it were a static declare. For example, if :Text contains SELECT * FROM Employee ORDER BY name we can make a cursor with the following:

```
DECLARE Cursor5 SCROLL CURSOR FOR Curdef1
PREPARE Curdef1 FROM :Text
```

18.14 Dynamic ALLOCATE CURSOR

The dynamic allocate cursor is similar to a dynamic declare cursor but it takes an already prepared statement and turns it into a cursor declaration. The syntax is slightly different and has the following form:

ALLOCATE <extended cursor name> [INSENSITIVE] [SCROLL] CURSOR
FOR <extended statement name>

You will notice that we have <extended cursor name> and <extended statement name> instead of <cursor name> and <statement identifier>, the difference being that the latter are <identifier>s and the former are <parameter>s or <embedded variable>s, i.e. extended names (*see Section 3.4 Names*). Otherwise the statement performs the same function as the dynamic declare cursor. The cursor name remains associated with the prepared statement until a DEALLOCATE PREPARE is implicitly or explicitly executed. For example if `:Text` contains ‘ `SELECT * FROM Dept` ’ we can make a cursor with the following:

```
PREPARE :statmnt1 FROM :Text
DECLARE 'Cur6' SCROLL CURSOR FOR :statmnt1
```

or

```
PREPARE 'statmnt2' FROM :Text
DECLARE :cur7 SCROLL CURSOR FOR 'statmnt2'
```

18.15 Dynamic OPEN CURSOR

The dynamic open statement permits the opening of cursors declared using the dynamic declare cursor or allocate cursor statements. It is very similar to the normal open statement and takes the following form:

OPEN <dynamic cursor name> [<using clause>]

The dynamic cursor name must identify a prepared statement through a previous execution of a dynamic declare cursor or allocate cursor statement. The dynamic cursor name has the format:

<dynamic cursor name> ::=
<cursor name>
| <extended cursor name>

If the <using clause> is omitted there must be no dynamic parameters in the prepared statement. If the using clause is specified then the number of parameters specified in the using clause must match the number of ?'s in the prepared statement. Otherwise it opens the identified cursor in the same way as the static open, but using the arguments or the descriptor area specified by the using clause as the source of the parameters to substitute. For example:

```
OPEN Cursor1
OPEN :Cur7
OPEN :Cur3 USING :val1, :val2
OPEN :Cur4 USING SQL DESCRIPTOR :desc1
```

18.16 Dynamic CLOSE CURSOR

The dynamic close statement permits the closing of cursors opened by a dynamic open cursor statement. It is very similar to the normal close statement and takes the following form:

CLOSE <dynamic cursor name>

The dynamic cursor name must identify a cursor previously opened by a dynamic open statement. For example:

```
CLOSE Cursor1
CLOSE :Cur3
```

18.17 Dynamic FETCH CURSOR

This command which has the format:

FETCH [[<fetch orientation>] FROM] <dynamic cursor name> <using clause>

operates on a cursor in exactly the same way as the normal fetch statement except that instead of having an ‘ `INTO` <fetch target list> ’ it has a <using clause> which specifies the destination of the values retrieved.

18.18 Dynamic DELETE Positioned

The <dynamic delete statement: positioned> is identical to the static <delete statement: positioned> as regards functionality and is almost identical in syntax except that the cursor name is a dynamic cursor name and may thus be an extended name in addition to an identifier. The syntax is thus:

DELETE FROM <table name> WHERE CURRENT OF <dynamic cursor name>

For example:

```
DELETE FROM Dept WHERE CURRENT OF :Cur7
```

18.19 Dynamic UPDATE Positioned

The <dynamic update statement: positioned> is identical to the static <update statement: positioned> as regards functionality and is almost identical in syntax except that the cursor name is a dynamic cursor name and may thus be an extended name in addition to an identifier. The syntax is thus:

UPDATE <table name>
    SET <object column name> = { <value expression> | NULL }
    [, { <object column name> = { <value expression> | NULL } }...]
    WHERE CURRENT OF <dynamic cursor name>

For example:

```
UPDATE Dept
  SET Name = Code || '_' || Name,
      Code = SUBSTRING (Name FROM 1 FOR 3)
  WHERE CURRENT OF :Cur7
```

18.20 Preparable Dynamic DELETE Positioned

The <preparable dynamic delete statement: positioned> is identical to the static <delete statement: positioned> as regards functionality and is almost identical in syntax except that the name of the table is optional. If the table name is not specified it is assumed to be the single underlying table of the cursor. The syntax is thus:

DELETE [FROM <table name>] WHERE CURRENT OF <cursor name>

For example:

```
DELETE WHERE CURRENT OF Cursor1
```

Note that this statement cannot be prepared until the <dynamic select statement> associated with the cursor has itself been prepared.

18.21 Preparable Dynamic UPDATE Positioned

The <preparable dynamic update statement: positioned> is identical to the static <update statement: positioned> as regards functionality and is almost identical in syntax except that the name of the table is optional. If the table name is not specified it is assumed to be the single underlying table of the cursor. The syntax is thus:

UPDATE [<table name>]
    SET <object column name> = { <value expression> | NULL }
    [, { <object column name> = { <value expression> | NULL } }...]
    WHERE CURRENT OF <cursor name>

For example:

```
UPDATE
  SET Name = Code || '_' || Name,
      Code = SUBSTRING (Name FROM 1 FOR 3)
  WHERE CURRENT OF Cursor1
```

Note that this statement cannot be prepared until the <dynamic select statement> associated with the cursor has itself been prepared.

18.22 A Complete Example

The following example demonstrates how dynamic SQL may be used in a fairly simple program. The example accepts a query from the user and checks that the query needs no additional parameters and that all fields returned are character strings or exact numerics. The exact numerics are forced into character strings using the SET DESCRIPTOR (we assume that the implementation defined default character set has a fixed single octet encoding for simplicity). The query is then transformed into a cursor. The rows of the cursor are read, crudely formatted and presented to the user. The program has very little error checking and is designed merely to show some of the dynamic SQL commands in context.

```
IDENTIFICATION DIVISION.
PROGRAM-ID. DYNSQL.
DATA DIVISION.
WORKING-STORAGE SECTION.
01  FAIL PICTURE 9.
01  TOTLENG PICTURE 9(3).
01  STRINGPOS PICTURE 9(3).
01  MAXLEN.
    02 MAXLENITEM PICTURE 9(3) OCCURS 30.
EXEC SQL BEGIN DECLARE SECTION END-EXEC.
01  SQLSTATE PICTURE X(5).
01  SQL_STATEMENT PICTURE X(500).
01  INPAR_COUNTER PICTURE 9(5) USAGE DISPLAY
             SIGN LEADING SEPARATE.
01  OUTPAR_COUNTER PICTURE 9(5) USAGE DISPLAY
             SIGN LEADING SEPARATE.
01  OUTSTRING PICTURE X(500).
01  INSTRING PICTURE X(500).
01  SQLS1 PICTURE X(500).
01  INDESC PICTURE X(128) VALUE 'INDESC'.
01  OUTDESC PICTURE X(128) VALUE 'OUTDESC'.
01  L1 PICTURE 9(5) USAGE DISPLAY SIGN LEADING SEPARATE.
01  L2 PICTURE 9(3) USAGE DISPLAY SIGN LEADING SEPARATE.
01  L3 PICTURE 9(3) USAGE DISPLAY SIGN LEADING SEPARATE.
01  TEMP PICTURE 9(3) USAGE DISPLAY SIGN LEADING SEPARATE.
EXEC SQL END DECLARE SECTION END-EXEC.

PROCEDURE DIVISION.
STARTING SECTION.
PARA1.
  EXEC SQL
    DECLARE CURSOR1 CURSOR FOR :SQLS1
  END-EXEC.
  EXEC SQL
    WHENEVER SQLERROR GO TO :ABORT
  END-EXEC.
  MOVE '00000' TO SQLSTATE.
  EXEC SQL
    ALLOCATE DESCRIPTOR :INDESC WITH MAX 10
  END-EXEC.
  EXEC SQL
    ALLOCATE DESCRIPTOR :OUTDESC WITH MAX 30
  END-EXEC.
```

```
LOOP SECTION.
PARA2.
  ACCEPT SQL_STATEMENT FROM CARD-READER.
  EXEC SQL
    PREPARE :SQLS1 FROM SQL_STATEMENT.
  END-EXEC.
  EXEC SQL
    DESCRIBE INPUT :SQLS1 USING SQL DESCRIPTOR :INDESC
  END-EXEC.
  EXEC SQL
    GET DESCRIPTOR :INDESC INPAR_COUNTER = COUNT
  END-EXEC.
  IF INPAR_COUNTER = Ø GOTO PARA3.
  DISPLAY 'No selection parameters (?) allowed - reenter'.
  GOTO PARA2.
PARA3.
  EXEC SQL
    DESCRIBE OUTPUT :SQLS1 USING SQL DESCRIPTOR :INDESC
  END-EXEC.
  EXEC SQL
    GET DESCRIPTOR :OUTDESC OUTPAR_COUNTER = COUNT
  END-EXEC.
  MOVE Ø TO FAIL.
  MOVE Ø TO TOTLENG.
  PERFORM TEST1 VARYING L1 FROM 1 BY 1
    UNTIL L1 > OUTPAR_COUNTER.
  IF FAIL = Ø GOTO PARA4.
  DISPLAY 'Output column not character string'.
  DISPLAY 'or exact numeric'.
  DISPLAY 'or total length exceeds 5ØØ characters'.
  DISPLAY '- reenter'.
  GOTO PARA1.
PARA4.
  EXEC SQL
    OPEN CURSOR1
  END-EXEC.
PARA5.
  EXEC SQL
    FETCH NEXT FROM CURSOR1 INTO SQL DESCRIPTOR :OUTDESC
  END-EXEC.
  IF SQLSTATE NOT = 'ØØØØØ'
    IF SQLSTATE = 'ØØ1ØØ' GOTO FINISH
      ELSE GOTO ABORT.
  MOVE 1 TO STRINGPOS.
  MOVE SPACES TO OUTSTRING.
  PERFORM OUT1 VARYING L1 FROM 1 BY 1
    UNTIL L1 > OUTPAR_COUNTER.
  GOTO PARA5.
```

```
FINISH SECTION.
PARA6.
  EXEC SQL
    CLOSE CURSOR1
  END-EXEC.
  EXEC SQL
    DEALLOCATE PREPARE :SQLS1
  END-EXEC.
  EXEC SQL
    DEALLOCATE DESCRIPTOR :INDESC
  END-EXEC.
  EXEC SQL
    DEALLOCATE DESCRIPTOR :OUTDESC
  END-EXEC.
  EXEC SQL
    EXECUTE IMMEDIATE 'COMMIT WORK'
  END-EXEC.
  STOP RUN.

ABORT SECTION.
PARA7.
  EXEC SQL
    EXECUTE IMMEDIATE 'ROLLBACK WORK'
  END-EXEC.
  STOP RUN.

TEST1 SECTION.
PARA8.
  EXEC SQL
    GET DESCRIPTOR :OUTDESC VALUES :L1
       :TEMP = TYPE, :L2 = OCTET_LENGTH, :L3 = PRECISION
  END-EXEC.
  IF TEMP > Ø AND TEMP < 6 GOTO PARA9.
  MOVE 1 TO FAIL.
  GOTO ENDTEST1.
PARA9.
  IF TEMP = 1 GOTO PARA1Ø.
  ADD 2 TO L3.
  EXEC SQL
    SET DESCRIPTOR :OUTDESC VALUES :L1
       TYPE = 1, LENGTH = :L3
       -- the default character set is used
  END-EXEC.
  MOVE L3 TO L2.
PARA1Ø.
  ADD L2 TO TOTLENG.
  IF TOTLENG > 5ØØ MOVE 1 TO FAIL.
  MOVE L2 TO MAXLENITEM(L1).
  ADD 1 TO MAXLENITEM(L1).
ENDTEST1.
  EXIT
```

```
OUT1 SECTION.
PARA11.
  EXEC SQL
    GET DESCRIPTOR :OUTDESC VALUES :L1
       :INSTRING = DATA
  END-EXEC.
  MOVE STRINGPOS TO TEMP.
  STRING INSTRING INTO OUTSTRING WITH POINTER STRINGPOS.
  MOVE TEMP TO STRINGPOS.
  ADD MAXLENITEM(L1) TO STRINGPOS.
```

19

Direct Invocation of SQL

Direct Invocation is the form of execution that is most commonly thought of when considering SQL. It is, however, the least well defined. SQL is, as we have said, a database *sub*-language and thus must operate in conjunction with some other language or environment. In the case of the module and embedded methods of use the context is supplied by the SQL procedure or by the standard programming language. In the case of Direct Invocation there is a context, but the context is non-standard and implementation defined. Indeed, even for one SQL implementation which has been ported to several environments there may be variations in the Direct Invocation context depending on the host operating system.

There are two major aspects of the SQL language that are implementation defined for Direct Invocation. The first is the way in which the SQLSTATE and associated diagnostic information are returned to the user; the second is the way in which the derived table that results from the direct select statement is returned or displayed to the user.

As in dynamic SQL, the rules for the completion of unqualified names and the default character set for identifers and character literals differ from those for the module and embedded languages. Like dynamic SQL, direct SQL makes use of the SET CATALOG, SET SCHEMA and SET NAMES commands (*see Chapter 13 Environment Management*) to control the substitution values and character set defaults. As in the other methods of use of SQL an implementation may supply additional SQL-like, but non-standard, statements for use by the user.

19.1 Permitted Statements

Direct Invocation permits any of the following SQL commands to be executed:

<SQL schema statement>
<SQL transaction statement>
<SQL session statement>
<SQL environment statement>
<insert statement>
<update statement: searched>
<delete statement: searched>
<direct select statement: multiple rows>
<temporary table declaration>
<direct implementation-defined statement>

All the above statements must be terminated by a semicolon, ';'. These are all the commands described in Chapters 4 Data Definition, 5 Schema Manipulation, 8 Access Control; 12 Transaction Management; 13 Environment Management and 14 Session Management, together with all of the commands described in Chapter 6 Non-Cursor Operations with the exception of Single Row SELECT (which is functionally replaced by <direct select statement: multiple rows>), the <temporary table declaration> described in Chapter 16 The Module Language and any implementation defined extensions. Naturally these statements cannot contain any parameters or references to host language variables.

19.2 Direct Select : Multiple Rows

This command is similar to the Single Row SELECT statement but without the single row restriction and with the ordering capability of the declare cursor statement. It has the format:

<query expression> [<order by clause>]

For example:

```
SELECT * FROM Employee ORDER BY name
SELECT name, address FROM Travel_Agent
Order NATURAL JOIN Order_line
ORDER BY suppliernr, product_code
```

20

The Information Schema

The meta data structure, or catalog, has been standardized in such a way that the user only has access to views that provide information specific to a user's circumstances. These views are provided in a schema called INFORMATION_SCHEMA, along with a number of domain definitions, one base table, an assertion and all the implementation defined or standard character sets, collations, translations and conversions supported by the implementation. This schema is referred to as the 'Information Schema'. It must be noted that only the Information Schema is standardized and not the base tables on which the views are themselves based, which exist in a separate schema, DEFINITION_SCHEMA, known as the 'Definition Schema'. The standardized information consists of the identities and characteristics of all domains, tables, views and columns accessible to a user, together with the privileges associated with these objects. Information is also provided on the relationships between objects in order that definitional dependencies can be extracted by the user who is the owner of the object.

We describe first the Definition Schema (the base tables), as given in the standard, so that the later view definitions will make sense. No implementation is required to define base tables in this way, and indeed it is unlikely that any implementation will ever do so as they will also need to record physical aspects, such as indexes, etc., which are outside the scope of the standard.

We then proceed to describe the Information Schema (primarily the views on these base tables), which are available in any conforming implementation. Lastly, we give some examples of the kind of queries that can usefully be made on the catalog.

20.1 The Definition Schema

The base tables are defined in a schema called DEFINITION_SCHEMA. The data definitions are intended to be as complete as the definitional power of SQL reasonably allows. In addition to numerous table constraints, a number of assertions are defined where appropriate.

We first give a diagrammatic data structure diagram of the catalog (*see Figure 20.1*) and this is followed by the various pieces of syntax that define the catalog together with a small amount of explanatory comment where necessary. In general the schema is taken to be self-explanatory, given an understanding of the language as described in the rest of this book or the standard ISO 9075.

A number of the base tables have plural names whereas the normal convention is to use the singular. This is done because in those cases the singular names are also key words and would have needed to be delimited identifiers.

The INFORMATION_SCHEMA, as we shall see, restricts access to information about objects defined in one catalog only. The underlying Definition Schema therefore needs to contain all the relevant information about that catalog and any objects in other catalogs referenced by these objects. Despite the fact that the Definition Schema never needs to be materialized, a number of implementors were concerned that a single Definition Schema might need to be materialized for the universe of catalogs reachable from a given single catalog, a so-called Universal Definition Schema, because of the foreign keys and other check clauses present in the base table definitions. In order to overcome their (unnecessary) concerns the standards body agreed at the last moment to change these constraints so that they implied a clearly bounded Definition Schema. As a result the definitions of the base tables given in the standard contain some strange check clauses, such as DATA_TYPE_CHECK_REFERENCES_COLLATION in the DATA_TYPE_DESCRIPTOR table, which is:

```
CONSTRAINT DATA_TYPE_DESCRIPTOR_REFERENCES_COLLATION
 CHECK (COLLATION_CATALOG <> ANY
         (SELECT DISTINCT CATALOG_NAME FROM SCHEMATA)
        OR
        (COLLATION_CATALOG, COLLATION_SCHEMA, COLLATION_NAME) IN
          (SELECT COLLATION_CATALOG, COLLATION_SCHEMA,
                  COLLATION_NAME
             FROM COLLATIONS)),
```

The bounding works in that only objects defined in the catalog itself are required to fulfil the constraints, as can be seen in the example given. For clarity in this book we have not adopted these last-minute changes. For example the above CHECK constraint is represented in this book as:

```
CONSTRAINT DATA_TYPE_DESCRIPTOR_REFERENCES_COLLATIONS
  FOREIGN KEY (COLLATION_CATALOG, COLLATION_SCHEMA, COLLATION_NAME)
    REFERENCES COLLATIONS,
```

which is much easier to understand.

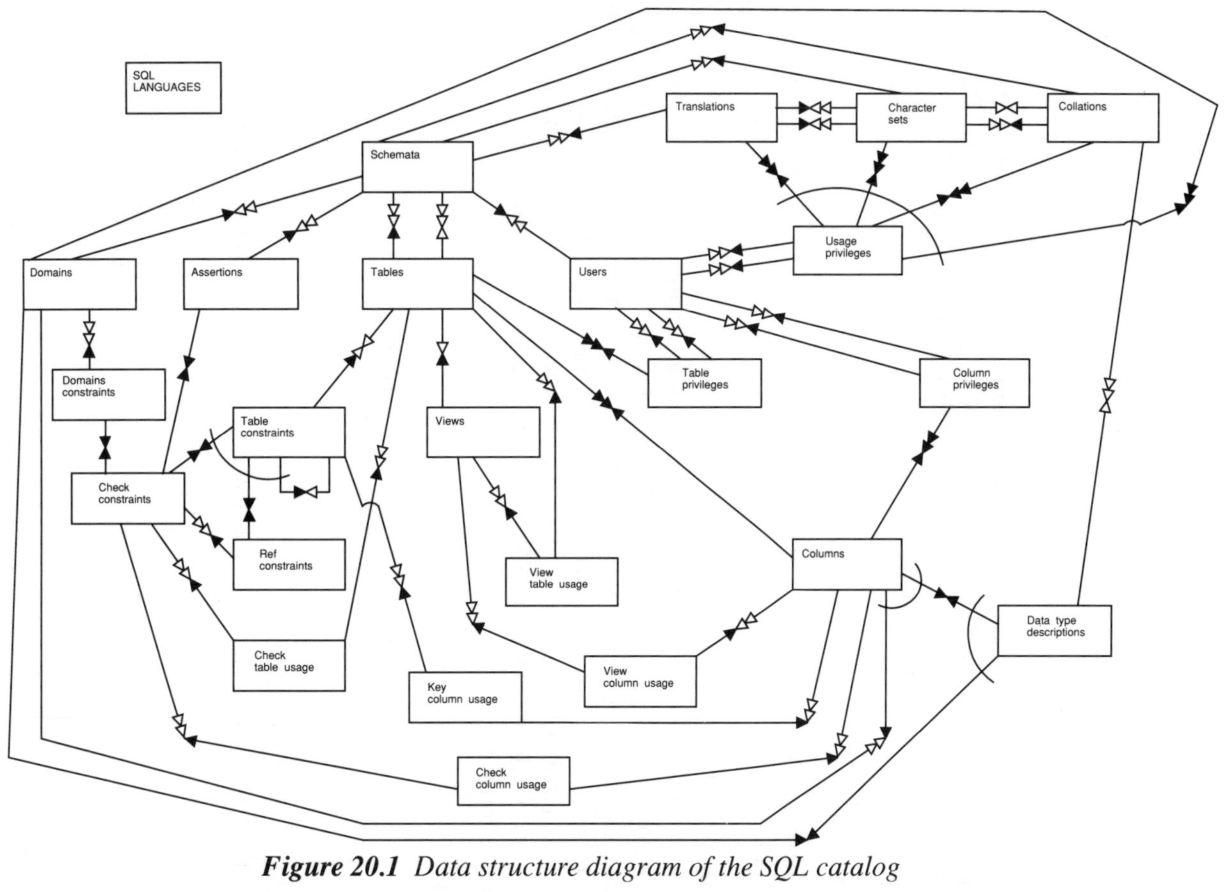

***Figure 20.1** Data structure diagram of the SQL catalog*

The schema definition begins:

```
CREATE SCHEMA DEFINITION_SCHEMA
    AUTHORIZATION DEFINITION_SCHEMA
```

20.1.1 The Domains

Three domains are used to define the columns in all of the tables. These three domains are SQL_IDENTIFIER, CARDINAL_NUMBER and CHARACTER_DATA and are defined in the INFORMATION_SCHEMA not in the DEFINITION_SCHEMA.

20.1.2 The Tables

There are 24 base tables. These are described separately in the following sections.

20.1.2.1 USERS

The USERS table has one row for each authorization identifier known to this catalog in the SQL environment. These represent all those users who may grant or receive privileges on objects in this catalog. These naturally include those who may create a schema in the catalog and those who currently own a schema in the catalog. These users must include the user PUBLIC (representing all users) and the special user _SYSTEM (representing the system that grants privileges to owners):

```
CREATE TABLE USERS
(
USER_NAME    INFORMATION_SCHEMA.SQL_IDENTIFIER
  CONSTRAINT USERS_PRIMARY_KEY PRIMARY KEY
)
```

20.1.2.2 SCHEMATA

The SCHEMATA table has one row for each schema in the catalog:

```
CREATE TABLE SCHEMATA
(
CATALOG_NAME                  INFORMATION_SCHEMA.SQL_IDENTIFIER,
SCHEMA_NAME                   INFORMATION_SCHEMA.SQL_IDENTIFIER,
SCHEMA_OWNER                  INFORMATION_SCHEMA.SQL_IDENTIFIER
  CONSTRAINT SCHEMA_OWNER_NOT_NULL NOT NULL,
DEFAULT_CHARACTER_SET_CATALOG INFORMATION_SCHEMA.SQL_IDENTIFIER,
DEFAULT_CHARACTER_SET_SCHEMA  INFORMATION_SCHEMA.SQL_IDENTIFIER,
DEFAULT_CHARACTER_SET_NAME    INFORMATION_SCHEMA.SQL_IDENTIFIER,
CONSTRAINT SCHEMATA_PRIMARY_KEY
  PRIMARY KEY (CATALOG_NAME, SCHEMA_NAME),
CONSTRAINT SCHEMATA_FOREIGN_KEY_USERS
  FOREIGN KEY (SCHEMA_OWNER)
    REFERENCES USERS
)
```

20.1.2.3 DATA_TYPE_DESCRIPTOR

This table has one row for each domain in the catalog and one row for each column in the catalog that is not defined in terms of a domain. The COLUMN_NAME column is used to determine whether the data type described is that of a domain or of a column. If the length of the string in COLUMN_NAME is zero then the row describes a domain:

```
CREATE TABLE DATA_TYPE_DESCRIPTOR
(
TABLE_OR_DOMAIN_CATALOG  INFORMATION_SCHEMA.SQL_IDENTIFIER,
TABLE_OR_DOMAIN_SCHEMA   INFORMATION_SCHEMA.SQL_IDENTIFIER,
TABLE_OR_DOMAIN_NAME     INFORMATION_SCHEMA.SQL_IDENTIFIER,
COLUMN_NAME              INFORMATION_SCHEMA.SQL_IDENTIFIER,
DATA_TYPE                INFORMATION_SCHEMA.CHARACTER_DATA
  CONSTRAINT TABLE_OR_DOMAIN_DATA_TYPE_NOT_NULL NOT NULL,
CHARACTER_MAXIMUM_LENGTH INFORMATION_SCHEMA.CARDINAL_NUMBER,
CHARACTER_OCTET_LENGTH   INFORMATION_SCHEMA.CARDINAL_NUMBER,
COLLATION_CATALOG        INFORMATION_SCHEMA.SQL_IDENTIFIER,
COLLATION_SCHEMA         INFORMATION_SCHEMA.SQL_IDENTIFIER,
COLLATION_NAME           INFORMATION_SCHEMA.SQL_IDENTIFIER,
NUMERIC_PRECISION        INFORMATION_SCHEMA.CARDINAL_NUMBER,
NUMERIC_PRECISION_RADIX  INFORMATION_SCHEMA.CARDINAL_NUMBER,
NUMERIC_SCALE            INFORMATION_SCHEMA.CARDINAL_NUMBER,
DATETIME_PRECISION       INFORMATION_SCHEMA.CARDINAL_NUMBER,
CONSTRAINT DATA_TYPE_DESCRIPTOR_PRIMARY_KEY
 PRIMARY KEY (TABLE_OR_DOMAIN_CATALOG, TABLE_OR_DOMAIN_SCHEMA,
             TABLE_OR_DOMAIN_NAME, COLUMN_NAME),
CONSTRAINT DATA_TYPE_DESCRIPTOR_REFERENCES_COLLATIONS
 FOREIGN KEY (COLLATION_CATALOG, COLLATION_SCHEMA, COLLATION_NAME)
   REFERENCES COLLATIONS,
CONSTRAINT TABLE_OR_DOMAIN_CHECK_COMBINATIONS
  CHECK (
    DATA_TYPE IN
        ('CHARACTER', 'CHARACTER VARYING', 'BIT', 'BIT VARYING')
    AND (CHARACTER_MAXIMUM_LENGTH, CHARACTER_OCTET_LENGTH,
        COLLATION_CATALOG, COLLATION_SCHEMA, COLLATION_NAME)
          IS NOT NULL
    AND (NUMERIC_PRECISION, NUMERIC_PRECISION_RADIX,
       NUMERIC_SCALE, DATETIME_PRECISION) IS NULL
  OR
    DATA_TYPE IN ('REAL', 'DOUBLE PRECISION', 'FLOAT')
    AND (CHARACTER_MAXIMUM_LENGTH, CHARACTER_OCTET_LENGTH,
         COLLATION_CATALOG, COLLATION_SCHEMA, COLLATION_NAME)
           IS NULL
    AND NUMERIC_PRECISION IS NOT NULL
    AND NUMERIC_PRECISION_RADIX = 2
    AND NUMERIC_SCALE IS NULL
    AND DATETIME_PRECISION IS NULL
  OR
    DATA_TYPE IN ('INTEGER', 'SMALLINT', 'NUMERIC', 'DECIMAL')
```

```
    AND (CHARACTER_MAXIMUM_LENGTH, CHARACTER_OCTET_LENGTH,
         COLLATION_CATALOG, COLLATION_SCHEMA, COLLATION_NAME)
            IS NULL
    AND NUMERIC_PRECISION IS NOT NULL
    AND NUMERIC_SCALE IS NOT NULL
    AND (NUMERIC_SCALE <> 0 AND NUMERIC_PRECISION_RADIX = 10
         OR
         NUMERIC_SCALE = 0 AND NUMERIC_PRECISION_RADIX IN (2, 10))
    AND DATETIME_PRECISION IS NULL
  OR
    DATA_TYPE IN ('DATE', 'TIME', 'TIMESTAMP',
                  'TIME WITH TIME ZONE',
                  'TIMESTAMP WITH TIME ZONE', 'INTERVAL')
    AND (CHARACTER_MAXIMUM_LENGTH, CHARACTER_OCTET_LENGTH,
         COLLATION_CATALOG, COLLATION_SCHEMA, COLLATION_NAME)
            IS NULL
    AND (NUMERIC_PRECISION, NUMERIC_PRECISION_RADIX) IS NULL
    AND NUMERIC_SCALE IS NULL
    AND DATETIME_PRECISION IS NOT NULL),
CONSTRAINT DATA_TYPE_DESCRIPTOR_CHECK_USED
  CHECK (
    (TABLE_OR_DOMAIN_CATALOG, TABLE_OR_DOMAIN_SCHEMA,
     TABLE_OR_DOMAIN_NAME, COLUMN_NAME) IN
    (SELECT TABLE_CATALOG, TABLE_SCHEMA, TABLE_NAME, COLUMN_NAME
       FROM COLUMNS
     UNION
     SELECT DOMAIN_CATALOG, DOMAIN_SCHEMA, DOMAIN_NAME, ''
       FROM DOMAINS))
)
```

20.1.2.4 DOMAINS

The DOMAINS table has one row for each domain in the catalog. The value of DOMAIN_DEFAULT is null if the domain has no default value; otherwise it is a character representation of the <default option>:

```
CREATE TABLE DOMAINS
(
DOMAIN_CATALOG INFORMATION_SCHEMA.SQL_IDENTIFIER,
DOMAIN_SCHEMA  INFORMATION_SCHEMA.SQL_IDENTIFIER,
DOMAIN_NAME    INFORMATION_SCHEMA.SQL_IDENTIFIER,
DOMAIN_DEFAULT INFORMATION_SCHEMA.CHARACTER_DATA,
CONSTRAINT DOMAINS_PRIMARY_KEY
 PRIMARY KEY (DOMAIN_CATALOG, DOMAIN_SCHEMA, DOMAIN_NAME),
CONSTRAINT DOMAINS_FOREIGN_KEY_SCHEMATA
 FOREIGN KEY (DOMAIN_CATALOG, DOMAIN_SCHEMA) REFERENCES SCHEMATA,
CONSTRAINT DOMAIN_CHECK_DATA_TYPE
 CHECK ((DOMAIN_CATALOG, DOMAIN_SCHEMA, DOMAIN_NAME, '')
       IN (SELECT TABLE_OR_DOMAIN_CATALOG, TABLE_OR_DOMAIN_SCHEMA,
                  TABLE_OR_DOMAIN_NAME, COLUMN_NAME
             FROM DATA_TYPE_DESCRIPTOR))
)
```

20.1.2.5 DOMAIN_CONSTRAINTS

The DOMAIN_CONSTRAINTS table has one row for each domain constraint in the catalog:

```
CREATE TABLE DOMAIN_CONSTRAINTS
(
CONSTRAINT_CATALOG INFORMATION_SCHEMA.SQL_IDENTIFIER,
CONSTRAINT_SCHEMA  INFORMATION_SCHEMA.SQL_IDENTIFIER,
CONSTRAINT_NAME    INFORMATION_SCHEMA.SQL_IDENTIFIER,
DOMAIN_CATALOG     INFORMATION_SCHEMA.SQL_IDENTIFIER
  CONSTRAINT DOMAIN_CATALOG_NOT_NULL NOT NULL,
DOMAIN_SCHEMA      INFORMATION_SCHEMA.SQL_IDENTIFIER
  CONSTRAINT DOMAIN_SCHEMA_NOT_NULL NOT NULL,
DOMAIN_NAME        INFORMATION_SCHEMA.SQL_IDENTIFIER
  CONSTRAINT DOMAIN_NAME_NOT_NULL NOT NULL,
IS_DEFERRABLE      INFORMATION_SCHEMA.CHARACTER_DATA
  CONSTRAINT DOMAIN_CONSTRAINTS_DEFERRABLE_NOT_NULL NOT NULL,
INITIALLY_DEFERRED INFORMATION_SCHEMA.CHARACTER_DATA
  CONSTRAINT DOMAIN_CONSTRAINTS_INITIALLY_DEFERRED_NOT_NULL
                   NOT NULL,
CONSTRAINT DOMAIN_CONSTRAINTS_PRIMARY_KEY
 PRIMARY KEY (CONSTRAINT_CATALOG, CONSTRAINT_SCHEMA,
             CONSTRAINT_NAME),
CONSTRAINT DOMAIN_CONSTRAINT_FOREIGN_KEY_SCHEMATA
 FOREIGN KEY (CONSTRAINT_CATALOG, CONSTRAINT_SCHEMA)
   REFERENCES SCHEMATA,
CONSTRAINT DOMAIN_CONSTRAINT_FOREIGN_KEY_DOMAINS
 FOREIGN KEY (DOMAIN_CATALOG, DOMAIN_SCHEMA, DOMAIN_NAME)
   REFERENCES DOMAINS,
CONSTRAINTS DOMAIN_CONSTRAINTS_FOREIGN_KEY_CHECK_CONSTRAINTS
 FOREIGN KEY (CONSTRAINT_CATALOG, CONSTRAINT_SCHEMA,
             CONSTRAINT_NAME)
   REFERENCES CHECK_CONSTRAINTS,
CONSTRAINTS DOMAIN_CONSTRAINTS_CHECK_DEFERRABLE
  CHECK ((IS_DEFERRABLE, INITIALLY_DEFERRED)
        IN (VALUES ('NO',  'NO'),
                   ('YES', 'NO'),
                   ('YES', 'YES')))
)
```

20.1.2.6 TABLES

The TABLES table contains one row for each table, including views and created temporary tables, in the catalog:

```
CREATE TABLE TABLES
(
TABLE_CATALOG INFORMATION_SCHEMA.SQL_IDENTIFIER,
TABLE_SCHEMA  INFORMATION_SCHEMA.SQL_IDENTIFIER,
TABLE_NAME    INFORMATION_SCHEMA.SQL_IDENTIFIER,
TABLE_TYPE    INFORMATION_SCHEMA.CHARACTER_DATA
  CONSTRAINT TABLE_TYPE_NOT_NULL NOT NULL,
CONSTRAINT TABLE_TYPE_CHECK
```

```
   CHECK (TABLE_TYPE IN
     ('BASE TABLE', 'VIEW', 'GLOBAL TEMPORARY', 'LOCAL TEMPORARY')),
 CONSTRAINT TABLES_PRIMARY_KEY
  PRIMARY KEY (TABLE_CATALOG, TABLE_SCHEMA, TABLE_NAME),
 CONSTRAINT TABLES_FOREIGN_KEY_SCHEMATA
  FOREIGN KEY (TABLE_CATALOG, TABLE_SCHEMA) REFERENCES SCHEMATA,
 CONSTRAINT CHECK_TABLE_IN_COLUMNS
  CHECK ((TABLE_CATALOG, TABLE_SCHEMA, TABLE_NAME)
         IN (SELECT  TABLE_CATALOG, TABLE_SCHEMA, TABLE_NAME
               FROM COLUMNS)),
 CONSTRAINT TABLES_CHECK_NOT_VIEW
  CHECK (NOT EXISTS
          (SELECT TABLE_CATALOG, TABLE_SCHEMA, TABLE_NAME
             FROM TABLES
             WHERE TABLE_TYPE = 'VIEW'
           EXCEPT
           SELECT TABLE_CATALOG, TABLE_SCHEMA, TABLE_NAME
             FROM VIEWS))
 )
```

20.1.2.7 VIEWS

The VIEWS table contains one row for each view in the catalog. The value of VIEW_DEFINITION is a character representation of the <query expression> in the <view definition> provided that this can be represented without truncation. If not then the column is NULL:

```
CREATE TABLE VIEWS
(
TABLE_CATALOG   INFORMATION_SCHEMA.SQL_IDENTIFIER,
TABLE_SCHEMA    INFORMATION_SCHEMA.SQL_IDENTIFIER,
TABLE_NAME      INFORMATION_SCHEMA.SQL_IDENTIFIER,
VIEW_DEFINITION INFORMATION_SCHEMA.CHARACTER_DATA,
CHECK_OPTION    INFORMATION_SCHEMA.CHARACTER_DATA
  CONSTRAINT CHECK_OPTION_NOT_NULL NOT NULL,
  CONSTRAINT CHECK_OPTION_CHECK
   CHECK (CHECK_OPTION IN ('NONE', 'LOCAL', 'CASCADED')),
IS_UPDATABLE    INFORMATION_SCHEMA.CHARACTER_DATA
  CONSTRAINT IS_UPDATABLE_NOT_NULL NOT NULL,
  CONSTRAINT IS_UPDATABLE_CHECK
   CHECK (IS_UPDATABLE IN ('YES', 'NO')),
CONSTRAINT VIEWS_PRIMARY_KEY
 PRIMARY KEY (TABLE_CATALOG, TABLE_SCHEMA, TABLE_NAME),
CONSTRAINT IS_UPDATABLE_CHECK_OPTION_CHECK
 CHECK ((IS_UPDATABLE, CHECK_OPTION)
        NOT IN (VALUES ('NO', 'CASCADED'),
                       ('NO', 'LOCAL'))),
CONSTRAINT VIEWS_IN_TABLES
 CHECK ((TABLE_CATALOG, TABLE_SCHEMA, TABLE_NAME)
        IN (SELECT TABLE_CATALOG, TABLE_SCHEMA, TABLE_NAME
              FROM TABLES
              WHERE TABLE_TYPE = 'VIEW'))
)
```

20.1.2.8 COLUMNS

The COLUMNS table has one row for each column of every table, including views and created temporary tables, in the catalog. The values of DOMAIN_CATALOG, DOMAIN_SCHEMA and DOMAIN_NAME have values only if the column is defined using a domain. The value of ORDINAL_POSITION is the ordinal position of the column in the table. The value of COLUMN_DEFAULT is null if the column has no default value specified at the column level. Note that a column may inherit a default value from a domain, if it is indeed based on a domain; default values derived from domains are not recorded in the COLUMNS table but in the DOMAINS table. Otherwise, the value of COLUMN_DEFAULT is a character representation of <default option>:

```
CREATE TABLE COLUMNS
(
TABLE_CATALOG     INFORMATION_SCHEMA.SQL_IDENTIFIER,
TABLE_SCHEMA      INFORMATION_SCHEMA.SQL_IDENTIFIER,
TABLE_NAME        INFORMATION_SCHEMA.SQL_IDENTIFIER,
COLUMN_NAME       INFORMATION_SCHEMA.SQL_IDENTIFIER,
ORDINAL_POSITION  INFORMATION_SCHEMA.CARDINAL_NUMBER
 CONSTRAINT COLUMN_POSITION_NOT_NULL NOT NULL,
DOMAIN_CATALOG    INFORMATION_SCHEMA.SQL_IDENTIFIER,
DOMAIN_SCHEMA     INFORMATION_SCHEMA.SQL_IDENTIFIER,
DOMAIN_NAME       INFORMATION_SCHEMA.SQL_IDENTIFIER,
COLUMN_DEFAULT    INFORMATION_SCHEMA.CHARACTER_DATA,
IS_NULLABLE       INFORMATION_SCHEMA.CHARACTER_DATA,
CONSTRAINT COLUMNS_PRIMARY_KEY
 PRIMARY KEY (TABLE_CATALOG, TABLE_SCHEMA, TABLE_NAME, COLUMN_NAME),
CONSTRAINT COLUMNS_UNIQUE
 UNIQUE (TABLE_CATALOG, TABLE_SCHEMA, TABLE_NAME, ORDINAL_POSITION),
CONSTRAINT COLUMNS_FOREIGN_KEY_TABLES
 FOREIGN KEY (TABLE_CATALOG, TABLE_SCHEMA, TABLE_NAME)
   REFERENCES TABLES,
CONSTRAINT COLUMNS_CHECK_REFERENCES_DOMAINS
 FOREIGN KEY (DOMAIN_CATALOG, DOMAIN_SCHEMA, DOMAIN_NAME)
   REFERENCES DOMAINS,
CONSTRAINT COLUMN_CHECK_DATA_TYPE
 CHECK (
   (DOMAIN_CATALOG, DOMAIN_SCHEMA, DOMAIN_NAME) IS NOT NULL
   AND
   (TABLE_CATALOG, TABLE_SCHEMA, TABLE_NAME, COLUMN_NAME)
    NOT IN (SELECT TABLE_OR_DOMAIN_CATALOG, TABLE_OR_DOMAIN_SCHEMA,
                   TABLE_OR_DOMAIN_NAME, COLUMN_NAME
              FROM DATA_TYPE_DESCRIPTOR)
   OR
   (DOMAIN_CATALOG, DOMAIN_SCHEMA, DOMAIN_NAME) IS NULL
   AND
   (TABLE_CATALOG, TABLE_SCHEMA, TABLE_NAME, COLUMN_NAME)
    IN (SELECT TABLE_OR_DOMAIN_CATALOG, TABLE_OR_DOMAIN_SCHEMA,
               TABLE_OR_DOMAIN_NAME, COLUMN_NAME
          FROM DATA_TYPE_DESCRIPTOR))
)
```

20.1.2.9 VIEW_TABLE_USAGE

The VIEW_TABLE_USAGE table has one row for each table name contained in the view definition of each view in the catalog:

```
CREATE TABLE VIEW_TABLE_USAGE
(
VIEW_CATALOG  INFORMATION_SCHEMA.SQL_IDENTIFIER,
VIEW_SCHEMA   INFORMATION_SCHEMA.SQL_IDENTIFIER,
VIEW_NAME     INFORMATION_SCHEMA.SQL_IDENTIFIER,
TABLE_CATALOG INFORMATION_SCHEMA.SQL_IDENTIFIER,
TABLE_SCHEMA  INFORMATION_SCHEMA.SQL_IDENTIFIER,
TABLE_NAME    INFORMATION_SCHEMA.SQL_IDENTIFIER,
CONSTRAINT VIEW_TABLE_USAGE_PRIMARY_KEY
 PRIMARY KEY (VIEW_CATALOG, VIEW_SCHEMA, VIEW_NAME, TABLE_CATALOG,
              TABLE_SCHEMA, TABLE_NAME),
CONSTRAINT VIEW_TABLE_USAGE_FOREIGN_KEY_VIEWS
 FOREIGN KEY (VIEW_CATALOG, VIEW_SCHEMA, VIEW_NAME)
   REFERENCES VIEWS,
CONSTRAINT VIEW_TABLE_USAGE_CHECK_REFERENCES_TABLES
 FOREIGN KEY (TABLE_CATALOG, TABLE_SCHEMA, TABLE_NAME)
   REFERENCES TABLES
)
```

20.1.2.10 VIEW_COLUMN_USAGE

The VIEW_COLUMN_USAGE table has one row for each column referenced by a view in the catalog:

```
CREATE TABLE VIEW_COLUMN_USAGE
(
VIEW_CATALOG  INFORMATION_SCHEMA.SQL_IDENTIFIER,
VIEW_SCHEMA   INFORMATION_SCHEMA.SQL_IDENTIFIER,
VIEW_NAME     INFORMATION_SCHEMA.SQL_IDENTIFIER,
TABLE_CATALOG INFORMATION_SCHEMA.SQL_IDENTIFIER,
TABLE_SCHEMA  INFORMATION_SCHEMA.SQL_IDENTIFIER,
TABLE_NAME    INFORMATION_SCHEMA.SQL_IDENTIFIER,
COLUMN_NAME   INFORMATION_SCHEMA.SQL_IDENTIFIER,
CONSTRAINT VIEW_COLUMN_USAGE_PRIMARY_KEY
 PRIMARY KEY (VIEW_CATALOG, VIEW_SCHEMA, VIEW_NAME, TABLE_CATALOG,
              TABLE_SCHEMA, TABLE_NAME, COLUMN_NAME),
CONSTRAINT VIEW_COLUMN_USAGE_CHECK_REFERENCES_COLUMNS
 FOREIGN KEY (TABLE_CATALOG, TABLE_SCHEMA, TABLE_NAME, COLUMN_NAME)
   REFERENCES COLUMNS,
CONSTRAINT VIEW_COLUMN_USAGE_FOREIGN_KEY_VIEWS
 FOREIGN KEY (VIEW_CATALOG, VIEW_SCHEMA, VIEW_NAME) REFERENCES VIEWS
)
```

20.1.2.11 TABLE_CONSTRAINTS

The TABLE_CONSTRAINTS table has one row for each table constraint in the catalog. The values of CONSTRAINT_CATALOG, CONSTRAINT_SCHEMA and CONSTRAINT_NAME constitute the name of the constraint being described. If the constraint definition did not specify a <constraint name>, then the value of CONSTRAINT_NAME is implementation defined; the values of CONSTRAINT_CATALOG and CONSTRAINT_SCHEMA are derived from the table in which the constraint is defined:

```
CREATE TABLE TABLE_CONSTRAINTS
(
CONSTRAINT_CATALOG INFORMATION_SCHEMA.SQL_IDENTIFIER,
CONSTRAINT_SCHEMA  INFORMATION_SCHEMA.SQL_IDENTIFIER,
CONSTRAINT_NAME    INFORMATION_SCHEMA.SQL_IDENTIFIER,
CONSTRAINT_TYPE    INFORMATION_SCHEMA.CHARACTER_DATA
 CONSTRAINT TABLE_CONSTRAINTS_CONSTRAINT_TYPE_NOT_NULL NOT NULL,
TABLE_CATALOG      INFORMATION_SCHEMA.SQL_IDENTIFIER
 CONSTRAINT TABLE_CONSTRAINTS_TABLE_CATALOG_NOT_NULL NOT NULL,
TABLE_SCHEMA       INFORMATION_SCHEMA.SQL_IDENTIFIER
 CONSTRAINT TABLE_CONSTRAINTS_TABLE_SCHEMA_NOT_NULL NOT NULL,
TABLE_NAME         INFORMATION_SCHEMA.SQL_IDENTIFIER
 CONSTRAINT TABLE_CONSTRAINTS_TABLE_NAME_NOT_NULL NOT NULL,
IS_DEFERRABLE      INFORMATION_SCHEMA.CHARACTER_DATA
 CONSTRAINT TABLE_CONSTRAINTS_IS_DEFERRABLE_NOT_NULL NOT NULL,
INITIALLY_DEFERRED INFORMATION_SCHEMA.CHARACTER_DATA
 CONSTRAINT TABLE_CONSTRAINTS_INITIALLY_DEFERRED_NOT_NULL NOT NULL,
CONSTRAINT TABLE_CONSTRAINT_PRIMARY_KEY
 PRIMARY KEY (CONSTRAINT_CATALOG, CONSTRAINT_SCHEMA,
              CONSTRAINT_NAME),
CONSTRAINT TABLE_CONSTRAINTS_CHECK_REFERENCES_TABLES
 FOREIGN KEY (TABLE_CATALOG, TABLE_SCHEMA, TABLE_NAME)
   REFERENCES TABLES,
CONSTRAINT CONSTRAINT_TYPE_CHECK
 CHECK (CONSTRAINT_TYPE
        IN ('UNIQUE', 'PRIMARY_KEY', 'FOREIGN KEY', 'CHECK')),
CONSTRAINT TABLE_CONSTRAINTS_DEFERRED_CHECK
 CHECK ((IS_DEFERRABLE, INITIALLY_DEFERRED)
         IN (VALUES ('NO',  'NO'),
                    ('YES', 'NO'),
                    ('YES', 'YES'))),
CONSTRAINT TABLE_CONSTRAINTS_CHECK_VIEWS
 CHECK ((TABLE_CATALOG, TABLE_SCHEMA, TABLE_NAME)
        IN (SELECT TABLE_CATALOG, TABLE_SCHEMA, TABLE_NAME
              FROM TABLES
              WHERE TABLE_TYPE <> 'VIEW')),
CONSTRAINT TABLE_CONSTRAINTS_UNIQUE_CHECK
 CHECK (1 = (SELECT COUNT (*)
               FROM (SELECT CONSTRAINT_CATALOG, CONSTRAINT_SCHEMA,
                            CONSTRAINT_NAME
                       FROM TABLE_CONSTRAINTS
                       WHERE CONSTRAINT_TYPE
                             IN ('UNIQUE', 'PRIMARY_KEY')
                     UNION ALL
                     SELECT CONSTRAINT_CATALOG, CONSTRAINT_SCHEMA,
                            CONSTRAINT_NAME
                       FROM REFERENTIAL_CONSTRAINTS
                     UNION ALL
```

```
                    SELECT CONSTRAINT_CATALOG, CONSTRAINT_SCHEMA,
                           CONSTRAINT_NAME
                      FROM CHECK_CONSTRAINTS) AS X
              WHERE (CONSTRAINT_CATALOG, CONSTRAINT_SCHEMA,
                     CONSTRAINT_NAME)
                     = (X.CONSTRAINT_CATALOG, X.CONSTRAINT_SCHEMA,
                        X.CONSTRAINT_NAME))),
CONSTRAINT TABLE_CONSTRAINTS_UNIQUE_PRIMARY_KEY_CHECK
 CHECK (UNIQUE (SELECT TABLE_CATALOG, TABLE_SCHEMA, TABLE_NAME
                FROM TABLE_CONSTRAINTS
                WHERE CONSTRAINT_TYPE = 'PRIMARY_KEY'))
)
```

20.1.2.12 KEY_COLUMN_USAGE

The KEY_COLUMN_USAGE table has one or more rows for each row in the TABLE_CONSTRAINTS table which represents a UNIQUE, PRIMARY KEY or FOREIGN KEY constraint. The values listed are the column names that constitute each unique constraint and the referencing column names in each foreign key constraint. The value of ORDINAL_POSITION is the ordinal position of the specific column in the constraint being described:

```
CREATE TABLE KEY_COLUMN_USAGE
(
CONSTRAINT_CATALOG INFORMATION_SCHEMA.SQL_IDENTIFIER,
CONSTRAINT_SCHEMA  INFORMATION_SCHEMA.SQL_IDENTIFIER,
CONSTRAINT_NAME    INFORMATION_SCHEMA.SQL_IDENTIFIER,
TABLE_CATALOG      INFORMATION_SCHEMA.SQL_IDENTIFIER
 CONSTRAINT KEY_COLUMN_USAGE_TABLE_CATALOG_NOT_NULL NOT NULL,
TABLE_SCHEMA       INFORMATION_SCHEMA.SQL_IDENTIFIER
 CONSTRAINT KEY_COLUMN_USAGE_TABLE_SCHEMA_NOT_NULL NOT NULL,
TABLE_NAME         INFORMATION_SCHEMA.SQL_IDENTIFIER
 CONSTRAINT KEY_COLUMN_USAGE_TABLE_NAME_NOT_NULL NOT NULL,
COLUMN_NAME        INFORMATION_SCHEMA.SQL_IDENTIFIER
 CONSTRAINT KEY_COLUMN_USAGE_COLUMN_NAME_NOT_NULL,
ORDINAL_POSITION   INFORMATION_SCHEMA.CARDINAL_NUMBER
 CONSTRAINT KEY_COLUMN_USAGE_ORDINAL_POSITION_NOT_NULL NOT NULL,
CONSTRAINT KEY_COLUMN_USAGE_PRIMARY_KEY
 PRIMARY KEY (CONSTRAINT_CATALOG, CONSTRAINT_SCHEMA,
              CONSTRAINT_NAME, COLUMN_NAME),
CONSTRAINT KEY_COLUMN_USAGE_UNIQUE
 UNIQUE (CONSTRAINT_CATALOG, CONSTRAINT_SCHEMA, CONSTRAINT_NAME,
         ORDINAL_POSITION),
CONSTRAINT KEY_COLUMN_USAGE_FOREIGN_KEY_COLUMNS
 FOREIGN KEY (TABLE_CATALOG, TABLE_SCHEMA, TABLE_NAME, COLUMN_NAME)
   REFERENCES COLUMNS,
CONSTRAINT KEY_COLUMN_CONSTRAINT_TYPE_CHECK
 CHECK ((CONSTRAINT_CATALOG, CONSTRAINT_SCHEMA, CONSTRAINT_NAME)
         IN (SELECT CONSTRAINT_CATALOG, CONSTRAINT_SCHEMA,
                    CONSTRAINT_NAME
               FROM TABLE_CONSTRAINTS
               WHERE CONSTRAINT_TYPE
                     IN ('UNIQUE', 'PRIMARY_KEY', 'FOREIGN KEY')))
)
```

20.1.2.13 REFERENTIAL_CONSTRAINTS

The REFERENTIAL_CONSTRAINTS table has one row for each row in the TABLE_CONSTRAINTS table that represents a referential constraint. The values of UNIQUE_CONSTRAINT_CATALOG, UNIQUE_CONSTRAINT_SCHEMA and UNIQUE_CONSTRAINT_NAME represent the name of the unique constraint applied to the referenced column list:

```
CREATE TABLE REFERENTIAL_CONSTRAINTS
(
CONSTRAINT_CATALOG          INFORMATION_SCHEMA.SQL_IDENTIFIER,
CONSTRAINT_SCHEMA           INFORMATION_SCHEMA.SQL_IDENTIFIER,
CONSTRAINT_NAME             INFORMATION_SCHEMA.SQL_IDENTIFIER,
UNIQUE_CONSTRAINT_CATALOG INFORMATION_SCHEMA.SQL_IDENTIFIER
 CONSTRAINT UNIQUE_CONSTRAINTS_CATALOG_NOT_NULL NOT NULL,
UNIQUE_CONSTRAINT_SCHEMA    INFORMATION_SCHEMA.SQL_IDENTIFIER
 CONSTRAINT UNIQUE_CONSTRAINTS_SCHEMA_NOT_NULL NOT NULL,
UNIQUE_CONSTRAINT_NAME      INFORMATION_SCHEMA.SQL_IDENTIFIER
 CONSTRAINT UNIQUE_CONSTRAINTS_NAME_NOT_NULL NOT NULL,
MATCH_OPTION                INFORMATION_SCHEMA.CHARACTER_DATA
 CONSTRAINT REFERENTIAL_MATCH_OPTION_NOT_NULL NOT NULL
CONSTRAINT REFERENTIAL_MATCH_OPTION_CHECK
 CHECK (MATCH_OPTION IN ('NONE', 'PARTIAL', 'FULL')),
UPDATE_RULE                 INFORMATION_SCHEMA.CHARACTER_DATA
 CONSTRAINT REFERENTIAL_UPDATE_RULE_NOT_NULL
 CONSTRAINT REFERENTIAL_UPDATE_RULE_CHECK
  CHECK (UPDATE_RULE IN
      ('CASCADE', 'SET NULL', 'SET DEFAULT', 'NO ACTION')),
DELETE_RULE                 INFORMATION_SCHEMA.CHARACTER_DATA
 CONSTRAINT REFERENTIAL_DELETE_RULE_NOT_NULL
 CONSTRAINT REFERENTIAL_DELETE_RULE_CHECK
  CHECK (DELETE_RULE IN
      ('CASCADE', 'SET NULL', 'SET DEFAULT', 'NO ACTION')),
CONSTRAINT REFERENTIAL_CONSTRAINTS_PRIMARY_KEY
 PRIMARY KEY (CONSTRAINT_CATALOG, CONSTRAINT_SCHEMA,
             CONSTRAINT_NAME)
CONSTRAINT REFERENTIAL_CONSTRAINTS_CONSTRAINT_TYPE_CHECK
 CHECK ((CONSTRAINT_CATALOG, CONSTRAINT_SCHEMA, CONSTRAINT_NAME)
        IN (SELECT CONSTRAINT_CATALOG, CONSTRAINT_SCHEMA,
                   CONSTRAINT_NAME
             FROM TABLE_CONSTRAINTS
             WHERE CONSTRAINT_TYPE = 'FOREIGN_KEY')),
CONSTRAINT UNIQUE_CONSTRAINT_CHECK_REFERENCES_UNIQUE_CONSTRAINT
 CHECK ((UNIQUE_CONSTRAINT_CATALOG, UNIQUE_CONSTRAINT_SCHEMA,
        UNIQUE_CONSTRAINT_NAME)
        IN (SELECT CONSTRAINT_CATALOG, CONSTRAINT_SCHEMA,
                   CONSTRAINT_NAME
             FROM TABLE_CONSTRAINTS
             WHERE CONSTRAINT_TYPE IN ('UNIQUE', 'PRIMARY_KEY')))
)
```

20.1.2.14 CHECK_CONSTRAINTS

The CHECK_CONSTRAINTS table has one row for each check constraint contained in a domain constraint, a table constraint or an assertion. The value of CHECK_CLAUSE is a character representation of the <search condition> in the check constraint, provided this can be represented without truncation. If not then the column is NULL:

```
CREATE TABLE CHECK_CONSTRAINTS
(
CONSTRAINT_CATALOG INFORMATION_SCHEMA.SQL_IDENTIFIER,
CONSTRAINT_SCHEMA  INFORMATION_SCHEMA.SQL_IDENTIFIER,
CONSTRAINT_NAME    INFORMATION_SCHEMA.SQL_IDENTIFIER,
CHECK_CLAUSE       INFORMATION_SCHEMA.CHARACTER_DATA,
CONSTRAINT CHECK_CONSTRAINTS_PRIMARY_KEY
 PRIMARY KEY (CONSTRAINT_CATALOG, CONSTRAINT_SCHEMA,
             CONSTRAINT_NAME),
CONSTRAINT CHECK_CONSTRAINTS_SOURCE_CHECK
 CHECK ((CONSTRAINT_CATALOG, CONSTRAINT_SCHEMA, CONSTRAINT_NAME)
       IN (SELECT *
             FROM (SELECT CONSTRAINT_CATALOG, CONSTRAINT_SCHEMA,
                          CONSTRAINT_NAME
                     FROM ASSERTIONS
                   UNION
                   SELECT CONSTRAINT_CATALOG, CONSTRAINT_SCHEMA,
                          CONSTRAINT_NAME
                     FROM TABLE_CONSTRAINTS
                   UNION
                   SELECT CONSTRAINT_CATALOG, CONSTRAINT_SCHEMA,
                          CONSTRAINT_NAME
                     FROM DOMAIN_CONSTRAINTS)))
)
```

20.1.2.15 CHECK_TABLE_USAGE

The CHECK_TABLE_USAGE table has one row for each table referenced by a check constraint or an assertion:

```
CREATE TABLE CHECK_TABLE_USAGE
(
CONSTRAINT_CATALOG INFORMATION_SCHEMA.SQL_IDENTIFIER,
CONSTRAINT_SCHEMA  INFORMATION_SCHEMA.SQL_IDENTIFIER,
CONSTRAINT_NAME    INFORMATION_SCHEMA.SQL_IDENTIFIER,
TABLE_CATALOG      INFORMATION_SCHEMA.SQL_IDENTIFIER,
TABLE_SCHEMA       INFORMATION_SCHEMA.SQL_IDENTIFIER,
TABLE_NAME         INFORMATION_SCHEMA.SQL_IDENTIFIER,
CONSTRAINT CHECK_TABLE_USAGE_PRIMARY_KEY
 PRIMARY KEY (CONSTRAINT_CATALOG, CONSTRAINT_SCHEMA,
             CONSTRAINT_NAME, TABLE_CATALOG, TABLE_SCHEMA,
             TABLE_NAME),
CONSTRAINT CHECK_TABLE_USAGE_FOREIGN_KEY_CHECK_CONSTRAINTS
 FOREIGN KEY (CONSTRAINT_CATALOG, CONSTRAINT_SCHEMA,
             CONSTRAINT_NAME)
```

```
      REFERENCES CHECK_CONSTRAINTS,
   CONSTRAINT CHECK_TABLE_USAGE_CHECK_REFERENCES_TABLES
    FOREIGN KEY (TABLE_CATALOG, TABLE_SCHEMA, TABLE_NAME)
      REFERENCES TABLES
   )
```

20.1.2.16 CHECK_COLUMN_USAGE

The CHECK_COLUMN_USAGE table has one row for each column referenced by a check constraint or an assertion:

```
CREATE TABLE CHECK_COLUMN_USAGE
(
CONSTRAINT_CATALOG INFORMATION_SCHEMA.SQL_IDENTIFIER,
CONSTRAINT_SCHEMA  INFORMATION_SCHEMA.SQL_IDENTIFIER,
CONSTRAINT_NAME    INFORMATION_SCHEMA.SQL_IDENTIFIER,
TABLE_CATALOG      INFORMATION_SCHEMA.SQL_IDENTIFIER,
TABLE_SCHEMA       INFORMATION_SCHEMA.SQL_IDENTIFIER,
TABLE_NAME         INFORMATION_SCHEMA.SQL_IDENTIFIER,
COLUMN_NAME        INFORMATION_SCHEMA.SQL_IDENTIFIER,
CONSTRAINT CHECK_COLUMN_USAGE_PRIMARY_KEY
 PRIMARY KEY (CONSTRAINT_CATALOG, CONSTRAINT_SCHEMA,
              CONSTRAINT_NAME, TABLE_CATALOG, TABLE_SCHEMA,
              TABLE_NAME, COLUMN_NAME),
CONSTRAINT CHECK_COLUMN_USAGE_FOREIGN_KEY_CHECK_CONSTRAINTS
 FOREIGN KEY (CONSTRAINT_CATALOG, CONSTRAINT_SCHEMA,
              CONSTRAINT_NAME)
   REFERENCES CHECK_CONSTRAINTS,
CONSTRAINT CHECK_COLUMN_USAGE_CHECK_REFERENCES_COLUMNS
 FOREIGN KEY (TABLE_CATALOG, TABLE_SCHEMA, TABLE_NAME, COLUMN_NAME)
   REFERENCES COLUMNS
)
```

20.1.2.17 ASSERTIONS

The ASSERTIONS table has one row for each assertion in the catalog:

```
CREATE TABLE ASSERTIONS
(
CONSTRAINT_CATALOG INFORMATION_SCHEMA.SQL_IDENTIFIER,
CONSTRAINT_SCHEMA  INFORMATION_SCHEMA.SQL_IDENTIFIER,
CONSTRAINT_NAME    INFORMATION_SCHEMA.SQL_IDENTIFIER,
IS_DEFERRABLE      INFORMATION_SCHEMA.CHARACTER_DATA
 CONSTRAINT ASSERTIONS_IS_DEFERRABLE_NOT_NULL NOT NULL,
INITIALLY_DEFERRED INFORMATION_SCHEMA.CHARACTER_DATA
 CONSTRAINT ASSERTIONS_INITIALLY_DEFERRED_NOT_NULL NOT NULL,
CONSTRAINT ASSERTIONS_DEFERRED_CHECK
 CHECK ((IS_DEFERRABLE, INITIALLY_DEFERRED)
       IN (VALUES ('NO',  'NO')
                  ('YES', 'NO')
                  ('YES', 'YES'))),
CONSTRAINT ASSERTIONS_PRIMARY_KEY
 PRIMARY KEY (CONSTRAINT_CATALOG, CONSTRAINT_SCHEMA,
              CONSTRAINT_NAME),
```

```
CONSTRAINT ASSERTIONS_FOREIGN_KEY_CHECK_CONSTRAINTS
 FOREIGN KEY (CONSTRAINT_CATALOG, CONSTRAINT_SCHEMA,
              CONSTRAINT_NAME)
   REFERENCES CHECK_CONSTRAINTS,
CONSTRAINT ASSERTIONS_FOREIGN_KEY_SCHEMATA
 FOREIGN KEY (CONSTRAINT_CATALOG, CONSTRAINT_SCHEMA)
   REFERENCES SCHEMATA
)
```

20.1.2.18 TABLE_PRIVILEGES

The TABLE_PRIVILEGES table has one row for each table privilege in the catalog. It can be thought of as a representation of the table privilege descriptors. A GRANTOR value of _SYSTEM indicates that this privilege was granted to the owner when the table was created. A GRANTEE value of PUBLIC indicates that this privilege is granted to all users:

```
CREATE TABLE TABLE_PRIVILEGES
(
GRANTOR        INFORMATION_SCHEMA.SQL_IDENTIFIER,
GRANTEE        INFORMATION_SCHEMA.SQL_IDENTIFIER,
TABLE_CATALOG  INFORMATION_SCHEMA.SQL_IDENTIFIER,
TABLE_SCHEMA   INFORMATION_SCHEMA.SQL_IDENTIFIER,
TABLE_NAME     INFORMATION_SCHEMA.SQL_IDENTIFIER,
PRIVILEGE_TYPE INFORMATION_SCHEMA.CHARACTER_DATA
 CONSTRAINT TABLE_PRIVILEGES_TYPE_CHECK
  CHECK (PRIVILEGE_TYPE IN
    ('SELECT', 'INSERT', 'DELETE', 'UPDATE', 'REFERENCES')),
IS_GRANTABLE   INFORMATION_SCHEMA.CHARACTER_DATA
 CONSTRAINT TABLE_PRIVILEGES_GRANTABLE_NOT_NULL NOT NULL
 CONSTRAINT TABLE_PRIVILEGES_GRANTABLE_CHECK
  CHECK (IS_GRANTABLE IN ('YES', 'NO')),
CONSTRAINT TABLE_PRIVILEGES_PRIMARY_KEY
 PRIMARY KEY (GRANTEE, TABLE_CATALOG, TABLE_SCHEMA, TABLE_NAME,
              GRANTOR, PRIVILEGE_TYPE),
CONSTRAINT TABLE_PRIVILEGES_FOREIGN_KEY_TABLES
 FOREIGN KEY (TABLE_CATALOG, TABLE_SCHEMA, TABLE_NAME)
   REFERENCES TABLES,
CONSTRAINT TABLE_PRIVILEGES_GRANTOR_FOREIGN_KEY_USER
 FOREIGN KEY (GRANTOR) REFERENCES USERS,
CONSTRAINT TABLE_PRIVILEGES_GRANTEE_FOREIGN_KEY_USER
 FOREIGN KEY (GRANTEE) REFERENCES USERS
)
```

20.1.2.19 COLUMN_PRIVILEGES

The COLUMN_PRIVILEGES table has one row for each column privilege in the catalog. It can be thought of as a representation of the column privilege descriptors. A GRANTOR value of _SYSTEM indicates that this privilege was granted to the owner when the column was created. A GRANTEE value of PUBLIC indicates that this privilege is granted to all users:

```
CREATE TABLE COLUMN_PRIVILEGES
(
GRANTOR         INFORMATION_SCHEMA.SQL_IDENTIFIER,
GRANTEE         INFORMATION_SCHEMA.SQL_IDENTIFIER,
TABLE_CATALOG   INFORMATION_SCHEMA.SQL_IDENTIFIER,
TABLE_SCHEMA    INFORMATION_SCHEMA.SQL_IDENTIFIER,
TABLE_NAME      INFORMATION_SCHEMA.SQL_IDENTIFIER,
COLUMN_NAME     INFORMATION_SCHEMA.SQL_IDENTIFIER,
PRIVILEGE_TYPE INFORMATION_SCHEMA.CHARACTER_DATA
 CONSTRAINT COLUMN_PRIVILEGE_TYPE_CHECK
  CHECK (PRIVILEGE_TYPE IN
    ('SELECT', 'INSERT', 'UPDATE', 'REFERENCES')),
IS_GRANTABLE     INFORMATION_SCHEMA.CHARACTER_DATA
 CONSTRAINT COLUMN_PRIVILEGES_IS_GRANTABLE_NOT_NULL NOT NULL
 CONSTRAINT COLUMN_PRIVILEGES_IS_GRANTABLE_CHECK
  CHECK (IS_GRANTABLE IN ('YES', 'NO')),
CONSTRAINT COLUMN_PRIVILEGES_PRIMARY_KEY
 PRIMARY KEY (GRANTEE, TABLE_CATALOG, TABLE_SCHEMA, TABLE_NAME,
             GRANTOR, PRIVILEGE_TYPE, COLUMN_NAME),
CONSTRAINT COLUMN_PRIVILEGES_FOREIGN_KEY_COLUMNS
FOREIGN KEY (TABLE_CATALOG, TABLE_SCHEMA, TABLE_NAME, COLUMN_NAME)
  REFERENCES COLUMNS,
CONSTRAINT COLUMN_PRIVILEGES_GRANTOR_FOREIGN_KEY_USER
FOREIGN KEY (GRANTOR) REFERENCES USERS,
CONSTRAINT COLUMN_PRIVILEGES_GRANTEE_FOREIGN_KEY_USER
FOREIGN KEY (GRANTEE) REFERENCES USERS
)
```

20.1.2.20 USAGE_PRIVILEGES

The USAGE_PRIVILEGES table has one row for each usage privilege in the catalog. It can be thought of as a representation of the usage privilege descriptors. A GRANTOR value of _SYSTEM indicates that this privilege was granted to the owner when the object was created. A GRANTEE value of PUBLIC indicates that this privilege is granted to all users:

```
CREATE TABLE USAGE_PRIVILEGES
(
GRANTOR         INFORMATION_SCHEMA.SQL_IDENTIFIER,
GRANTEE         INFORMATION_SCHEMA.SQL_IDENTIFIER,
OBJECT_CATALOG INFORMATION_SCHEMA.SQL_IDENTIFIER,
OBJECT_SCHEMA   INFORMATION_SCHEMA.SQL_IDENTIFIER,
OBJECT_NAME     INFORMATION_SCHEMA.SQL_IDENTIFIER,
OBJECT_TYPE     INFORMATION_SCHEMA.CHARACTER_DATA
 CONSTRAINT USAGE_PRIVILEGES_OBJECT_TYPE_NOT_NULL NOT NULL,
CONSTRAINT USAGE_PRIVILEGES_OBJECT_TYPE_CHECK
 CHECK (OBJECT_TYPE IN
   ('DOMAIN', 'CHARACTER SET', 'COLLATION', 'TRANSLATION')),
IS_GRANTABLE    INFORMATION_SCHEMA.CHARACTER_DATA
 CONSTRAINT USAGE_PRIVILEGES_IS_GRANTABLE_NOT_NULL NOT NULL
 CONSTRAINT USAGE_PRIVILEGES_IS_GRANTABLE_CHECK
```

```
  CHECK (IS_GRANTABLE IN ('YES', 'NO')),
CONSTRAINT USAGE_PRIVILEGES_PRIMARY_KEY
 PRIMARY KEY (GRANTEE, OBJECT_CATALOG, OBJECT_SCHEMA, OBJECT_NAME,
              OBJECT_TYPE, GRANTOR),
CONSTRAINT USAGE_PRIVILEGES_CHECK_REFERENCES_OBJECT
 CHECK ((OBJECT_CATALOG, OBJECT_SCHEMA, OBJECT_NAME, OBJECT_TYPE)
        IN (SELECT DOMAIN_CATALOG, DOMAIN_SCHEMA, DOMAIN_NAME,
                   'DOMAIN'
              FROM DOMAINS
            UNION
            SELECT CHARACTER_SET_CATALOG, CHARACTER_SET_SCHEMA,
                   CHARACTER_SET_NAME, 'CHARACTER SET'
              FROM CHARACTER_SETS
            UNION
            SELECT COLLATION_CATALOG, COLLATION_SCHEMA,
                   COLLATION_NAME, 'COLLATION'
              FROM COLLATIONS
            UNION
            SELECT TRANSLATION_CATALOG, TRANSLATION_SCHEMA,
                   TRANSLATION_NAME, 'TRANSLATION'
              FROM TRANSLATIONS)),
CONSTRAINT USAGE_PRIVILEGES_GRANTOR_FOREIGN_KEY_USERS
FOREIGN KEY (GRANTOR) REFERENCES USERS,
CONSTRAINT USAGE_PRIVILEGES_GRANTEE_FOREIGN_KEY_USERS
FOREIGN KEY (GRANTEE) REFERENCES USERS
)
```

20.1.2.21 CHARACTER_SETS

The CHARACTER_SETS table has one row for each character set, i.e. combination of character repertoire and form-of-use in the catalog. If CHARACTER_SET_NAME identifies a character repertoire, then the value of FORM_OF_USE is the implicit form-of-use of the character repertoire. Otherwise, the value of FORM_OF_USE is the same as CHARACTER_SET_NAME. If the default collation for the character set is the order of characters in the repertoire, then the values of DEFAULT_COLLATE_CATALOG, DEFAULT_COLLATE_SCHEMA and DEFAULT_COLLATE_NAME are null. Otherwise, the values represent the name of the default collation. A row always exists in this table for the character set SQL_TEXT. That row contains the definition of the character set that contains all the implementation supported characters:

```
CREATE TABLE CHARACTER_SETS
(
CHARACTER_SET_CATALOG    INFORMATION_SCHEMA.SQL_IDENTIFIER,
CHARACTER_SET_SCHEMA     INFORMATION_SCHEMA.SQL_IDENTIFIER,
CHARACTER_SET_NAME       INFORMATION_SCHEMA.SQL_IDENTIFIER,
FORM_OF_USE              INFORMATION_SCHEMA.SQL_IDENTIFIER,
NUMBER_OF_CHARACTERS     INFORMATION_SCHEMA.CARDINAL_NUMBER,
```

```
DEFAULT_COLLATE_CATALOG INFORMATION_SCHEMA.SQL_IDENTIFIER
 CONSTRAINT CHARACTER_SETS_DEFAULT_COLLATE_CATALOG_NOT_NULL
   NOT NULL,
DEFAULT_COLLATE_SCHEMA  INFORMATION_SCHEMA.SQL_IDENTIFIER
 CONSTRAINT CHARACTER_SETS_DEFAULT_COLLATE_SCHEMA_NOT_NULL NOT NULL,
DEFAULT_COLLATE_NAME    INFORMATION_SCHEMA.SQL_IDENTIFIER
 CONSTRAINT CHARACTER_SETS_DEFAULT_COLLATE_NAME_NOT_NULL  NOT NULL,
CONSTRAINT CHARACTER_SETS_PRIMARY_KEY
 PRIMARY KEY (CHARACTER_SET_CATALOG, CHARACTER_SET_SCHEMA,
             CHARACTER_SET_NAME),
CONSTRAINT CHARACTER_SETS_FOREIGN_KEY_SCHEMATA
 FOREIGN KEY (CHARACTER_SET_CATALOG, CHARACTER_SET_SCHEMA)
   REFERENCES SCHEMATA,
CONSTRAINT CHARACTER_SETS_CHECK_REFERENCES_COLLATIONS
 FOREIGN KEY (DEFAULT_COLLATE_CATALOG, DEFAULT_COLLATE_SCHEMA,
             DEFAULT_COLLATE_NAME)
   REFERENCES COLLATIONS
)
```

20.1.2.22 COLLATIONS

The COLLATIONS table has one row for each character collation in the catalog. A row always exists in this table for the collation SQL_TEXT. That row represents the definition of the collation corresponding to SQL_TEXT character set:

```
CREATE TABLE COLLATIONS
(
COLLATION_CATALOG      INFORMATION_SCHEMA.SQL_IDENTIFIER,
COLLATION_SCHEMA       INFORMATION_SCHEMA.SQL_IDENTIFIER,
COLLATION_NAME         INFORMATION_SCHEMA.SQL_IDENTIFIER,
CHARACTER_SET_CATALOG INFORMATION_SCHEMA.SQL_IDENTIFIER
 CONSTRAINT COLLATIONS_CHARACTER_SET_CATALOG_NOT_NULL NOT NULL,
CHARACTER_SET_SCHEMA  INFORMATION_SCHEMA.SQL_IDENTIFIER
 CONSTRAINT COLLATIONS_CHARACTER_SET_SCHEMA_NOT_NULL NOT NULL,
CHARACTER_SET_NAME    INFORMATION_SCHEMA.SQL_IDENTIFIER
 CONSTRAINT COLLATIONS_CHARACTER_SET_NAME_NOT_NULL NOT NULL,
PAD_ATTRIBUTE         INFORMATION_SCHEMA.CHARACTER_DATA
 CONSTRAINT COLLATIONS_PAD_ATTRIBUTE_CHECK
  CHECK (PAD_ATTRIBUTE IN ('NO PAD','PAD SPACE')),
CONSTRAINT COLLATIONS_PRIMARY_KEY
 PRIMARY KEY (COLLATION_CATALOG, COLLATION_SCHEMA, COLLATION_NAME),
CONSTRAINT COLLATIONS_FOREIGN_KEY_SCHEMATA
 FOREIGN KEY (COLLATION_CATALOG, COLLATION_SCHEMA)
   REFERENCES SCHEMATA,
CONSTRAINT COLLATIONS_CHECK_REFERENCES_CHARACTER_SETS
 FOREIGN KEY (CHARACTER_SET_CATALOG, CHARACTER_SET_SCHEMA,
             CHARACTER_SET_NAME)
   REFERENCES CHARACTER_SETS
)
```

20.1.2.23 TRANSLATIONS

The TRANSLATIONS table has one row for each character translation in the catalog. The values of SOURCE_CHARACTER_SET_CATALOG, SOURCE_CHARACTER_SET_SCHEMA and SOURCE_CHARACTER_SET_NAME represent the name of the character set specified as the source for the translation. The values of TARGET_CHARACTER_SET_CATALOG, TARGET_CHARACTER_SET_SCHEMA and TARGET_CHARACTER_SET_NAME represent the name of the character set specified as the target for the translation:

```
CREATE TABLE TRANSLATIONS
(
TRANSLATION_CATALOG          INFORMATION_SCHEMA.SQL_IDENTIFIER,
TRANSLATION_SCHEMA           INFORMATION_SCHEMA.SQL_IDENTIFIER,
TRANSLATION_NAME             INFORMATION_SCHEMA.SQL_IDENTIFIER,
SOURCE_CHARACTER_SET_CATALOG INFORMATION_SCHEMA.SQL_IDENTIFIER
 CONSTRAINT TRANSLATIONS_SOURCE_CHARACTER_SET_CATALOG_NOT_NULL
   NOT NULL,
SOURCE_CHARACTER_SET_SCHEMA  INFORMATION_SCHEMA.SQL_IDENTIFIER
 CONSTRAINT TRANSLATIONS_SOURCE_CHARACTER_SET_SCHEMA_NOT_NULL
   NOT NULL,
SOURCE_CHARACTER_SET_NAME    INFORMATION_SCHEMA.SQL_IDENTIFIER
 CONSTRAINT TRANSLATIONS_SOURCE_CHARACTER_SET_NAME_NOT_NULL
   NOT NULL,
TARGET_CHARACTER_SET_CATALOG INFORMATION_SCHEMA.SQL_IDENTIFIER
 CONSTRAINT TRANSLATIONS_TARGET_CHARACTER_SET_CATALOG_NOT_NULL
   NOT NULL,
TARGET_CHARACTER_SET_SCHEMA  INFORMATION_SCHEMA.SQL_IDENTIFIER
 CONSTRAINT TRANSLATIONS_TARGET_CHARACTER_SET_SCHEMA_NOT_NULL
   NOT NULL,
TARGET_CHARACTER_SET_NAME    INFORMATION_SCHEMA.SQL_IDENTIFIER
 CONSTRAINT TRANSLATIONS_TARGET_CHARACTER_SET_NAME_NOT_NULL
   NOT NULL,
CONSTRAINT TRANSLATIONS_PRIMARY_KEY
 PRIMARY KEY (TRANSLATION_CATALOG, TRANSLATION_SCHEMA,
             TRANSLATION_NAME),
CONSTRAINT TRANSLATIONS_FOREIGN_KEY_SCHEMATA
 FOREIGN KEY (TRANSLATION_CATALOG, TRANSLATION_SCHEMA)
   REFERENCES SCHEMATA,
CONSTRAINTS TRANSLATIONS_CHECK_REFERENCES_SOURCE
 FOREIGN KEY (SOURCE_CHARACTER_SET_CATALOG,
             SOURCE_CHARACTER_SET_SCHEMA,
             SOURCE_CHARACTER_SET_NAME)
   REFERENCES CHARACTER_SETS,
CONSTRAINTS TRANSLATIONS_CHECK_REFERENCES_TARGET
 FOREIGN KEY (TARGET_CHARACTER_SET_CATALOG,
             TARGET_CHARACTER_SET_SCHEMA,
             TARGET_CHARACTER_SET_NAME)
   REFERENCES CHARACTER_SETS
)
```

20.1.2.24 SQL_LANGUAGES

The SQL_LANGUAGES table has one row for each SQL language dialect supported by the implementation:

```
CREATE TABLE SQL_LANGUAGES
(
SQL_LANGUAGE_SOURCE                INFORMATION_SCHEMA.CHARACTER_DATA
 CONSTRAINT SQL_LANGUAGES_SOURCE_NOT_NULL NOT NULL,
SQL_LANGUAGE_YEAR                  INFORMATION_SCHEMA.CHARACTER_DATA,
SQL_LANGUAGE_CONFORMANCE           INFORMATION_SCHEMA.CHARACTER_DATA,
SQL_LANGUAGE_INTEGRITY             INFORMATION_SCHEMA.CHARACTER_DATA,
SQL_LANGUAGE_IMPLEMENTATION        INFORMATION_SCHEMA.CHARACTER_DATA,
SQL_LANGUAGE_BINDING_STYLE         INFORMATION_SCHEMA.CHARACTER_DATA,
SQL_LANGUAGE_PROGRAMMING_LANGUAGE INFORMATION_SCHEMA.CHARACTER_DATA,
CONSTRAINT SQL_LANGUAGES_STANDARD_VALID_CHECK
 CHECK ((     SQL_LANGUAGE_SOURCE = 'ISO 9075'
          AND SQL_LANGUAGE_YEAR IS NOT NULL
          AND SQL_LANGUAGE_CONFORMANCE IS NOT NULL
          AND SQL_LANGUAGE_IMPLEMENTATION IS NULL
          AND ((     SQL_LANGUAGE_YEAR = '1987'
                AND SQL_LANGUAGE_CONFORMANCE IN ('1', '2')
                AND SQL_LANGUAGE_INTEGRITY IS NULL
                AND ((BINDING = 'DIRECT'
                     AND SQL_LANGUAGE_PROGRAMMING_LANGUAGE IS NULL)
              OR
               (     SQL_LANGUAGE_BINDING_STYLE IN
                     ('EMBEDDED','MODULE')
                AND SQL_LANGUAGE_PROGRAMMING_LANGUAGE
                    IN ('COBOL', 'FORTRAN','PASCAL','PLI'))))
          OR
               (     SQL_LANGUAGE_YEAR = '1989'
                AND SQL_LANGUAGE_CONFORMANCE IN ('1', '2')
                AND SQL_LANGUAGE_INTEGRITY IN ('YES', 'NO')
                AND ((BINDING = 'DIRECT'
                     AND SQL_LANGUAGE_PROGRAMMING_LANGUAGE IS NULL)
             OR
              (     SQL_LANGUAGE_BINDING_STYLE IN
                    ('EMBEDDED','MODULE')
               AND SQL_LANGUAGE_PROGRAMMING_LANGUAGE
                    IN ('COBOL', 'FORTRAN','PASCAL','PLI'))))
          OR
               (     SQL_LANGUAGE_YEAR = '1992'
                AND SQL_LANGUAGE_CONFORMANCE
                    IN ('ENTRY','INTERMEDIATE','FULL')
                AND SQL_LANGUAGE_INTEGRITY IS NULL
                AND ((BINDING = 'DIRECT'
                      AND SQL_LANGUAGE_PROGRAMMING_LANGUAGE IS NULL)
             OR
              (     SQL_LANGUAGE_BINDING_STYLE IN
                    ('EMBEDDED','MODULE')
               AND SQL_LANGUAGE_PROGRAMMING_LANGUAGE
                    IN ('ADA','C','COBOL',
                        'FORTRAN','MUMPS','PASCAL','PLI'))))
```

```
          OR
           (SQL_LANGUAGE_SOURCE <> 'ISO 9075')))
   )
```

20.1.3 The Assertions

Three assertions follow that check cross table constraints.

20.1.3.1 UNIQUE_CONSTRAINT_NAME

The UNIQUE_CONSTRAINT_NAME assertion ensures that the same constraint name is not used by more than one table constraint, domain constraint and assertion:

```
CREATE ASSERTION UNIQUE_CONSTRAINT_NAME
  CHECK (1 =
    (SELECT MAX (OCCURRENCES)
       FROM (SELECT COUNT (*) AS OCCURRENCES
               FROM (SELECT CONSTRAINT_CATALOG, CONSTRAINT_SCHEMA,
                            CONSTRAINT_NAME
                       FROM DOMAIN_CONSTRAINTS
                     UNION ALL
                     SELECT CONSTRAINT_CATALOG, CONSTRAINT_SCHEMA,
                            CONSTRAINT_NAME
                       FROM TABLE_CONSTRAINTS
                     UNION ALL
                     SELECT CONSTRAINT_CATALOG, CONSTRAINT_SCHEMA,
                            CONSTRAINT_NAME
                       FROM ASSERTIONS)
               GROUP BY CONSTRAINT_CATALOG, CONSTRAINT_SCHEMA,
                        CONSTRAINT_NAME))
        )
```

20.1.3.2 EQUAL_KEY_DEGREES

The assertion EQUAL_KEY_DEGREES ensures that every foreign key has the same number of columns as the corresponding unique constraint:

```
CREATE ASSERTION EQUAL_KEY_DEGREES
  CHECK (NOT EXISTS (
    SELECT *
      FROM (SELECT COUNT (DISTINCT FK.COLUMN_NAME),
                   COUNT (DISTINCT PK.COLUMN_NAME)
              FROM KEY_COLUMN_USAGE AS FK,
                   REFERENTIAL_CONSTRAINTS AS RF,
                   KEY_COLUMN_USAGE AS PK
              WHERE
                  (FK.CONSTRAINT_CATALOG, FK.CONSTRAINT_SCHEMA,
                   FK.CONSTRAINT_NAME)
                  =
                  (RF.CONSTRAINT_CATALOG, RF.CONSTRAINT_SCHEMA,
                   RF.CONSTRAINT_NAME)
```

```
              AND
                 (PK.CONSTRAINT_CATALOG, PK.CONSTRAINT_SCHEMA,
                  PK.CONSTRAINT_NAME)
                 =
                 (RF.UNIQUE_CONSTRAINT_CATALOG,
                  RF.UNIQUE_CONSTRAINT_SCHEMA,
                  RF.UNIQUE_CONSTRAINT_NAME)
      GROUP BY
              RF.CONSTRAINT_CATALOG, RF.CONSTRAINT_SCHEMA,
              RF.CONSTRAINT_NAME
          ) AS REF (FK_DEGREE, PK_DEGREE)
      WHERE FK_DEGREE <> PK_DEGREE))
```

20.1.3.3 KEY_DEGREE_GREATER_THAN_OR_EQUAL_TO_1

The assertion KEY_DEGREE_GREATER_THAN_OR_EQUAL_TO_1 ensures that every unique constraint and referential constraint has at least one column:

```
CREATE ASSERTION KEY_DEGREE_GREATER_THAN_OR_EQUAL_TO_1
  CHECK (NOT EXISTS (
    SELECT *
      FROM TABLE_CONSTRAINTS
           FULL OUTER JOIN
           KEY_COLUMN_USAGE
             USING (CONSTRAINT_CATALOG, CONSTRAINT_SCHEMA,
                    CONSTRAINT_NAME)
      WHERE COLUMN_NAME IS NULL
        AND CONSTRAINT_TYPE IN
           ('UNIQUE', 'PRIMARY KEY', 'FOREIGN KEY')))
```

20.2 The Information Schema

The views, which are the only standardized part of the Information Schema, are viewed tables defined in terms of the base tables described in the first part of this chapter. The views are so constructed that they provide information only about objects defined in the catalog in which the Information Schema itself resides. This information may include the names of objects in other catalogs but these objects themselves are not visible through that particular instance of the Information Schema. The information is naturally available in the Information Schema of the catalog in which they are defined.

An implementation need do no more than provide access to tables, base or viewed, that act like these views. If the tables provided are views then there is no requirement that the view definitions should be anything like those given here. These definitions are given only to make clear what the intent of the views is. They also provide examples of both simple and complex queries as additional tutorial material.

The information schema views are defined as belonging to a schema called INFORMATION_SCHEMA, enabling them to be accessed in the same way as any other tables, in any other schema. A SELECT privilege is granted on all these tables to PUBLIC, but no other privilege is granted on them, so they can never be updated, even when the view definition would otherwise so allow. These Information Schema views and other objects are assumed to be represented in the base tables in the same way as any other tables, etc., and are thus self-describing.

The schema definition begins:

```
CREATE SCHEMA INFORMATION_SCHEMA
    AUTHORIZATION INFORMATION_SCHEMA
```

20.2.1 The Domains

Three domains are defined and these are used to define the columns in all of the base tables in DEFINITION_SCHEMA. The three domains are SQL_IDENTIFIER, CARDINAL_NUMBER and CHARACTER_DATA and are described in separate sections following. The domains are defined in the INFORMATION_SCHEMA rather than the DEFINITION_SCHEMA so that they are guaranteed to be available to users who might want them to access or manipulate the data in the views.

20.2.1.1 SQL_IDENTIFIER

This domain is intended to contain only valid SQL identifiers. The character set used is SQL_TEXT which is implementation defined but must hold every character that the implementation supports. There is in fact no way to specify in SQL a <domain constraint> that could be applied to this domain so as to fulfil the complete modelling requirements, i.e. one that would allow only valid identifiers. The 'L' which is given as the length of the character string is taken to be the implementation defined maximum length of <identifier>. This must be at least 128 but may be longer if the implementation so desires:

```
CREATE DOMAIN SQL_IDENTIFIER
    AS CHARACTER VARYING (L) CHARACTER SET SQL_TEXT

GRANT USAGE ON DOMAIN SQL_IDENTIFIER TO PUBLIC
```

20.2.1.2 CARDINAL_NUMBER

This domain is intended to contain any non-negative number that is less than the implementation defined maximum for INTEGER (i.e. the implementation-defined value of NUMERIC_PRECISION_RADIX raised to the power of implementation-defined NUMERIC_PRECISION):

```
CREATE DOMAIN CARDINAL_NUMBER
    AS INTEGER
    CONSTRAINT CARDINAL_NUMBER_DOMAIN_CHECK CHECK (VALUE >= 0)

GRANT USAGE ON DOMAIN CARDINAL_NUMBER TO PUBLIC
```

20.2.1.3 CHARACTER_DATA

This domain is intended to contain any character data. The 'ML' which is given as the length of the character string is taken to be the implementation-defined maximum length of a varying character string:

```
CREATE DOMAIN CHARACTER_DATA
    AS CHARACTER VARYING (ML) CHARACTER SET SQL_TEXT

GRANT USAGE ON DOMAIN CHARACTER_DATA TO PUBLIC
```

20.2.2 INFORMATION_SCHEMA_CATALOG_NAME

This *base* table has a single row which defines the name of the catalog in which the Information Schema resides:

```
CREATE TABLE INFORMATION_SCHEMA_CATALOG_NAME
(
CATALOG_NAME     SQL_IDENTIFIER,
CONSTRAINT INFORMATION_SCHEMA_CATALOG_NAME_PRIMARY_KEY
  PRIMARY KEY (CATALOG_NAME)
)
```

20.2.3 SCHEMATA

This view identifies the schemata that are owned by the current user:

```
CREATE VIEW SCHEMATA
  AS SELECT CATALOG_NAME, SCHEMA_NAME, SCHEMA_OWNER,
            DEFAULT_CHARACTER_SET_CATALOG,
            DEFAULT_CHARACTER_SET_SCHEMA,
            DEFAULT_CHARACTER_SET_NAME
       FROM DEFINITION_SCHEMA.SCHEMATA
       WHERE SCHEMA_OWNER = CURRENT_USER
             AND CATALOG_NAME
                 = (SELECT CATALOG_NAME
                      FROM INFORMATION_SCHEMA_CATALOG_NAME)

GRANT SELECT ON SCHEMATA TO PUBLIC
```

20.2.4 DOMAINS

This view identifies all the domains in the catalog that are accessible to a user. This includes not only the domains that the user is entitled to use in column definitions but also all those domains that have been used in the column definitions of columns to which the user has access:

```
CREATE VIEW DOMAINS
  AS SELECT DISTINCT
            DOMAIN_CATALOG, DOMAIN_SCHEMA, DOMAIN_NAME, DATA_TYPE,
            CHARACTER_MAXIMUM_LENGTH, CHARACTER_OCTET_LENGTH,
            COLLATION_CATALOG, COLLATION_SCHEMA, COLLATION_NAME,
```

```
          CHARACTER_SET_CATALOG, CHARACTER_SET_SCHEMA,
          CHARACTER_SET_NAME,
          NUMERIC_PRECISION, NUMERIC_PRECISION_RADIX,
          NUMERIC_SCALE, DATETIME_PRECISION, DOMAIN_DEFAULT
     FROM DEFINITION_SCHEMA.DOMAINS
          JOIN
          DEFINITION_SCHEMA.DATA_TYPE_DESCRIPTOR AS D
             LEFT JOIN
             DEFINITION_SCHEMA.COLLATION AS S
               USING (COLLATION_CATALOG, COLLATION.SCHEMA,
                      COLLATION_NAME)
           ON (DOMAIN_CATALOG, DOMAIN_SCHEMA, DOMAIN_NAME, '')
              = (TABLE_OR_DOMAIN_CATALOG, TABLE_OR_DOMAIN_SCHEMA,
                 TABLE_OR_DOMAIN_NAME, COLUMN_NAME)
     WHERE
     ((DOMAIN_CATALOG, DOMAIN_SCHEMA, DOMAIN_NAME, 'DOMAIN')
      IN (SELECT OBJECT_CATALOG, OBJECT_SCHEMA, OBJECT_NAME,
                 OBJECT_TYPE
            FROM DEFINITION_SCHEMA.USAGE_PRIVILEGES
            WHERE GRANTEE IN ('PUBLIC', CURRENT_USER))
     OR
      (DOMAIN_CATALOG, DOMAIN_SCHEMA, DOMAIN_NAME)
      IN (SELECT DOMAIN_CATALOG, DOMAIN_SCHEMA, DOMAIN_NAME
            FROM COLUMNS))
     AND DOMAIN_CATALOG
         = (SELECT CATALOG_NAME
              FROM INFORMATION_SCHEMA_CATALOG_NAME)

GRANT SELECT ON DOMAINS TO PUBLIC
```

20.2.5 DOMAIN_CONSTRAINTS

This view identifies all the domain constraints in the catalog that are owned by a user:

```
CREATE VIEW DOMAIN_CONSTRAINTS
  AS SELECT DISTINCT
            CONSTRAINT_CATALOG, CONSTRAINT_SCHEMA, CONSTRAINT_NAME,
            DOMAIN_CATALOG, DOMAIN_SCHEMA, DOMAIN_NAME,
            IS_DEFERRABLE, INITIALLY_DEFERRED
       FROM DEFINITION_SCHEMA.DOMAIN_CONSTRAINTS
            JOIN
            DEFINITION_SCHEMA.SCHEMATA S
              ON ((CONSTRAINT_CATALOG, CONSTRAINT_SCHEMA)
                  = (S.CATALOG_NAME, S.SCHEMA_NAME))

       WHERE SCHEMA_OWNER = CURRENT_USER
             AND CONSTRAINT_CATALOG
                 = (SELECT CATALOG_NAME
                      FROM INFORMATION_SCHEMA_CATALOG_NAME)

GRANT SELECT ON DOMAIN_CONSTRAINTS TO PUBLIC
```

20.2.6 TABLES

This view identifies all the tables in the catalog that are accessible to a user. This is basically all tables for which the user has at least one privilege, either on the table itself or on at least one column of the table:

```
CREATE VIEW TABLES
  AS SELECT TABLE_CATALOG, TABLE_SCHEMA, TABLE_NAME, TABLE_TYPE
       FROM DEFINITION_SCHEMA.TABLES
       WHERE (TABLE_CATALOG, TABLE_SCHEMA, TABLE_NAME)
               IN (SELECT TABLE_CATALOG, TABLE_SCHEMA, TABLE_NAME
                     FROM DEFINITION_SCHEMA.TABLE_PRIVILEGES
                     WHERE GRANTEE IN ('PUBLIC', CURRENT_USER)
                   UNION
                   SELECT TABLE_CATALOG, TABLE_SCHEMA, TABLE_NAME
                     FROM DEFINITION_SCHEMA.COLUMN_PRIVILEGES
                     WHERE GRANTEE IN ('PUBLIC', CURRENT_USER))
             AND TABLE_CATALOG
                 = (SELECT CATALOG_NAME
                      FROM INFORMATION_SCHEMA_CATALOG_NAME)

GRANT SELECT ON TABLES TO PUBLIC
```

20.2.7 VIEWS

This view identifies all the views in the catalog that are accessible to a user. This is basically all views that occur in the TABLES view for the user:

```
CREATE VIEW VIEWS
  AS SELECT TABLE_CATALOG, TABLE_SCHEMA, TABLE_NAME,
            CASE WHEN (TABLE_CATALOG, TABLE_SCHEMA, CURRENT_USER)
                      IN (SELECT CATALOG_NAME, SCHEMA_NAME,
                                 SCHEMA_OWNER
                            FROM DEFINITION_SCHEMA.SCHEMATA)
                 THEN VIEW_DEFINITION
                 ELSE NULL
            END AS VIEW_DEFINITION,
            CHECK_OPTION, IS_UPDATABLE
       FROM DEFINITION_SCHEMA.VIEWS
       WHERE (TABLE_CATALOG, TABLE_SCHEMA, TABLE_NAME)
               IN (SELECT TABLE_CATALOG, TABLE_SCHEMA, TABLE_NAME
                     FROM TABLES)
             AND TABLE_CATALOG
                 = (SELECT CATALOG_NAME
                      FROM INFORMATION_SCHEMA_CATALOG_NAME)

GRANT SELECT ON VIEWS TO PUBLIC
```

20.2.8 COLUMNS

This view identifies the columns of tables in the catalog that are accessible to a user. This is basically all columns for which the user has at least one privilege, either explicitly on the column or through a SELECT privilege on the whole table:

```
CREATE VIEW COLUMNS
  AS SELECT DISTINCT
            TABLE_CATALOG, TABLE_SCHEMA, TABLE_NAME, C.COLUMN_NAME,
            ORDINAL_POSITION,
            CASE WHEN (TABLE_CATALOG, TABLE_SCHEMA, CURRENT_USER)
                       IN (SELECT CATALOG_NAME, SCHEMA_NAME,
                                  SCHEMA_OWNER
                             FROM DEFINITION_SCHEMA.SCHEMATA)
                 THEN COLUMN_DEFAULT
                 ELSE NULL
            END AS COLUMN_DEFAULT,
            IS_NULLABLE,
            COALESCE(D1.DATA_TYPE, D2.DATA_TYPE) AS DATA_TYPE,
            COALESCE(D1.CHARACTER_MAXIMUM_LENGTH,
                     D2.CHARACTER_MAXIMUM_LENGTH)
              AS CHARACTER_MAXIMUM_LENGTH,
            COALESCE(D1.CHARACTER_OCTET_LENGTH,
                     D2.CHARACTER_OCTET_LENGTH)
              AS CHARACTER_OCTET_LENGTH,
            COALESCE(D1.NUMERIC_PRECISION, D2.NUMERIC_PRECISION)
              AS NUMERIC_PRECISION,
            COALESCE(D1.NUMERIC_PRECISION_RADIX,
                     D2.NUMERIC_PRECISION_RADIX)
              AS NUMERIC_PRECISION_RADIX,
            COALESCE(D1.NUMERIC_SCALE, D2.NUMERIC_SCALE)
              AS NUMERIC_SCALE,
            COALESCE(D1.DATETIME_PRECISION, D2.DATETIME_PRECISION)
              AS DATETIME_PRECISION,
            COALESCE(C1.CHARACTER_SET_CATALOG,
                     C2.CHARACTER_SET_CATALOG)
              AS CHARACTER_SET_CATALOG,
            COALESCE(C1.CHARACTER_SET_SCHEMA,
                     C2.CHARACTER_SET_SCHEMA)
              AS CHARACTER_SET_SCHEMA,
            COALESCE(C1.CHARACTER_SET_NAME, C2.CHARACTER_SET_NAME)
              AS CHARACTER_SET_NAME,
            COALESCE(D1.COLLATION_CATALOG, D2.COLLATION_CATALOG)
              AS COLLATION_CATALOG,
            COALESCE(D1.COLLATION_SCHEMA, D2.COLLATION_SCHEMA)
              AS COLLATION_SCHEMA,
            COALESCE(D1.COLLATION_NAME, D2.COLLATION_NAME)
              AS COLLATION_NAME,
            DOMAIN_CATALOG, DOMAIN_SCHEMA, DOMAIN_NAME
```

```
        FROM DEFINITION_SCHEMA.COLUMNS AS C
             LEFT JOIN
             DEFINITION_SCHEMA.DATA_TYPE_DESCRIPTOR AS D1
               LEFT JOIN
               DEFINITION_SCHEMA.COLLATIONS AS C1
                 ON (D1.COLLATION_CATALOG, D1.COLLATION.SCHEMA,
                     D1.COLLATION_NAME)
                    = (C1.COLLATION_CATALOG, C1.COLLATION.SCHEMA,
                       C1.COLLATION_NAME)
               ON (C.TABLE_CATALOG, C.TABLE_SCHEMA, C.TABLE_NAME,
                   C.COLUMN_NAME)
                   = (D1.TABLE_OR_DOMAIN_CATALOG,
                      D1.TABLE_OR_DOMAIN_SCHEMA,
                      D1.TABLE_OR_DOMAIN_NAME, D1.COLUMN_NAME)
               LEFT JOIN
               DEFINITION_SCHEMA.DATA_TYPE_DESCRIPTOR AS D2
                 LEFT JOIN
                 DEFINITION_SCHEMA.COLLATION AS C2
                   ON (D2.COLLATION_CATALOG, D2.COLLATION.SCHEMA,
                       D2.COLLATION_NAME)
                      = (C2.COLLATION_CATALOG, C2.COLLATION.SCHEMA,
                         C2.COLLATION_NAME)
                 ON (C.DOMAIN_CATALOG, C.DOMAIN_SCHEMA,
                     C.DOMAIN_NAME)
                    = (D2.TABLE_OR_DOMAIN_CATALOG,
                       D2.TABLE_OR_DOMAIN_SCHEMA,
                       D2.TABLE_OR_DOMAIN_NAME)
        WHERE
         (C.TABLE_CATALOG, C.TABLE_SCHEMA, C.TABLE_NAME,
          C.COLUMN_NAME)
           IN (SELECT TABLE_CATALOG, TABLE_SCHEMA, TABLE_NAME,
                      COLUMN_NAME
                 FROM DEFINITION_SCHEMA.COLUMN_PRIVILEGES
                 WHERE GRANTEE IN ('PUBLIC', CURRENT_USER))
         AND C.TABLE_CATALOG
             = (SELECT CATALOG_NAME
                  FROM INFORMATION_SCHEMA_CATALOG_NAME)

  GRANT SELECT ON COLUMNS TO PUBLIC
```

20.2.9 TABLE_PRIVILEGES

This view identifies the privileges on tables defined in this catalog that have either been granted to the user or the user has granted to others. This includes the privileges that the user acquires as a result of creating a table. These table privileges are those that have been granted without an associated column list. Those with a column list create column privileges:

```
CREATE VIEW TABLE_PRIVILEGES
  AS SELECT GRANTOR, GRANTEE, TABLE_CATALOG, TABLE_SCHEMA,
            TABLE_NAME, PRIVILEGE_TYPE, IS_GRANTABLE
       FROM DEFINITION_SCHEMA.TABLE_PRIVILEGES
       WHERE GRANTEE IN ('PUBLIC', CURRENT_USER)
             OR GRANTOR = CURRENT_USER
         AND TABLE_CATALOG
             = (SELECT CATALOG_NAME
                  FROM INFORMATION_SCHEMA_CATALOG_NAME)
GRANT SELECT ON TABLE_PRIVILEGES TO PUBLIC
```

20.2.10 COLUMN_PRIVILEGES

This view identifies the privileges on columns of tables defined in this catalog that have either been granted to the user or the user has granted to others. This includes the privileges that the user acquires as a result of creating a table or subsequently adding a column. These column privileges are those that have been granted with an associated column list:

```
CREATE VIEW COLUMN_PRIVILEGES
  AS SELECT GRANTOR, GRANTEE, TABLE_CATALOG, TABLE_SCHEMA,
            TABLE_NAME, COLUMN_NAME, PRIVILEGE_TYPE, IS_GRANTABLE
       FROM DEFINITION_SCHEMA.COLUMN_PRIVILEGES
       WHERE GRANTEE IN ('PUBLIC', CURRENT_USER)
             OR GRANTOR = CURRENT_USER
         AND TABLE_CATALOG
             = (SELECT CATALOG_NAME
                  FROM INFORMATION_SCHEMA_CATALOG_NAME)
GRANT SELECT ON COLUMN_PRIVILEGES TO PUBLIC
```

20.2.11 USAGE_PRIVILEGES

This view identifies the privileges on domains, character sets, translations and collations defined in this catalog that have either been granted to the user or the user has granted to others. This includes the privileges that the user acquires as a result of creating the object:

```
CREATE VIEW USAGE_PRIVILEGES
  AS SELECT GRANTOR, GRANTEE, OBJECT_CATALOG, OBJECT_SCHEMA,
            OBJECT_NAME, OBJECT_TYPE, 'USAGE' AS PRIVILEGE_TYPE,
            IS_GRANTABLE
       FROM DEFINITION_SCHEMA.USAGE_PRIVILEGES
       WHERE GRANTEE IN ('PUBLIC', CURRENT_USER)
             OR GRANTOR = CURRENT_USER
         AND OBJECT_CATALOG
             = (SELECT CATALOG_NAME
                  FROM INFORMATION_SCHEMA_CATALOG_NAME)
GRANT SELECT ON USAGE_PRIVILEGES TO PUBLIC
```

20.2.12 TABLE_CONSTRAINTS

This view identifies all table constraints in a catalog that are owned by a user. This includes column constraints as these are syntactically transformed into table constraints:

```
CREATE VIEW TABLE_CONSTRAINTS
  AS SELECT CONSTRAINT_CATALOG, CONSTRAINT_SCHEMA, CONSTRAINT_NAME,
            TABLE_CATALOG, TABLE_SCHEMA, TABLE_NAME,
            CONSTRAINT_TYPE, IS_DEFERRABLE, INITIALLY_DEFERRED
       FROM DEFINITION_SCHEMA.TABLE_CONSTRAINTS
            JOIN
            DEFINITION_SCHEMA.SCHEMATA S
              ON (CONSTRAINT_CATALOG, CONSTRAINT_SCHEMA)
                 = (S.SCHEMA_CATALOG, S.SCHEMA_NAME)
       WHERE SCHEMA_OWNER = CURRENT_USER
             AND CONSTRAINT_CATALOG
                 = (SELECT CATALOG_NAME
                      FROM INFORMATION_SCHEMA_CATALOG_NAME)

GRANT SELECT ON TABLE_CONSTRAINTS TO PUBLIC
```

20.2.13 REFERENTIAL_CONSTRAINTS

This view identifies all table constraints (which are also referential constraints) in a catalog that are owned by a user. This includes column referential constraints:

```
CREATE VIEW REFERENTIAL_CONSTRAINTS
  AS SELECT CONSTRAINT_CATALOG, CONSTRAINT_SCHEMA, CONSTRAINT_NAME,
            UNIQUE_CONSTRAINT_CATALOG, UNIQUE_CONSTRAINT_SCHEMA,
            UNIQUE_CONSTRAINT_NAME, MATCH_OPTION, UPDATE_RULE,
            DELETE_RULE
       FROM DEFINITION_SCHEMA.REFERENTIAL_CONSTRAINTS
            JOIN
            DEFINITION_SCHEMA.SCHEMATA S
              ON (CONSTRAINT_CATALOG, CONSTRAINT_SCHEMA)
                 = (S.SCHEMA_CATALOG, S.SCHEMA_NAME)
       WHERE SCHEMA_OWNER = CURRENT_USER
             AND CONSTRAINT_CATALOG
                 = (SELECT CATALOG_NAME
                      FROM INFORMATION_SCHEMA_CATALOG_NAME)

GRANT SELECT ON REFERENTIAL_CONSTRAINTS TO PUBLIC
```

20.2.14 CHECK_CONSTRAINTS

This view identifies all table constraints (which are also check constraints) in a catalog, together with the check constraints of assertions and domains that are owned by a user. This includes column check constraints:

```
CREATE VIEW CHECK_CONSTRAINTS
  AS SELECT CONSTRAINT_CATALOG, CONSTRAINT_SCHEMA, CONSTRAINT_NAME,
            CHECK_CLAUSE
       FROM DEFINITION_SCHEMA.CHECK_CONSTRAINTS
            JOIN
            DEFINITION_SCHEMA.SCHEMATA S
              ON (CONSTRAINT_CATALOG, CONSTRAINT_SCHEMA)
                 = (S.SCHEMA_CATALOG, S.SCHEMA_NAME)
       WHERE SCHEMA_OWNER = CURRENT_USER
             AND CONSTRAINT_CATALOG
                 = (SELECT CATALOG_NAME
                      FROM INFORMATION_SCHEMA_CATALOG_NAME)
GRANT SELECT ON CHECK_CONSTRAINTS TO PUBLIC
```

20.2.15 KEY_COLUMN_USAGE

This view identifies all the columns in tables owned by a user that are constrained as keys, e.g. have UNIQUE, PRIMARY KEY or FOREIGN KEY constraints:

```
CREATE VIEW KEY_COLUMN_USAGE
  AS SELECT CONSTRAINT_CATALOG, CONSTRAINT_SCHEMA, CONSTRAINT_NAME,
            TABLE_CATALOG, TABLE_SCHEMA, TABLE_NAME, COLUMN_NAME,
            ORDINAL_POSITION
       FROM DEFINITION_SCHEMA.KEY_COLUMN_USAGE
            JOIN
            DEFINITION_SCHEMA.SCHEMATA S
              ON (CONSTRAINT_CATALOG, CONSTRAINT_SCHEMA)
                 = (S.SCHEMA_CATALOG, S.SCHEMA_NAME)
       WHERE SCHEMA_OWNER = CURRENT_USER
             AND CONSTRAINT_CATALOG
                 = (SELECT CATALOG_NAME
                      FROM INFORMATION_SCHEMA_CATALOG_NAME)
GRANT SELECT ON KEY_COLUMN_USAGE TO PUBLIC
```

20.2.16 ASSERTIONS

This identifies all the assertions in a catalog that are owned by a user:

```
CREATE VIEW ASSERTIONS
  AS SELECT CONSTRAINT_CATALOG, CONSTRAINT_SCHEMA, CONSTRAINT_NAME,
            IS_DEFERRABLE, INITIALLY_DEFERRED
       FROM DEFINITION_SCHEMA.ASSERTIONS
            JOIN
            DEFINITION_SCHEMA.SCHEMATA S
              ON (CONSTRAINT_CATALOG, CONSTRAINT_SCHEMA)
                 = (S.SCHEMA_CATALOG, S.SCHEMA_NAME)
       WHERE SCHEMA_OWNER = CURRENT_USER
             AND CONSTRAINT_CATALOG
```

```
                  = (SELECT CATALOG_NAME
                       FROM INFORMATION_SCHEMA_CATALOG_NAME)

GRANT SELECT ON ASSERTIONS TO PUBLIC
```

20.2.17 CHARACTER_SETS

This view identifies all the character sets in a catalog owned by a user:

```
CREATE VIEW CHARACTER_SETS
  AS SELECT CHARACTER_SET_CATALOG, CHARACTER_SET_SCHEMA,
            CHARACTER_SET_NAME, FORM_OF_USE, NUMBER_OF_CHARACTERS,
            DEFAULT_COLLATE_CATALOG, DEFAULT_COLLATE_SCHEMA,
            DEFAULT_COLLATE_NAME
       FROM DEFINITION_SCHEMA.CHARACTER_SETS
       WHERE (CHARACTER_SET_CATALOG, CHARACTER_SET_SCHEMA,
              CHARACTER_SET_NAME, 'CHARACTER SET')
               IN (SELECT OBJECT_CATALOG, OBJECT_SCHEMA,
                   OBJECT_NAME, OBJECT_TYPE
                     FROM DEFINITION_SCHEMA.USAGE_PRIVILEGES
                     WHERE GRANTEE IN ('PUBLIC', CURRENT_USER))
         AND CHARACTER_SET_CATALOG
             = (SELECT CATALOG_NAME
                  FROM INFORMATION_SCHEMA_CATALOG_NAME)

GRANT SELECT ON CHARACTER_SETS TO PUBLIC
```

20.2.18 COLLATIONS

This view identifies all of the collating sequences in a catalog that are owned by a user:

```
CREATE VIEW COLLATIONS
  AS SELECT COLLATION_CATALOG, COLLATION_SCHEMA, COLLATION_NAME,
            CHARACTER_SET_CATALOG, CHARACTER_SET_SCHEMA,
            CHARACTER_SET_NAME, PAD_ATTRIBUTE
       FROM DEFINITION_SCHEMA.COLLATIONS
       WHERE (COLLATION_CATALOG, COLLATION_SCHEMA, COLLATION_NAME,
              'COLLATION')
               IN (SELECT OBJECT_CATALOG, OBJECT_SCHEMA,
                          OBJECT_NAME, OBJECT_TYPE
                     FROM DEFINITION_SCHEMA.USAGE_PRIVILEGES
                     WHERE GRANTEE IN ('PUBLIC', CURRENT_USER))
         AND COLLATION_CATALOG
             = (SELECT CATALOG_NAME
                  FROM INFORMATION_SCHEMA_CATALOG_NAME)

GRANT SELECT ON COLLATIONS TO PUBLIC
```

20.2.19 TRANSLATIONS

This view identifies all of the character translations in a catalog that are owned by a user:

```
CREATE VIEW TRANSLATIONS
  AS SELECT TRANSLATION_CATALOG, TRANSLATION_SCHEMA,
            TRANSLATION_NAME, SOURCE_CHARACTER_SET_CATALOG,
            SOURCE_CHARACTER_SET_SCHEMA,
            SOURCE_CHARACTER_SET_NAME, TARGET_CHARACTER_SET_CATALOG,
            TARGET_CHARACTER_SET_SCHEMA, TARGET_CHARACTER_SET_NAME,
       FROM DEFINITION_SCHEMA.TRANSLATIONS
       WHERE (TRANSLATION_CATALOG, TRANSLATION_SCHEMA,
              TRANSLATION_NAME, 'TRANSLATION')
               IN (SELECT OBJECT_CATALOG, OBJECT_SCHEMA,
                          OBJECT_NAME, OBJECT_TYPE
                     FROM DEFINITION_SCHEMA.USAGE_PRIVILEGES
                     WHERE GRANTEE IN ('PUBLIC', CURRENT_USER))
         AND TRANSLATION_CATALOG
             = (SELECT CATALOG_NAME
                  FROM INFORMATION_SCHEMA_CATALOG_NAME)

GRANT SELECT ON TRANSLATIONS TO PUBLIC
```

20.2.20 VIEW_TABLE_USAGE

This view identifies all the views in a catalog that are dependent on a table in the catalog owned by the user. The views reported need not be owned by the user:

```
CREATE VIEW VIEW_TABLE_USAGE
  AS SELECT VIEW_CATALOG, VIEW_SCHEMA, VIEW_NAME,
            TABLE_CATALOG, TABLE_SCHEMA, TABLE_NAME
       FROM DEFINITION_SCHEMA.VIEW_TABLE_USAGE
            JOIN
            DEFINITION_SCHEMA.SCHEMATA S
              ON (TABLE_CATALOG, TABLE_SCHEMA)
                 = (S.SCHEMA_CATALOG, S.SCHEMA_NAME)
       WHERE SCHEMA_OWNER = CURRENT_USER
             AND VIEW_CATALOG
                 = (SELECT CATALOG_NAME
                      FROM INFORMATION_SCHEMA_CATALOG_NAME)

GRANT SELECT ON VIEW_TABLE_USAGE TO PUBLIC
```

20.2.21 VIEW_COLUMN_USAGE

This view identifies all the views in a catalog that are dependent on a column in a table in the catalog owned by the user. The views reported need not be owned by the user:

```
CREATE VIEW VIEW_COLUMN_USAGE
  AS SELECT VIEW_CATALOG, VIEW_SCHEMA, VIEW_NAME,
            TABLE_CATALOG, TABLE_SCHEMA, TABLE_NAME, COLUMN_NAME
       FROM DEFINITION_SCHEMA.VIEW_COLUMN_USAGE
            JOIN
            DEFINITION_SCHEMA.SCHEMATA S
              ON (TABLE_CATALOG, TABLE_SCHEMA)
                 = (S.SCHEMA_CATALOG, S.SCHEMA_NAME)
       WHERE SCHEMA_OWNER = CURRENT_USER
             AND VIEW_CATALOG
                 = (SELECT CATALOG_NAME
                      FROM INFORMATION_SCHEMA_CATALOG_NAME)

GRANT SELECT ON VIEW_COLUMN_USAGE TO PUBLIC
```

20.2.22 CONSTRAINT_TABLE_USAGE

This view identifies the tables in the catalog on which constraints owned by the user are dependent. The tables need not be owned by the same user:

```
CREATE VIEW CONSTRAINT_TABLE_USAGE
  AS SELECT TABLE_CATALOG, TABLE_SCHEMA, TABLE_NAME,
            CONSTRAINT_CATALOG, CONSTRAINT_SCHEMA, CONSTRAINT_NAME
       FROM ((SELECT TABLE_CATALOG, TABLE_SCHEMA, TABLE_NAME,
                     CONSTRAINT_CATALOG, CONSTRAINT_SCHEMA,
                     CONSTRAINT_NAME
                FROM DEFINITION_SCHEMA.CHECK_COLUMN_USAGE)
             UNION
             (SELECT PK.TABLE_CATALOG, PK.TABLE_SCHEMA,
                     PK.TABLE_NAME, FK.CONSTRAINT_CATALOG,
                     FK.CONSTRAINT_SCHEMA, FK.CONSTRAINT_NAME
                FROM DEFINITION_SCHEMA.REFERENTIAL_CONSTRAINTS AS FK
              JOIN
              DEFINITION_SCHEMA.TABLE_CONSTRAINTS AS PK
                ON (FK.UNIQUE_CONSTRAINT_CATALOG,
                    FK.UNIQUE_CONSTRAINT_SCHEMA,
                    FK.UNIQUE_CONSTRAINT_NAME)
                   = (PK.CONSTRAINT_CATALOG, PK.CONSTRAINT_SCHEMA,
                      PK.CONSTRAINT_NAME)))
            JOIN
            DEFINITION_SCHEMA.SCHEMATA S
              ON (TABLE_CATALOG, TABLE_SCHEMA)
                 = (S.CATALOG_NAME, S.SCHEMA_NAME)
       WHERE SCHEMA_OWNER = CURRENT_USER
             AND CONSTRAINT_CATALOG
                 = (SELECT CATALOG_NAME
                      FROM INFORMATION_SCHEMA_CATALOG_NAME)

GRANT SELECT ON CONSTRAINT_TABLE_USAGE TO PUBLIC
```

20.2.23 CONSTRAINT_COLUMN_USAGE

This view identifies the constraints, including assertions, in a catalog that are dependent on a column:

```
CREATE VIEW CONSTRAINT_COLUMN_USAGE
  AS SELECT TABLE_CATALOG, TABLE_SCHEMA, TABLE_NAME, COLUMN_NAME,
            CONSTRAINT_CATALOG, CONSTRAINT_SCHEMA, CONSTRAINT_NAME
       FROM ((SELECT TABLE_CATALOG, TABLE_SCHEMA, TABLE_NAME,
                     COLUMN_NAME, CONSTRAINT_CATALOG,
                     CONSTRAINT_SCHEMA, CONSTRAINT_NAME
                FROM DEFINITION_SCHEMA.CHECK_COLUMN_USAGE)
             UNION
             (SELECT K.TABLE_CATALOG, K.TABLE_SCHEMA, K.TABLE_NAME,
                     K.COLUMN_NAME, CONSTRAINT_CATALOG,
                     CONSTRAINT_SCHEMA, CONSTRAINT_NAME
                FROM DEFINITION_SCHEMA.TABLE_CONSTRAINTS
              JOIN
              DEFINITION_SCHEMA.KEY_COLUMN_USAGE AS K
                USING (CONSTRAINT_CATALOG, CONSTRAINT_SCHEMA,
                       CONSTRAINT_NAME)))
            JOIN
            DEFINITION_SCHEMA.SCHEMATA S
              ON (TABLE_CATALOG, TABLE_SCHEMA)
                 = (S.CATALOG_NAME, S.SCHEMA_NAME)
      WHERE SCHEMA_OWNER = CURRENT_USER
            AND CONSTRAINT_CATALOG
                = (SELECT CATALOG_NAME
                       FROM INFORMATION_SCHEMA_CATALOG_NAME)
GRANT SELECT ON CONSTRAINT_COLUMN_USAGE TO PUBLIC
```

20.2.24 COLUMN_DOMAIN_USAGE

This view identifies all the columns in a catalog owned by a user that are dependent on a domain:

```
CREATE VIEW COLUMN_DOMAIN_USAGE
  AS SELECT D.DOMAIN_CATALOG, D.DOMAIN_SCHEMA, D.DOMAIN_NAME,
            TABLE_CATALOG, TABLE_SCHEMA, TABLE_NAME, COLUMN_NAME
       FROM DEFINITION_SCHEMA.COLUMNS C
            JOIN
            DEFINITION_SCHEMA.DOMAINS D
              JOIN
              DEFINITION_SCHEMA.SCHEMATA S
                ON (DOMAIN_CATALOG, DOMAIN_SCHEMA)
                   = (S.CATALOG_NAME, S.SCHEMA_NAME)
              ON (D.DOMAIN_CATALOG, D.DOMAIN_SCHEMA, D.DOMAIN_NAME)
                 = (C.DOMAIN_CATALOG, C.DOMAIN_SCHEMA,
                    C.DOMAIN_NAME)
```

```
        WHERE SCHEMA_OWNER = CURRENT_USER
            AND C.DOMAIN_NAME IS NOT NULL
            AND D.DOMAIN_CATALOG
                 = (SELECT CATALOG_NAME
                      FROM INFORMATION_SCHEMA_CATALOG_NAME)

GRANT SELECT ON COLUMN_DOMAIN_USAGE TO PUBLIC
```

20.2.25 SQL_LANGUAGES

The SQL_LANGUAGES view has one row for each SQL language dialect supported by the implementation. It is in fact identical in content to the base table:

```
CREATE VIEW SQL_LANGUAGES
  AS SELECT SQL_LANGUAGE_SOURCE, SQL_LANGUAGE_YEAR,
            SQL_LANGUAGE_CONFORMANCE, SQL_LANGUAGE_INTEGRITY,
            SQL_LANGUAGE_IMPLEMENTATION, SQL_LANGUAGE_BINDING_STYLE,
            SQL_LANGUAGE_PROGRAMMING_LANGUAGE
       FROM DEFINITION_SCHEMA.SQL_LANGUAGES

GRANT SELECT ON SQL_LANGUAGES TO PUBLIC
```

20.2.26 INFORMATION_SCHEMA_CATALOG_NAME_CARDINALITY

This assertion ensures that there is exactly one row in the INFORMATION_SCHEMA_CATALOG_NAME table:

```
CREATE ASSERTION INFORMATION_SCHEMA_CATALOG_NAME_CARDINALITY
  CHECK (1= (SELECT COUNT(*)
               FROM INFORMATION_SCHEMA_CATALOG_NAME))
```

20.3 Extracting the Information

The views in the INFORMATION_SCHEMA schema may be accessed in precisely the same way as any other view to which you have access. The views may be used to discover what objects you own; for instance:

```
SELECT * FROM INFORMATION_SCHEMA.SCHEMATA
```

will tell you which schemata you own. A query such as:

```
SELECT *
  FROM INFORMATION_SCHEMA.TABLES
  WHERE (TABLE_CATALOG, TABLE_SCHEMA)
        IN (SELECT CATALOG_NAME, SCHEMA_NAME
              FROM INFORMATION_SCHEMA.SCHEMATA)
```

will tell you which tables you own, as opposed to which tables you have access to, which is simply the query:

```
SELECT * FROM INFORMATION_SCHEMA.TABLES
```

Not only can you discover what objects you possess or have access to but you may also discover the attributes of the objects. This information should be enough to enable you to reproduce the semantics, if not the precise syntax, of the original CREATE statement (as modified by any subsequent schema manipulation commands). For example, to determine the data type, etc. of the salary column in the Employee table in the Company schema of the TEST catalog you could say, assuming that you have the necessary access:

```
SELECT DATA_TYPE, NUMERIC_PRECISION,
       NUMERIC_PRECISION_RADIX, NUMERIC_SCALE
  FROM INFORMATION_SCHEMA.COLUMNS
  WHERE (TABLE_CATALOG, TABLE_SCHEMA, TABLE_NAME,
         COLUMN_NAME)
        = ('TEST', 'Company', 'Employee', 'salary')
```

Privileges may also be inspected; for example:

```
SELECT *
  FROM INFORMATION_SCHEMA.TABLE_PRIVILEGES
  WHERE GRANTOR NOT IN (CURRENT_USER, '_SYSTEM')
```

will return all the table privileges that you have been granted by other people. The _SYSTEM grantor is the special authorization identifier that identifies privileges you possess by reason of being the owner of an object. You may also inspect privileges that you have granted; for example:

```
SELECT *
  FROM INFORMATION_SCHEMA.USAGE_PRIVILEGES
  WHERE GRANTOR = USER AND OBJECT_TYPE = 'DOMAIN'
```

will list the USAGE privileges on domains that you have granted to other authorization identifiers. These may have been privileges granted on your own domains or on those of others for which you yourself have been granted the privilege with the WITH GRANT OPTION.

The views in the INFORMATION_SCHEMA may also be used to determine the impact of potential changes made using the schema manipulation commands. For instance, if you own a domain TEST.YOURS.POSTCODE and wish to know which columns would be affected if you alter or drop the domain, the following query will provide the answer:

```
SELECT TABLE_CATALOG, TABLE_SCHEMA, TABLE_NAME, COLUMN_NAME
  FROM INFORMATION_SCHEMA.COLUMN_DOMAIN_USAGE
  WHERE (DOMAIN_CATALOG, DOMAIN_SCHEMA, DOMAIN_NAME)
        = ('TEST', 'YOURS', 'POSTCODE')
```

The above are only a few of the queries that are possible on the tables of the INFORMATION_SCHEMA, designed to give a flavour of the options. The INFORMATION_SCHEMA is a major information resource within any SQL system and should be treated as such. Experience will determine what sort of information is of most value to you in any given circumstances.

Part III
Using the SQL Language

21

Database and Application Analysis

The database system plus the suite of application programs traditionally forms the information system offered to clients. Sales information systems, production scheduling information systems, management information systems and money transfer information systems are all systems for a particular purpose, designed to meet the requirements of the clients of the system.

In this chapter we will address some issues related to the analysis of the application programs and the database parts of the information system. At this level we are not interested in issues related to distributed databases or

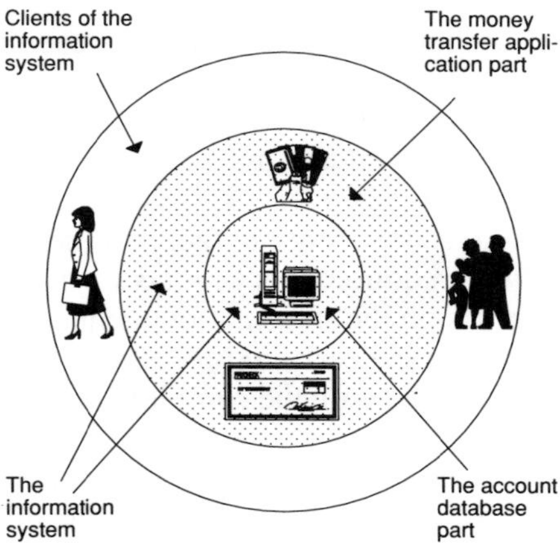

Figure 21.1 *The money transfer information system and some clients*

performance issues since these are treated as separate topics elsewhere in the book. We have chosen not to be exhaustive in our coverage of issues; nor do we treat every topic addressed in full detail.

21.1 From Conceptual to Physical Using Data and Function

When developing information systems the methods in use have some form of phasing from a conceptual or abstract idea of the requirements to a physical or concrete realization of these into system components. Whether this is done in a rigid sequence of steps with no or very little reiteration or in a very much more reiterative manner, i.e. a prototyping or a time-boxed approach, is irrelevant; we go from orientation via analysis into design and implementation.

Furthermore, all of our development work must result in concrete deliverables in the form of a database (the data definition as well as the data itself for manipulation) plus functionality encapsulated into application programs, modules and/or routines. In the world of expert systems the words for database and application suite may become knowledge base, containing rules, facts, frames; and expert application, built from inference engines, forward and backward reasoning and Bayesian logic. The paradigm for object-oriented or semantic worlds uses different words again, like object, inheritance, messages, generalization and specialization. Whatever the words used, the structure of the development process is essentially the same.

The two aspects, data and function, have been included in Figure 21.2 with the phasing top to bottom. Another example of phasing is found in 'A framework for information systems architecture' of J.A. Zachman (1987).

21.2 Database and Application Analysis Issues

Developing an information system from the results obtained in analysis work requires careful design. Modern and powerful tools which support and partially automate the work we need to perform in the various phases have arrived. These include CASE (Computer aided software engineering) tools, fourth generation environments (4GE) and many kinds of database and application code generators. This increase in capability plus the vastly improved performance and capacity of hardware components may give the impression that life has become easier for analysts and designers. This is not true. The need for proper analysis and careful design stems from the fact that the clients of the information systems increase their requirements in tandem if not more quickly than technological advancements on the information technology supply side.

The information systems of the early sixties, recording stock levels in single warehouses, cannot be compared with the complex information systems among suppliers and buyers today. A buyer's system assesses resupply requirements, automatically places an order with the preferred supplier through EDI (Electronic Data Interchange) and, once the goods have arrived and have satisfied quality controls, payment instructions are automatically issued to the bank.

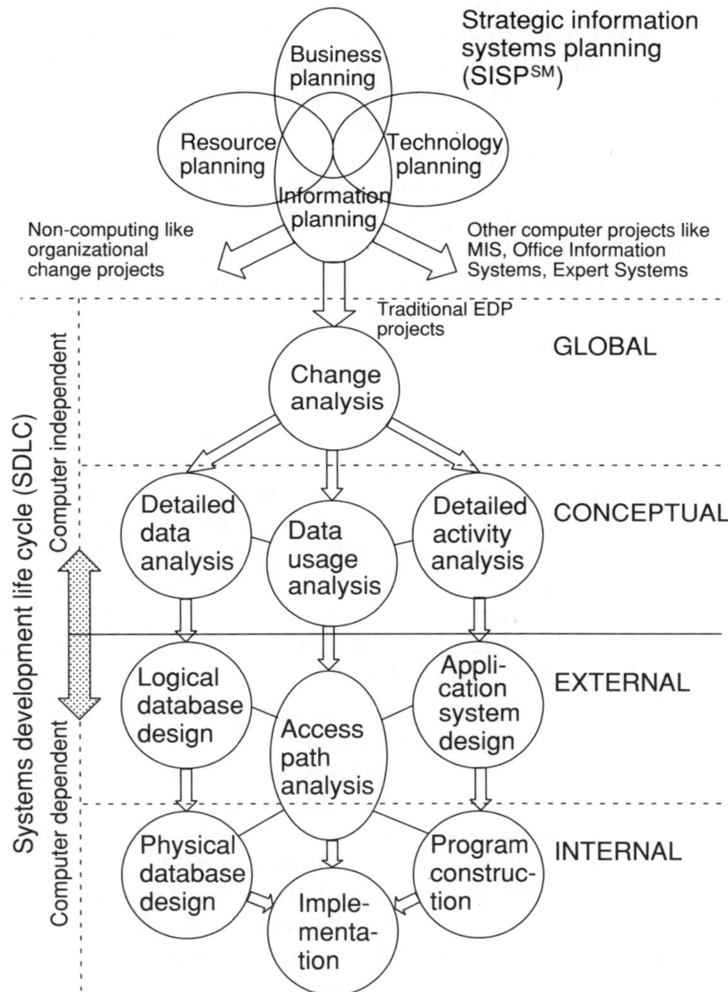

Figure 21.2 *An example of a systems development life cycle*

Another factor to keep in mind is that most hardware components have increased in capacity and improved in performance 100 to 100 000 fold for the same or often lower prices. Data storage on disk has not kept pace, especially in the area of speed. The increasing need to integrate application areas further leads to more people wanting access to the same data at the same time, leading to queues for service. Careful analysis and design can help in identifying solutions to these problems.

The increased capability of database management systems (DBMSs) allows us to negotiate between the application part of the information system and the database management part of the information system as to which will take on what work. Calculating the average salary per department, the total number of employees on projects, the total amount of time spent on a project and so on can be done by application programs using procedural logic to navigate the database or can simply be requested from the DBMS. Our general recommendation is to delegate the responsibility for all aspects of maintaining data to the DBMS as a matter of principle, since most of the time this delivers significant benefits.

Pushed by requirements of demanding clients and to some extent by evolving standards like SQL, suppliers increase the power and functionality of the DBMSs. Trust in the capability of the DBMS and the reengineering facilities of new versions of DBMS software will swing the balance continually towards the DBMS component of the information system. However, the ever-increasing demands of the clients will at the same time force the application part of the information system to become more and more complex and demand increased capabilities from the DBMS in the next release. This loop will never end. Obviously knowing what is to come in future releases provides criteria for application and database design. With the arrival of referential integrity in the SQL standard, certain checks, like verifying the existence of a `Department` with the same `deptcd` for the freshly entered `Employee`, could be delegated to the DBMS. Designing an application in such a way that all referential integrity checks are easily identified and removed from the application routines should make the task of upgrading an application suite far easier. *Chapter 28 Performance Aspects* should help in the choice of options to achieve and maintain good performance and sensible use of the DBMS.

When designing relational database structures we must trust the DBMS to perform the manipulation commands efficiently, effectively and above all correctly. A DBMS is a software processor reacting to structures and patterns; it has no knowledge of the semantics of the database structure it controls. As long as the defined data structure is in accordance with the principles built into the DBMS the requested functions will be performed correctly.

For the correct (and efficient) updating of data in the database the data needs to be structured in a particular manner, called normalized form. The originator of the relational model, E.F. Codd (1970), defined a technique for going from an unnormalized data structure to data structures in the third normal form. Many articles and books have been written on this subject (*see Rock-Evans, 1987a; Date, 1986a, 1986b*) so we will not describe the steps in detail. Further forms of normalization, such as fourth and fifth normal forms or the Boyce-Codd normal form (BCNF), dealing with more or less specialized situations, have also been written about. For our purpose a brief explanation of the three original normal forms will suffice.

Take a data structure of unspecified normalized form (*see Figure 21.3*) and simply assume it to be unnormalized. Assume we have found a tape-based application containing 'project data'. We now want to normalize the data, found on the tape, to meet the design of a relational database application. Step 1 is the removal of repeating groups to arrive at first normal form (1NF or FNF) (*see Figure 21.4*). Relational theory does not allow repeating groups of columns to

PROJECT_CD
budget
forecast
actual
resp_dept
sponsor_dept
resp_name
sponsor_name
empnr
name
sex
salary
date_of_birth
deptcd
deptnm
date_joining
job
prev_salary
start_dt_job
end_dt_job
project_role
start_date_asg
end_date_asg

Figure 21.3 *Project data TAPE*

appear in a table. The project details may not include repeating (groups of) columns describing the assignments or skills of employees working on the project. Some projects may have only one employee assignment and some may have many. The form of the project data tape would appear as a very irregular and not maintainable table for a relational DBMS. The solution is to split the table into two. The repeating group of columns pertaining to assignments are split off to form a table of their own and the remainder form a second table. To keep the original implicit relationship between project and assignment intact, the project_cd is duplicated and used as a column of the key of the assignment table. The process is repeated for any further repeating groups in each table, going from high order to low order and duplicating keys successively at lower levels. The end result is that all tables in the data structure are in 1NF. The structure is now regular in that each table consists of a number of columns, each with a single value, and a key made up of one or more columns.

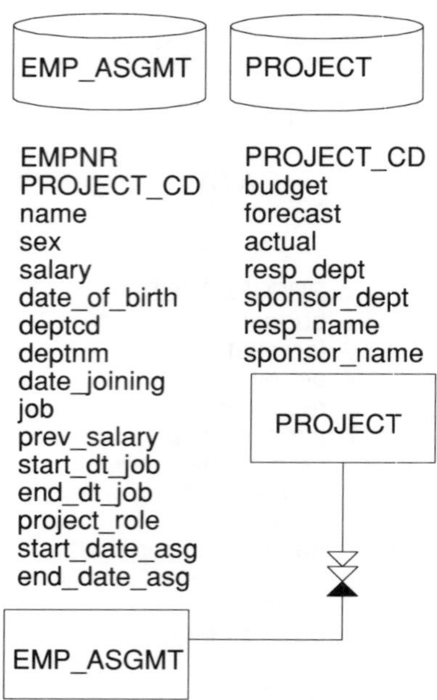

Figure 21.4 *A first try at 1NF*

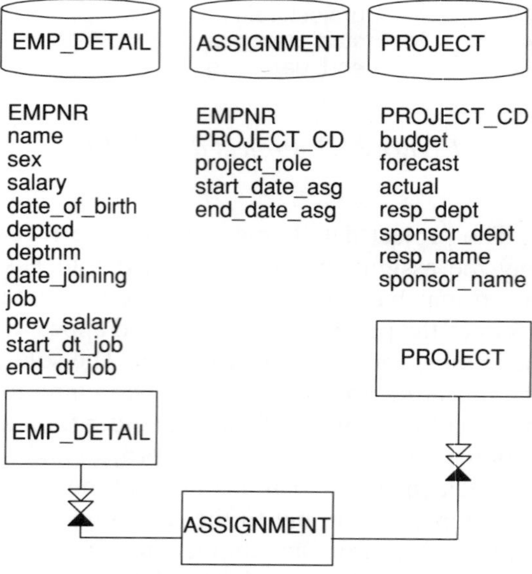

Figure 21.5 *Attempt at 2NF*

Step 2 is the removal of partial key dependencies to arrive at the second normal form (2NF or SNF) (*see Figure 21.5*). At this stage we must look at tables having composite keys, i.e. keys consisting of more than one column. For each such key we inspect the non-key columns of each table and verify that they are dependent upon the total composite key. Should we find one or more columns dependent only on part of the composite key we must split the table again. Each column dependent on a part of the composite key is removed from the original table to form a new table, with the part of the key on which it depends as the key of the new table. This must be done for each dependency found in the 1NF data structure. Look at the EMP_ASGMT table in our example and compare Figure 21.5 with Figure 21.4. Again the relationship is maintained between the upward extracted table containing the partial key dependent columns and part of the original key. This part of the key is still present in the key of the original table which has been left behind with fewer columns. Note that in the EMP_DETAIL table there is repeating data about the employee's previous jobs (functions). This implies that this table is not in the first normal form and we should split these columns 'downward' into JOB_HIST. This step is not shown separately.

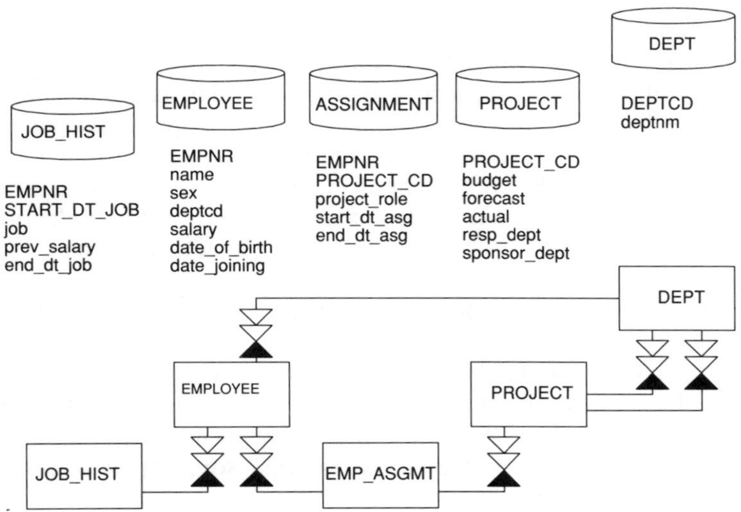

Figure 21.6 *Example of tables in 3NF*

Step 3 is the removal of transitively dependent columns. Such a dependency occurs when columns in a table do not describe the object being described by the table itself, but something else identified by a column that is not part of the key to the table, for instance columns in Employee describing features of the department they work for or projects describing departments for which they are scheduled. The original table, which contained the transitive dependencies, is split and retains the column(s) of the key of the new table as non-key column(s) so that the original relationship is preserved. The new table is formed by each of the data items that were dependent on the column(s) that now become(s) the key of the new table. Again, this process must be repeated as many times as is necessary. The result is a greater number of tables which are said to be in the third normal form (3NF or TNF) (*see Figure 21.6*). The normalized data structure can now simply be rewritten into SQL data definition statements to create the tables. The example we have developed here is almost equivalent to the Company database (*see Appendix A The Example Database*).

In designing databases you must be aware that the term database has changed meaning in recent years. In the seventies and early eighties a database was a single entity described by a single set of data definition language commands and under the control of a single DBMS. In the SQL standard this simple concept of a database is still possible, but more complex scenarios are also allowed. In fact, a lot of freedom is given to the implementors of DBMS software to move gradually towards truly distributed systems supported by heterogeneous DBMSs running on a multitude of hardware and operating system platforms. A database in SQL is a dynamic concept and can best be seen as the combination of tables visible to an application during the execution of a transaction.

An application may include a number of SQL modules that contain SQL commands and it is bound to a data description. Different modules may be bound to different data descriptions and may therefore access different data structures. As the application carries out processes on behalf of its clients it may activate more and different modules and extend the scope of its operation. The 'view' on the database becomes wider and the database expands. Parts of the database may reside on different computers. One way of expressing the capabilities of SQL is that the potential database is formed by the collection of all SQL-based databases in the entire world while the actual database is the particular subset activated by the application.

Under these circumstances no single application may see the entire database. A new application with access to its own private database, which is then given access to part of a new database, builds a bridge and expands the database. Obviously, the applications must understand the meaning of the data structures and the problems of redundancy and coding differences in heterogeneous environments are not simple to resolve. We discuss some of these problems in *Chapter 27 Distributed Databases.*

21.3 Correctness Aspects

Clients are often fully dependent in their work on the correct functioning of the information system. The process of database and application design must therefore ensure that the information system supports its clients adequately. The responsibility for correctly maintaining the data in the system is shared between various 'components' (*see Figure 21.7*).

Integrity maintenance is the responsibility of the DBMS. Our definition of integrity is the situation in which the data in the database is in accordance with the data definition as provided to the DBMS. All underlying physical aspects

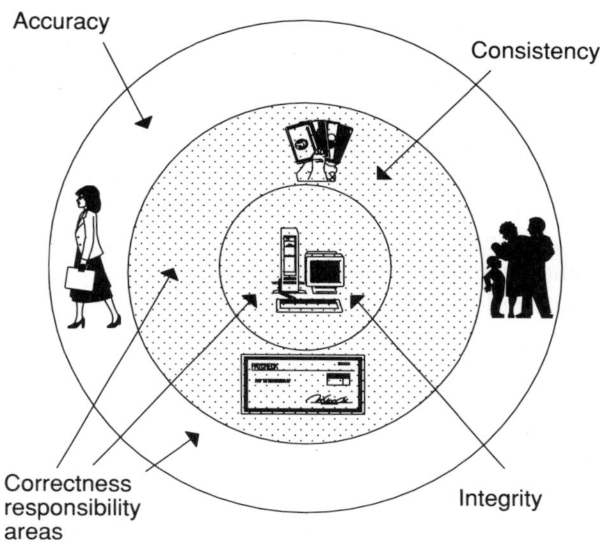

Figure 21.7 *Responsibility for correctness of data*

for which the DBMS may rely on other system components, like the operating system, are considered part of integrity control. For our company example (*see Appendix A The Example Database*) the database is considered to be in an integral state when each `Employee` has a `deptcd` that represents an existing `Department`, the `sex` for each `Employee` is represented by either an F or M, and also the indexes contain correct pointers, the disk blocks are properly allocated and pointer chains are not broken or incorrectly linked.

Consistency control is the responsibility of the collective application programs. The programmed consistency controls are checks and procedures that are additional to the integrity checks. Dynamic constraints particularly, such as the changes in marital status or complex changes in commission, may require complex programming. When booking a trip for an employee in our example database (*see Appendix A The Example Database*) a travel agent may need to adjust the flight details, hotel accommodation and other facilities such as hire cars according to the employee's profile. Checks on the consistency between the various portions of the itinerary can be placed in the **information system**. Such a control on the 'service level' might include items such as all flight seat allocations should be first class, window, non-smoking, rooms should be doubles in the four- or five-star category hotels and hire cars should possess a number of luxury options. Advantage should also be taken of any available frequent traveller or corporate discount programs. The described process of evaluation, selection and booking from the various portions of the itinerary on the basis of the employee's profile cannot, or at least not completely, be described in terms of integrity checks which can be placed under the control of the **DBMS**. This requires, therefore, a degree of consistency control being exercised by the **application program**.

The important difference between the two groups of rules is that the first group is completely prescriptive but the DBMS can simply ensure that there are no exceptions. The rules are of an absolute nature. For example, the duration of a flight may not be negative and neither can the price of an hotel room. The return flight cannot occur before the employee was born, etc. In the second group the rules are not all so absolute but may include rules with empirical boundaries or restrictions or concern deontological situations or other agreements. The weight of a passenger will probably never (empirically) exceed 200 kg, but even if our employee is exceedingly 'gravitationally challenged' he will not be rejected as a passenger. However, a passenger with overweight baggage (a commercial boundary) may indeed check the baggage in but it is undesirable that this should occur without a corresponding compensatory action such as the payment of an excess baggage fee or the unpacking of some items.

These last two groups of rules remain in the hands of the application and not in those of the DBMS. Similarly, with the recovery of errors, the application uses the SQL ROLLBACK statement to give information to the DBMS about the boundaries of transactions and the action it requires from the DBMS. Note that the DBMS uses techniques, like locking of rows, tables, etc., to guarantee that transactions for various clients outside the information system will not interfere with partially completed integrity and consistency units.

Accuracy control is the responsibility of the clients of the information system. This category includes the timeliness, accuracy and completeness of information. It is often only possible to verify correctness by checking the occurrence in the real world and making some kind of judgement on the possibility or plausibility. The weight of a person can be limited to between 0 and 125 kilograms, but choosing a 100 per cent safe upper limit may lead to foolishly unnecessary checking by the DBMS or the application. Integrity checking is absolutely black and white; consistency checks may involve logic and statistics by the application, but the final responsibility must reside with the client of the information system. Consider the judgement of the quality of wine. Colour, nose and taste differ from person to person and there will always be debate on the judgement of different connoisseurs. It remains the final responsibility of the client to deliver timely, accurate and complete and relevant information to the information system.

The borderlines between these areas of control are not fixed. The capability of the innermost circle in Figure 21.7 increases regularly, through the efforts of manufacturers and SQL standardization. The middle layer then initially contracts, but increased client requirements demand ever-increasing functionality. The final outer layer has to deal with any activities left. The delegation of responsibility is in a state of flux during the database and application design process while the designer negotiates with the client community the boundaries and functionality of the information system. Within the design process the delegation of responsibility is specified between application and DBMS. One way of increasing the speed of implementation and increasing the maintainability and reliability of an information system is by trying to make the application layer as small as possible and leaving the correctness checking entirely to the DBMS. The application responsibility is given, if possible, entirely to the DBMS or the information system contract is renegotiated between clients and the application so that the client takes the responsibility for correctness. This approach is very much favoured in 4GE application development to ensure speedy and simple implementations.

21.4 Security Aspects

Security of information systems deals with two major aspects: the maintenance of the operational service and its speedy reinstatement after any failure and the prevention of the unauthorized use of the information system components.

The first objective is maintained by having mechanisms available in the information system to collect necessary back-up information for use in recovery processes. According to the SQL standard the DBMS must have some of these mechanisms in place to maintain database integrity and to undo SQL commands in case the DBMS cannot achieve the desired post-SQL command condition in accordance with the DDL specification or a hardware or software failure occurs. Furthermore, the SQL standard describes the transaction concept (*see Chapter 12 Transaction Management*) and provides control statements in SQL for supporting this concept (*see Section 12.3 Control Statements in SQL*). All of this is aimed at controlling the correct functioning of the information system 'within the scope of the application transactions being processed'.

The SQL standard does not specify any of the mechanisms a manufacturer must implement or supply to provide this capability. Outside the transaction many things may go wrong — disks may fail, application programs or the DBMS may malfunction, inaccurate or simply 'wrong' data may have been entered by clients of the information system. All of these situations require some kind of repair. The recovery mechanisms — either supplied by the DBMS manufacturer or available in the form of dedicated application programs that perform the repair — need to concentrate on recovery at the consistency unit level, since the clients of the information system can only be interested in the information system complying with the contract at the level of consistency.

To meet the second objective SQL offers support in the form of access control facilities as described in *Chapter 8 Access Control*. SQL allows the specification of privileges that can be granted to and revoked from clients of the information system. Such a client is identified to SQL by an authorization identifier. The processes of identification and checking to see that the identified client is properly authenticated form part of some system-wide security arrangement and fall outside the scope of SQL. The linking pin is the authorization identifier which is supplied by the 'outside security agents' in the operating system, network management system or whatever to the SQL-based DBMS.

21.5 Current Trends

In this section we will briefly consider just a few trends and the effects on database and application analysis and design.

21.5.1 Batch versus On-line

Clients of information systems want more and more instantaneous access to data; they do not want to wait for batch processes to collect and provide the data to them next day. The arrival of terminals has led to an enormous growth in the on-line retrieval and updating of data, which has caused a shift from the traditional batch processing during the night to a larger amount of on-line processing. International, even global, networks have given people everywhere access to databases around the world at times convenient to them, so that on-line transactions may arrive at any time during the day. However, the need for batch processing has not disappeared; on the contrary, large processing requirements that were previously run on dedicated information systems have been integrated into database-oriented information systems that are shared with on-line clients. Long batch transactions now compete during the day with the on-line requirements for database access. Locking data in the database for a long time will increase queues of clients waiting for the release of resources reserved by the DBMS. The SQL commands `SET TRANSACTION <transaction access mode>` and `SET TRANSACTION ISOLATION LEVEL <level of isolation>` specify the intention of the transaction and the permitted impact on other transactions of the transaction issuing the commands (*see Section 12.3 Control Statements in SQL*). By allowing the DBMS not to block the access of batch programs to locked rows of tables reserved for concurrently processing transactions (the level of isolation is low) the throughput of the workload in the database may be increased at the expense of processing potentially inconsistent data.

21.5.2 Historic Data Handling

The concept of time is complex and to model databases so that time is handled correctly is more complicated than we have space in this book to cover but we offer a few guidelines and comments. SQL provides functionality in the form of datetime and interval data types, a predicate and time zone handling facilities (*see Chapter 23 Using the Datetime Facilities*).

Most current database implementations capture datetime in a snapshot sense. The event is recorded at a date and time and the history of events or changes over time are very seldom modelled correctly. Let us examine some analysis and design issues involved. Having designed a data structure and verified its being in 3NF (*see Section 21.2 Database and Application Analysis Issues*) further work needs to be done. We must validate the data structure to be valid over time, because we want it to be capable of handling every required business situation. Doing business is dynamic and it requires the information system to reflect changes accordingly. Looking at the business by taking a snapshot of the database means that the database must represent the state of the real world at any point in time. We may want to remember datetime details and periods of validity (intervals of time). These details must be checked and if necessary added to the data structure. In the snapshots of time not only do datetime columns need to be added to tables but also certain relationships may occur at certain time periods. Certain tables — usually tables of key importance, like patient, treatment, client, order — go through several phases, where certain relationships with other tables may, must or may not exist. Allowing an information system to have 'a memory' means that additional relationships and tables may be required to support that memory. An employee may only work for one department at a time, but he may work for multiple departments over time. One can see the same thing in, for example, patient's making, breaking, keeping and cancelling appointments (*see also Rock-Evans' (1987b) second volume on 'Data Analysis — the methods'*). Each fact is supported by a corresponding event that needs to be recorded in the database. The data structure should cater for this memory.

A more complex problem is making corrections over time and keeping track of when which fact was known. The fact that Employee 'Cannan', with empnr 04711, was assigned to a Project, with project_cd 'MKTG03', last Monday for 4 hours will have been stored in the Timesheet table in our Company database. Today, Thursday '1991:04:25' we discover that the Employee 'Cannan' actually worked on Project 'MKTG03' on Monday for 6 hours. We do not simply overwrite the original information on the Timesheet, but record an additional event saying that today we registered the revised hours. Several questions could now be framed:

1. On Wednesday we ask: How long did Employee 'Cannan' actually work?
2. On Friday we ask: How long did Employee 'Cannan' actually work?
3. On Friday we ask: How long did we think at Wednesday noon Employee 'Cannan' worked?
4. We may even add questions like 'Who did we give the wrong information to?' in order to allow people or information systems to correct a possible wrong decision made on the basis of the original information.

The corresponding SQL queries for these natural language questions lead to fairly complex constructs. The queries and answers are as follows. Query 1 on Wednesday will be:

```
SELECT hours FROM Timesheet
  WHERE   empnr = 04711
    AND   project_cd = 'MKTG03'
    AND   timestamp_end =
          TIMESTAMP'9999-12-31 23:59:59.999999'
```

The answer to this query will be `'04:00'`. Query 2 on Friday will be identical to query 1, but the answer will be `'06:00'`. Query 3 on Friday will be:

```
SELECT hours FROM Timesheet
  WHERE  empnr = Ø4711
    AND  project_cd = 'MKTGØ3'
    AND  (timestamp_start >=
          TIMESTAMP'1991-Ø4-24 ØØ:ØØ:ØØ' AND
          timestamp_start <
          TIMESTAMP'1991-Ø4-25 ØØ:ØØ:ØØ') OR
         (TIMESTAMP'1991-Ø4-24 ØØ:ØØ:ØØ' >=
          timestamp_start AND
          TIMESTAMP'1991-Ø4-24 ØØ:ØØ:ØØ' < timestamp_end)
```

The answer to this query will be `'Ø4:ØØ'`. Note that had 'Cannan' modified his timesheet several times on Wednesday multiple rows would have been returned by this query. An alternative syntax for this query is:

```
SELECT hours FROM Timesheet
  WHERE   empnr = Ø4711
    AND   project_cd = 'MKTGØ3'
    AND   (timestamp_start,timestamp_end) OVERLAPS
          (TIMESTAMP'1991-Ø4-24 ØØ:ØØ:ØØ',
           TIMESTAMP'1991-Ø4-25 ØØ:ØØ:ØØ')
```

Further information on time-related issues can be found in *Chapter 23 Using the Datetime Facilities.*

21.5.3 Client–Server Concepts

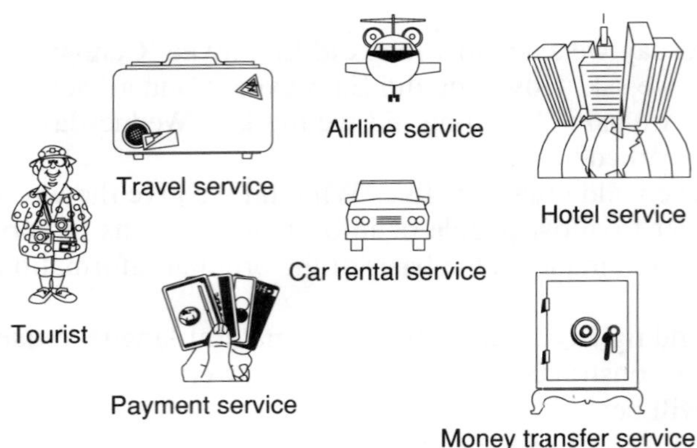

Figure 21.8 *Client–server applications*

The SQL standard is moving away from the concept of a single environment in which data processing takes place. An application program may use many modules which can each access the same or different databases (*see Chapter 27 Distributed Databases*). By adding modules new data can be made available to the application program. The application program is the client of the called modules, but the modules called may act as clients and call upon other servers for further details. Each server isolates the client from knowledge about where the data is and how it is structured. The requested data is returned by the server to the client. Take the example in Figure 21.8 where the tourist is a client of the server dealing with travel services when he wants to schedule travel and a client of the payment server which arranges payments. The travel service is in its own right a client of servers providing airline, car rental and hotel services and can possibly call upon the payment service on behalf of the tourist. The payment server has access to the money transfer services of various financial institutions. In this manner each client calls upon the server to satisfy a request and relies on the knowledge of the server to deal with the question. SQL currently offers commands so that a client can set up communications with servers. These commands are described in *Chapter 14 Session Management* and you will observe that a lot of the real power is left to the implementor. SQL allows you to establish multiple sessions between a client and different servers, but only a single session may be active at one time. Before switching sessions you must COMMIT or ROLLBACK the transaction for that session first. This is a severe limitation which makes it difficult to co-ordinate updates across multiple servers or to support multiple levels of client-server applications efficiently. Further work is needed on two-phase commit handling and control and in allowing ROLLBACK of selective parts of work.

21.6 Data Driven Programming

In designing applications the objective is to make use of components of the system in such a way that they do the work they are good at. Having a powerful data management capability available through SQL to define and manipulate data and regulate proper access to the data makes it worth while to look for other applications. Data driven programming means that in programming we try to move all the data definitions and lists in programs to database storage and make the programs more generally applicable. This is exactly the way fourth generation environments (4GEs) have developed.

21.6.1 Help Modules

Providing on-line help to users from within the application can be made simpler to handle and maintain by having generalized routines available for saving and restoring images on the terminal screen and retrieving help data from one or more tables in the database. The application program only needs to transfer control and context dependent information when a certain keyboard key has been depressed. In many system architectures the definition of keys is handled in a common user interface component. The handling of paging forward and backward through help screens and switching to other help topics is now managed by a sub-system accessing the help tables in the database.

21.6.2 Menu Screen Options

Providing flexible and sophisticated access to programs in a comprehensive application environment can also be designed by having a generalized sub-system using data from database tables. Based on the authorization identifier the menu sub-system may paint a menu screen for the client behind the terminal, which contains only options he is allowed to use. Shortcuts to other parts of the menu network or hierarchy may be provided and client dependent homonym and synonym handling may be provided.

21.6.3 Error Handling

Providing correct error messages with useful hints on how to repair the situation and how to proceed or otherwise provide help in narrative texts from the help system is a luxury many application systems do not offer. In the case of layered application software the structuring of error handling is vital. Inner components of the system may give very cryptic and not very helpful messages. A generalized and uniform error handling procedure plus information being passed to the client behind the terminal on how to deal with initial error recovery actions makes applications simpler and allows programmers to get on with the real task.

22

Integrity Control

In Part II on 'The SQL Language', we have seen the facilities available in SQL for integrity control. In this chapter we will investigate further the concepts of integrity control and the use of the facilities provided for defining integrity constraints in an SQL database as well as those available to simplify and control the maintenance of the defined integrity rules. We will look first at the four kinds of integrity as described in the relational model, then at the different types of relationships that can exist between entities and how these can be implemented in SQL. We will concentrate on binary relationships as these are the most common, but will also touch on unary relationships as well as the concepts of inclusivity and exclusivity. Finally, we will look at the management aspects of integrity control, specifically the relationship between business rules and triggered actions and the problems of cyclic constraints.

22.1 Definition

In a database environment we can imagine three levels of correctness. The database can be in an 'integral', a 'consistent' or an 'accurate' state.

The first level, integrity, has to do with whether the data is self-consistent and agrees with its definition. This covers not only the physical aspects of the database, i.e. is it correctly structured with regard to the rules of the database management system, i.e. such areas as the indexes being consistent with the table data, overflow chains being unbroken, etc., but also covers the facilities at the 'logical' level, i.e. the column and table constraints and the assertions that can be specified in SQL to require the DBMS to control the logical aspects of the database. A DBMS guarantees that in an integral database it is not possible to discover any inconsistency within the data itself, e.g. if there exists an order line for a given order there also exists an order with the same order number, or if data is redundantly stored all copies have the same value. Integrity, however, says nothing about whether the contents of the database were arrived at by a series of consistent changes.

The second level, consistency, deals with correctness which cannot be, at least currently, enforced by the database management system and is the responsibility of the application programs. Checks on valid state changes are examples of the kind of change that must currently be controlled by the application. The sum of the integrity and consistency levels forms in fact the contract between an **information system** and its users with regard to guarantees of correctness. Consistency says nothing about the accuracy of the information stored that is covered by the next level.

The highest level, accuracy, deals with the facts. This is always the responsibility of the information provider. The old GIGO principle (garbage in / garbage out) still applies.

The physical aspects of the first level is the exclusive concern of the database management software and provided that this software is adequate the user need not be concerned with that aspect. The logical aspects of the first level is the area with which we will concern ourselves in this chapter. This area is the responsibility of the data modeller. It is frequently the case that not all necessary constraints are available in a given implementation. In this case the constraints will need to migrate to the second level, consistency. For performance reasons it may also not be possible to implement all of the constraints or some of them may need to be implemented in the application software, consistency, and some in the database definition, integrity. It is our contention that even if not all of the constraints are implemented in the DBMS it is a good idea to define them all in terms of SQL as a reference model for application programmers and subsequent maintainers of the system. SQL provides a concise and unambiguous definition which can be of great benefit in the development and maintenance phases of systems.

The relational model defines four kinds of integrity:

Domain Integrity
Entity Integrity
Referential Integrity
User Integrity

We will describe these in the following sections.

22.2 Domain Integrity

Domain integrity is concerned with the values that may be contained within a particular column. As we have seen the concept of domain is sometimes implicit and sometimes optional in SQL. All columns have an implicit domain derived from their data type, but more explicit domain integrity can be supported either by the use of defined domains (*see Section 4.3 CREATE*

DOMAIN) or by the use of the column or table constraints, CHECK and NOT NULL.

Let us look at part of the Employee table:

```
CREATE TABLE Employee
(
empnr              NUMERIC (5),
name               CHARACTER (40) NOT NULL,
address            CHARACTER VARYING (200),
sex                CHARACTER NOT NULL,
job                job NOT NULL,
home_telno         telno,
deptcd             CHARACTER (3),
work_telno         telno UNIQUE,
salary             NUMERIC (6) NOT NULL,
...
CHECK (sex IN ('M','F')),
PRIMARY KEY (empnr)
)
```

Here we can see several mechanisms at work. First, on the name, sex, job and salary columns we have NOT NULL specified. This means that every row in the table must contain a value in these columns, i.e. we cannot register a person as being employed by the company unless we know their name, sex, what they are going to do and how much we are going to pay them to do it. We are not so concerned with values for address and home telephone number, for example; these latter columns may or may not contain actual values. Columns without actual values are said to be null, a kind of state rather than a value. This constraint is not really a *domain constraint* as it does not constrain the values that are legal in a column, only the fact that some value is required. We have included it here for completeness and because the concept of null, or not null, is important for some of the other constraints discussed later.

Real domain constraints are defined with a CHECK clause. This check clause can be specified for a column or can form part of a domain definition. An example of the first case can be seen with the sex column. Here the table definition contains '`CHECK (sex IN ('M','F'))`', which ensures that the values in the sex column are either the character 'M' or the character 'F'. Other values that would have been permissible with just the implicit data type constraints of CHARACTER, such as 'H' (hermaphrodite), are now impossible. The CHECK clause may contain any predicate or search condition with only minor restrictions. No set functions may be used except in subqueries (they would have no meaning in the context of controlling the values of a column) and nor may constructs that might vary over time, such as the functions that return the date and time or key words such as USER. This is necessary since otherwise a database that was integer on day 1 might cease to be integer on day 2 or might be integer for user A but not for user B, without in either case any changes being made. Thus it is possible to set up tables that hold the legal values for the domain and reference this table in the CHECK clause (this is similar to a foreign key constraint).

The preferred method of defining domain constraints using the CHECK clause is with the CREATE DOMAIN statement. In our example schema we have:

```
CREATE DOMAIN telno AS CHARACTER (14)
    CHECK (     VALUE LIKE '+%(_)%-%-%'
            OR VALUE LIKE '+%-%-%-%'
            OR VALUE LIKE '%-%'
            OR VALUE LIKE '___')
```

The definition of a domain 'telno' we have used in the column definitions for home_telno and work_telno has the advantage that the definition of the data type, check clause and any aspects of the domain need only be made once and all columns defined with this domain will have a guaranteed consistent definition. The domain constraint that we have defined requires that any column using this domain must contain values such as '+31-20-659-7751', '+31(0)20-659-7751' or ones with a similar form (i.e. with the exception of special numbers like 100, 999, it makes an attempt to ensure the accepted international form of the number). We also have the domain 'job' which is used in the definition of the 'job' column and that looks like:

```
CREATE DOMAIN job AS CHARACTER (20)
    CHECK (VALUE IN (SELECT * FROM Valid_Jobs))
```

This defines the permissible values by reference to another table.

22.3 Entity Integrity

Entity integrity is concerned with the ability to uniquely identify a row in a table. We can see the use of entity integrity in the Dept table:

```
CREATE TABLE Dept
(
deptcd      CHARACTER (3) PRIMARY KEY,
deptnm      CHARACTER (12)
)
```

Here every row in the department table must have a 'deptcd' and that 'deptcd' must be different from the 'deptcd' of any other row in the table. Thus if we know a 'deptcd' we can uniquely identify the row in the Dept table that describes the department where it exists. If a row does not exist then we *know* that the department does not exist or is not described in our database. There is no possibility that another row might describe it.

The PRIMARY KEY clause is equivalent to the combination of a NOT NULL constraint and a UNIQUE constraint on the column identified as the primary key, and of course vice versa. In its simplest form the key words PRIMARY KEY are used as a column constraint. Naturally this is only possible if the primary key is a single column.

If the primary key consists of more than one column as in the Travel_Req table:

```
CREATE TABLE Travel_Req
(
empnr                   NUMERIC (5),
request_date            DATE,
destination             CHARACTER (40),
travel_date             DATE,
stay                    NUMERIC (2),
PRIMARY KEY (empnr, request_date),
)
```

we can use the key words, PRIMARY KEY, with a column list as a separate clause within the table definition. As for a single column, the same effect can be achieved with NOT NULL and UNIQUE constraints, i.e.:

```
CREATE TABLE Travel_Req
(
empnr                NUMERIC (5) NOT NULL,
request_date         DATE NOT NULL,
destination          CHARACTER (40),
travel_date          DATE NOT NULL,
stay                 NUMERIC (2),
UNIQUE (empnr, request_date),
)
```

but the intention of the constraints is no longer clear. This latter form must be used if there is more than one 'candidate key' for a table and we wish to control all of them. Since PRIMARY KEY may be specified only once per table it can be used to control only one of the candidate keys. An example of a non-primary candidate key can be seen in the Itinerary table elsewhere in this chapter.

22.4 Referential Integrity

Referential integrity is concerned with the relationships between values in two tables. It is supported by either the column constraint REFERENCES or the table constraint FOREIGN KEY. A referential constraint requires that the values contained in a column or a list of columns (called the referencing columns) be the same as the values of a corresponding set of columns (called the referenced columns) in another table if none of the referencing columns are null.

There are several examples of referential integrity constraints in our example schema. One of the most common examples is the relationship between an employee and a department in a company which we define as:

```
CREATE TABLE Dept
(
deptcd          CHARACTER (3) PRIMARY KEY,
deptnm          CHARACTER (12)
)

CREATE TABLE Employee
(
empnr           NUMERIC (5),
name            CHARACTER (40) NOT NULL,
address         CHARACTER VARYING (200),
sex             CHARACTER NOT NULL,
home_telno      telno,
deptcd          CHARACTER (3),
work_telno      telno UNIQUE,
salary          NUMERIC (6) NOT NULL,
commission      NUMERIC (6,2),
vehicleid       CHARACTER (7),
constituency    CHARACTER (4),
CHECK (sex IN ('M','F')),
PRIMARY KEY (empnr),
UNIQUE (vehicleid),
FOREIGN KEY (empnr) REFERENCES Emp_Ext,
FOREIGN KEY (deptcd) REFERENCES Dept,
FOREIGN KEY (vehicleid) REFERENCES Vehicle,
FOREIGN KEY (constituency) REFERENCES Constituency
)
```

The *italicized text* shows the foreign key clause which enforces the referential constraint that all values in the column deptcd in the Employee table must correspond to values of the deptcd column in the Dept table. This is the simplest possible constraint, but the constraint may also cover a set of columns, as in the foreign key of the Itinerary table which relates to the primary key of the Travel_Req table:

```
CREATE TABLE Travel_Req
(
empnr           NUMERIC (5),
request_date    DATE,
destination     CHARACTER (40),
stay            NUMERIC (2),
PRIMARY KEY (empnr, request_date),
FOREIGN KEY (empnr) REFERENCES Employee
)
```

```
CREATE TABLE Itinerary
(
itinerary_no    NUMERIC (5),
empnr           NUMERIC (5) NOT NULL,
request_date    DATE NOT NULL,
travel_agent_id CHARACTER (10),
flight_no_out   CHARACTER (6) NOT NULL,
hotel           CHARACTER (40),
flight_no_back  CHARACTER (6) NOT NULL,
PRIMARY KEY (itinerary_no),
UNIQUE (empnr, request_date),
FOREIGN KEY (empnr,request_date) REFERENCES Travel_Req,
FOREIGN KEY (travel_agent_id) REFERENCES Travel_Agent
)
```

Both of these examples use a primary key to define the referenced columns, but this is not a requirement. The only requirement for the referenced columns is that they be the subject of a UNIQUE constraint. In the Employee table the column work_telno would be a possible target for a referential constraint and we could define a table, to identify contact points into the company, that makes use of that, e.g.:

```
CREATE TABLE Contact_Point
(
contact_point  CHARACTER (15) PRIMARY KEY,
telephone_no   telno,
FOREIGN KEY (telephone_no) REFERENCES Employee (work_telno)
)
```

In this case we have had to specify the referenced column explicitly; in the previous cases it was implicitly the columns of the primary key.

22.4.1 The MATCH Option

In cases where the foreign key consists of more than one column the default situation is such that the constraint is satisfied if any of the columns in the foreign key is null. It may well be that we do not wish to permit such partially null foreign keys to exist and some experts, e.g. E.F. Codd and C.J. Date, would prefer not to do so. SQL as now specified allows you the choice. If you wish to follow Codd's advice, you will always specify the MATCH FULL option on any multi-column foreign key constraints. Our example database contains only one multi-column foreign key constraint and that is in the Itinerary table. We could attach the option as shown below:

```
CREATE TABLE Itinerary
(
itinerary_no     NUMERIC (5),
empnr            NUMERIC (5) NOT NULL,
request_date     DATE NOT NULL,
travel_agent_id  CHARACTER (10),
flight_no_out    CHARACTER (6) NOT NULL,
hotel            CHARACTER (40),
flight_no_back   CHARACTER (6) NOT NULL,
PRIMARY KEY (itinerary_no),
UNIQUE (empnr, request_date),
FOREIGN KEY (empnr,request_date) REFERENCES Travel_Req
   MATCH FULL
)
```

In fact in this case it is redundant because both columns, empnr and request_date, are defined as NOT NULL but the syntax is still valid.

Where we do want to allow partially null foreign keys, but also want to ensure that there is always a value that can be substituted for each remaining null such that a match will be possible, we can then specify MATCH PARTIAL instead of MATCH FULL. This ensures that there is always a 'candidate' row in the referenced table that could be used.

22.5 User Integrity

User integrity is concerned with all the other forms of integrity constraint that a user may require but which are not covered by the other three. It is supported by the CHECK clause, the UNIQUE constraint and the ASSERTION statement. The most common user integrity constraint is the UNIQUE clause. The unique constraint is implicit in primary key constraints or may be used in combination with NOT NULL constraints to form a candidate key constraint. These aspects were discussed above (*see Section 22.3 Entity Integrity*).

UNIQUE may also be used independently, as in the column definition for work_telno in the Employee table. This clause ensures that no two values in the column are identical, i.e. no two employees have the same work telephone number. This does not prevent a value or several values from being null since null is not strictly a value but a state and one null is not generally considered as being equal to another. This definition allows one or more employees to exist without the benefit of modern communications facilities, a situation that will certainly be attractive to some!

Another possible case where we might have wanted to use a UNIQUE constraint on a non-key column would be if we had included a column 'driving_licence_no' in the Employee table. Some employees may not be in possession of a licence so the column must allow for nulls, but the regulatory authorities usually ensure that one person's licence does not have the same number as another's. To reflect this situation we can, and probably should, define the column with the UNIQUE constraint, thereby ensuring that detectable errors do not creep into our database.

Another case of a user integrity constraint is the check clause. We have seen this clause several times before in these discussions in relation to the permissible values in a domain or column. The same clause may be used to implement constraints that have to do with the relationship between values in more than one column in a row or that relate to more than one table (excluding referential constraints) or control the cardinality of tables, etc. The range of possible constraints that may be implemented by this means is virtually endless. In fact, apart from the referential constraint, the standard defines all other constraints in terms of check constraints. Even there, the constraint aspects of the referential constraint definition can be simulated by a check clause, but the clause also permits certain associated actions that preclude use of the check clause in the internal definition (*see Section 22.8.2 Triggered Actions*).

We will look at the intra-row constraints now and discuss the other possibilities in the next topic. If we consider the Emp_Ext table:

```
CREATE TABLE Emp_Ext
(
empnr                NUMERIC (5),
date_of_birth        DATE NOT NULL,
date_of_joining      DATE NOT NULL,
previous_employer    CHARACTER (40),
p_e_address          CHARACTER VARYING (200),
CHECK (date_of_birth < date_of_joining),
PRIMARY KEY (empnr),
FOREIGN KEY (empnr) REFERENCES Employee
)
```

we can see that we have a check constraint, in *italicized text*, which ensures that no one is recorded as employed before they are born. A more reasonable constraint might have been:

```
CHECK (date_of_birth + INTERVAL '15' YEAR < date_of_joining)
```

which would prevent the record showing employment of people who should still be at school.

User integrity checks frequently range over more than one table and although it does not matter to which table the constraint is attached it makes the schema difficult to read and check. In these cases a better alternative is the ASSERTION statement which is a self-standing constraint, independent of the table definition. We can see this in the Information Schema, where the following assertion is defined:

```
CREATE ASSERTION EQUAL_KEY_DEGREES
  CHECK (NOT EXISTS (
    SELECT *
      FROM (SELECT COUNT (DISTINCT FK.COLUMN_NAME),
                   COUNT (DISTINCT PK.COLUMN_NAME)
              FROM KEY_COLUMN_USAGE AS FK,
                   REFERENTIAL_CONSTRAINTS AS RF,
                   KEY_COLUMN_USAGE AS PK
              WHERE
                  (FK.CONSTRAINT_CATALOG,
                   FK.CONSTRAINT_SCHEMA,
                   FK.CONSTRAINT_NAME)
                  =
                  (RF.CONSTRAINT_CATALOG,
                   RF.CONSTRAINT_SCHEMA,
                   RF.CONSTRAINT_NAME)
               AND
                  (PK.CONSTRAINT_CATALOG,
                   PK.CONSTRAINT_SCHEMA,
                   PK.CONSTRAINT_NAME)
                  =
                  (RF.UNIQUE_CONSTRAINT_CATALOG,
                   RF.UNIQUE_CONSTRAINT_SCHEMA,
                   RF.UNIQUE_CONSTRAINT_NAME)
               GROUP BY
              RF.CONSTRAINT_CATALOG, RF.CONSTRAINT_SCHEMA,
              RF.CONSTRAINT_NAME
          ) AS REF (FK_DEGREE, PK_DEGREE)
     WHERE FK_DEGREE <> PK_DEGREE))
```

This assertion checks the number of columns in a foreign key constraint against the number of keys in the corresponding unique constraint to ensure that there are the same number. This could have been done in any of the three tables involved, but it is more obvious and easier to maintain as a separate entity.

The facilities provided in SQL are such that virtually any static constraint can be defined, although for performance reasons many are likely to remain as documentation or as part of the specification for update programs. This latter use is not to be underestimated as the SQL constraint is much more formal and unambiguous than any natural language text and its use in specifications can significantly reduce misunderstandings and consequent errors.

We will consider one last example of a user-defined integrity check before we move on to look at the implementation of relationships. You will find a column called minimum_order in the Product_Supply table, but there is no check in the Order_Line table that the ordered quantity is greater than or equal to the specified minimum. If we wished to add such a constraint then the following addition to the Order_Line table would suffice:

```
CHECK (quantity >=
         (SELECT minimum_order
            FROM Product_Supply PS
            WHERE PS.product_code = Order_Line.product_code
                  AND
                  PS.suppliernr =
                     (SELECT suppliernr
                         FROM Order
                         WHERE Order.ordernr
                              = Order_Line.ordernr)))
```

22.6 The Implementation of Relationships — Examples

We want to discuss in this section the various kinds of relationships that can exist between entities and how we can express these relationships in terms of SQL integrity constraints. First, what are the characteristics of a relationship? The first major way in which we can distinguish a relationship is by class. The class of the relationship is given by the number of entity types participating in the relationship. The most important of these is the binary class involving two different entity types. We will deal first with this class of relationship and then look at unary relationships. Other classes are not considered in this book.

The second way of classifying a relationship is by degree. We can identify three degrees of relationship, namely:

1 : 1
1 : N
M : N

Each relationship of a particular degree can have optionality on one or other side or on both sides. Thus, for binary relationships we can enumerate 12 differing kinds of relationship. These are:

1	to 1	
0 or 1	to 1	
1	to 0 or 1	
0 or 1	to 0 or 1	
1	to *n*	(*n* = 1 or more)
0 or 1	to *n*	(*n* = 1 or more)
1	to 0 or *n*	(*n* = 1 or more)
0 or 1	to 0 or *n*	(*n* = 1 or more)
m	to *n*	(*m* = 1 or more; *n* = 1 or more)
0 or *m*	to *n*	(*m* = 1 or more; *n* = 1 or more)
m	to 0 or *n*	(*m* = 1 or more; *n* = 1 or more)
0 or *m*	to 0 or *n*	(*m* = 1 or more; *n* = 1 or more)

Of these 12 there are two pairs that are duplicates if the left and right sides of one from each pair are reversed. Therefore we will ignore, in the following discussion, the two redundant duplicates (1 to 0 or 1 and *m* to 0 or *n*).

When 'more' is mentioned there are two sub-types possible, one where 'more' is unlimited and the other where 'more' is greater than 1 but less than some other higher number. We will deal first with the unlimited case and then show how this cardinality constraint can be applied.

In the examples given below we use the tables from our example schema 'Company' but in some cases not all the columns or constraints that belong to the table are shown, though all the columns and constraints relevant to the relationship under discussion are.

Italicized text shows, for each example, the actual clauses required to implement the relationship.

22.6.1 Binary 1 : 1

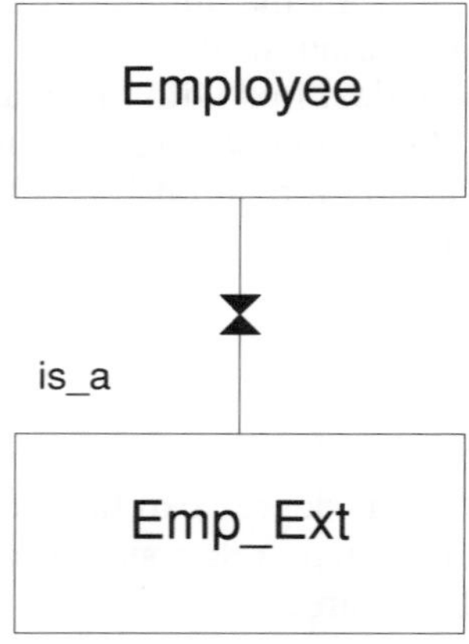

Figure 22.1 *Binary 1 : 1*

If there are two tables T1 and T2 this relationship says that for each row in T1 there is a single corresponding row in T2 and vice versa. In our example database there exists such a relationship between Employee and Emp_Ext (*see Figure 22.1*). This symmetric relationship is of very limited value in an SQL database where one would generally combine the two tables into one since both will normally have the same primary key. There may, however, be situations where for purely technical or performance reasons a single logical table is split into two or more physical tables. For example, a particular SQL implementation may not support more than X columns in any one table and if the analysis has identified a table with Y columns where Y > X then a construction such as the above may be required. Alternatively, it may be that several columns in a table are rarely referenced while the remainder are frequently referenced. In that case, in order to increase the performance to acceptable levels, the infrequently used columns can be hived off into a separate, extension, table. We will assume the latter case in our example and define the relationship between the Employee table and the Emp_Ext table by adding a pair of foreign key constraints which together with the primary keys define the relationship:

```
CREATE TABLE Employee
(
empnr               NUMERIC (5),
name                CHARACTER (40) NOT NULL,
address             CHARACTER VARYING (200),
sex                 CHARACTER NOT NULL,
home_telno          telno,
deptcd              CHARACTER (3),
work_telno          telno UNIQUE,
salary              NUMERIC (6) NOT NULL,
commission          NUMERIC (6,2),
vehicleid           CHARACTER (7),
constituency        CHARACTER (4),
CHECK (sex IN ('M','F')),
PRIMARY KEY (empnr),
FOREIGN KEY (empnr) REFERENCES Emp_Ext
)

CREATE TABLE Emp_Ext
(
empnr                  NUMERIC (5),
date_of_birth          DATE NOT NULL,
date_of_joining        DATE NOT NULL,
previous_employer      CHARACTER (40),
p_e_address            CHARACTER VARYING (200),
CHECK (date_of_birth < date_of_joining),
PRIMARY KEY (empnr),
FOREIGN KEY (empnr) REFERENCES Employee
)
```

22.6.2 Binary 0 or 1 : 1

If there are two tables T1 and T2 this relationship says that for each row in T1 there may or may not be a single corresponding row in T2 but there is never more than one corresponding row in T2, while for every row in T2 there must be a single corresponding row in T1. In our example database there exists such a relationship between Travel_Req and Itinerary (*see Figure 22.2*). Here each itinerary is related to one and only one travel requisition (Travel_Req) but, of course, not every travel requisition is approved, so in these cases there is no related itinerary.

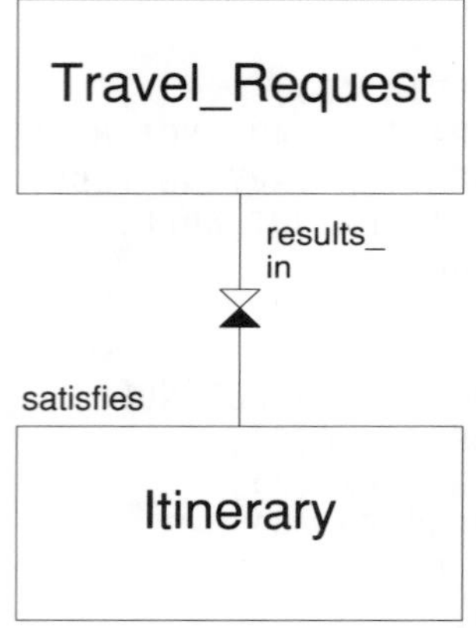

Figure 22.2 *Binary 0 or 1 : 1*

This relationship is very much akin to the generalization/specialization concept that forms a basic part of object-oriented databases. It could be said that Itinerary *is a* travel requisition that has been approved and implemented. Direct support for this concept is currently defined in the SQL3 working draft. The relationship is implemented in current standard SQL by means of a FOREIGN KEY and NOT NULL and UNIQUE constraints defined in the 'sub-table', in our example — the itinerary table. The NOT NULL UNIQUE combination defines a 'candidate key', i.e. one of a number of possible primary keys but not in this case the chosen one. We may only choose one candidate key as the primary key:

```
CREATE TABLE Travel_Req
(
empnr               NUMERIC (5),
request_date        DATE,
destination         CHARACTER (40),
stay                NUMERIC (2),
PRIMARY KEY (empnr, request_date),
)

CREATE TABLE Itinerary
(
itinerary_no        NUMERIC (5),
empnr               NUMERIC (5) NOT NULL,
request_date        DATE NOT NULL,
travel_agent_id     CHARACTER (10),
flight_no_out       CHARACTER (6) NOT NULL,
hotel               CHARACTER (40),
flight_no_back      CHARACTER (6) NOT NULL,
PRIMARY KEY (itinerary_no),
UNIQUE (empnr, request_date),
FOREIGN KEY (empnr,request_date) REFERENCES Travel_Req
)
```

Here we have defined a separate primary key, itinerary_no, for the Itinerary table. If we had not done so then the primary key would have been (empnr, request_date) and the two additional NOT NULL constraints and the UNIQUE constraint would have been subsumed by the primary key clause.

22.6.3 Binary 0 or 1 : 0 or 1

If there are two tables T1 and T2 this relationship says that for each row in T1 there may or may not be a single corresponding row in T2 but that there is never more than one corresponding row in T2 and vice versa. In our example database there exists such a relationship between Employee and Vehicle (*see Figure 22.3*). Here a vehicle, owned by the company, may or may not be assigned to an employee (e.g. a company car). Similarly, not every employee is assigned a company car. Thus we have the situation where a relationship may or may not exist between two occurrences but such a relationship can only exist between one employee and one vehicle, i.e. no employee is assigned more than one company car. The relationship is implemented with symmetrical pairs of CHECK constraints containing a MATCH predicate:

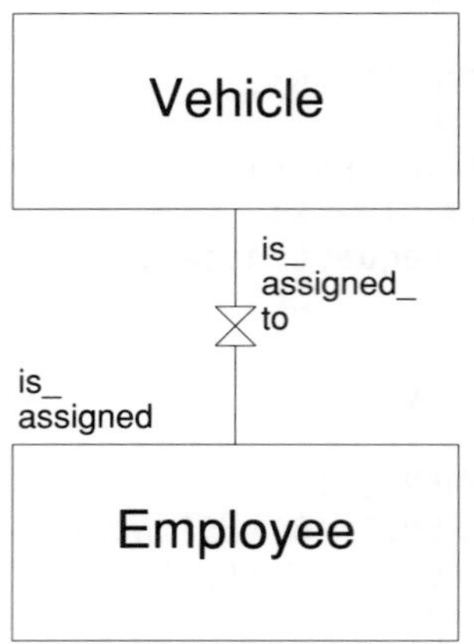

Figure 22.3 *Binary 0 or 1 : 0 or 1*

```
CREATE TABLE Employee
(
empnr                NUMERIC (5),
name                 CHARACTER (40) NOT NULL,
...
vehicleid            CHARACTER (7),
constituency         CHARACTER (4),
...
PRIMARY KEY (empnr),
CHECK ((vehicleid, empnr) MATCH
    (SELECT vehicleid, empnr FROM Vehicle))
)

CREATE TABLE Vehicle
(
vehicleid            NUMERIC (5),
empnr                NUMERIC (5),
acquisition_date     DATE NOT NULL,
PRIMARY KEY (vehicleid),
CHECK ((empnr, vehicleid) MATCH
    (SELECT empnr, vehicleid FROM Employee))
)
```

It would have been possible to define the relationship using a symmetrical pair of FOREIGN KEY constraints (' `FOREIGN KEY (vehicleid, empnr) REFERENCES Vehicle` ' and ' `FOREIGN KEY (empnr, vehicleid) REFERENCES Employee` ') between the two tables if we also defined the pair of redundant UNIQUE constraints (' `UNIQUE (vehicleid, empnr)` ' and ' `UNIQUE (empnr, vehicleid)` ') which are necessary to support the FOREIGN KEYs. Remember that UNIQUE does not imply or require a NOT NULL constraint. The presence of such a NOT NULL constraint would remove the optionality that we desire. We think, however, that the definition of redundant UNIQUE constraints is a bad practice and have thus chosen the solution using the MATCH predicate.

22.6.4 Binary 1 : n

If there are two tables T1 and T2 this relationship says that for each row in T1 there is always exactly one corresponding row in T2 and for every row in T2 there is at least one corresponding row, and possibly more than one corresponding row in T1. In our example database there exists such a relationship between Order_Line and Order (*see Figure 22.4*). Here every order is required to have at least one order line; it may have many order lines but it may not exist without at least one. Conversely, every order line must belong to one and only one order. The relationship is implemented by a combination of a FOREIGN KEY constraint on a part of the PRIMARY KEY and a CHECK constraint which uses a subquery:

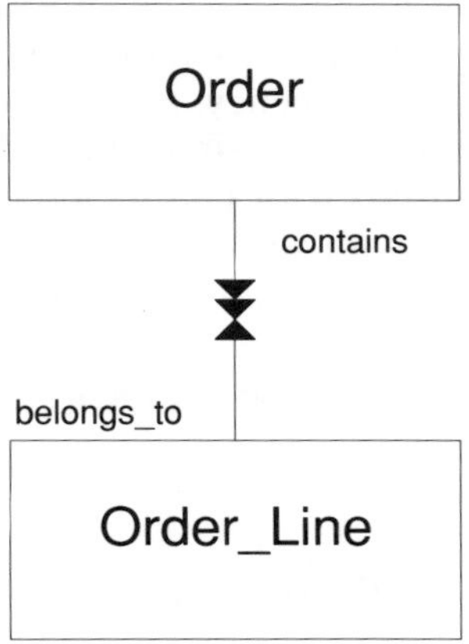

Figure 22.4 *Binary 1 : n*

```
CREATE TABLE Order
(
ordernr             NUMERIC (5),
suppliernr          NUMERIC (5) NOT NULL,
date_issued         DATE NOT NULL,
PRIMARY KEY (ordernr),
CHECK (ordernr IN
    (SELECT ordernr FROM Order_line))
)
```

```
CREATE TABLE Order_Line
(
ordernr             NUMERIC (5),
order_linenr        NUMERIC (5),
product_code        NUMERIC (5) NOT NULL,
quantity            NUMERIC (5) NOT NULL,
PRIMARY KEY (ordernr, order_linenr),
FOREIGN KEY (ordernr) REFERENCES order
)
```

22.6.5 Binary 0 or 1 : n

If there are two tables T1 and T2 this relationship says that for each row in T1 there may or may not be a corresponding row in T2 but that if there is then there is exactly one such row and that for every row in T2 there is at least one corresponding row in T1. In our example database there exists such a relationship between Employee and Constituency (*see Figure 22.5*). In our fictitious company there is a workers representative council. In order to be able to conduct elections the employees are divided into constituencies. All employees belong to exactly one constituency, except for senior managers who are not eligible to vote and thus belong to no constituency. Furthermore, a constituency without voters is meaningless and thus not possible. From this it can be seen that every constituency has a relationship with one or more employees and that each employee has a relationship with zero or one constituencies. The example is somewhat contrived as the relationship is rare in practice and it is difficult to find good examples. It is included here for completeness and to show that there is indeed an SQL solution should it be required.

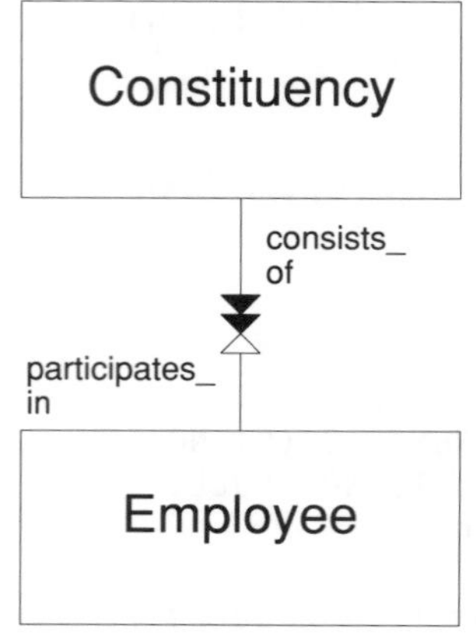

Figure 22.5 *Binary 0 or 1 : n*

The relationship is implemented by a FOREIGN KEY in the Employee table and a CHECK constraint in the Constituency table:

```
CREATE TABLE Employee
(
empnr           NUMERIC (5),
name            CHARACTER (40) NOT NULL,
...
constituency    CHARACTER (4),
...
PRIMARY KEY (empnr),
...
FOREIGN KEY (constituency) REFERENCES Constituency
)

CREATE TABLE Constituency
(
constituency    CHARACTER (4),
representative NUMERIC (5),
PRIMARY KEY (constituency),
FOREIGN KEY (representative) REFERENCES Employee,
CHECK (constituency IN (SELECT constituency FROM employee))
)
```

22.6.6 Binary 1 : 0 or n

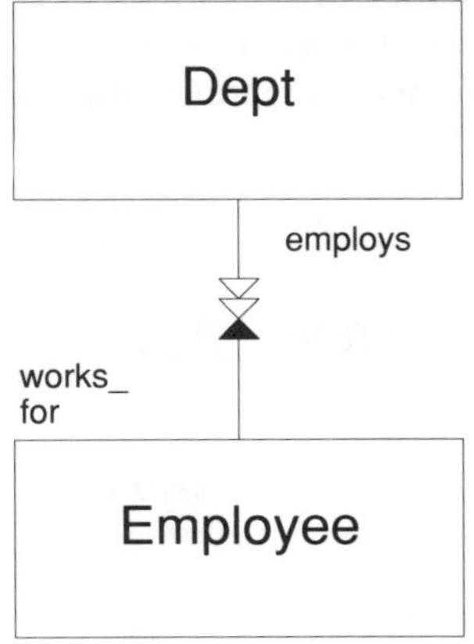

Figure 22.6 *Binary 1 : 0 or n*

If there are two tables T1 and T2 this relationship says that for each row in T1 there are zero or more corresponding rows in T2 but for every row in T2 there is one and only one corresponding row in T1. For example in our example database there exists such a relationship between Employee and Dept (*see Figure 22.6*). Here each department may have zero, one or more employees but each employee must work for one and only one department. This relationship is implemented by a NOT NULL constraint and a FOREIGN KEY in the Employee table:

```
CREATE TABLE Employee
(
empnr      NUMERIC (5),
name       CHARACTER (40) NOT NULL,
...
deptcd     CHARACTER (3) NOT NULL,
...
PRIMARY KEY (empnr),
...
FOREIGN KEY (deptcd) REFERENCES dept
)

CREATE TABLE Dept
(
deptcd     CHARACTER (3) PRIMARY KEY,
deptnm     CHARACTER (12)
)
```

22.6.7 Binary 0 or 1 : 0 or n

If there are two tables T1 and T2 this relationship says that for each row in T1 there is at most one corresponding row in T2 and that for each row in T2 there are zero or more corresponding rows in T1. In our example database there exists such a relationship between Itinerary and Travel_Agent (*see Figure 22.7*). An itinerary for a travel request may be arranged by a travel agent

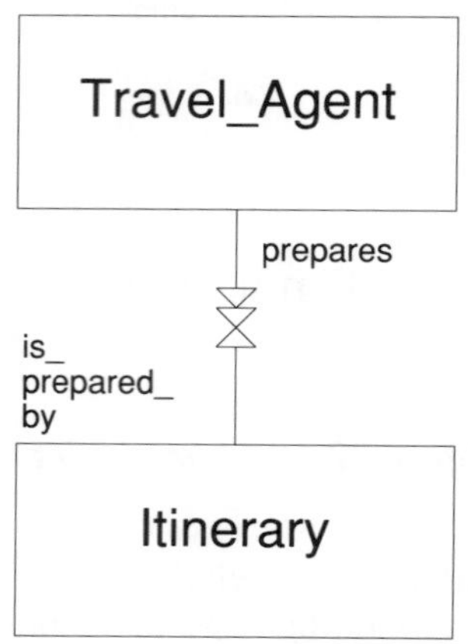

Figure 22.7 *Binary 0 or 1 : 0 or n*

or it may be arranged internally by the company itself. In the former case the itinerary is related to the single travel agent who makes the arrangements and in the latter case there is, of course, no relationship. A travel agent may arrange several itineraries. The relationship is implemented by a simple FOREIGN KEY in the itinerary table:

```
CREATE TABLE Itinerary
(
itinerary_no     NUMERIC (5),
empnr            NUMERIC (5) NOT NULL,
request_date     DATE NOT NULL,
travel_agent_id  CHARACTER (10),
flight_no_out    CHARACTER (6) NOT NULL,
hotel            CHARACTER (40),
flight_no_back   CHARACTER (6) NOT NULL,
PRIMARY KEY (itinerary_no),
UNIQUE (empnr, request_date),
FOREIGN KEY (empnr, request_date)
  REFERENCES Travel_Req,
FOREIGN KEY (travel_agent_id)
  REFERENCES Travel_Agent
)

CREATE TABLE Travel_Agent
(
travel_agent_id  CHARACTER (10),
name             CHARACTER (40),
address          CHARACTER VARYING (200),
PRIMARY KEY (travel_agent_id)
)
```

Because there is no NOT NULL constraint on the travel_agent_id column in the Itinerary table the relationship remains optional on the Itinerary side.

22.6.8 Binary m : n

If there are two tables T1 and T2 this relationship says that for each row in T1 there is at least one corresponding row in T2 and vice versa. In our example database there exists such a relationship between Supplier and Product (*see Figure 22.8*). This kind of relationship is impossible to model directly in SQL as it would require the existence of columns whose values were themselves multi-values, i.e. non-atomic. This would make the tables of a non-first normal form which is a basic requirement for SQL. The other higher normal forms, though desirable, are not explicitly required by the SQL language.

To model this kind of relationship we need to generate a new table to represent the relationship itself. In our example, we have called this table Product_Supply. In principle the table need only contain columns to support the primary keys taken from the original tables, Product and Supplier. The combination of these two primary keys forms the primary key of our relationship table.

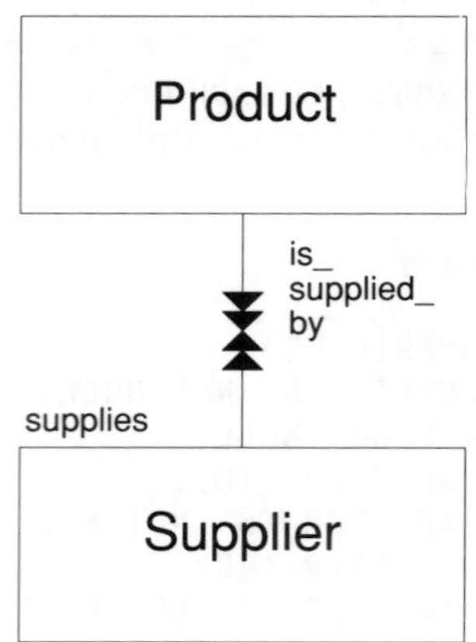

Figure 22.8 Binary *m* : *n*

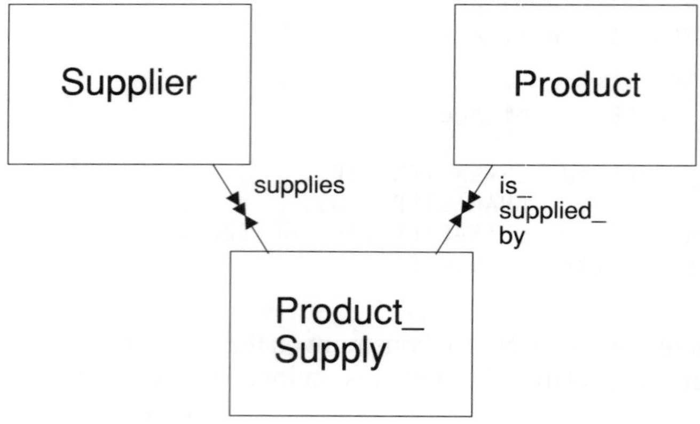

Figure 22.9 Implementation *m* : *n*

The relationship has been reformed such that it now appears as in Figure 22.9. This is identical to a pair of 1 : *n* relationships which can be seen in the example table definitions below:

```
CREATE TABLE Product
(
product_code  NUMERIC (5),
name          CHARACTER (20) NOT NULL,
PRIMARY KEY (product_code),
CHECK (product_code IN
    (SELECT product_code
        FROM Product_Supply))
)
```

```
CREATE TABLE Supplier
(
suppliernr     NUMERIC (5),
name           CHARACTER (20) NOT NULL,
address        CHARACTER VARYING (200),
PRIMARY KEY (suppliernr),
CHECK (suppliernr IN
    (SELECT suppliernr
       FROM Product_Supply))
)

CREATE TABLE Product_Supply
(
product_code  NUMERIC (5),
suppliernr    NUMERIC (5),
minimum_order NUMERIC (10),
PRIMARY KEY (product_code, suppliernr),
FOREIGN KEY (product_code) REFERENCES Product,
FOREIGN KEY (suppliernr) REFERENCES Supplier
)
```

However, we have added an extra column 'minimum_order' to represent additional information that might be identified on the relationship itself. It is frequently the case with many-to-many relationships that further study will reveal additional data that can be captured in this extra table. The presence or absence of such additional data is, however, not of importance with regard to our ability to represent the relationship in SQL.

22.6.9 Binary 0 or m : n

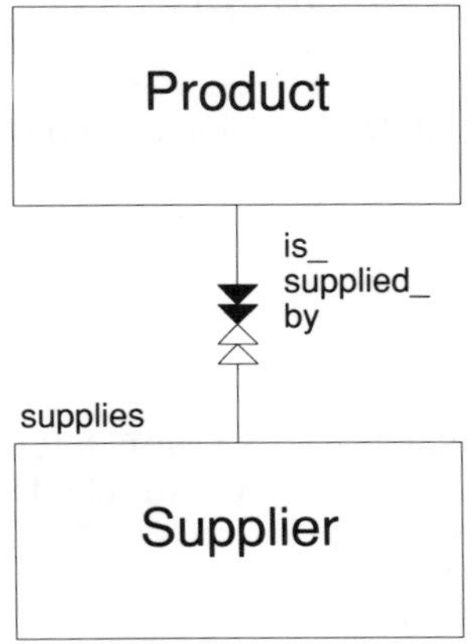

Figure 22.10 *Binary 0 or m : n*

If there are two tables T1 and T2 this relationship says that for each row in T1 there is at least one corresponding row in T2 while a row in T2 may or may not have corresponding rows in T1. No such relationship exists in our example database so we will consider a variation of the relationship between Supplier and Product (*see Figure 22.10*). This kind of relationship is impossible to model directly in SQL for the same reasons as were given for the *m* : *n* case, but we can reform it in a similar way (*see Figure 22.11*). This is identical to a 1 : 0 to *n* relationship and a 1 : *n* relationship. The appropriate example table definitions can be seen below:

```
CREATE TABLE Product
(
product_code    NUMERIC (5),
name            CHARACTER (20) NOT NULL,
PRIMARY KEY (product_code),
)
```

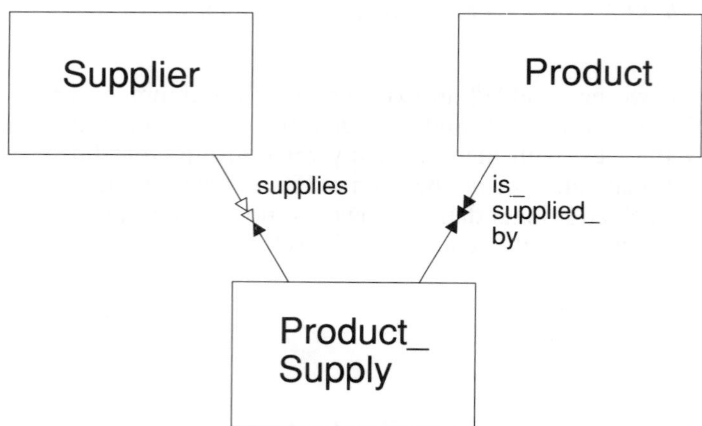

Figure 22.11 *Implementation 0 or m : n*

```
CREATE TABLE Supplier
(
suppliernr      NUMERIC (5),
name            CHARACTER (20) NOT NULL,
address         CHARACTER VARYING (200),
PRIMARY KEY (suppliernr),
CHECK (suppliernr IN
    (SELECT suppliernr
        FROM Product_Supply))
)
```

```
CREATE TABLE Product_Supply
(
product_code     NUMERIC (5),
suppliernr       NUMERIC (5),
minimum_order    NUMERIC (10),
PRIMARY KEY (product_code, suppliernr),
FOREIGN KEY (product_code) REFERENCES Product,
FOREIGN KEY (suppliernr) REFERENCES Supplier
)
```

22.6.10 Binary 0 or m : 0 or n

If there are two tables T1 and T2 this relationship says that for each row in T1 there may or may not be a corresponding row in T2 and vice versa. No such relationship exists in our example database so we will consider a variation of the relationship between Supplier and Product (*see Figure 22.12*). This kind of relationship is impossible to model directly in SQL for the same reasons given in the *m* : *n* case. We can reform it in a similar manner (*see Figure 22.13*). We can see that this is identical to a pair of 1 : 0 to *n* relationships. The appropriate example table definitions can be seen below:

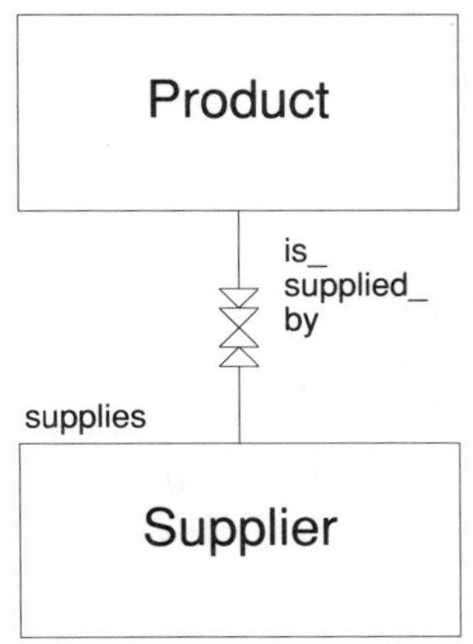

Figure 22.12 *Binary 0 or m : 0 or n*

```
CREATE TABLE Product
(
product_code     NUMERIC (5),
name             CHARACTER (20) NOT NULL,
PRIMARY KEY (product_code),
)
```

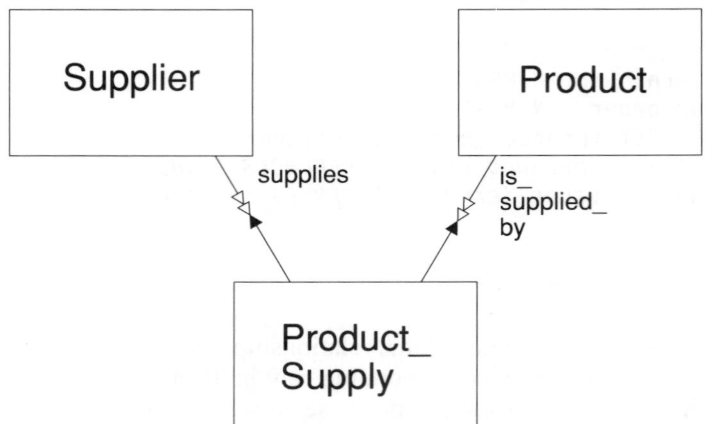

Figure 22.13 *Implementation 0 or m : 0 or n*

```
CREATE TABLE Supplier
(
suppliernr      NUMERIC (5),
name            CHARACTER (20) NOT NULL,
address         CHARACTER VARYING (200),
PRIMARY KEY (suppliernr),
)

CREATE TABLE Product_Supply
(
product_code    NUMERIC (5),
suppliernr      NUMERIC (5),
minimum_order   NUMERIC (10),
PRIMARY KEY (product_code, suppliernr),
FOREIGN KEY (product_code) REFERENCES Product,
FOREIGN KEY (suppliernr) REFERENCES Supplier
)
```

22.6.11 Additional Cardinality Constraints

In all of the above examples we have assumed that *n* or *m* can be any number from 1 to infinity. In many cases that is not true. If we assume that our Order and Order_Line tables represent some actual physical form which is filled in and sent to the supplier, then that form will have only a limited number of possible 'lines' that may be completed. Fortunately, the CHECK constraint allows us not only to check for values but also to check the number of rows in a table that meet certain criteria. For instance, if there was a rule that an order might not have more than 10 order items we would have to introduce the additional check constraint into the Order table as follows:

```
CHECK (10 >= (SELECT COUNT(*)
              FROM Order_Line
              WHERE Order.ordernr = Order_Line.ordernr))
```

22.6.12 Unary Relationships

A unary relationship is a relationship between an entity type and itself. In principle all and any of the 10 kinds of relationships we have just discussed for binary relationships could be devised for unary ones by simply using the same entity on both sides of the relationship. In practice it is hard to find sensible examples of many of the possible unary relationships, but in the example schema we have provided two kinds to give the general idea. Both of these are related to the Employee entity and have been implemented in the Emp_Ext table.

The first is a unary 0 or 1 : 0 or 1 relationship called marriage. For some reason the company wishes to know which of its employees are married to other employees. The table elements that support the relationship are shown in *italicized text* in the following table definition:

```
CREATE TABLE Emp_Ext
(
empnr                NUMERIC (5),
date_of_birth        DATE NOT NULL,
date_of_joining      DATE NOT NULL,
spouse               NUMERIC (5),
manager              NUMERIC (5),
previous_employer    CHARACTER (40),
p_e_address          CHARACTER VARYING (200),
CHECK (date_of_birth < date_of_joining),
PRIMARY KEY (empnr),
CHECK ((empnr, spouse) MATCH (SELECT spouse,
        empnr FROM Emp_Ext)),
FOREIGN KEY (empnr) REFERENCES Employee,
FOREIGN KEY (manager) REFERENCES Emp_Ext
)
```

If we compare this to the binary example we can see that the binary example needed two CHECK clauses, one in each table, but here the two CHECK clauses are identical and would occur in the same table so only one is needed.

The second example is a unary 0 or 1 : 0 or *n* relationship which represents the management hierarchy in the company. The table elements that support the relationship are again shown in *italicized text* in the following table definition:

```
CREATE TABLE Emp_Ext
(
empnr                NUMERIC (5),
date_of_birth        DATE NOT NULL,
date_of_joining      DATE NOT NULL,
spouse               NUMERIC (5),
manager              NUMERIC (5),
previous_employer    CHARACTER (40),
p_e_address          CHARACTER VARYING (200),
CHECK (date_of_birth < date_of_joining),
PRIMARY KEY (empnr),
CHECK ((empnr, spouse) MATCH (SELECT spouse,
        empnr FROM Emp_Ext)),
FOREIGN KEY (empnr) REFERENCES Employee,
FOREIGN KEY (manager) REFERENCES Emp_Ext
)
```

If we compare this to the binary example we can see that it is virtually the same; the only difference is that the referenced table is the same table as the referencing table.

22.7 Combinations of Relationships

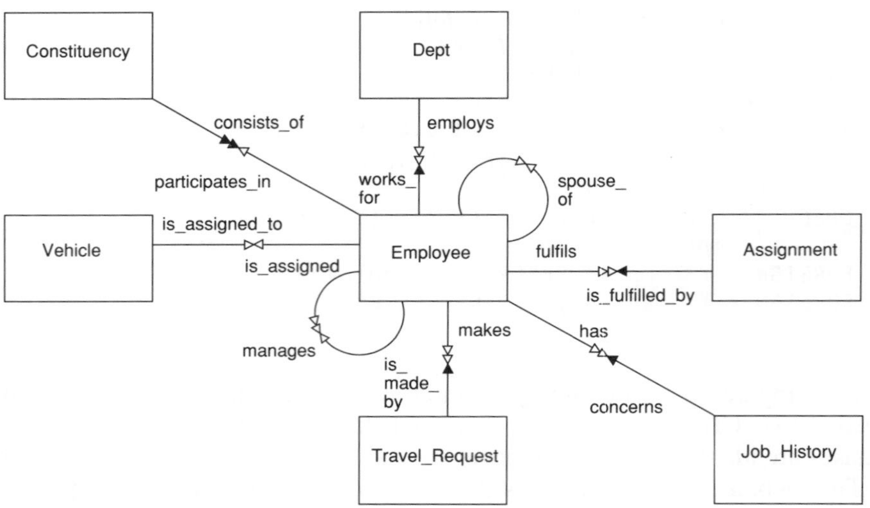

Figure 22.14 *Relationships for the Employee entity*

Relationships between entities may also have a relationship with each other. The normal situation for SQL is for relationships to be independent of each other. If we consider the relationships that Employee has (*see Figure 22.14*) it is obvious that the relationships between Employee and Vehicle are independent of the relationship with Travel_Request, Job_History, Assignment, etc. Whether an employee is assigned a vehicle has nothing to do with having a specific job history or assignment. Even the required relationship with Dept can be considered independent of the others. This is not always the case and we will look at three types of relationships that a relationship may have with one or more other relationships.

22.7.1 Exclusivity

Exclusivity is the situation where a relationship potentially exists between an entity and two or more other entities but the entity may only be in one of the potential relationships at any one time. In other words, one relationship *excludes* the other relationships. We can see several examples of such exclusive relationships in the Information Schema. One obvious case is a column that may be defined in terms of a data type or in terms of a domain but not both.

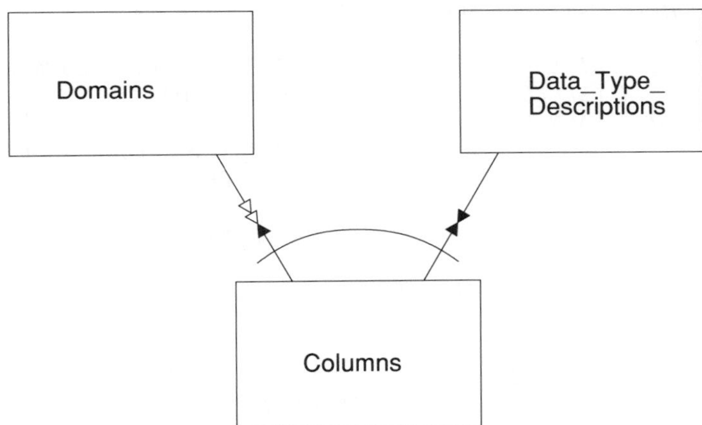

Figure 22.15 *Exclusive relationships*

In Figure 22.15 the exclusivity is shown as an arc crossing the relationships which are mutually exclusive. If we examine the table definition we can see how the exclusivity is achieved. The relevant elements that define the relationships and enforce the exclusivity are marked in *italicized text*:

```
CREATE TABLE COLUMNS
(
TABLE_CATALOG    INFORMATION_SCHEMA.SQL_IDENTIFIER,
TABLE_SCHEMA     INFORMATION_SCHEMA.SQL_IDENTIFIER,
TABLE_NAME       INFORMATION_SCHEMA.SQL_IDENTIFIER,
COLUMN_NAME      INFORMATION_SCHEMA.SQL_IDENTIFIER,
ORDINAL_POSITION INFORMATION_SCHEMA.CARDINAL_NUMBER
 CONSTRAINT COLUMN_POSITION_NOT_NULL NOT NULL,
DOMAIN_CATALOG   INFORMATION_SCHEMA.SQL_IDENTIFIER,
```

```
DOMAIN_SCHEMA      INFORMATION_SCHEMA.SQL_IDENTIFIER,
DOMAIN_NAME        INFORMATION_SCHEMA.SQL_IDENTIFIER,
COLUMN_DEFAULT     INFORMATION_SCHEMA.CHARACTER_DATA,
IS_NULLABLE        INFORMATION_SCHEMA.CHARACTER_DATA,
CONSTRAINT COLUMNS_PRIMARY_KEY
 PRIMARY KEY (TABLE_CATALOG, TABLE_SCHEMA, TABLE_NAME,
             COLUMN_NAME),
CONSTRAINT COLUMNS_UNIQUE
 UNIQUE (TABLE_CATALOG, TABLE_SCHEMA, TABLE_NAME,
         ORDINAL_POSITION),
CONSTRAINT COLUMNS_FOREIGN_KEY_TABLES
 FOREIGN KEY (TABLE_CATALOG, TABLE_SCHEMA, TABLE_NAME)
   REFERENCES TABLES,
CONSTRAINT COLUMNS_CHECK_REFERENCES_DOMAINS
 FOREIGN KEY (DOMAIN_CATALOG, DOMAIN_SCHEMA, DOMAIN_NAME)
   REFERENCES DOMAINS,
CONSTRAINT COLUMN_CHECK_DATA_TYPE
 CHECK (
   (DOMAIN_CATALOG, DOMAIN_SCHEMA, DOMAIN_NAME) IS NOT NULL
   AND
   (TABLE_CATALOG, TABLE_SCHEMA, TABLE_NAME, COLUMN_NAME)
    NOT IN (SELECT TABLE_OR_DOMAIN_CATALOG,
TABLE_OR_DOMAIN_SCHEMA,
                   TABLE_OR_DOMAIN_NAME, COLUMN_NAME
              FROM DATA_TYPE_DESCRIPTOR)
   OR
   (DOMAIN_CATALOG, DOMAIN_SCHEMA, DOMAIN_NAME) IS NULL
   AND
   (TABLE_CATALOG, TABLE_SCHEMA, TABLE_NAME, COLUMN_NAME)
    IN (SELECT TABLE_OR_DOMAIN_CATALOG,
TABLE_OR_DOMAIN_SCHEMA,
               TABLE_OR_DOMAIN_NAME, COLUMN_NAME
          FROM DATA_TYPE_DESCRIPTOR))
)
```

There are several ways of implementing exclusivity depending on the relationship types. In the above example one relationship is implemented by a foreign key and the other by an IN predicate. The second cannot be implemented as a foreign key because what would be the foreign key is also the primary key, which could never be optional. If all the exclusive relationships are implemented using foreign keys the exclusivity is simply a check that more than one foreign key is never entirely non-null.

A different technique, using a cardinality check for mutually exclusive one-to-one relationships, can be seen in the TABLE_CONSTRAINTS table which is also in the Information Schema (*see Section 20.1.2.11 TABLE_CONSTRAINTS*).

22.7.2 *Inclusivity*

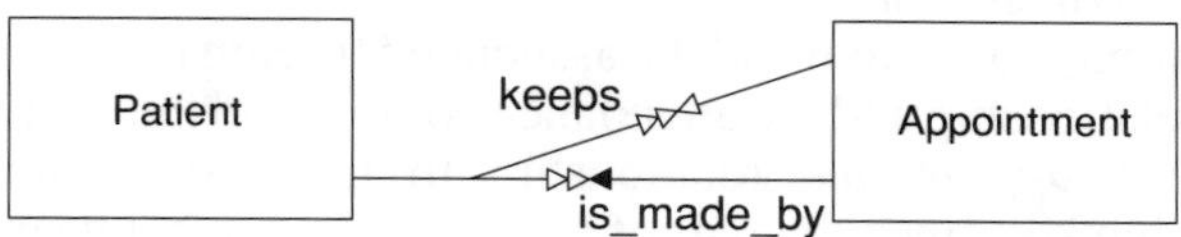

Figure 22.16 *Inclusive relationships*

Inclusivity is the situation where a relationship between one entity and another may exist only if another relationship exists between the entity and some other entity (the same or different from that of the first relationship). One example is that of a hospital out-patient who *makes* an appointment with a clinic (the first relationship) and then later *keeps* that appointment (the second inclusive relationship). The patient obviously cannot keep appointments that were never made.

In Figure 22.16 the inclusivity is shown by the fact that the line indicating the inclusive relationship terminates on the line of the other relationship and not on the box indicating the entity. If we examine the table definitions we can see how the inclusivity is achieved. The relevant elements that define the relationships and enforce the inclusivity are marked in *italicized text*:

```
CREATE TABLE Patient
(
registration_no  INTEGER,
name             CHARACTER(40),
address          CHARACTER VARYING (400),
PRIMARY KEY (registration_no)
)

CREATE TABLE Appointment
(
clinic           CHARACTER(20),
session_date     DATE,
session_time     TIME,
registration_no  INTEGER,
attendance       CHARACTER,
PRIMARY KEY (clinic, session_date, session_time),
FOREIGN KEY (registration_no) REFERENCES Patient,
CHECK (attendance IS NULL OR registration_no IS NOT NULL)
)
```

The CHECK clause in the table Appointment is derived from

```
CHECK (attendance IS NULL
   OR (registration_no IS NOT NULL AND
       attendance IS NOT NULL))
```

a form that clearly states the intention of the constraint, by means of a number of transformation rules, (R13), (R6) and (R1) which can be found in *Section 25.5.3 Boolean Transformation Rules*.

The registration_no column and the associated foreign key support the *makes appointment* relationship and the attendance column and the CHECK constraint support the *keeps appointment* relationship. In this case it is not necessary to repeat the foreign key since the pair of relationships are between the same two entities, namely the same patient for the same appointment. The style is similar to that of the exclusive relationship checks in that we look to see if the foreign key is filled or not, the difference being that in an exclusive relationship it may not be filled and in an inclusive relationship it must be filled.

22.7.3 Mutual Dependency

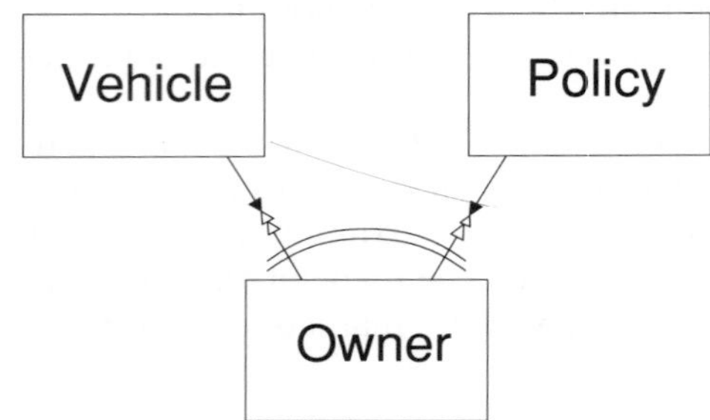

Figure 22.17 *Mutually dependent relationships*

Mutual dependency is the situation where two or more relationships must either all exist or none of them may exist. If we try to model the situation where the owner of a vehicle is required to have insurance cover and insurance companies will only insure vehicle owners, then assuming that everybody is not required to own a car we have a mutual dependency between the two relationships. The relationship is *mutual* because the existence of each relationship depends on the existence of the other. In Figure 22.17 the mutual dependency is shown as a pair of arcs crossing the relationships that are mutually dependent.

If we examine the table definitions we can see how the mutual dependency is achieved. The relevant elements that define the relationships and enforce the mutual dependency are marked in *italicized text*:

```
CREATE TABLE Vehicle
(
vehicle_id          INTEGER,
person_id           INTEGER NOT NULL,
acquisition_date    DATE NOT NULL,
...
PRIMARY KEY (vehicle_id),
FOREIGN KEY (person_id) REFERENCES Person
)
```

```
CREATE TABLE Policy
(
policy_no          INTEGER,
person_id          INTEGER NOT NULL,
premium            NUMERIC(6,2) NOT NULL,
...
PRIMARY KEY (policy_no),
FOREIGN KEY (person_id) REFERENCES Person
)

CREATE TABLE Person
(
person_id          INTEGER,
name               CHARACTER (40) NOT NULL,
...
PRIMARY KEY (person_id),
CHECK (
    (SELECT COUNT(*)
       FROM Policy
       WHERE Person.person_id = Policy.person_id)
    +
    (SELECT COUNT(*)
       FROM Vehicle
       WHERE Person.person_id = Vehicle.person_id) = 0
  OR
    ((SELECT COUNT(*)
        FROM Policy
        WHERE Person.person_id = Policy.person_id) > 0
      AND
     (SELECT COUNT(*)
        FROM Vehicle
        WHERE Person.person_id = Vehicle.person_id) > 0))
)
```

22.8 Management

22.8.1 Problems with Loops

With foreign keys and check clauses it is possible to generate cycles of constraints that make it impossible to insert new data into a database if the constraints are checked at the end of each SQL command. Of the relationships discussed in the preceding sections three inherently have this problem, the 1 : 1, the 1 : n and the n : m relationships, i.e. all those that do not have optionality on one side or the other. It is true that we define the transaction as the basic unit of success and are thus, in principle, not concerned if the database is not entirely consistent during the life of a transaction, only that it is guaranteed to be consistent at the end of the transaction. However, it is also normally useful to keep the database as consistent as possible at all times and the constraints are therefore by default checked after every command. As we have seen in Part II on

'The SQL Language', there is a <set constraints mode statement> available in SQL to control the time at which constraints are checked which permits the filling of otherwise unfillable databases (*see 13.5 SET CONSTRAINTS MODE*).

Therefore before storing an Employee, Emp_Ext, Order, Order_Line, Product, Supplier or Product_Supply we need to manipulate the constraints. Let us take, for example, the storing of an Order and an associated Order_Line. To store these rows we must first disable the check constraint in the Order table or the foreign key on ordernr in Order_Line. To do this we must name at least one of the constraints and in this case we have chosen the check in the Order table:

```
CREATE TABLE Order
(
ordernr        NUMERIC (5),
suppliernr     NUMERIC (5) NOT NULL,
date_issued    DATE NOT NULL,
PRIMARY KEY (ordernr),
CONSTRAINT Order_contains_at_least_one_order_line
  CHECK (ordernr IN (SELECT ordernr FROM Order_line))
)

CREATE TABLE Order_Line
(
ordernr        NUMERIC (5),
order_linenr   NUMERIC (5),
product_code   NUMERIC (5) NOT NULL,
quantity       NUMERIC (5) NOT NULL,
PRIMARY KEY (ordernr, order_linenr),
FOREIGN KEY (ordernr) REFERENCES order
)
```

Good practice would probably call for explicit labelling of all constraints, but the system will supply a name that can be used if necessary. In the example we have restricted ourselves to naming explicitly only one of the minimal set of constraints that must be manipulated in order to populate the database.

The correct sequence of operations to store the rows is thus:

```
SET CONSTRAINTS Order_contains_at_least_one_order_line
    DEFERRED
INSERT INTO Order VALUES (:ordernr, :suppliernr,
                          CURRENT_DATE)
INSERT INTO Order_Line VALUES (:ordernr, 1, :product,
                               :quantity)
SET CONSTRAINTS Order_contains_at_least_one_order_line
    IMMEDIATE
...
```

This defers the constraint for the minimum period possible. Once the first order line is stored the constraint can be reintroduced and any subsequent order lines inserted without problems.

22.8.2 Triggered Actions

As we have seen in Part II on 'The SQL Language', SQL has facilities geared to assist in the maintenance of integrity. These facilities are the 'referential triggered actions' which are only specifiable in <referential constraint definition>s (*see Section 4.2.2.2 References*).

These triggered actions allow us to specify certain consequent actions as part of the database definitions, thus freeing the programmer or direct user from having to take care of integrity maintenance. For instance, there is an implicit requirement in the relationship definitions that the deletion of an Employee row should always be accompanied by the deletion of the associated Emp_Ext row. To achieve that using data manipulation commands we have the same problem as with insertion. This can, of course, be solved as described in the preceding section (*see Section 22.8.1 Problems with Loops*), but triggered actions provide a much more elegant solution. We can extend the <referential constraint definition> of the Emp_Ext table to delete the Emp_Ext row automatically when the associated Employee row is deleted. This is shown in the following table definitions:

```
CREATE TABLE Employee
(
empnr          NUMERIC (5),
name           CHARACTER (40) NOT NULL,
address        CHARACTER VARYING (200),
...
PRIMARY KEY (empnr),
FOREIGN KEY (empnr) REFERENCES Emp_Ext
)

CREATE TABLE Emp_Ext
(
empnr          NUMERIC (5),
...
PRIMARY KEY (empnr),
FOREIGN KEY (empnr) REFERENCES Employee
    ON DELETE CASCADE
)
```

While it is always the case that deletion of a referenced row should lead to the deletion of the referencing rows in cases where the two tables are representing a single (possibly compound) object in the real world (as was the case above and in the case of Order and Order_Line), it is not always the case. Take, for example, the case of the Dept and Employee tables. It would be rather drastic for a company to appear to fire all employees just because a department closed — which would be the case if we added an ON DELETE CASCADE to the foreign key on 'deptcd' in the Employee table. A more likely scenario is that the employees are attached to a reserve department or the personnel department while awaiting reassignment. To achieve this we need to add the following phrase to the foreign key clause for deptcd in the employee table definition:

```
ON DELETE SET DEFAULT
```

If we wish to be able to change the department code and have that automatically reflected in the rows associated with employees who work in that department we can again add a phrase to the foreign key clause for deptcd in the Employee table definition:

```
ON UPDATE CASCADE
```

This would give us a table definition like the following:

```
CREATE TABLE Employee
(
empnr          NUMERIC (5),
name           CHARACTER (40) NOT NULL,
address        CHARACTER VARYING (200),
sex            CHARACTER NOT NULL,
home_telno     telno,
deptcd         CHARACTER (3) NOT NULL DEFAULT 'PER',
work_telno     telno UNIQUE,
job            job NOT NULL,
salary         NUMERIC (6) NOT NULL,
commission     NUMERIC (6,2),
vehicleid      CHARACTER (7),
constituency   CHARACTER (4),
CHECK (sex IN ('M','F')),
PRIMARY KEY (empnr),
CHECK ((vehicleid, empnr) MATCH
  (SELECT vehicleid, empnr FROM Vehicle)),
CONSTRAINT Employee_link_to_extension
  FOREIGN KEY (empnr) REFERENCES Emp_Ext,
FOREIGN KEY (deptcd) REFERENCES Dept
    ON DELETE SET DEFAULT
    ON UPDATE CASCADE,
FOREIGN KEY (constituency) REFERENCES Constituency
)
```

23

Using the Datetime Facilities

In Part II of this book we have described the datetime data types and some examples of their use in column definition. In this chapter we will look not so much at what facilities are available but at how certain aspects of the real world that are concerned with dates and times may be modelled in SQL databases. We will quickly review the facilities available and then discuss the concept of time, the various kinds of time-related constructions and how these can be represented in SQL. For further study of this topic we recommend Snodgrass and Ahn, 1985, Snodgrass, 1989 and Sarda, 1990 as good starting points.

23.1 Basic Facilities

The basic special facilities that SQL offers in the area of date and time, over and above the normal facilities that also apply to date and time, are as follows:

three datetime data types
    DATE, TIME and TIMESTAMP
one interval data type
    INTERVAL
four date time value functions
    CURRENT_DATE, CURRENT_TIME, CURRENT_TIMESTAMP,
        EXTRACT
one predicate
    OVERLAPS
one time zone modifier
    AT ...
one set statement for the default time zone
    SET TIME ZONE ...

23.2 A Taxonomy of Time

The concept of time, including the concept of date, is not generally very well understood. We all know, or think we know, what we mean when we talk about time, but we very rarely bother to define our terms of reference clearly or to think through the implications of the way we use time. In this chapter we will look at the various ways in which time can be used and how that affects the way in which we have to define tables in SQL.

We generally use time in one of two ways: either to define the moment an event occurred or to define a period of validity. In the first case, for example, a person's birth is an event and we refer to that moment (with a certain degree of precision) as the date of birth. We have an example of precisely that in our example database in the Emp_Ext table:

```
CREATE TABLE Emp_Ext
(
empnr               NUMERIC (5),
date_of_birth       DATE NOT NULL,
date_of_joining     DATE NOT NULL,
previous_employer   CHARACTER (40),
p_e_address         CHARACTER VARYING (200),
CHECK (date_of_birth < date_of_joining),
PRIMARY KEY (empnr),
FOREIGN KEY (empnr) REFERENCES Employee
)
```

In fact, in this table we have two such events, as joining the company is also an event and is recorded in the column 'date_of_joining'. This example uses the data type DATE as we are not interested in the time of day that a person was born (although for applications such as astrology it may be of vital importance).

In the Itinerary table we have two events, the outward and return flights, and the times of these events are recorded in the columns highlighted below:

```
CREATE TABLE Itinerary
(
itinerary_no        NUMERIC (5),
empnr               NUMERIC (5) NOT NULL,
request_date        DATE NOT NULL,
travel_agent_id     CHARACTER (10),
outward_date        DATE,
flight_no_out       CHARACTER (6) NOT NULL,
outward_time        TIME,
hotel               CHARACTER (40),
return_date         DATE,
flight_no_back      CHARACTER (6) NOT NULL,
return_time         TIME,
PRIMARY KEY (itinerary_no),
UNIQUE (empnr, request_date),
FOREIGN KEY (empnr,request_date) REFERENCES Travel_Req,
FOREIGN KEY (travel_agent_id) REFERENCES Travel_Agent
)
```

Here we have used a pair of columns for each event but we could have defined single columns for each event as:

```
outward_time    TIMESTAMP(0),
```

and

```
return_time     TIMESTAMP(0),
```

If we had been recording scientific measurements in some real-time monitoring system then we might possibly want a much greater precision with regard to the time of the event. We could then use TIMESTAMP(9) to capture the time to nanosecond precision.

In the second case, that of the definition of a period of validity, the most common one we all experience is life itself. We have already considered the event 'date of birth'; if we also consider the event 'date of death', these two events define the period that is the life span of the person concerned. In our example database this period is not represented but we do have an equivalent for the life span of a project:

```
CREATE TABLE Project
(
project_cd      projcd,
start_date      DATE NOT NULL,
end_date        DATE,
resp_dept       NUMERIC (5) NOT NULL,
sponsor_dept    NUMERIC (5) NOT NULL,
budget          DECIMAL (6,2),
forecast        DECIMAL (6,2),
actual          DECIMAL (6,2),
description     CHARACTER VARYING (2000),
PRIMARY KEY (project_cd),
FOREIGN KEY (resp_dept) REFERENCES Dept,
FOREIGN KEY (sponsor_dept) REFERENCES Dept
)
```

Here the two columns 'start_date' and 'end_date' define the period of validity or life span of the project. This is the first of three types of 'period of validity' time period which we have already referred to as 'life span' data. In this type the entity can only have a single period of validity; we do not allow the same project to exist twice (and reincarnated humans are treated as separate people!). A noticeable attribute of this kind of period is that neither event is considered part of the primary key.

Unfortunately, life is not always so simple. If we consider the relationship between employees and projects we can see that an employee may work for several projects and a project may have several employees. If we defined the table as follows:

```
CREATE TABLE Assignment
(
empnr           NUMERIC (5),
project_cd      projcd,
project_role    CHARACTER (15),
start_date      DATE NOT NULL,
end_date        DATE,
PRIMARY KEY (empnr, project_cd),
FOREIGN KEY (empnr) REFERENCES Employee,
FOREIGN KEY (project_cd) REFERENCES Project
)
```

then the contents of the table might look like that shown in Figure 23.1. If we execute the command

```
SELECT empnr
  FROM Assignment
  WHERE DATE'1991-04-20' BETWEEN start_date AND end_date
        AND project_cd = 'BREN02'
```

in order to discover who worked on the BREN02 project on 16 April 1991 we would get the answer:

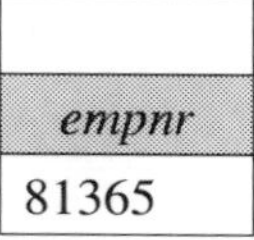

empnr
81365

Assignment				
empnr	*project_cd*	*project_role*	*start_date*	*end_date*
81365	BREN02	Worker	1991-04-05	9999-12-31
23792	SULL01	Worker	1991-05-17	1991-07-01
74188	BNFL01	Quality Assurance	1991-04-21	1991-05-15
74188	BREN02	Project Leader	1991-06-01	9999-12-31
...	...		...	...

Figure 23.1 *Contents of the Assignment table*

This might be a misleading result since employee 74188 might have worked on BREN02 before 1991-06-01 but we have no way of representing that in the table as defined because we would violate the primary key constraint. The table does not tell us who worked on which project but what was the last period that someone worked on a project. Thus we can see whether someone has worked on a project or not, but if they have we can only record one period (say the last). Over time, the relationship between employees and projects might well have looked like Figure 23.2 and the answer we really wanted to the question 'Who worked on the BREN02 project on 16 April 1991?' is:

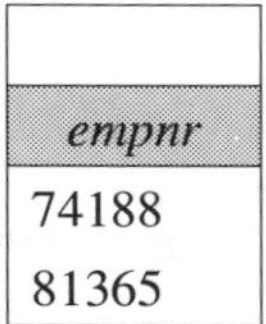

empnr
74188
81365

In order to achieve this we must alter the table definition slightly to include the start_date in the primary key:

```
CREATE TABLE Assignment
(
empnr       NUMERIC (5),
project_cd    projcd,
project_role CHARACTER (15),
start_date    DATE NOT NULL,
end_date      DATE,
PRIMARY KEY (empnr, project_cd, start_date),
FOREIGN KEY (empnr) REFERENCES Employee,
FOREIGN KEY (project_cd) REFERENCES Project
)
```

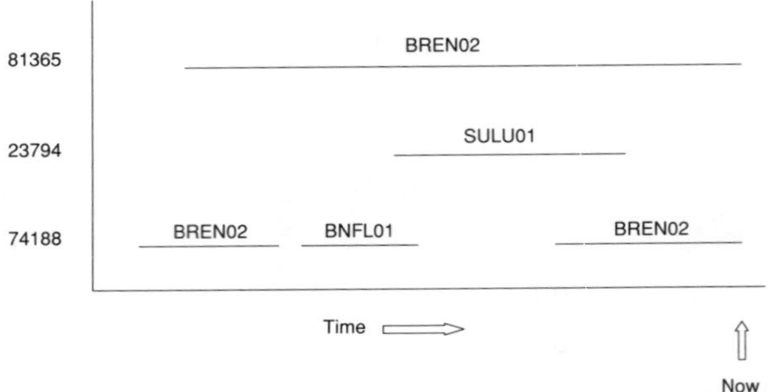

Figure 23.2 *Timeline — employees working on projects*

Assignment				
empnr	*project_cd*	*project_role*	*start_date*	*end_date*
81365	BREN02	Worker	1991-04-05	9999-12-31
23792	SULL01	Worker	1991-05-17	1991-07-01
74188	BNFL01	Quality Assurance	1991-04-21	1991-05-15
74188	BREN02	Worker	1991-03-01	1991-04-20
74188	BREN02	Project Leader	1991-06-01	9999-12-31
...	...		...	...

Figure 23.3 *Altered contents of the Assignment table*

Then the contents of the table can be as shown in Figure 23.3 and the query will return the desired result.

You may have noticed the strange date '9999-12-31' in the end date column for some rows. This date, well into the future, is the maximum permitted value for a DATE data type column and is used here to represent 'not yet ended'. We could have chosen to represent this as NULL, but the use of a large future date simplifies the writing of queries. If we had used nulls then the select statement would have had to look like:

```
SELECT empnr
  FROM Assignment
  WHERE (DATE'1991-04-20' BETWEEN start_date AND end_date
         OR
         DATE'1991-04-20' >= start_date
         AND end_date IS NULL)
    AND project_cd = 'BREN02'
```

or

```
SELECT empnr
  FROM Assignment
  WHERE   DATE'1991-04-20' >= start_date
          AND (DATE'1991-04-20' <= end_date
               OR
               end_date IS NULL)
    AND project_cd = 'BREN02'
```

or some such variation.

In the above we added the start_date to the primary key but the end_date would have been just as suitable, except that the use of null to represent open periods would obviously not be permitted. In practice many searches are done on the most recent periods, so using a fixed value (e.g. 9999-12-31) for open periods and using the end_date instead of the start_date in the PRIMARY KEY is usually best. Another reason for using '9999-12-31' instead of NULL is that should we ever want to sort the rows on the basis of the end_date then '9999-12-31' will always sort in the correct place whereas the sort order of NULL is implementation defined and our application would not be portable across different database systems.

We have assumed that the end_date column is filled with the last date of the period, but in practice, and especially because of the way in which the OVERLAPS predicate works, it is more convenient to fill the column with the last day *plus 1*; i.e. if an employee stops working on a project on 10 June 1990 then we would record the end date as 11 June 1990.

The query above involved just the one date but if we need to search for a period, say list the employees who worked on projects in May 1991, then we can use the OVERLAPS predicate so:

```
SELECT empnr
   FROM Assignment
   WHERE (DATE'1991-05-01, INTERVAL 1 MONTH)
         OVERLAPS (start_date, end_date)
     AND  project_cd = 'BREN02'
```

We have not provided all the necessary constraints on the Assignment table, but in principle we should ensure that there are no overlapping periods where the same employee works for the same project. To do this we need to define a CHECK clause as follows:

```
CREATE TABLE Assignment
(
empnr        NUMERIC (5),
project_cd   projcd,
project_role CHARACTER (15),
start_date   DATE NOT NULL,
end_date     DATE,
CHECK (NOT EXISTS (
    SELECT *
      FROM Assignment AS W1 JOIN Assignment AS W2
           USING (empnr, project_cd)
      WHERE (W1.start_date, W1.end_date)
           OVERLAPS (W2.start_date, W2.end_date)
           AND W1.start_date <> W2.start_date)),
PRIMARY KEY (empnr, project_cd, end_date),
FOREIGN KEY (empnr) REFERENCES Employee,
FOREIGN KEY (project_cd) REFERENCES Project
)
```

This CHECK clause and others like it in the example are theoretically correct, but it is not suggested that they be implemented in all circumstances. Frequently these constraints are implicit in the code of the routines (possibly, and hopefully, only a single routine) that stores and updates them. However, if an integral database is to be maintained in the face of direct on-line updates from human users these kinds of constraints may be very necessary.

There is an alternative method for representing the period in a table, which is to use the data type INTERVAL. This construction is frequently more difficult to handle but in principle we can replace any pair of dates defining a period by a single start or end date and a period length (or interval). If we were to use this method the Assignment table might have been defined as:

```
CREATE TABLE Assignment
(
empnr          NUMERIC (5),
project_cd     projcd,
start_date     DATE NOT NULL,
period_length  INTERVAL DAY(3),
CHECK (NOT EXISTS (
    SELECT *
      FROM Assignment AS W1 JOIN Assignment AS W2
           USING (empnr, project_cd)
      WHERE (W1.start_date, W1.period_length)
           OVERLAPS (W2.start_date, W2.period_length)
           AND W1.start_date <> W2.start_date)),
PRIMARY KEY (empnr, project_cd, end_date),
FOREIGN KEY (empnr) REFERENCES Employee,
FOREIGN KEY (project_cd) REFERENCES Project
)
```

We call this kind of data 'periodic' data to distinguish it from 'life span' data. Periodic data represents something that can repeat over time whereas life span data only ever has a single occurrence. In fact the preceding kind of data is only one of two possible kinds of 'periodic' data — 'interruptible periodic' data — as the periods do not need to be contiguous. In the example data given above it was clear that gaps existed between each period for the combination of employee and project. Interruptible is not intended to mean that the gaps must exist, only that they *may* exist.

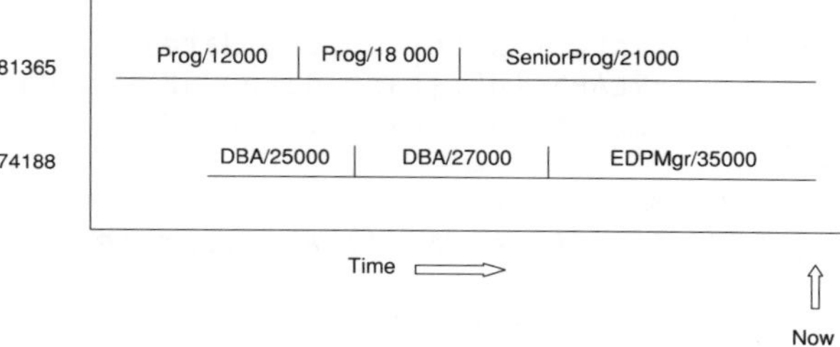

Figure 23.4 *Timeline – employee's job titles*

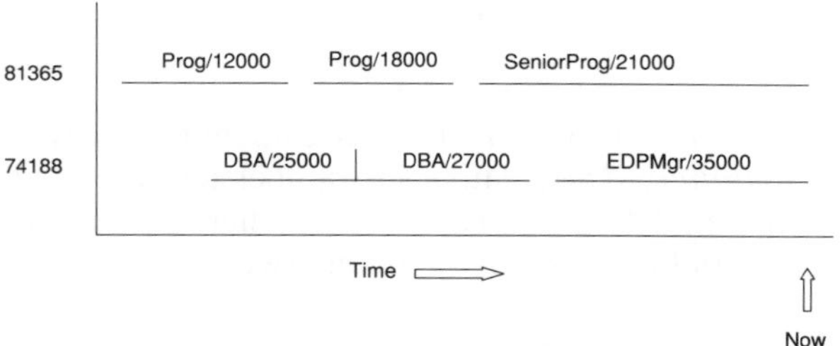

Figure 23.5 *Illegal Timeline – employee's job titles*

There is, however, another kind of periodic data — 'un-interruptible periodic' data in which gaps may not exist. An example of this kind can be seen in the Job_History table. Every employee has zero or more Job_History rows depending on the number of times his or her salary or job title has changed during the period of employment, but there can be no time during that period where the employee has been without a job or salary. The relationship between the employee and job/salary over time will always have the form shown in Figure 23.4. A construction such as that given in Figure 23.5 would not make sense.

The necessary definition of the table is as follows:

```
CREATE TABLE Job_History
(
empnr          NUMERIC (5),
job            job NOT NULL,
salary         NUMERIC (6) NOT NULL,
start_date     DATE,
end_date       DATE,
CHECK (NOT EXISTS (
       SELECT *
         FROM Job_History AS J1 JOIN Job_History AS J2
              USING (empnr)
         WHERE (J1.start_date, J1.end_date)
                OVERLAPS (J2.start_date, J2.end_date)
           AND J1.start_date <> J2.start_date)),
CHECK (1 =
         (SELECT MAX (occurrences)
            FROM (SELECT COUNT(*) AS occurrences
            FROM Job_History AS J1 LEFT JOIN
                 Job_History AS J2
              ON J1.empnr = J2.empnr
              AND J1.end_date = J2.start_date
           WHERE J2.empnr IS NULL
           GROUP BY J1.empnr))),
PRIMARY KEY (empnr, end_date),
FOREIGN KEY (empnr) REFERENCES Employee
)
```

This has the same basic format as the Assignment table except for the additional constraint in *italicized text*. This constraint checks that for each employee there is only one row that does not have an immediate successor, and thus there are no gaps. A gap would necessarily generate two rows without an immediate successor.

In general, the fact that columns with date, time or timestamp data types are now prevalent in the primary keys can lead to problems defining referential integrity unless there are some non-periodic data to which to refer. In the above example this is indeed the case but it becomes complicated when a hierarchy of references includes periodic data other than at the lowest level.

Furthermore, the period of a periodic datum is frequently independent of the period of other periodic data, even when the data themselves (without consideration of time aspects) are dependent on the same keys. In the above case the salary and job title are both dependent on empnr and on 'a' start_date but not necessarily dependent on the same start date as the other. In these cases it might be thought better to split the table into a job title history table and a salary history table. This leads to one table for every attribute which is logically correct but mostly unacceptable from both an understanding and a performance point of view. Normally some application specific compromises need to be made.

There is a third way in which we use time which is related to both the kind of event and the kind of period discussed at the beginning of the chapter. The events we discussed then were single events in the real world that we were recording. The variation that we will now look at has to do with things in the real world which are continuous but of which we take measurements. These measurements are themselves the events whose times are recorded, but the event is of less importance than the thing being measured. A good example of this is temperature measurement. If we are recording temperatures at various places then we might record the information in a table like:

```
CREATE TABLE Temperature
(
location   CHARACTER(20),
instant    TIMESTAMP,
degrees    NUMERIC(4,2) NOT NULL,
PRIMARY KEY (location, instant)
)
```

Unlike the previous event times these event times always form part of the primary key of the table. This is not to say that the earlier events never form part of the primary key but it is not commonly so.

An interesting aspect of these 'measurement' event times is that it is possible to interpolate values for the intermediate instances. If we extend the table to include a flag to say whether the value was measured or interpolated as in:

```
CREATE TABLE Temperature
(
location   CHARACTER(20),
instant    TIMESTAMP,
degrees    NUMERIC(4,2) NOT NULL,
sort CHARACTER,
CHECK (sort IN ('M', 'I')),
PRIMARY KEY (location, instant)
)
```

Temperature			
location	*instant*	*degrees*	*sort*
De Bilt	1990-08-16 11:00:00	18.00	M
De Bilt	1990-08-16 11:30:00	18.98	M
De Bilt	1990-08-16 12:00:00	19.86	M
De Bilt	1990-08-16 12:30:00	20.52	M
De Bilt	1990-08-16 13:00:00	20.92	M
De Bilt	1990-08-16 13:30:00	20.99	M
De Bilt	1990-08-16 14:00:00	20.73	M

Figure 23.6 *The Temperature table*

Temperature			
location	*instant*	*degrees*	*sort*
De Bilt	1990-08-16 11:00:00	18.00	M
De Bilt	1990-08-16 11:15:00	18.50	I
De Bilt	1990-08-16 11:30:00	18.98	M
De Bilt	1990-08-16 11:45:00	19.44	I
De Bilt	1990-08-16 12:00:00	19.86	M
De Bilt	1990-08-16 12:15:00	20.22	I
De Bilt	1990-08-16 12:30:00	20.52	M
De Bilt	1990-08-16 12:45:00	20.76	I
De Bilt	1990-08-16 13:00:00	20.92	M
De Bilt	1990-08-16 13:15:00	20.99	I
De Bilt	1990-08-16 13:30:00	20.99	M
De Bilt	1990-08-16 13:45:00	20.73	I
De Bilt	1990-08-16 14:00:00	20.73	M

Figure 23.7 *The Temperature table with interpolated values*

and we had a table with the values given in Figure 23.6 we could interpolate intermediate values for the quarter hours and store them in the table to obtain the values given in Figure 23.7.

We have now covered the various uses of time as regards the real world and the way we model it in an SQL database, but there is still one serious problem remaining. In all of the above we assume that the values in the database are correct representations of the real-world values and that if they turn out to be incorrect then the original values are overwritten and thus lost. In a great many systems this is not a problem but there are systems where it is important to know not only what the state of the world actually was at a given point in time but also what we thought the state of the world at that point in time was at another point in time. These other systems include ones where decisions are made on the basis of the available information and if that database state is lost it becomes impossible to see why certain decisions were made. Another example of such a system is one where it must be possible to track the sequence of changes for audit purposes. In our example database we have assumed that the timesheet records need to be audited. What we need to be able to do is to recreate the database as it was at any given point in time and in order to do that we must keep track of the times that records were inserted into the database and the times that the information in the record was replaced or deleted.

Consider the timesheet records for employees 81365 and 74188 for the BREN02 project for hours worked on 1 July 1991. Assume that the records were inserted on 1 August 1991 and that the hours for 81365 were corrected on 5 August; then the situation is as shown in Figure 23.8. This looks very similar to uninterruptible periodic data, and indeed it is, the difference being that the periodic data uses a different time axis. One can apply this (database) historical time axis both to data that is real-world time independent and data that is dependent on any of the real-world time sorts. To implement we need to add start and end times, and because we must normally allow for the situation where several updates occur in a day we use timestamp data types with a precision as close as possible to that of the system clock.

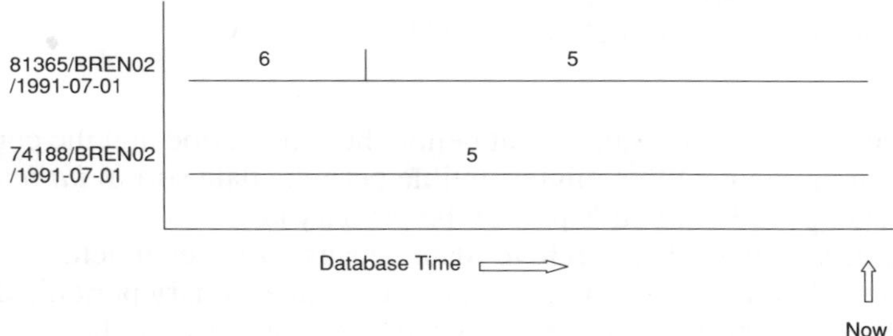

Figure 23.8 *Database Timeline — timesheet hours*

The timesheet table is defined thus:

```
CREATE TABLE Timesheet
(
empnr               NUMERIC (5),
project_cd          projcd,
work_date           DATE,
hours               INTERVAL HOUR TO MINUTE,
overtime_hours      INTERVAL HOUR TO MINUTE,
timestamp_start     TIMESTAMP NOT NULL DEFAULT CUR-
                    RENT_TIMESTAMP,
timestamp_end       TIMESTAMP NOT NULL
   DEFAULT TIMESTAMP'9999-12-31 23:59:59.999999',
CHECK (NOT EXISTS (
   SELECT *
      FROM Timesheet AS T1 JOIN Timesheet AS T2
           USING (empnr, project_cd, work_date)
      WHERE (T1.timestamp_start, T1.timestamp_end)
             OVERLAPS (T2.timestamp_start, T2.timestamp_end)
        AND T1.timestamp_start <> T2.timestamp_start)),
```

```
CHECK (1 =
   (SELECT MAX (occurrences)
       FROM (SELECT COUNT(*) AS occurrences
             FROM Timesheet AS T1 LEFT JOIN Timesheet AS T2
                ON (T1.empnr, T1.project_cd, T1.work_date) =
                   (T2.empnr, T2.project_cd, T2.work_date)
               AND T1.timestamp_end = T2.timestamp_start
            WHERE T2.empnr IS NULL
          GROUP BY T1.empnr, T1.project_cd, T1.work_date))),
PRIMARY KEY (empnr, project_cd, work_date, timestamp_end),
FOREIGN KEY (empnr) REFERENCES Employee,
FOREIGN KEY (project_cd) REFERENCES Project
)
```

and we can see the two columns that define the time period and the constraints necessary to implement the uninterruptible periodic data sort in *italicized text*. The timestamp_end column is part of the primary key.

We call this kind of data 'archive' data because it is never actually deleted. The major difference between this archive data and ordinary periodic data is in the way an application must operate on it. For normal periodic data we can simply use the SQL insert, delete and update commands to insert, delete and update the data. However, in the case of archive data this is not always so.

For Insert we can indeed use the insert command ensuring that the 'timestamp_start' column is filled with the current system time (we can use a default clause as above) and that the 'timestamp_end' column is filled with the maximum possible date (again we can use the default clause). However, we should check that there are no existing rows with the same primary key values (ignoring the timestamp_start) as that would be a logical duplicate of the real-world object.

For Delete we cannot actually delete the row as we could then never recreate the database state as it was before that deletion. Instead, we must update the row and change the 'timestamp_end' column to the current system time. We may only change the 'timestamp_end' value if it is currently the maximum value. It is not permitted to change history!

For Update we can again not simply update the record as we must have access to both the old and the new values. To achieve this we must logically delete the old row (change the 'timestamp_end' to the current time) and insert a new record with the new values (with the relevant columns filled as for a normal insert, we should ensure that the end time of the old row and the start time of the new row are identical). Again, we may only update the row whose 'timestamp_end' value is the maximum value.

It is unfortunate that the standard SQL language does not offer any mechanism to hide this process from the application program. There are, however, commercial products that have implemented a trigger mechanism that does allow this process to be hidden and the applications to use the normal insert, delete and update commands.

For retrieval of data from tables that contain archive data we must take special precautions. In order to see the latest state of the database we must add the following to each and every WHERE clause:

```
AND timestamp_end = TIMESTAMP'9999-12-31 23:59:59.999999'
```

To inspect the archive data we can make use of the OVERLAPS predicate in the same way as we did with the periodic data to select rows that existed at a particular time or within a particular period.

23.3 Time Zones

Railways have had an immensely important influence on time. In fact, the modern obsession with time probably stems from the railway timetables. The Netherlands had existed quite happily (except for the occasional natural or political disaster) without a common idea of what time it was until the coming of the railways. Then came railway timetables and although in the beginning timetables were published showing both local and 'standard' (Amsterdam) railway time, in the end the whole country had to conform and adopt standard railway time for the convenience of everyone. In larger countries the railways were unable to insist on a single national time, and since the sun declined to alter its ways, they had to devise something else. The solution was discovered in the late 1870s by Sir Sandford Fleming, a Canadian railway planner and engineer. This solution was the next best thing to a single standard time — multiple standard times. This system of time zones, invented by the railways, was adopted by 27 nations at a conference in Washington, D.C., USA in 1884 and the world has been stuck with it ever since.

For those systems that operate around the globe, or are used to produce railway timetables (in large countries) or nowadays airline timetables, SQL has the necessary provisions. Two datetime data types have a WITH TIME ZONE option, namely TIME WITH TIME ZONE and TIMESTAMP with TIME ZONE. In our example schema we have the table Itinerary. We could modify its definition to add time zone information as follows:

```
CREATE TABLE Itinerary
(
itinerary_no        NUMERIC (5),
empnr               NUMERIC (5) NOT NULL,
request_date        DATE NOT NULL,
travel_agent_id     CHARACTER (10),
flight_no_out       CHARACTER (6) NOT NULL,
outward_departure   TIMESTAMP(0) WITH TIME ZONE,
outward_arrival     TIMESTAMP(0) WITH TIME ZONE,
hotel               CHARACTER (40),
flight_no_back      CHARACTER (6) NOT NULL,
return_departure    TIMESTAMP(0) WITH TIME ZONE,
return_arrival      TIMESTAMP(0) WITH TIME ZONE,
PRIMARY KEY (itinerary_no),
UNIQUE (empnr, request_date),
FOREIGN KEY (empnr,request_date) REFERENCES Travel_Req,
FOREIGN KEY (travel_agent_id) REFERENCES Travel_Agent
)
```

Here we have replaced the pair of columns, DATE and TIME, for each event with single TIMESTAMP columns for each event and added the WITH TIME ZONE option. We have also renamed the columns and added columns to record the arrival as well as the departure times.

Assume that somebody is going on a round trip to Singapore starting from Schipol (Amsterdam). We might populate the table with an insert statement:

```
INSERT INTO Itinerary (
   itinerary_no, empnr, request_date, travel_agent_id,
   flight_no_out, outward_departure, outward_arrival, hotel,
   flight_no_back, return_departure, return_arrival)
VALUES (
   02794, 23456, DATE'1989-07-24', 'AMEX',
   'SQ 23', TIMESTAMP'1989-08-05 18:15:00+02:00',
   TIMESTAMP'1989-08-06 17:25:00+08:00', 'RAFFLES',
   'SQ 24', TIMESTAMP'1989-08-29 23:00:00+08:00',
   TIMESTAMP'1989-08-30 08:00:00+02:00')
```

In this case we have stored the departure and arrival times in local time, Amsterdam in the summer being 2 hours ahead of GMT (or Universal Coordinated Time, to be absolutely correct) and Singapore 8 hours ahead. We could have stored all the times in GMT as in:

```
INSERT INTO Itinerary (
   itinerary_no, empnr, request_date, travel_agent_id,
   flight_no_out, outward_departure, outward_arrival, hotel,
   flight_no_back, return_departure, return_arrival)
VALUES (
   02794, 23456, DATE'1989-07-24', 'AMEX',
   'SQ 23', TIMESTAMP'1989-08-05 16:15:00+00:00',
   TIMESTAMP'1989-08-06 09:25:00+00:00', 'RAFFLES',
   'SQ 24', TIMESTAMP'1989-08-29 15:00:00+00:00',
   TIMESTAMP'1989-08-30 06:00:00+00:00')
```

The advantage of the former is that on retrieval we know what the time zone originally was, i.e. we can see directly that departure took place in a +2:00 time zone and arrival in a +8:00 time zone. When we retrieve the values from the columns we see precisely what we put in. Calculations, such as the length of journeys, remain the same; thus:

```
SELECT
  (outward_arrival-outward_departure) HOUR TO MINUTE
   AS outward_time,
  (return_arrival-return_departure) HOUR TO MINUTE
   AS return_time
  FROM Itinerary
  WHERE itinerary_no = 02794
```

will yield the same table with two interval columns as a result, regardless of which method of storage is used (*see Figure 23.9*).

outward_time	*return_time*
17:10	15:00

Figure 23.9 *Result of a SELECT on the Itinerary table*

In dealing with time zones we must be careful to ensure that the correct time zone is always explicitly or implicitly specified. An insert statement such as:

```
INSERT INTO Itinerary (
   itinerary_no, empnr, request_date, travel_agent_id,
   flight_no_out, outward_departure, outward_arrival, hotel,
   flight_no_back, return_departure, return_arrival)
VALUES (
   02794, 23456, DATE'1989-07-24', 'AMEX',
   'SQ 23', TIMESTAMP'1989-08-05 18:15:00',
   TIMESTAMP'1989-08-06 17:25:00', 'RAFFLES',
   'SQ 24', TIMESTAMP'1989-08-29 23:00:00',
   TIMESTAMP'1989-08-30 08:00:00')
```

will work but will store all times as if they had an explicit time zone equal to that specified for the current session. If we were working in Amsterdam that might well be +2:00, or we might have set it explicitly with a set time zone statement as in:

```
SET TIME ZONE INTERVAL'+02:00' HOUR TO MINUTE
```

This, however, would still mean that two of the times specified would be wrong. We could, of course, make some use of this as in:

```
INSERT INTO Itinerary (
   itinerary_no, empnr, request_date, travel_agent_id,
   flight_no_out, outward_departure, outward_arrival, hotel,
   flight_no_back, return_departure, return_arrival)
VALUES (
   02794, 23456, DATE'1989-07-24', 'AMEX',
   'SQ 23', TIMESTAMP'1989-08-05 18:15:00',
   TIMESTAMP'1989-08-06 17:25:00+08:00', 'RAFFLES',
   'SQ 24', TIMESTAMP'1989-08-29 23:00:00+08:00',
   TIMESTAMP'1989-08-30 08:00:00')
```

which does yield the correct answer.

Once the times are stored with the time zones we can manipulate them into other time zones. Assume we want to know what time, in Amsterdam, the person will arrive in Singapore. We can do that, assuming the current time zone is set as above with:

```
SELECT outward_arrival AT LOCAL
  FROM Itinerary
  WHERE itinerary_no = 02794
```

If we are not sure of the current time zone or wish to use a different one we might say:

```
SELECT outward_arrival AT TIME ZONE
  INTERVAL'+2:00' HOUR TO MINUTE
  FROM Itinerary
  WHERE itinerary_no = 02794
```

If we were in a program we might first retrieve the correct offset, from a table of time zone offsets, into a host language variable and then use that variable as in:

```
SELECT time_zone INTO :time_zone
  FROM Time_Zone_Offsets
  WHERE airport = 'Singapore'

SELECT outward_arrival AT TIME ZONE :time_zone
  FROM Itinerary
  WHERE itinerary_no = 02794
```

24

Handling Missing Information

In real life missing information is very common; for instance people do not fill in forms completely because they do not know the answer to the question, they do not understand the question, the question does not apply to them, they do not think that the question applies to them, or because the questionnaire does not contain all the questions or information that it should. Somehow or other we seem to cope but we doubt if many of us ever think about how we do actually manage. Opinion polling organizations and other users of statistical analysis have naturally developed explicit procedures to cope with these problems, but the general computing community has not.

Missing information is one factor that is all too often forgotten when databases are designed or queried. SQL provides some explicit support for the concept of missing information, the NULL state, but this support is clearly inadequate in many situations. Do we really need to concern ourselves? Some authors, such as C.J. Date (Date, 1986a), seem to want to abandon any use of NULL to represent missing information while others suggest that we wait until the academic researchers have finally solved all of the problems. These seem to represent an attitude similar to that of the proverbial ostrich, with its head in the sand. The problem of missing information is real (i.e. not missing) and will not go away even if we ignore it. We strongly suggest that even if our attempts to handle missing information lead in some cases to errors of interpretation, the errors caused are more likely to be detectable and correctable than if we attempt to build databases and systems in which the problem is completely eliminated by pretending that it does not exist. Further research is certainly needed. So is the implementation of some of the ideas that have already been researched, so that we can build less error-prone and more complete systems pending the final solution (always assuming that there is one). In the meantime we should attempt to understand the problems and devise ways of minimizing them in current information systems.

24.1 Missing: Applicable and Inapplicable Markings

E.F. Codd in several of his papers on missing information (Codd, 1986, 1987) points out that we can have missing information of two kinds, missing rows and missing values in rows that are present. Missing rows may represent either potentially valid events or objects that never happened or do not exist, events or objects that happened or exist but are not known to the database (i.e. the database is incomplete) or, finally, events or objects that are not valid (i.e. impossible or, using his own words, 'inapplicable') and that are thus, correctly, not represented. Codd goes on to say that we do not need to consider the consequences of this class of missing information as the database just models a 'micro-world'. This may be true, but it is worth bearing in mind that in interpreting answers to queries on the database we need to consider the completeness of the database as well as its validity.

Correctly reflecting missing information provides the scope of this chapter and this primarily pertains to missing information in, effectively, columns. Let us first try and tidy up the terminology. A column either has a value or it does not. Thus the null value is, in fact, not a value but a status and a column has one of two statuses, one of which is the status 'VALUED' and the other is the status 'NULL'. In principle a column could have any one of a number of statuses but current SQL only allows for these two. An ANSI committee is believed to have once listed 13 different non-valued states but we think most of us can survive with somewhat fewer, though SQL's one is probably too few.

One can argue that in the case of inapplicable values the database design could or even should be upgraded to correctly reflect structurally such reality and in doing so reduce the need for inapplicably missing information. Employees can be subdivided into those who do not earn commission and those who do. Such a technique calls for the either excessive subdivision of data into small tables, with the corresponding problems of recombining them in queries, or the availability of specialization/generalization facilities with the inheritance of properties. SQL does not, yet (*see Section F.3 Features Still to be Developed in Appendix F*), provide this latter facility so we still need databases designed such that fields may need to represent missing or inapplicable values.

24.2 SQL and Three-Valued Logic

Let us first look at current SQL (the simplest case) where we have in principle a three-valued logic in operation. This logic can be shown in the truth tables of Figure 24.1. In this case SQL does not make any further distinction in the different kinds of NULL or missing information. The above logic is used for the NULL state regardless of any finer distinctions. Let us take the following example and examine some more variations in NULL states. We define an example table called Employee and populate some rows with personal details,

AND	*T*	*?*	*F*
T	T	?	F
?	?	?	F
F	F	F	F

OR	*T*	*?*	*F*
T	T	T	T
?	T	?	?
F	T	?	F

NOT	
T	F
?	?
F	T

Figure 24.1 *Truth tables for three-valued logic*

as shown in Figure 24.2. The table contains several fields showing '?', being a representation for the NULL status reflecting 'unknown'. The current SQL recognizes only one NULL status and the database designer can attach the meaning he or she would like it to represent. Looking at the three-valued logic the most logical meaning seems to be that the value is applicable but currently unknown.

Employee							
empnr	*name*	*address*	*sex*	*home_telno*	*work_telno*	*salary*	*commis-sion*
12345	Brown	13 Forest Approach	M	+44(0)71-349-9906	+44(0)71-211-3013	11300	0
23456	Smith	12 Greenbank Avenue	?	+44(0)81-332-8793	+44(0)71-211-8998	?	?
34567	Patel	5 Lauder Road	F	+44(0)71-222-2222	+44(0)71-211-1357	25000	800
56789	Jones	71 High Street	M	+44(0)71-765-2132	+44(0)71-211-3014	9000	?

Figure 24.2 *Employee table containing various NULL field information*

24.2.1 Comparisons with Unknown Markings in Search Expressions

If 'x' is taken to be '`sex = 'M'`' then the names corresponding to the true answer to the kinds of tests on sex which we can make are as given in Table 24.1.

The fact that there are six alternative tests means that we must be very clear about what we mean when we query the database. Take, for example, a query:

```
SELECT * FROM Person WHERE <search condition>
```

Table 24.1 Test results with NULL status involved

Test performed	*Answer provided*
KNOWN TO BE x	Brown, Jones
POSSIBLY x	Brown, Jones, Smith
KNOWN NOT TO BE x	Patel
NOT (KNOWN TO BE x)	Smith, Patel
UNKNOWN	Smith
NOT UNKNOWN	Brown, Patel, Jones

The equivalent <search condition>s for each of these tests are given in Table 24.2.

Table 24.2 Tests and SQL search conditions with NULL status involved

Test performed	*SQL search condition*
KNOWN TO BE x	sex = 'M'
POSSIBLY x	sex = 'M' OR sex IS NULL
KNOWN NOT TO BE x	sex <> 'M'
NOT (KNOWN TO BE x)	sex <> 'M' OR sex IS NULL
UNKNOWN	sex IS NULL
NOT UNKNOWN	sex IS NOT NULL

This is fine when we have very simple search conditions, as in the above example, but if the question is of the second (POSSIBLY x) or the fourth (NOT (KNOWN TO BE x)) type it quickly becomes very tedious when the search condition is more complex, e.g. if it tests more than one column. SQL has some help to offer in this area with tests on any boolean expression, including a search condition of the form:

```
<search condition> ::=
    <boolean expression> IS [ NOT ] { TRUE | FALSE | UNKNOWN }
```

We can thus rewrite the above as shown in Table 24.3.

Table 24.3 Tests and alternative SQL search conditions with NULL status involved

Test performed	*SQL search condition*
KNOWN TO BE x	sex = 'M'
POSSIBLY x	sex = 'M' IS NOT FALSE
KNOWN NOT TO BE x	sex = 'M' IS FALSE
NOT (KNOWN TO BE x)	sex = 'M' IS NOT TRUE
UNKNOWN	sex = 'M' IS UNKNOWN
NOT UNKNOWN	sex = 'M' IS NOT UNKNOWN

We can now replace ' `sex = 'M'` ' by any arbitrary expression. This makes the formulation of a query much more straightforward. However, SQL still does not recognize the distinction between various kinds of NULL states.

24.3 Predicates and Missing Information

We have looked primarily at the simple comparison predicate and seen how careful we must be when formulating queries since it is three-valued. SQL has a number of other predicates, BETWEEN, IN, LIKE, NULL, Quantified (SOME, ALL), MATCH, UNIQUE and EXISTS. We might expect that these also would have all been three-valued like the comparison predicate but some SQL predicates, namely the NULL, UNIQUE, MATCH and EXISTS predicates, are two valued and not three-valued and this can lead to mistakes in query formulation. While this is not an error in the specification of SQL it is obviously an area in which users of SQL must be extremely careful. The NULL predicate is the least likely to be a problem as it is intuitively two valued. The two new predicates, UNIQUE and MATCH, are not a problem if one remembers that they are equivalent to the unique and referential constraints, which by the nature of constraints must be either true or false. With the others it pays to be careful; Kocharekar (1989) discusses cases where combinations of predicates can evaluate to unknown even when a correct answer of false can be arrived at by careful consideration of the database contents.

24.4 Set Functions and Missing Information

One further problem area for the unwary is that of the statistical, or set, functions — COUNT, SUM, AVG, MIN and MAX. These work by effectively discarding the NULLs from the set and operating on the remaining values. In some cases, this may be what is required. If we had only used NULL in the Employee table to mean 'Does Not Have A Salary', for example, then the query ' `SELECT COUNT(salary) FROM Employee` ' would correctly return a count of the people with a value for salary, in our case 3. The query ' `SELECT COUNT(*) FROM Employee` ' would return 4. A query ' `SELECT AVG(salary) FROM Employee` ' actually means 'What is the average salary of the people whose salary I know?', giving 15100 as an answer, and the question 'What is the average salary of all employees?' is in general unanswerable. Depending on the query it is sometimes valuable to substitute a value for a null. SQL has a substitution capability in its conditional value expression which lets you write such things as '`SELECT AVG(CASE WHEN salary IS NULL THEN 15000 ELSE salary END) FROM Employee`', giving as an answer 15075. There is, of course, a shorthand version available for the simple case but the general case will allow, for example, substituting the minimum salary for a job grade in place of an applicable null marking so that the value substituted is not a simple constant but a more intelligent value.

In summary, within the limits of the three-valued logic, most of the desirable results can be achieved in SQL, but care must always be exercised because seemingly simple queries are not always what they seem. This is not a problem with SQL but with humanity's predilection for not being precise.

24.5 More Than Three-Valued Logic

We have now dealt with SQL and three-valued logic; the most common classifications of missing information divide it into 'missing — not applicable' and 'missing — applicable, but unknown' but to these we might want to add a third class 'missing — not known if applicable or not' with the respective short names 'N/A', '?' and 'unsure'. The difference between these classes can be understood if we consider our example table. In any given row the column may contain an amount (of commission), it may be NULL because that person does not have a commission ('missing — not applicable'), it may be NULL because we know that the person is entitled to a commission but we do not know how much it is ('missing — applicable, but unknown') or, possibly, it may be NULL because we do not know whether the person is entitled to a commission or not ('missing — not known if applicable or not'). This gives us four- (or possibly five-) valued logic.

Our example table might now contain the values given in Figure 24.3. In this table we observe three non-valued states, ?, unsure and N/A. These are only three different possibilities. In this example we will assign ? to the NULL state, meaning there is a value applicable but we do not know what it is. Smith certainly has a sex and is also entitled to a commission but we do not know the applicable values. Brown is also entitled to a commission but has not managed to earn one. For N/A we know that there is no applicable value and thus we may assume that Jones is not entitled to a commission, maybe because he does not work for the sales department. For unsure we do not know whether an applicable value exists or not. Employee Smith may or may not have a home phone number; we simply do not know. The truth sequence from absolutely true to certainly not applicable would therefore be: T, ?, F, unsure, N/A. SQL only knows T, F, NULL, where NULL could be any of ?, unsure or N/A. If we ignore the notion of unsure, the remaining four statuses can be treated fairly consistently. The statuses T, ? and F are all within the scope of applicable repre-

Employee							
empnr	*name*	*address*	*sex*	*home_telno*	*work_telno*	*salary*	*commis-sion*
12345	Brown	13 Forest Ap-proach	M	+44(0)71-349-9906	+44(0)71-211-3013	11300	0
23456	Smith	12 Greenbank Avenue	?	unsure	+44(0)71-211-8998	?	?
34567	Patel	5 Lauder Road	F	+44(0)71-222-2222	+44(0)71-211-1357	25000	800
56789	Jones	71 High Street	M	+44(0)71-765-2132	+44(0)71-211-3014	9000	N/A

Figure 24.3 *Employee table containing three-valued NULL field information*

sentations, where T and F have to do with an evaluation on a proper value and ? is based on the fact that a value is applicable, like Employee.sex, but the real-world value is simply unknown. The status N/A represents a status for inapplicable (what Codd (1986, 1987) calls an I-mark), representing the fact that the given field cannot hold a value because none applies, like the commission for Jones. The filling in of a value for the applicable but ? status (Codd's A-mark) can be performed by any database user having normal update rights. The changing of N/A into ? or a proper value is a different issue, since the N/A condition can usually be avoided by redesigning the database structure. Splitting up the Employee table into Non_Commissioned_Employees and Commissioned_Employees would allow us to store Employee information in the appropriate table without the N/A status ever being needed. If this allocation into one or the other table can be derived from a clear-cut rule then this rule can be used as a CHECK constraint.

For operations on data types the outcome is dependent on the values and statuses operated upon. Taking the sequence value, ? and N/A, the result of an operation will be determined by the 'lowest' component in the operation. Adding a value to a ? will result in a ?. The table is as given in Table 24.4.

Table 24.4 Operations with values, unknown status and N/A status

Result of operation	*Value*	*?*	*N/A*
value	value	?	N/A
?	?	?	N/A
N/A	N/A	N/A	N/A

Having multiple null statuses we also need to assess the implications for unary operators and truth tables for four-valued logic. A good treatment of this matter is given in Gessert (1990). Negating may be interpreted in the sense that true and false are swapped but N/A and ? remain where they are. Alternatively, when we rank from 'most true' to 'least true' the sequence should be reversed. In a table all this looks as shown in Table 24.5.

Table 24.5 Negation and boolean operators in four-valued logic

p	*INV(p)*
T	N/A
?	F
F	?
N/A	T

p	*NOT(p)*
T	F
?	?
F	T
N/A	N/A

AND	*T*	*?*	*F*	*N/A*
T	T	?	F	N/A
?	?	?	F	N/A
F	F	F	F	F
N/A	N/A	N/A	F	N/A

OR	*T*	*?*	*F*	*N/A*
T	T	T	T	T
?	T	?	?	?
F	T	?	F	F
N/A	T	?	F	N/A

The kind of tests that we can now make on commission are greatly expanded and for the moment SQL provides no support for the distinctions. In the working draft for a follow-on SQL standard the concept of NULL has been expanded to allow a user specified list of 'states' to be defined for a domain or column and to be individually tested. This work is not yet complete but SQL appears to be moving in the right direction; there still remains no sign of similar action on the programming languages front.

24.6 Tautological and Absurd Queries

In the treatment of missing information there are still more traps for the unwary in that, for example, expressions involving two unknowns may evaluate to ? when there can never be a single substitute value that would result in true and thus the expression is, strictly speaking, false. Similarly, tautologies may evaluate to ? when the correct answer is, of course, always true.

Examples of the above two situations are where the commission of a given Employee is unknown and the query expression is '`(Employee.commission < 500) OR (Employee.commission >= 500)`'. In two-valued logic this is a tautology as one or the other side must evaluate to true (the other is then by definition false). SQL using three-valued logic would evaluate this query expression as '? AND ?' and thus ?, i.e. not true. This reasoning is obviously valid in those cases where we are sure that there is an applicable value, since in the case where a value is inapplicable the search expression should evaluate to something else, like N/A. An example of an absurd query is '`(Employee.sex = 'M') AND (Employee.sex = 'F')`'. Here the answer in two-valued logic is always false but SQL in the case of Smith returns the result of the evaluation as ?.

In the area of 'silly' queries, i.e. those outside the area of discourse covered by the database, SQL is unable to provide sensible error handling. Suppose we have a query on a aircraft manufacturers database such as:

```
SELECT sum(Employee.salary)
  FROM Employee E, Dept D
  WHERE E.deptcd = D.deptcd AND
        D.deptnm = 'Worm Farming'
```

This query will most likely return the answer 0, since the DBMS would not find any employee working for a department named 'Worm Farming'. More to the point, in the case where this whole department does not exist at all, the whole department is 'missing' and the answer should therefore not be 0, the query not being appropriate and thus no value is applicable. However, this conclusion can only be made if via referential integrity constraints it is impossible for an Employee to exist without the corresponding Department. In assessing queries there seems to be an hierarchy of evaluation that cannot be supported by SQL but which it is worth while to observe when designing applications. Firstly, each query is considered, syntactically, to eliminate tautologies and absurdities as discussed above. Secondly, queries need to be checked against the data structure as represented in the SQL catalog to detect impossible or 'silly queries'. Finally, the query is executed against the database and the matching against database values, unknowns and N/As.

24.7 DEFAULT <literal> or CASE for NULL

Given the problems NULL causes it is worth while investigating under which conditions NULL may be replaced by a DEFAULT clause providing a <literal>. The syntax for column definition defaults is '`DEFAULT` <literal>' (*see Section 4.2.1.1 Defaults*). We present situations where this construct may be used.

When a column always needs a value, i.e. it has a column constraint '`NOT NULL`' (*see Section 4.2.1.2 Column Constraints*) or equivalent, then it requires a proper value. In certain cases we may allow the application not to supply a value when it is clear that the initial value upon creation of a row is obvious. In the example of the creation of a new bank account we may assume that the column containing the balance may be set to the default value zero if no other value was provided. The concept of NULL would certainly not be acceptable to the bank. The column definition would look like:

```
balance    NUMERIC (12,2) NOT NULL DEFAULT 0
```

Another example of actively dealing with missing information is the situation where we want to simulate a multi-valued NULL condition (*see Section 24.5 More Than Three-Valued Logic*). When we want to know why a value for `commission` is missing and therefore commission may receive the `NULL` status, we can add a column called `commission_null` explaining which NULL applies, 'missing — not applicable', 'missing — applicable, but not known' or 'missing — not known if applicable or not'. If our example company (*see Appendix A The Example Database*) decides to use the following rules for commission we can then provide a reason for not supplying the value for commission. Every person in the sales department 'SLS' will receive a commission and therefore commission may only have a NULL status of 'missing — applicable, but not known' or value '‼'. Employees working in the marketing department 'MKT' may have a commission dependent upon the contract they have negotiated and thus we can only record 'missing — not known if applicable or not' or value '?' when registering an employee and afterwards verify and correct. Finally, remaining employees will never get a commission and the NULL status should reflect 'missing — not applicable' or value 'ϕ'. In the case where `commission` is not `NULL`, `commission_null` will have the value '√'. This assignment cannot be done using SQL DDL, but we can define a `CHECK` clause to limit the values to the allowable range:

```
deptcd            CHARACTER (3) NOT NULL DEFAULT 'PER',
commission        NUMERIC (6,2),
commission_null   CHARACTER (1)
CHECK (commission_null in ('√', '‼', '?', 'ϕ')
       AND
       ((commission IS NOT NULL AND commission_null = '√')
        OR
        (deptcd = 'SLS' AND commission_null = '‼')
        OR
        (deptcd = 'MKT' AND commission_null in
                                  ('‼', '?', 'ϕ'))
        OR
        (commission_null = 'ϕ')))
```

The retrieval of all Employees not having a commission who are entitled to one could be achieved with the following SQL query:

```
SELECT E.empnr, E.name
  FROM Employee E
  WHERE commission_null = '‼'
```

The display of the commission status could be made more readable by providing users with the following VIEW when retrieving Employee information:

```
CREATE VIEW Employee-commission
   (number, name, salary, commission,
    commission_entitlement)
AS
SELECT E.empnr, E.name, E.salary, E.commission,
       CASE commission_null
       WHEN '√' THEN 'Applicable and value known'
       WHEN '!!' THEN 'Applicable and value not known'
       WHEN '?' THEN 'Not known if applicable'
       WHEN 'φ' THEN 'Not applicable'
       END
  FROM Employee E
```

24.8 Replace NULL by Value Always

There are some who want to dispose of NULL by insisting that a suitable value can always be found. No column in pure relational theory can assume the NULL value. C.J. Date (1985) advocates such a situation. We believe that the real world has many situations where information is missing and humans can properly deal with such a situation. It is a matter of education and training to understand the concepts of missing information and act appropriately.

In information systems we model the real world and as system designers we should never assume certain events do not happen or conditions do not arise, unless nature or some other authority is in command which allows no exceptions. Usually we have to cater for exceptions and we cannot be sure that for a column certain values will never occur and so we can reserve these values to represent one or the other kind of missing information. In many cases the domain of the column may be completely required to capture the real-world situation. Furthermore, should we reserve a specific value for NULL then it may be the case that many different columns may have different characteristics for the values they legitimately need to allow and therefore each column may need different values to specify the NULL status — not an easy task for implementors and programmers to keep track of consistently.

Another issue is the violation of the closure of the SQL language. Closure means that when you operate against a table then the resulting table has the same characteristics. When we would like to execute an `OUTER JOIN` using Dept and Employee this will give us a table with rows containing columns of departments and their employees, and for the departments having no employees we would find the employee columns set to NULL. This useful command would not give us the additional value without the concept of NULL. We are quite happy to deal with NULL.

[illegible]

[illegible] Celsius

[illegible]

[illegible] value [illegible]

[illegible] value [illegible]

[illegible]

24.8 [illegible] NULLs [illegible]

There are [illegible] who want to [illegible] NULL by [illegible] [illegible] theory can [illegible] NULL [illegible] (1985) [illegible] We [illegible] real world [illegible] is missing [illegible] to deal with [illegible] to understand the concept [illegible] and [illegible] people [illegible]

[illegible] should [illegible] or [illegible] unless [illegible] which allows [illegible] tion. [illegible] we have [illegible] example, and [illegible] column [illegible] will [illegible] and [illegible] we [illegible] missing [illegible] domain of the [illegible] required [illegible] capture [illegible] situation [illegible] value for NULL [illegible] may [illegible] constraint [illegible] for the [illegible] and [illegible] each column [illegible] implementation and programmers [illegible] consistency.

[illegible] SQL [illegible] table [illegible] same [illegible] NULL [illegible] and [illegible] table with [illegible] columns [illegible] no [illegible] would [illegible] NULL. This useful [illegible] not give us the [illegible] without the concept of NULL [illegible] badly [illegible] with NULL.

25

Translating Natural Language Queries

The purpose of this chapter is to present a method[1] of arriving at a correctly formulated query in SQL given a problem statement in natural language. The method is a rather general purpose one and as such can be used for formulation of computer language syntax in general.

The term 'user friendliness' is often used in discussions concerning computer languages and the design and use of information systems. There is, apparently, no single correct answer available to satisfy all the points raised but by the end of this chapter the reader should have an impression of the arguments used in such discussions.

25.1 The Steps in the Query Formulation Method

In defining a method for the unambiguous and correct formulation of a query in a query language there are two major phases. The first is aimed at the formulation of the query in an unambiguous manner within the scope of the universe of discourse of the relevant information system. We will use our Company database model as an example (*see Appendix A The Example Database*). The second phase is aimed at producing a correctly formulated and hopefully readable query in a computer language, in our case SQL.

We would expect the query to be formulated by someone — whom we will call the user — having a knowledge of the universe of discourse and the user query to be translated into computer language by someone — whom we will

1. This chapter is based on previous work done in the Netherlands Database Club, a working group of the NGI and described in an article in *Informatie* (de Jonge *et al.*, 1988).

call the information analyst — with information analysis capabilities. To what extent knowledge of the universe of discourse and information analysis capabilities can be united in a single person is up to the reader to determine. We feel there are not many people who possess both elements of this equation.

The method consists of four steps, each transforming the query from one format into another format. The syntax or representation of each format is different but of increasing formality while preserving the semantic equivalence.

The method is such that we concentrate in each step on a single aspect of the problem of formulation of natural language queries into SQL. Once familiar with all aspects in each step, it may be possible to perform some transformations, for not too complex queries, in a single action involving the logic of multiple steps. However, to acquire this skill intensive collaboration between the user and the information analyst is necessary to transform the user query into a format suitable for a query language processor. After a while the user should acquire an increasing degree of independence from the information analyst. Figure 25.1 shows the steps in the method.

Steps in the method to create correct SQL!

Step name	*Actions required*	*Participants*
Interpret	Clarify and make more explicit the natural language query of the user — typically by giving real-world examples	User in conjunction with the information analyst
Shape	Transform free natural language into natural language using a prescribed style such as the simple, unique expressions in the business language of the information system	User in conjunction with the information analyst
Formalize	Transform into the formalism of 'tuple calculus' using the tables, columns and referential integrity information maintained by the DBMS	Information analyst
Generate	Translate into the syntax of the chosen query language (in our case SQL) according to fixed transformation rules	Information analyst or a translation programme

Figure 25.1 *Steps in the method of formulating natural language queries into SQL*

Step 1 forms the first (natural language) phase, steps 2 to 4, the second (formalization) phase. In steps 1 to 3 a description of the database in the information system is required, but step 4 is purely mechanical. *Section 25.4* contains background information for this process, *Section 25.4.1* describing the database schema DDL and *Section 25.4.2* the corresponding **data structure diagram**. At the level of a relational database implementation this represents the tables contained in the database and their relationships. Since the connection is arranged through **foreign key** relationships, for each of the 'arrows' in the data structure diagram, we have added the columns in the **referencing table** that support the foreign key. We have also added the meaning of the reference, so the data structure diagram also contains some semantic information.

25.1.1 Step 1: Interpret

Here the user formulates, in natural language, the question to which an answer is required from the information system. The user and the information analyst, in co-operation, try to understand and eradicate all ambiguity from the query. Take, for example, the question 'Which specialist operates on heart patients alone?'. The word 'alone' could indicate 'he carries out only the operations on heart patients' *or* 'he operates completely on his own' *or* 'he works exclusively with heart patients'. During the dialogue between them the user must make clear to the information analyst which meaning is intended. Even linguistically incorrect interpretations must be considered, since no one, users or information analysts, command natural languages perfectly and natural languages of themselves are imperfect for our purposes.

For complete and unambiguous understanding of the query the intended meaning of each term of the query formulation needs to be explored. Since the information system is expected to provide the answer, all terms used in the query have to be related to the terms and definitions of the information system. The information analyst must therefore understand the meaning of all the terms known to the information system as laid down in the thesaurus, catalog, data dictionary system, information schema or whatever the repository for meta-data about the information system is called. Such a catalog contains the description, the definition of all terms used in the information system plus their meaning and provides insight into homonyms and synonyms. For this step the definitions are of greater importance than the terms themselves.

From the summary description of the Company information system, in *Section 25.4.1 Database Schema DDL*, the meaning of resp_dept for a project is not clear. Does it mean the department initially requesting the project? Is it the department responsible for the project right now, or does it indicate the department supplying the project leader to the project?

Even if the catalog does not distinguish between multiple meanings for a specific term, we have to realize that the user might have another meaning in mind which was not documented during the information systems design. We recommend the use of examples during this step to clarify meanings, especially in difficult cases or situations where knowledge of the information system and the universe of discourse do not sufficiently overlap in the information analyst and the user.

This step concluded that the query is still formulated in terms natural to the user, not in tables, fields and relationships. The result is an agreed natural language text that is 100 per cent understood by the two parties.

25.1.2 Step 2: Shape

After having reached agreement about the nature and meaning of the query, the information analyst will transform (shape) the natural language text into simple and singular terms and conditions. Complex terms and conditions must be broken down.

During this step all the terms in the query as posed by the user must be replaced by (synonymous) terms from the database definition of the information system. Although step 1 may have clarified some terms in the query, we now need to replace them all. In the interpretation stage we might have concluded that the term 'age' is unambiguously derivable from information present in the information system (such as birth date and today's date), but during the second step we need to understand exactly how this derivation takes place. Once the second step is completed the reshaped query should only contain terms known to or expressible within the structure of the information system.

It is obvious that, during the design period and also during the operational lifetime, user-specific terms have to be added to the dictionary system to facilitate the recognition of semantic equivalence of user query elements and information system constructs for the user or the information systems query processor. In particular there is a need for terms that represent a complex structure in themselves but are an easily understood concept for the user.

In shaping the query we structure and formalize it a little by using key words from a limited set, like FOR-WHICH-IS-TRUE, THERE-EXISTS-A, FOR-ALL, NEVER, ONLY, ALWAYS, etc. We are gradually moving towards a language structure that matches tuple calculus (Date, 1986b, Chapter 14), but the end product of this step is still natural language which the user must understand fully.

25.1.3 Step 3: Formalize

Once the query has been shaped the remainder of the process becomes much more mechanical and the transformation into a formal specification can begin. We suggest using tuple calculus for this formal notation and then applying a number of transformation rules to arrive at a standard notation called prenex normal form. The method does not prescribe a particular notation, though we have SQL as a target database language. If we always intended to translate into QBE (Query By Example) domain calculus (Date, 1986b) would be better. Both choices are based on predicate logic, because database operations must be described simply and clearly.

The significant characteristics of predicate logic are that we can reference entities (tables) and their relationships (referential integrity), and over and above that we can express general truths such as THERE-EXISTS-A, FOR-ALL as well as expressions that can be built up using AND, OR and NOT (*see Gamut, 1982 and Chang and Lee, 1973*).

The prenex normal form is a specific form of expression in first-order predicate logic. This format positions all quantifiers (THERE-EXISTS-A and FOR-ALL) at the beginning of the query (Date, 1986b and Chang and Lee, 1973) but it does not limit expressive power and has the advantage of great unambiguity of expression.

25.1.4 Step 4: Generate

The information analyst, or even a translation program, can now transform the tuple calculus expression, in our case in prenex normal form, into the syntax of the chosen database language, such as SQL. Since such a program simulates the 'intelligent behaviour' of the information analyst, some prefer to call such a program an expert system; others simply use the word compiler.

Relational query language processors often require some kind of mapping from the tuple calculus format to the peculiarities of the syntax and semantics of languages like SQL and QUEL. In SQL, for example, the quantifier FOR-ALL is missing. Thus for the expression FOR-ALL (x): (x>0) a transformation is necessary to the logically equivalent NOT (THERE-EXISTS-A (x): NOT (x>0)). The language QUEL, on the other hand, only knows the quantifier THERE-EXISTS-A implicitly; and one may not put NOT in front. If the tuple calculus expression contains NOT THERE-EXISTS-A (...) then we must transform this into something like COUNT (...) = 0.

25.2 A Query Transformation Example

Suppose a user poses the following question: 'Which employees have a colleague working as project leader on a project managed by the same department as is managing a project financed by R&D?' This is a very artificial question but we have chosen it since it illustrates several aspects we want to show in a complex query. *Section 25.4.3 Some Additional Questions to Try*, has some more complex questions.

25.2.1 Interpreting the Question

The first question the information analyst may ask the user is what is meant by 'Which employees?' Does the information analyst just want the name or other information as well — even the department name and manager? In this case the names and empnr's of the employees are sufficient. The query is reformulated as follows: 'Give the name and empnr of employees who have a colleague working as project leader on a project managed by the same department as is managing a project financed by R&D!'

Points the information analyst should bring in are what is intended by 'a project managed by' and 'department as is managing a project'. The term managing a project is unknown to the information system. Even were such a term known to the information system it would be a good idea to verify that the user has the same definition in mind.

Alternative interpretations may be generated from the data structure diagram (*see Section 25.4.2 Data Structure Diagram*) such as:

- A project is managed by a department that has responsibility over a project, or
- A project is managed by the department sponsoring the project, or
- A project is managed by the department that currently supplies the employee performing the role of project leader for the project, or
- A project is managed by the department that originally supplied the employee who performed the role of project leader for the project.

The user agrees that the department currently responsible for a project is understood to be the one managing it.

Note that some of the possible definitions above introduced the concept of time. In *Chapter 23 Using the Datetime Facilities* we give examples on dealing with time-dependent information such as that referred to in the last two definitions above. Similarly the phrase 'have a colleague working' is substituted by 'have a member of their own department working as'.

The query now reads: 'Give the name and empnr of employees who have a member of their own department working as project leader on a project for which the department responsible was also responsible for a project financed by R&D!'

25.2.2 Shaping the Question into Business Language

The query, still in natural language, is gradually transformed into a more formal notation. First, we try to reshape the structure of the sentence into:

```
<requested information>
FROM <things we ask information about>
FOR-WHICH-IS-TRUE <a group of conditions>
```

The requested information and the conditions are either simple (i.e. directly mappable on to conditions or terms known in the information system, such as two columns having the same value) or have the form THERE-EXISTS-A or NOT THERE-EXISTS-A (or THERE-EXISTS-NO). For each of these subconditions the same transformation rules must be applied.

Let us look at what information is requested about the employees and try to shape the conditions into something like:

```
name, empnr FROM employees
FOR-WHICH-IS-TRUE THERE-EXISTS-A department
   which same department employs an employee
   AND
   which particular employee worked as project leader on a
      project
   AND
   which particular project fell under the responsibility of
      a department
   AND
   this specific department was also responsible for a
      project
   AND
   that specific project was financed by the department R&D
```

We can still have a readable but reasonably precise query by replacing the references ('which same', 'this specific' and 'that particular') by allocating names to the ' `thing we ask information about` '. By doing so, we make absolutely clear which things we want to refer to and it becomes obvious when we are talking about the same or different (collections of) projects and departments. The construction now takes the form:

```
name, empnr FROM employee E1
FOR-WHICH-IS-TRUE THERE-EXISTS-A department
   where that particular department employs employee E1
   AND
   where ...
```

By introducing symbolic names for the department and other items and reformulating the associated subqueries we obtain:

```
name, empnr FROM employee E1
FOR-WHICH-IS-TRUE
   THERE-EXISTS-A department D1
   FOR-WHICH-IS-TRUE
      department D1 employs employee E1
      THERE-EXISTS-A employee E2
      FOR-WHICH-IS-TRUE
         department D1 employs employees E2
         ...
```

In the above formulation we are using the convention that conditions aligned under each other are connected via an AND unless we use the term OR. We can continue to process each sub-condition into the form FOR-WHICH-IS-TRUE until we obtain:

```
name, empnr FROM employee E1
FOR-WHICH-IS-TRUE
   THERE-EXISTS-A department D1
   FOR-WHICH-IS-TRUE
      department D1 employs employee E1
      FOR-WHICH-IS-TRUE
      THERE-EXISTS-A employee E2
      FOR-WHICH-IS-TRUE
         department D1 employs employees E2
         FOR-WHICH-IS-TRUE
         THERE-EXISTS-A project P1
         FOR-WHICH-IS-TRUE
         employee E2 is a project leader for project P1
            FOR-WHICH-IS-TRUE
            THERE-EXISTS-A department D2 AND project P2
            FOR-WHICH-IS-TRUE
               project P1 was sponsored by department D2
               project P2 was sponsored by department D2
               FOR-WHICH-IS-TRUE
               THERE-EXISTS-A department D3
               FOR-WHICH-IS-TRUE
                  department D3 financed project P2
                  department D3 is R&D
```

We find the expression ‘ `employee E2 is a 'project leader' for project P1` ’ which we cannot simply map on to the database structure. In agreement with the user's interpretation we replace ‘ `employee E2 is a 'project leader' for project P1` ’ by the equivalent formulation ‘ `there is an assignment scheduled for project P1 that is fulfilled by employee E2` ’ and ‘ `the role in the assignment is 'project leader'` ’. More formally, this leads to:

```
THERE-EXISTS-A assignment A
FOR-WHICH-IS-TRUE
   employee E fulfils assignment A
   assignment A is scheduled for project P
   the role of assignment A is R
```

If we substitute the above structure, with appropriate fresh substitutions for A, E, P and R, for the construction ‘employee E is an R for project P’ in the correct place or places (in our case only once), we obtain the following definition:

```
name, empnr FROM employee E1
FOR-WHICH-IS-TRUE
   THERE-EXISTS-A department D1
   FOR-WHICH-IS-TRUE
   department D1 employs employee E1
   FOR-WHICH-IS-TRUE
   THERE-EXISTS-A employee E2
   FOR-WHICH-IS-TRUE
   department D1 employs employees E2
   FOR-WHICH-IS-TRUE
      THERE-EXISTS-A project P1 AND assignment A1
      FOR-WHICH-IS-TRUE
      employee E2 fulfils assignment A1
      assignment A1 is scheduled for project P1
      the role of assignment A1 is "project leader"
      FOR-WHICH-IS-TRUE
         THERE-EXISTS-A department D2 AND project P2
         FOR-WHICH-IS-TRUE
         department D2 was responsible for project P1
         department D2 was responsible for project P2
         FOR-WHICH-IS-TRUE
            THERE-EXISTS-A department D3
            FOR-WHICH-IS-TRUE
            department D3 sponsored project P2
            department D3 is R&D
```

25.2.3 Formalize the Syntax

In the previous section we have not only shaped the query, trying to disassemble the question to obtain a clear and explicit understanding of what the user wanted to ask, but have also formalized it. What we need to do now is to carry out the 'context-switch', where terms like department, assignment, financed, employs must be replaced by the corresponding names of tables, columns and foreign key relationships of the database. One could also say that the terms from the dictionary part (the descriptive part) of the encyclopaedia are substituted for terms from the directory part (the schema definition part), and all simple conditions are replaced by conditions between columns in the database.

At the same time we switch to a more compact, mathematical notation. The result expressed in tuple calculus looks as follows:

```
{(E1.name, E1.empnr) ¦
   E1 ∈ Employee
   and
   ∃ D1 ∈ Dept: D1.deptcd = E1.deptcd
   and
   ∃ E2 ∈ Employee: D1.deptcd = E2.deptcd
   and
   ∃ P1 ∈ Project: (∃ A1 ∈ Assignment:
           E2.empnr = A1.empnr
           and
           P1.project_cd = A1.project_cd
           and
           A1.project_role = "Project Leader"
           and
           (∃ D2 ∈ Dept: (∃ P2 ∈ Project:
                   D2.deptcd = P1.resp_dept
                   and
                   D2.deptcd = P2.resp_dept
                   and
                   (∃ D3 ∈ Dept:
                      P2.sponsor_dept= D3.deptcd
                      and
                      D3.deptnm = "R&D")))) }
```

This expression can be transformed to prenex normal form (*see Section 25.3.3 Rewrite Rules for Obtaining Prenex Normal Form*) with the following result:

```
{(E1.name, E1.empnr) ¦
   E1 ∈ Employee and ∃ D1 ∈ Dept: ∃ E2 ∈ Employee: ∃ P1 ∈
   Project: ∃ A1 ∈ Assignment: ∃ D2 ∈ Dept: ∃ P2 ∈ Project:
   ∃ D3 ∈ Dept:
      D1.deptcd = E1.deptcd
   and  D1.deptcd = E2.deptcd
   and  E2.empnr = A1.empnr
   and  P1.project_cd = A1.project_cd
   and  A1.project_role = "Project Leader"
   and  D2.deptcd = P1.resp_dept
   and  D2.deptcd = P2.resp_dept
   and  P2.sponsor_dept= D3.deptcd
   and  D3.deptnm = "R&D" }
```

25.2.4 Generating the SQL Query

The tuple calculus expression in prenex normal form can now be transformed in a straightforward manner into SQL giving:

```
SELECT E1.name, E1.empnr
FROM    Employee AS E1, Dept AS D1, Employee AS E2, Project
        AS P1, Assignment AS A1, Dept AS D2, Project AS P2,
        Dept AS D3
WHERE   D1.deptcd = E1.deptcd
   AND  D1.deptcd = E2.deptcd
   AND  E2.empnr = A1.empnr
   AND  P1.project_cd = A1.project_cd
   AND  A1.project_role = "Project Leader"
   AND  D2.deptcd = P1.resp_dept
   AND  D2.deptcd = P2.resp_dept
   AND  P2.sponsor_dept= D3.deptcd
   AND  D3.deptnm = "R&D"
```

In general we recommend using better descriptive names for database identifiers and alias names, but in complex queries it often takes a lot of effort to obtain a neat layout.

25.3 General Remarks

Some remarks on the processes used to resolve various issues in the previous paragraphs follow.

25.3.1 The Chosen Steps

The subdivision into four steps is obviously an arbitrary choice. We could have included a separate step between formalize and generate to carry out the transformation into prenex normal form. The separation between steps is not always clear-cut — during the shaping we begin formalizing as well. Apart from the 'context-switch', the formalizing step is really just the transformation into a more formal, mathematical notation. In our particular example one could argue that the steps shape and formalize should be combined into a single step. However, we have represented shaping as a separate step, since during this step the transformation of the query is transformed into simpler conditions connected by boolean operators like AND and OR. Since we did not use very complex conditions the simplification does not show very clearly.

25.3.2 Macro Facilities

In *Section 25.2.2 Shaping the Question into Business Language* we saw an expression of the form ' `employee X is a R for project Y` '. In that instance, X was E2, R was 'project leader' and Y was P1. This expression was not directly mappable on to terms from the data dictionary. The interpretation we chose, however, was expressible as a more complex condition, namely ' `there is an assignment scheduled ' for project Y that is fulfilled by employee X` ' and ' `the role in the assignment is R` '.

The last action in the shaping step in our example is the substitution of each occurrence of such a complex condition. In fact, this action is not very much more than the replacement of a macro-call by the corresponding macro-body. The use of such macros can be very handy. The question is where such a facility may reside. A panel-driven query facility on top of SQL is one option.

25.3.3 Rewrite Rules for Obtaining Prenex Normal Form

One particular query can often be expressed in many different ways in a single language. The benefit of standardization is a more uniform formulation. In our case we chose prenex normal form for a number of reasons.

Apart from uniformity, we find prenex normal form more 'readable'. For example, as a result of steps 3 and 4 it is pretty easy to contrive simpler formulations, which are usually more efficient to execute by short-cutting some of the equations. When we replace ' `D1.deptcd = E1.deptcd and D1.deptcd = E2.deptcd` ' by the more directly formulated ' `E1.deptcd = E2.deptcd` ' and ' `D2.deptcd = P1.resp_dept and D2.deptcd = P2.resp_dept` ' by ' `P1.resp_dept = P2.resp_dept` ' the result of step 3 becomes:

```
{(E1.name, E1.empnr) |
   E1 ∈ Employee: ∃ D1 ∈ Dept: ∃ E2 ∈ Employee: ∃ P1 ∈ Pro-
   ject: ∃ A1 ∈ Assignment: ∃ D2 ∈ Dept: ∃ P2 ∈ Project: ∃
   D3 ∈ Dept:
        E1.deptcd = E2.deptcd
   and  E2.empnr = A1.empnr
   and  P1.project_cd = A1.project_cd
   and  A1.project_role = "Project Leader"
   and  P1.resp_dept = P2.resp_dept
   and  P2.sponsor_dept= D3.deptcd
   and  D3.deptnm = "R&D" }
```

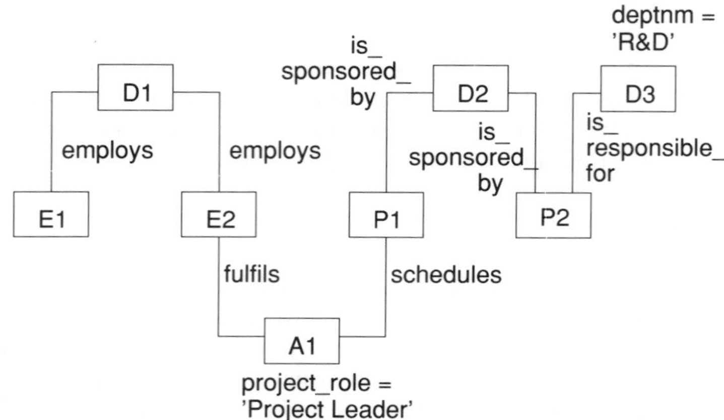

Figure 25.2 *Query structure diagram for complex queries*

However, this simpler and more direct formulation is only truly equivalent when the relationships involved have referential integrity constraints in place. Projects always have a resp_dept and a sponsor_dept; thus we need not refer to the project when stepping from one project to another; similarly, every employee has a deptcd.

Not only the prenex normal form itself is more readable but also the resulting SQL query. Generating SQL syntax from our step 3 result gives us a 'flat' query formulation in SQL instead of a 'nested' query. A nested query is one where subqueries exist with, perhaps, further sub-subqueries and so on. A 'flat' query is one where there are few, if possible no, subqueries.

If we had generated SQL from the expression at the beginning of *Section 25.2.3 Formalize the Syntax* we would have had a query in SQL with seven 'nested' SELECTs. This is awkward to represent on paper so we will leave it to your imagination.

To make the reading and interpretation of complex queries easier Remmen (1985) introduced diagrammatic representation in the form of query relationship diagrams which were further enhanced in de Jonge *et al.* (1988). A variation on the representation of the query structure is presented in the query structure diagram in Figure 25.2.

25.3.4 Flat Versus Nested SQL Queries

In the previous section we distinguished between 'flat' and 'nested' queries, and we showed a preference for the 'flat' formulation. To show the reasons for this try to 'reverse engineer' the original natural language query from the two SQL queries below. An example of a nested query is:

```
SELECT  E1.name
FROM    Employee AS E1
WHERE   E1.empnr =
        (SELECT    A1.empnr
        FROM       Assignment AS A1
        WHERE      A1.deptcd =
                   (SELECT    P1.deptcd
                   FROM       Project AS P1
                   WHERE      P1.project_cd = 'SQLØ1'))
AND     E1.empnr =
        (SELECT    E2.empnr
        FROM       Employee AS E2
        WHERE      E2.empnr =
                   (SELECT    A2.empnr
                   FROM       Assignment AS A2
                   WHERE      A2.deptcd =
                              (SELECT P2.deptcd
                              FROM Project AS P2
                              WHERE P2.project_cd = 'SQLØ2')))
```

An example of a flat query is:

```
SELECT  E1.name
FROM    Employee AS E1, Employee AS E2, Assignment AS A1,
          Assignment AS A2, Project AS P1, Project AS P2
WHERE   E1.empnr = A1.empnr
   AND  A1.project_cd = P1.project_cd
   AND  P1.project_cd = 'SQL01'
   AND  E2.empnr = A2.empnr
   AND  A2.project_cd = P2.project_cd
   AND  P2.project_cd = 'SQL02'
   AND  E1.empnr = E2.empnr
```

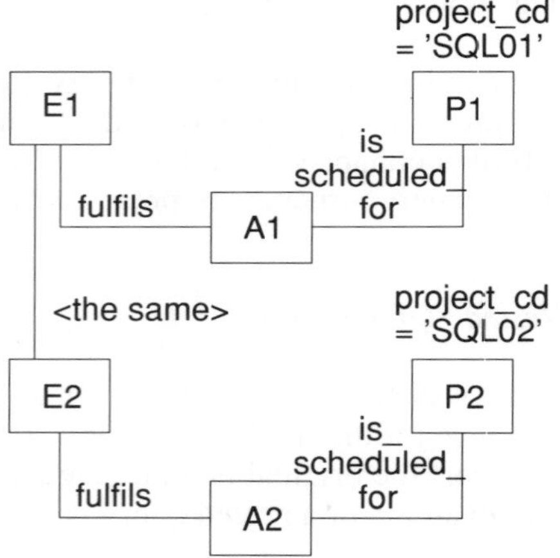

Figure 25.3 *Query structure diagram for SQL project*

The query structure diagram is shown in Figure 25.3. The actual natural language query on which the two equivalent SQL queries above are based is question 6 from the questions in *Section 25.4.3 Some Additional Questions to Try.*

In our view readability is an important issue, because it contributes to correct and maintainable coding. A second benefit of 'flat' SQL is the ability of optimizers in database management systems to generate more efficient code. Certain optimizers always operate inside out in 'nested' SQL queries and thereby frequently cannot achieve an optimal solution.

25.3.5 Aliasing

In *Section 25.2.4 Generating the SQL Query* we have mentioned all the tables used in the FROM part of the SELECT command and used aliasing everywhere. Always using the alias, or **correlation name**, option, even when not strictly required, has a number of benefits. Firstly, those cases where it is absolutely necessary cease to become exceptions and thus potentially more confusing to read. Secondly, the query itself becomes very much more readable given the choice of clear identifiers. Finally, its shows explicitly that every SQL query uses tuple variables. Also the format:

```
SELECT ...
FROM P
WHERE ...
```

implies that all Ps in the WHERE-part are occurrences of an implicitly declared tuple variable which incidently was named 'P'.

Referencing in the FROM clause all of the tables used also brings benefits. We can see directly which tables are used and how often, and we can obtain a formulation with as few as possible EXISTSs enhancing the flatness of the query. Not having EXISTSs also helps users to understand the final SQL query as they frequently do not understand the existential quantifier — EXISTS.

25.3.6 Top-Down Versus Bottom-Up

Finally, we would like to make it clear that our approach is top-down. Putting the original question in the form of a clause using the 'who/which-construct' we get 'Which employees have a colleague, who is working as project leader on a project, which is managed by a department, which is also managing a project, which is financed by R&D?' or even 'Which employees work for a department, which has an employee, who is working as project leader on a project, which is managed by a department, which is also managing a project, which is financed by R&D?'

Looking at the buildup of the sentence it is clear that we have worked from left to right, from start to finish. More generally, if a query is formulated as a main clause with subordinate clauses (and subordinate clauses within subordinate clauses, etc.) we start with the main clause and subsequently process the subordinate clauses and so on. Alternatively, if the query is expressed in a tree-like structure, we start processing from the top, the root, and proceed downward via the branches (giving more details) to the leaves (revealing more detailed information).

In the bottom-up approach one needs to recognize the various subsets for which one creates the computer language representation, and finally all pieces are built together into a single (chunk of the) query. We would start by identifying the R&D department before finding the projects that R&D finances, which is required before one can find the department(s) managing these projects.

25.4 Background Information

This section provides background material for the examples in this chapter.

25.4.1 Database Schema DDL

The following DDL statements describe the relevant part of the Company schema for this chapter. The *italicized* parts in the schema have been added to refer explicitly to the relationships in the data structure diagram in the next section:

```
CREATE SCHEMA Company AUTHORIZATION cannan

CREATE TABLE Dept
(
deptcd        CHARACTER (3) PRIMARY KEY,
deptnm        CHARACTER (12)
)

CREATE TABLE Employee
(
empnr         NUMERIC (5),
name          CHARACTER (40) NOT NULL,
address       CHARACTER VARYING (200),
sex           CHARACTER NOT NULL,
home_telno    CHARACTER (14),
deptcd        CHARACTER (3) NOT NULL DEFAULT 'PER',
work_telno    CHARACTER (14) UNIQUE,
job           CHARACTER (20) NOT NULL,
salary        NUMERIC (6) NOT NULL,
...
commission    NUMERIC (6,2),
CHECK (sex IN ('M','F')),
PRIMARY KEY (empnr),
...
CONSTRAINT employs FOREIGN KEY (deptcd) REFERENCES Dept
   ON DELETE SET DEFAULT
   ON UPDATE CASCADE
)

CREATE TABLE Project
(
project_cd    CHARACTER (6),
start_date    DATE NOT NULL,
end_date      DATE,
resp_dept     NUMERIC (5) NOT NULL,
sponsor_dept  NUMERIC (5) NOT NULL,
budget        DECIMAL (6,2),
forecast      DECIMAL (6,2),
actual        DECIMAL (6,2),
description   CHARACTER VARYING (2000),
PRIMARY KEY (project_cd),
CONSTRAINT responsible_for FOREIGN KEY (resp_dept)
   REFERENCES Dept,
CONSTRAINT sponsors FOREIGN KEY (sponsor_dept)
   REFERENCES Dept
)
```

```
CREATE TABLE Assignment
(
empnr          NUMERIC (5),
project_cd     CHARACTER (6),
project_role CHARACTER (15),
start_date     DATE NOT NULL,
end_date       DATE,
CHECK (NOT EXISTS (
   SELECT *
     FROM Assignment AS W1 JOIN Assignment AS W2
          USING (empnr, project_cd)
     WHERE (W1.start_date, W1.end_date)
           OVERLAPS
           (W2.start_date, W2.end_date)
           AND W1.start_date <> W2.start_date)),
CHECK (project_role IN (
      'Project Leader',
      'Quality Assurance',
      'Worker',
      'Planner')),
PRIMARY KEY (empnr, project_cd, start_date),
CONSTRAINT fulfils FOREIGN KEY (empnr) REFERENCES Employee,
CONSTRAINT scheduled_for FOREIGN KEY (project_cd)
   REFERENCES Project
)
```

25.4.2 Data Structure Diagram

The data structure diagram of the relevant part of the Company schema has been reproduced in Figure 25.4 with the names of the relationships inserted clockwise. As an example, a Department employs an Employee.

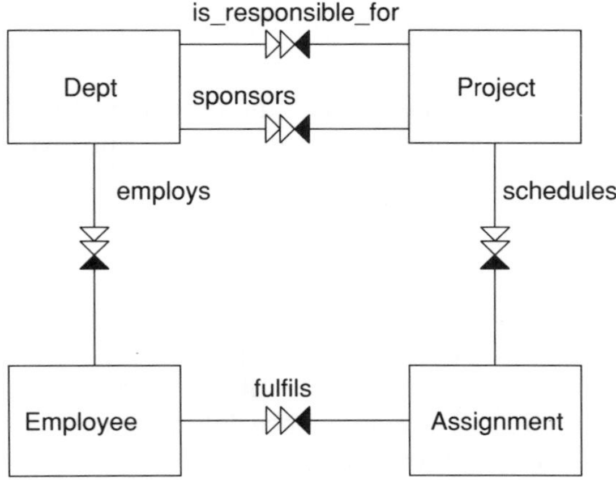

Figure 25.4 *Partial data structure diagram for natural language query examples*

25.4.3 Some Additional Questions to Try

Using the method described in this chapter you should be able to formulate correct SQL statements for the following questions:

1. Give the name of all employees from department R&D who participate in more than two assignments.
2. Give the names of all employees who have (had) an assignment in project SQL02.
3. Give the names of all employees who have never had an assignment in project SQL02.
4. Give the names of all employees who have (had) an assignment in projects SQL02 and SQL03 but who have never had an assignment in project SQL01.
5. Give the names and project roles of employees who had an assignment scheduled for the SQL02 project between 1990-10-01 and 1991-02-28.
6. Give the names of all employees who have worked for both the SQL01 and SQL02 projects.
7. Give the names of all projects that have had assigned to them employees who have also worked on project SQL02.
8. Give the names of all employees who have worked on at least two different projects.
9. Give the names of all employees who have worked in at least two different roles on the same project.
10. Give the names of the projects for which, in the period 1991-02-01 to 1991-02-28, no employees were assigned who were working for the R&D department.

25.5 Additional Information for Natural Language Translation

25.5.1 Truth Tables and Boolean Logic

To make the analysis and evaluation of the outcome of boolean expressions easier we provide some elementary transformation rules which will help you simplify the expressions.

25.5.2 Truth Tables for Boolean Expressions

The truth tables in Table 25.1 will help to determine the outcome of boolean expressions and to modify existing ones into formats more suitable for presentation in steps 3 'formalise' and 4 'generate' of the method for translating natural language queries into SQL. The equivalence definitions are provided in the next section, Boolean Transformation Rules.

Table 25.1 Truth tables for boolean expressions

a	b	$a \wedge b$	$\neg a$	$\neg b$	$(\neg a) \wedge (\neg b)$	$a \vee b \equiv \neg(\neg a \wedge \neg b)$	$a \Rightarrow b \equiv \neg a \vee b$	$b \Rightarrow a$	$a \Leftrightarrow b \equiv (a \Rightarrow b) \wedge (b \Rightarrow a) \equiv (a \wedge b) \vee (\neg a \wedge \neg b)$
0	0	0	1	1	1	0	1	1	1
0	1	0	1	0	0	1	1	0	0
1	0	0	0	1	0	1	0	1	0
1	1	1	0	0	0	1	1	1	1

A single example of the type $a \Rightarrow b$ should help you understand the table:

```
If the moon is made of 'green cheese', then I am more than 5
metres tall.
```

This expression is true, because the premise is not true; that is $a \Rightarrow b$ is surely true, if a is false!

25.5.3 Boolean Transformation Rules

In essence only two boolean operators are required, $\wedge$ and $\neg$. All other operators can be avoided by using transformation rules as described in this section, reformulating existing expressions into equivalent expressions that are syntactically different. This enables us to rewrite boolean expressions into a set of symbols we (or some database software such as SQL or QUEL based systems) can better understand. The following are the basic rules for transforming boolean expressions:

(R1) $1 \wedge a \equiv a$
(R2) $0 \wedge a \equiv 0$
(R3) $1 \vee a \equiv 1$
(R4) $0 \vee a \equiv a$
(R5) $a \wedge (\neg a) \equiv 0$
(R6) $a \vee (\neg a) \equiv 1$
(R7) $\neg(\neg a) \equiv a$

The following rules describe, in pairs, the commutative, the associative, the distributive and the de Morgan rules for transformation of boolean expressions:

Commutative rules:
(R8) $a \wedge b \equiv b \wedge a$ (R9) $a \vee b \equiv b \vee a$

Associative rules:
(R10) $a \wedge (b \wedge c) \equiv (a \wedge b) \wedge c$ (R11) $a \vee (b \vee c) \equiv (a \vee b) \vee c$

Distributive rules:
(R12) $a \wedge (b \vee c) \equiv (a \wedge b) \vee (a \wedge c)$ (R13) $a \vee (b \wedge c) \equiv (a \vee b) \wedge (a \vee c)$

De Morgan rules:
(R14) $\neg(a \wedge b) \equiv (\neg a) \vee (\neg b)$ (R15) $\neg(a \vee b) \equiv (\neg a) \wedge (\neg b)$

The following transformations are also allowable:
(R16) $a \vee b \equiv \neg(\neg a \wedge \neg b)$ (R17) $a \Rightarrow b \equiv \neg a \vee b$
(R18) $a \Leftrightarrow b \equiv (a \Rightarrow b) \wedge (b \Rightarrow a) \equiv (a \wedge b) \vee (\neg a \wedge \neg b)$

Some examples of the application of the rules just presented can be seen in the following transformations. The transformation rule used is indicated in superscript after each ≡ symbol:

1. $a \vee b \equiv^{(R7)} \neg\neg(a \vee b) \equiv^{(R15)} \neg(\neg a \wedge \neg b)$ *(see also definition (R16))*
2. $a \Rightarrow b \equiv^{(R17)} (\neg a) \vee b \equiv^{(R7)} \neg\neg((\neg a) \vee b) \equiv^{(R15)} \neg((\neg(\neg a)) \wedge \neg b) \equiv^{(R7)} \neg(a \wedge \neg b)$
3. $a \Leftrightarrow b \equiv^{(R18)} (a \Rightarrow b) \wedge (b \Rightarrow a) \equiv^{(R17)} (\neg a \vee b) \wedge (\neg b \vee a)$
$\equiv^{(R12)} ((\neg a \vee b) \wedge \neg b) \vee ((\neg a \vee b) \wedge a) \equiv^{(R8)} (\neg b \wedge (\neg a \vee b)) \vee (a \wedge (\neg a \vee b))$
$\equiv^{(R12)} ((\neg b \wedge \neg a) \vee (\neg b \wedge b)) \vee ((a \wedge \neg a) \vee (a \wedge b))$
$\equiv^{(R5)} ((\neg b \wedge \neg a) \vee 0) \vee (0 \vee (a \wedge b)) \equiv^{(R4)} (\neg b \wedge \neg a) \vee (a \wedge b) \equiv^{(R8) \text{ and } (R9)}$
$(a \wedge b) \vee (\neg a \wedge \neg b)$

25.5.4 Prenex Normal Form Translation Rules

The following rules may be used in the transformation of formulae:

1. $\neg(\neg f) = f$
2. if f then $g = f \Rightarrow g = (\neg f) \vee g$
3. $f \vee g = g \vee f$
4. $f \wedge g = g \wedge f$
5. $\neg(f \vee g) = (\neg f) \wedge (\neg g)$
6. $\neg(f \wedge g) = (\neg f) \vee (\neg g)$
7. $\neg(\forall x \in A\text{: f}(x)) = \exists x \in A\text{: }(\neg \text{f}(x))$
8. $\neg(\exists x \in A\text{: f}(x)) = \forall x \in A\text{: }(\neg \text{f}(x))$
9. $(\forall x \in A\text{: f}(x)) \wedge (\forall x \in A\text{: g}(x)) = \forall x \in A\text{: }(\text{f}(x) \wedge \text{g}(x))$
10. $(\exists x \in A\text{: f}(x)) \vee (\exists x \in A\text{: g}(x)) = \exists x \in A\text{: }(\text{f}(x) \vee \text{g}(x))$
11. $\text{Q } x \in A\text{: f}(x) = \text{Q } y \in A\text{: f}(y/x)$
12. $(\text{Q } x \in A\text{: f}(x)) \bullet g = \text{Q } x \in A\text{: }(\text{f}(x) \bullet g)$
13. $(\text{Q}_1\ x \in A\text{: f}(x)) \bullet (\text{Q}_2\ y \in B\text{: g}(y)) = \text{Q}_1\ x \in A\text{: Q}_2\ y \in B\text{: }(\text{f}(x) \bullet \text{g}(y))$

where:

- f and g stand for formulae.
- f(x) and g(x) stand for formulae where at least one of the free variables is x.
- Q stands for a quantifier and can thus be either ∃ or ∀. Thus transformation rule 11 stands for two rules, one where both Qs are replaced by ∃ and one where both are replaced by ∀.

- f(y/x) stands for the formula that is obtained if all free occurrences of x are replaced by y in the formula f(x).
- • stands either for the operator $\wedge$ or the operator $\vee$. Thus rule 12 stands for four rules depending on the substitutions for • and Q, and rule 13 for eight rules.

In rule 12 the formula g may not contain any free occurrences of x and in rule 13 the formula f(x) must not contain any free y's and the formula g(y) must not contain any free x's.

26

Usage of Views

The view mechanism is a very powerful concept which can be used for many different purposes, some of which we will explore in this chapter. A full description of the create view statement is given elsewhere (*see Section 4.4 CREATE VIEW*); however, the syntax for creating a view is:

```
CREATE VIEW <table name> [ ( <view column list> ) ]
    AS <query expression>
    [ WITH [ CASCADED | LOCAL ] CHECK OPTION ]
```

In the following sections we present some of the significant benefits of using the view concept, and highlight some important side effects to be aware of.

26.1 Enhancing Accessibility and User Access

Let us first recall a few important characteristics of the view concept. The result of a view is in essence a table, a so-called derived table, combining portions of one or more (different) tables into this single table. This does not mean that the data available through a view is to be regarded as a separate permanent storage structure, though the actual implementation is left to the SQL software supplier. The portions are effectively a selection of rows and/or a projection of columns. The derived table can always be perceived as having been generated from the underlying base tables. Views may be referenced in the <query expression> to create another view.

This allows the presentation of data stored in a database in forms more suitable for differing groups of users. These may be users invoking SQL directly from their terminals to produce reports or may be programmers coding modules using the SQL module language.

26.1.1 Structure Simplification

An SQL database is usually structured to minimize maintenance efforts while providing good performance overall which places a tremendous burden on it. For some strong advocates of the relational model, this always results in a database structure which is normalized to at least the third normal form (3NF). Many papers in the previous decade have devised yet further forms of normalization. Kent (1983) gives a clear and concise description of these.

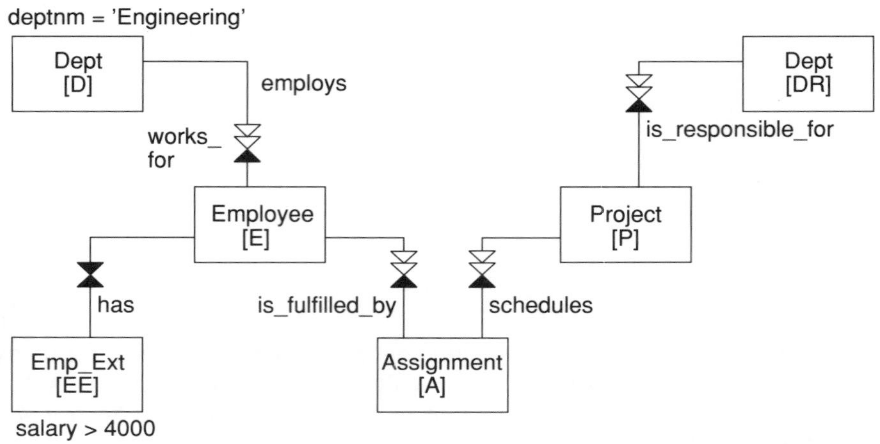

Figure 26.1 *Query structure diagram for VIEW Works_on_project*

By definition, normalizing a data structure leads to an increased number of tables, since normalization is primarily concerned with understanding the dependencies of data elements and establishing a data structure that is easy to handle in terms of insertions, deletions and updates. This does not mean — in fact it usually means exactly the opposite — that it is easy to understand how to extract data from or browse through such structures. The view mechanism allows the bringing together of separate tables into a single derived table via the formulation of the <query expression>. Using set operators such as UNION, EXCEPT, INTERSECT and JOIN in its different forms, we can process and group multiple sets of rows from different tables. The resulting denormalized view may be very straightforward to understand but on the other hand it may lack the characteristics required to enable updating to take place through such a view. Take, for example, the following view definition:

```
CREATE VIEW Works_on_project
    (e_name, e_dob, d_worksfor,
     ep_start, p_code,
     d_name_responsible)
AS
SELECT E.name,
       EE.date_of_birth,
       D.deptnm, A.start_date,
       P.project_cd, DR.deptnm
  FROM Employee E, Emp_Ext EE,
       Dept D, Assignment A,
       Project P, Dept DR
  WHERE E.deptcd = D.deptcd
    AND EE.empnr = E.empnr
    AND A.empnr = E.empnr
    AND A.project_cd = P.project_cd
    AND P.resp_dept = DR.deptcd
    AND D.deptnm = 'Engineering'
    AND EE.salary > 13000
```

This view returns a table of project and employee data for all employees in the engineering department earning a salary of more than 13 000. Figure 26.1 shows a query structure diagram for this view definition (*see Chapter 25 Translating Natural Language Queries and in particular Figure 25.2*).

26.1.2 Making only Relevant Parts of the Database Visible

'Out of sight, out of mind' — this phrase exemplifies the purpose of limiting the data visible through the view created. Essentially by selecting positively those portions offered to users irrelevant data is filtered out. Once the structure is simplified, as explained in the previous section, underlying tables are selected in an intelligent manner to reduce the size of the derived table. One aspect of this is the selection of relevant rows which is shown in the WHERE clause here; the other is the projection of a subset of columns from the set of underlying, possibly also derived, tables. The first aspect of the algorithm for this selection process is specified in the WHERE clause of the <query expression>, in the example above, where the first five conditions join the tables involved and the last two conditions reflect a (further) selection of relevant rows. The WHERE clause has two similar but distinctive roles: on the one hand it specifies connections between underlying tables and thus selects rows that qualify; on the other hand it provides further limiting criteria.

The second aspect, projection, is reflected in the six column names specified in the SELECT statement and is shown with more user-friendly names between the parentheses after the view name in the CREATE VIEW command. This is a subset of columns available from the underlying tables in the FROM clauses in the <query expression>.

26.1.3 Derivation Support

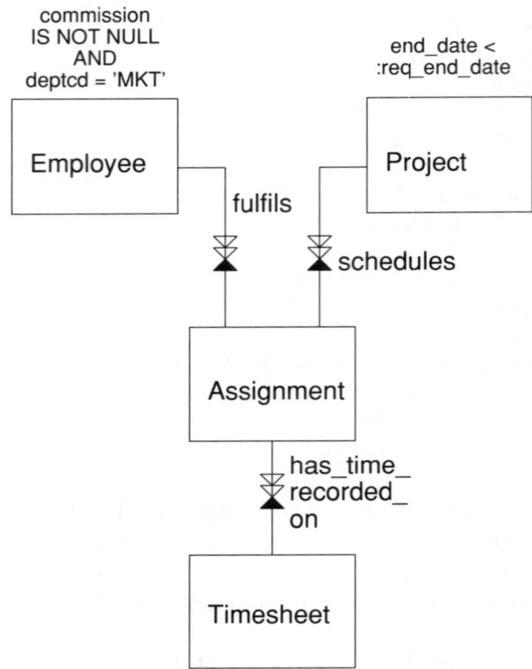

Figure 26.2 *Query structure diagram for Project_times view*

A further way of pleasing the user is to provide assistance with the derivation of values from the selected rows and columns in the view. We can specify in the view definition the calculation of minima, maxima, averages or counts based on sets of rows. We could specify a view with columns containing the results of operations performed on other, visible or invisible, columns of the view. The concatenation of name and address for all employees belonging to the department of the person issuing the query could be given in a single column, their total salary and commission, the duration of each project they participated in, in days as calculated from start_date to end_date and the total number of hours each employee worked on that project are also examples of this. The resulting view definition looks like:

```
CREATE VIEW Project_times
  AS
  SELECT E.name || ',' || E.address,
         E.salary + E.commission, A.project_cd,
         SUM(T.hours + T.overtime_hours),
         ((P.end_date-P.start_date) + 1 DAY)
           DAY
  FROM Employee AS E, Assignment AS A,
       Project AS P, Timesheet AS T
  WHERE E.empnr = A.empnr
    AND P.project_cd = A.project_cd
    AND A.empnr = T.empnr
    AND A.project_cd = T.project_cd
    AND E.deptcd = 'MKT'
    AND E.commission IS NOT NULL
    AND P.end_date < :req_end_date
  GROUP BY A.project_cd
```

Figure 26.2 opposite shows the query structure diagram for the view Project_ times. *Appendix A The Example Database* shows more opportunities for views containing derived columns.

26.2 Limiting Access to Data

In the SQL standard access to data is arranged via the GRANT and REVOKE statements (*see Chapter 8 Access Control*). This access control is based on objects known to the SQL DBMS and views belong to the list of objects access control operates on.

By its nature the view mechanism limits very precisely the scope and visibility of data in the database. As such, this characteristic can be used to select and project a specific portion of available data into a derived table. Being a table, the access control mechanism for tables is itself available to the security designer of the database.

The view mechanism offers control over rows as well as columns, thereby allowing effective control at the record and field occurrence level. This would obviously require the definition of many views and so there will always be a trade-off between precision and fine-tuning on the one hand and resource usage and practicality on the other. Real life in our universe of discourse is complex and that is what we have to reflect. An example of control of a view is that a project manager may only be allowed to see the job history of employees currently assigned to the project or those due to start within one month. We could define a view to provide project managers with this data:

```
CREATE VIEW Project_worker_details
  AS
  SELECT empnr, E1.*, JH1.*
    FROM Employee AS E1 LEFT JOIN Job_History AS JH1
    USING (empnr)
    WHERE EXISTS ( SELECT *
                     FROM Assignment AS A1,
                          Assignment AS A2,
                          Employee AS E2, Project AS P
                     WHERE E2.empnr = A2.empnr
                       AND A2.project_cd = P.project_cd
                       AND E1.empnr = A1.empnr
                       AND A1.project_cd = P.project_cd
                       AND E2.empnr = CURRENT_USER
                       AND A2.project_role =
                              'Project Manager'
                       AND (A1.start_date, A1.end_date)
                              OVERLAPS
                             (CURRENT_DATE + 1 MONTH))
    GROUP BY empnr
```

Figure 26.3 shows the view Project_workers_details in the format of a query structure diagram.

In many applications access control is also used to keep some information invisible to certain users. Security regulations or sensitive data may require protection. This requirement may simply be fulfilled through access constraints or by the definition of a view that is granted to the target users of the information system. Examples of shielding may be found in the queries described in Figure 26.2 and in Figure 26.3. This shielding, however, has to be distinguished

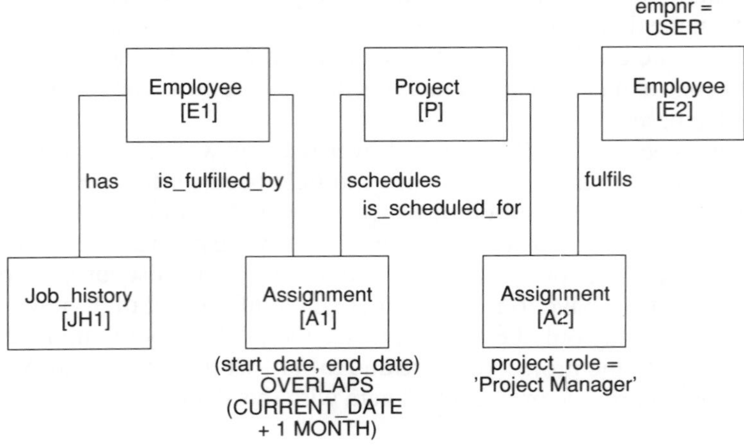

Figure 26.3 *Query structure diagram for Project_workers_details view*

from information that is missing. The dilemma here is what the SQL DBMS should reply to a query using a view that excludes some data from the user.

26.3 Mapping to Host Language Conventions

An SQL database may need to serve many application programmes written in many different languages. The current SQL supports many standardized computer languages with SQL acting as a data sub-language. *Chapter 17 The Embedded Languages* provides a more detailed description of this.

The programming language standardization committees have been fighting over definitions of data types for use across the board for years. The database community has been striving to support the information requirements of applications in different computer languages and has found ways around some of the problems. It appears that we may now expect a standard on a common set of language-independent data types within a reasonable time frame. For the moment, though, we need to allow for mappings taking place in SQL and *Chapter 11 Functions and Expressions* offers some insight into possible transformations and manipulations of data types.

Items that need attention in SQL are naming conventions, data types and precision requirements. The naming of objects like tables, columns and constraints must obey the rules of the embedded language. Special characters and limited lengths of names are only two of the considerations. The view mechanism helps by offering renaming facilities for columns in the <view column list> clause and for table names in the <table name> clause. In the example below we define the view such that the column minimum_order, which is defined as NUMERIC (10) in the database, appears as the NUMERIC (6,2) column and with the additional property that a NULL status is replaced by the value 0:

```
CREATE VIEW No_nulls_ps (prdcd, splcd, minord)
  AS
  SELECT product_code, supplier_code,
         CASE minimum_order
           WHEN NULL THEN CAST (0 AS NUMERIC (6,2))
           ELSE CAST (minimum_order AS NUMERIC (6,2))
         END
  FROM Product_supply
```

26.4 Enhanced Physical Environment Support

SQL is a language that is aimed at offering facilities to the user of the DBMS. Tuning and physical design facilities are not intended to be part of it and are left to the implementors to define. Certain inherent SQL functions and mechanisms, like the view mechanism, can be used implicitly or explicitly to enhance the performance of the physical environment in terms of memory usage, disk utilization and data independence.

26.4.1 Physical Data Independence

Many tools and constructs can be used to enhance the performance of the (database) system, but they are primarily discussed in *Chapter 28 Performance Aspects*. The lack of an explicit data storage definition language, which ANSI advocated in the ANSI SPARC 3 schema architecture 1977, requires some extra restructuring in the schema using SQL DDL commands. A proposal for a standard 'SQL Data Storage Description Language' can be found in BCS/CODASYL (1987). In our example database we have split the entity Employee into two tables called Employee and Emp_Ext (*see Appendix A The Example Database*). Usually such splitting and setting up of a one-to-one relationship takes place in order to use layered storage devices (selection of different speeds) or to allow better clustering of data into single I/O blocks or pages (selection of smaller rows).

This design decision obviously makes the joining of two tables necessary for each and every query that involves columns from each of the tables involved. A view that defines this joining of the tables makes life much easier for the application programs involved. Better maintainability is also achieved as it allows isolation of changes to the schema definitions, e.g. columns may be moved between the two tables with no application effort. This conclusion may not be true for all one-to-one relationships between tables. See *Section 22.6 The Implementation of Relationships — Examples* for a more detailed discussion on examples such as Travel_Req to Itinerary and Employee and Vehicle.

For example, switching between columns between Employee and Emp_Ext remains invisible for programs using a view, providing access to both tables through the view:

```
CREATE VIEW Complete_employee
  AS
  SELECT *
    FROM Employee NATURAL LEFT JOIN Emp_Ext ON (empnr)
```

26.4.2 Reduction of Dataflow

Defining views that contain only the columns required in the application makes it possible for the SQL DBMS to project the required data alone into the memory buffers. This allows more data requested by applications to be held in memory, so making a higher hit rate possible and reducing costly I/O operations, although at the expense of increased CPU usage for the selection of the appropriate data.

26.5 Using the WITH CHECK Options

Another interesting feature of views is the '`WITH CHECK OPTION`'. This has two sub-options, CASCADED and LOCAL. A simple '`WITH CHECK OPTION`' is equivalent to '`WITH CASCADED CHECK OPTION`'. In its simplest sense a

'WITH CHECK OPTION' ensures that any row updated through the view remains a member of the set of rows visible in the view.

We frequently see views as a way in which access to data can be controlled, but we often consider only read access and ignore write access. Consider the following view:

```
CREATE VIEW Prd_emps
  AS
  SELECT (empnr, name, deptcd, salary, sex)
    FROM Employee
    WHERE deptcd = 'PRD'
  WITH CHECK OPTION
```

Prd_emps					
empnr	*name*	*deptcd*	*salary*	...	*sex*
21347	De Vries	PRD	8500	...	M
65732	Jansen	PRD	9750	...	F
94376	van de Kraak	PRD	10500	...	M

Figure 26.4 *The Prd_emps view*

This view (*see Figure 26.4*) allows a user, say the manager of the production department (PRD), to see and manipulate data on all employees in his or her department. The 'WITH CHECK OPTION' restricts the update of the deptcd column value to its existing value, as any other value would automatically be excluded from the view by the WHERE clause.

Using this view we can define further ones until we have achieved a hierarchy. Consider the following two views:

```
CREATE VIEW Prd_low_paid_emps
  AS
  SELECT *
    FROM Prd_emps
    WHERE salary < 8900

CREATE VIEW Prd_low_paid_me
  AS
  SELECT *
    FROM Prd_low_paid_emps
    WHERE name = USER
  WITH CHECK OPTION
```

The Prd_low_paid_emps view allows a user to see employees in the production department who have low salaries. The user may then update the data on them, with the exception of the deptcd column. Updating the salary of an employee to 8900 or more would make that employee invisible to this view.

The Prd_low_paid_me view allows a low paid employee to see the data recorded about him or herself. That data may be updated, but again the column appearing in the WHERE clause, name, is controlled by the ' WITH CHECK OPTION ' and may not be changed. The ' WITH CHECK OPTION ' is actually a ' WITH CASCADED CHECK OPTION ' since neither option was specified. Salary and deptcd from the underlying WHERE clauses are therefore also controlled.

The rules simply state that, where a view contains a ' WITH CASCADED CHECK OPTION ', no updates to a row done through that view shall cause the row to become no longer visible through that view. Also, if any view definition, say VD1, is based even indirectly on a view, say VD2, which contains a ' WITH CASCADED CHECK OPTION ', then no updates to a row through view VD1 shall cause the row on which the row is based to be no longer visible in VD2 or any view subordinate to VD2.

The meaning of the LOCAL option can best be seen in an example. Observe the view hierarchy in the views V1, V2 and V3 below:

```
CREATE VIEW V1
  AS
  SELECT *
    FROM V2
    WHERE deptcd = (SELECT deptcd
                      FROM Employee E
                      WHERE E.name = USER)
  WITH LOCAL CHECK OPTION

CREATE VIEW V2
  AS
  SELECT *
    FROM V3
    WHERE  salary * 1.1 < (SELECT target_salary
                             FROM Guidelines G
                             WHERE  V3.job =  G.job)

CREATE VIEW V3
  AS
  SELECT *
    FROM Employee
    WHERE address LIKE '*Amsterdam*'
  WITH CHECK OPTION
```

The bottom view, V3, selects employees with an address in Amsterdam and has a non-specific ' WITH CHECK OPTION '. This is equivalent to a ' WITH CASCADED CHECK OPTION ', and means that any row materialized in that view may not disappear from the view as the result of updates done through it or any other view derived from it (the original situation). The middle view, V2, selects Amsterdam employees whose salaries are more than 10 per cent below the target for their type of job. This view has no ' WITH CHECK OPTION ' and thus rows may come and go as requested. The top view, V1, selects low paid

Amsterdam employees who work in the user's own department. This view has a ' WITH LOCAL CHECK OPTION ' which means that a row may not disappear from it as the result of an update if it still appears in the view (or table) from which it is derived, i.e. V2. Thus the check is local to the view; it depends only on the WHERE clause of the view itself and does not take into account the WHERE clauses of any views from which it is derived. Note that once a CASCADED check is encountered in a hierarchy the presence, absence or type of a ' WITH CHECK OPTION ' clause in any underlying view is irrelevant. This facility enables us to devise views that describe unwanted situations and allows them to be corrected using that view, whilst maintaining control of other factors. This is not possible with the CASCADED option alone. In the example the user may not change the deptcd or the location in order to remove a row from the view but may change the salary.

26.6 Conclusions on Views

The above sections show many reasons for developing views. From the perspective of maintainable and secure application design limiting of the scope of the data available for applications is valid and desirable. Views can not only help users access the database more easily but also control access to inappropriate data. However, while views can be effective and are often necessary we need to realize why we are choosing this mechanism. Benefits can also cause unwanted side effects. The enhanced physical data independence or access control may result in excessive CPU overhead. The use of views for access control may blur the insight into the data structure and the referential integrity between tables.

27

Distributed Databases

The popularity of SQL type languages is now so great that nowadays almost every computing platform, from the smallest PC to the biggest mainframe, has an SQL implementation available. The more the requirements for increased complexity in data processing solutions, the more likely these solutions will want to (re-)use existing data on multiple computers.

Computers with processing and storage capacity linked in a computer network constitute open distributed processing systems where three components are recognized as essential. The first, the communications function, takes care of the exchange and transport of data among computer nodes, the memory function takes care of definition and manipulation of data (and its associated rules) and the third, the processing function, provides processing capability and also manages the communications and memory complexes. All three functions are influenced by the requirement of sharing data on multiple computer nodes. The sheer time delay involved in transportation over distance demands extra measures to ensure secure and reliable data processing.

Distribution may be desirable from various points of view. The user wants to have data available at his or her own working location and many different jobs may require the same data at their respective locations. From the perspective of memory, replication of data may be required as security against failure or loss or for ease of access or ease of storage. From the processing point of view data may be required at parallel processing nodes to improve throughput or be available at differently scaled multiple processors to increase efficiency and costs.

SQL is aimed at logical data definition and logical data manipulation so that in the standard, all physical characteristics of data storage have been removed. *Chapter 28 Performance Aspects* shows which physical characteristics are involved in designing and implementing databases. The design and implementation of distributed databases are another mode of physical optimization. We will use SQL as a high level language here to show what functionality is necessary to support distributed database management, concentrating on the memory function and the requirements for distributed environments. We will look first at some aspects of data distribution and then see how SQL deals with it.

27.1 Definition of Terms in Distributed Databases

When talking about the distributed memory function we must first define the various components that play a role within it. A *distributed database* is one, which holds data distributed across the storage media of at least two computers (also called sites or nodes) connected by some form of communications network. Within the distributed database relationships that have been defined in terms of integrity constraints are consistently maintained within the data which resides on the storage media of the participating computers at the various locations in the network. This consistency is maintained during `INSERT`, `UPDATE` and `DELETE` operations. Each node is a database system in its own right, but sites have agreed to work together so that a user at one node can access all data in the distributed database as if it were stored at the user's local node.

A *distributed application* is one, which has autonomous processing capabilities for the local database and that also contains at least one function that uses the parts of the distributed database which are located on different nodes. Such a function manipulates data in the distributed database.

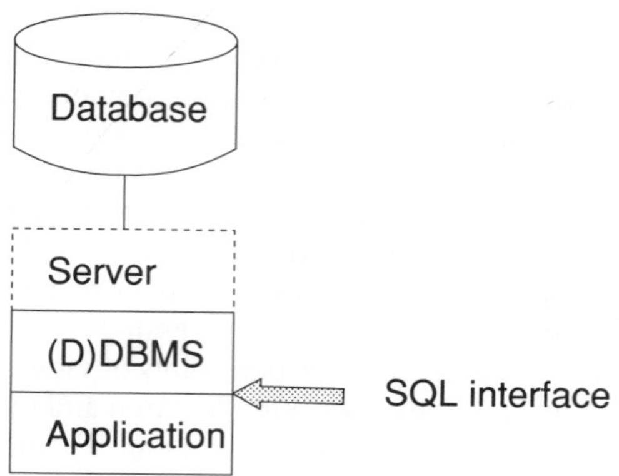

Figure 27.1 *Application to DBMS SQL interface*

A *distributed DBMS* (DDBMS) is a software system that supports the definition and manipulation of a distributed database for a distributed application. The distributed database is presented by the DDBMS to the distributed application as if it were a single, local database. A DBMS in this context is a software system that supports the definition and manipulation of a local database at a single computer node in the network. When considering distributed database systems there can be several distinctions made regarding the degree of distribution permitted and the placement among the components of an **information system** of the responsibility for controlling the various facets. In IBM documentation a distinction is made between the following four scenarios:

1. Remote Request. An application program running on a local node has the ability to submit an SQL command (request) to another node to be processed against data at that remote node. An important aspect is that each individual remote SQL request is also a separate transaction and an implicit commit takes place after each successful request.
2. Remote Unit of Work. In this scenario, the restriction on a single SQL request per transaction is relaxed. An application program may submit several SQL requests to the same node before requesting the end of the transaction.
3. Distributed Unit of Work. Here an application program may submit different SQL requests belonging to the same transaction to different nodes. The application program can therefore process data from several locations in a secure manner.
4. Distributed Request. In this last scenario a single SQL command may itself process data that resides on several different nodes.

In SQL at the moment the Remote Request and the Remote Unit of Work scenarios are supported. The third scenario, Distributed Unit of Work, is not required to be supported because a transaction within SQL need only be able to process data from a single node. Implementations may, however, support Distributed Unit of Work in a standard manner if they so choose (*see Chapter 14 Session Management*). Support for the Distributed Request scenario is buried within the **DBMS** and is therefore transparent to the SQL language. However, in this chapter we discuss a number of problems that distributed request poses as if it was indeed visible at the SQL interface between the DBMS and application program.

In treating SQL as a language we are interested in the complexities of data management by the DBMS which supports SQL as a data sub-language. We will ignore any form of data distribution carried out by servers whose functions are called on by the DBMS. These forms of distribution are invisible to the application and so they have no influence on the SQL statements issued by the application. Servers, such as (network) operating systems, parallel processing firmware, disk sub-system control software, may have the capabilities to replicate, distribute and recombine data in many different forms. Looking at the three components Application, (D)DBMS and Disk-server it is the interface between Application and (D)DBMS that requires our attention for the sake of understanding SQL and its capabilities (*see Figure 27.1*). The implementation of the SQL functionality into services provided by the (D)DBMS and its underlying components lies beyond the scope of this book.

27.2 A Four-Step Method for Data Distribution

For a general understanding of the principles involved in data distribution we will use a simple model. This describes four layers of data distribution and prescribes four steps by which data distribution can be achieved. Stefano Ceri and Giuseppe Pelagatti (1988) have written many papers on distribution of data and the four-step model originates with them. They are structured as follows: first, the design of a global database and the application description with no distribution implications, second, the specification of fragments of data which are identified and clustered for efficient processing, third, the allocation of these fragments to nodes in the network supporting the distributed application and, fourth, the processing at each node of incoming requests against database data under local responsibility and the return of the requested data in (derived) table format. C.J. Date (1987b) has specified 12 criteria which must be fulfilled by a 'full function' distributed system and these criteria are further explored in relation to a number of major DBMS implementations in NGI (1990).

27.2.1 Global Distributed Data Processing

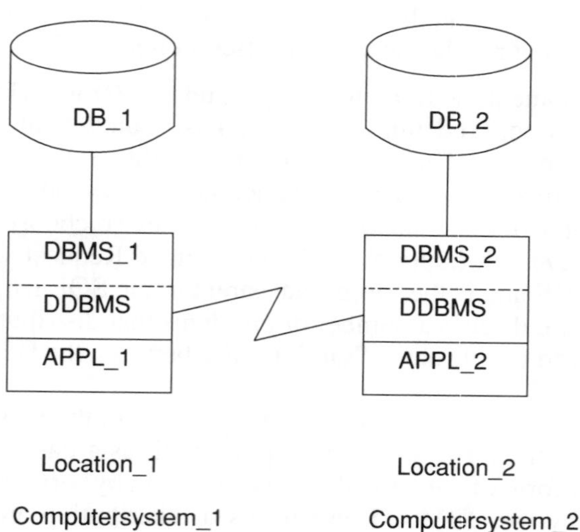

Figure 27.2 *Global distributed application*

Under ideal conditions an application requiring data from a distributed database does not need to know how exactly the data is retrieved from its distributed storage media. The purpose of relational database technology is for the application to express via 'SQL' operations what data is required. The database system software (DBMS) will then work out how to get this data to the application. In distributed data processing where the DBMS is operating on a distributed database it provides services to an application requiring data from many different locations. This is known as a global application to keep it distinct from a local application which just processes data from the local database. Figure 27.2 shows a global distributed application. At this level a global schema describing the structure of the entire database would be desirable so that we would not see any effects of storage media distribution or computer node configuration.

For multiple global applications to communicate in an understandable form the traffic between computers in the network must be in 'global language'. The format and the meaning of messages must be understood by the local DBMSs at the participating nodes. In the case of an SQL environment this requirement is supported by 'remote data access' protocols (RDA) which specify the formulation and format of queries issued by the client and the response — data in the form of a table plus accompanying status information — given by the server. The SQL Access group — manufacturers of SQL database management software — are specifying how the SQL and RDA standards may be used in conjunction with their software.

27.2.2 Fragmentation of Portions of Data

In a relational database data is stored in tables of rows and columns. In a distributed relational database sets of tables, sets of rows and/or sets of columns may need to be constructed for distribution. This step specifies such sets, called fragments, which should possess certain characteristics.

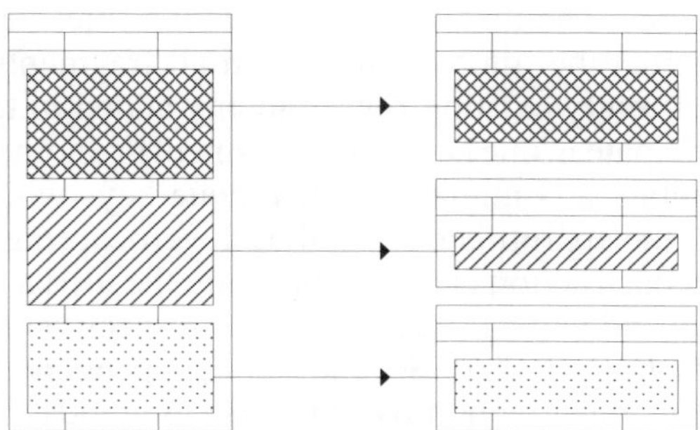

Figure 27.3 *Horizontal fragmentation scheme*

A fragment is a section from a relational table. Horizontal fragmentation (*see Figure 27.3*) selects rows from a table, vertical fragmentation selects columns. An example of horizontal fragmentation is the selection of employees of an organization according to the department where they work. Each fragment could be allocated to department computers to have data about local employees available without further communication costs. The aim is that rows are selected on the basis of the values of a (set of) column(s) such that all rows are assigned to a fragment and all fragments are disjunct, i.e. no row exists in more than one fragment.

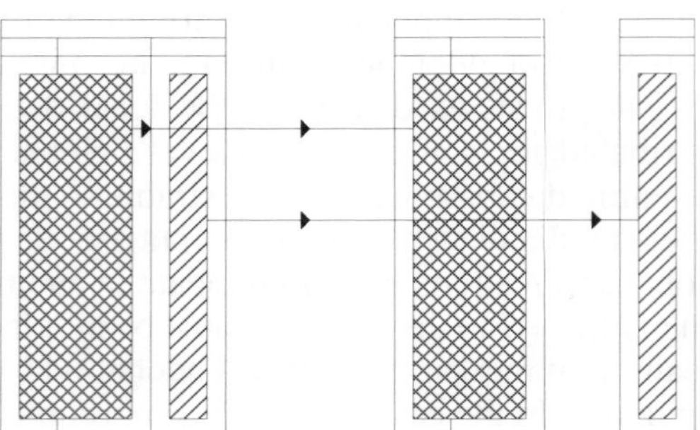

Figure 27.4 *Vertical fragmentation scheme*

An example of vertical fragmentation (*see Figure 27.4*) is the selection of employees of an organization by the type of data required per job function. The accounts application would require financial data while project management would require job history plus education and training records. The columns providing this information are selected and allocated to the appropriate fragments on the basis of their content according to their DDL specification. Each column of the table must be assigned to at least one fragment and fragments must be disjunct if possible. A similar example of vertical fragmentation can be seen in the split of entity Employee into the tables Employee and Emp_Ext (*see Appendix A The Example Database*).

Ceri and Pelagatti (1988) specify three rules that must be adhered to in distributed environments. The first, the reconstruction rule, states that it must be possible to reconstruct the 'global table' from all fragments. This means that every row, both currently existing rows and any added in the future, must be guaranteed to participate in one horizontal fragment or another and each vertical fragment must contain a configuration of unique keys which will enable the joining together of the appropriate rows of each vertical fragment into the logical whole. This reconstruction can be done using the `UNION` and `JOIN` set operators for horizontal and vertical fragmentations respectively (*see the examples in Figure 27.5 and Figure 27.6*). Second, the independence rule requires that horizontal fragments must be non-overlapping; they must be disjunct. This is comparable to normalization where the aim is to avoid update inconsistencies. If one specifies fragments containing overlapping data, fragments allocated to different computer nodes may contain the same logical data. Since this allocation may not involve replication the DBMS may not necessarily recognize inconsistencies taking place during updates. If the DBMS does recognize that overlap exists an alternative might be to replicate each entire fragment to all involved computer nodes. However, this would result in large redundancies. Third, the completeness rule requires for vertical fragmentation that each column must participate in at least one fragment. In constructing vertical fragments we must ensure that each column in the global table definition is included in at least one fragment definition so that the JOIN can amalgamate all vertical fragments using the unique keys required by the reconstruction rule.

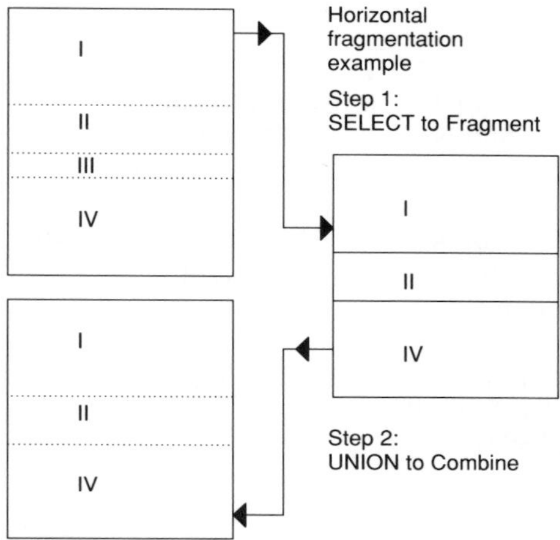

Figure 27.5 SELECT to fragment, UNION to combine

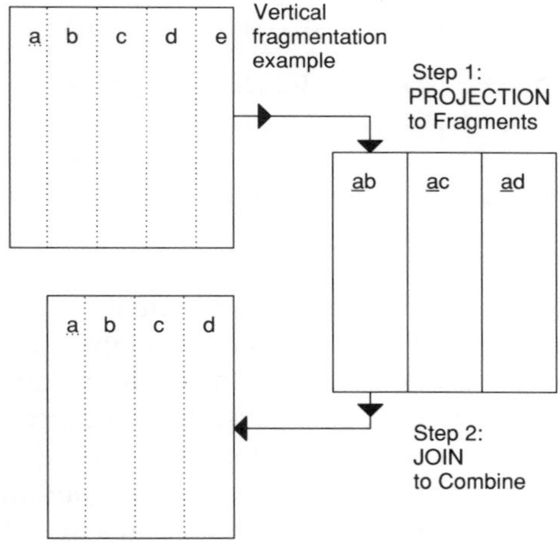

Figure 27.6 PROJECT to fragment, JOIN to combine

27.2.2.1 Horizontal Fragmentation

Essentially horizontal fragmentation can be achieved by defining tables for each fragment and defining a check clause for the column(s) involved. The original table definition is:

```
CREATE TABLE Employee
(
empnr           NUMERIC (5),
name            CHARACTER (40) NOT NULL,
salary          NUMERIC (6) NOT NULL,
home_telno      CHARACTER (14),
...
deptcd          CHARACTER (3) NOT NULL DEFAULT 'PER',
work_telno      CHARACTER (14) UNIQUE,
PRIMARY KEY (empnr),
...
FOREIGN KEY (deptcd) REFERENCES Dept
   ON DELETE SET DEFAULT
   ON UPDATE CASCADE
)
```

Employee						
empnr	*name*	*salary*	*home_telno*	...	*deptcd*	*work_telno*
12345	Brown	11300	+44-71-349-9906	...	SLS	+44-71-211-3013
23456	Smith	12000	?	...	PRD	+44-71-211-8998
34567	Patel	25000	+44-71-222-2222	...	SLS	+44-71-211-1357
56789	Jones	9000	+44-71-765-2132	...	SLS	+44-71-211-3014

Figure 27.7 *Horizontal fragmentation — original Employee table*

and the table itself looks like that shown in Figure 27.7.

To define a fragment in SQL we must define a table to contain it. The division can be considered as a case construct, the qualification conditions for each fragment explicitly 'enumerated', with possibly an 'otherwise' as a catch-all at the end. This can be seen as a `SELECT` statement on the rows of the original table. Since the `CHECK` clause allows for a search condition we can specify exactly the same conditions as for a `WHERE` clause in a `SELECT` statement. In our case we are using the values of the deptcd column, the 'enumerated' fragment; in this case for the sales department it is defined as:

```
CREATE TABLE Employee_SLS
(
empnr          NUMERIC (5),
name           CHARACTER (40) NOT NULL,
salary         NUMERIC (6) NOT NULL,
...
home_telno     CHARACTER (14),
deptcd         CHARACTER (3) NOT NULL DEFAULT 'SLS',
work_telno     CHARACTER (14) UNIQUE,
PRIMARY KEY (empnr),
CHECK (deptcd IN ('SLS')),
...
FOREIGN KEY (deptcd) REFERENCES Dept
)
```

Note that we have deleted the `ON DELETE SET DEFAULT` and `ON UPDATE CASCADE` clauses and modified the `DEFAULT` for deptcd. This has repercussions since the original default was intended to revert people to the 'PER' department if their department was deleted. However, SQL cannot automatically migrate rows between fragments. A similar problem exists with `ON UPDATE CASCADE`

Employee_SLS						
empnr	*name*	*salary*	*home_telno*	...	*deptcd*	*work_telno*
12345	Brown	11300	+44-71-349-9906	...	SLS	+44-71-211-3013
34567	Patel	25000	+44-71-222-2222	...	SLS	+44-71-211-1357
56789	Jones	9000	+44-71-765-2132	...	SLS	+44-71-211-3014

Figure 27.8 *Horizontal fragmentation – Employee table fragment for SLS department*

since changing the value of the deptcd would violate the `CHECK` clause. The only solution is to modify the table definition temporarily. This problem has already been solved in many implementations but since SQL is intended for high-level logical description of data definitions and manipulations this is not possible. The above definition produces the table in Figure 27.8.

The 'otherwise' fragment would allow any row to be inserted in it that does not contain any value for the department mentioned in an 'enumerated' fragment. Obviously we would prefer SQL to process such consistency checks in a simpler manner but for now we have to define this fragment as follows:

```
CREATE TABLE Employee_otherwise
(
empnr       NUMERIC (5),
name     CHARACTER (40) NOT NULL,
salary      NUMERIC (6) NOT NULL,
home_telno    CHARACTER (14),
...
deptcd      CHARACTER (3) NOT NULL DEFAULT 'PER',
work_telno    CHARACTER (14) UNIQUE,
PRIMARY KEY (empnr),
CHECK (deptcd NOT IN ('SLS')),
...
FOREIGN KEY (deptcd) REFERENCES Dept
   ON DELETE SET DEFAULT
   ON UPDATE CASCADE
)
```

Employee_otherwise						
empnr	*name*	*salary*	*home_telno*	...	*deptcd*	*work_telno*
23456	Smith	12000	?	...	PRD	+44-71-211-8998

Figure 27.9 *Horizontal fragmentation — Employee table fragment for 'otherwise' department*

Similar restrictions apply as for the Employee_SLS fragment, since referential actions do not work across tables and so cannot be used in high-level horizontal fragmentation (*see Figure 27.9*).

27.2.2.2 Vertical Fragmentation

Here the tables involved are defined containing only the columns appropriate for the fragment. The vertical fragment containing 'financial details' would be defined as follows:

```
CREATE TABLE Employee_FD
(
empnr         NUMERIC (5),
salary        NUMERIC (6) NOT NULL,
home_telno    CHARACTER (14),
PRIMARY KEY (empnr),
...
CONSTRAINT Employee_fd_to_wd
   FOREIGN KEY (empnr) REFERENCES Employee_WD
)
```

This would result in the table in Figure 27.10.

Another fragment could contain the remaining columns with 'work details' plus a corresponding primary or candidate key — in our case the primary key empnr — for the one-to-one match on each row in both fragments:

Employee_FD			
empnr	*name*	*salary*	*home_telno*
12345	Brown	11300	+44-71-349-9906
23456	Smith	12000	?
34567	Patel	25000	+44-71-222-2222
56789	Jones	9000	+44-71-765-2132

Figure 27.10 *Vertical fragmentation — Employee table fragment financial details*

```
CREATE TABLE Employee_WD
(
empnr          NUMERIC (5),
name           CHARACTER (40) NOT NULL,
...
deptcd         CHARACTER (3) NOT NULL DEFAULT 'PER',
work_telno     CHARACTER (14) UNIQUE,
PRIMARY KEY (empnr),
...
CONSTRAINT Employee_wd_to_fd
   FOREIGN KEY (empnr) REFERENCES Employee_FD,
FOREIGN KEY (deptcd) REFERENCES Dept
)
```

This would result in the table in Figure 27.11.

Employee_WD				
empnr	*name*	...	*deptcd*	*work_telno*
12345	Brown	...	SLS	+44-71-211-3013
23456	Smith	...	PRD	+44-71-211-8998
34567	Patel	...	SLS	+44-71-211-1357
56789	Jones	...	SLS	+44-71-211-3014

Figure 27.11 *Vertical fragmentation — Employee table fragment work details*

27.2.2.3 Combined Horizontal and Vertical Fragmentation

Obviously, both horizontal and vertical fragmentation can be combined in a single table (*see Figure 27.12*). The employee data may be vertically fragmented to provide financial data on all employees while the remaining job history and education and training data could be horizontally fragmented on a

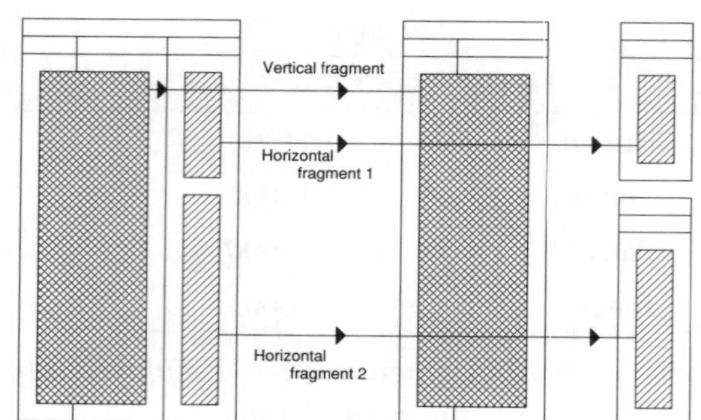

Figure 27.12 *Combined fragmentation scheme*

departmental basis. Each department could then have this data for its own employees in a fragment.

The fragment containing 'financial details' would be defined as before:

```
CREATE TABLE Employee_FD_all
(
empnr         NUMERIC (5),
home_telno    CHARACTER (14),
salary        NUMERIC (6) NOT NULL,
PRIMARY KEY (empnr),
...
CONSTRAINT Employee_fd_to_wd
   CHECK (empnr MATCH
      (SELECT empnr
      FROM (TABLE Employee_WD_SLS
            UNION
            TABLE Employee_WD_otherwise)))
)
```

Employee_FD_all			
empnr	*name*	*salary*	*home_telno*
12345	Brown	11500	+44-71-349-9906
23456	Smith	12000	?
34567	Patel	25000	+44-71-222-2222
56789	Jones	9000	+44-71-765-2132

Figure 27.13 *Vertical plus horizontal fragmentation — Employee table vertical fragment financial details*

Changing the `FOREIGN KEY` into a `CHECK` clause is necessary because the `FOREIGN KEY` clause does not allow the referencing of more than one table. The `CHECK` clause combines the two tables and defines a `MATCH` on the referencing column which would have been the foreign key. Note that the foreign key in the SQL standard has been defined in terms of the MATCH predicate. This would result in the table given in Figure 27.13.

The first horizontal fragment would contain the remaining columns with 'work details' plus empnr:

```
CREATE TABLE Employee_WD_SLS
(
empnr          NUMERIC (5),
name           CHARACTER (40) NOT NULL,
...
deptcd         CHARACTER (3) NOT NULL DEFAULT 'SLS',
work_telno     CHARACTER (14) UNIQUE,
PRIMARY KEY (empnr),
...
CHECK (deptcd IN ('SLS')),
CONSTRAINT Employee_wd_to_fd
   FOREIGN KEY (empnr) REFERENCES Employee_FD,
FOREIGN KEY (deptcd) REFERENCES Dept
)
```

This would result in the table given in Figure 27.14.

Employee_WD_SLS				
empnr	*name*	...	*deptcd*	*work_telno*
12345	Brown	...	SLS	+44-71-211-3013
34567	Patel	...	SLS	+44-71-211-1357
56789	Jones	...	SLS	+44-71-211-3014

Figure 27.14 *Vertical plus horizontal fragmentation — Employee table fragment work details for SLS department*

Note again that we have deleted the ON DELETE SET DEFAULT and ON UPDATE CASCADE clauses and modified the DEFAULT for deptcd. For the same reasons as before (*see Section 27.2.2.1 Horizontal Fragmentation*) this has repercussions since the original default was intended to revert people to the 'PER' department after their department was deleted.

The second and last horizontal fragment would contain the remaining columns with 'work details' plus empnr for the 'otherwise' departments:

```
CREATE TABLE Employee_WD_otherwise
(
empnr          NUMERIC (5),
name           CHARACTER (40) NOT NULL,
...
deptcd         CHARACTER (3) NOT NULL DEFAULT 'PER',
work_telno     CHARACTER (14) UNIQUE,
PRIMARY KEY (empnr),
...
CHECK (deptcd NOT IN ('SLS')),
CONSTRAINT Employee_wd_to_fd
   FOREIGN KEY (empnr) REFERENCES Employee_FD,
FOREIGN KEY (deptcd) REFERENCES Dept
)
```

This would result in the table given in Figure 27.15. In short, for the purpose of distribution management, a fragment can be seen as a view on a table.

Employee_WD_otherwise				
empnr	*name*	...	*deptcd*	*work_telno*
23456	Smith	...	PRD	+44-71-211-8998

Figure 27.15 *Vertical plus horizontal fragmentation — Employee table fragment work details for otherwise departments*

27.2.3 Allocation of Fragments of Data

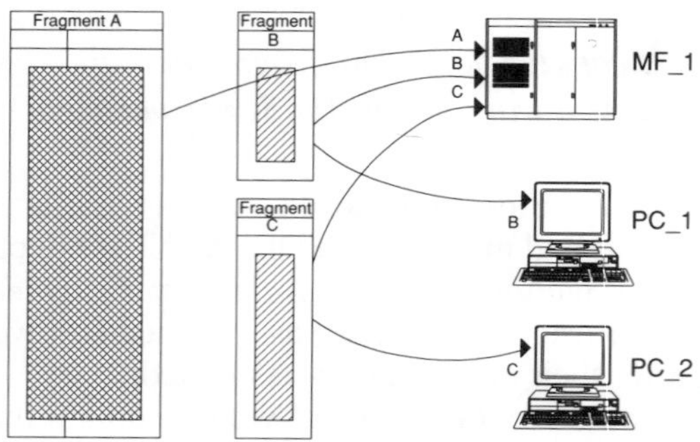

Figure 27.16 *Fragment allocation scheme*

In a distributed database data is stored on the storage media of multiple computers in a computer network. The DBMS must maintain a registration of which fragments, as defined in the previous section, are to be allocated to which computers in the network. Such a specification is called the fragment allocation; each fragment must be allocated to at least one computer node in the network, though in some cases one fragment may be allocated to multiple computers — replication. In Figure 27.16 the two smaller, horizontal fragments are each allocated to a PC, as well as to the mainframe. These are called replicated fragments, since they have a 1:*n* allocation of fragment to computer node in the network storing the fragment. The DBMS must cater for maintaining the redundant allocations of the same fragment so that updating remains in step. The larger vertical fragment is 1:1 allocated to the mainframe. The DBMS has no need to worry about redundancy of data in this case. The mainframe effectively holds all three fragments making up the entire table, while each PC has a small dedicated fragment.

With SQL we must define a schema for each computer in the network which will hold data for the distributed application. The various fragments as described above will have to be included in the appropriate schema. The fragments in Figure 27.16, A — Employee_FD_all, B — Employee_WD_SLS and C — Employee_WD_otherwise, are all included in the schema for the mainframe MF_1. Employee_WD_SLS and Employee_WD_otherwise are incorporated in the schemata for the PCs PC_1 and PC_2 respectively.

Note that Ceri's four step method does allow for redundant allocation of fragments. This redundancy must be controlled by the DDBMS, so that all update manipulation commands can be directed to the appropriate fragments to maintain integrity of data in the distributed database. This controlled and minimal redundancy is equivalent to the three normalization steps used on data structures during database design. There is, however, a case for other forms of redundancy that can be controlled during vertical and horizontal fragment definition. The name of an employee could be included during the vertical fragmentation of the Employee_FD and Employee_WD fragments. This would make retrieval easier but updating the name would involve the DDBMS in accessing the other vertical fragment (assuming the access privileges are given) to update the corresponding row. Horizontal fragmentation could allow overlap in the definition of fragments which in practice means redundancy. Allowing marketing employees (deptcd = 'MKT') to reside in both Employee_SLS and Employee_otherwise means duplicate tasks for the DDBMS. Architecturally it is questionable to allow redundancy in both fragmentation and in allocation.

27.2.4 Local Data Processing

At the local computer where a local DBMS manages the local database — which is the sum of the allocated fragments — the network format query must be transformed into local conventions. In a neatly setup database the names of tables and columns, the formats of data in 'similar' columns, the agreements about codes (like country codes) all match. In a heterogeneous and autonomous environment there may be different DBMSs involved and the database structures may differ. Local mapping caters for the adaptation of database names, database semantics, data formats, mapping of codes, constraint support, data manipulation semantics to the agreed global or network format and meaning. Using standard SQL and distributed database designs at all the involved nodes will help significantly. This may not be feasible in large federated networks of information processing systems, and small alliances and bridges may be a better way to build up pools of distributed database systems.

27.3 A Worked Example

SQL provides only limited provisions to manage distributed databases for distributed applications where the SQL database management system takes responsibility for all features mentioned. In this section we are going to work through a simple example of a distributed database and a simple application program to remove the office phone from employees Jones and Smith.

27.3.1 Fragmenting and Allocation

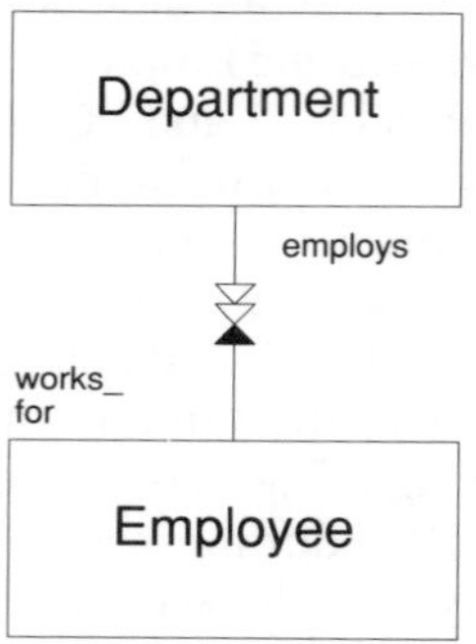

Figure 27.17 *Employee works_for Department*

One portion of the example database deals with Employee works_for Department (*see Figure 27.17*). In our distributed database we have chosen a combined fragmentation of the Employee table (*see Section 27.2.2.3 Combined Horizontal and Vertical Fragmentation*). The Department table is allocated to MF_1, while fragments of the Employee tables conform to Figure 27.16 resulting in table Employee_WD_SLS being replicated on to MF_1 and PC_1 and table Employee_WS_otherwise being replicated on to MF_1 and PC_2. This is depicted in detail in Figure 27.18. The schemata for the various nodes would look as follows. The mainframe schema MF_1 is:

```
CREATE SCHEMA mf_1 AUTHORIZATION otten

CREATE TABLE Dept
(
deptcd          CHARACTER (3) PRIMARY KEY,
deptnm          CHARACTER (12)
)
```

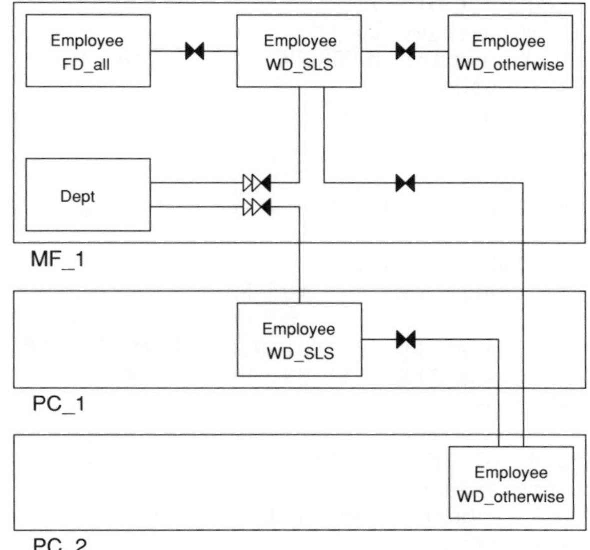

Figure 27.18 SQL schemata per node

```
CREATE TABLE Employee_FD_all
(
empnr          NUMERIC (5),
home_telno     CHARACTER (14),
salary         NUMERIC (6) NOT NULL,
PRIMARY KEY (empnr),
...
CONSTRAINT Employee_fd_to_wd
   CHECK (empnr MATCH
      (SELECT empnr
         FROM (
           TABLE Employee_WD_SLS
           UNION
           TABLE Employee_WD_otherwise)))
)

CREATE TABLE Employee_WD_SLS
(
empnr          NUMERIC (5),
name           CHARACTER (40) NOT NULL,
...
deptcd         CHARACTER (3) NOT NULL DEFAULT 'SLS',
work_telno     CHARACTER (14) UNIQUE,
PRIMARY KEY (empnr),
...
```

```
CHECK (deptcd IN ('SLS')),
CONSTRAINT Employee_wd_to_fd
   FOREIGN KEY (empnr) REFERENCES Employee_FD,
FOREIGN KEY (deptcd)
   REFERENCES Dept
)

CREATE TABLE Employee_WD_otherwise
(
empnr          NUMERIC (5),
name           CHARACTER (40) NOT NULL,
...
deptcd         CHARACTER (3) NOT NULL DEFAULT 'PER',
work_telno     CHARACTER (14) UNIQUE,
PRIMARY KEY (empnr),
...
CHECK (deptcd NOT IN ('SLS')),
CONSTRAINT Employee_wd_to_fd
   FOREIGN KEY (empnr) REFERENCES Employee_FD,
FOREIGN KEY (deptcd)
   REFERENCES Dept
)

CREATE VIEW Employee
   AS
   SELECT empnr, salary, home_telno, name, deptcd, work_telno
   FROM Employee_FD_all NATURAL JOIN (TABLE Employee_WD_SLS
      UNION TABLE Employee_WD_otherwise)
```

The PC_1 schema is:

```
CREATE SCHEMA pc_1 AUTHORIZATION otten

CREATE TABLE Employee_WD_SLS
(
empnr          NUMERIC (5),
name           CHARACTER (40) NOT NULL,
...
deptcd         CHARACTER (3) NOT NULL DEFAULT 'SLS',
work_telno     CHARACTER (14) UNIQUE,
PRIMARY KEY (empnr),
...
CHECK (deptcd IN ('SLS')),
CONSTRAINT Employee_wd_to_fd
   FOREIGN KEY (empnr) REFERENCES Employee_FD,
FOREIGN KEY (deptcd) REFERENCES Dept
)
```

The PC_2 schema is:

```
CREATE SCHEMA pc_2 AUTHORIZATION otten

CREATE TABLE Employee_WD_otherwise
(
empnr          NUMERIC (5),
name           CHARACTER (40) NOT NULL,
...
deptcd         CHARACTER (3) NOT NULL DEFAULT 'PER',
work_telno     CHARACTER (14) UNIQUE,
PRIMARY KEY (empnr),
...
CHECK (deptcd NOT IN ('SLS')),
CONSTRAINT Employee_wd_to_fd
   FOREIGN KEY (empnr) REFERENCES Employee_FD,
FOREIGN KEY (deptcd) REFERENCES Dept
)
```

27.3.2 Locating the Data

Before we can modify the work_telno column to remove the office phone from the selected employees we must first know which fragment contains the column. SQL provides no transparency for fragment definitions, since the only way to implement fragments in current SQL is to specify a table per fragment. The information can be obtained from the catalog, dependent upon location and the actual implementation. At node PC_1 there may be no information available about schema MF_1 and PC_2, in which case the application must hold this information.

The work_telno is actually present in the two horizontal fragments Employee_WD_SLS and Employee_WD_otherwise. The data for Jones and Smith must be in one of those fragments, but which? We cannot begin to derive the answer from the question, since the fragmentation algorithm is based on deptcd, which is unspecified in the question. The only option is to search both fragments and we need to use the allocation information to find out at which node and in which schema the required data is to be found. One possible strategy is to query the Employee view at MF_1 to find out for which departments Jones and Smith work. We would then know which horizontal fragment(s) we need. We must then update all fragments involved at all the nodes to which they have been allocated, since SQL does not help us with replication of updates.

To isolate the application program from all this navigation and separate the distribution knowledge we may incorporate a client–server approach in our solution (*see Figure 27.19*). The concept of maintaining a connection between the client and server is very powerful since the server may in its own right call upon the services of another server. In this manner a certain level of independence and transparency can be introduced. Each combination of client and server(s) forms a level of isolation and independence. Each line between the

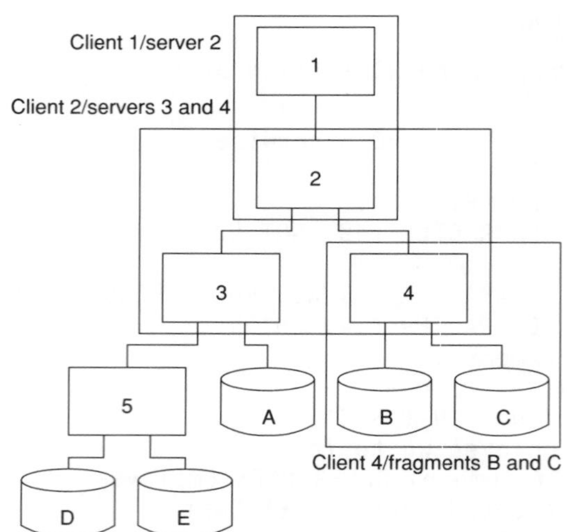

Figure 27.19 *Client–server processes and data fragments*

client and server signifies an SQL_session as described in *Chapter 14 Session Management*.

The following SQL principles must be kept in mind when designing clients and servers into the structure of an application:

1. A session is a connection between an application program in an SQL_Client and an SQL_Server.
2. An application program may establish sessions to several SQL_Servers and switch between them.
3. The establishment of a session and any switch of session must occur between transactions.

Currently, SQL has a number of tools in place to allow implementations to offer distributed functionality, but in emerging SQL standards further functionality must be added.

27.3.3 The SQL Coding for the Operation

The simplest manner is to connect to each node individually and try to perform the update on each applicable fragment for both names. This is the simplest method when we are trying to show distributed characteristics using logical high-level SQL, which is only capable of operating a single SQL command against a single table (or fragment). SQL itself has no capability of migrating updates across tables (or fragments). In SQL, the update of the deptcd requires deletion in one fragment and insertion in the other appropriate fragment under control of the distributed application. Many implementations will have supporting logic at the physical DBMS level to do this kind of migration automatically and provide isolation to the distributed application from the level of fragmentation, or even global distributed data processing:

```
CONNECT TO SQL_server_mf_1 AS SSMF1

UPDATE mf_1.Employee_WD_SLS
   SET work_telno = NULL
   WHERE name = 'Jones' or name = 'Smith'
UPDATE Employee_WD_otherwise
   SET work_telno = NULL
   WHERE name = 'Jones' or name = 'Smith'
COMMIT
CONNECT TO SQL_server_pc_1 AS SSPC1

UPDATE pc_1.Employee_WD_SLS
   SET work_telno = NULL
   WHERE name = 'Jones' or name = 'Smith'
COMMIT
CONNECT TO SQL_server_pc_2 AS SSPC2

UPDATE pc_2.Employee_WD_otherwise
   SET work_telno = NULL
   WHERE name = 'Jones' or name = 'Smith'
COMMIT
DISCONNECT ALL
```

In the above example each session starts with the first `UPDATE` statement after `CONNECT` and ends with the subsequent `COMMIT`.

28

Performance Aspects

SQL is primarily aimed at defining and manipulating data at the logical level. Performance is the art or skill of optimizing information systems. This involves looking at all the components in the realization of the information system. These range from the application programs, routines and modules and the way they use SQL DML to the data structures that have been specified to the DBMS through SQL DDL. There are also the many database related features available from implementors of DBMS and operating system software, plus areas such as hardware settings, the configuration of disk sub-systems, the bandwidth of communication lines between terminals and computers and many more. We will discuss some 30 points in the following four sections: the physical data and application design approach, disk access structures, disk storage and main memory organization and query access planning. Some of the points address SQL, but many deal with options and features that are not applicable at the logical level of data design but are more in the realm of physical data design and tuning. Particular implementations often offer a range of such options. The art is in choosing a selection of options that will not affect the design of the programs, since one of the main advantages of relational systems is that navigation and the physical location of data are shielded from the application.

Performance upgrading is done during physical database design once data and activity analysis and logical database and application design have taken place. This does not bar design methods from considerable iteration between the analysis and the logical design and the physical design. It is fair to say that even while analysing the requirements you must have a fair idea of what the various hardware and software components of the system are capable.

Given a correct set of deliverables in the analysis phase of a systems development methodology (*see Figure 28.1 for an overview of the method used*

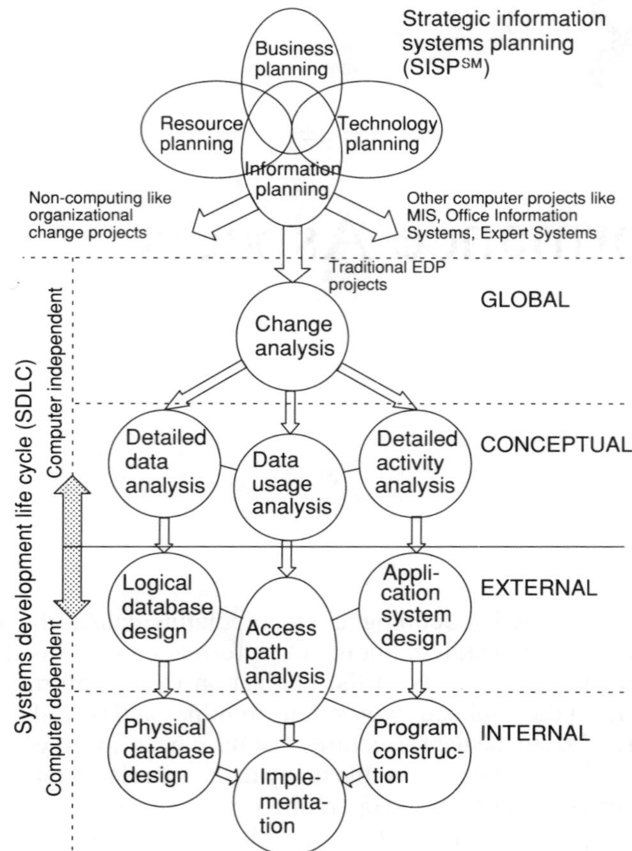

Figure 28.1 *An example of a systems development life cycle*

in DCE) and the mapping of the analysis findings on to information system components, the main task is to choose from the many options available while observing a few key principles:

1. The analysis results should match the logical and physical design as closely as possible. The fewer distortions introduced after a correct analysis the quicker and easier it is to redesign and reoptimize if (structural) changes to the analysis are required. Having started by allowing the DBMS to perform as many functions as it is technically capable of in a logical design, during detailed physical design some things may be found to work more efficiently if you program them into your application or tune the DBMS and operating system in various ways.
2. When changing parameters and options during the physical design process in order to better the performance always document the reasons for your

decisions, which alternatives you have rejected and why. Your elaborate theorizing and extensive testing of the performance hypotheses is often nullified by the next maintenance job done on the system. Increasing performance requirements for systems frequently leads to choices whose repercussions are difficult to hypothesize.
3. Before making a modification that will improve the performance of the information system, check possible alternatives. Some alterations are simple and do not have far-reaching consequences; others require a whole chain of adaptations, like additional medication to counteract the adverse effect of the initial set of pills prescribed.

In each of the following sections we present a number of topics with suggestions on how to improve performance within them. We do not claim to be comprehensive and we will not discuss particular system options in depth. When applying changes during the physical design to enhance performance of the initial logical design the following checks and balances often form the basis for decision making. Though by occupying more disk space or allowing more disk I/O operations you may save main memory or computing power, the reverse is also true. Taking more time to design the database and the application and to exploit the available options for performance enhancement may shorten the running time of the application significantly. When making extensive use of multiple performance options the capability of the DBMS to optimize the system automatically is usually severely reduced. Always weigh up the conflicting benefits when deciding whether to optimize or not. We would advise that if you do not need to, do not do it, since DBMSs become smarter all the time. When your expertise is requested to improve an unacceptable performance it is good to have many different options to choose from, but remember the saying ‘In der Beschränkung zeigt sich der Meister’, which means ‘Don’t overdo it’.

28.1 Physical Data and Application Design Approach

With the results of the analysis in hand we have to bear in mind that we start with a one-to-one mapping of these on to the chosen hardware software environment. A properly normalized data structure (*see Section 21.2 Database and Application Analysis Issues*) can easily be mapped into SQL DDL commands. Limitations in packages you are using — like the number of columns in a table — may force you to take action — such as vertically fragmenting tables — to make a solution work. Always assume that the next release of the package will have improvements and make sure you are able to undo any such deviation or enhancement you introduced for the sake of performance improvement.

A fully normalized data structure contains many tables, since the essence of normalization is to split tables into ones with fewer columns. Applications by their very nature collect and associate data and thus need to join tables while retrieving from the database. The process of denormalization involves the storing of joined tables in the database such that the application can simply retrieve the appropriate rows from the table. Updating, however, becomes more cumbersome since denormalization introduces redundancy. We may also denormalize tables for an application by providing a view that presents the data in a joined format. The data itself still resides in normalized form on disk.

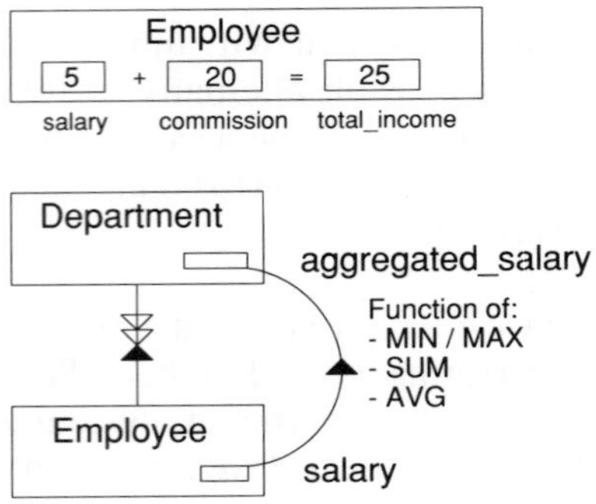

Figure 28.2 *Derived actual and virtual data*

There has always been a big debate about derived data. This is data derivable from base data in the database, such as calculations of values in single or multiple tables like the total income from salary plus commission for employees or averages, totals, minimums and maximums using data across relationships or counts of rows (*see Figure 28.2*). Asking the DBMS to collect these details means far less programming for the application, but does mean extra work for the DBMS. With frequent retrievals and few updates it often pays to define the derived items within the database as real stored and maintained columns. When the retrieval–update ratio is reversed we can more efficiently produce a view specifying a derived column that is not stored in the database and is materialized with each retrieval. Unfortunately, SQL does not allow the storage of these derived values as actual columns in the database and provides the view mechanism for virtual derived data only. The standard does not, however, prohibit an implementor from physically storing view information in the database and many implementations offer support for this feature. In a future standard for SQL a trigger mechanism may be provided which, under predefined conditions, allows some DML-like manipulation to take place. For example, in updating a salary or commission, the total_income column for that employee can be automatically derived and stored. Similarly the aggregated_salary column for the corresponding Dept will be updated upon the modification of an employee's salary. The SQL standard only allows the actual representation of derived data to be maintained by application programs. The view mechanism for a virtual derived representation for the total_income calculation would have a view definition as follows:

```
CREATE VIEW Employee_financials (nr, name, total_income)
   AS    SELECT empnr, name, salary+commission
           FROM Employee
```

The view definition for the aggregated_salary information would look like:

```
CREATE VIEW Employee_aggregation (dept, e_cnt, total_sal,
min_sal)
   AS   SELECT D.deptnm, COUNT(E.empnr), SUM(E.salary),
             MIN(E.salary)
          FROM Dept D NATURAL LEFT JOIN Employee E
               USING (deptcd)
          GROUP BY D.deptcd, D.deptnm
```

An alternative syntax would be:

```
CREATE VIEW Employee_aggregation (dept, e_cnt, total_sal,
min_sal)
   AS   SELECT  D.deptnm,
           (SELECT COUNT(E.empnr) FROM Employee E
              WHERE E.deptcd = D.deptcd),
           (SELECT SUM(E.salary) FROM Employee E
              WHERE E.deptcd = D.deptcd),
           (SELECT MIN(E.salary) FROM Employee E
             WHERE E.deptcd = D.deptcd)
        FROM Dept D
```

The general message from this section is to let the DBMS take care of as much as it can handle and only take things away if performance suffers. Early releases of DBMS software — even famous packages from renowned manufacturers — providing sophisticated facilities like optimizers and query plan developers may not work efficiently or accurately. The next release of the DBMS is likely to have been improved enough to deliver better results than your specific modifications. You might then want to undo your modifications and revert to a simpler physical implementation.

Query optimizers frequently develop different access plans for query processing in the case of nested subqueries as opposed to flat queries, even when both express the same query (*see Section 25.3.4 Flat Versus Nested SQL Queries*). While we would not recommend arbitrarily modifying query formulation to optimize query processing performance, flat queries usually achieve a better performance in DBMSs and are sometimes also more readable. Where you need to do something strange to get a query processed correctly or speedily always document what you did and for what reason.

Another example is the introduction of referential integrity in the SQL Addendum in ISO 9075:1989(E), which caused checks programmed in application programs to become redundant and consume unnecessary resources. Inadequately designed applications required significant restructuring. *Appendix F Differences between SQL-1992 and SQL-1989* discusses not only the differences but also other features that are expected in the future. We recommend taking these into account when designing applications so that major restructuring may be avoided.

28.2 Disk Access Structures

Data on storage media, typically disks, must be organized in a way that makes access simple and quick. Groups like the BCS DBAWG (the Data Base Administration Working Group of the British Computer Society) have worked along-

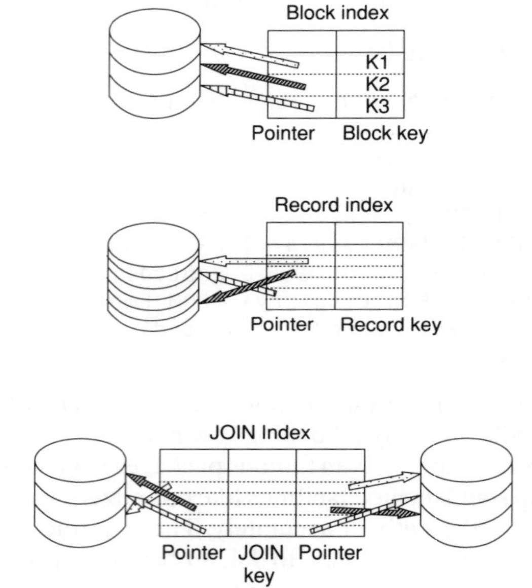

Figure 28.3 *Block index, row index and JOIN index*

side CODASYL (Conference on Data System Languages) to specify a DSDL (Data Storage Definition Language) for network databases (BCS/CODASYL Data Base Administration Working Group, 1981). The DSDL is described in a three-schema architecture (*see ANSI/X3/SPARC (1975) for how a logical database definition as specified by the DDL could be mapped on to storage*). Features like record fragmentation, clustering, pointer configurations, indexes, virtual/actual data items, block sizes and more were specified, but these are not now considered to be in the area of standardization and are left to the manufacturers of packages. One disk access structure is the availability of an index. This is invisible in SQL since it is a physical entity. There are many kinds of index (*see Figure 28.3*): a row index containing the disk location of a row in a table given its column value (for unique (sets of) columns or for columns allowing duplicates) or governing the sequencing of rows in key sequence; a block index maintaining only the lowest/highest key value per block; and an index for joining two tables with the key values plus the disk locations for each of the two rows involved (such an index is particularly useful when you have a vertically fragmented table and the index contains the primary key with, for each key, the disk locations of the rows for all corresponding fragments) (*see Appendix A The Example Database, for the tables Employee and Emp_Ext*).

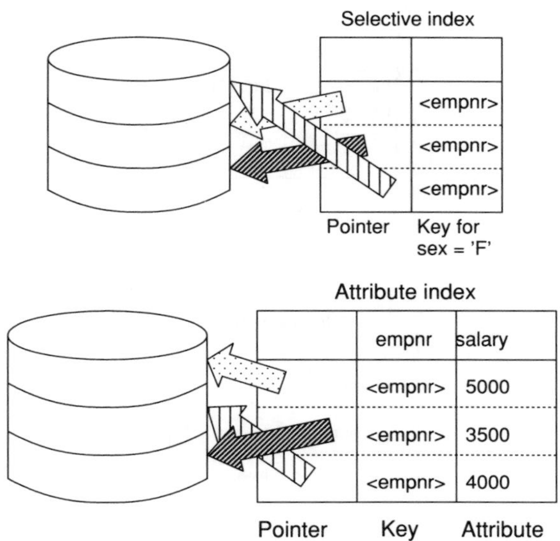

Figure 28.4 *Selective index and attribute index*

A selective index is one containing rows based on column values which is automatically maintained by the DBMS for those rows that satisfy certain criteria, e.g. all female employees (*see Figure 28.4*). Stonebraker (1989) provides a good justification for this kind of index. Attribute indexes hold, besides the key, some extra information as specified by the database administrator (such as the sex column being added to an index based on empnr) so that the DBMS can efficiently evaluate a query involving sex selections as part of a join without having to access unnecessary employee data in the table itself. Essentially this is a vertical fragmentation outside the scope of SQL DDL. A much-used variation on indexing is the B-tree access structure. The B-tree takes a key and walks through the branches to reach the leaves, which can be blocks of pointers to blocks or records in a data file or may themselves contain the actual data. A B-tree mechanism is based on the principle that data and key information is stored in blocks or pages of disk storage and the B-tree acts as a mechanism to find out in which block the target record resides. Many different varieties of B-tree have been researched (*see Wiederhold (1977) for further information on storage structures*).

One mechanism for finding rows quickly with no or few extra disk I/O operations is hashing, or calculating, the disk location of rows by applying a distribution calculation based on column values (*see Figure 28.5*). Using the value to calculate the location during storage and retrieval helps to find the row almost immediately. The snag with this approach is that it relies on you knowing the key value of the row you want. If not, you must locate the row by some other means. In the worst case this can mean a scan of the whole disk area in which the rows can reside.

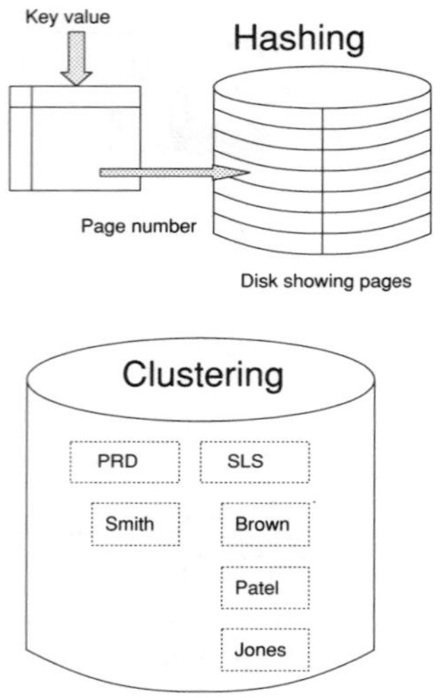

Figure 28.5 *Hashing and clustering*

Another mechanism is clustering rows of the same or different tables (*see Figure 28.5*). Rows with the same or adjacent key values may be placed together using indexing, or hashing, or by specifying physical proximation based on keys (e.g. having all Job_History rows near the relevant Employee). Some implementations offer sophisticated key compression techniques which are very useful in reducing index size and key space in records that are clustered and stored physically adjacent to one another. Accessing stored information in top-down index sequence or scanning disk space means that key information can be built up from incrementally collected portions of the key.

To optimize disk I/O and main memory space one effective technique is to fragment tables vertically. Columns that are frequently used together are a prime target for performance improvement. The frequently used columns are placed in one fragment, the less frequently used in another fragment. The resulting vertical fragments can then be distributed on to different areas of disk and when columns are needed only pages from the relevant fragment will be loaded into main memory. Also, since the fragment is smaller, more rows will fit into the same page. Should an implementation not support such an option invisibly in the application you can create it yourself (*see Section 27.2.2 Fragmentation of Portions of Data for an example*).

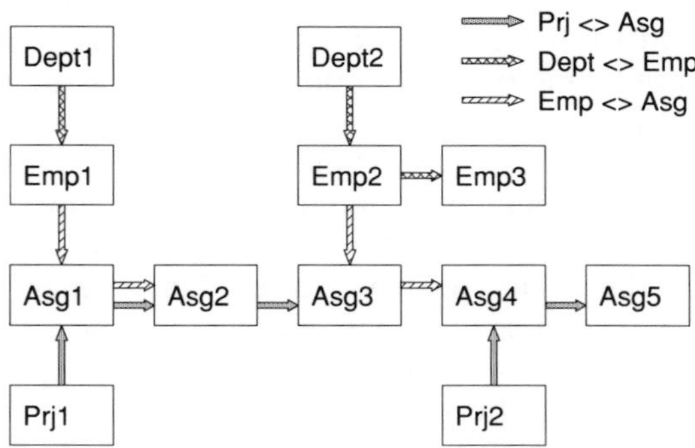

Figure 28.6 *Direct pointers*

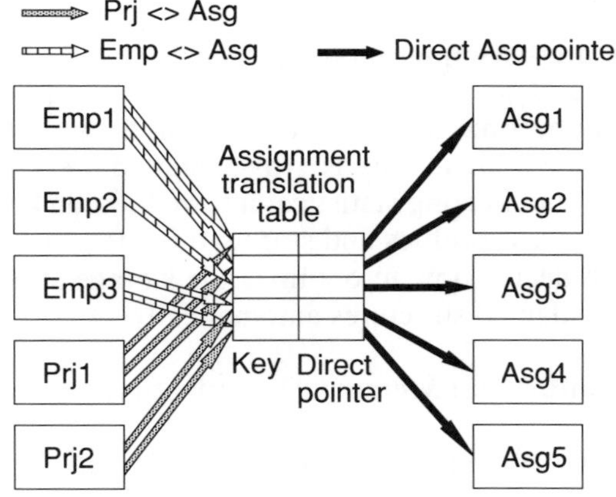

Figure 28.7 *Indirect pointers*

Some implementations use pointers of various kinds for relationships within storage structures supporting fragments of rows, pointers from indexes and linking rows with the same column values (*see Figure 28.6*). Pointers may indicate the exact disk location of a row, or a block plus an offset entry number in that page, where the page may contain a mini index to find the row. Having multiple pointers pointing to a single row means that any reorganization of disk storage and relocation of rows on disk will require the updating of all pointers to the new location of that row. One alternative sometimes offered is the use of an indirect pointer (*see Figure 28.7*) which is then translated to the direct pointer using a table. Reorganizations only need to update the translation table, but extra access to the translation table is required before accessing the row. Complex schemes of peer-to-peer (next and prior) or first-last-member-to-owner, etc. have been designed to speed up access. These configurations often require detailed insight into the behaviour of the application and can be applied to the physical database structure by the database administrator while remaining completely shielded from logic of the application program. Note that some implementations use a kind of indirect pointer mechanism in their indexes by having a primary key index that provides a direct pointer into the table, often as a block index, and then alternate key and foreign key indexes providing the primary key which acts as an indirect pointer into the primary key index at the leaves. Upon reorganization of the data in the target table only the primary key index needs to be updated. However, with a very long primary key this mechanism takes up a great deal of space in the leaves of the indirect index.

Part of the physical database design effort is in obtaining a good insight into the manner in which the application, both generally and specifically, uses the database. Once we know about specific update times or prolonged retrieval operations, it may be worth while to modify some of the above aids just before a change in access pattern occurs, like creating/dropping an index before a specific end of month program and then dropping/creating the index again afterwards.

Implementations are becoming more and more sophisticated and with the arrival of optimizers and query access path planning algorithms which are part of the DBMS it may become increasingly difficult to find out what is really happening in the storage area. This is why manufacturers implement functionality in DBMSs for collecting statistical information on key value distribution and transaction access profiles and storing the information in the catalog. The DBMS can then decide how to optimize the storage structures and make the best use of these adapted structures automatically.

28.3 Disk Storage and Main Memory Organization

The DBMS is a software program that organizes the transfer of data between disk storage and main memory storage. A major item for consideration is the block or page size. Disks are physically organized into cylinders, tracks, segments and logically into things like data spaces and files. The smallest unit of disk I/O is the block or page. Organizing tables or groups of tables on to disks with particular page sizes allows larger rows of tables with many columns to fit on to bigger pages. In calculated clustering mechanisms the loading percentage of pages goes up as the number of rows on the page increases. In a database structure with both small and large rows, variation in page size may give better loading and less overflow, leading to better disk utilization and quicker access. On the other hand, the management of different page sizes causes fragmentation in the swapping of pages from disk to and from main memory.

In database systems disk storage is often a serious problem area. Disk speed has greatly increased and many read/write heads per disk surface make the tracing of data faster. Other techniques include reading data ahead from a complete track or cylinder. Given a smaller page size, data from multiple pages will be maintained in main memory where it is available for subsequent sequential read operations from application programs. This is a good strategy for a DBMS, while in the situation of many concurrent application programs reading individual records the smaller pages require little capacity of internal memory. Another technique is to store pages across different disk units. This latter avoids congestion and queuing for each single component. Queuing on a single disk can often be solved by splitting the data across multiple disks. This can also happen with components like disk controllers, data paths from disk controller to disk, from I/O channel to disk controller and so on.

Different types of storage media should be considered, when the time comes for adding them to the configuration. Small but fast disks, very large disks, robot-handled tape cassettes in a carousel, optical write-once-read-many disks, memory chips in disk controllers to arrange caching, all these techniques are available at the DBMS or operating system level. You may feel that the co-ordination of all these resources adds to the problems and you are correct. Caching and paging mechanisms for the DBMS, operating system and disk subsystem often need co-ordination that is more easily arranged in an architecture made up of components of a single manufacturer.

When adding disks you may also add extra disks to contain extra copies of data. This feature, sometimes called dual or mirror disks, may decrease retrieval time if traffic is high and add a little to update expenses only. This option may also offer a speedy solution to the problem of recovery in certain hardware failures. High-volume transaction environments and fault-tolerant systems rely on such principles.

Holding frequently used data in main memory as well as the small tables often found in application programs, like country code translation tables or frequently used currency exchange rates, will cost main memory but save significantly on retrieval I/O. Updates also need to be written to permanent storage, i.e. the disks.

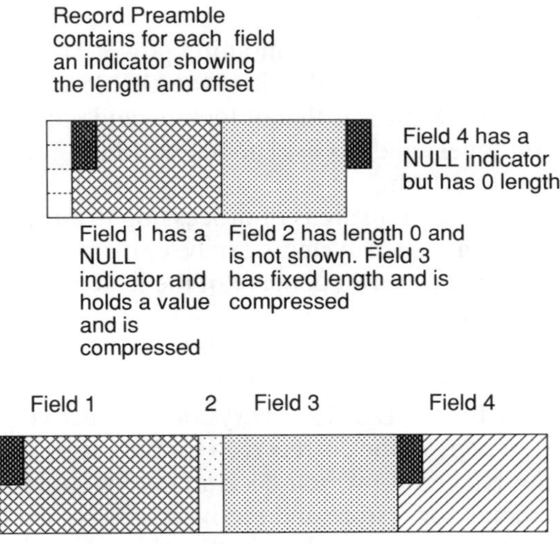

Figure 28.8 *Compressed storage of data*

Note that certain implementations have different ways of solving problems. The handling of NULL or variable length strings requires extra bytes in some implementations whereas others use clever storage features to minimize space requirements (*see Figure 28.8*).

Other features we will not discuss include working page sets, multiple memory buffers, page read ahead on sequential scans, concurrent I/O to multiple disks and downloading query clauses on to the micro chips of disk heads and controllers to minimize the amounts of data on the paths into main memory.

28.4 Query Access Planning

Apart from the mere manipulation of the disk there are many opportunities to enhance the performance of the query processing itself, such as flattening the query (*see Chapter 25 Translating Natural Language Queries*). Many optimizers work more efficiently on flat queries than on nested ones. In the same chapter you will also find rewrite rules to specify the same query in a different format which is easier for SQL programmers and the optimizer to understand.

SQL offers static and dynamic SQL execution. The static SQL execution offers the DBMS the possibility of analysing the query and creating a plan of attack for it. This can be done on first execution or through some kind of program registration. These access plans can then be stored in the program or module library or somewhere in the catalog. Obviously if the database structure changes the access plan must be regenerated, either at the next execution after the restructuring or by using some utility program. When the spread of values of a column changes, the optimizer may want to select a different route. When a query involves three tables each with a select on columns, it is advantageous to cut down the intermediate results by starting with the table having the smallest number of rows.

In relational implementations the computing power of the system is increasingly used, because of the many evaluations the DBMS must make. One of the time consuming areas in DBMSs is that of locking and recovery. Setting proper transaction isolation levels and access modes will help reduce the amount of work the DBMS must perform.

By analysing carefully certain areas of processing in an application or during maintenance the performance of systems can be enhanced. The golden rule that 20 per cent of the coding causes 80 per cent of the load is probably well known. Some areas for careful analysis include:

1. Recovery of data. Setting unnecessarily stringent recovery options will cause a lot of extra work for the DBMS. Every form of recovery relies on having previously made a copy of the correct data for later use. The synchronization of the data being backed up which costs many valuable on-line resources, and the requirements for restore and recovery always need attention.
2. Reorganization of data. Putting data in the spot where it belongs. Indexes become unbalanced, pages become crowded and overflow, pointer chains get longer and out of sequence. Many other things can and do go wrong.

Leaving a system to itself will automatically induce chaos. Periodic maintenance to reoptimize storage structures may involve specialized utilities or application programs. High volume transaction environments need careful attention and often require specific design decisions. Defining data that logically belongs together into recovery sets and ensuring a synchronized approach to reorganization will decrease the duration of any reorganization.

3. Loading data into the database. Initially data needs to be loaded into the database and during reorganization significant amounts may need to be reloaded. Offering data in a particular sequence, or in a random sequence, may greatly improve loading times. Off-line sorting is usually quicker than sorting as part of the loading into the DBMS.
4. Conversion. The actual conversion of data from the old application into the newly designed database is often seen as a one-off job, but in many cases systems are not allowed to go off-line and a new version of an application system which requires restructuring or conversion of some data from the old database must be introduced gradually. In such cases the application and/or the DBMS must be designed to do the conversion on the fly. Possessing the option of stopping on-line conversion during busy periods will improve the performance of the application.

Other ways to improve systems performance are to introduce extra servers for each client requesting a service or to have specialized servers, organized such that each request is dealt with by the appropriate server. Finally, several utilities offered by manufacturers will optimize the database or collect statistics for future use.

Appendices

The Example Database

Nearly all the examples in this book are based on a single database consisting of a single catalog containing two schemata, one called INFORMATION_SCHEMA and one that contains the example and is based on the internal administration of a fictitious company. We will assume that our data analysis of the company has resulted in the identification of the following entities. We give a brief description of each entity and identify its attributes and their associated characteristics.

Entity: Employee

An employee is a person who works for the company in some capacity

Attributes :

empnr	every employee is given a unique 5 digit number which is used to identify the employee within the company (employee number)
name	the employee's name
address	the employee's address
sex	the sex of the employee. The company uses the code 'M' to identify a male and the code 'F' to identify a female
job	the job title currently held by the employee
home telephone number	the employee's home telephone number, an 11 digit telephone number consisting of the country code, the area code and the number itself. The complete number begins with a + and each part is separated from the others by a –, i.e. in international format
work telephone number	the employee's work telephone number, an 11 digit telephone number consisting of the country code, the area code and the number itself. The complete number begins with a + and each part is separated from the others by a –, i.e. in international format
salary	the employee's annual salary
commission	the commission earned to date by the employee
date of birth	the employee's date of birth
date of joining	the date on which the employee joined the company
previous employer	the name of the employee's immediately previous employer
previous employer's address	the address of the employee's immediately previous employer

Entity : Department

A department or functional group within the company

Attributes :

department code	a unique three character code used internally in the company to identify the department
department name	the official name of the department

Entity : Constituency

An electoral group within the company which elects a representative to the staff council. All employees except senior managers are members of a constituency

Attributes :

constituency code	a unique four character code used internally in the company to identify the constituency
representative	the employee number of the elected representative for this constituency

Entity: Vehicle

A motor vehicle owned by the company, i.e. a company car. These are assigned to individual employees

Attributes :

vehicle identifier	the registration number of the vehicle
date of acquisition	the date on which it was acquired by the company

Entity : Travel Request

A request by an employee to travel to a particular destination on a given date and to remain there for so many days

Attributes :

date of request	the date on which the travel request is made
destination	the name of the location to which the employee wishes to travel
date of travel	the date on which travel is requested
length of stay	the number of days that the employee wishes to remain at the destination

Entity : Travel Agent

An agent, external to the company, who makes travel arrangements

Attributes :

travel agent identifier	a unique identifier within the company of the external travel agent
name	the real name of the travel agent
address	the postal address of the travel agent

Entity : Itinerary

The details of the actual travel arrangements made as the result of a travel request

Attributes :

itinerary number	a unique identifier within the company of the itinerary
date of outward travel	the date on which the outward travel will take place
outward flight number	the flight number of the outward flight, if any
time of outward flight	the departure time of the outward flight
hotel	the hotel, if any, that has been booked for the stay
date of return travel	the date on which the return travel will take place
return flight number	the flight number of the return flight, if any
time of return flight	the departure time of the return flight

Entity : Order

A composite request for goods or material made to another company

Attributes :

order number	a unique identifier within the company of the order
supplier	the identifier of the external company to whom the request is made
date of issue	the date on which the order is issued to the other company

Entity : Order Line

The detailed request for a single item or material made to another company as part of an order

Attributes :

order line number	a unique identifier within the order of the order line
product code	the identifier of the product that is being ordered
quantity	the quantity of the product that is being ordered

Entity : Product

An item or material that the company purchases

Attributes :

product code	a unique numeric code used internally in the company to identify the product
product name	the usual name of the product

Entity : Supplier

An external company that supplies goods or material to the company

Attributes :

supplier number	a unique identifier within the company for the external company
name	the real name of the external company
address	the postal address of the external company

Entity : Job History

A record of the previous job titles and salary that an employee has held or received during his or her employment by the company

Attributes :	
employee number	a unique identifier within the company of the employee
job	the job title held by the employee during the period
salary	the salary received by the employee during the period
start_date	the first day of a period during which the employee held the job title at the given salary
end_date	the day immediately following the last day of the period during which the employee held the job title at the given salary

Entity : Project

An activity that is carried out by the company for a specified period of time. This activity can be internal but is usually an activity carried out for a client company

Attributes :	
project identifier	the unique identifier that is used to identify the project
start date	the date on which the project started or is to start
end date	the day immediately following the date on which the project ended
responsible department	the department within the company that is responsible for carrying out the project
sponsoring department	the department within the company that is responsible for sponsoring, or financing, the project
budget	the original budgeted cost of the project
forecast	the forecast total cost of the project
actual	the actual cost of the project to date
description	a brief textual description of the project

Entity : Assignment

A relationship between an employee and a project that defines the period during which the employee worked on the project

Attributes :	
employee number	the unique identification of the employee
project role	the task within the project that is fulfilled by this person
project number	the unique identification of the project
start date	the first day of a period during which the employee worked for the project
end date	the date immediately following the last day of a period during which the employee worked for the project

Entity : Timesheet	
A record of the number of hours that an employee charged against a project on a given date	
Attributes :	
employee number	the unique identifier that is used to identify the employee
project identifier	the unique identifier that is used to identify the project
work date	the date on which the work was carried out
hours	the number of normal hours (and minutes) worked on that day for the project
overtime hours	the number of overtime hours (and minutes) worked on that day for the project
timestamp start	the timestamp when this entity was stored in the database
timestamp end	the timestamp when this entity was logically deleted from the database

The relationships between the various entities are shown in the data structure diagram in Figure A.

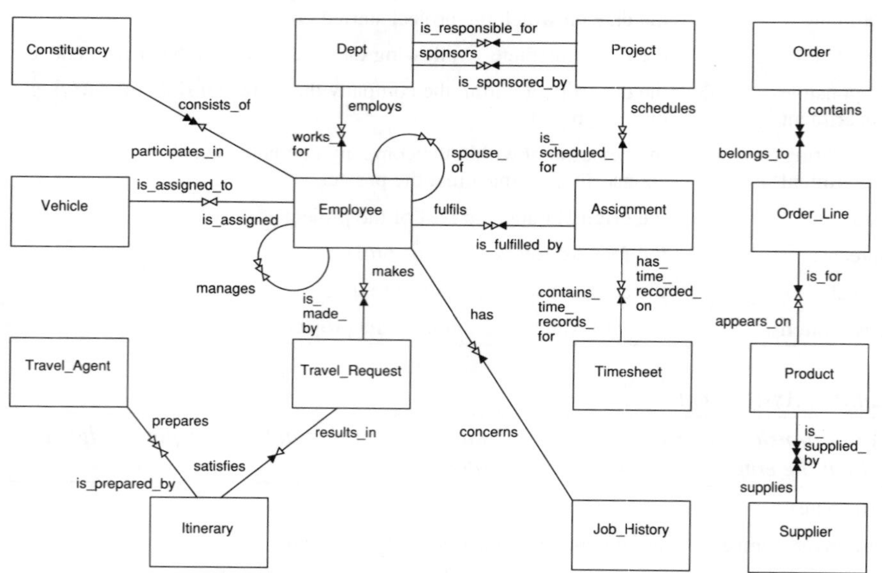

***Figure A** Data structure diagram of the example database*

The complete schema used in the book for most of the example is:

```
CREATE SCHEMA Company AUTHORIZATION cannan

CREATE DOMAIN telno AS CHARACTER (14)
   CHECK (    VALUE LIKE '+%(_)%-%-%'
          OR  VALUE LIKE '+%-%-%-%'
          OR  VALUE LIKE '%-%'
          OR  VALUE LIKE '___')

CREATE DOMAIN job AS CHARACTER (20)
   CHECK (VALUE IN (SELECT * FROM Valid_Jobs))

CREATE DOMAIN acquisition_date AS DATE DEFAULT CURRENT_DATE

CREATE DOMAIN projcd AS CHARACTER (6)
   CHECK ((SUBSTRING(VALUE FROM 5 FOR 1) BETWEEN '0' AND '9')
     AND (SUBSTRING(VALUE FROM 6 FOR 1) BETWEEN '0' AND '9'))

CREATE TABLE Dept
(
deptcd  CHARACTER (3) PRIMARY KEY,
deptnm  CHARACTER (12)
)
```

```
CREATE TABLE Employee
(
empnr               NUMERIC (5),
name                CHARACTER (40) NOT NULL,
address             CHARACTER VARYING (200),
sex                 CHARACTER NOT NULL,
home_telno          telno,
deptcd              CHARACTER (3) NOT NULL DEFAULT 'PER',
work_telno          telno UNIQUE,
job                 job NOT NULL,
salary              NUMERIC (6) NOT NULL,
commission          NUMERIC (6,2),
vehicleid           CHARACTER (7),
constituency        CHARACTER (4),
CHECK(sex IN ('M','F')),
PRIMARY KEY (empnr),
CHECK ((vehicleid, empnr) MATCH
   (SELECT vehicleid, empnr FROM Vehicle)),
CONSTRAINT Employee_link_to_extension
   FOREIGN KEY (empnr) REFERENCES Emp_Ext,
FOREIGN KEY (deptcd) REFERENCES Dept
   ON DELETE SET DEFAULT
   ON UPDATE CASCADE,
FOREIGN KEY (constituency) REFERENCES Constituency
)

CREATE TABLE Emp_Ext
(
empnr               NUMERIC (5),
date_of_birth       DATE NOT NULL,
date_of_joining     DATE NOT NULL,
spouse              NUMERIC (5),
manager             NUMERIC (5),
previous_employer   CHARACTER (40),
p_e_address         CHARACTER VARYING (200),
CHECK (date_of_birth < date_of_joining),
PRIMARY KEY (empnr),
CHECK ((empnr, spouse) MATCH
        (SELECT spouse, empnr FROM Emp_Ext)),
FOREIGN KEY (empnr) REFERENCES Employee
   ON DELETE CASCADE,
FOREIGN KEY (manager) REFERENCES Emp_Ext
)
```

```
CREATE TABLE Valid_Job
(
job_title            CHARACTER (20) PRIMARY KEY
)

CREATE TABLE Job_History
(
empnr                NUMERIC (5),
job                  job NOT NULL,
salary               NUMERIC (6) NOT NULL,
start_date           DATE,
end_date             DATE,
CHECK (NOT EXISTS (
   SELECT *
     FROM Job_History AS J1 JOIN Job_History AS J2
         USING (empnr)
     WHERE (J1.start_date, J1.end_date)
        OVERLAPS
        (J2.start_date, J2.end_date)
      AND J1.start_date <> J2.start_date)),
CHECK (1 =
    (SELECT MAX (occurrences)
      FROM (SELECT COUNT(*) AS occurrences
           FROM Job_History AS J1 LEFT JOIN Job_History AS J2
            ON J1.empnr = J2.empnr
             AND J1.end_date = J2.start_date
           WHERE J2.empnr IS NULL
           GROUP BY J1.empnr))),
PRIMARY KEY (empnr, start_date),
FOREIGN KEY (empnr) REFERENCES Employee
)

CREATE TABLE Project
(
project_cd           projcd,
start_date           DATE NOT NULL,
end_date             DATE,
resp_dept            NUMERIC (5) NOT NULL,
sponsor_dept         NUMERIC (5) NOT NULL,
budget               DECIMAL (6,2),
forecast             DECIMAL (6,2),
actual               DECIMAL (6,2),
description          CHARACTER VARYING (2000),
PRIMARY KEY (project_cd),
FOREIGN KEY (resp_dept) REFERENCES Dept,
FOREIGN KEY (sponsor_dept) REFERENCES Dept
)
```

```
CREATE TABLE Assignment
(
empnr               NUMERIC (5),
project_cd          projcd,
project_role        CHARACTER (15),
start_date          DATE NOT NULL,
end_date            DATE,
CHECK (NOT EXISTS (
   SELECT *
     FROM Assignment AS W1 JOIN Assignment AS W2
      USING (empnr, project_cd)
     WHERE (W1.start_date, W1.end_date)
           OVERLAPS
           (W2.start_date, W2.end_date)
       AND W1.start_date <> W2.start_date)),
CHECK (project_role IN (
         'Project Leader',
         'Quality Assurance',
         'Worker',
         'Planner')),
PRIMARY KEY (empnr, project_cd, start_date),
FOREIGN KEY (empnr) REFERENCES Employee,
FOREIGN KEY (project_cd) REFERENCES Project
)
```

```
CREATE TABLE Timesheet
(
empnr               NUMERIC (5),
project_cd          projcd,
work_date           DATE,
hours               INTERVAL HOUR TO MINUTE,
overtime_hours      INTERVAL HOUR TO MINUTE,
timestamp_start     TIMESTAMP NOT NULL
                    DEFAULT CURRENT_TIMESTAMP,
timestamp_end       TIMESTAMP NOT NULL
   DEFAULT TIMESTAMP'9999-12-31-23:59:59.999999',
CHECK (NOT EXISTS (
   SELECT *
     FROM Timesheet AS T1 JOIN Timesheet AS T2
       USING (empnr, project_cd, work_date)
       WHERE (T1.timestamp_start, T1.timestamp_end)
             OVERLAPS
             (T2.timestamp_start, T2.timestamp_end)
         AND T1.timestamp_start <> T2.timestamp_start)),
CHECK (1 = (SELECT MAX (occurrences)
   FROM (SELECT COUNT(*) AS occurrences
       FROM Timesheet AS T1 LEFT JOIN Timesheet AS T2
         ON (T1.empnr, T1.project_cd, T1.work_date) =
            (T2.empnr, T2.project_cd, T2.work_date)
            AND T1.timestamp_end = T2.timestamp_start
       WHERE T2.empnr IS NULL
       GROUP BY T1.empnr, T1.project_cd, T1.work_date))),
PRIMARY KEY (empnr, project_cd, work_date, timestamp_start),
FOREIGN KEY (empnr) REFERENCES Employee,
FOREIGN KEY (project_cd) REFERENCES Project
)

CREATE TABLE Vehicle
(
vehicleid           NUMERIC (5),
empnr               NUMERIC (5),
acquisition_date    acquisition_date NOT NULL,
PRIMARY KEY (vehicleid),
CHECK ((empnr, vehicleid) MATCH
   (SELECT empnr, vehicleid FROM Employee))
)
```

```
CREATE TABLE Constituency
(
constituency        CHARACTER (4),
representative      NUMERIC (5),
PRIMARY KEY (constituency),
FOREIGN KEY (representative) REFERENCES Employee,
CHECK (constituency IN (SELECT constituency FROM Employee))
)

CREATE TABLE Order
(
ordernr             NUMERIC (5),
suppliernr          NUMERIC (5) NOT NULL,
date_issued         DATE NOT NULL,
PRIMARY KEY (ordernr),
CONSTRAINT Order_contains_at_least_one_order_line
   CHECK (ordernr IN (SELECT ordernr FROM Order_Line))
)

CREATE TABLE Order_Line
(
ordernr             NUMERIC (5),
order_linenr        NUMERIC (5),
product_code        NUMERIC (5) NOT NULL,
quantity            INTEGER NOT NULL,
PRIMARY KEY (ordernr, order_linenr),
FOREIGN KEY (ordernr) REFERENCES Order,
FOREIGN KEY (product_code) REFERENCES Product
)

CREATE TABLE Travel_Req
(
empnr               NUMERIC (5),
request_date        DATE,
destination         CHARACTER (40),
travel_date         DATE,
stay                SMALLINT,
PRIMARY KEY (empnr, request_date),
FOREIGN KEY (empnr) REFERENCES Employee
)
```

```
CREATE TABLE Itinerary
(
itinerary_no        NUMERIC (5),
empnr               NUMERIC (5) NOT NULL,
request_date        DATE NOT NULL,
travel_agent_id     CHARACTER (10),
outward_date        DATE,
flight_no_out       CHARACTER (6) NOT NULL,
outward_time        TIME,
hotel               CHARACTER (40),
return_date         DATE,
flight_no_back      CHARACTER (6) NOT NULL,
return_time         TIME,
PRIMARY KEY (itinerary_no),
UNIQUE (empnr, request_date),
FOREIGN KEY (empnr, request_date) REFERENCES Travel_Req,
FOREIGN KEY (travel_agent_id) REFERENCES Travel_Agent
)

CREATE TABLE Travel_Agent
(
travel_agent_id     CHARACTER (10),
name                CHARACTER (40),
address             CHARACTER VARYING (200),
PRIMARY KEY (travel_agent_id)
)

CREATE TABLE Product
(
product_code        NUMERIC (5),
name                CHARACTER (20) NOT NULL,
PRIMARY KEY (product_code),
CONSTRAINT Product_must_be_supplied
   CHECK (product_code IN
      (SELECT product_code FROM Product_Supply))
)

CREATE TABLE Supplier
(
suppliernr          NUMERIC (5),
name                CHARACTER (20) NOT NULL,
address             CHARACTER VARYING (200),
PRIMARY KEY (suppliernr),
CONSTRAINT Supplier_must_supply_something
   CHECK (suppliernr IN (SELECT suppliernr FROM
   Product_Supply))
)
```

```
CREATE TABLE Product_Supply
(
product_code      NUMERIC (5),
suppliernr        NUMERIC (5),
minimum_order     NUMERIC (10),
PRIMARY KEY (product_code, suppliernr),
FOREIGN KEY (product_code) REFERENCES Product,
FOREIGN KEY (suppliernr) REFERENCES Supplier
)

CREATE ASSERTION Max_Order_Lines
CHECK (10 >=
   (SELECT MAX(lines)
       FROM (SELECT COUNT(*) AS lines
             FROM Order_line
             GROUP BY ordernr)))

CREATE VIEW Hq_Tel_List (name, telno, staffnr)
   AS
   SELECT name, telno, empnr
     FROM Employee
     WHERE deptcd = 'HDQ'
```

B

BNF Syntax Notation

B.1 Introduction and Purpose

The syntactic notation used in this book is an extended version of 'Backus normal form' or 'Backus Naur form' (BNF). The purpose of BNF notation is to describe how character strings may be produced, using a substitution process, so as to correctly represent commands in the language.

In BNF, each syntactic element of the language is defined by means of a 'production rule'. This defines the element in terms of a formula consisting of the characters, character strings and syntactic elements that can be used to form an instance of it.

B.2 Symbols

The version of BNF used makes use of the following symbols:

Symbol	*Meaning*
< >	Angle brackets delimit character strings that are the names of syntactic elements, the non-terminal symbols of the SQL language.
::=	The definition operator. This is used in a production rule to separate the element defined by the rule from its definition. The element being defined appears to the left of the operator and the formula that defines the element appears to the right.
[ ]	Square brackets indicate optional elements in a formula. The portion of the formula within the brackets may be explicitly specified or may be omitted.

{ } Braces group elements in a formula. The portion of the formula within the braces must be explicitly specified.

| The alternative operator. The vertical bar indicates that the portion of the formula following the bar is an alternative to the portion preceding the bar. If the vertical bar occurs at a position where it is not enclosed in braces or square brackets, it specifies a complete alternative for the element defined by the production rule. If the vertical bar occurs in a portion of a formula enclosed in braces or square brackets, it specifies alternatives for the contents of the innermost pair of such braces or brackets.

... The ellipsis indicates that the preceding element of a formula may be repeated. If the ellipsis occurs immediately after a portion of a formula enclosed in braces, the repetition is of the whole of the formula enclosed within those braces. Otherwise it applies only to the immediately preceding element.

!! Introduces normal English text. This is used when the definition of a syntactic element is not expressed in BNF. In the standard it is a reference to syntax rules that defines the element. In this book it is used to point to the place in the book where the production is explained; for example:

<preparable implementation-defined statement> ::= !! (*see Section 18.4 PREPARE*)

Since this is implementation defined the syntax cannot properly be specified by the standard.

Spaces and line breaks are ignored. Apart from those symbols to which special functions are ascribed above, other characters and character strings in a formula stand for themselves. In addition, if the symbols to the right of the definition operator in a production consist entirely of BNF symbols, then those symbols stand for themselves and do not take on their special meaning. For example, the definition of the not equals operator is:

<not equals operator> ::= <>

In this case <> means <> and is not the non-terminal symbol with an empty name.

Pairs of braces and square brackets may be nested to any depth, and the alternative operator may appear at any depth within such a nest.

B.3 The Substitution Process

A character string that forms an instance of any syntactic element may be generated from the BNF definition of that syntactic element by application of the following steps:

1. Select any one option from those defined on the right-hand side of a production rule for the element and replace the element by this option.
2. Replace each ellipsis and the object to which it applies by one or more instances of this object.
3. For each portion of the string enclosed in square brackets, either delete the brackets and their contents or change the brackets to braces.
4. For each portion of the string enclosed in braces, apply steps 1 to 5 to the sub-string between the braces, then remove the braces.
5. Apply steps 1 to 5 to any non-terminal syntactic element (i.e. name enclosed in angle brackets) that remains in the string.

The expansion or production is complete when no further non-terminal symbols remain in the character string.

C

BNF Syntax Diagrams

This appendix contains an abbreviated form of the BNF syntax definitions used in the SQL standard. All SQL statements are described in sufficient detail to enable syntactically correct SQL to be written without problem. There are nine distinct syntax trees in the SQL language. Of these trees two, (<token> and <separator>), are concerned with lexical aspects, one (<module>) is concerned with the module language, four (<embedded SQL host program>, <embedded SQL declare section>, <embedded SQL statement> and <embedded exception declaration>) are concerned with the embedded SQL languages, one (<preparable>) is concerned with the syntax that must be supplied as data to dynamic commands and the last one (<direct SQL statement>) is concerned with SQL which may be directly invoked. The BNF is presented in alphabetic order of the production name.

<action> ::=
    SELECT
  | DELETE
  | INSERT [(<privilege column list>)]
  | UPDATE [(<privilege column list>)]
  | REFERENCES [(<privilege column list>)]
  | USAGE
!! (*see Chapter 8 Access Control*)

<action list> ::= <action> [{ , <action> }...]
!! (*see Chapter 8 Access Control*)

<actual identifier> ::=
<regular identifier>
| <delimited identifier>
!! (*see Section 3.3 Identifiers*)

<Ada host identifier> ::= !! (*see Section 17.1.1 Ada*)

<Ada initial value> ::=
:= <character representation>...
!! (*see Section 17.1.1 Ada*)

<Ada qualified type specification> ::=
CHAR [CHARACTER SET [IS]
<character set specification>]
(1 : <length>)
| SQL_STANDARD.BIT (1 : <length>)
| SQL_STANDARD.SMALLINT
| SQL_STANDARD.INT
| SQL_STANDARD.REAL
| SQL_STANDARD.DOUBLE_PRECISION
| SQL_STANDARD.SQLCODE_TYPE
| SQL_STANDARD.SQLSTATE_TYPE
| SQL_STANDARD.INDICATOR_TYPE
!! (*see Section 17.1.1 Ada*)

<Ada type specification> ::=
<Ada qualified type specification>
| <Ada unqualified type specification>
!! (*see Section 17.1.1 Ada*)

<Ada unqualified type specification> ::=
CHAR (1 : <length>)
| BIT (1 : <length>)
| SMALLINT
| INT
| REAL
| DOUBLE_PRECISION
| SQLCODE_TYPE
| SQLSTATE_TYPE
| INDICATOR_TYPE
!! (*see Section 17.1.1 Ada*)

<Ada variable definition> ::=
<Ada host identifier>
[{ , <Ada host identifier> }...] :
<Ada type specification> [<Ada initial value>]
!! (*see Section 17.1.1 Ada*)

<add column definition> ::=
    ADD [COLUMN] <column definition>
!! (*see Section 5.2.2.1 Add Column*)

<add domain constraint definition> ::=
    ADD <domain constraint>
!! (*see Section 5.2.1.3 Add Domain Constraint*)

<add table constraint definition> ::=
    ADD <table constraint definition>
!! (*see Section 5.2.2.3 Add Table Constraint*)

<allocate cursor statement> ::=
    ALLOCATE <extended cursor name>
        [INSENSITIVE] [SCROLL] CURSOR
        FOR <extended statement name>
!! (*see Section 18.14 Dynamic ALLOCATE CURSOR*)

<allocate descriptor statement> ::=
    ALLOCATE DESCRIPTOR <descriptor name>
        [WITH MAX <occurrences>]
!! (*see Section 18.8 ALLOCATE DESCRIPTOR*)

<alter column action> ::=
      <set column default clause>
    | <drop column default clause>
!! (*see Section 5.2.2.5 Set Column Default and Section 5.2.2.6 Drop Column Default*)

<alter column definition> ::=
    ALTER [COLUMN] <column name> <alter column action>
!! (*see Section 5.2.2.5 Set Column Default and Section 5.2.2.6 Drop Column Default*)

<alter domain action> ::=
      <set domain default clause>
    | <drop domain default clause>
    | <add domain constraint definition>
    | <drop domain constraint definition>
!! (*see Section 5.2.1 ALTER DOMAIN*)

<alter domain statement> ::=
    ALTER DOMAIN <domain name> <alter domain action>
!! (*see Section 5.2.1 ALTER DOMAIN*)

<alter table action> ::=
      <add column definition>
    | <alter column definition>
    | <drop column definition>
    | <add table constraint definition>
    | <drop table constraint definition>
!! (*see Section 5.2.2 ALTER TABLE*)

<alter table statement> ::=
ALTER TABLE <table name> <alter table action>
!! (*see Section 5.2.2 ALTER TABLE*)

<approximate numeric literal> ::= <mantissa> E <exponent>
!! (*see Section 3.7.8 Approximate Numeric Literals*)

<approximate numeric type> ::=
FLOAT [(<precision>)]
| REAL
| DOUBLE PRECISION
!! (*see Section 3.7.7 The Approximate Numeric Data Type*)

<argument> ::= <target specification>
!! (*see Section 18.7 USING*)

<as clause> ::= [AS] <column name>
!! (*see Section 9.5 Query Specification*)

<assertion check> ::=
CHECK (<search condition>)
!! (*see Section 4.5 CREATE ASSERTION*)

<assertion definition> ::=
CREATE ASSERTION <constraint name> <assertion check>
[<constraint attributes>]
!! (*see Section 4.5 CREATE ASSERTION*)

<authorization identifier> ::= <identifier>
!! (*see Section 3.4 Names*)

<between predicate> ::=
<row value constructor> [NOT] BETWEEN
<row value constructor> AND
<row value constructor>
!! (*see Section 10.2.2 Between Predicate*)

<bit> ::= 0 | 1
!! (*see Section 3.7.4 Bit String Literals*)

<bit length expression> ::=
BIT_LENGTH (<string value expression>)
!! (*see Section 11.2.2.4 BIT_LENGTH*)

<bit primary> ::=
<common primary> | <string value function>
!! (*see Section 11.1.2 String Value Expressions*)

<bit string literal> ::=
B' [<bit>...] '
[{ <separator>...
' [<bit>...] ' }...]
!! (*see Section 3.7.4 Bit String Literals*)

<bit string type> ::=
BIT [(<length>)]
| BIT VARYING (<length>)
!! (*see Section 3.7.3 The Bit Data Type*)

<bit substring function> ::=
SUBSTRING (<bit value expression>
FROM <start position>
[FOR <string length>])
!! (*see Section 11.2.2.1 SUBSTRING*)

<bit value expression> ::=
<bit value expression> <concatenation operator>
<bit primary>
| <bit primary>
!! (*see Section 11.1.2 String Value Expressions*)

<bit value function> ::=
<bit substring function>
!! (*see Section 11.1.2 String Value Expressions*)

<boolean factor> ::=
[NOT] <boolean test>
!! (*see Section 10.1 Search Conditions*)

<boolean primary> ::=
<predicate>
| (<search condition>)
!! (*see Section 10.1 Search Conditions*)

<boolean term> ::=
<boolean factor>
| <boolean term> AND <boolean factor>
!! (*see Section 10.1 Search Conditions*)

<boolean test> ::=
<boolean primary> [IS [NOT]
{ TRUE | FALSE | UNKNOWN }]
!! (*see Section 10.1 Search Conditions*)

<C array specification> ::=
<left bracket> <length> <right bracket>
!! (*see Section 17.1.2 C*)

```
<C bit variable> ::=
    BIT <C host identifier>
        <C array specification> [ <C initial value> ]
        [ { , <C host identifier>      <C array specification>
            [ <C initial value> ] }... ]
!! (see Section 17.1.2 C)

<C character variable> ::=
    char
        [ CHARACTER SET [ IS ]
            <character set specification> ]
        <C host identifier>
        <C array specification> [ <C initial value> ]
        [ { , <C host identifier>      <C array specification>
            [ <C initial value> ] }... ]
!! (see Section 17.1.2 C)

<C class modifier> ::= const | volatile
!! (see Section 17.1.2 C)

<C derived variable> ::=
      <C VARCHAR variable>
    | <C bit variable>
!! (see Section 17.1.2 C)

<C host identifier> ::= !! (see Section 17.1.2 C)

<C initial value> ::=
    = <character representation>...
!! (see Section 17.1.2 C)

<C numeric variable> ::=
    { long | short | float | double }
        <C host identifier> [ <C initial value> ]
            [ { , <C host identifier>
                [ <C initial value> ] }... ]
!! (see Section 17.1.2 C)

<C storage class> ::= auto | extern | static
!! (see Section 17.1.2 C)

<C VARCHAR variable> ::=
    VARCHAR [ CHARACTER SET [ IS ]
            <character set specification> ]
        <C host identifier> <C array specification>
            [ <C initial value> ]
        [ { , <C host identifier>
            <C array specification>
            [ <C initial value> ] }... ]
!! (see Section 17.1.2 C)
```

<C variable definition> ::=
[<C storage class>]
[<C class modifier>]
<C variable specification>
;
!! (*see Section 17.1.2 C*)

<C variable specification> ::=
<C numeric variable>
| <C character variable>
| <C derived variable>
!! (*see Section 17.1.2 C*)

<case abbreviation> ::=
NULLIF (<value expression> , <value expression>)
| COALESCE (<value expression>
{ , <value expression> }...)
!! (*see SECTION 11.3.2 NULLIF and Section 11.3.3 COALESCE*)

<case expression> ::=
<case abbreviation>
| <case specification>
!! (*see Section 11.3.1 CASE*)

<case operand> ::= <value expression>
!! (*see Section 11.3.1 CASE*)

<case specification> ::=
<simple case>
| <searched case>
!! (*see Section 11.3.1 CASE*)

<cast operand> ::=
<value expression>
| NULL
!! (*see Section 11.2.4 CAST*)

<cast specification> ::=
CAST (<cast operand> AS <cast target>)
!! (*see Section 11.2.4 CAST*)

<cast target> ::=
<domain name>
| <data type>
!! (*see Section 11.2.4 CAST*)

<catalog name> ::= <identifier>
!! (*see Section 3.4 Names*)

<char length expression> ::=
{ CHAR_LENGTH | CHARACTER_LENGTH }
(<string value expression>)
!! (*see Section 11.2.2.2 CHARACTER_LENGTH*)

<character factor> ::=
<character primary> [<collate clause>]
!! (*see Section 11.1.2 String Value Expressions*)

<character primary> ::=
<common primary> | <string value function>
!! (*see Section 11.1.2 String Value Expressions*)

<character representation> ::=
<nonquote character>
| <quote symbol>
!! (*see Section 3.7.2 Character Literals*)

<character set definition> ::=
CREATE CHARACTER SET <character set name>
[AS] <character set source>
[<collate clause>
| <limited collation definition>]
!! (*see Section 4.6 CREATE CHARACTER SET*)

<character set name> ::=
[<schema name> .] <SQL language identifier>
!! (*see Section 3.4 Names*)

<character set source> ::=
GET <existing character set name>
!! (*see Section 4.6 CREATE CHARACTER SET*)

<character set specification> ::=
<standard character repertoire name>
| <implementation-defined character repertoire name>
| <user-defined character repertoire name>
| <standard universal character form-of-use name>
| <implementation-defined universal form-of-use name>
!! (*see Section 4.1.2 Schema Default Character Set*)

<character string literal> ::=
[<introducer><character set specification>]
' [<character representation>...] '
[{ <separator>...
' [<character representation>...] ' }...]
!! (*see Section 3.7.2 Character Literals*)

<character string type> ::=
CHARACTER [(<length>)]
| CHAR [(<length>)]
| CHARACTER VARYING (<length>)
| CHAR VARYING (<length>)
| VARCHAR (<length>)
!! (*see Section 3.7.1 The Character Data Type*)

<character substring function> ::=
SUBSTRING (<character value expression>
FROM <start position>
[FOR <string length>])
!! (*see Section 11.2.2.1 SUBSTRING*)

<character translation> ::=
TRANSLATE (<character value expression>
USING <translation name>)
!! (*see Section 11.2.3.5 TRANSLATE*)

<character value expression> ::=
<concatenation>
| <character factor>
!! (*see Section 11.1.2 String Value Expressions*)

<character value function> ::=
<character substring function>
| <fold>
| <form-of-use conversion>
| <character translation>
| <trim function>
!! (*see Section 11.1.2 String Value Expressions*)

<check constraint definition> ::=
CHECK (<search condition>)
!! (*see Section 4.2.1.2.4 Check*)

<close statement> ::=
CLOSE <cursor name>
!! (*see Section 7.6 CLOSE*)

<COBOL binary integer> ::=
{ PIC | PICTURE } [IS] S<COBOL nines>
[USAGE [IS]] BINARY
!! (*see Section 17.1.3 COBOL*)

<COBOL bit type> ::=
{ PIC | PICTURE } [IS] { B [(<length>)] }...
!! (*see Section 17.1.3 COBOL*)

```
<COBOL character type> ::=
    [ CHARACTER SET [ IS ]
        <character set specification> ]
    { PIC | PICTURE } [ IS ] { X [ ( <length> ) ] }...
!! (see Section 17.1.3 COBOL)

<COBOL computational integer> ::=
    { PIC | PICTURE } [ IS ] S<COBOL nines>
    [ USAGE [ IS ] ] { COMP | COMPUTATIONAL }
!! (see Section 17.1.3 COBOL)

<COBOL host identifier> ::= !! (see Section 17.1.3 COBOL)

<COBOL integer type> ::=
      <COBOL computational integer>
    | <COBOL binary integer>
!! (see Section 17.1.3 COBOL)

<COBOL nines> ::= { 9 [ ( <length> ) ] }...
!! (see Section 17.1.3 COBOL)

<COBOL nines specification> ::=
      <COBOL nines> [ V [ <COBOL nines> ] ]
    | V <COBOL nines>
!! (see Section 17.1.3 COBOL)

<COBOL numeric type> ::=
    { PIC | PICTURE } [ IS ]
    S <COBOL nines specification>
    [ USAGE [ IS ] ] DISPLAY SIGN LEADING SEPARATE
!! (see Section 17.1.3 COBOL)

<COBOL type specification> ::=
      <COBOL character type>
    | <COBOL bit type>
    | <COBOL numeric type>
    | <COBOL integer type>
!! (see Section 17.1.3 COBOL)

<COBOL variable definition> ::=
    {01|77} <COBOL host identifier>
    <COBOL type specification>
    [ <character representation>... ] .
!! (see Section 17.1.3 COBOL)

<collate clause> ::= COLLATE <collation name>
!! (see Section 4.2.1.3 Collation)
```

<collating sequence definition> ::=
<external collation>
| <schema collation name>
| DESC (<collation name>)
| DEFAULT
!! (*see Section 4.7 CREATE COLLATION*)

<collation definition> ::=
CREATE COLLATION <collation name>
FOR <character set specification>
FROM <collation source> [NO PAD | PAD SPACE]
!! (*see Section 4.7 CREATE COLLATION*)

<collation name> ::= <qualified name>
!! (*see Section 4.7 CREATE COLLATION*)

<collation source> ::=
<collating sequence definition>
| <translation collation>
!! (*see Section 4.7 CREATE COLLATION*)

<column constraint> ::=
NOT NULL
| <unique specification>
| <references specification>
| <check constraint definition>
!! (*see Section 4.2.1.2 Column Constraints*)

<column constraint definition> ::=
[<constraint name definition>]
<column constraint>
[<constraint attributes>]
!! (*see Section 4.2.1.2 Column Constraints*)

<column definition> ::=
<column name> { <data type> | <domain name> }
[<default clause>]
[<column constraint definition>...]
[<collate clause>]
!! (*see Section 4.2.1 Column Definition*)

<column name> ::= <identifier>
!! (*see Section 3.4 Names*)

<column name list> ::=
<column name> [{ , <column name> }...]
!! (*see Section 9.3.1 Table References*)

<column reference> ::= [<qualifier> .] <column name>
!! (*see Section 11.1 Value Expressions*)

<comment> ::=
<comment introducer> [<comment character>...]
<newline>
!! (*see Section 3.2 Tokens*)

<comment character> ::=
<nonquote character> | '
!! (*see Section 3.2 Tokens*)

<comment introducer> ::= -- [{ - }...]
!! (*see Section 3.2 Tokens*)

<commit statement> ::=
COMMIT [WORK]
!! (*see Section 12.3.1 The COMMIT Statement*)

<common primary> ::=
<unsigned value specification>
| <column reference>
| <set function specification>
| <scalar subquery>
| <case expression>
| (<value expression>)
| <cast specification>
!! (*see Section 11.1 Value Expressions*)

<comparison operator> ::=
=
| <not equals operator>
| <less than operator>
| <greater than operator>
| <less than or equals operator>
| <greater than or equals operator>
!! (*see Section 10.2.1 Comparison Predicate*)

<comparison predicate> ::=
<row value constructor>
<comparison operator> <row value constructor>
!! (*see Section 10.2.1 Comparison Predicate*)

<concatenation> ::=
<character value expression>
<concatenation operator>
<character factor>
!! (*see Section 11.1.2 String Value Expressions*)

<concatenation operator> ::= ||
!! (*see Section 11.1.2 String Value Expressions*)

<condition> ::= SQLERROR | NOT FOUND
!! (*see Section 17.2 Exception Control*)

<condition information> ::=
EXCEPTION <condition number>
<condition information item>
[{ , <condition information item> }...]
!! (*see Chapter 15 Error Handling and Diagnostics*)

<condition information item> ::=
<simple target specification> =
<condition information item name>
!! (*see Chapter 15 Error Handling and Diagnostics*)

<condition information item name> ::=
CONDITION_NUMBER | RETURNED_SQLSTATE | CLASS_ORIGIN |
SUBCLASS_ORIGIN | SERVER_NAME | CONNECTION_NAME |
CONSTRAINT_CATALOG | CONSTRAINT_SCHEMA |
CONSTRAINT_NAME | CATALOG_NAME | SCHEMA_NAME |
TABLE_NAME | COLUMN_NAME | CURSOR_NAME | MESSAGE_TEXT |
MESSAGE_LENGTH | MESSAGE_OCTET_LENGTH
!! (*see Chapter 15 Error Handling and Diagnostics*)

<condition number> ::= <simple value specification>
!! (*see Chapter 15 Error Handling and Diagnostics*)

<connect statement> ::=
CONNECT TO
{ <SQL-Server>
[AS <connection name>] [USER <user name>] }
| DEFAULT
!! (*see Section 14.1 CONNECT*)

<connection name> ::= <simple value specification>
!! (*see Section 14.1 CONNECT*)

<connection object> ::=
DEFAULT
| <connection name>
!! (*see Section 14.2 SET CONNECTION*)

<constraint attributes> ::=
<constraint check time> [[NOT] DEFERRABLE]
| [NOT] DEFERRABLE [<constraint check time>]
!! (*see Section 4.2.1.2 Column Constraints*)

<constraint check time> ::=
INITIALLY DEFERRED
| INITIALLY IMMEDIATE
!! (*see Section 4.2.1.2 Column Constraints*)

<constraint name> ::= <qualified name>
!! (*see Section 4.2.1.2 Column Constraints*)

<constraint name definition> ::=
    CONSTRAINT <constraint name>
!! (*see Section 4.2.1.2 Column Constraints*)

<constraint name list> ::=
      ALL
    | <constraint name> [{ , <constraint name> }...]
!! (*see Section 13.5 SET CONSTRAINTS MODE*)

<conversion name> ::= <qualified name>
!! (*see Section 11.2.3.6 CONVERT*)

<correlation name> ::= <identifier>
!! (*see Section 9.3.1 Table References*)

<corresponding column list> ::= <column name list>
!! (*see Section 9.3 Query Expression*)

<corresponding spec> ::=
    CORRESPONDING [BY (<corresponding column list>)]
!! (*see Section 9.3 Query Expression*)

<cross join> ::=
    <table reference> CROSS JOIN <table reference>
!! (*see Section 9.3.2.4 JOIN*)

<cursor name> ::= <identifier>
!! (*see Section 7.1 DECLARE CURSOR*)

<cursor specification> ::=
    <query expression> [<order by clause>]
    [<updatability clause>]
!! (*see Section 7.1 DECLARE CURSOR*)

<data type> ::=
      <character string type>
        [CHARACTER SET <character set specification>]
    | <national character string type>
    | <bit string type>
    | <numeric type>
    | <datetime type>
    | <interval type>
!! (*see Section 3.7 Data Types*)

<date literal> ::= DATE <date string>
!! (*see Section 3.7.10 Datetime Literals*)

<date string> ::= ' <date value> '
!! (*see Section 3.7.10 Datetime Literals*)

<date value> ::=
<years value> - <months value> - <days value>
!! (*see Section 3.7.10 Datetime Literals*)

<datetime field> ::=
<non-second datetime field>
| SECOND
!! (*see Section 11.2.1.4 EXTRACT*)

<datetime literal> ::=
<date literal>
| <time literal>
| <timestamp literal>
!! (*see Section 3.7.10 Datetime Literals*)

<datetime primary> ::=
<common primary> | <datetime value function>
!! (*see Section 11.1.3 Datetime Value Expressions*)

<datetime term> ::=
<datetime primary> [<time zone>]
!! (*see Section 11.1.3 Datetime Value Expressions*)

<datetime type> ::=
DATE
| TIME [(<time precision>)] [WITH TIME ZONE]
| TIMESTAMP [(<timestamp precision>)]
[WITH TIME ZONE]
!! (*see Section 3.7.9 The Datetime Data Type*)

<datetime value> ::= <unsigned integer>
!! (*see Section 3.7.10 Datetime Literals*)

<datetime value expression> ::=
<datetime term>
| <interval value expression> + <datetime term>
| <datetime value expression> + <interval term>
| <datetime value expression> – <interval term>
!! (*see Section 11.1.3 Datetime Value Expressions*)

<datetime value function> ::=
CURRENT_DATE
| CURRENT_TIME [(<time precision>)]
| CURRENT_TIMESTAMP [(<timestamp precision>)]
!! (*see Sections 11.2.1 Datetime Functions; 11.2.1.1 CURRENT_DATE; 11.2.1.2 CURRENT_TIME and 11.2.1.3 CURRENT_TIMESTAMP*)

<day-time interval> ::=
<days value> [<space> <hours value>
[: <minutes value> [: <seconds value>]]]
!! (*see Section 3.7.12 Interval Literals*)

<day-time literal> ::=
<day-time interval> | <time interval>
!! (*see Section 3.7.10 Datetime Literals*)

<days value> ::= <datetime value>
!! (*see Section 3.7.10 Datetime Literals*)

<deallocate descriptor statement> ::=
DEALLOCATE DESCRIPTOR <descriptor name>
!! (*see Section 18.9 DEALLOCATE DESCRIPTOR*)

<deallocate prepared statement> ::=
DEALLOCATE PREPARE <SQL statement name>
!! (*see Section 18.5 DEALLOCATE PREPARE*)

<declare cursor> ::=
DECLARE <cursor name>
[INSENSITIVE] [SCROLL] CURSOR
FOR <cursor specification>
!! (*see Section 7.1 DECLARE CURSOR*)

<default clause> ::= DEFAULT <default option>
!! (*see Section 4.2.1.1 Defaults*)

<default option> ::=
<literal>
| <datetime value function>
| USER
| CURRENT_USER
| SESSION_USER
| SYSTEM_USER
| NULL
!! (*see Section 4.2.1.1 Defaults*)

<delete rule> ::= ON DELETE <referential action>
!! (*see Section 4.2.2.2 References*)

<delete statement: positioned> ::=
DELETE FROM <table name>
WHERE CURRENT OF <cursor name>
!! (*see Section 7.5 DELETE Positioned*)

<delete statement: searched> ::=
DELETE FROM <table name>
[WHERE <search condition>]
!! (*see Section 6.4 DELETE Searched*)

<delimited identifier> ::=
" <delimited identifier body>... "
!! (*see Section 3.3 Identifiers*)

<delimited identifier body> ::=
<nondoublequote character>
| ""
!! (*see Section 3.3 Identifiers*)

<delimiter token> ::=
<character string literal>
| <date string>
| <time string>
| <timestamp string>
| <interval string>
| <delimited identifier>
| <SQL special character>
| <not equals operator>
| <greater than or equals operator>
| <less than or equals operator>
| <concatenation operator>
| :
| <left bracket>
| <right bracket>
!! (*see Section 3.2 Tokens*)

<derived column> ::= <value expression> [<as clause>]
!! (*see Section 9.5 Query Specification*)

<derived column list> ::= <column name list>
!! (*see Section 9.3.1 Table References*)

<derived table> ::= <table subquery>
!! (*see Section 9.3.1 Table References*)

<describe input statement> ::=
DESCRIBE INPUT <SQL statement name>
<using descriptor>
!! (*see Section 18.6 DESCRIBE*)

<describe output statement> ::=
DESCRIBE [OUTPUT] <SQL statement name>
<using descriptor>
!! (*see Section 18.6 DESCRIBE*)

<describe statement> ::=
  <describe input statement>
 | <describe output statement>
!! (*see Section 18.6 DESCRIBE*)

<descriptor item name> ::=
 TYPE | LENGTH | RETURNED_LENGTH | OCTET_LENGTH |
 RETURNED_OCTET_LENGTH | PRECISION | SCALE |
 DATETIME_INTERVAL_CODE | DATETIME_INTERVAL_PRECISION |
 NULLABLE | INDICATOR | DATA | NAME | UNNAMED |
 COLLATION_CATALOG | COLLATION_SCHEMA | COLLATION_NAME |
 CHARACTER_SET_CATALOG | CHARACTER_SET_SCHEMA |
 CHARACTER_SET_NAME
!! (*see Section 18.10 GET DESCRIPTOR and
 Section 18.11 SET DESCRIPTOR*)

<descriptor name> ::=
 [<scope option>] <simple value specification>
!! (*see Section 18.8 ALLOCATE DESCRIPTOR*)

<diagnostics size> ::=
 DIAGNOSTICS SIZE <number of conditions>
!! (*see Section 12.3.3 The SET TRANSACTION Statement*)

<digit> ::= 0 | 1 | 2 | 3 | 4 | 5 | 6 | 7 | 8 | 9
!! (*see Section 3.1 Characters*)

<direct implementation-defined statement> ::=
!! (*see Chapter 19 Direct Invocation of SQL*)

<direct select statement: multiple rows> ::=
 <query expression> [<order by clause>]
!! (*see Section 19.2 Direct Select : Multiple Rows*)

<direct SQL data statement> ::=
  <delete statement: searched>
 | <direct select statement: multiple rows>
 | <insert statement>
 | <update statement: searched>
 | <temporary table declaration>
!! (*see Chapter 19 Direct Invocation of SQL*)

<direct SQL statement> ::=
 <directly executable statement> ;
!! (*see Chapter 19 Direct Invocation of SQL*)

<directly executable statement> ::=
<direct SQL data statement>
| <SQL schema statement>
| <SQL transaction statement>
| <SQL session statement>
| <SQL environment statement>
| <direct implementation-defined statement>
!! (*see Chapter 19 Direct Invocation of SQL*)

<disconnect object> ::=
<connection object>
| ALL
| CURRENT
!! (*see Section 14.3 DISCONNECT*)

<disconnect statement> ::=
DISCONNECT <disconnect object>
!! (*see Section 14.3 DISCONNECT*)

<domain constraint> ::=
[<constraint name definition>]
<check constraint definition>
[<constraint attributes>]
!! (*see Section 4.3 CREATE DOMAIN*)

<domain definition> ::=
CREATE DOMAIN <domain name> [AS] <data type>
[<default clause>]
[<domain constraint>...]
[<collate clause>]
!! (*see Section 4.3 CREATE DOMAIN*)

<domain name> ::= <qualified name>
!! (*see Section 4.3 CREATE DOMAIN*)

<drop assertion statement> ::=
DROP ASSERTION <constraint name>
!! (*see Section 5.1.4 DROP ASSERTION*)

<drop behaviour> ::= CASCADE | RESTRICT
!! (*see Section 5.1 The DROP Statements*)

<drop character set statement> ::=
DROP CHARACTER SET <character set name>
!! (*see Section 5.1.8 DROP CHARACTER SET*)

<drop collation statement> ::=
DROP COLLATION <collation name>
!! (*see Section 5.1.6 DROP COLLATION*)

<drop column definition> ::=
DROP [COLUMN] <column name> <drop behaviour>
!! (*see Section 5.2.2.2 Drop Column*)

<drop column default clause> ::=
DROP DEFAULT
!! (*see Section 5.2.2.6 Drop Column Default*)

<drop domain constraint definition> ::=
DROP CONSTRAINT <constraint name>
!! (*see Section 5.2.1.4 Drop Domain Constraint*)

<drop domain default clause> ::= DROP DEFAULT
!! (*see Section 5.2.1.2 Drop Domain Default*)

<drop domain statement> ::=
DROP DOMAIN <domain name> <drop behaviour>
!! (*see Section 5.1.2 DROP DOMAIN*)

<drop schema statement> ::=
DROP SCHEMA <schema name> <drop behaviour>
!! (*see Section 5.1.1 DROP SCHEMA*)

<drop table constraint definition> ::=
DROP CONSTRAINT <constraint name> <drop behaviour>
!! (*see Section 5.2.2.4 Drop Table Constraint*)

<drop table statement> ::=
DROP TABLE <table name> <drop behaviour>
!! (*see Section 5.1.3 DROP TABLE*)

<drop translation statement> ::=
DROP TRANSLATION <translation name>
!! (*see Section 5.1.7 DROP TRANSLATION*)

<drop view statement> ::=
DROP VIEW <table name> <drop behaviour>
!! (*see Section 5.1.5 DROP VIEW*)

<dynamic close statement> ::=
CLOSE <dynamic cursor name>
!! (*see Section 18.16 Dynamic CLOSE CURSOR*)

<dynamic cursor name> ::=
<cursor name>
| <extended cursor name>
!! (*see Section 18.15 Dynamic OPEN CURSOR*)

<dynamic declare cursor> ::=
DECLARE <cursor name>
[INSENSITIVE] [SCROLL] CURSOR
FOR <statement name>
!! (*see Section 18.13 Dynamic DECLARE CURSOR*)

<dynamic delete statement: positioned> ::=
DELETE FROM <table name>
WHERE CURRENT OF <dynamic cursor name>
!! (*see Section 18.18 Dynamic DELETE Positioned and Section 18.20 Preparable Dynamic DELETE Positioned*)

<dynamic fetch statement> ::=
FETCH [[<fetch orientation>]
FROM] <dynamic cursor name>
<using clause>
!! (*see Section 18.17 Dynamic FETCH CURSOR*)

<dynamic open statement> ::=
OPEN <dynamic cursor name> [<using clause>]
!! (*see Section 18.15 Dynamic OPEN CURSOR*)

<dynamic parameter specification> ::= ?
!! (*see Section 18.3 EXECUTE IMMEDIATE and Section 3.6 Values and Targets*)

<dynamic select statement> ::= <cursor specification>
!! (*see Section 18.4 PREPARE*)

<dynamic single row select statement> ::=
<query specification>
!! (*see Section 18.4 PREPARE*)

<dynamic update statement: positioned> ::=
UPDATE <table name>
SET <set clause> [{ , <set clause> }...]
WHERE CURRENT OF <dynamic cursor name>
!! (*see Section 18.19 Dynamic UPDATE Positioned and Section 18.21 Preparable Dynamic UPDATE Positioned*)

<else clause> ::= ELSE <result>
!! (*see Section 11.3.1 CASE*)

<embedded character set declaration> ::=
SQL NAMES ARE <character set specification>
!!(*see Chapter 17 The Embedded Languages*)

<embedded exception declaration> ::=
WHENEVER <condition> <exception action>
!! (*see Section 17.2 Exception Control*)

<embedded SQL Ada program> ::=
!! (*see Chapter 17 The Embedded Languages*)

<embedded SQL begin declare> ::=
<SQL prefix> BEGIN DECLARE SECTION
[<SQL terminator>]
!! (*see Chapter 17 The Embedded Languages*)

<embedded SQL C program> ::=
!! (*see Chapter 17 The Embedded Languages*)

<embedded SQL COBOL program> ::=
!! (*see Chapter 17 The Embedded Languages*)

<embedded SQL declare section> ::=
<embedded SQL begin declare>
[<embedded character set declaration>]
[<host language variable definition>...]
<embedded SQL end declare>
| <embedded SQL MUMPS declare>
!! (*see Chapter 17 The Embedded Languages*)

<embedded SQL end declare> ::=
<SQL prefix> END DECLARE SECTION
[<SQL terminator>]
!! (*see Chapter 17 The Embedded Languages*)

<embedded SQL FORTRAN program> ::=
!! (*see Chapter 17 The Embedded Languages*)

<embedded SQL host program> ::=
<embedded SQL Ada program>
| <embedded SQL C program>
| <embedded SQL COBOL program>
| <embedded SQL FORTRAN program>
| <embedded SQL MUMPS program>
| <embedded SQL Pascal program>
| <embedded SQL PL/I program>
!! (*see Chapter 17 The Embedded Languages*)

<embedded SQL MUMPS declare> ::=
<SQL prefix> BEGIN DECLARE SECTION
[<embedded character set declaration>]
[<MUMPS variable definition>...]
END DECLARE SECTION <SQL terminator>
!!(*see Chapter 17 The Embedded Languages*)

<embedded SQL MUMPS program> ::=
!! (*see Chapter 17 The Embedded Languages*)

<embedded SQL Pascal program> ::=
!! (*see Chapter 17 The Embedded Languages*)

<embedded SQL PL/I program> ::=
!! (*see Chapter 17 The Embedded Languages*)

<embedded SQL statement> ::=
<SQL prefix> <statement or declaration>
[<SQL terminator>]
!! (*see Chapter 17 The Embedded Languages*)

<embedded variable name> ::= : <host identifier>
!! (*see Chapter 17 The Embedded Languages*)

<end field> ::=
<non-second datetime field>
| SECOND [(<fractional seconds precision>)]
!! (*see Section 3.7.11 The Interval Data Type*)

<escape character> ::= <character value expression>
!! (*see Section 10.2.3 Like Predicate*)

<exact numeric literal> ::=
<unsigned integer> [. [<unsigned integer>]]
| . <unsigned integer>
!! (*see Section 3.7.6 Exact Numeric Literals*)

<exact numeric type> ::=
NUMERIC [(<precision> [, <scale>])]
| DECIMAL [(<precision> [, <scale>])]
| DEC [(<precision> [, <scale>])]
| INTEGER
| INT
| SMALLINT
!! (*see Section 3.7.5 The Exact Numeric Data Type*)

<exception action> ::= CONTINUE | <go to>
!! (*see Section 17.2 Exception Control*)

<execute immediate statement> ::=
EXECUTE IMMEDIATE <SQL statement variable>
!! (*see Section 18.3 EXECUTE IMMEDIATE*)

<execute statement> ::=
EXECUTE <SQL statement name>
[<result using clause>]
[<parameter using clause>]
!! (*see Section 18.12 EXECUTE*)

<existing character set name> ::=
<standard character repertoire name>
| <implementation-defined character repertoire name>
| <schema character set name>
!! (*see Section 4.6 CREATE CHARACTER SET*)

<exists predicate> ::= EXISTS <table subquery>
!! (*see Section 10.2.9 Exists Predicate*)

<explicit table> ::= TABLE <table name>
!! (*see Section 9.3 Query Expression*)

<exponent> ::= <signed integer>
!! (*see Section 3.7.8 Approximate Numeric Literals*)

<extended cursor name> ::=
[<scope option>] <simple value specification>
!! (*see Section 18.14 Dynamic ALLOCATE CURSOR*)

<extended statement name> ::=
[<scope option>] <simple value specification>
!! (*see Section 18.14 Dynamic ALLOCATE CURSOR*)

<external collation> ::=
EXTERNAL (' <external collation name> ')
!! (*see Section 4.7 CREATE COLLATION*)

<external collation name> ::=
<standard collation name>
| <implementation-defined collation name>
!! (*see Section 4.7 CREATE COLLATION*)

<external translation> ::=
EXTERNAL (' <external translation name> ')
!! (*see Section 4.8 CREATE TRANSLATION*)

<external translation name> ::=
<standard translation name>
| <implementation-defined translation name>
!! (*see Section 4.8 CREATE TRANSLATION*)

<extract expression> ::=
EXTRACT (<extract field> FROM <extract source>)
!! (*see Section 11.2.1.4 EXTRACT*)

<extract field> ::=
<datetime field>
| <time zone field>
!! (*see Section 11.2.1.4 EXTRACT*)

<extract source> ::=
<datetime value expression>
| <interval value expression>
!! (*see Section 11.2.1.4 EXTRACT*)

<factor> ::=
[+ | –] <numeric primary>
!! (*see Section 11.1.1 Numeric Value Expressions*)

<fetch orientation> ::=
NEXT
| PRIOR
| FIRST
| LAST
| { ABSOLUTE | RELATIVE }
<simple value specification>
!! (*see Section 7.3 FETCH*)

<fetch statement> ::=
FETCH [[<fetch orientation>] FROM]
<cursor name> INTO <fetch target list>
!! (*see Section 7.3 FETCH*)

<fetch target list> ::=
<target specification>
[{ , <target specification> }...]
!! (*see Section 7.3 FETCH*)

<fold> ::=
{ UPPER | LOWER } (<character value expression>)
!! (*see Section 11.2.3.3 UPPER and Section 11.2.3.4 LOWER*)

<form-of-use conversion> ::=
CONVERT (<character value expression>
USING <conversion name>)
!! (*see Section 11.2.3.6 CONVERT*)

<FORTRAN host identifier> ::=
!! (*see Section 17.1.4 FORTRAN*)

<FORTRAN type specification> ::=
CHARACTER [* <length>]
[CHARACTER SET [IS]
<character set specification>]
| BIT [* <length>]
| INTEGER
| REAL
| DOUBLE PRECISION
!! (*see Section 17.1.4 FORTRAN*)

```
<FORTRAN variable definition> ::=
    <FORTRAN type specification>
    <FORTRAN host identifier>
        [ { , <FORTRAN host identifier> }... ]
!! (see Section 17.1.4 FORTRAN)

<fractional seconds precision> ::= <unsigned integer>
!! (see Section 3.7.9 The Datetime Data Type)

<from clause> ::=
    FROM <table reference>
        [ { , <table reference> }... ]
!! (see Section 9.4.1 FROM)

<general literal> ::=
      <character string literal>
    | <national character string literal>
    | <bit string literal>
    | <hex string literal>
    | <datetime literal>
    | <interval literal>
!! (see Section 3.5 Literals)

<general set function> ::=
    AVG | MAX | MIN | SUM | COUNT
        ( [ <set quantifier> ] <value expression> )
!! (see Section 11.4 Set Functions)

<general value specification> ::=
      <parameter specification>
    | <dynamic parameter specification>
    | <variable specification>
    | USER
    | CURRENT_USER
    | SESSION_USER
    | SYSTEM_USER
    | VALUE
!! (see Section 3.6 Values and Targets)

<get descriptor information> ::=
      <get information>
    | VALUE <item number>
        <get item information>
            [ { , <get item information> }... ]
!! (see Section 18.10 GET DESCRIPTOR)

<get descriptor statement> ::=
    GET DESCRIPTOR <descriptor name>
        <get descriptor information>
!! (see Section 18.10 GET DESCRIPTOR)
```

<get diagnostics statement> ::=
GET DIAGNOSTICS <SQL diagnostics information>
!! (*see Chapter 15 Error Handling and Diagnostics*)

<get information> ::=
<simple target specification 1> = COUNT
!! (*see Section 18.10 GET DESCRIPTOR*)

<get item information> ::=
<simple target specification 2>
= <descriptor item name>
!! (*see Section 18.10 GET DESCRIPTOR*)

<go to> ::= { GOTO | GO TO } <goto target>
!! (*see Section 17.2 Exception Control*)

<goto target> ::=
: <host label identifier>
| <unsigned integer>
| <host PL/I label variable>
!! (*see Section 17.2 Exception Control*)

<grant statement> ::=
GRANT <privileges> ON <object name>
TO <grantee> [{ , <grantee> }...]
[WITH GRANT OPTION]
!! (*see Section 8.1 GRANT*)

<grantee> ::=
PUBLIC
| <authorization identifier>
!! (*see Chapter 8 Access Control*)

<greater than operator> ::= >
!! (*see Section 10.2.1 Comparison Predicate*)

<greater than or equals operator> ::= >=
!! (*see Section 10.2.1 Comparison Predicate*)

<group by clause> ::
GROUP BY <grouping column reference list>
!! (*see Section 9.4.3 GROUP BY*)

<grouping column reference> ::=
<column reference> [<collate clause>]
!! (*see Section 9.4.3 GROUP BY*)

<grouping column reference list> ::=
<grouping column reference>
[{ , <grouping column reference> }...]
!! (*see Section 9.4.3 GROUP BY*)

<having clause> ::= HAVING <search condition>
!! (*see Section 9.4.4 HAVING*)

<hex string literal> ::= X' [<hexdigit>...] '
[{ <separator>...
' [<hexdigit>...] ' }...]
!! (*see Section 3.7.4 Bit String Literals*)

<hexdigit> ::=
<digit>
| A | B | C | D | E | F | a | b | c | d | e | f
!! (*see Section 3.7.4 Bit String Literals*)

<host identifier> ::=
<Ada host identifier>
| <C host identifier>
| <COBOL host identifier>
| <FORTRAN host identifier>
| <MUMPS host identifier>
| <Pascal host identifier>
| <PL/I host identifier>
!! (*see Chapter 17 The Embedded Languages*)

<host label identifier> ::=
!! (*see Section 17.2 Exception Control*)

<host language variable definition> ::=
<Ada variable definition>
| <C variable definition>
| <COBOL variable definition>
| <FORTRAN variable definition>
| <MUMPS variable definition>
| <Pascal variable definition>
| <PL/I variable definition>
!! (*see Chapter 17 The Embedded Languages*)

<host PL/I label variable> ::=
!! (*see Section 17.2 Exception Control*)

<hours value> ::= <datetime value>
!! (*see Section 3.7.10 Datetime Literals*)

<identifier> ::=
[<introducer><character set specification>]
<actual identifier>
!! (*see Section 3.3 Identifiers*)

<identifier body> ::=
<identifier start>
[{ _ | <identifier part> }...]
!! (*see Section 3.3 Identifiers*)

<identifier part> ::= <identifier start> | <digit>
!! (*see Section 3.3 Identifiers*)

<identifier start> ::=
!! (*see Section 3.3 Identifiers*)

<implementation-defined character repertoire name> ::=
<character set name>
!! (*see Section 4.6 CREATE CHARACTER SET*)

<implementation-defined collation name> ::=
<collation name>
!! (*see Section 4.7 CREATE COLLATION*)

<implementation-defined translation name> ::=
<translation name>
!! (*see Section 4.8 CREATE TRANSLATION*)

<implementation-defined universal form-of-use name> ::=
<character set name>
!! (*see Section 4.6 CREATE CHARACTER SET*)

<in predicate> ::=
<row value constructor>
[NOT] IN <in predicate value>
!! (*see Section 10.2.5 In Predicate*)

<in predicate value> ::=
<table subquery>
| (<in value list>)
!! (*see Section 10.2.5 In Predicate*)

<in value list> ::=
<value expression> { , <value expression> }...
!! (*see Section 10.2.5 In Predicate*)

<indicator parameter> ::=
[INDICATOR] <parameter name>
!! (*see Section 3.6 Values and Targets*)

<indicator variable> ::=
[INDICATOR] <embedded variable name>
!! (*see Section 3.6 Values and Targets*)

<insert column list> ::= <column name list>
!! (*see Section 6.1 INSERT*)

<insert columns and source> ::=
[(<insert column list>)] <query expression>
| DEFAULT VALUES
!! (*see Section 6.1 INSERT*)

<insert statement> ::=
INSERT INTO <table name>
<insert columns and source>
!! (*see Section 6.1 INSERT*)

<interval factor> ::=
[+ | –] <common primary> [<interval qualifier>]
!! (*see Section 11.1.4 Interval Value Expressions*)

<interval leading field precision> ::= <unsigned integer>
!! (*see Section 3.7.11 The Interval Data Type*)

<interval literal> ::=
INTERVAL [+ | –] <interval string>
<interval qualifier>
!! (*see Section 3.7.12 Interval Literals*)

<interval qualifier> ::=
<start field> TO <end field>
| <single datetime field>
!! (*see Section 3.7.12 Interval Literals*)

<interval string> ::=
' { <year-month literal> | <day-time literal> } '
!! (*see Section 3.7.12 Interval Literals*)

<interval term> ::=
<interval factor>
| <interval term 2> * <factor>
| <interval term 2> / <factor>
| <term> * <interval factor>
!! (*see Section 11.1.4 Interval Value Expressions*)

<interval term 1> ::= <interval term>
!! (*see Section 11.1.4 Interval Value Expressions*)

<interval term 2> ::= <interval term>
!! (*see Section 11.1.4 Interval Value Expressions*)

<interval type> ::= INTERVAL <interval qualifier>
!! (*see Section 3.7.11 The Interval Data Type*)

<interval value expression> ::=
<interval term>
| <interval value expression 1> + <interval term 1>
| <interval value expression 1> – <interval term 1>
| (<datetime value expression> –
<datetime term>) <interval qualifier>
!! (*see Section 11.1.4 Interval Value Expressions*)

<interval value expression 1> ::=
<interval value expression>
!! (*see Section 11.1.4 Interval Value Expressions*)

<introducer> ::= _
!! (*see Section 3.3 Identifiers*)

<isolation level> ::=
ISOLATION LEVEL <level of isolation>
!! (*see Section 12.3.3 The SET TRANSACTION Statement*)

<item number> ::= <simple value specification>
!! (*see Section 18.10 GET DESCRIPTOR*)

<join column list> ::= <column name list>
!! (*see Section 9.3.2.4 JOIN*)

<join condition> ::= ON <search condition>
!! (*see Section 9.3.2.4 JOIN*)

<join specification> ::=
<join condition>
| <named columns join>
!! (*see Section 9.3.2.4 JOIN*)

<join type> ::=
INNER
| <outer join type> [OUTER]
| UNION
!! (*see Section 9.3.2.4 JOIN*)

<joined table> ::=
<cross join>
| <qualified join>
| (<joined table>)
!! (*see Section 9.3.2.4 JOIN*)

<key word> ::=
  <reserved word>
 | <non-reserved word>
!! (*see Section 3.2 Tokens*)

<language clause> ::=
 LANGUAGE <language name>
!! (*see Section 16.1 Modules*)

<language name> ::=
 ADA | C | COBOL | FORTRAN | MUMPS | PASCAL | PLI
!! (*see Section 16.1 Modules*)

<left bracket> ::= [
!! (*see Section 3.2 Tokens*)

<length> ::= <unsigned integer>
!! (*see Section 3.7 Data Types*)

<length expression> ::=
  <char length expression>
 | <octet length expression>
 | <bit length expression>
!! (*see Section 11.2.2 String Functions*)

<less than operator> ::= <
!! (*see Section 10.2.1 Comparison Predicate*)

<less than or equals operator> ::= <=
!! (*see Section 10.2.1 Comparison Predicate*)

<level of isolation> ::=
  READ UNCOMMITTED
 | READ COMMITTED
 | REPEATABLE READ
 | SERIALIZABLE
!! (*see Section 12.3.3 The SET TRANSACTION Statement*)

<like predicate> ::=
 <match value> [NOT] LIKE <pattern>
  [ESCAPE <escape character>]
!! (*see Section 10.2.3 Like Predicate*)

<limited collation definition> ::=
 COLLATION FROM <collation source>
!! (*see Section 4.6 CREATE CHARACTER SET*)

<literal> ::=
<signed numeric literal>
| <general literal>
!! (*see Section 3.5 Literals*)

<local table name> ::= <qualified identifier>
!! (*see Section 3.4 Names*)

<mantissa> ::= <exact numeric literal>
!! (*see Section 3.7.8 Approximate Numeric Literals*)

<match predicate> ::=
<row value constructor> MATCH [UNIQUE]
[PARTIAL | FULL] <table subquery>
!! (*see Section 10.2.8 Match Predicate*)

<match value> ::= <character value expression>
!! (*see Section 10.2.3 Like Predicate*)

<minutes value> ::= <datetime value>
!! (*see Section 3.7.10 Datetime Literals*)

<module> ::=
<module name clause>
<language clause>
<module authorization clause>
[<temporary table declaration>...]
<module contents>...
!! (*see Section 16.1 Modules*)

<module authorization clause> ::=
SCHEMA <schema name>
| AUTHORIZATION <module authorization identifier>
| SCHEMA <schema name>
AUTHORIZATION <module authorization identifier>
!! (*see Section 16.1 Modules*)

<module authorization identifier> ::=
<authorization identifier>
!! (*see Section 16.1 Modules*)

<module character set specification> ::=
NAMES ARE <character set specification>
!! (*see Section 16.1 Modules*)

<module contents> ::=
<declare cursor>
| <dynamic declare cursor>
| <procedure>
!! (*see Section 16.1 Modules*)

<module name> ::= <identifier>
!! (*see Section 16.1 Modules*)

<module name clause> ::=
    MODULE [<module name>]
        [<module character set specification>]
!! (*see Section 16.1 Modules*)

<months value> ::= <datetime value>
!! (*see Section 3.7.10 Datetime Literals*)

<MUMPS character variable> ::=
    VARCHAR <MUMPS host identifier>
        <MUMPS length specification>
        [{ , <MUMPS host identifier>
            <MUMPS length specification> }...]
!! (*see Section 17.1.5 MUMPS*)

<MUMPS host identifier> ::= !! (*see Section 17.1.5 MUMPS*)

<MUMPS length specification> ::= (<length>)
!! (*see Section 17.1.5 MUMPS*)

<MUMPS numeric variable> ::=
    <MUMPS type specification>
        <MUMPS host identifier>
            [{ , <MUMPS host identifier> }...]
!! (*see Section 17.1.5 MUMPS*)

<MUMPS type specification> ::=
      INT
    | DEC [(<precision> [, <scale>])]
    | REAL
!! (*see Section 17.1.5 MUMPS*)

<MUMPS variable definition> ::=
    { <MUMPS numeric variable>
     | <MUMPS character variable> } ;
!! (*see Section 17.1.5 MUMPS*)

<named columns join> ::= USING (<join column list>)
!! (*see Section 9.3.2.4 JOIN*)

<national character string literal> ::=
    N' [<character representation>...] '
        [{ <separator>...
            ' [<character representation>...] '
            }...]
!! (*see Section 3.7.2 Character Literals*)

<national character string type> ::=
NATIONAL CHARACTER [(<length>)]
| NATIONAL CHAR [(<length>)]
| NCHAR [(<length>)]
| NATIONAL CHARACTER VARYING (<length>)
| NATIONAL CHAR VARYING (<length>)
| NCHAR VARYING (<length>)
!! (*see Section 3.7.1 The Character Data Type*)

<newline> ::=
!! implementation-defined end-of-line indicator
!! (*see Section 3.2 Tokens*)

<non-join query expression> ::=
<non-join query term>
| <query expression> UNION
[ALL] [<corresponding spec>] <query term>
| <query expression> EXCEPT
[ALL] [<corresponding spec>] <query term>
!! (*see Section 9.3 Query Expression*)

<non-join query primary> ::=
<simple table>
| (<non-join query expression>)
!! (*see Section 9.3 Query Expression*)

<non-join query term> ::=
<non-join query primary>
| <query term> INTERSECT [ALL]
[<corresponding spec>] <query primary>
!! (*see Section 9.3 Query Expression*)

<non-reserved word> ::= !! (*see Appendix D Key Words*)
!! (*see Section 3.2 Tokens*)

<non-second datetime field> ::=
YEAR | MONTH | DAY | HOUR | MINUTE
!! (*see Section 3.7.11 The Interval Data Type*)

<nondelimiter token> ::=
<regular identifier>
| <key word>
| <unsigned numeric literal>
| <national character string literal>
| <bit string literal>
| <hex string literal>
!! (*see Section 3.2 Tokens*)

<nondoublequote character> ::=
!! (*see Section 3.3 Identifiers*)

<nonquote character> ::=
!! (*see Section 3.2 Tokens*)

<not equals operator> ::= <>
!! (*see Section 10.2.1 Comparison Predicate*)

<null predicate> ::=
<row value constructor> IS [NOT] NULL
!! (*see Section 10.2.4 Null Predicate*)

<number of conditions> ::= <simple value specification>
!! (*see Section 12.3.3 The SET TRANSACTION Statement*)

<numeric primary> ::=
<common primary> | <numeric value function>
!! (*see Section 11.1.1 Numeric Value Expressions*)

<numeric type> ::=
<exact numeric type>
| <approximate numeric type>
!! (*see Section 3.7.5 The Exact Numeric Data Type and Section 3.7.7 The Approximate Numeric Data Type*)

<numeric value expression> ::=
<term>
| <numeric value expression> + <term>
| <numeric value expression> – <term>
!! (*see Section 11.1.1 Numeric Value Expressions*)

<numeric value function> ::=
<position expression>
| <extract expression>
| <length expression>
!! (*see Section 11.1.1 Numeric Value Expressions*)

<object column> ::= <column name>
!! (*see Section 6.3 UPDATE Searched*)

<object name> ::=
[TABLE] <table name>
| DOMAIN <domain name>
| COLLATION <collation name>
| CHARACTER SET <character set name>
| TRANSLATION <translation name>
!! (*see Chapter 8 Access Control*)

<occurrences> ::= <simple value specification>
!! (*see Section 18.8 ALLOCATE DESCRIPTOR*)

<octet length expression> ::=
OCTET_LENGTH (<string value expression>)
!! (*see Section 11.2.2.3 OCTET_LENGTH*)

<open statement> ::=
OPEN <cursor name>
!! (*see Section 7.2 OPEN*)

<order by clause> ::=
ORDER BY <sort specification list>
!! (*see Section 7.1 DECLARE CURSOR*)

<ordering specification> ::= ASC | DESC
!! (*see Section 7.1 DECLARE CURSOR*)

<outer join type> ::=
LEFT
| RIGHT
| FULL
!! (*see Section 9.3.2.4 JOIN*)

<overlaps predicate> ::=
<row value constructor 1> OVERLAPS
<row value constructor 2>
!! (*see Section 10.2.7 Overlaps Predicate*)

<parameter> ::=
| SQLCODE
| SQLSTATE
!! (*see Section 16.3 Procedures*)

<parameter declaration list> ::=
(<parameter> [{ , <parameter> }...])
| <parameter>...
!! (*see Section 16.3 Procedures*)

!! (*see Section 16.4 Parameters*)

<parameter specification> ::=
<parameter name> [<indicator parameter>]
!! (*see Section 3.6 Values and Targets*)

!! (*see Section 18.7 USING*)

<Pascal host identifier> ::= !! (*see Section 17.1.6 Pascal*)

<Pascal type specification> ::=
PACKED ARRAY
<left bracket> 1 : <length> <right bracket>
OF CHAR [CHARACTER SET [IS]
<character set specification>]
| PACKED ARRAY
<left bracket> 1 : <length> <right bracket>
OF BIT
| INTEGER
| REAL
| CHAR [CHARACTER SET [IS]
<character set specification>]
| BIT
!! (*see Section 17.1.6 Pascal*)

<Pascal variable definition> ::=
<Pascal host identifier>
[{ , <Pascal host identifier> }...] :
<Pascal type specification> ;
!! (*see Section 17.1.6 Pascal*)

<pattern> ::= <character value expression>
!! (*see Section 10.2.3 Like Predicate*)

<PL/I host identifier> ::= !! (*see Section 17.1.7 PL/I*)

<PL/I type fixed binary> ::=
{ BIN | BINARY } FIXED
| FIXED { BIN | BINARY }
!! (*see Section 17.1.7 PL/I*)

<PL/I type fixed decimal> ::=
{ DEC | DECIMAL } FIXED
| FIXED { DEC | DECIMAL }
!! (*see Section 17.1.7 PL/I*)

<PL/I type float binary> ::=
{ BIN | BINARY } FLOAT
| FLOAT { BIN | BINARY }
!! (*see Section 17.1.7 PL/I*)

<PL/I type specification> ::=
{ CHAR | CHARACTER } [VARYING] (<length>)
[CHARACTER SET [IS]
<character set specification>]
| BIT [VARYING] (<length>)
| <PL/I type fixed decimal> (<precision>
[, <scale>])
| <PL/I type fixed binary> [(<precision>)]
| <PL/I type float binary> (<precision>)
!! (*see Section 17.1.7 PL/I*)

<PL/I variable definition> ::=
{DCL | DECLARE}
{ <PL/I host identifier>
| (<PL/I host identifier>
[{ , <PL/I host identifier> }...]) }
<PL/I type specification>
[<character representation>...] ;
!! (*see Section 17.1.7 PL/I*)

<position expression> ::=
POSITION (<character value expression>
IN <character value expression>)
!! (*see Section 11.2.3.1 POSITION*)

<precision> ::= <unsigned integer>
!! (*see Section 3.7 Data Types*)

<predicate> ::=
<comparison predicate>
| <between predicate>
| <in predicate>
| <like predicate>
| <null predicate>
| <quantified comparison predicate>
| <exists predicate>
| <unique predicate>
| <match predicate>
| <overlaps predicate>
!! (*see Section 10.2 Predicates*)

<preparable dynamic delete statement: positioned> ::=
DELETE [FROM <table name>]
WHERE CURRENT OF <cursor name>
!! (*see Section 18.4 PREPARE*)

<preparable dynamic update statement: positioned> ::=
  UPDATE [<table name>]
    SET <set clause list>
    WHERE CURRENT OF <cursor name>
!! (*see Section 18.4 PREPARE*)

<preparable implementation-defined statement> ::=
!! (*see Section 18.4 PREPARE*)

<preparable SQL data statement> ::=
   <delete statement: searched>
  | <dynamic single row select statement>
  | <insert statement>
  | <dynamic select statement>
  | <update statement: searched>
  | <preparable dynamic delete statement: positioned>
  | <preparable dynamic update statement: positioned>
!! (*see Section 18.4 PREPARE*)

<preparable statement> ::=
   <preparable SQL data statement>
  | <SQL schema statement>
  | <SQL transaction statement>
  | <SQL environment statement>
  | <preparable implementation-defined statement>
!! (*see Section 18.4 PREPARE*)

<prepare statement> ::=
  PREPARE <SQL statement name>
    FROM <SQL statement variable>
!! (*see Section 18.4 PREPARE*)

<privilege column list> ::= <column name list>
!! (*see Chapter 8 Access Control*)

<privileges> ::=
   ALL PRIVILEGES
  | <action list>
!! (*see Chapter 8 Access Control*)

<procedure> ::=
  PROCEDURE <procedure name>
    <parameter declaration list> ;
    <SQL statement> ;
!! (*see Section 16.3 Procedures*)

<procedure name> ::= <identifier>
!! (*see Section 16.3 Procedures*)

<qualified identifier> ::= <identifier>
!! (*see Section 3.4 Names*)

<qualified join> ::=
<table reference> [NATURAL] [<join type>] JOIN
<table reference> [<join specification>]
!! (*see Section 9.3.2.4 JOIN*)

<qualified local table name> ::=
MODULE . <local table name>
!! (*see Section 3.4 Names*)

<qualified name> ::=
[<schema name> .] <qualified identifier>
!! (*see Section 3.4 Names*)

<qualifier> ::=
<table name>
| <correlation name>
!! (*see Section 3.4 Names*)

<quantified comparison predicate> ::=
<row value constructor> <comparison operator> <quantifier>
<table subquery>
!! (*see Section 10.2.6 Quantified Comparison Predicate*)

<quantifier> ::= ALL | { SOME | ANY }
!! (*see Section 10.2.6 Quantified Comparison Predicate*)

<query expression> ::=
<non-join query expression>
| <joined table>
!! (*see Section 9.3 Query Expression*)

<query primary> ::=
<non-join query primary>
| <joined table>
!! (*see Section 9.3 Query Expression*)

<query specification> ::=
SELECT [<set quantifier>] <select list>
<table expression>
!! (*see Section 9.5 Query Specification*)

<query term> ::=
<non-join query term>
| <joined table>
!! (*see Section 9.3 Query Expression*)

<quote> ::= '
!! (*see Section 3.1 Characters*)

<quote symbol> ::= <quote><quote>
!! (*see Section 3.7.2 Character Literals*)

<reference column list> ::= <column name list>
!! (*see Section 4.2.2.2 References*)

<referenced table and columns> ::=
    <table name> [(<reference column list>)]
!! (*see Section 4.2.2.2 References*)

<references specification> ::=
    REFERENCES <referenced table and columns>
        [MATCH { PARTIAL | FULL }]
        [<referential triggered action>]
!! (*see Section 4.2.2.2 References*)

<referencing columns> ::=
    <reference column list>
!! (*see Section 4.2.2.2 References*)

<referential action> ::=
      CASCADE
    | SET NULL
    | SET DEFAULT
    | NO ACTION
!! (*see Section 4.2.2.2 References*)

<referential constraint definition> ::=
    FOREIGN KEY (<referencing columns>)
        <references specification>
!! (*see Section 4.2.2.2 References*)

<referential triggered action> ::=
      <update rule> [<delete rule>]
    | <delete rule> [<update rule>]
!! (*see Section 4.2.2.2 References*)

<regular identifier> ::= <identifier body>
!! (*see Section 3.3 Identifiers*)

<reserved word> ::= !! (*see Appendix D Key Words*)

<result> ::= <result expression> | NULL
!! (*see Section 11.3.1 CASE*)

<result expression> ::= <value expression>
!! (*see Section 11.3.1 CASE*)

<result using clause> ::= <using clause>
!! (*see Section 18.7 USING*)

<revoke statement> ::=
REVOKE [GRANT OPTION FOR] <privileges>
ON <object name>
FROM <grantee> [{ , <grantee> }...]
<drop behaviour>
!! (*see Section 8.2 REVOKE*)

<right bracket> ::=]
!! (*see Section 3.2 Tokens*)

<rollback statement> ::=
ROLLBACK [WORK]
!! (*see Section 12.3.2 The ROLLBACK Statement*)

<row subquery> ::= <subquery>
!! (*see Section 9.6 Subqueries*)

<row value constructor> ::=
<row value constructor element>
| (<row value constructor list>)
| <row subquery>
!! (*see Section 9.1 Row Value Constructors*)

<row value constructor 1> ::= <row value constructor>
!! (*see Section 10.2.7 Overlaps Predicate*)

<row value constructor 2> ::= <row value constructor>
!! (*see Section 10.2.7 Overlaps Predicate*)

<row value constructor element> ::=
<value expression> | NULL | DEFAULT
!! (*see Section 9.1 Row Value Constructors*)

<row value constructor list> ::=
<row value constructor element>
[{ , <row value constructor element> }...]
!! (*see Section 9.1 Row Value Constructors*)

<scalar subquery> ::= <subquery>
!! (*see Section 9.6 Subqueries*)

<scale> ::= <unsigned integer>
!! (*see Section 3.7 Data Types*)

<schema authorization clause> ::=
<schema name>
| AUTHORIZATION <authorization identifier>
| <schema name>
AUTHORIZATION <authorization identifier>
!! (*see Section 4.1.1 Authorization*)

<schema character set name> ::= <character set name>
!! (*see Section 4.6 CREATE CHARACTER SET*)

<schema character set specification> ::=
DEFAULT CHARACTER SET <character set specification>
!! (*see Section 4.1.2 Schema Default Character Set*)

<schema collation name> ::= <collation name>
!! (*see Section 4.7 CREATE COLLATION*)

<schema definition> ::=
CREATE SCHEMA <schema authorization clause>
[<schema character set specification>]
[<schema element>...]
!! (*see Section 4.1 CREATE SCHEMA*)

<schema element> ::=
<domain definition>
| <table definition>
| <view definition>
| <grant statement>
| <assertion definition>
| <character set definition>
| <collation definition>
| <translation definition>
!! (*see Section 4.1.3 Schema Elements*)

<schema name> ::=
[<catalog name> .] <unqualified schema name>
!! (*see Section 4.1 CREATE SCHEMA*)

<schema translation name> ::= <translation name>
!! (*see Section 4.8 CREATE TRANSLATION*)

<scope option> ::= GLOBAL | LOCAL
!! (*see Section 3.4 Names*)

<search condition> ::=
<boolean term>
| <search condition> OR <boolean term>
!! (*see Section 10.1 Search Conditions*)

<searched case> ::=
CASE
<searched when clause>...
[<else clause>]
END
!! (*see Section 11.3.1 CASE*)

<searched when clause> ::=
WHEN <search condition> THEN <result>
!! (*see Section 11.3.1 CASE*)

<seconds fraction> ::= <unsigned integer>
!! (*see Section 3.7.12 Interval Literals*)

<seconds integer value> ::= <unsigned integer>
!! (*see Section 3.7.10 Datetime Literals*)

<seconds value> ::=
<seconds integer value> [. [<seconds fraction>]]
!! (*see Section 3.7.10 Datetime Literals*)

<select list> ::=
*
| <select sublist> [{ , <select sublist> }...]
!! (*see Section 9.5 Query Specification*)

<select statement: single row> ::=
SELECT [<set quantifier>] <select list>
INTO <select target list>
<table expression>
!! (*see Section 6.2 Single Row SELECT*)

<select sublist> ::=
<derived column>
| <qualifier> . *
!! (*see Section 9.5 Query Specification*)

<select target list> ::=
<target specification>
[{ , <target specification> }...]
!! (*see Section 6.2 Single Row SELECT*)

<separator> ::= { <comment> | <space> | <newline> }...
!! (*see Section 3.2 Tokens*)

<set authorization identifier statement> ::=
SET SESSION AUTHORIZATION <value specification>
!! (*see Section 13.4 SET SESSION AUTHORIZATION*)

<set catalog statement> ::=
SET CATALOG <value specification>
!! (*see Section 13.1 SET CATALOG*)

<set clause> ::=
<object column> = <update source>
!! (*see Section 6.3 UPDATE Searched*)

<set clause list> ::=
<set clause> [{ , <set clause> }...]
!! (*see Section 6.3 UPDATE Searched*)

<set connection statement> ::=
SET CONNECTION <connection object>
!! (*see Section 14.2 SET CONNECTION*)

<set constraints mode statement> ::=
SET CONSTRAINTS <constraint name list>
{ DEFERRED | IMMEDIATE }
!! (*see Section 13.5 SET CONSTRAINTS MODE*)

<set column default clause> ::=
SET <default clause>
!! (*see Section 5.2.2.5 Set Column Default*)

<set descriptor information> ::=
<set information>
| VALUE <item number>
<set item information>
[{ , <set item information> }...]
!! (*see Section 18.11 SET DESCRIPTOR*)

<set descriptor statement> ::=
SET DESCRIPTOR <descriptor name>
<set descriptor information>
!! (*see Section 18.11 SET DESCRIPTOR*)

<set domain default clause> ::= SET <default clause>
!! (*see Section 5.2.1.1 Set Domain Default*)

<set function specification> ::=
COUNT (*)
| <general set function>
!! (*see Section 11.4 Set Functions*)

<set information> ::=
COUNT = <simple value specification 1>
!! (*see Section 18.11 SET DESCRIPTOR*)

<set item information> ::=
<descriptor item name> =
<simple value specification 2>
!! (*see Section 18.11 SET DESCRIPTOR*)

<set time zone statement> ::=
SET TIME ZONE <set time zone value>
!! (*see Section 13.6 SET TIME ZONE*)

<set names statement> ::=
SET NAMES <value specification>
!! (*see Section 13.3 SET NAMES*)

<set quantifier> ::= DISTINCT | ALL
!! (*see Section 9.5 Query Specification*)

<set schema statement> ::=
SET SCHEMA <value specification>
!! (*see Section 13.2 SET SCHEMA*)

<set time zone value> ::=
<interval value expression>
| LOCAL
!! (*see Section 13.6 SET TIME ZONE*)

<set transaction statement> ::=
SET TRANSACTION <transaction mode>
[{ , <transaction mode> }...]
!! (*see Section 12.3.3 The SET TRANSACTION Statement*)

<signed integer> ::= [+ | –] <unsigned integer>
!! (*see Section 3.7.6 Exact Numeric Literals*)

<signed numeric literal> ::=
[+ | –] <unsigned numeric literal>
!! (*see Section 3.7.6 Exact Numeric Literals*)

<simple case> ::=
CASE <case operand>
<simple when clause>...
[<else clause>]
END
!! (*see Section 11.3.1 CASE*)

<simple Latin letter> ::=
<simple Latin upper case letter>
| <simple Latin lower case letter>
!! (*see Section 3.1 Characters*)

```
<simple Latin lower case letter> ::=
      a | b | c | d | e | f | g | h | i | j | k | l | m | n | o | p | q | r | s | t | u |
        v | w | x | y | z
!! (see Section 3.1 Characters)

<simple Latin upper case letter> ::=
      A | B | C | D | E | F | G | H | I | J | K | L | M | N | O | P | Q | R | S | T | U |
        V | W | X | Y | Z
!! (see Section 3.1 Characters)

<simple table> ::=
      <query specification>
    | <table value constructor>
    | <explicit table>
!! (see Section 9.3 Query Expression)

<simple target specification> ::=
      <parameter name>
    | <embedded variable name>
!! (see Section 3.6 Values and Targets)

<simple target specification 1> ::=
    <simple target specification>
!! (see Section 18.10 GET DESCRIPTOR)

<simple target specification 2> ::=
    <simple target specification>
!! (see Section 18.10 GET DESCRIPTOR)

<simple value specification> ::=
      <parameter name>
    | <embedded variable name>
    | <literal>
!! (see Section 3.6 Values and Targets)

<simple value specification 1> ::=
    <simple value specification>
!! (see Section 18.11 SET DESCRIPTOR)

<simple value specification 2> ::=
    <simple value specification>
!! (see Section 18.11 SET DESCRIPTOR)

<simple when clause> ::=
    WHEN <when operand> THEN <result>
!! (see Section 11.3.1 CASE)
```

<single datetime field> ::=
<non-second datetime field>
[(<interval leading field precision>)]
| SECOND [(<interval leading field precision>
[, <fractional seconds precision>])]
!! (*see Section 3.7.11 The Interval Data Type*)

<sort key> ::=
<column name> | <unsigned integer>
!! (*see Section 7.1 DECLARE CURSOR*)

<sort specification> ::=
<sort key> [<ordering specification>]
!! (*see Section 7.1 DECLARE CURSOR*)

<sort specification list> ::=
<sort specification>
[{ , <sort specification> }...]
!! (*see Section 7.1 DECLARE CURSOR*)

<source character set specification> ::=
<character set specification>
!! (*see Section 4.8 CREATE TRANSLATION*)

<space> ::= !! space character
!! (*see Section 3.1 Characters*)

<SQL data change statement> ::=
<delete statement: positioned>
| <delete statement: searched>
| <insert statement>
| <update statement: positioned>
| <update statement: searched>
!! (*see Chapter 7 Cursor Operations and Chapter 6 Non-Cursor Operations*)

<SQL data statement> ::=
<open statement>
| <fetch statement>
| <close statement>
| <select statement: single row>
| <SQL data change statement>
!! (*see Chapter 7 Cursor Operations and Chapter 6 Non-Cursor Operations*)

<SQL diagnostics information> ::=
<statement information>
| <condition information>
!! (*see Chapter 15 Error Handling and Diagnostics*)

<SQL diagnostics statement> ::=
<get diagnostics statement>
!! (*see Chapter 15 Error Handling and Diagnostics*)

<SQL dynamic data statement> ::=
<allocate cursor statement>
| <dynamic open statement>
| <dynamic fetch statement>
| <dynamic close statement>
| <dynamic delete statement: positioned>
| <dynamic update statement: positioned>
!! (*see Chapter 18 Dynamic SQL*)

<SQL dynamic statement> ::=
<system descriptor statement>
| <prepare statement>
| <deallocate prepared statement>
| <describe statement>
| <execute statement>
| <execute immediate statement>
| <SQL dynamic data statement>
!! (*see Chapter 18 Dynamic SQL*)

<SQL embedded character> ::=
<left bracket>
| <right bracket>
!! (*see Section 3.1 Characters*)

<SQL environment statement> ::=
<set catalog statement>
| <set schema statement>
| <set names statement>
| <set authorization identifier statement>
| <set time zone statement>
!! (*see Chapter 13 Environment Management*)

<SQL language character> ::=
<simple Latin letter>
| <digit>
| <SQL special character>
!! (*see Section 3.1 Characters*)

<SQL language identifier> ::=
<SQL language identifier start>
[{ _ | <SQL language identifier part> }...]
!! (*see Section 3.4 Names*)

<SQL language identifier part> ::=
<simple Latin letter>
| <digit>
!! (*see Section 3.4 Names*)

<SQL language identifier start> ::= <simple Latin letter>
!! (*see Section 3.4 Names*)

<SQL prefix> ::= EXEC SQL | &SQL(
!! (*see Chapter 17 The Embedded Languages*)

<SQL schema definition statement> ::=
<schema definition>
| <table definition>
| <view definition>
| <grant statement>
| <domain definition>
| <character set definition>
| <collation definition>
| <translation definition>
| <assertion definition>
!! (*see Chapter 4 Data Definition and Chapter 8 Access Control*)

<SQL schema manipulation statement> ::=
<drop schema statement>
| <alter table statement>
| <drop table statement>
| <drop view statement>
| <revoke statement>
| <alter domain statement>
| <drop domain statement>
| <drop character set statement>
| <drop collation statement>
| <drop translation statement>
| <drop assertion statement>
!! (*see Chapter 5 Schema Manipulation and Chapter 8 Access Control*)

<SQL schema statement> ::=
<SQL schema definition statement>
| <SQL schema manipulation statement>
!! (*see Chapter 4 Data Definition; Chapter 5 Schema Manipulation and Chapter 8 Access Control*)

<SQL session statement> ::=
<connect statement>
| <set connection statement>
| <disconnect statement>
!! (*see Chapter 14 Session Management*)

<SQL special character> ::=
. | ; | (|) | , | : | % | _ | ? | ' | " | + | –
| * | / | <space> | <less than operator>
| <greater than operator> | = | &
| <vertical bar>
!! (*see Section 3.1 Characters*)

<SQL statement> ::=
<SQL schema statement>
| <SQL data statement>
| <SQL transaction statement>
| <SQL environment statement>
| <SQL session statement>
| <SQL dynamic statement>
| <SQL diagnostics statement>
!! (*see Section 16.3 Procedures*)

<SQL statement name> ::=
<statement name>
| <extended statement name>
!! (*see Section 18.4 PREPARE*)

<SQL statement variable> ::=
<simple target specification>
!! (*see Section 18.3 EXECUTE IMMEDIATE*)

<SQL terminal character> ::=
<SQL language character>
| <SQL embedded language character>
!! (*see Section 3.1 Characters*)

<SQL terminator> ::= END-EXEC | ; |)
!! (*see Chapter 17 The Embedded Languages*)

<SQL transaction statement> ::=
<set transaction statement>
| <set constraints mode statement>
| <commit statement>
| <rollback statement>
!! (*see Chapter 12 Transaction Management*)

<SQL-Server> ::=
<simple value specification>
!! (*see Section 14.1 CONNECT*)

<standard character repertoire name> ::=
<character set name>
!! (*see Section 4.6 CREATE CHARACTER SET*)

<standard collation name> ::= <collation name>
!! (*see Section 4.7 CREATE COLLATION*)

<standard translation name> ::= <translation name>
!! (*see Section 4.8 CREATE TRANSLATION*)

<standard universal character form-of-use name> ::=
<character set name>
!! (*see Section 4.6 CREATE CHARACTER SET*)

<start field> ::=
<non-second datetime field>
[(<interval leading field precision>)]
!! (*see Section 3.7.11 The Interval Data Type*)

<start position> ::= <numeric value expression>
!! (*see Section 11.2.2.1 SUBSTRING*)

<statement information> ::=
<statement information item>
[{ , <statement information item> }...]
!! (*see Chapter 15 Error Handling and Diagnostics*)

<statement information item> ::=
<simple target specification> =
<statement information item name>
!! (*see Chapter 15 Error Handling and Diagnostics*)

<statement information item name> ::=
NUMBER | MORE | COMMAND_FUNCTION | DYNAMIC_FUNCTION |
ROW_COUNT
!! (*see Chapter 15 Error Handling and Diagnostics*)

<statement name> ::= <identifier>
!! (*see Section 18.4 PREPARE*)

<statement or declaration> ::=
<declare cursor>
| <dynamic declare cursor>
| <temporary table declaration>
| <embedded exception declaration>
| <SQL statement>
!! (*see Chapter 17 The Embedded Languages*)

<string length> ::= <numeric value expression>
!! (*see Section 11.2.2.1 SUBSTRING*)

<string value expression> ::=
<character value expression>
| <bit value expression>
!! (*see Section 11.1.2 String Value Expressions*)

<string value function> ::=
<character value function>
| <bit value function>
!! (*see Section 11.1.2 String Value Expressions*)

<subquery> ::= (<query expression>)
!! (*see Section 9.6 Subqueries*)

<system descriptor statement> ::=
<allocate descriptor statement>
| <deallocate descriptor statement>
| <set descriptor statement>
| <get descriptor statement>
!! (*see Chapter 18 Dynamic SQL*)

<table constraint> ::=
<unique constraint definition>
| <referential constraint definition>
| <check constraint definition>
!! (*see Section 4.2.2 Table Constraints*)

<table constraint definition> ::=
[<constraint name definition>]
<table constraint>
[<constraint attributes>]
!! (*see Section 4.2.2 Table Constraints*)

<table definition> ::=
CREATE [{ GLOBAL | LOCAL } TEMPORARY]
TABLE <table name>
<table element list>
[ON COMMIT { DELETE | PRESERVE } ROWS]
!! (*see Section 4.2 CREATE TABLE*)

<table element> ::=
<column definition>
| <table constraint definition>
!! (*see Section 4.2 CREATE TABLE*)

<table element list> ::=
(<table element> [{ , <table element> }...])
!! (*see Section 4.2 CREATE TABLE*)

<table expression> ::=
<from clause>
[<where clause>]
[<group by clause>]
[<having clause>]
!! (*see Section 9.4 Table Expression*)

<table name> ::=
<qualified name>
| <qualified local table name>
!! (*see Section 3.4 Names*)

<table reference> ::=
<table name> [[AS] <correlation name>
[(<derived column list>)]]
| <derived table> [AS] <correlation name>
[(<derived column list>)]
| <joined table>
!! (*see Section 9.3.1 Table References*)

<table subquery> ::= <subquery>
!! (*see Section 9.6 Subqueries*)

<table value constructor> ::=
VALUES <table value constructor list>
!! (*see Section 9.2 Table Value Constructors*)

<table value constructor list> ::=
<row value constructor>
[{ , <row value constructor> }...]
!! (*see Section 9.2 Table Value Constructors*)

<target character set specification> ::=
<character set specification>
!! (*see Section 4.8 CREATE TRANSLATION*)

<target specification> ::=
| <variable specification>
!! (*see Section 3.6 Values and Targets*)

<temporary table declaration> ::=
DECLARE LOCAL TEMPORARY TABLE
<qualified local table name>
<table element list>
[ON COMMIT { PRESERVE | DELETE } ROWS]
!! (*see Section 16.2 DECLARE LOCAL TEMPORARY TABLE*)

<term> ::=
<factor>
| <term> * <factor>
| <term> / <factor>
!! (*see Section 11.1.1 Numeric Value Expressions*)

<time interval> ::=
<hours value> [: <minutes value>
[: <seconds value>]]
| <minutes value> [: <seconds value>]
| <seconds value>
!! (*see Section 3.7.12 Interval Literals*)

<time literal> ::= TIME <time string>
!! (*see Section 3.7.10 Datetime Literals*)

<time precision> ::= <fractional seconds precision>
!! (*see Section 3.7.9 The Datetime Data Type*)

<time string> ::=
' <time value> [<time zone interval>] '
!! (*see Section 3.7.10 Datetime Literals*)

<time value> ::=
<hours value> : <minutes value> : <seconds value>
!! (*see Section 3.7.10 Datetime Literals*)

<time zone> ::= AT <time zone specifier>
!! (*see Section 11.1.3 Datetime Value Expressions*)

<time zone field> ::= TIMEZONE_HOUR | TIMEZONE_MINUTE
!! (*see Section 11.2.1.4 EXTRACT*)

<time zone interval> ::=
{ + | – } <hours value> : <minutes value>
!! (*see Section 3.7.10 Datetime Literals*)

<time zone specifier> ::=
LOCAL
| TIME ZONE <simple value specification>
!! (*see Section 11.1.3 Datetime Value Expressions*)

<timestamp literal> ::= TIMESTAMP <timestamp string>
!! (*see Section 3.7.10 Datetime Literals*)

<timestamp precision> ::= <fractional seconds precision>
!! (*see Section 3.7.9 The Datetime Data Type*)

<timestamp string> ::=
    ' <date value> <space> <time value>
        [<time zone interval>] '
!! (*see Section 3.7.10 Datetime Literals*)

<token> ::=
      <nondelimiter token>
    | <delimiter token>
!! (*see Section 3.2 Tokens*)

<transaction access mode> ::= READ ONLY | READ WRITE
!! (*see Section 12.3.3 The SET TRANSACTION Statement*)

<transaction mode> ::=
      <transaction access mode>
    | <isolation level>
    | <diagnostics size>
!! (*see Section 12.3.3 The SET TRANSACTION Statement*)

<translation collation> ::=
    TRANSLATION <translation name>
        [THEN COLLATION <collation name>]
!! (*see Section 4.7 CREATE COLLATION*)

<translation definition> ::=
    CREATE TRANSLATION <translation name>
        FOR <source character set specification>
        TO <target character set specification>
        FROM <translation source>
!! (*see Section 4.8 CREATE TRANSLATION*)

<translation name> ::= <qualified name>
!! (*see Section 4.8 CREATE TRANSLATION*)

<translation source> ::=
      <external translation>
    | IDENTITY
    | <schema translation name>
!! (*see Section 4.8 CREATE TRANSLATION*)

<trim character> ::= <character value expression>
!! (*see Section 11.2.3.2 TRIM*)

<trim function> ::=
    TRIM ([[{ LEADING | TRAILING | BOTH }]
        [<trim character>] FROM] <trim source>)
!! (*see Section 11.2.3.2 TRIM*)

<trim source> ::= <character value expression>
!! (*see Section 11.2.3.2 TRIM*)

<unique column list> ::= <column name list>
!! (*see Section 4.2.1.2.2 Unique*)

<unique constraint definition> ::=
{ UNIQUE | PRIMARY KEY } (<unique column list>)
!! (*see Section 4.2.1.2.2 Unique*)

<unique predicate> ::= UNIQUE <table subquery>
!! (*see Section 10.2.10 Unique Predicate*)

<unqualified schema name> ::= <identifier>
!! (*see Section 3.4 Names*)

<unsigned integer> ::= <digit>...
!! (*see Section 3.7.6 Exact Numeric Literals*)

<unsigned literal> ::=
<unsigned numeric literal>
| <general literal>
!! (*see Section 3.5 Literals*)

<unsigned numeric literal> ::=
<exact numeric literal>
| <approximate numeric literal>
!! (*see Section 3.5 Literals*)

<unsigned value specification> ::=
<unsigned literal>
| <general value specification>
!! (*see Section 3.6 Values and Targets*)

<updatability clause> ::=
FOR { READ ONLY | UPDATE [OF <column name list>] }
!! (*see Section 7.1 DECLARE CURSOR*)

<update rule> ::= ON UPDATE <referential action>
!! (*see Section 4.2.2.2 References*)

<update source> ::=
<value expression> | NULL | DEFAULT
!! (*see Section 6.3 UPDATE Searched*)

<update statement: positioned> ::=
UPDATE <table name>
SET <set clause list>
WHERE CURRENT OF <cursor name>
!! (*see Section 7.4 UPDATE Positioned*)

<update statement: searched> ::=
UPDATE <table name>
SET <set clause list>
[WHERE <search condition>]
!! (*see Section 6.3 UPDATE Searched*)

<user name> ::= <simple value specification>
!! (*see Section 14.1 CONNECT*)

<user-defined character repertoire name> ::=
<character set name>
!! (*see Section 4.6 CREATE CHARACTER SET*)

<using arguments> ::=
{ USING | INTO } <argument> [{ , <argument> }...]
!! (*see Section 18.7 USING*)

<using clause> ::=
<using arguments>
| <using descriptor>
!! (*see Section 18.7 USING*)

<using descriptor> ::=
{ USING | INTO } SQL DESCRIPTOR <descriptor name>
!! (*see Section 18.7 USING*)

<value expression> ::=
<numeric value expression>
| <string value expression>
| <datetime value expression>
| <interval value expression>
!! (*see Section 11.1 Value Expressions*)

<value specification> ::=
<literal>
| <general value specification>
!! (*see Section 3.6 Values and Targets*)

<variable specification> ::=
<embedded variable name> [<indicator variable>]
!! (*see Section 3.6 Values and Targets*)

<vertical bar> ::= |
!! (*see Section 3.1 Characters*)

<view column list> ::= <column name list>
!! (*see Section 4.4 CREATE VIEW*)

<view definition> ::=
  CREATE VIEW <table name> [(<view column list>)]
    AS <query expression>
    [WITH [CASCADED | LOCAL] CHECK OPTION]
!! (*see Section 4.4 CREATE VIEW*)

<when operand> ::= <value expression>
!! (*see Section 11.3.1 CASE*)

<where clause> ::= WHERE <search condition>
!! (*see Section 9.4.2 WHERE*)

<year-month literal> ::=
   <years value>
  | [<years value> –] <months value>
!! (*see Section 3.7.12 Interval Literals*)

<years value> ::= <datetime value>
!! (*see Section 3.7.10 Datetime Literals*)

D

Key Words

Key words are words that have a special significance for SQL. They are divided into two classes, reserved words and non-reserved words. Reserved words are words that a user may not use in writing SQL commands except within character literals. Non-reserved words have a special significance but their context within the language is such that they never conflict with user assigned names. Examples of non-reserved words are the key words used in accessing the Diagnostics area. In this Appendix we provide a third list which are those words that at the time of going to press had already been included in the SQL3 working draft and thus may become reserved words in a future revision of the SQL language. There is no guarantee that all of these will indeed become reserved words but you would be well advised to avoid their use, or use them only in the delimited identifiers form, just in case. It is highly likely that most of them will.

D.1 Reserved Words

ABSOLUTE | ACTION | ADD | ALL | ALLOCATE | ALTER | AND | ANY | ARE | AS | ASC | ASSERTION | AT | AUTHORIZATION | AVG |

BEGIN | BETWEEN | BIT | BIT_LENGTH | BOTH | BY |

CASCADE | CASCADED | CASE | CAST | CATALOG | CHAR | CHARACTER | CHAR_LENGTH | CHARACTER_LENGTH | CHECK | CLOSE | COALESCE | COLLATE | COLLATION | COLUMN | COMMIT | CONNECT | CONNECTION | CONSTRAINT | CONSTRAINTS | CONTINUE | CONVERT | CORRESPONDING | COUNT | CREATE | CROSS | CURRENT | CURRENT_DATE | CURRENT_TIME | CURRENT_TIMESTAMP | CURRENT_USER | CURSOR |

DATE | DAY | DEALLOCATE | DEC | DECIMAL | DECLARE | DEFAULT | DEFERRABLE | DEFERRED | DELETE | DESC | DESCRIBE | DESCRIPTOR | DIAGNOSTICS | DISCONNECT | DISTINCT | DOMAIN | DOUBLE | DROP |

ELSE | END | END-EXEC | ESCAPE | EXCEPT | EXCEPTION | EXEC | EXECUTE | EXISTS | EXTERNAL | EXTRACT |

FALSE | FETCH | FIRST | FLOAT | FOR | FOREIGN | FOUND | FROM | FULL |

GET | GLOBAL | GO | GOTO | GRANT | GROUP |

HAVING | HOUR |

IDENTITY | IMMEDIATE | IN | INDICATOR | INITIALLY | INNER | INPUT | INSENSITIVE | INSERT | INT | INTEGER | INTERSECT | INTERVAL | INTO | IS | ISOLATION |

JOIN |

KEY |

LANGUAGE | LAST | LEADING | LEFT | LEVEL | LIKE | LOCAL | LOWER |

MATCH | MAX | MIN | MINUTE | MODULE | MONTH |

NAMES | NATIONAL | NATURAL | NCHAR | NEXT | NO | NOT | NULL | NULLIF | NUMERIC |

OCTET_LENGTH | OF | ON | ONLY | OPEN | OPTION | OR | ORDER | OUTER | OUTPUT | OVERLAPS |

PAD | PARTIAL | POSITION | PRECISION | PREPARE | PRESERVE | PRIMARY | PRIOR | PRIVILEGES | PROCEDURE | PUBLIC |

READ | REAL | REFERENCES | RELATIVE | RESTRICT | REVOKE | RIGHT | ROLLBACK | ROWS |

SCHEMA | SCROLL | SECOND | SECTION | SELECT | SESSION | SESSION_USER | SET | SIZE | SMALLINT | SOME | SPACE | SQL | SQLCODE | SQLERROR | SQLSTATE | SUBSTRING | SUM | SYSTEM_USER |

TABLE | TEMPORARY | THEN | TIME | TIMESTAMP | TIMEZONE_HOUR | TIMEZONE_MINUTE | TO | TRAILING | TRANSACTION | TRANSLATE | TRANSLATION | TRIM | TRUE |

UNION | UNIQUE | UNKNOWN | UPDATE | UPPER | USAGE | USER | USING |

VALUE | VALUES | VARCHAR | VARYING | VIEW |

WHEN | WHENEVER | WHERE | WITH | WORK | WRITE |

YEAR |

ZONE

D.2 Non-reserved Words

ADA |

C | CATALOG_NAME | CHARACTER_SET_CATALOG | CHARACTER_SET_NAME | CHARACTER_SET_SCHEMA | CLASS_ORIGIN | COBOL | COLLATION_CATALOG | COLLATION_NAME | COLLATION_SCHEMA | COLUMN_NAME | COMMAND_FUNCTION | COMMITTED | CONDITION_NUMBER | CONNECTION_NAME | CONSTRAINT_CATALOG | CONSTRAINT_NAME | CONSTRAINT_SCHEMA | CURSOR_NAME |

DATA | DATETIME_INTERVAL_CODE | DATETIME_INTERVAL_PRECISION | DYNAMIC_FUNCTION |

FORTRAN |

LENGTH |

MESSAGE_LENGTH | MESSAGE_OCTET_LENGTH | MESSAGE_TEXT | MORE | MUMPS |

NAME | NULLABLE | NUMBER |

PASCAL | PLI |

REPEATABLE | RETURNED_LENGTH | RETURNED_OCTET_LENGTH | RETURNED_SQLSTATE | ROW_COUNT |

SCALE | SCHEMA_NAME | SERIALIZABLE | SERVER_NAME | SUBCLASS_ORIGIN |

TABLE_NAME | TYPE |

UNCOMMITTED | UNNAMED

D.3 Possible Future Reserved Words

ACTOR | AFTER | ALIAS | ASYNC |

BEFORE | BEGIN | BOOLEAN | BREADTH |

CALL | CLASS | COMPLETION | CONSTRUCTOR | CYCLE |

DATA | DEPTH | DEREF | DESTROY | DESTRUCTOR | DICTIONARY |

EACH | ELSEIF | EQUALS |

FUNCTION |

GENERAL |

IF | IGNORE |

LEAVE | LESS | LIMIT | LOOP |

MAKE | MODIFY |

NEW | NONE |

OBJECT | OFF | OID | OLD | OPERATION | OPERATORS | OTHERS |

PARAMETERS | PENDANT | PREORDER | PRIVATE | PROTECTED |

RECURSIVE | REF | REFERENCING | REMOVE | REPLACE | REPRESENTATION | RESIGNAL | RETURN | RETURNS | ROLE | ROUTINE | ROW |

SAVEPOINT | SEARCH | SENSITIVE | SEQUENCE | SIGNAL | SIMILAR | SQLEXCEPTION | SQLWARNING | STRUCTURE |

TEST | THAN | THERE | TRIGGER | TUPLE | TYPE |

UNDER |

VARIABLE | VIRTUAL | VISIBLE |

WAIT | WHILE | WITHOUT

Levels and Conformance

E.1 Levels

The SQL standard defines three levels for the language, representing a nested hierarchy of functionality. The three levels are:

Entry
Intermediate
Full

The Entry level is the most restricted and the Full level is the complete level. The Intermediate level contains all of the functionality of the Entry level but is not as complete as the Full level.

The Entry level is roughly equivalent to the functionality defined in the 1989 standard and includes all corrections to that standard. In addition to the facilities of the 1989 standard, the Entry level includes the embedded language interfaces to seven different programming languages (the 1989 standard included advisory text for four languages), new facilities to replace those that have been designated 'deprecated' (i.e. liable to be removed at the next revision of the standard) and facilities that will aid conversion to the new standard. These additional facilities include:

The SQLSTATE parameter and error codes
Commas and parentheses in parameter list
Renaming columns in a select list
Delimited identifiers
Direct invocation of SQL

The Intermediate level includes many new features such as:

The Schema Manipulation commands
Dynamic SQL
Transaction Isolation levels
Multiple module support
Referential actions
Outer Join, Outer Union, Intersect and Difference set operators
Domains
The CASE expression
The CAST function
Diagnostics
Basic Datetime and Interval data types
Varying length character strings
Multiple character sets
etc.

Notable features which are missing from the Intermediate level include:

Assertions
Constraint names
GLOBAL temporary tables
Deferred constraint checking
Self Referencing inserts, updates and deletes
Subqueries in check clauses
The BIT data type
Full Datetime and Interval support including precision and time zones
Limited character set definition
Character collating sequences
Character translations
Scrolled cursors
etc.

The Full level includes all the facilities of the language. The Full level is the one dealt with in this book.

E.2 Conformance

An implementation may claim several different forms of conformance. There are approximately 2289 different conforming SQL implementations possible. This large number derives from the various possible combinations of languages supported, but ignoring these only 21 variants are possible.

Each conforming implementation must state which:

1. Level of conformance is claimed (i.e. Full, Intermediate or Entry).
2. Binding styles are supported (i.e. Module, Embedded or Direct).
3. Languages are supported for binding styles Module and Embedded.

Implementations claiming conformance to the Intermediate level must provide a flagger capable of optionally diagnosing syntax that does not conform to the Entry level or to the Intermediate level. An implementation claiming conformance to the Full level must be capable of optionally diagnosing syntax that does not conform to any of the three levels and provide a further option for checking at each level that involves going further than just a syntax check and accessing the catalog to diagnose such things as data type mismatches, etc.

In addition the conforming implementation must supply definitions for all of the characteristics of the SQL language that the standard declares to be implementation defined.

F

Differences between SQL-1992 and SQL-1989

F.1 Incompatibilities

The 1992 standard for SQL is almost entirely upwards compatible with the original standards (ISO 9075:1987(E) and ISO 9075:1989(E). There are only 10 known incompatibilities, one of which is a long list of additional key words. Of the others three can properly be considered to be mistakes in the original SQL and most of the remainder are unfortunate wordings which led to potentially undesirable interpretations.

The known incompatibilities are:

1. It is no longer a requirement that multiple openings of an unordered cursor within a single transaction return the rows in the same order every time. In the 1992 standard, the order of rows returned for an unordered cursor is always implementation dependent.
2. Previously <parameter name>s were simple <identifier>s. In the 1992 standard, colons are now required to delimit <parameter name>s.
3. The specification of the enforcement of WITH CHECK OPTION for a view was ambiguous. The 1992 standard clarifies the intent of WITH CHECK OPTION and adds options that provide the two useful interpretations of the previous situation.
4. The <unique constraint definition> had no rule to prevent the definition of two unique constraints with identical unique column lists on a table. The 1992 standard requires that all unique column lists be distinct within a table.

5. There was no requirement that users have SELECT privileges on tables referenced in contexts other than <select statement: single row> or <fetch statement>. The 1992 standard requires that users have SELECT privileges on tables referenced in various <query expression>s, <table expression>s, <search condition>s and <value expression>s.
6. There was no rule to prevent the specification of a view from referencing itself. The 1992 standard forbids such self-referencing.
7. There was no rule to prevent the use of outer references in <set function specification>s of <search condition>s of <having clause>s. The 1992 standard forbids usage as the semantics are not defined.
8. The module associated with an embedded SQL program had an implementation defined <module authorization identifier> which could be bound at either run time or compile time. The 1992 standard defines such a module to have no <module authorization identifier> and thus the appropriate authorization identifier is always determined at run-time.
9. If the current row of the cursor is deleted, then the situation was that the cursor was always positioned before the next row (if any). The 1992 standard makes the situation undefined if the deletion is not done through the cursor.
10. A number of additional reserved words have been added to the language. The complete reserved word list can be found in *Appendix D Key Words*.

F.2 New Features

The major new features in the language are:

Support for additional data types
Support for multiple character sets
Support for schema manipulation capabilities
Additional privilege capabilities
Additional integrity facilities
Definition of the Information Schema
Improved diagnostic facilities
Facilities to support Remote Data Access, e.g. session statements and schema name qualification
Additional relational operators
Support for dynamic SQL
Definition of direct SQL
Standardization of support for embedded SQL
Support for additional language bindings
Support for increased orthogonality

F.3 Features Still to be Developed

ISO has specified the following areas to be considered in any revision of the SQL standard.

Additional requirements of RDA standardization
Additional requirements of IRDS standardization
Enhanced schema and constraint definitions
Additional data manipulation capabilities
Database services interface
Additional programming language interfaces
Support for database utilities
Interfaces for database distribution
Support for object-oriented database systems
Support for knowledge-based systems
Support for other high-level tools of modern information management

Some features already drafted when the 1992 standard was finalized, go some way to filling in these areas:

An enumerated data type
An abstract data type definition capability
Primitive Object Management
A new form of referential action, PENDANT.
Enhanced assertions
Triggers
Multiple null states
Sub-tables and generalizations
External functions
Recursive union
A SIMILAR predicate
Asynchronous SQL
Relaxed update rules
Persistent modules

G

Glossary

Note that in this glossary the terms are to be found under the singular form although references to terms in this glossary may have been made using the plural form.

Access control Access Control (*see Chapter 8*) supervises access to objects managed by an SQL **DBMS**. These objects are **domain**, **table** (including a view), **column**, **character set**, **collation** and **translation**. Usage is controlled by granting or revoking rights. Users of the database on whose behalf SQL commands are executed need to have obtained appropriate **privileges** (*see Table 8.1 in Section 8.4 Cascade effects of the REVOKE statement for the privileges required to create schema objects*). The specification of such rights is reflected in privilege descriptors which are stored in the catalogue (*see Section 20.1.2.18 TABLE_PRIVILEGES, Section 20.1.2.19 COLUMN_PRIVILEGES and Section 20.1.2.20 USAGE_PRIVILEGES*).

Accuracy A concept specifying that the **clients** of an **information system** must ensure the correctness of data by taking responsibility for its rightness, timeliness and completeness in transactions with the information system. Some checks can be delegated to the information system and are labelled **integrity** and **consistency** (*see Section 21.3 Correctness Aspects*).

Application An application is a set of **application programs** designed to support a portion of the business of an organization. It is part of an **information system** and takes responsibility for the **consistency** of the data.

Application program An application program provides automated support for part of an application. It may contain **SQL statements**, such as **DML**,

DDL or other **SQL control** statements, which instruct the **DBMS** to carry out actions. These statements may take the form of the module language, **embedded language** or appear as **Direct SQL** statements.

Assertion An assertion is an **integrity** constraint not directly coupled to a **table** but functionally equivalent to a **check** constraint for a **base table** (*see Section 4.5 CREATE ASSERTION and Section 4.2.2.3 Check*). Assertions allow the delegation of complex conditions to the **DBMS** to hold true. The specification of some of the behaviour of SQL has been done using assertions (*see Section 20.1.3 The Assertions*).

Attribute An attribute is a characteristic of an **entity** about which we have decided to record data in the database. During the conceptual phase of a **Systems Development Life Cycle** data requirements are represented as **entities**, **attributes** and **relationships**. In our database (*see Appendix A The Example Database*) we see many attributes described including name, salary, home_telno, project_cd, budget, forecast, work_date, overtime_hours, request_date, destination, travel_date.

Authorization identifier An authorization identifier is an identifier holding a unique reference to a user of the **DBMS**. Such a user can be a person or an **application program** executing on behalf of a person. The authorization identifier is inherited by the **server** from the calling **client** and finally passed to the SQL DBMS via the **modules** containing the SQL **data definition** and/or **data manipulation** commands. The process of identifying a client (person or program) and the authentication of that identity is outside the scope of SQL and remains the responsibility of the computing environment (*see Chapter 8 Access Control*).

Base table A base table can be thought of as a two-dimensional storage space (a file) on persistent storage (typically a disk). It holds a particular part of the data in a database. For further explanation of the table concept *see Section 2.5.1 Table and Section 2.7 Conventions Used*. Examples of tables can be found in our database (*see Appendix A The Example Database*). Data from a base table may be used to create **derived tables** of any kind, like **views**. The SQL standard does not prescribe how implementors must store data in base tables.

BNF BNF is the syntax notation called 'Backus normal form' or 'Backus Naur form'. An extended version is used in the SQL standard and in this book (*see Appendix B BNF Syntax Notation*). The purpose of BNF is to describe how formulations of valid language in terms of character strings may be produced. From the SQL language description (*see Appendix C BNF Syntax Diagrams*) we use the BNF production rules to obtain correctly formatted SQL statements.

Boolean Boolean logic is the two-valued logic of true and false. In SQL we use a three-valued logic introducing unknown (or **null**) into the equation.

Predicates can generally assume the three values mentioned and play an important function in query formulation.

Candidate key A candidate key is a non-**null unique key** for a **table**. A unique key need not be non-null though this is a requirement for a candidate key in relational theory. The SQL standard gives the freedom to specify ' `UNIQUE` ' or ' `UNIQUE NOT NULL` ', the combination specifying a candidate key (*see Sections 4.2.1.2.2 Unique, 4.2.2.1 Unique and Section 22.3 Entity Integrity*). See also **foreign key**. A candidate key has the role of uniquely identifying a row in a table. Providing the value for a candidate key implies that the **DBMS** can find a single occurrence or row in the table. See also **primary key**.

Cardinality Cardinality is the property of a table or a relationship describing the number of objects involved. The cardinality of a table indicates the number of rows in the table. The cardinality of a relationship specifies how many objects of each of the two types are involved. For a detailed description of how to control the cardinality of the relationship *see Chapter 22 Integrity Control*.

Cascade Cascading in general means propagation of some action or property. In SQL the following cascade options are provided. When defining a referential constraint for a column (*see Section 4.2.1.2.3 References*) or table (*see Section 4.2.2.2 References*) we may specify the execution of a referential triggered action (see **referential action**) which allows for the specification of a cascade option. When specifying various kinds of DROP commands (*see Section 5.1 The DROP statements*) as part of the **schema manipulation** part of SQL, cascading may be specified to drop associated objects. When defining a view (*see Section 4.4 CREATE VIEW*) the cascade option of the WITH CHECK OPTION clause causes the same clause to be effectively applied to the underlying views as well. When revoking **privileges** (*see Section 8.4 Cascade effects of the Revoke statement*) the cascade option will revoke a chain of privileges.

Catalog A catalog is a named collection of one or more **schemata** grouped together for various reasons. The catalog may be seen as a **database** of schemata that describe application databases (*see Section 2.5.3 Catalog and the example of catalog reference in Section 4.1 CREATE SCHEMA*). Each SQL database is itself therefore described in the catalog which is represented as the DEFINITION_SCHEMA (*see Chapter 20 The Information Schema, in particular Figure 20.1 Data structure diagram of the SQL catalog*). The concepts like table, column, view are treated just like entities at the dictionary or catalog level (*see Section 2.5.3 Catalog*). The catalog database describes the features of SQL, such that a **column** belongs to a **table**, and that a column may have a domain defined and may have a column default (*see Section 20.1.2.8 COLUMNS*).

Character repertoire A character repertoire is a defined set of characters as supported by an implementation of SQL. Various character repertoires may be available and can be used in building up a **character set** (*see Section 3.7.1 The Character Data Type*). The character repertoire has a default collating sequence.

Character set A set of characters is a defined set of characters, a **character repertoire** and a physical encoding (*see Section 4.6 CREATE CHARACTER SET*). Characters from a specified character set may be used in **identifiers**, character **literals** and the character **data type** (*see Section 3.7.1 The Character Data Type*). A collating sequence may be specified for a character set. See also **collation**.

Check A check constraint can be specified for a **column** (*see Section 4.2.1.2.4 Check*) or for a **table** (*see Section 4.2.2.3 Check*) and allows the specification of an arbitrary **search condition** that the **DBMS** must hold true. When creating a **view** we may specify the check option. This feature may only be specified if the view is updatable and provides a degree of control on the updates which may be done through the view (*see Section 4.4 CREATE VIEW*).

Client SQL allows the setting up of a client–**server** construction where the client calls on the server to provide services. For connecting an application program to a session *see Chapter 14 Session Management*, for a more general introduction to the client–server approach *see Section 21.5.3 Client-Server Concepts* and for an example of a client server application in distributed databases *see Section 27.3.2 Locating the Data.*

Coalesce The COALESCE option is one of the **conditional value expressions**. COALESCE selects from a list of values the first non-null values. COALESCE is used in the SQL language specification itself for the NATURAL option on the JOIN (*see Section 9.3.2.4.5 The NATURAL option*).

Conditional value expression A conditional value expression is a **value expression** selecting a value to return based on one or a number of conditions. In *Section 11.3 Conditional Value Expressions*, the CASE, NULLIF and **COALESCE** expressions are explained.

Coercibility Coercibility describes which collating sequence to use when comparing <character value expression>s with different collating sequences (*see Section 4.7 CREATE COLLATION and Table 4.3 Coercibility and collating sequences resulting from operations and for use in comparisons*).

Collation A collation (or collating sequence) can be defined for a character repertoire (*see Section 4.7 CREATE COLLATION*) and can be used in a **column** definition (*see Section 4.2.1.3 Collation*). It specifies the rules for the **comparison** and the sequencing of character strings.

Column A column is the vertical dimension of a **table**, a **row** being the horizontal dimension. A column represents an **attribute** of the **entity** modelled by a table. The salary (the attribute or column) of an Employee (the entity or table) offers the possibility of holding salary data for each Employee. The field at the intersection of the row and column holds the value in accordance with the **data type** specified for the column. Such a column may have a **domain** defined and may have a column default (*see Section 20.1.2.8 COLUMNS*).

Compare equal The <equals operator> (=) compares two values and determines equality (*see Section 10.2.1 Comparison Predicate*). In the case of a character **data type** the values need not be identical to be equal since the **collation** and **coercibility** affect the order of values to be compared (*see Section 4.7 CREATE COLLATION*).

Comparison When comparing values of the same or different data types several operators can be used (*see Section 10.2.1 Comparison Predicate*). For character strings the **collation** plays a role in the comparison. The **compare equal** operator is probably the most valuable since it allows the specification of **referential integrity** and many of the **check** constraints (*see Sections 4.2.1.2.3 References, and Section 4.2.1.2.4 Check*) and allows the collecting data from various **table**s in the **database** during join commands. When reasoning with missing information a comparison may involve three or 'more' valued logic (*see Section 24.2.1 Comparisons with Unknown Markings in Search Expressions*).

Conformance The International SQL standard specifies conforming SQL language and conforming SQL implementations. Conforming SQL language shall abide by the BNF format, associated syntax rules and access rules, definitions and descriptions in the SQL standard. A conforming SQL implementation shall process conforming SQL language according to the associated general rules, definitions and descriptions in the SQL standard. Conformance is dependent upon the level of SQL specification, the host languages and the binding style supported (*see Appendix E Levels and Conformance*).

Connection The CONNECT command establishes a session to an SQL_Server. The SET CONNECTION command selects and activates a session from those already established (*see Chapter 14 Session Management*).

Consistency A concept specifying that the **application** will ensure that data is consistent in the eyes of the user of the **information system**. During the development of the information system the users have agreed a 'contract' for correctness for which the application is responsible. To a large extent the **DBMS** will support the application by providing data **integrity** and offering tools for concurrency and recovery at the consistency level (*see Chapter 12 Transaction Management*). See also **integrity** and **accuracy** (*Section 21.3 Correctness Aspects*).

Constraint A constraint is a specification in the **DDL** which the **DBMS** must not violate. Constraints can be specified on **columns**, on **tables** and for **domains**. The column and domain constraints control values in a single column whereas the table constraint can check values for groups of columns.

Referential integrity checks (also called the **foreign key** constraint) allow the specification of a **referential action** to be performed when rows are modified or deleted. Checks are usually performed after each SQL command, but the moment of checking is given to **application** control, and will in any case take place before the **transaction** ends. See also **assertion**.

Constructor In SQL there is a <Row Value Constructor> and a <Table Value Constructor>, with which we can derive values for a single row or combine several <Row Value Constructor>s into a <Table Value Constructor> creating a derived table (*see Chapter 9 Derived Tables*).

Correlation name A correlation name is an alias for the name of a **table** in a **table reference** in a **query expression** or **table expression**. In a single query it is frequently necessary to refer to the same table several times but to be able to distinguish these references from each other, as each is being used to identify a different subset of the table. This can only be done if each subset can be given a temporary name (a correlation name or alias or perhaps local variable). For more information *see Section 9.3.1 Table References and Section 25.3.5 Aliasing*.

Cursor A cursor is a mechanism that allows a **module** of an **application program** to step through the rows of a table, whether a base table, a view or any other arbitrarily derived table. This mechanism is necessary since the programming languages available for use with SQL work in principle on a record at a time basis and not on a set basis. For an overview of the programming languages *see Chapter 16 The Module Language*. Cursors provide an interface between the set orientation of SQL and the record orientation of programming languages (*see Chapter 7 Cursor Operations*).

Data model A data model is a way of representing the data part of the **Universe of Discourse**. The most quoted data models are the hierarchical, the network and the relational. Each such model has a set of rules which must be obeyed when modelling the Universe of Discourse. A pictorial representation of such a model of the Universe of Discourse can be made using a **data structure diagram**.

Data definition Data Definition is the execution of DDL commands by the **DBMS** upon request by users (usually the database administrator) or by **application programs**. These commands are executed against the **catalog**, but in certain cases the content of the **database** is checked or updated to verify or ensure **consistency** between the specification of the database in the catalog (in the form of meta-data) and the content of the database itself *see Chapter 4 Data Definition and Chapter 5 Schema Manipulation*.

Data manipulation Data manipulation is the execution of DML commands by the **DBMS** upon the request of **application programs**. These commands are executed against the **database** (*see Chapter 6 Non-Cursor Operations and Chapter 7 Cursor Operations*). The **catalog** prescribes behaviour by supplying information to the DBMS about the structure of the database, the names of columns, tables, etc., and providing **constraints** and **checks** to be performed.

Data structure diagram A data structure diagram (DSD) is a pictorial representation of the data structure within our **Universe of Discourse**. Such a diagrammatic picture usually gives an insight into the data (to be) maintained in the **database**. The diagrams are usually augmented by definitions for each of the objects shown. We have provided DSDs for SQL (of the relational **data model** type) at the conceptual and the logical levels of the **SDLC** using a specific notation (*see Figure 2.6 in Section 2.7 Conventions Used*) which we developed during our work on a large project.

Data type A data type is the specification of permissible values allowed. SQL recognizes the following data types: character, bit, exact numeric, approximate numeric, datetime, Interval (*see Section 3.7 Data Types*). A data type is basically a kind of **domain** which limits the permissible values. Every value in a column must belong to a domain as specified in a domain definition or inherent to the data type.

Database A database is a collection of data maintained by a **DBMS** via **SQL statements**. It is part of an **information system**. The meaning of the term database has changed considerably over the years, and in the SQL standard a database is not simply some set of data described by a simple **data definition** but encompasses a much wider connotation (*see Section 2.4 Database*).

DBMS A DBMS (database management system) is a software package providing functionality to maintain data in **databases**. The SQL language describes the **SQL statements** with which such a software package can be addressed, i.e. which syntax to use when communicating with a DBMS and which functionality may be expected. See also **conformance**.

DDL The DDL is the subset of **data definition** language commands in SQL. These commands describe to the **DBMS** the characteristics of the data structure (probably as indicated in a **data structure diagram**) which needs to be maintained so that data **integrity** is ensured. The DDL commands effectively populate the **catalog** with rows of meta-data which prescribe the behaviour of the DBMS.

Default The concept of defaults deals with the provision of a predefined alternative in the case where something is missing. This may apply to many different things. For a value that is missing at the time of inserting a row in a table an alternative value may be supplied through a **column** default or a **domain** default. For a schema a default character set may be specified that acts as the character set for columns and domains that have no character set specified. When specifying a **collation** the sequence of characters in the set may be according to the default or some other sequence. For examples of all these instances *see Chapter 4 Data Definition*. The schema manipulation language allows modification or the dropping of defaults (*see Chapter 5 Schema Manipulation*).

Definition schema The definition schema (DEFINITION_SCHEMA) are a collection of base tables thought to be supporting the **information schema**. The definition schema supplied in *Section 20.1 The Definition Schema* provides only a model of the base tables that are required and does not imply that an implementation shall provide the functionality of SQL as described in that particular way.

Derived table A derived table is a result (originally) obtained from a **base table**. SQL offers many language constructs to specify such derivation (*see Chapter 9 Derived Tables*). The <row value constructor> and <table value constructor> produce a row (a single row table) and **table** (a single or multi row table) respectively. A **query expression** is the basic way of defining a derived table. It is the starting point for the declaration of **views**, **cursors** and **subqueries**. SQL offers many recursive capabilities, leading to recursive specifications of derived tables and allowing often equivalent operations on those data structures. For example, a view can be defined on a base table, but subsequently the view itself can be used in view definition.

Diagnostics SQL offers diagnostics capabilities for analysing errors and determining corrective actions (*see Chapter 15 Error Handling and Diagnostics*). The new status parameter SQLSTATE provides information about the error. SQL now has extensive, standardized codes for error reporting, allowing much better analysis.

Direct SQL Direct SQL indicates a situation where SQL statements can be issued directly to the **DBMS**, generally using a presentation device such as a terminal where the result is also provided (*see Chapter 19 Direct Invocation of SQL*).

Distinct Two values are said to be distinct if they are both not **null** and do not **compare equal**.

Distributed database A distributed database is a database that holds data that are distributed across storage media of at least two computers (also called sites or nodes) connected by some form of communications network (*see Chapter 27 Distributed Databases*). The definition of **database** in SQL is quite different from what was common in the past decade.

DML The DML is the subset of **data manipulation** commands in SQL. These commands invoke actions from the **DBMS** to manipulate data in the **database**. The actions in the database are guaranteed by the DBMS to maintain the **integrity** of the data in the database. The **application programs** issue DML commands to change the contents of the database to reflect changes in the **Universe of Discourse**.

Domain A domain is a set of permissible values. Every value in a column must belong to a domain as specified in a domain definition (*see Section 4.3 CREATE DOMAIN*) or be inherent to the **data type**.

DSD See **data structure diagram**.

Duplicate Two values are duplicates if they are not **distinct**. Two rows are duplicates if all their corresponding values are not distinct.

Dynamic SQL Dynamic SQL is a functionality where an SQL command is offered to the **DBMS** by an **application program** where the SQL command is constructed during the execution of the program (*see Chapter 18 Dynamic SQL*).

Embedded language An embedded language is an extension to a standard programming language offering SQL functionality (*see Chapter 17 The Embedded Languages*). An alternative to embedded language is the **module language**.

Entity An entity is a thing, event or concept in our **Universe of Discourse** we deem of sufficient importance and/or interest to maintain data about. A **DSD** will show the entities of interest to our information system. The term entity is associated with the conceptual phase of the **SDLC**. We have many examples of entities in our Company Database (*see Appendix A The Example Database*); they include Employee, Project, Timesheet, Travel_Req.

Environment The SQL environment of a session includes the **catalog**, **schema**, **authorization identifier**, details about **constraint** checking and time zone information. It does not include **session** management details. The statements in environment management form part of the **SQL control** statements (*see Chapter 13 Environment Management*).

Extended name An extended name is a parameter or a host language variable containing a character string that has the format of an identifier and that takes the place of a normal identifier in the case of descriptor names (*see Section 18.8 ALLOCATE DESCRIPTOR*). In the case of an SQL statement identifier (*see Section 18.4 PREPARE*) and a dynamic cursor name (*see Section 18.15 Dynamic OPEN CURSOR*) extended names may be used as well as normal identifiers. In addition an extended name may have a scope declaration of GLOBAL or LOCAL. A LOCAL scope is the **module** in which the extended name is defined and a GLOBAL scope is all modules being used in an SQL **session**. The default is LOCAL (*see also Section 3.4 Names*).

Foreign key A foreign key is a key specification in a **referencing table** referencing a **primary key** or **candidate key** (more particularly a **unique key**) in the referenced table. This is the primary mechanism in SQL to relate (rows in) one table to (rows in) another though potentially the same table.

Fragmentation Fragmentation is the concept of splitting up a table into fragments (horizontally and/or vertically). Each such fragment can then be allocated to a node in the communications network supporting a **distributed database** (*see Section 27.2.2 Fragmentation of Portions of Data*). In designing a high-performance database the same principle of fragmentation may be used (*see Chapter 28 Performance Aspects*).

Function A function in SQL takes a scalar value (*see Section 11.2 Scalar Functions*) or a set of scalar values (*see Section 11.4 Set Functions*) and returns a scalar value. A scalar value is in principle any value that can be assigned to a column. Functions are available for manipulation of values for various data types. The current date, time and time-stamp may be obtained and the string and substring location, case conversion and manipulation can be performed. The CAST function converts a value from one data type into a value for another data type where also a representation of NULL can be made to your own liking. For an example of the CAST function *see Section 26.3 Mapping to Host Language Conventions*.

Host language A programming language which caters for the use of SQL. Programming languages can call SQL modules (*see Chapter 16 The Module Language*) or offer embedded extensions that interface with SQL, called **embedded languages**. For related topics see **dynamic SQL** and **direct SQL**.

Host language variable When SQL is used in a **host language** environment, the exchange of data values is performed via variables that are defined in the host language and are available in SQL. Several examples of host language variables used in conjunction with various SQL statements are given. For an example using cursor operations *see Section 7.1 Declare Cursor*. *See Section 15.1 The Get Diagnostics Command* for passing parameters for error handling and see *Chapter 18 Dynamic SQL* for passing parameters to and obtaining values from a dynamic SQL environment.

Identifier An identifier is a name or a part of a name. Such names serve to identify the various objects in an SQL **database**, for example the **tables**, **columns** and **views**. There are many kinds of names in SQL but they are all made up of one or more identifiers linked together with periods (*see Section 3.3 Identifiers*).

Information Schema The Information Schema is a set of views defined in a schema called ' `INFORMATION_SCHEMA` ' (*see Section 20.2 The Information Schema*). The information schema views are derived from the base tables as they are described for **definition schema**.

Information system An automated system consisting primarily of a **database** part and an **application** part, supported by **DBMS**, operating system, network software, compilers, hardware, communication network, etc. (*see Chapter 21 Database and Application Analysis*). An information system acts as a **server** providing information services to **clients** of the system (*see Section 21.5.3 Client–Server Concepts, and page 434 on Client–Server design in distributed database applications*). The information system as a whole is responsible for supplying information in a **consistent** state.

Integrity A concept specifying that the **DBMS** is responsible for maintaining the data in accordance with the **database definition** as recorded in the **catalog**. See also **consistency** and **accuracy** (*see Section 21.3 Correctness Aspects*).

Key A key is a very basic and important concept in relational theory. Different kinds of keys serve different specific purposes in relational database management. A first distinction is unique versus non-unique keys. Unique keys are **primary keys**, **candidate keys** and **unique keys**. Non-unique keys include **foreign keys**. The purpose of the unique keys is to identify a single **row** in a **table** based on the key value. The role of the non-unique key is primarily to maintain **relationships** among rows of tables. It also offers storage mechanisms the possibility of using linking access mechanisms for quick retrieval and clustered storage (*see Chapter 28 Performance Aspects*).

Key word A key word is a word (a string) in the SQL language (*see Appendix D Key Words*). When looking at the BNF notation of SQL (*see Appendix B BNF Syntax Notation*) the formulation of a correct SQL statement takes place by a substitution process until no further non-terminal BNF symbols remain (*see Appendix C BNF Syntax Diagrams*). The character string produced is a syntactically correct SQL statement. A key word is a character string (or word) that forms an essential structural part of the SQL language. Some key words are also reserved words; examples of reserved words are CREATE, SCHEMA, SELECT, FROM, WHERE. Examples of key words that are not reserved words are C, MORE, COBOL and SCALE.

Literal A literal is a way of representing a value, each of which has a **data type**. For each data type there is a corresponding literal specification. Literals are a very basic part of the SQL language and anywhere a value is required the literal may be used. Literals may be used in **value expressions** (*see Section 3.5 Literals*). For examples of the use of literals *see Section 3.7.2 Character Literals, Section 3.7.4 Bit String Literals, Section 3.7.6 Exact Numeric Literals, Section 3.7.8 Approximate Numeric Literals and Section 3.7.10 Datetime Literals*.

Missing information Information may be missing in a database for many reasons (*see Chapter 24 Handling Missing Information*). SQL offers the possibility of **null** to record that a value is missing. This property belongs to a column and during **table** definition the characteristic of allowing null is attached (*see Section 4.2.1.2.1 NOT NULL and Section 4.2.2.3 Check*). The property may be inherited by columns of **derived tables** (*see Section 18.8 ALLOCATE DESCRIPTOR*). Note that in some cases values are not allowed to be missing; e.g. in **primary keys** none of the participating **columns** in the key may assume the null status.

Module A module has a name, is specified for a **host language** and has one or more **procedures**. A module may be associated with zero, one or more compilation units, each calling only one such module. An **application program** can consist of many compilation units (*see Chapter 16 The Module*

Language). An alternative to the module language is an **embedded language**.

Normalization Normalization is a process described by E.F. Codd with the purpose of giving (unnormalized) data structure a more regular form. A data structure in a (sufficiently) normalized form allows the **DBMS** to maintain the **consistency** of the data in the supporting database using a limited set of **DML** commands, typically INSERT, UPDATE, SELECT and DELETE. For a description of the steps in the normalization process (*see Section 21.2 Database and Application Analysis Issues*).

Null Null is a concept in SQL that reflects missing information. Null is not really a value but more of a status, indicating that a value is not present. We can specify for each column whether we would allow missing information or not (*see Section 4.2.1.2.1 NOT NULL*). We may also want to distinguish between various reasons for not providing a value (*see Chapter 24 Handling Missing Information*). In other cases there must always be a (valid) value. These cases include **primary keys**, **candidate keys** or columns that always need a value (also called mandatory fields) though they are not necessarily unique (*see Appendix A The Example Database*). A separate but useful concept is **defaults**.

Outer reference A reference to a column outside the current **table expression**. Table expressions can be nested within one another and any reference to a column of a table whose scope is wider than the current table expression is called an outer reference. The outer reference is thus always in an expression lower in the nesting hierarchy than the table referenced.

Parameter A parameter is a construct allowing information to pass between a caller and the called. In the SQL context the caller is an **application program** (compilation unit) and the called is a **procedure** of a **module** (*see Chapter 16 The Module Language, specifically Section 16.4 Parameters for the Definition, Section 16.5 A Complete Example*).

Predicate A <predicate> is a simple statement which can be true, false or sometimes unknown. The available predicates are: comparison, between, like, null, in, quantified comparison, overlaps, match, exists and Unique (*see Chapter 10 Predicates and Search Conditions*). Examples of predicates can be found throughout the book (*see Section 23.2 A Taxonomy of Time for between and overlaps predicates, Section 26.2 Limiting Access to Data for exists predicate*). Note that a predicate is a very powerful concept since being used in a **search condition** it can specify a <table **subquery**> which is the new start of an SQL query.

Predicate logic Predicate logic is a formal (mathematical) language sufficient to describe the behaviour of a **Universe of Discourse**. Not only the semantics need to be captured but also the syntax needed to communicate with computer systems. SQL allows the specification of **SQL statements** in predicate logic format. Predicate logic is based on the uttering of **predicates** and maintaining truth. See also **integrity**.

Prenex normal form Prenex normal form is a query notation that makes the mechanical execution of transformation rules easier. Since SQL does not support the universal ($\forall$) quantifier, we need rewrite rules. These are easier to apply when the query is in prenex normal form (*see Section 25.5.4 Prenex Normal Form Translation Rules*).

Primary key The primary key is the **candidate key** promoted to be the main key for the **table**. The choice of the primary key is made from among the candidate keys. This choice may, in some circumstances, be arbitrary. On the one hand the DBMS implementation would like to see a kind of cryptic — perhaps internally assigned — sequence number as the primary key with the assumption that the value of this key would never change and so be an ideal object for foreign keys of associated tables. Keys of this type are called surrogates. On the other hand we would like the user of the system to be able to remember the key value easily for simple access to the rows of a table. In that case the value of the primary key may change and needs a referential action — cascading on update — for associated tables. For an example of cascade on update *see Section 4.2.2.2 References*. In the Itinerary table in our example database we have a choice of two candidates for the primary key (*see Section 22.4 Referential Integrity and Section 22.6.2 Binary 0 or 1 : 1*).

Privilege A privilege is the right to perform a specific action (INSERT, UPDATE, DELETE, SELECT, REFERENCE, USAGE) on an object (domain, table, column, character set, collation or translation).

Privilege descriptor A privilege descriptor describes who has provided whom with the privilege of performing a specific action on a specific object, with or without the ability to grant the same privilege to others. These descriptors are stored in the catalog and form the basis for access control in SQL (*see Section 8 Access Control*).

Procedure A procedure is part of a **module** and contains an **SQL statement**. The procedure may be called from a **host language** where information to and from calling modules is exchanged via **parameters**.

Production A production is the transformation of a BNF definition leading to a character string if iteratively repeated (*see Section B.3 The Substitution Process*).

Quantifier The quantifiers 'For All' ($\forall$) and 'There Exists' ($\exists$) are available in relational calculus. SQL has an explicit language construct for 'There Exists' in the form of the exists predicate, but for 'For All' we need a transformation into the exists predicate. An overview of rules for such a transformation is given in *Section 25.5.4 Prenex Normal Form Translation Rules*.

Query expression A query expression is the basic way of defining a **derived table** from the **database**. From this starting point we can declare **views**, **cursors** and **subqueries**. We can specify **set operators** (like JOINs of various kinds, a UNION or EXCEPT or an INTERSECT) or specify a **query specification**.

Query specification A query specification is basically the SELECT clause plus the list of selected columns (directly from tables specified in the FROM clause or otherwise derived) followed by a **table expression**.

Referenced table When specifying a **referential integrity** constraint the table name in the references clause is the referenced table. **Referential integrity** is implemented by including a **foreign key** in the referencing table which relates a row in the referencing table to a row in the referenced table. Note that the match predicate is a form of temporary referential integrity where the <table subquery> behind the key word MATCH designates the referenced table (*see Section 4.2.2.2 References*).

Referencing table When specifying a **referential integrity** constraint as part of a column **constraint** or a table **constraint** the table for which the references clause is specified is the referencing table. **Referential integrity** is implemented by including a **foreign key** in the referencing table which relates a row in the referencing table to a row in the referenced table. Note that the match predicate is a form of temporary referential integrity where the <row value constructor> before the key word MATCH designates the referencing table (*see Section 4.2.2.2 References*).

Referential action A referential action (and triggered action and referential triggered action) is specified in a references clause in **schema definition**. Upon update or delete of a row of the **referenced table** all eligible rows in the **referencing table** will undergo the referential action. This may be **CASCADE** the update or delete action, SET **NULL** or SET **DEFAULT**.

Referential integrity Referential integrity is the functionality in SQL supporting relationships among (rows of) **referencing tables** and **referenced tables**. The References clauses in the column and table allow the specification of referential integrity constraints and the MATCH predicate offers temporary referential integrity. For column and table constraints containing the references clause *see Chapter 4 Data Definition* and *Chapter 22 Integrity Control*.

Relationship A relationship is an association between two **entities** (*see Section 2.7 Conventions Used*). The relationship is represented as a line connecting the two entities in a data structure diagram and with various arrowheads to highlight some aspects of the relationship, such as optionality and cardinality. A relationship formed in the conceptual phase of a **systems development life cycle** will need to be translated into an SQL construct (*see Chapter 22 Integrity Control*).

Row A row is the representation of a single fact, event, thing (i.e. **entity**) in the **Universe of Discourse**. It is the horizontal subdivision of a **table**. See also **column**. Employee Patel is represented as a single row in the Employee table in our Company database (*see Appendix A The Example Database*); for some examples of employee Patel *see Section 2.5.1 Table and Section 24.5 More than Three-Valued Logic*.

Schema The schema is the collection of SQL objects (tables, views, domains, etc.) that are in some way related to one another. All the objects in the database are described in one schema or another (*see Section 2.5.2 Schema*).

Schema manipulation SQL offers the capability of modifying the existing definition of a schema. Objects (such as table, view, domain, etc.) may be added, dropped or modified (*see Chapter 5 Schema Manipulation*).

SDLC See **systems development life cycle**.

Search condition A search condition is a statement or group of statements joined together by boolean operators resulting in a true, false or unknown condition (*see Section 10.1 Search Conditions*). Such search conditions are used in the WHERE and HAVING clauses of **data manipulation** statements or specify the JOIN condition (*see Section 25.3.4 Flat Versus Nested SQL Queries*). Search conditions may also appear in **data definition** statements in **check** clauses (*see Section 4.2.2.3 Check*), **assertion** checks (*see Section 20.1.3 The Assertions*) and **view** definitions (*see Section 26.2 Limiting Access to Data*) to select desired rows from the database. A powerful construct to be used in search conditions are **predicates**, which allow an array of options for validating or evaluating database content.

Server A server can be seen like an engine providing some service. A client calls the server, resulting in the service being performed. See also **client** and **session**.

Session A session is a connection between an application program in an SQL **client** and an SQL **server** (*see Chapter 14 Session Management*).

Set function A set function is an operation on a set of values in a column of a table or all values from a column in a group of rows in a table. Apart from the COUNT(*) all other set functions will ignore the null status but will return a warning if any such nulls are ignored. Set functions are: COUNT, AVG, MAX, MIN, SUM (*see Section 11.4 Set Functions*).

Set operator A set operator takes two sets of rows and produces a resulting table. The set operators in SQL are UNION, EXCEPT (difference), INTERSECT and JOIN. SQL does not support DIVIDE directly but using the NOT EXISTS predicate the DIVIDE set operator can be simulated. For further explanation and details *see Section 9.3.2 Set Operators*.

SQL control SQL control statements are a group of statements including Access Control, Transaction Management, Environment Management,

Session Management, Error Handling and Diagnostics, Dynamic SQL (*see similarly named chapters for more information*).

SQL statement SQL statements can be categorized as **data manipulation**, **data definition** or **SQL control** statements.

SQLSTATE SQLSTATE is one of the status parameters in SQL. The other is SQLCODE which is no longer recommended. Every SQL procedure call must provide a status parameter to obtain error and warning statuses which are all defined in the SQL standard including the values exchanged. Implementor defined codes are catered for as distinctly separate (*see Section 15.3 SQLSTATE*).

Static SQL Static SQL are SQL statements that are known at the program specification time. The implementor can check syntax and a fair amount of the semantics at preprocessing or compilation time of the **application program**. See also **dynamic SQL**.

Subquery A subquery is primarily specified in **predicates** to search the database for values. A subquery is essentially a nested **query expression**, so the next level of query starts.

Systems development life cycle A systems development life cycle (SDLC) is a phased approach to systems development in which the data and activities in the **Universe of Discourse** are modelled into **data structure diagrams** and activity structure diagrams. During the various phases of the SDLC we progress from a complete but abstract representation in the conceptual phase (**entities**, **attributes** and **relationships** to express data-related concepts) to a very concrete representation in the logical and physical design phases (**tables**, **rows**, **columns**, **domains**, index structures, files) leading to the actual **database** on disk. The conceptual phase highlights which data we are interested in and how we want it structured for our **application**. The logical design introduces the particular **data model** that the target **DBMS** belongs to and the physical design allows representation of the more performance-related features.

Table A table is a very basic and important concept of SQL. You can think of it as a rectangular sheet with **columns** and **rows**. Each intersection (cell) can contain a value, represented by a **literal**, or can have the status **null**.

Table expression The table expression forms the second part of a **query expression** following on from the **query specification**. It contains the FROM clause and the optional WHERE, GROUP BY and HAVING clauses. These clauses themselves are constructed using lower level construct. The FROM clause uses **table reference**s.

Table reference A table reference specifies a **table** reference of one or the other kind. Examples are **base tables**, **views**, **derived tables** from **subqueries**. A table reference basically specifies table name, an optional correlation name (like a local variable) and optional derived column list which allows renaming of the columns in the table referenced.

Temporary table SQL supports the creation of global and local temporary tables (*see Section 4.2 CREATE TABLE*). These tables are effectively materialized when referenced in a **session**. Every module in every session that references a local temporary table causes a distinct instance to be materialized which cannot be shared between sessions or even modules in the same session (*see also Section 16.2 DECLARE LOCAL TEMPORARY TABLE*). Any module in every session that references a global temporary table causes a distinct instance to be materialized, which is then shared between all modules of the same session. See also **base table**, **view** and **derived table**.

Time zone A time zone is the concept of shifting time backwards or forwards with a specified number of hours and minutes for all modules and transactions in the session executing the SET TIME ZONE command. This command is described in *Section 13.6 SET LOCAL TIME ZONE*, and is part of the SQL control statements. For an example of handling time zones *see Section 23.3 Time Zones.*

Transaction A transaction is a unit of work as specified by an **application program** through SQL commands (COMMIT, ROLLBACK, SET TRANSACTION). The purpose of a transaction is to combine a sequence of operations, including SQL **data definition** and/or **data manipulation** statements into a single unit which is atomic with respect to recovery (*see Chapter 12 Transaction Management*). The specification of such units of work by the application allows the **DBMS** to organize concurrency control and recovery and makes it possible for the **application** to maintain the contents of the database in a **consistent** state.

Translation Translation is a character **function** offering the capability to translate characters from one **character set** into another character set. Note that TRANSLATE is a logical character replacement and different from CONVERT which is concerned with mapping from one to another physical representation of characters (*see Section 11.2.3.5 TRANSLATE and Section 11.2.3.6 CONVERT*).

Triggered action A triggered action can be specified when we define a referential constraint for a column (*see Section 4.2.1.2.3 References*) or for a table (*see Section 4.2.2.2 References*). See also **referential action** and **cascade**.

Universe of Discourse The Universe of Discourse is the part of the 'real world' that we consider to be within the scope of an **information system**.

Unique key A unique specification for a column means that the **DBMS** must ensure that, for each row in the table, that column has a distinct and unique value, i.e. no **duplicates** are allowed. The uniqueness may be specified for an individual column (*see Section 4.2.1.2.2 Unique*) or for a group of columns in a table (*see Section 4.2.2 Table Constraints*). Such a set of columns is named a **candidate key** or a **primary key** if NOT **NULL** has also been specified. Note that many implementations require a specific storage or access mechanism (typically an index) for unique constraints. This falls outside the scope of the SQL standard.

Value expression A value expression is a construct returning a single value. Examples of value expressions are column references, **literals**, a **parameter** or variable, a **set function**, a **function** or a **conditional value expression**.

View A view is basically a table. A view is not a physical or **base table** but a named **derived table** defined in terms of a query expression on one or more base tables or, recursively, on views (*see Section 4.4 CREATE VIEW*). Unlike other derived tables, **query expressions** and **search conditions**, a view definition is a permanent object to which **privileges** are associated. The data specified by a view definition, however, may not exist as a separate, persistent storage structure but is generated from the underlying permanent base tables.

H

References

ANSI/X3/SPARC Study Group on Data Base Management Systems (1975) Interim Report, *FDT (Bulletin of ACM SIGMOD)*, 7(2).

BCS/CODASYL Data Base Administration Working Group (1981) CODASYL Data Description Language Committee, Journal of Development 1981, Appendix A.

BCS/CODASYL Data Base Administration Working Group Draft (1987) SQL Data Storage Description Language, BCS report DBAWG–SP–24, January (unpublished, available from BCS).

Ceri, Stefano and Giuseppe Pelagatti (1988) *Distributed Databases, Principles and Systems*, McGraw-Hill International Editions, New York.

Chang, C.L. and R.C.T. Lee (1973) *Symbolic Logic and Mechanical Theorem Proving*, Academic Press, San Diego.

Codd, E.F. (1970) 'A relational model for large shared data banks', *Communications of the ACM*, 13(6), June.

Codd, E.F. (1986) 'Missing information (applicable and inapplicable) in relational databases', *SIGMOD RECORD*, 15(4), December, 53–78.

Codd, E.F. (1987) 'More commentary on missing information in relational databases (applicable and inapplicable)', *SIGMOD RECORD*, 16(1), March.

Coulouris, G.F. and J. Dollimore (1988) *Distributed Systems: Concepts and Design*, Addison-Wesley, Wokingham.

Date, C.J. (1985) *An Introduction to Database Systems*, vol. II, Addison-Wesley, Reading, Mass.

Date, C.J. (1986a) *Relational Databases: Selected Writings*, Addison-Wesley, Reading, Mass.

Date, C.J. (1986b) *An Introduction to Database Systems*, vol. I, 4th edn, Addison-Wesley, Reading, Mass.

Date, C.J. (1987a) *A Guide to the SQL Standard*, Addison-Wesley, Reading, Mass.

Date, C.J. (1987b) 'What is a Distributed Database System? Parts I and II', *The Relational Journal*, 1(1 and 2), June and October.

de Jonge, W., W. Schoemaker, J. Bruijning and G.A.M. Otten (1988) 'Het formuleren van opdrachten in een relationele vraagtaal', *Informatie*, 6, 407–416.

Eswaran, K.P., J.N. Gray, R.A. Lorie and I.L. Traiger (1976) 'The notions of consistency and predicate locks in a database system', *Communications of the ACM*, 19(11), November, 624–633.

Gamut, L.T.F. (1982) *Logica, Taal en Betekenis*, 2 volumes, Het Spectrum, Utrecht.

Gessert, G.H. (1990) 'Four valued logic for relational database systems', *SIGMOD RECORD*, 19(1), March, 29–35.

Gray, Jim (1981) 'The transaction concept: virtues and limitations', Proceedings 7th International Conference on Very Large Data Bases, September, Cannes, France, Computer Society Press/IEEE, Los Angeles, Ca.

Gretton-Watson, P. (1988) 'Distributed Database Development', *Computer Communications*, 11(5), October, 275–280.

ISO 9075:1987(E) (1987) *Database Language SQL*, The International Organization for Standardization.

ISO 9075:1989(E) (1989) *Database Language SQL*, The International Organization for Standardization.

ISO 9075:1992(E) (1992a) *Database Language SQL*, The International Organization for Standardization.

ISO DIS 10032:1992(E) (1992b) *The Reference Model for Data Management*, The International Organization for Standardization.

Kent, William (1983) 'A simple guide to five normal forms in relational database theory', *Communications of the ACM*, 26(2), February, 120–125.

Kocharekar, Raju (1989) 'Nulls in Relational Databases — Revisited', *SIGMOD RECORD*, 18(1), March, 68–73.

NGI (1990) 'DatabaseClub NGI — Werkgroep DDBMS gedistribueerde databases: concept, mythe en werkelijkheid', Stichting Informatica Congressen NGI, Amsterdam.

Remmen, F. (1985) 'Hoe vriendelijk zijn vraagtalen in het gebruik?', *Informatie*, 7/8, 666–673.

Rock-Evans, R. (ed.) (1987a) *State of the Art Report No 15/1 on Analyst Workbenches*, Pergamon Infotech Ltd, Maidenhead.

Rock-Evans, R. (1987b) *Analysis within the Systems Development Life Cycle*, 4 volumes, Pergamon Infotech Ltd, Maidenhead.

Rock-Evans, R. (1989) *A Simple Introduction to Data and Activity Analysis*, Computer Weekly Publications, Sutton.

Sarda, N.L. (1990) 'Algebra and query language for a historical data model', *Computer Journal*, 33(1), 11–18.

Snodgrass, R. (1989) 'Correspondence from R. Snodgrass', *SIGMOD Record*, 18(3), September, 102–103.

Snodgrass, R. and I. Ahn (1985) 'A taxonomy of time in databases', Proceedings of ACM SIGMOD International Conference on Management of Data, May, Austin, Texas, ACM, New York.

Stonebraker, Michael (1989) 'The case for partial indexes', *SIGMOD Record*, 18(4), December, 4–11.

Wiederhold, G. (1977) *Database Design*, McGraw-Hill Kogakusha Ltd, Tokyo.

Zachman, J.A. (1987) 'A framework for information systems architecture', *IBM Systems Journal*, 26(3).

I

Analytical Table of Contents

1 Introduction **3**

1.1 What is SQL? 3
1.2 The History of SQL 4
1.3 Why a Standard? 5
1.4 The Standardization Process 6
1.5 The Importance of SQL 8
1.6 How to Read this Book 9
1.6.1 The Structure of the Book 9
1.6.1.1 Introduction 9
1.6.1.2 The SQL Language 9
1.6.1.3 Using the SQL Language 11
1.6.1.4 Appendices 11
1.6.2 Access Mechanisms 11

2 Some Basic Concepts **15**
2.1 Environment 16
2.2 Information System 16
2.3 Database Management System 16
2.4 Database 16
2.5 Database Definition 17
2.5.1 Table 17
2.5.2 Schema 20
2.5.3 Catalog 20
2.6 Database Manipulation 21
2.7 Conventions Used 21

3 Basic Language Elements **27**
3.1 Characters 27
3.2 Tokens 28
3.3 Identifiers 29
3.4 Names 31
3.5 Literals 33
3.6 Values and Targets 33
3.7 Data Types 34
3.7.1 The Character Data Type 34
3.7.2 Character Literals 36
3.7.3 The Bit Data Type 37
3.7.4 Bit String Literals 38
3.7.5 The Exact Numeric Data Type 38
3.7.6 Exact Numeric Literals 39
3.7.7 The Approximate Numeric Data Type 40
3.7.8 Approximate Numeric Literals 41
3.7.9 The Datetime Data Type 41
3.7.10 Datetime Literals 43
3.7.11 The Interval Data Type 44
3.7.12 Interval Literals 46

4 Data Definition **49**
4.1 CREATE SCHEMA 49
4.1.1 Authorization 50
4.1.2 Schema Default Character Set 50
4.1.3 Schema Elements 51
4.2 CREATE TABLE 52
4.2.1 Column Definition 55
4.2.1.1 Defaults 55
4.2.1.2 Column Constraints 56
4.2.1.3 Collation 60
4.2.2 Table Constraints 60
4.2.2.1 Unique 61
4.2.2.2 References 62
4.2.2.3 Check 65
4.3 CREATE DOMAIN 66
4.3.1 Defaults 67
4.3.2 Collation 68
4.3.3 Domain Constraints 68
4.4 CREATE VIEW 68
4.5 CREATE ASSERTION 70
4.6 CREATE CHARACTER SET 71
4.7 CREATE COLLATION 72
4.8 CREATE TRANSLATION 75

5 Schema Manipulation **77**
5.1 The DROP Statements 77
5.1.1 DROP SCHEMA 78
5.1.2 DROP DOMAIN 79
5.1.3 DROP TABLE 81
5.1.4 DROP ASSERTION 81
5.1.5 DROP VIEW 82
5.1.6 DROP COLLATION 82
5.1.7 DROP TRANSLATION 83
5.1.8 DROP CHARACTER SET 84
5.2 The ALTER Statements 84
5.2.1 ALTER DOMAIN 84
5.2.1.1 Set Domain Default 85
5.2.1.2 Drop Domain Default 85
5.2.1.3 Add Domain Constraint 86
5.2.1.4 Drop Domain Constraint 86
5.2.2 ALTER TABLE 87
5.2.2.1 Add Column 87
5.2.2.2 Drop Column 87
5.2.2.3 Add Table Constraint 88
5.2.2.4 Drop Table Constraint 89
5.2.2.5 Set Column Default 89
5.2.2.6 Drop Column Default 90

6 Non-Cursor Operations **91**
6.1 INSERT 91
6.2 Single Row SELECT 93
6.3 UPDATE Searched 93
6.4 DELETE Searched 95
6.5 Data Assignment Rules 96
6.5.1 Retrieval Assignment 96
6.5.2 Store Assignment 96

7 Cursor Operations **99**
7.1 DECLARE CURSOR 101
7.2 OPEN 104
7.3 FETCH 104
7.4 UPDATE Positioned 105
7.5 DELETE Positioned 108
7.6 CLOSE 109

8 Access Control **111**
8.1 GRANT 113
8.2 REVOKE 116
8.3 Ripple Effects of the GRANT Statement 117
8.4 Cascade Effects of the REVOKE Statement 117
8.5 Checking the Privileges 119

9 Derived Tables **121**
9.1 Row Value Constructors 121
9.2 Table Value Constructors 122
9.3 Query Expression 122
9.3.1 Table References 125
9.3.2 Set Operators 126
9.3.2.1 UNION 126
9.3.2.2 EXCEPT 128
9.3.2.3 INTERSECT 129
9.3.2.4 JOIN 130
9.3.2.5 DIVIDE — the missing option 137
9.3.3 Set Operations Result Data Types 137
9.4 Table Expression 138
9.4.1 FROM 139
9.4.2 WHERE 139
9.4.3 GROUP BY 140
9.4.4 HAVING 141
9.5 Query Specification 141
9.6 Subqueries 144

10 Predicates and Search Conditions **145**
10.1 Search Conditions 145
10.2 Predicates 147
10.2.1 Comparison Predicate 147
10.2.2 Between Predicate 150
10.2.3 Like Predicate 150
10.2.4 Null Predicate 151
10.2.5 In Predicate 152
10.2.6 Quantified Comparison Predicate 153
10.2.7 Overlaps Predicate 154
10.2.8 Match Predicate 155
10.2.9 Exists Predicate 156
10.2.10 Unique Predicate 157

11 Functions and Expressions **159**
11.1 Value Expressions 159
11.1.1 Numeric Value Expressions 160
11.1.2 String Value Expressions 161
11.1.3 Datetime Value Expressions 162
11.1.4 Interval Value Expressions 164
11.2 Scalar Functions 165
11.2.1 Datetime Functions 165
11.2.1.1 CURRENT_DATE 165
11.2.1.2 CURRENT_TIME 166
11.2.1.3 CURRENT_TIMESTAMP 166
11.2.1.4 EXTRACT 166
11.2.2 String Functions 167
11.2.2.1 SUBSTRING 167
11.2.2.2 CHARACTER_LENGTH 168
11.2.2.3 OCTET_LENGTH 169
11.2.2.4 BIT_LENGTH 169
11.2.3 Character Functions 169
11.2.3.1 POSITION 169
11.2.3.2 TRIM 170
11.2.3.3 UPPER 170
11.2.3.4 LOWER 171
11.2.3.5 TRANSLATE 171
11.2.3.6 CONVERT 172
11.2.4 CAST 172
11.3 Conditional Value Expressions 176
11.3.1 CASE 176
11.3.2 NULLIF 177
11.3.3 COALESCE 177
11.4 Set Functions 178
11.4.1 COUNT 179
11.4.2 AVG 179
11.4.3 MIN 179
11.4.4 MAX 179
11.4.5 SUM 180

12 Transaction Management **181**
12.1 Some Basic Concepts 181
12.1.1 Transaction 181
12.1.2 Atomicity 182
12.1.3 Recovery 183
12.1.4 Concurrency 183
12.1.5 Serializability 184
12.2 Initiating a Transaction 184
12.3 Control Statements in SQL 185
12.3.1 The COMMIT Statement 185

12.3.2 The ROLLBACK Statement 186
12.3.3 The SET TRANSACTION Statement 186

13 Environment Management **189**
13.1 SET CATALOG 189
13.2 SET SCHEMA 190
13.3 SET NAMES 190
13.4 SET SESSION AUTHORIZATION 191
13.5 SET CONSTRAINTS MODE 191
13.6 SET TIME ZONE 192

14 Session Management **195**
14.1 CONNECT 196
14.2 SET CONNECTION 197
14.3 DISCONNECT 197

15 Error Handling and Diagnostics **199**
15.1 The GET DIAGNOSTICS Command 200
15.2 Diagnostic Area 200
15.3 SQLSTATE 204
15.4 SQLSTATE Codes 205
15.5 Whatever Happened to SQLCODE? 208

16 The Module Language **209**
16.1 Modules 210
16.2 DECLARE LOCAL TEMPORARY TABLE 211
16.3 Procedures 212
16.4 Parameters 214
16.5 A Complete Example 218

17 The Embedded Languages **221**
17.1 The Supported Languages 223
17.1.1 Ada 223
17.1.2 C 224
17.1.3 COBOL 225
17.1.4 FORTRAN 226
17.1.5 MUMPS 226
17.1.6 Pascal 226
17.1.7 PL/I 227
17.2 Exception Control 227
17.3 Inserting SQL Commands into the Host Language 228
17.4 A Complete Example 229

18 Dynamic SQL **233**
18.1 Why Dynamic SQL? 233
18.2 The Basic Structure of Dynamic SQL 234
18.3 EXECUTE IMMEDIATE 235
18.4 PREPARE 235
18.5 DEALLOCATE PREPARE 237
18.6 DESCRIBE 237
18.7 USING 238
18.8 ALLOCATE DESCRIPTOR 239
18.9 DEALLOCATE DESCRIPTOR 243
18.10 GET DESCRIPTOR 244
18.11 SET DESCRIPTOR 245
18.12 EXECUTE 247
18.13 Dynamic DECLARE CURSOR 247
18.14 Dynamic ALLOCATE CURSOR 247
18.15 Dynamic OPEN CURSOR 248
18.16 Dynamic CLOSE CURSOR 248
18.17 Dynamic FETCH CURSOR 249
18.18 Dynamic DELETE Positioned 249
18.19 Dynamic UPDATE Positioned 249
18.20 Preparable Dynamic DELETE Positioned 250
18.21 Preparable Dynamic UPDATE Positioned 250
18.22 A Complete Example 250

19 Direct Invocation of SQL **255**
19.1 Permitted Statements 256
19.2 Direct Select : Multiple Rows 256

20 The Information Schema **257**
20.1 The Definition Schema 258
20.1.1 The Domains 260
20.1.2 The Tables 260
20.1.2.1 USERS 260
20.1.2.2 SCHEMATA 260
20.1.2.3 DATA_TYPE_DESCRIPTOR 261
20.1.2.4 DOMAINS 262
20.1.2.5 DOMAIN_CONSTRAINTS 263
20.1.2.6 TABLES 263
20.1.2.7 VIEWS 264
20.1.2.8 COLUMNS 265
20.1.2.9 VIEW_TABLE_USAGE 266
20.1.2.10 VIEW_COLUMN_USAGE 266
20.1.2.11 TABLE_CONSTRAINTS 266
20.1.2.12 KEY_COLUMN_USAGE 268
20.1.2.13 REFERENTIAL_CONSTRAINTS 269
20.1.2.14 CHECK_CONSTRAINTS 270

20.1.2.15	CHECK_TABLE_USAGE	270
20.1.2.16	CHECK_COLUMN_USAGE	271
20.1.2.17	ASSERTIONS	271
20.1.2.18	TABLE_PRIVILEGES	272
20.1.2.19	COLUMN_PRIVILEGES	272
20.1.2.20	USAGE_PRIVILEGES	273
20.1.2.21	CHARACTER_SETS	274
20.1.2.22	COLLATIONS	275
20.1.2.23	TRANSLATIONS	276
20.1.2.24	SQL_LANGUAGES	277
20.1.3	The Assertions	278
20.1.3.1	UNIQUE_CONSTRAINT_NAME	278
20.1.3.2	EQUAL_KEY_DEGREES	278
20.1.3.3	KEY_DEGREE_GREATER_THAN_OR_EQUAL_TO_1	279
20.2	The Information Schema	279
20.2.1	The Domains	280
20.2.1.1	SQL_IDENTIFIER	280
20.2.1.2	CARDINAL_NUMBER	280
20.2.1.3	CHARACTER_DATA	281
20.2.2	INFORMATION_SCHEMA_CATALOG_NAME	281
20.2.3	SCHEMATA	281
20.2.4	DOMAINS	281
20.2.5	DOMAIN_CONSTRAINTS	282
20.2.6	TABLES	283
20.2.7	VIEWS	283
20.2.8	COLUMNS	284
20.2.9	TABLE_PRIVILEGES	285
20.2.10	COLUMN_PRIVILEGES	286
20.2.11	USAGE_PRIVILEGES	286
20.2.12	TABLE_CONSTRAINTS	287
20.2.13	REFERENTIAL_CONSTRAINTS	287
20.2.14	CHECK_CONSTRAINTS	287
20.2.15	KEY_COLUMN_USAGE	288
20.2.16	ASSERTIONS	288
20.2.17	CHARACTER_SETS	289
20.2.18	COLLATIONS	289
20.2.19	TRANSLATIONS	290
20.2.20	VIEW_TABLE_USAGE	290
20.2.21	VIEW_COLUMN_USAGE	290
20.2.22	CONSTRAINT_TABLE_USAGE	291
20.2.23	CONSTRAINT_COLUMN_USAGE	292
20.2.24	COLUMN_DOMAIN_USAGE	292
20.2.25	SQL_LANGUAGES	293
20.2.26	INFORMATION_SCHEMA_CATALOG_NAME_ CARDINALITY	293
20.3	Extracting the Information	293

21 Database and Application Analysis **297**
21.1 From Conceptual to Physical Using Data and Function 298
21.2 Database and Application Analysis Issues 298
21.3 Correctness Aspects 304
21.4 Security Aspects 307
21.5 Current Trends 308
21.5.1 Batch versus On-line 308
21.5.2 Historic Data Handling 308
21.5.3 Client–Server Concepts 310
21.6 Data Driven Programming 311
21.6.1 Help Modules 311
21.6.2 Menu Screen Options 312
21.6.3 Error Handling 312

22 Integrity Control **313**
22.1 Definition 313
22.2 Domain Integrity 314
22.3 Entity Integrity 316
22.4 Referential Integrity 317
22.4.1 The MATCH Option 319
22.5 User Integrity 320
22.6 The Implementation of Relationships — Examples 323
22.6.1 Binary 1 : 1 324
22.6.2 Binary 0 or 1 : 1 326
22.6.3 Binary 0 or 1 : 0 or 1 327
22.6.4 Binary 1 : *n* 329
22.6.5 Binary 0 or 1 : *n* 330
22.6.6 Binary 1 : 0 or *n* 331
22.6.7 Binary 0 or 1 : 0 or *n* 332
22.6.8 Binary *m* : *n* 333
22.6.9 Binary 0 or *m* : *n* 335
22.6.10 Binary 0 or *m* : 0 or *n* 337
22.6.11 Additional Cardinality Constraints 338
22.6.12 Unary Relationships 339
22.7 Combinations of Relationships 340
22.7.1 Exclusivity 341
22.7.2 Inclusivity 343
22.7.3 Mutual Dependency 344
22.8 Management 345
22.8.1 Problems with Loops 345
22.8.2 Triggered Actions 347

23 Using the Datetime Facilities **351**
23.1 Basic Facilities 351
23.2 A Taxonomy of Time 352
23.3 Time Zones 365

24 Handling Missing Information **369**
24.1 Missing: Applicable and Inapplicable Markings 370
24.2 SQL and Three-Valued Logic 370
24.2.1 Comparisons with Unknown Markings in Search Expressions 371
24.3 Predicates and Missing Information 373
24.4 Set Functions and Missing Information 373
24.5 More Than Three-Valued Logic 374
24.6 Tautological and Absurd Queries 376
24.7 DEFAULT <literal> or CASE for NULL 377
24.8 Replace NULL by Value Always 379

25 Translating Natural Language Queries **381**
25.1 The Steps in the Query Formulation Method 381
25.1.1 Step 1: Interpret 383
25.1.2 Step 2: Shape 384
25.1.3 Step 3: Formalize 384
25.1.4 Step 4: Generate 385
25.2 A Query Transformation Example 385
25.2.1 Interpreting the Question 385
25.2.2 Shaping the Question into Business Language 386
25.2.3 Formalize the Syntax 389
25.2.4 Generating the SQL Query 390
25.3 General Remarks 391
25.3.1 The Chosen Steps 391
25.3.2 Macro Facilities 391
25.3.3 Rewrite Rules for Obtaining Prenex Normal Form 392
25.3.4 Flat Versus Nested SQL Queries 393
25.3.5 Aliasing 394
25.3.6 Top-Down Versus Bottom-Up 395
25.4 Background Information 395
25.4.1 Database Schema DDL 396
25.4.2 Data Structure Diagram 397
25.4.3 Some Additional Questions to Try 398
25.5 Additional Information for Natural Language Translation 398
25.5.1 Truth Tables and Boolean Logic 398
25.5.2 Truth Tables for Boolean Expressions 398
25.5.3 Boolean Transformation Rules 399
25.5.4 Prenex Normal Form Translation Rules 400

26 Usage of Views **403**
26.1 Enhancing Accessibility and User Access 403
26.1.1 Structure Simplification 404
26.1.2 Making only Relevant Parts of the Database Visible 405
26.1.3 Derivation Support 406
26.2 Limiting Access to Data 407

26.3 Mapping to Host Language Conventions 409
26.4 Enhanced Physical Environment Support 409
26.4.1 Physical Data Independence 410
26.4.2 Reduction of Dataflow 410
26.5 Using the WITH CHECK Options 410
26.6 Conclusions on Views 413

27 Distributed Databases **415**
27.1 Definition of Terms in Distributed Databases 416
27.2 A Four-Step Method for Data Distribution 418
27.2.1 Global Distributed Data Processing 418
27.2.2 Fragmentation of Portions of Data 419
27.2.2.1 Horizontal Fragmentation 421
27.2.2.2 Vertical Fragmentation 424
27.2.2.3 Combined Horizontal and Vertical Fragmentation 425
27.2.3 Allocation of Fragments of Data 428
27.2.4 Local Data Processing 429
27.3 A Worked Example 430
27.3.1 Fragmenting and Allocation 430
27.3.2 Locating the Data 433
27.3.3 The SQL Coding for the Operation 434

28 Performance Aspects **437**
28.1 Physical Data and Application Design Approach 439
28.2 Disk Access Structures 442
28.3 Disk Storage and Main Memory Organization 446
28.4 Query Access Planning 448

A The Example Database **453**

B BNF Syntax Notation **467**
B.1 Introduction and Purpose 467
B.2 Symbols 467
B.3 The Substitution Process 468

C BNF Syntax Diagrams **471**

D Key Words **531**
D.1 Reserved Words 531
D.2 Non-reserved Words 533
D.3 Possible Future Reserved Words 534

E Levels and Conformance **535**
E.1 Levels 535
E.2 Conformance 536

F Differences between SQL-1992 and SQL-1989 **539**
F.1 Incompatibilities 539
F.2 New Features 540
F.3 Features Still to be Developed 541

G Glossary **543**

H References **561**

I Analytical Table of Contents **565**

Index **577**

Index

The syntax diagrams in Appendix C, the Glossary in Appendix G and the individual key words in Appendix D have not been indexed and in general only the first occurrence of a term within the same section has been indexed.

ABSOLUTE, 104
Access control, 17, 33, 111, 116, 211, 213, 236, 256, 307, 407
  checking privileges, 119
  granting privileges, 113
  revoking privileges, 116
Accuracy:
  definition of, 306, 314
Ada, 210, 215, 223, 277, 533
  host language variable definition, 223
  parameter data types, 216
  SQL_STANDARD package for, 214
ADD:
  column, 87
  domain constraint, 86
  table constraint, 88
ALL, 93, 123, 126, 128, 129, 141, 153, 178
ALLOCATE CURSOR, 247
ALLOCATE DESCRIPTOR, 239
ALTER
  domain, 84
AND, 145
  truth table for, 146
ANY, 153
Approximate numeric data types, 40
  literals, 41
ASC, 101
Assertion:
  CREATE, 70
  DROP, 79, 81
ASSERTIONS:
  base table, 271
  view, 288
AT, 163
Atomicity, 182
Authorization:
  current, 33, 56, 77, 91, 94, 95, 106, 108, 111, 119, 196, 200
  module, 33, 56, 119, 211
  schema, 50, 77, 111
  session, 33, 56, 191, 197, 211
AVG, 178, 179

Between predicate, 150
BIT, 37
Bit data types, 37
  literals, 38
BIT VARYING, 37
BIT_LENGTH, 160, 169

BNF notation, 467

C, 210, 215, 223
  host language variable definition, 224
  parameter data types, 216
Candidate key, 19
CARDINAL_NUMBER domain, 280
CASCADE, 63
CASE, 160, 176
CAST, 160, 172
Catalog:
  basic concept of, 20
CHAR, 36
CHARACTER, 35
CHARACTER_DATA domain, 281
Character data types, 34
  literals, 36
Character functions, 169–172
CHARACTER_LENGTH, 160, 168
Character set:
  CREATE, 71
  default for schema, 50
  DROP, 79, 84
Characters:
  used in SQL, 27
CHARACTER_SETS:
  base table, 274
  view, 289
CHARACTER VARYING, 35
CHECK, 60, 65, 70
CHECK_COLUMN_USAGE:
  base table, 271
Check constraint, 60, 65
CHECK_CONSTRAINTS:
  base table, 270
  view, 288
CHECK_TABLE_USAGE:
  base table, 270
CLOSE, 109
  dynamic, 248
COALESCE, 136, 177
COBOL, 210, 215, 223
  host language variable definition, 225
  parameter data types, 216
Coercibility, 73
COLLATE, 60, 68, 71, 161
COLLATION, 71
  column, 60
  CREATE, 72
  domain, 68
  DROP, 79, 82
  usage in character set definition, 71
COLLATIONS:
  base table, 275
  view, 289
Column:
  basic concept of, 18
  collation, 60
  constraints, 56–60
  defaults, 55
  definition of, 55, 87
  DROP, 87
COLUMN_DOMAIN_USAGE:
  view, 292
COLUMN_PRIVILEGES:
  base table, 273
  view, 286
COLUMNS:
  base table, 265
  view, 284
COMMAND_FUNCTION, 203
Comments, 28
COMMIT WORK, 185
Comparison:
  coercibility, 73
  compare equals, 148
  padding of character strings, 72
Comparison predicate, 147
Concatenation, 161, 162
Concurrency, 183
Conditional value expressions, 176
  CASE, 176
  COALESCE, 177
  NULLIF, 177
Conformance, 536
CONNECT, 196
Consistency:
  definition of, 305, 314
CONSTRAINT_COLUMN_USAGE:
  view, 292
Constraints:
  cardinality, 338
  check, 60, 65
  column, 56–60
  defer options, 57
  domain, 68, 86
  DROP, 86, 89
  foreign key, 59, 62
  management of loops, 345
  NOT NULL, 57
  primary key, 58
  set mode of, 191
  table, 60–62, 65, 88
  triggered actions, 62, 347
  unique, 58, 61
CONSTRAINT_TABLE_USAGE:
  view, 291
Context information, 196
CONTINUE, 228
CONVERT, 161, 172

Correlation names:
  usage of, 394
CORRESPONDING, 123
COUNT, 178, 179, 244
CREATE:
  assertion, 70
  character set, 71
  collation, 72
  domain, 66
  schema, 49
  table, 52
  translation, 75
  view, 68
CROSS, 131
CURRENT_DATE, 163, 165
CURRENT_TIME, 163, 166
CURRENT_TIMESTAMP, 163, 166
CURRENT_USER, 56
Cursor, 100
Cursors:
  close, 100, 109, 185, 186
  declare, 211
  declare cursor, 99, 101, 247
  delete, 100, 108
  dynamic allocate, 247
  fetch, 99, 104
  open, 99, 104
  order by, 101
  scroll, 102, 105
  sensitive, 101, 104
  updatability, 102
  update, 100, 105

Data assignment rules:
  retrieval, 96
  store, 96
Database:
  definition of, 16
  physical design, 439
Database management system:
  definition of, 16
Databases:
  indexes, 442
DATA_TYPE_DESCRIPTOR:
  base table, 261
Data types, 34
  approximate numeric, 40
  bit, 37
  casting to, 172
  character, 34
  codes for dynamic descriptors, 242
  datetime, 41
  exact numeric, 38
  interval, 44
  result of set operations, 137
DATE, 42
Datetime data types, 41
  literals, 43
  usage of, 352
Datetime functions, 165, 166
Datetime value expressions, 162, 164
DAY, 41, 44
DEALLOCATE DESCRIPTOR, 243
DEALLOCATE PREPARE, 237
DEC, 39
DECIMAL, 38
DECLARE CURSOR, 101
  dynamic, 247
Declared temporary table:
  name of, 32, 212
DECLARE LOCAL TEMPORARY
    TABLE, 211
DEFAULT, 56, 72, 93, 121, 196, 197
  use of, 377
Defaults:
  catalog name, 189, 190
  character set for dynamic and direct
    SQL, 190
  character set for module, 211
  collating sequence, 71
  column, 55, 89
  descriptor value, 246
  domain, 67, 85
  DROP, 85, 90
  inserting in rows, 91
  schema name, 190
  SQL_Server, 196
DEFAULT VALUES, 91
DEFERRED, 191
Definition schema, 258
DELETE:
  dynamic positioned, 249, 250
  positioned, 108
  searched, 95
DESC, 72, 101
DESCRIBE, 237
Descriptors:
  allocating, 239
  contents of, 240
  deallocating, 243
  default values for, 246
  extracting values from, 244
  filling, 237
  setting values in, 245
  using, 238
Diagnostics area:
  exception information, 202
  size, 199
  size of, 188
  statement information, 201

Diagnostics area:
  values of COMMAND_FUNCTION in, 203
Direct SQL:
  permitted statements, 256
DISCONNECT, 197
DISTINCT, 93, 141, 178
Distributed database:
  definition of, 416
Distributed databases:
  types of usage, 416
Domain:
  ALTER, 84
  basic concept of, 19
  casting to, 172
  collation, 68
  constraints, 68
  CREATE, 66
  defaults, 67
  DROP, 78, 79
  integrity of, 314
DOMAIN_CONSTRAINTS:
  base table, 263
  view, 282
DOMAINS:
  base table, 262
  view, 281
DOUBLE PRECISION, 40
DROP:
  assertion, 79, 81
  character set, 79, 84
  collation, 79, 82
  column, 87
  column default, 90
  domain, 78, 79
  domain constraint, 86
  domain default, 85
  options, 78
  schema, 78
  table, 78, 81
  table constraint, 89
  translation, 79, 83
  view, 78, 82
Dynamic SQL:
  necessity for, 233
  preparable statements, 236
  relationship of commands in, 234

ELSE, 176
Embedded languages, 221
  declaratives, 221
  exception handling, 227
  host language variables, 222
  prefixes and terminators for, 223
  supported languages, 223
Entry level, 535
Environment:
  definition of, 16
EQUAL_KEY_DEGREES assertion, 278
Error codes:
  SQLCODE, 208
  SQLSTATE, 205
ESCAPE, 150
Exact numeric data types, 38
  literals, 39
Examples (complete):
  dynamic SQL, 250
  embedded language, 229
  module language, 218
  schemata, 260, 280, 459
EXCEPT, 123, 128
Exception handling, 227
EXECUTE, 247
EXECUTE IMMEDIATE, 235
Exists predicate, 156
Extended names, 32
Extended Pascal, 223
EXTERNAL, 72, 75
EXTRACT, 160, 166

FALSE, 145
Features:
  new, 540
  still to be developed, 541
FETCH, 104
  dynamic, 249
FIRST, 104
FLOAT, 40
Foreign key, 20, 59, 62, 317
FORTRAN, 210, 215, 223, 228
  host language variable definition, 226
  parameter data types, 216
FROM, 139
FULL, 59, 62, 130, 155
Full level, 536

GET DESCRIPTOR, 244
GET DIAGNOSTICS, 200
GO TO, 228
GRANT:
  ripple effects of, 117
GROUP BY, 140

HAVING, 141
Host language variables:
  Ada definitions, 223
  C definitions, 224
  COBOL definitions, 225
  FORTRAN definitions, 226
  MUMPS definitions, 226

Host language variables:
  Pascal definitions, 226
  PL/I definitions, 227
  references to, 222
HOUR, 41, 44

Identifiers, 29
IDENTITY, 75
IMMEDIATE, 191
Incompatibilities, 539
Indexes, 442
Information schema, 279
  usage of, 293
INFORMATION_SCHEMA_
    CATALOG_NAME:
  base table, 281
INFORMATION_SCHEMA_
    CATALOG_NAME_
    CARDINALITY:
  assertion, 293
Information systems:
  definition of, 16
  design of, 298
  handling time in, 308
  security of, 307
INNER, 130, 132
In predicate, 152
INSENSITIVE, 101, 104, 247
INSERT, 91
INT, 39
INTEGER, 38
Integrity:
  definition of, 304, 313
  domain, 314
  entity, 316
  referential, 317
  user, 320
Intermediate level, 536
INTERSECT, 123, 129
Interval data types, 44
  day–time, 44
  literals, 46
  year–month, 44
Interval value expressions, 164, 192
IS, 145
  truth table for, 146
Isolation levels, 187

JOIN, 122, 130

Key:
  basic concept of, 19
  candidate, 19
  foreign, 20
  primary, 20
  primary key, 241
KEY_COLUMN_USAGE:
  base table, 268
  view, 288
KEY_DEGREE_GREATER_
    THAN_OR_EQUAL_TO_1:
  assertion, 279
Key words, 531
  non–reserved words, 533
  possible future reserved words, 534
  reserved words, 531
Known not nullable, 241

LAST, 104
LEFT, 130
Levels, 535
Like predicate, 150
Literals, 33
  approximate numeric, 41
  bit, 38
  character, 36
  datetime, 43
  exact numeric, 39
  interval, 46
LOCAL, 163, 193
LOWER, 161, 171

MATCH, 59, 62, 155, 319
Match predicate, 155
MAX, 178, 179
MIN, 178, 179
MINUTE, 41, 44
Missing information:
  handling of, 369
  types of, 370, 374
  use of NULL, 370
Module language, 209
Modules:
  contents of, 211
MONTH, 41
MUMPS, 210, 215, 222, 223
  host language variable definition, 226
  parameter data types, 217

Names, 31
  correlation, 125
  extended, 32
  qualified by INFORMATION_
    SCHEMA, 32
  scope of, 32
NATIONAL CHARACTER, 36
NATURAL, 130
NCHAR, 36
NEXT, 104
NO ACTION, 63, 64

Normalization, 300
NOT, 145
  truth table for, 146
NOT FOUND, 228
NOT NULL constraint, 57
NULL, 56, 93, 121, 172, 176
NULLIF, 177
Null predicate, 151
NUMERIC, 38
Numeric value expressions, 160

OCTET_LENGTH, 169
  <octet, 160
OPEN, 104
  dynamic, 248
OR, 145
  truth table for, 146
ORDER BY, 101
OUTER, 130, 132
OVERLAPS, 356
Overlaps predicate, 154, 356

Parameters, 214
PARTIAL, 59, 62, 155
PASCAL, 210, 215, 223
  host language variable definition, 226
  parameter data types, 217
PL/I, 210, 215, 223
  host language variable definition, 227
  parameter data types, 217
POSITION, 160, 169
Predicate:
  between, 150
Predicates, 147
  comparison, 147
  exists, 156
  in, 152
  like, 150
  match, 155
  null, 151
  overlaps, 154
  quantified comparison, 153
  unique, 157
Prenex normal form, 392
PREPARE, 235
Primary key, 20, 58, 61, 241
PRIOR, 104
Privilege descriptors:
  definition of, 112
Procedures, 212

Quantified comparison predicate, 153
Query expressions, 91, 122
Query specifications, 141

READ ONLY, 186
READ WRITE, 186
REAL, 40
Recovery, 183
REFERENCES, 59, 62
REFERENTIAL_CONSTRAINTS:
  base table, 269
  view, 287
Referential integrity, 59, 62
Relationships:
  binary, 324, 326, 327, 329–333, 335, 337
  exclusive, 341
  inclusive, 343
  mutually dependent, 344
  taxonomy of, 323
  unary, 339
RELATIVE, 104
RESTRICT, 78
REVOKE, 80–84, 88
  cascade effects of, 117
RIGHT, 130
ROLLBACK WORK, 186
Row:
  basic concept of, 18
Row value constructor, 121, 122, 147, 150–153

Scalar functions, 165
  CAST, 172
  character, 169–172
  datetime, 165, 166
  string, 167–169
Schema:
  authorization, 50
  basic concept of, 20
  CREATE, 49
  default character set for, 50
  DROP, 78
  elements of, 51
SCHEMATA:
  base table, 260
  view, 281
Scope:
  of correlation names, 125
  of names, 32
  of table names, 125
  of temporary tables, 52
SCROLL, 101, 105, 247
Search conditions, 145
SECOND, 41, 44
SELECT, 141
  multiple row, 256
  single row, 93
Serializability, 184

Sessions:
connecting to, 196, 213
context information, 196
definition of, 195
disconnecting from, 197
switching between, 197
SESSION_USER, 56
SET:
column default, 89
domain default, 85
values in columns, 93
SET CATALOG, 189
SET CONNECTION, 197
SET CONSTRAINTS, 185
SET CONSTRAINTS MODE, 191
SET DEFAULT, 63
SET DESCRIPTOR, 245
Set functions, 160, 178
AVG, 179
COUNT, 179
effect of NULL on, 373
MAX, 179
MIN, 179
SUM, 180
SET NAMES, 190
SET NULL, 63
Set Operators, 126
corresponding option, 123, 124
CROSS JOIN, 131
DIVIDE, 137
EXCEPT, 128
INNER JOIN, 132
INTERSECT, 129
JOIN, 130
natural option, 130, 135
OUTER JOIN, 132
UNION, 126
UNION JOIN, 135
SET SCHEMA, 190
SET SESSION AUTHORIZATION, 191, 211
SET TIME ZONE, 192
SET TRANSACTION, 186
SMALLINT, 38
SOME, 153
SQLCODE, 208, 212, 228
parameter data type of, 215
SQLERROR, 228
SQL_IDENTIFIER domain, 280
SQL_LANGUAGES:
base table, 277
view, 293
SQLSTATE, 204, 212, 228
parameter data type of, 215
SQL_TEXT:
definition of, 27
String functions, 167–169
String value expressions, 161
Subqueries, 121, 144, 152, 153, 156, 157, 160
SUBSTRING, 161, 162, 167
SUM, 178, 180
SYSTEM_USER, 56

TABLE, 123
basic concept of, 17
constraints, 60–62, 65
CREATE, 52
DROP, 78, 81
temporary, 52
usage in constraints, 61
TABLE_CONSTRAINTS:
base table, 267
view, 287
Table expressions, 138
FROM, 139
GROUP BY, 140
HAVING, 141
WHERE, 139
TABLE_PRIVILEGES:
base table, 272
view, 286
Table references, 125
TABLES:
base table, 263
updatability of derived, 142
view, 283
Table value constructor, 122, 123
Target specification, 34
Temporary table:
usage in constraints, 61
Temporary tables:
definition of local, 211
TIME, 42
database vs real–world, 362
interruptible vs uninterruptible periods, 358
measurement of continuous processes, 360
moments of, 352
periods of, 352
taxonomy of, 352
TIMESTAMP, 42
TIME ZONE, 163
TIMEZONE_HOUR, 41
TIMEZONE_MINUTE, 41
Time zones, 364
setting of, 192

Time zones:
  TIMEZONE_HOUR, 41
  TIMEZONE_MINUTE, 41
Tokens:
  used in SQL, 28
Transaction:
  basic concept of, 181–184
  control of, 185, 186
  initiating, 184
TRANSLATE, 161, 171
TRANSLATION, 72
  CREATE, 75
  DROP, 79, 83
TRANSLATIONS:
  base table, 276
  view, 290
Triggered actions, 62, 347
TRIM, 170
TRUE, 145

UNION, 123, 126
UNION JOIN, 130, 135
UNIQUE, 58, 61, 155
Unique constraint, 58, 61
UNIQUE_CONSTRAINT_NAME assertion, 278
Unique predicate, 157
UNKNOWN, 145
UPDATE:
  dynamic positioned, 249, 250
  positioned, 105
  searched, 93
UPPER, 161, 170
USAGE_PRIVILEGES:
  base table, 273
  view, 286
USER, 56
USERS:
  base table, 260
USING, 238

VALUE, 68
Value expressions, 159
Value specification, 33
Value specifications, 160
VALUES, 122
VARCHAR, 36
View:
  as access control device, 405, 407
  as derived data support, 406
  as interface support for 3GLs, 409
  as performance enhancer, 409
  as structural simplifier, 404
  CREATE, 68
  DROP, 78, 82
VIEW_COLUMN_USAGE:
  base table, 266
  view, 291
VIEWS:
  base table, 264
  view, 283
VIEW_TABLE_USAGE:
  base table, 266
  view, 290

WHEN, 176
WHENEVER, 228
WHERE, 93, 95, 139
WITH CHECK OPTION, 68
  usage of, 410

YEAR, 41, 44